Scottish Record Society

Parish Registers of Dunfermline 1561-1700

Editor: Henry Paton

Alpha Editions

This edition published in 2020

ISBN : 9789354034213

Design and Setting By
Alpha Editions
email - alphaedis@gmail.com

EXPLANATORY NOTE.

———◆◆◆———

THE date given is that of baptism or marriage.

The first few pages are copied from the Register *verbatim et literatim.*

The ensuing entries are abridged, the form being in most cases a repetition of these specimens.

The baptisms and marriages are recorded in the Register in parallel columns—and in the transcription the marriages are placed month by month immediately after the baptisms. Where no marriages are recorded for the month, this fact is indicated.

The original spelling of surnames and place names is retained; but in the abridgement Christian names are modernised, except that some of a peculiar nature are given as they stand.

In the first few pages of the Register the record of marriages is impaired by the outer edge of the page having been cut away.

It should be kept in mind that prior to 1600 the year is reckoned from 25th March.

PARISH REGISTERS OF DUNFERMLINE

1561-1700.

1561. JULY.

B[aptisms].—The 16 day Alexr. Marschall had a man chyld born to him of his wyff, Effie Etown, baptizit and callit Patrik.

The 20 day Jhone Sauderis had a woman chyld born to him of his wyff, Besse Bwrn, baptizit and callit Jonat.

The 27 day Jhone Langlandis had a man chyld born to him of his wyff, Besse Bad, baptizit and callit James.

M[arriages].—The 6 of July H . . . .¹ wes mariet to Jea . . . ; George Philip to Bar . . . .

The 13 Hector Wilso[n] . . . . to Jonat . . . ; Wilzem Walker (?) . . . .

The 27 M. James . . . . mariet to Jonat . . . ; Wilzem Henderson to . . . .

AUGUST.

B.   The 3 day Wilzem Thomson had a woman chyld born to him of his wyff, Katerin Steinson, baptizit and callit Katerin.

That day Cutbert Richartson had a woman chyld born to him of his wyff, Jonat Fyff, baptizit and callit Marjorie.

The 10 day James Cois had a man chyld born to him of his wyff, Katerin Clevie, baptizit and callit Richart.

The 14 day Thomas Monqwhur had a man chyld born to him of his wyff, Marjori Andirson, baptizit and callit Jhone.

That day Jhone Boswell had a man chyld born to him of his wyff, Jonat Dagleich, baptizit and callit Tomas.

That day Robert Legat had a woman child born to him of his wyff, Jonat Andirson, baptizit and callit Jonat.

That day Jhone Walwod had a man chyld born to him of his wyff, Girsel Mastirtoun, baptizit and callit James.

The 17 day Adam Stoby had a man chyld born to him of his wyff, Katerin Mastirtoun, baptizit and callit James.

That day Jhone Doncan had a man chyld born to him of his wyff, Jonat Ranalt, baptizit and callit Jhone.

The 31 day Wilzem Wilson had a man chyld born to him of his wyff, Jonat Mudie, baptizit and callit James.

That day Wilzem Yowng had a man chyld born to him of his wyff, Katerin Brand, baptizit and callit Jhone.

M.   The 3 of August . . . . wes mariet to . . . .

The 10 Jhone . . . . in Kyngorn wes [mariet] to Elein Keir.

The 17 day Tho[mas] . . . . wes mariet to . . . ; Wilzem Wilson to . . . .

SEPTEMBER.

B.   The 7 day Waltir Stronge had a woman chyld born to him of his wyff, Elein Lyall, baptizit and callit Katerin.

That day Robert Wylson had a woman chyld, begottin in fornication of Maran Tomson, baptizit and callit David.

The 14 day Tomas Mudy had a woman chyld born to him of his wyff, Kirsten Harper, baptizit and callit Katerin.

¹ The leaf has been cut short at the side.

That day Jhone Potter had a man chyld born to him of his wyf, Katerin Wylson, baptizit and callit Tomas.

That day Wilzem Schortes had a woman chyld born to him of his wyff, Jonat Crystie, baptizit and callit Katerin.

That day James Brwis had a woman chyld born to him of his wyff, Marjorie Gibbon, baptizit and callit Margaret.

The 17 day Wilzem Wilsone had a man chyld born to him off his wyff, Katerin Crysteson, baptizit and callit Wilziam.

The 21 day Jhone Walwood had a man chyld born to him of his wyff, Helein Wardlaw, baptizit and callit Abraham.

That day Jhone Car had a woman chyld born to him of his wyff, Kirsten Car, baptizit and callit Margaret.

That day Jhone Blakater had a man chyld born to him of his wyff, Isbell Balfour, baptizit and callit Abraham.

That day Jhone Bwrn had a woman chyld born to him of his wyff, Jonat Steinson, baptizit and callit Elspet.

The 28 Jhone Wardlaw had a man chyld born to him off his wyff, Jonat Murray, baptizit and callit Jhone.

That day David Workman had a man chyld born to him of his wyff, Marjori Schortes, baptizit and callit James.

That day Jhone Scherair had a woman chyld born to him of his wyff, Nans Cunninghame, baptizit and callit Kirsten.

M. [*None.*]

OCTOBER.

B. The 1 day Peter Robertson had a man chyld born to him of his wyff, Jonat Wrycht, baptizit and callit James.

The 5 day Jhone Huton had a woman chyld born to him of his wyff, Jonat Paton, baptizit and callit Isbell.

That day Henry Reid had a man chyld born to him off his wyff, Margaret Stoby, baptizit and callit James.

That day Wilzem Andirson had a man chyld born to him of his wyff, Jonet Yonger, baptizit and callit David.

The 8 day Robert Dagleich had a man chyld born to him of his wyff, Jonet Etown, baptizit and callit Robert.

That day Jhone Potter had a woman chyld born to him of his wyff, Isbell Walker, baptizit and callit Isobell.

The 19 day Richart Potter had a man chyld born to him of his wyff, Katerin Walker, baptizit and callit Richart.

The 29 day Jhone Walwood had a woman chyld born to him of his wyff, Meg Sanderis, baptizit and callit Girsell.

M. The 5 day Androw Brown wes mariet to Kirsten Andirsone.

That day Jhone Strange wes mariet to Jonat Malcom.

The 12 day Jhone Watsone wes mariet to Nans Dewer.

NOVEMBER.

B. The 2 day Wilzem Durie had a man chyld born to him of his wyff, Jonet Gurlay, baptizit and callit Patrik.

That day Jhone Davidsone had a man chyld born to him of his wyf, Katerin Simsone, baptizit and callit Tomas.

. . . . day[1] James Keir had a man chyld born to [him] of his wyf, Nans Brown, baptizit and callit Jhone.

[The] 9 day Johne Huton had a man chyld born to him [of his] wyff, Besse Langlandis, baptizit and callit Robert.

The 12 day Jhone Steinsone had a man chyld, begotten in fornication of Margaret Craik, baptizit and callit Jhone.

The 16 day Wilzem Schortes in Lethems had a man chyld born to him of his wyff, Margarat Jonsone, baptizit and callit Androw.

[1] Torn.

That day Wilzem Boswell had a woman chyld born to him of his wyff, Elein Kellok, baptizit and callit Effie.

The 19 day Jhone Brown had a woman chyld born to him off his wyff, Isobell Mudie, baptizit and callit Katerin.

That day Androw Foster had a man chyld born to him of his wyff, Elein Wardlaw, baptizit and callit Androw.

That day Wilzem Cragie had a woman chyld born to him of his wyff, Elein Steinson, baptizit and callit Jonat.

The 26 day Richart Huton had a man chyld born to him of his wyff, Isobell Bwrn, baptizit and callit Alexander.

M. The 2 day Laurence Tomson wes mariet to Elein Huton.

The 9 day Laurenc Smyth wes mariet to Margaret Edison

DECEMBER.

B. The 7 day Andrew Pacok had a woman child born to him of his wife, Janet Blak, baptized and called Janet.

That day John Man had, &c.,[1] of his wife, Mæg Flokart, baptized and called Marjory.

The 10 day Arche Cuninghame and Isobel Sandis had Isobel baptized.[1]

The 14 day James Harrowair and Janet Cois had Janet.

The 24 day John Andirsone and Mæg Flokhart had Isobel.

The 28 day William Walkar and Madie Strong had David.

That day Andrew Walkar and Margaret Burt had Rosina.

M. The 7 day William . . . .[2] married to Bessie . . . .

That day Andrew . . . . married to Janet . . . .

The 21 day Richard . . . . [in] Aberdour was married [to] Madie Fleming.

John Makdonald (?) and Janet Dixon married.

John Furd to Janet . . . .

John Hodgs to Isobel . . . .

JANUARY [1561-2].

B. The 4 day Robert Watson and Margaret Millair had Margaret.

The 11 day James Dewer and Janet Law had David.

The 14 day David Bruis and Janet Doncain had James (in fornication).

The 18 day Loury Peirson and Margaret Brand had Margaret.

That day Thomas Huton and Marjory Eli had Janet.

That day John Andirson and Janet Walker had Elspet.

That day Henry Glas and Maws Weild had Alexander.

The 25 day Cuthbert Geddie and Mege Mwire had Patrick.

The 28 day John Flokcart and Janet Wilson had Effie.

That day Nicol Balfour and Bessie Duri had John.

M. [*None.*]

FEBRUARY.

B. The 1 day John Cunninghame and Katherine Walwood had Robert.

The 8 day Thomas Andirson and Christian Wilson had Andrew.

That day John Mudie and Janet Davidsone had Girsell (Grizel).

That day John Bull and Marjory Doncane had John.

That day John Peirson and Mege Watsone had David.

The 15 day John Elder and Effie Smeton had John.

That day David Qwariour and Christian Donald had Marion.

That day John Smart and Margaret Kirk had John.

That day William Mudie and Marjory Burn had Elspet (Elizabeth).

The 25 day William Brown and Elspet Gilmor had Elspet.

---

[1] Hereafter the entries are abridged, the form in most cases being a repetition of the above specimens.

[2] Edge cut off.

M.   The 8 day James Walker was married to Annie Henry.
The 15 day John Gardiner was married to Bessie Hutcheon.
The 22 day Charles Makmun was married to Christian Broun.

MARCH.

B.   The 8 day Hector Wilson and Janet Chalmer had Katherine.
That day John Mudie and Helen Cowe had Patrick.
That day James Burn and Janet Makkie had Bessie.
That day John Crychtoun and Bessie Mutray had Harry.
That day Alexander Scotland and Margaret Hendirson had Margaret.
That day James Clerk and Janet Banks had Margaret.
The 11 day William Robertson and Janet Boswell had Archibald.
The 15 day Tom Westwood and Effie Moyes had Robert.
That day Thomas Logtoun and Janet Philp had Christian.
That day Thomas Huton and Ellen Kellok had Patrick.
The 29 day [1562] James Cusin and Christian Paton had . . . . [*name not
filled in*].

M.   The 8 day Walter Clune was married to Katherine Nevin.

APRIL [1562].

B.   The 8 day David Scortes (Schortes) and Janet Watson had John (in
fornication).
That day James Mories and Mag Paton had Effie.
The 12 day Robert Logtoun and Katherine Ædison had David.
That day Thomas Davidson and Janet Keir had Isobel.
That day Peter Andirson and Marain Fargus had George.
The 19 day David Logton and Christian Mudie had George.
The 26 day William Eson and Margaret Person had John.

M.   The 12 day Alexander Kininmont was married to Margaret Dowe (?).
That day John Robertsone married to Marjory Steinson.
John Brown to Margaret Mu[die?].
The 19 day John Bruis was married to Marion Hutso[n].
That day John Edison was married to Isobel Stewart.

MAY.

B.   The 3 day of May Henry Peirson and Bessie Reid had John.
That day John Gib and Katherine Angus had John.
The 20 day Adam Stewart and Janet Blakater had Patrick.
That day John Smyth and Isobel Kellok had Katherine.
That day John Murray and Ellen Dangzeill had John.
The 24 day Henry Wilson and Janet Portar had Christian.
That day John Brown and Christian Andirson had Robert.
The 31 day David Fargusson and Isobel Durham had Margaret.   (In the
margin against this entry is written " minister of the Evangell.")
That day William Morgain and Janet Dewar had David.
That day John Mutray and Janet Andirson had Alexander.

M.   The 3 day John R . . . . married to Margaret Bl . . . .
The 10 day James Find (?) . . . . was married to Elein . . . .
That day Robert Tomson was married to Isobel . . . .
The 24 day Thomas . . . . was married to . . . . Meldrum.
The 31 day Thomas . . . . was married to . . . . ; and Andrew . . . . to
Margaret . . . .
That day [William] Mikilj[on] was married to Bessie [Baxter].   (*Cf.* 1563,
Sept. 19th.)

JUNE.

B.   The 7 day of June Laurence Wallwod and Janet Hendirson had William
(in fornication).

That day Thomas Garvan and Janet Makinon had Bessie.
The 10 day Andrew Harrowair and Madi Horn had Isobel.
The 21 day John Wilson and Janet Banks had Janet.
The 24 day Robert Howburn and Marion Dempstertoun had Henry (in fornication).

M. The 14 day John Dangzell was married to Nans Craik.
That day Robert Kilgour was married to Marjory West.
The 21 day Andrew Anderson to Bessie Kellok.

JULY.

B. The first of July James Mabray and Bessie Dennestoun had Phillip.
That day Abraham Walwod and Isobel Dagleich had Grizel.
The 5 of July William Moris and Margaret Anderson had Robert.
That day John Skirling and Effie Morphi had Margaret.
The 8 day Patrick Wilson and Bessie Breidheid had George.
That day David Andirsone and Margaret Hayik had Richard.
The 12 day Tom Broun and Janet Lilson (? Wilson) had William.
That day William Martin and Meg Austin had Adam (in fornication).
That day Robert Bennie and Isobel Andirson had Elspet.
That day Thomas Donald and Ellen Bruse had Robert.
The 19 day Wat Crystie and Janet Watson had Margaret.
That day John Andirsone and Margaret Hendirson had Margaret.

M. The 5 day Robert Davidson was married to Isobel Banks.
The 12 day Andrew Law, "sumtym a popish priest," was married to Bessie Burn.
That day James Hendirson was married to Margaret Logtoun.
The 19 day John Miller was married to Christian Andirson.

AUGUST.

B. The 8[1] day William Couper and Janet Keir had Bessie.
The 5[1] day Richard Walker and Janet Kennedy had Bessie.
The 9 day William Walwood and Ket Cini had Robert.
That day Tom Scharp and Janet Kaven had Margaret.
That day Andrew Jonson and Bessie Liddell had John.
The 16 day Andrew Smyth and Bessie Couston had Andrew.
The 19 day David Bull and Meg Curry had John.
The 23 day William[2] Schortes and Bessie Cryste had Janet.
That day Lourie Tomson and Ellen Huton had Loure (*i.e.*, Laurence).
That day John Watson and Nans Dewar had John.
The 26 day Tom Hendin and Janet Barklay had John.
That day John Tomson and Begy Stokis had Hester.

M. The 23 day Thomas Mar[k?] was married to Janet Lond[ie?].

SEPTEMBER.

B. The 6 day David Cunnand and Kaet Alison had Christian.
That day William Symson and Kaet Bennet had Patrick.
The 9 John Knox and Marion Stalker had Bessie.
That day George Jonson and Effie Beveraig had John.
The 13 day Robert Phillen and Janet Couper had Effie.
The 16 day James Wemis and Janet Durie had Isobel.
That day David Michaell and Betereig (Beatrice) Kellok had John.
The 23 day Walter Lyndsay and Janet Clark had Janet.
That day John Lathreis and Janet Duncan had Margaret (in fornication).

M. The 6 day John Ste . . . . was married to Janet P . . . .
The 13 day Andrew Hunter was married to Nans Scherper.
That day John Reid was married to Janet Tomson.

[1] So in the register.
[2] An asterisk is placed over this word *William* in the register, and in the margin is written " Wobster."

OCTOBER.

B.   The 4 day James Blak and Christian Peirson had Bessie.
The 11 day Andrew Cim and Janet Heich had Elspet.
The 14 day Thomas Murdo and Christian Harper had Margaret.
That day George Mutray and Margaret Person had Bessie.
The 25 day George Fleming and Tissabe Duglas had Janet.

M.   The 11 day John Aldistoun was married to Bessie Warkman.
The 14 day James King was married to Janet Wellison.
Robert Paton to Janet Dagleich.
William Wricht to Christian Tomson.

NOVEMBER.

B.   The 8 day Robert Andirson and Nans Miller had Elspet.
The 22 day John Car and Christian Car had Janet.
The 25 day Arche Cuninghame and Janet Davidson had Alexander.
That day John Fillen and Janet Matheson had Margaret (in fornication).

M.   The 1 [day] Andrew Forfair was married to Ellen Schortes.
The 22 day Andrew Moris was married to Isobel Edisone.
James Whyt to Janet Mudie.

DECEMBER.

B.   The 6 day Patrick Chalmers and Janet Curre (?) had George.
The 13 day William Boswell and Ellen Kellok had Henry.
That day Robert Dewar and Catherine Law had Nicol.
That day Malcolm Makinon and Janet Bell had William.
That day George Sanders and Margaret Duri had George.
That day Andrew Stodwart and Elison Gillis had Katherine.[1]
The 20 day William Walkar and Bessie Trumbill had Thomas.
The 27 day Cuthbert Wardlaw and Katherine Dagleich had Ester.
That day Richard Uterly and Margaret Dempstertoun had Jacob.
That day Adam Burn and Elspet Huntair had John.
That day George Barnard and Mege Angus had Patrick.

M.   The 6 day Laurence Bonalay was married to Ellen Andirson.
The 20 day Thomas Beveraig was married to Janet Cuninghame.

JANUARY [1562-3].

B.   The 13 day David Murray and Christian Travell (or Cravell) had Patrick
(in fornication).
The 17 day Hector Bredhed and Elspet Bowes had Katherine.
That day Robert Stenhus and Janet Tomson had John.
The 24 day John Liddell and Christian Miche had Adam.
The 31 day William Wilson at Pitliver and Elspet Donat had Abraham and
Jacob.
That day Tom Huton and Marjory Eli had Andrew.

M.   The 17 day Andrew Cim was married to Bege Bell.

FEBRUARY.

B.   The 7 day of Februair David Wilson had 3 barnis born at one tyme of his
wyf, Katerin Stewart, baptizit, ane callit Josep[h], ane uthir Margaret
and the thrid . . .
That day Andrew Law and Bessie Burn had Janet.
The 14 day John Huntair and Christian Robertsone had Nicol.
That day Thomas Stevin and Janet Bull had William.
That day Charles Edison and Isobel Tomson had Andrew.
That day John Kellok and Bessie Person had James.

[1] *Aberdour* in margin.

The 24 day John Lennox and Mege Patirson had John (in fornication).
The 28 day James Huton and Nans Steinson had George.
That day John Brown and Margaret Muir had Nicol.

M. The 21 day David Fergus was married to Ellen Wricht.

MARCH.

B. The 7 day John Edison and Isobel Stewart had Marjory.
That day William Sanders and Margaret Lamb had Katherine.
That day John Dangzell and Nans Craik had Katherine.
That day Robert Roxburch and Janet Michell had Elspet (in fornication).[1]
The 10 day Robert Wilson and Janet Pert had Gelis.
That day David Henry and Christian Lyall had Marjory.
The 14 day Patrick Murray and Marjory Wallet had William.
That day John Makalzeon and Marion Lyndsay had Marjory.
That day David Andirson and Janet Wat had Christian.
The 17 day Thomas Brechin and Christian Stenson had William.
The 21 day David Bankis and Janet Weild had Thomas.
That day William Horn and Margaret Stenhous had Adam.
That day John Steinson and Janet Pacok had Ellen.
The 28 day [1563] Nicol Dewer and Katherine Kellok had Thomas.
That day Thomas Blak and Christian Meldrum had Elspet.

M. [*None.*]

APRIL [1563].

B. The 4 day William Durie and Janet Gurlay had Marjory.
That day William Tomsone[2] and Nans Schortus had Robert.
That day John Patersone and Bessie Dangzeill had [*name and sex not filled in*].
The 11 day James Atkin and Bessie Malcolm had Alexander.
That day Nicol Andirson and Maws Brand had Laurence.
The 14 day Robert Angus and Christian Beverag had Nicol (in fornication).
The 25 day Nicol Peirson and Katherine Hendirson had Robert.
That day Robert Crafurd and Christian Colzear had Effie.
That day Walter Strong and Ellen Lyall had John.

M. The 18 day John Millar was married to Nans Craik.
Adam Clevis (*or* Clevie) to Margaret P . . . .

MAY.

B. The 2 day John Angus and Mege Kellok had John.
That day Lourie Tod and Christian Wilzemson had David.
That day John Gibsone and Bessie Stewart had Janet.
The 16 day John Keir and Christian Henderson had Christian.
That day John Dulie and Isobel Gray had Andrew.
The 30 day Robert Davidson and Isobel Bankis had Janet.

M. The 2 day John Be . . . . was married to Margaret C[all]ender (?).
The 9 day Andrew Mutray was married to Ellen Wardlaw.
Lowrie Steinson to Bessie Mutray.
John Steinson to Marjory Trumbill.

JUNE.

B. The 6 day Lowrie Kirk and Mege Bennet had Thomas.
The 20 day Allan Horne and Janet Davidsone had Margaret.
That day Gilbert Colzear and Christian Malcom had Christian.

M. The 6 day Thomas Doncane was married to Isobel Waich.
The 27 day Patrick Keir was married to Gelis Peirsone.

---

[1] *Rossyth* in margin.
[2] In margin against this entry *Inglis Wille*, evidently a soubriquet.

James Watchman to Margaret Kevell.
John Wilzemsone to Alison Atkin.

JULY.

B.   The 4 day James Knox and Christian Brwis had James.
That day William Makkie and Katherine Steinsone had Nicol.
The 7 day Michael Stewart and Gelis Andirson had a daughter called . . . .
(in fornication).
The 11 day James Findlaw and Janet Muir had William.
That day David Burne and Janet Whyt had Janet.
The 14 day Arche Angus and Bessie Dewer had Katherine.
That day James Whyt and Janet Mudie had Christian.
The 18 day Thomas Andirsone and Elein Peirson had Christian.
The 21 day John Aldstoun and Bessie Workman had James.
That day John Martiall and Nans Angus had Nans.
The 25 day James Immerie and Elison Pacok had Elein.
The 28 day David Lawta and Isobel Mutray had Nans.

M.   The 18 day Thom Edison was married to Isobel Robertson.
The 25 day John Atkin was married to Isobel Burn.
Robert Crysteson to Margaret Dagleich.

AUGUST.

B.   The 1 day Richard Potter and Kate Walker had James.
That day Andrew Andirsone, "ane indweller of Perth, had a man chyld born
in fornication to him of Besse Gray, receivit at hir handis heir aftir her
repentance, baptizit and callit Jhone."
The 8 day Tome Wostwood (*sic*) and Effie Moyes had Robert.
That day Thomas Yowng and Marjory Hunnon had Margaret.
The 15 day Alexander Carson and Margaret Reid had Christian.
That day Nicol Cant and Kat Kellok had Christian.
That day John Bull and Isobel Watson had Janet (in fornication).[1]
That day John Brown and Christian Eson had Andrew.
The 18 day Alexander Andirsone and Bessie Steinson had Maws.
The 22 day John Patersone and Begs Huchie had William.
The 29 day John Millair and Christian Andirson had Nans.

M.   The 29 day John Bull was married to Isobel Watsone.

SEPTEMBER.

B.   The 5 day John Robertsone and Marjory Steinson had Margaret.
That day Robert Peris and Janet Gray had Christian.
The 12 day Alexander Cuninghame and Margaret Kemp had Kate.
The 19 day William Mikiljone and Bessie Baxter had Janet.
The 26 day John Smyth[2] and Maige Kellok had Bessie.
That day Alexander Marschaell and Effie Ætoun had Margaret.

M.   [*None.*]

OCTOBER.

B.   The 3 day Tom Steinson and Kate Dagleich had David.
That day Henry Fynlason and Margaret Scharp had Henry.
The 6 day Henry Reid and Mage Stobie had Margaret.
The 10 day William Wrycht and Christian Tomson had William.
The 13 day Gilbert Martyn and Katherine Gray had Katherine.
That day John Robertsone and Janet Crafurd had Katherine.[3]
The 17 day John Kellok and Janet Durie had Katherine.

[1] *Rossyth* in margin.   [2] *Caiger* (*i.e.*, probably cadger) in margin.
[3] *Of Carnok* in margin.

That day William Huton and Effie Karkettill had John (in fornication).
The 31 day Thomas Wilson and Bessie Wilson had Elein.

M. [*None.*]

NOVEMBER.

B. The 7 day John Murray and Christian Spens had Edward.
That day John Reid and Janet Tomson had George.
The 21 day Arche Cuningham and Isobel Sandis had John.
That day Henry Jonson and Bessie Bankis had Abraham.
That day Tom Merlzeon and Christian Whyt had a daughter (in fornication). [1]
The 28 day Rob Wilson and Bessie Reid had James.

M. The 14 day David Pacok was married to Janet Chalmer.
Charles Cuninghame to Kate Walwod.
The 21 day William Keir was married to Janet Ranold.
Robert Andirson to Janet Walker.

DECEMBER.

B. The 1 day William Kent and Katherine Hodgs had Robert.
The 5 day John Huntar and Christian Matheson had Janet.
The 15 day John Miller and Nans Orack had Andrew.
The 19 day James Young and Marion Purraik had Patrick.
That day John Potter, younger, and Isobel Walker had Janet.
The 26 Gilbert Kennedy and Margaret Brady had Margaret.
That day James Symson and Isobel Henderson had James.
That day James Dewer and Janet Law had Bessie.
That day David Fzergus and Ellen Wrycht had Ellen.

M. The 5 day Robert Roxbruch was married to Janet Mitchell.
That day Thom Wilson was married to Elison Chalmers.
The 26 day William Young was married to Bessie Burn.

JANUARY [1563-4].

B. The 2 day John Smeton and Katherine Stobie had William.
That day John Bull and Nans Symson had David.
The 9 day John Brown and Christian Andirson had David.
The 19 day John Alisone and Janet Cim had John.
That day John Mudie and Ellen Cowie had Robert.
The 26 day John Chrychtoun and Bessie Mutray had Janet.
The 30 day George Warkman and Maus Hendirsone had Christian.

M. [*None.*]

FEBRUARY.

B. The 2 day John Walker and Margaret Walker had Kat.
That day David Eson and Annie Wardlaw had David.
The 9 day William Schortus and Janet Crystie had Adam.
The 13 day Nicol Dewer and Helen Horne had Robert.
That day Tom Smyth and Katherine Chalmer had John.
The 20 day John Davidsone and Katherine Cimson had Robert.
The 27 day John Murie and Kat Smeton had Katherine.
That day John Stenhous and Kate Dewer had John.

M. The 6 day William Wilson, younger, was married to Nans Donald.
That day Andrew Curre was married to Janet Piers.
The 13 day Walter Harper was married to Janet Dagleich.

MARCH.

B. The 1 day David Warkman and Marjory Schortous had Janet.

---

[1] *Rosyth* in margin.

The 5 day David Paycolk and Isobel Cuningham had Margaret (in fornication).
That day David Michell and Beatrix Kellok had James.
That day John Mudie and Janet Davidson had Margaret.
The 19 day John Cuninghame and Katherine Walwod had John.
That day John Walwod and Mege Sanders had Tissabe.
That day John Huton and Janet Paton had Christian.
That day John Man and Mege Flokert had David.
The 22 day Allan Tomson and Nans Aedison had John.
The 29 day [1564] William Boswell and Ellen Kellok had John.

M. The 12 day Thomas Smyth was married to Made Walker.
The 19 day Tom Andirson was married to Bessie Patirson.

APRIL [1564].

B. The 2 day William Mudie and Marjory Burne had John.
The 16 day William Tomson and Katherine Steinson had John.
The 23 day Robert Esplein and Marjory Logtoun had Marjory.
The 30 day Robert Dagleich and Katherine Russell had Arche and Marjory.

M. The 2 day James Cuthbert was married to Iden Huton.
And James Logtoun to Margaret Brand.
The 9 day David Paycok was married to Isobel Cuninghame.
And Robert Straqwhin to Isobel Warkman.
John Chatir to Janet Martiall.
James Schew to Kate Atkin.
The 16 day William Keir was married to Anapill Lowrie.
David Strang to Grizel Spittell.
John Rae to Margaret Direnoch.
The 23 day John Andirson was married to Isobel Gib.
The 30 day Rob Peirson was married to Janet Brown.

MAY.

B. The 7 day Thomas Hending and Janet Barklay had Christian.
That day Robert Car and Ellen Huton had John
That day Henry Huton and Margaret Murray had Marion.
The 10 day John Gib and Kate Angus had Isobel.
The 21 day Robert Andirson and Janet Walker had . . . , "begottin in fornication befoir they wer mariet."

M. The 21 day David Miche was married to Katherine Sanders.
The 28 day Adam Robertson was married to Kaete Bennat.

JUNE.

B. The 4 day John Muire and Bessie Grant had John.
The 18 day William Andirsone and Janet Yonger had a daughter.
That day John Elder and Effie Smeton had Arche.
The 25 day John Robertsone and Keit Stenhus had John.

M. The 4 day Adam Fairlie was married to Marjory Lundyn.
James Harrowair to Margaret Blyth.
The 11 day John Bruis was married to Maus Scot.
The 25 day John Burn of the Roddis was married to Emmellie Cuming.

JULY.

B. The 5 day[1] John Symerwaell and Janet Gillies had Isobel.
That day William Mackie and Katherine Steinson had Robert.
The 9 day John Peirsone and Margaret Watson had John.
The 16 day Patrick Cryste and Janet Burn had Thomas.

[1] *Alias Scull* in margin.

That day Tom Huton and Marjory Henderson had Isobel.
The 23 day John Mutray and Janet Anderson had Bessie.
The 30 day James Cois and Kate Clevie had Bessie.

M.   The 2 day James Wilson was married to Isobel Kirk.
The 23 day John Sanderis was married to Margaret Lourie.
George Warkman to Marjory Symson.
The 30 day John Cuningham was married to Bessie Peirson.
Alexander Hadan to Janet Inglis.
Henry Cosser to Effie Huton.

AUGUST.

B.   The 9 day John Bell and Margaret Calander had Andrew.
The 13 day Robert Stenhus and Janet Tomson had Janet.
That day Robert Logtoun and Kate Edison had Christian.
The 21 day John Potter and Katherine Wilson had William.
The 27 day David Strong and Grizel Spittell had Bessie.
That day William Eson and Margaret Peirson had Andrew.

M.   The 13 day Robert Mastirtoun was married to Janet Dullie.
John Hodgs to Christian Dewer.
The 27 day William Donaldson was married to Annie Matheson.
John Car to Annie Sibbet.

SEPTEMBER.

B.   The 10 day David Fergusson[1] and Isobel Durhame had William.
That day John Wallet and Grizel Mastertoun had Robert.
That day Robert Davidson and Isobel Bankis had Margaret.
The 17 day William Walwod and Kat Cim had Bessie.
The 20 day James Keir and Bessie Burn had Thomas.
The 24 day Lowrie Tod and Christian Wilzemson had Catherine.
That day Patrick Keir and Gelis Peirson had Christian.

M.   The 17 day Alexander Forester, "minister of the ewangell at Gedburch,"
was married to Bessie Bodwell.
Arche Jonson "indwellair at Abirdour," was married to Janet Burn.

OCTOBER.

B.   The 1 day Abraham Walwod and Isobel Dagleich had Isobel.
That day William Sanderis and Margaret Lamb had George.
The 8 day William Durie and Janet Gurlay had James.
That day John Burn and Janet Steinson had John.
That day James Burn and Janet Makkie had James.
The 15 day John Watsone and Nans Dewer had Harry.
That day William Edison and Janet Grant had Marjory.
The 22 day James Watchman and Margaret Kævell had Isobel.
The 29 day Robert Phillen and Janet Couper had William.
That day Robert Aedison and Janet Kellok had James.
That day John Bull and Marjory Doncan had Harri (Harry).

M.   The 15 day Andrew Walwod was married to Isobel Chalmer.

NOVEMBER.

B.   The 5 day Hector Breidheid and Elizabeth Bruis had Annie.
The 8 day James Cusyng and Christian Paton had Isobel.
That day William Anderson and Margaret Norie had Nans.
The 12 day James Wemis and Margaret Wemis had Margaret.
That day James Cutbert and Iden Huton had Patrick.
That day Tom Logtoun and Janet Philp had a son.[2] . . .

[1] *Minister* in margin.
[2] Occasionally, though the child's name is omitted, the sex is indicated by " woman
child " or " man child."

The 19 day William Cragie and Ellen Steinson had Christian.
The 26 day William Wrycht and Christian Tomson had Janet.
That day James Schew and Kate Atkin had . . .
The 29 day Patrick Chalmers and Janet Curie had Janet.

M. The 12 day Peter Trumbill was married to Janet Horn.
John Brown to Christian Dewer.
The 26 day Andrew Wilson married to Marion Meldrum.

DECEMBER.

B. The 3 day John Steinson and Marjory Trumbill had . . .
The 6 day Andrew Currour and Janet Piers had . . .
The 10 day Henry Deis and Bessie Arnat had William.
The 17 day Andrew Dagleich and Janet Cusin had James.
The 20 day Rob Peirsoun and Janet Broun had Bessie.
The 31 day William Colzear and Margaret Broun had a son . . .
That day William Robertson and Janet Boswell had James.
That day Alexander Hammiltoun and Annie Logtoun had William.
That day Peter Cuninghame and . . . had . . . [*wife's and child's name omitted*].
That day William Walker and Mage Stronge had Rosyna.

M. The 10 day James Bwist was married to Janet Huton.
John Lawrie to Margaret Wrycht.
The 24 day George Cowentrie was married to Maige Kellok.
The 31 day William Smyth was married to Nans Brown.
Henry Keir to Marjory Edison.

JANUARY [1564-5].

B. The 3 day John Millair and Janet Adamson had Robert.
That day John Kellok and Janet Wilson had Emmie.
The 10 day John Potter and Isobel Walker had Richard.
The 14 day William Burn and Janet Mutray ("who deit in hir travaill") had William.
That day Tom Blak and Christian Meldrum had Robert.
That day David Bull and Maeg Curry had Patrick.
The 17 day Tom Smyth and Made Walker had a daughter . . .
That day Maurice Paycok and Christian Blaik had David.
The 21 day "Robert Fryssar had a woman chyld born to him of his wyf, Margaret Denistoun (presentit be fait[h]full men, he remaining onpenitent for the presente and singing at the Qwenis mes aftir he had communicat with the kirk), baptizit and callit Margaret." [Three names in the margin against this entry, viz. "Johne Bwrn, P. Blakater, F. Cowane."]
That day William Maurice and Margaret Andirsone had George.
That day William Hendirsone and Begs Oraik had William (in fornication).
That day William Morgain and Janet Dewer had Elizabeth.
The 28 day John Lawson and Christian Tempilman had Christian.
That day Alexander Scotland and Marjory Hendirson had Alexander.
That day Andrew Paycok and Janet Blak had Ellen.

M. The 7 day Andrew Riche was married to Effie Cwik.
The 21 day William Mubray was married to Elspet Whitson.

FEBRUARY.

B. The 4 day James Mubray and Bessie Denistoun had William.
The 7 day Richard Walkar and Janet Kennedy had Richard.
That day Robert Smyth and Isobel Wilson had Rosina.
The 11 day Wille Burn and Mege Clark had James.
That day George Sanders and Margaret Durie had George.
That day John Aldstoun and Bessie Warkman had Effie.
The 21 day David Swenton and Marjory Ewin had Janet.

M. The 4 William Burn was married to Marjory Logtoun.
The 18 day Tom Marlzeon was married to Nans Whyt.
George Andirsone to Bessie Blak.
The 25 day David Watson was married to Bessie Sanders.

MARCH.

B. The 4 day Laurence Bonalay and Ellen Andirsone had Margaret.
That day George Fleming and Janet Burn had Marjory.
That day David Miche and Katherine Sanders had Robert.
That day Richard Spens and Maus Couper had Henry.
That day James Speir and Marjory Sibbet had Lowrence.
That day Robert Patrik and Marion Andirson had William.
That day Tom Huton and Marjory Elie had Gilbert.
That day John Chattu (*sic*) and Janet Martiall had William.
The 7 day Andrew Harrowar and Made Horn had Effie.
That day Walter Young and Janet Man had Effie.
The 11 day Adam Clevie and Margaret Purrok had Janet.
That day Harry Murray and Christian Levistoun had Nans.
That day Thomas Donald and Ellen Brwis had John.
That day William Pullour and Meg Wostwattir had Bessie.
The 14 day David Wilson and Kæt Stewart had Peter.[1]
The 18 day John Schera and Annie Cuninghame had Andrew.
That day James Dewer and Janet Law had John.
That day John Millar and Christian Anderson had Margaret.
That day Thomas Murdo and Janet Kirk had Robert.
That day Nicol Cant and Katherine Kellok had Robert.
The 25 day [1565] Patrick Murray and Marjory Wallwod had Robert.
That day James Brwis and Marjory Gibbon had James.
That day Tom Mudie and Christian Harper had Christian.

M. The 18 day David Mortimer was married to Janet Walkar.

APRIL [1565].

B. The 1 day William Keir and Janet Ranald had Bessie.
That day James Logtoun and Margaret Brand had Andrew.
The 8 day William Brown and Elizabeth Gilmor had Grizel.
That day William Roxburch and Isobel Andirson had Andrew.
That day Lowrie Tomson and Ellen Huton had Katherine.
That day Wille Burn in Gellat and Janet Brown had Robert.
The 15 day Thomas Cuming and Mæg Bard had James.
The 18 day James Drysdeill "had a woman chyld born in fornication of
Margaret Donaldson *alias* Whyt Wyndo, baptizit and callit Kirsten."[2]
The 22 day John Brown and Mæge Man had David.
That day John Tomson and Elison Horn had Janet.
The 29 day Tom Wilson and Elison Chalmer had Effie.
That day Alexander Forfair and Katherine Tomson had Margaret.

M. The 1 day John Ramsay was married to Bessie Symson.
The 29 day John Wricht was married to Bessie Brown.
Thomas Murdo to Katherine Scherair.

MAY.

B. The 6 day Tom Proud and Margaret Ros had John (in fornication).
The 16 day Andrew Smyth and Bessie Coustoun had Nans.
That day Cuthbert Wardlaw and Katherine Dagleich had Harry.
That day William Wilson and Nans Donald had Effie.
The 20 day Andrew Jonsone and Bessie Liddell had Christian.
That day Andrew Moris and Isobel Edison had James and William.
The 27 day James Harrowar and Margaret Blyth had Bessie.

---

[1] *Barndy* in margin.   [2] *Lochlevin* in margin.

That day John Greig and Mege Hutcheon had Christian.

M. The 6 day David Schortus was married to Janet Andirsone.
The 27 John Gardiner was married to Kete Findlasone.

JUNE.

B. The 3 day Robert Bennie and Isobel Andirsone had George.
That day Henry Glass and Maws Weild had Harry.
The 6 day John Robertson and Marion Mutray had Rosina (in adultery).[1]
That day Peter Robertson and Janet Wrycht had Lowri.
That day Hector Greig and Janet Ranie had William.
The 10 day John Gib and Kæte Angus had Robert.
That day Tom Doncane and Isobel Waiche had Janet.
That day Rob Straqwhin and Isobel Workman had Harry.
That day John Brown and Isobel Andirsone had Allan.
That day Charles Wallang and Margaret Robertson had Kæte (in fornication).
The 20 day Robert Man and Margaret Stark had Marjory.
That day Henry Peirsone and Bessie Reid had Andrew.
The 24 day David Drysdell and Janet Champlet had Henry.
That day Tom Marlzeon and Nans Whyt had John.

M. The 3 day John Watsone was married to Janet Davidsone.
The 10 day Michael Tomson was married to Margaret Cutbert.
The 17 day John Andirsone was married to Kæt Huton.
William Burn to Violet Turc[an ?].
Tom Dugall to Janet Peirson.

JULY.

B. The 1 day William Tomson and Nans Shortes had James.
The 4 day John Sanders and Bessie Burn had Patrick.
The 8 day Andrew Cowbron and Mege Moir had William.
The 11 day William Mackie and Kete Steinson had Kæte.
That day Harry Knox and Kæt Mutray had George (in fornication).
The 15 day Robert Piers and Janet Gray had James.
That day John Robertson and Marjory Steinson had Janet.
The 18 day Pete Logtoun and Kete Row had Thomas (in fornication).
The 22 Robert Dewer and Kæte Law had Elspet.
That day Walter Strang and Ellen Lyall had David.
That day John Millair and Nans Oraik had Bessie.
The 25 day James Smyth and Kæte Paycock had Isobel.
The 29 day Antony Rutherfurd and Maws Fergussone had William.
That day Patrick Durie and Elizabeth Lundyn had George.
That day Richard Potter and Kete Walkar had John.
That day John Murray and Ellen Daingzell had William.
That day John Huntair and Christian Robertsone had James.
That day Michael Horn and Margaret Ramsay had Isobel.

M. The 8 day Adam Knox was married to Janet Doncane.
The 15 day Andrew Wemis was married to Kæte Man.

AUGUST.

B. The 5 day John Wilsone and Janet Bankis had Patrick.
That day John Richertsone and Alison Bell had Janet.
The 12 day Robe Cuninghame and Ellen Sleich had Isobel.
That day Robert Mastirtoun and Janet Dulie had Janet.
That day John Murie and Kæt Smeton had John.
The 19 day Robert Andirson and Nans Millair had a daughter.
The 26 day David Murray "the Capitan," and Janet Wemis had John.

[1] *Jok of Howadick* in margin.

That day William Horn and Margaret Stenhus had David.
The 29 day Alexander Bening and Mege Broun had David.

M.   The 5 day George Wilson was married to Kate Wilsone.
The 12 day William Cragie was married to Isobel Andirsone.
And William Blak to Margaret Robertsone.
The 26 day Richard Steinson was married to Margaret Wallet.

SEPTEMBER.

B.   The 2 day Lourie Smyth and Margaret Aedisone had John.
The 9 day Walter Flais and Bessie Peirsone had Bessie.[1]
That day William Walkar and Bessie Trumbill had Charles.
The 12 day William Mikiljon and Bessie Baxter had Patrick.
That day John Rae and Margaret Dyrenoch had Effie.
That day Patrick Wilson and Bessie Breidheid had Alexander.
That day Duncan Symson and Elspet Derenoch had Robert.   [In the
  margin against this entry is written, "This man fled to us from
  Comberie in the Heland for Macgregoir."]
The 16 day Tom Millair and Janet Keir had John.
That day Andrew Wilson and Marion Meldrum had Kate.
That day John Stirling and Effie Morphie had John.
That day John Tomsone and Bege Stokkis had Bessie.
That day John Cuninghame and Janet Talzeour had John (in fornication).
The 19 day George Warkman, younger, and Marjory Symson had George.
That day John Smyth[2] and Maige Kellok had Margaret.
The 23 day John Mackalzeon and Marion Lyndsay had Christian.
That day William Schortus in South Lethems and Margaret Jhonson had
  Christian.
The 26 day William Schortes[3] and Bessie Cryste had David.
The 30 day David Wobster and Janet Brown had Ellen.

M.   The 30 day Patrick Burn was married to Margaret Steinson.

OCTOBER.

B.   The 7 day Gilbert Kennedy and Margaret Bredie had Barbara.
The 14 day Wille Burn, cutler, and Ellen Wardlaw had Janet (in fornication).
The 21 day Nicol Dewer and Kate Kellok had William.
The 28 day Lowrie Steinson and Bessie Mutray had Margaret.

M.   The 7 day John Wat was married to Margaret Tomson.
The 21 day John Brown was married to Janet Walkar.

NOVEMBER.

B.   The 4 day John Inglis and Janet Atkin had Alexander.
That day William Stenhus and Margaret Elder had Patrick.
The 11 day John Kellok and Meg Hutson had a son.
That day Henry Reid and Mage Stobie had Gelis.
That day John Liddell and Christian Miche had Robert.[1]
That day David Paycok and Isobel Cuninghame had Andrew.
That day William Patirsone and Marjory Fleming had William (in fornication).
The 18 day Nicol Dagleich and Janet Carnis had Robert.
The 21 day William Mudie and Marjory Burn had Thomas.
The 25 day Andrew Trumbill and Margaret Andirsone had Andrew.

M.   The 11 day John Gamill was married to Bessie Donaldsone.
Robert Creich to Janet Elder.
The 18 day Tom Walwod was married to Bessie Spittell.
Thomas Davidson to Bessie Doncane.

---

[1] *Indweller of Leith* in margin.   [2] *Cagger* in margin.
[3] *Wobster* in margin.   [4] *Opressit* in margin.

DECEMBER.

B. The 2 day David Mortimer and Janet Walkar had David.
That day Alexander Carsan and Margaret Reid had Rosina.
The 9 day John Burn in Roddis and Emilie Cuming had Christian.
The 23 day Tom Moire "had a woman chyld born to him in fornication, baptizit and callit Jonat."

M. The 2 day William Steinsone was married to Marjory Sibbet.
The 16 day James Hutson was married to Janet Bonalley.
The 30 day Andrew Law was married to Janet Peirson.

JANUARY [1565-6].

B. The 6 day John Walwod and Christian Dagleich had Nicol.
That day Robin Wilson and Janet Pæt had Nans.
That day Gilbert Martin and Kæte Grey had William.
That day John Steinson and Janet Paycok had Isobel.
That day John Wilzemson and Elison Atkin had William.
The 9 day Arche Cuninghame and Mege Davidson had Maus.
The 20 day Tom Smyth and Katherine Chalmer had William.
That day John Meik and Christian Broun had Bege (in fornication).
The 27 day James Atkin and Bessie Malcom had Christian.

M. [*None.*]

FEBRUARY.

B. The 3 day John Sanderis and Margaret Lowrie had Clement.
That day Andrew Riche and Effie Cuik had Katherine.
That day James Huton and Nans Steinson had Nans.
The 10 day David Færgus and Ellen Wrycht had John.
The 17 day John Crychtoun and Bessie Mutray had Marjory.
That day John Hodgs and Christian Dewer had Robert.
That day Alexander Cuningham and Margaret Kemp had William.
The 27 day Patrick Keir and Gelis Peirson had Begs.
That day Robert Dagleich and Kæte Russall had Robert.
That day John Gardiner and Kæte Finlason had Ellen.

M. The 17 day Tom Doncan was married to Margaret Kæven.

MARCH.

B. The 6 day John Steinson and Marjory Trumbill had Ellen.
That day William Wilson and Christian Hunon had Janet.
That day Arche Cuninghame and Isobel Sands had Arche.
That day William Andirson and Janet Yonger had Patrick.
That day John Kellok and Margaret Peirson had Janet.
The 17 day John Smyth and Janet Dewer had Margaret (in fornication).
That day John Walkar and Mæg Walkar had Andrew.
That day Lowrie Schortes and Katherine Mill had Annie.
The 24 day James Cois and Bessie Fotringham had David.
That day John Smart and Margaret Kirk had Kæte.
The 27 day [1566] Robert Inglis and Christian Donaldson had Katherine and Margaret.
The 31 day Henry Strange and Male Dun had Robert (in fornication).
That day James Ywng and Marion Purrok had James.
That day Robert Dewer and Bessie Nicoll had Nicol (in fornication).
That day John Elder and Effie Smeton had Christian.

M. [*None.*]

APRIL [1566].

B. The 10 day John Car and Annie Sibbet had David.
The 14 day Robert Andirsone and Janet Walkar had Ellen

That day Lawrence Kirk and Margaret Bennait had William.
That day Robert Doncane and Annie Donaldson had Margaret (in fornication).
That day John Inche and Margaret Andirsone had Kaet.
That day John Wrycht and Bessie Broun had . . . .
The 17 day Patrick Blakater and Grizel Hammiltoun had Christian.[1]
The 21 day Henry Jonsone and Bessie Banks had John.
That day John Andirsone and Kaete Huton had Bessie.
That day William Tomsone and Kate Steinsone had Christian.
That day John Peirsone and Margaret Watsone had Harry.
The 28 day David Schortes and Janet Andirsone had Christian.

M.   The 7 day John Gray was married to Janet Archibald.

MAY.

B.   The 1 day Robert Logtoun and Kaet Ædison had Isobel.
The 12 day James Bwist and Janet Huton had Christian.
That day Nicol Westwood and Ellen Keirdoch had Bessie.
The 19 day Henry Finlawson and Margaret Scharp had Katherine.
That day John Murdo and Kete Scherair had Christian.
That day John Reid and Marjory Symsone had John.
The 26 day David Æson and Annie Wardlaw had John.
That day Cymne (*sic*) Dewer and Marjory Russall had Thomas (in fornication).

M.   [*None.*]

JUNE

B.   The 2 day James Wat and Bessie Broun had Ellen.[2]
That day Thomas Dugall and Janet Peirsone had Thomas.[2]
The 12 John Bull and Nans Symson had Marjory.
That day David Cunnand and Kaete Alison had Nans.
The 16 day John Patirson and Begs Huchie had Kaete.
The 23 day David Fergussone, "minister of the ewangell," and Isobel Durhame had Patrick.
The 30 day John Watsone and Janet Davison had David.

M.   That day [prob. the 2nd] James Stark was married to Ellen Drummond (parishioners of Abirdour).
The 9 day David Fyf married to Annie Hedgs.
That day Tom Sanderis was married to Janet Fothringham.
The 16 day Thomas Dangzeill was married to Marjory Dagleich.
And William Wels to Nans Currour.

JULY.

B.   The 7 day Alexander Andirson and Bessie Steinson had Bessie.
The 10 day John Grahame and Bessie Mill had Bessie.[3]
The 14 day Rob Peiris and Janet Gray had Janet.
That day John Potter and Kete Wilson had Bessie.
That day Andrew Jonsone and Bessie Liddell had Bessie.
That day Geordi Wilson and Kaete Wilson had Margaret.
That day Henry Elder (Innerkethin) and Margaret Clark had Thomas.
The 21 day John Bwll (Rossyth) and Isobel Watson had Nans.
The 24 day James Wilson and Isobel Kirk had Christian.
The 31 day Patrick Durie and Elizabeth Lundyn had John.
That day John Kellok and Ellen Wilson had John.

M.   [*None.*]

AUGUST.

B.   The 4 day William Durie and Janet Gurlay had Sara.

[1] *Then off Dinduff* in margin.
[2] *Innerkethin* against either or both of these entries, in margin.
[3] *Saline* in margin.

That day David Bouga and Mæg Russall had Ellen (in fornication.)
The 11 day John Stenhus and Nans Edison had Adam.[1]
The 14 day John Mutray and Janet Anderson had Ellen.
That day Adam Stewart and Janet Blakater had David.
That day John Reid and Janet Tomson had Isobel.
The 25 day William Cragie and Isabel Andirson had Christian.
That day Lawrence Smyth and Margaret Edison had Christian.
That day John Huton and Janet Paton had Bessie.

M. The 4 day William Kyninmont was married to Christian Angus.

SEPTEMBER.

B. The 1 day John Brown and Janet Walkar had Robert.
That day Wat Cryste and Janet Watsone had Janet.
That day James Symson and Isobel Henderson had Katherine.
That day David Scotland and Kete Atkin (Schew's wife) had John (in adultery).
The 8 day James Wemis and Margaret Wemis had Patrick.
That day David Warkman and Mage Schortus had Alexander.
The 11 day John Wallet and Grizel Mastertoun had John.
The 15 day David Michell and Bæto (*sic*) Kellok had Janet.
That day William Wrycht and Christian Tomson had Christian.
That day John Davidsone and Kæte Symson had Bessie.
That day David Jonson ("indwellar of Edinburch, twiching whois repentance we recevit a testimoniall from thence") and Isobel Horn had David (in fornication).
The 22 day James Knox and Christian Brwis had Ellen.
That day William Donaldson and Nans Matheson had Bessie.
The 25 day John Brown and Christian Andirson had George.

M. [*None.*]

OCTOBER.

B. The 6 day John Gamill and Bessie Donaldsone had Janet.
That day Nicol Donaldsone and Kæte Wilson had Christian.
The 13 day Nicol Makkie and Kæt Blæk had Bessie (in fornication).
That day John Rae and Margaret Direnoch had Alexander.
That day Captain David Murray and Janet Wemis had Robert.
That day Andrew Spittell and Katherine Logen had Andrew.
The 16 day George Jonson and Effie Beveraig had Margaret.
The 20 day Andrew Walwod and Isobel Chalmer had Margaret.
That day James Drummond and Janet Paterson had Henry.
The 27 day Andrew Law, cutler, and Janet Peirson had Bessie.

M. The 20 day John Muschat was married to Margaret Boqwhennan.

NOVEMBER.

B. The 3 day Abraham Walwod and Isobel Dagleich had Bessie.
That day Adam Robertson and Kæte Bennat had James.
That day George Mutray and Janet Tomson had Janet (in fornication).
The 13 day Anton Rutherfurd and Mase Fergusson had Janet.
That day William Steinson and Marjory Sibbet had Christian.
The 17 day Patrick Burn and Margaret Steinson had Bessie.
The 20 day Robert Paton and Janet Dagleich had Janet.

M. The 3 day George Mutray was married to Janet Tomson.
John Phillen to Janet Patirson.

DECEMBER.

B. The first day William Symson and Kæt Bennait had Christian.
The 4 day Andrew Currour and Janet Piers had Richard.

---

[1] *Inerkethen pratas* in margin.

The 8 day John Makkie and Margaret Jonson had James.
That day John Watsone and Nans Dewer had Elizabeth.
The 11 day Tom Westwood and Effie Moys had Edward.
That day James Whyt and Janet Mudie had John.
The 15 Robert Dagleich and Christian Boswell had David.
That day Tom Peirson and Bessie Wilson had Margaret.
That day " Jhone Liddels [1] woman's chyld was borne to him of his wyf Kirsten Miche, baptizit and callit Katerin."

M. [*None.*]

JANUARY [1566-7].

B. The 5 day John Man and Meg Flockart had Katherine.
That day Adam Andersone and Isobel Spens had John.
The 8 day Tom Andirson and Ellen Peirson had Andrew.
That day Robert Davidsone and Isobel Bankis had John.
The 15 day Robert Peirson and Janet Brown had Isobel.
That day Hector Breidheid and Elizabeth Brwis had Bessie.
The 19 day Tom Blak and Christian Meldrum had Nicol.
That day John Muir and Bessie Grant had Andrew.
The 22 day David Fyff and Annie Hodgs had Janet.
The 26 day Richard Potter and Kate Walkar had William.

M. The 26 Alexander Stewin was married to Janet Sibbet.

FEBRUARY.

B. The 2 day John Burn and Emilie Cuming had John.
That day Robert Straqwhin and Isobel Warkman had Janet.
The 5 day Richard Walkar and Janet Kennedy had Thomas.
The 9 day James Mubray and Bessie Dennistoun had James.
That day Gilbert Cowston and Mete Montheiht (*sic*) had Isobel.
That day James Cois and . . . . had David.
That day John Aldstoun and Bessie Warkman had Margaret.
That day John Alisone and Janet Cim had James.
That day Allan Tomson and . . . . had Charles.
That day Robert Fryssar and Margaret Dennistoun had Janet.
The 16 day Will Blak and Margaret Robertson had Bessie.
The 23 day Henry Glas and Maws Weild had William.
That day David Lawte and Isobel Mutray had Grizel.

M. The 2 day Henry Davidson was married to Keit Mutray.
The 9 day Henry Sempill was married to Margaret Goddye.

MARCH.

B. The second day Pete Blakater and Bessie Davidsone had James.[2]
That day John Kellok and Janet Durie had Beatris.
The 9 day Robert Leggat and Janet Andersone had Nans.
That day Patrick Chalmers and Janet Currie had James.
That day John Gray and Janet Archibald had John.
The 16 day William Mudie and Marjory Burn had Marjory.
That day Gilbert Colzear and Christian Malcolm had Christian.
The 23 day Cuthbert Wardlaw and Kate Dagleich had Robert.
That day Nicol Cant and Kate Kellok had Bessie.
That day George Sanderis and Margaret Durie had Janet.
That day Michael Tomson and Margaret Wynter had Nans.
That day John Blakater and Isobel Balfour had David.
The 26 day [1567] John Gibson and Bessie Stewart had Ellen.

M. [*None.*]

APRIL [1567].

B. The 9 day John Cuninghame and Kate Wallet had Nans.

[1] (Margin) " slaine in the Hewch."   [2] *Rossyth* in margin.

The 13 day William Roxburch and Isobel Andirsone had Robert.
That day William Tomson and Nans Schortes had Peter.
That day Robert Mastirtoun and Janet Dullie had Patrick.
That day Alexander Culrois and Isobel Levintoun had John.
The 20 day James Logtoun and Margaret Brand had Henry.
That day Tom Doncane and Margaret Kæven had twins, Margaret and
Isobel.
That day William Schortes and Janet Cryste had James.
The 27 day .   .   .   . Bull and Janet Curre had Charles.

M.   The 6 day David Fergus was married to Margaret Trumbill.
David Ben to Margaret Mudie.
The 27 day John Rae of Leith was married here to Catherine Cryste.

MAY.

B.   The 4 day Tom Steill and Janet Bull had Thomas.
That day John Bell and Margaret Callender had David.
The 11 day James Dewer and Janet Law had Adam.
That day William Morgan and Janet Dewer had William.
The 14 day William Robertson and Janet Boswell had Katherine.
The 21 day Robert Phillen and Janet Couper had David.
That day Robert Wilson and Rosina Ramsay had Patrick.
The 25 day David Wilzemson and Ellen Wilson, widow of Robert Cowan, had
Elison (in fornication).
That day John Phillen and Janet Paterson had David.
That day Robert Peirson and Kæte Colyn had Bessie (in fornication).
That day Andrew Harrowair and Made Horn had John.

M.   The 18 day Nicol Hart was married to Emmie Blaklok.
James Kirkwood to Janet Stenhus.
John Cutbert to Margaret Clark.
David Wilzemson to Janet Harrowair.

JUNE.

B.   The 1 day James Cois and Bessie Fothringhame had Andrew.
The 18 day Heri Knox and Kæte Mutray had Margaret (in fornication).
The 22 day Gilbert Kennedie and Margaret Bredie had Nans.
That day James Finlaw and Ellen Muir had Janet.
That day Lowrie Wallet and Janet Hendirson had William (in fornication).
The 29 day James Keir and Annie Broun had Christian.

M.   The 1 day Alexander Reid (Rossyth) was married to Janet Pyrnie.
Gilbert Colzear to Ellen Sanders.
David Cunningham to Margaret Steinson.
John Fyff to Marjory Reid.
James Hardy to Marion Clune.
David Sword to Elspet Gibson.
The 8 day Tom Brown was married to Christian Michie.
William Angus to Mege Dewer.

JULY.

B.   The 2 day John Whitsone and Isobel Andersone had Ellen.
The 13 day Robert Lyndsay (of Cavell) and Janet Kinros had Margaret (in
fornication).
The 16 day John Sanderis and Bessie Burn had William.
The 20 day Lourie Bonalay and Ellen Andirson had Robert.
That day James Immerri and Alison Paycok had Nans.
The 30 day John Bull and Marjory Doncane had Marjory.

M.   The 6 day Robert Kellok was married to Bessie Walwod.
The 13 day Andrew Eson was married to Elizabeth Bewie.

The 27 day Andrew Peirson was married to Christian Loudian.
David Wat in Markinch to Christian Gib here.

AUGUST.

B. The 3 day John Millar and Nans Oraik had Andrew.
The 10 day Tom Hendyn and Janet Barklay had . . . .
The 24 day John Stirlin and Effie Morphie had John.
The 27 day Andrew Fergusson (Innerkethin) and Janet Bar had William.
"That day the bastard woman chyld gottin in fornication betwix Mage
Murray and Jhone Blakater wes baptizit and callit Nicolas."
The 31 John Hodgs and Marion Bardi had Bessie.
That day John Gillespie and Margaret Pringill had Bessie.

M. The 3 day Alexander Marschall was married to Gelis Kelloik.
Henry Glas to Marion Greig.

SEPTEMBER.

B. The 3 day John Andirson and Kate Huton had Alison.
That day Tom Kellok (Beath) and Christian Marschall had Gelis.
The 7 day Michael Horn and Mage Ramsay had Gilbert.
The 14 day Patrick Durie and Elspet Lundyn had Robert.
That day John Smyth and Isobel Kellok had John.
The 24 day John Huntair and Christian Robertson had Robert.
The 28 day James Harowar and Mage Blyth had Marjory.
That day Andrew Spittell and Kete Logen had Margaret.

M. The 7 day Thomas Gib was married to Marjory Black.

OCTOBER.

B. The 1 day James Burn and Janet Macki had Marion.
The 5 day Wate Strong and Ellen Lyall had Ellen.
That day John Wrycht and Bessie Brown had Margaret.
The 8 day John Potter, younger, and Isobel Walkar had David.
The 12 day John Greig and Marjory Hutcheon had Abraham.
That day Tom Marlzeon and Nans Whyt had Margaret.
The 22 day George Flemin and Isobel Burn had John.
That day William Moris and Mage Anderson had Kete.

M. The 26 day John Miller in Rossyth was married to Janet Dewer.

NOVEMBER.

B. The 9 day Tom Huton and Marjory Ely had Margaret.
The 23 day Tom Mudie and Christian Harper had Margaret.
The 26 day Willam Mikiljon and Bessie Baxter had William.
That day John Mill and Marion Strageith had George.
That day James Moris and Mage Paton had Lawrence.
The 30 day Patrick Murray and Marjory Walwood had Effie.

M. The 9 day Charles Walker was married to Margaret Reid.
Andrew Peirson was married to Bessie Currour.
The 22 day John Brwis was married to Margaret Smyth.
The 30 day William Wilson was married to Janet Donald.

DECEMBER.

B. The 7 day Robert Roxburch and Janet Michall had John.
That day John Hodgs and Christian Dewer had Ellen.
That day Lowrie Tod and Christian Wilzemson had James.
That day William Keir and Annapill Lourie had John.
The 14 day John Smyth and Maige Kellok had Gelis.
That day Arche Angus and Bessie Dewer had Bessie.

That day John Kellok and Margaret Hutson had John.
The 21 day James Hendirson (Laird of Fordell) and Gene Murray had Annas.
That day Henry Sempill and Margaret Goddy had Marjory.
That day Tom Cunand and Kate Mudie had George.
The 28 George Andirsone and Bessie Blak had Grizel.
That day David Miche and Kete Sanders had Christian.

M. The 7 day John Davidson was married to Kate Symson.
Robert Doncane to Nans Donaldsone.
James Cryste to Isobel Gib.

JANUARY [1567-8].

B. The 4 day Andrew Moris and Isobel Edison had William.
That day Henry Reid and Mage Stobe had David.
That day James Young and Bessie Burn had John.
That day William Colzear and Margaret Brown had John.
That day Tom Robertson and Margaret Crafurd had Bessie.
That day Lowrie Kirk and Magi Bennat had Andrew.
That day John Car and Annie Sibbet had Michael.
The 11 day Alexander Forfair and Kete Tomson had David.
That day Andrew Smyth and Bessie Cowstoun had Abraham.
That day Andrew Trumbill and Margaret Andersone had Janet.
The 14 day Arche Cuninghame and Isobel Sandis had Isobel.
The 18 day Robert Esplein and Marjory Logtoun had John.
The 25 day William Mackie and Kate Steinson had Janet.
That day Henry Hart (Rossyth) and Malie Watson had Katherine.

M. The 4 day Tom Steill was married to Margaret Inglis.
That day John Dewer was married to Katherine Angus.
Patrick Gat to Bessie Edisone.

FEBRUARY.

B. The first day Captain David Murray and Janet Wemis had Margaret.
That day Anthony Rutherfurd and Mawse Fargussone had Patrick.
The 8 day James Brwis and Marjory Gibbon had Edward.
That day William Schortes and Barbara Duglas had James.
That day Tom Pullour and Mage Wostwood had Thomas.
That day Tom Duglas and Maws Burn had . . . .
The 15 day John Steinson and Marjory Trumbill had Patrick.
That day John Chattu and Janet Marschall had John.
That day William Burn and Janet Burn had William.
That day Lowrie Steinson and Bessie Mutray had Adam.
That day David Paycok and Isobel Cuninghame had Robert.
The 22 day John Andirson and Janet Ranat had Ellen.
That day Lowrie Tomson and Ellen Huton had Bessie.
That day John Fyff and Maige Reid had Gelis.
That day William Cragie and Isobel Andirsone had Bessie.
That day Robert Patrik and Marion Andersone had John.
That day Robert Andirsone and Nans Millair had Margaret.
That day John Fargusson (Innerkethin) and Janet Nevell had Margaret.
The 29 day William Steinson and Maige Sibbet had Marjory.
That day David Swenton and Annie Ewin had William.
That day Patrick Keir and Gelis Peirson had Janet.

M. The 8 day John Sandis was married to Janet Edisone.
The 29 day John Paton was married to Christian Nicoll.

MARCH.

B. The 7 day David Schortes and Janet Andirsone had John.
The 14 day William Wilson and Nans Donald had Bessie.
That day William Horn and Margaret Stenhus had William.

That day William Martin and Isobel Andirson had Ellen.
That day William Angus and Mege Dewer had Robert.
The 17 day Robert Friser and Margaret Denistoun had twins, William and Margaret.
The 21 day David Cunand and Kate Alison had Isobel.
The 28 day [1568] Henry Mill and Kete Harrowair had David.
That day John Crychteoun and Bessie Mutray had George.

M. [*None.*]

APRIL [1568].

B. The 4 day Andrew Law and Janet Peirson had Bessie.
That day David Wilzemson and Janet Harrowar had David.
That day John Speir and Marjory Sibbet had Bessie.
That day Robert Yowng and Bessie Burt had Henry.
The 11 day Henry Davidson and Kate Mutray had Andrew.
That day Andrew Wilson and Christian Meldrum had Bessie
That day John Burn and Emillie Cuming had Christian.
The 18 day John Peirson and Margaret Watson had Bessie.
That day John Murray and Ellen Daingzeil had Peter.
The 25 day Robert Dewer and Kate Law had Isobel.

M. [*None.*]

MAY.

B. The 2 day Alexander Reid and Janet Pirnie had Effie.
That day William Horn and Kat Blek had Katherine (in fornication).
That day Tom Huton and Christian Inglis had William (in fornication).
The 9 day Andrew Clark and Isobel Uterlie had Walter.
That day Andrew Peirson and Christian Loudian had Janet.
The 12 day John Meik and Ellen Watson had Andrew.
The 16 day William Tomsone and Nans Schortes had William.
The 23 day David Fyff and Annie Hodgs had Ellen.
The 30 day Tom Davidson and Janet Keir had Bessie
That day John Kellok and . . . . . Wilson had Janet.

M. The 23 day James Hendirson was married to Mag Meldrum.
The 30 day James Pacok was married to Ellen Whyt.
Andrew Wallet to Janet Andirsone.

JUNE.

B. The 9 day James Blak and Christian Peirson had John.
That day John Muschat and Margaret Boqwhennan had Lawrence.
The 13 day John Elder and Effie Smeton had Nans.
That day Robert Doncan and Ellen Mersar had Janet.
The 23 day John Watsone and Janet Davidsone had William.
The 27 day William Morgain and Janet Dewer had James.
That day James Cois and Bessie Fothringhame had Bessie.
The 30 day Patrick Wilsone and Bessie Bredheid had Marion.

M. The 13 day Alexander Robeson was married to Elison Spens.
Gilbert Tomson to Margaret Murray.

JULY.

B. The 11 day Tom Brechin and Christian Steinson had Alexander.
The 14 day Alexander Scotland and Marjory Hendirsone had Janet.
The 18 day John Mudie and Ellen Cowe had Nans.
That day William Symson and Kate Bennait had Robert.
That day James Smyth and Kate Paycok had Robert.
The 21 day John Steinson and Janet Paycok had Adam.
The 25 day John Inglis and Janet Atkin had Isobel.
That day George Mutray and Janet Tomson had Bessie.
That day William Walkar and Bessie Trumbill had George.

The 28 day Gilbert Colzear and Ellen Sanderis had Bessie.
That day Robert Smyth and Isobel Wilson had Nans.
That day Alexander Benning and Megi Brown had William.

M.   [*None.*]

AUGUST.

B.   The 8 day Pete Cryste and Janet Burn had twins, James and John.
That day Henry Finlason and Margaret Scharp had William.
That day Thomas Gib and Marjory Black had Isobel.
The 22 day David Burn and Kæte Durie had Patrick.

M.   The 8 day John Neill was married to Ellen Kellok.

SEPTEMBER.

B.   The 1 day James Wilson and Isobel Kirk had Laurence.
The 12 day William Keir and Janet Ranald had John.
The 19 day William Roxburch (Rossyth) and Isobel Andirsone had Isobel.
The 22 day Loury Schortes and Katherine Mill had William.
That day Richard Potter and Kæte Walkar had Janet.
The 26 day Robert Bennie and Isobel Andirson had James.

M.   The 19 day Charles Wallange was married to Margaret Durie.

OCTOBER.

B.   The 3 day David Færgusson, minister, and Isobel Durhame had Robert.
That day John Brwis and Mage Smyth had Marjory.
That day James Atkin and Bessie Malcolme had Elisabeth.
The 10 day Alexander Cuninghame and Margaret Kemp had Janet.
That day Robert Doncane and Ellen Donaldsone had Katherine.
The 17 day John Robertsone and Marjory Steinson had John.
That day David Wobster and Janet Brown had John.
That day John Wilsone and Christian Bankis had John.
The 24 day David Færgus and Margaret Trumbill had David.
The 27 day Charles Warkar (*sic*) and Margaret Reid had John.
The 31 James Bwist and Janet Huton had Charles.
That day Rob Logtoun and Kæte Edison had Tissabe.
That day Andrew Riche and Effie Cwik had Margaret.

M.   The 24 day George Smyth was married to Janet Angus.
William Tomson to Janet Walkar.

NOVEMBER.

B.   The 14 day John Dewer and Kæte Angus had James.
The 17 day John Browne and Janet Walkar had Andrew.
That day Arche Cunninghame and Mege Davidsone had Janet.
The 21 day John Kellok and Margaret Hutson had Janet.
That day John Burn and Janet Steinson had Bessie.
The 24 day Robert Dagleich and Kæte Russall had John.
The 28 day Andrew Peirson and Bessie Currour had Bessie.
That day Robert Wells and Grizel Michie had Bessie.

M.   The 7 day John Walkar was married to Margaret Tomson.
David Mudie to Isobel Paycok.
Henry Broun to Isobel Dagleich.
The 21 day John Sanderis was married to Grizel Hodgs.
The 28 day Robert Schortes was married to Janet Brown.

DECEMBER.

B.   The 8 day James Millair and Elspet Yongair had Gilbert.
The 21 day John Broun and Christian Andirson had Bessie.

That day Pete Burn and Margaret Steinson had Janet.
That day Andrew Andirson and Isobel Wilson had Margaret.
That day Tom Smyth and Katherine Chalmeris had Katherine.
The 15 day Michael Horn and Margaret Ramsay had John.
The 19 day Robert Mastirtoun and Janet Dulie had Nans.
The 22 day Rob Andirson and Janet Walkar had Alexander.
That day John Anderson and Kate Huton had Nans.
The 26 day Alexander Marschall and Gelis Kellok had Janet.
That day John Wilzemson and Elison Atkin had Janet.
That day Arche Angus and Bessie Dewer had Robert.

M.   The 5 day Andrew Duglas was married to Bessie Mudie.
The 19 day Patrick Mudie was married to Marjory Bennie.

JANUARY [1568-9].

B.   The 2 day John Man and Margaret Flockart had Nans.
That day William Dasone and Bessie Walkar had Marjory.[1]
The 9 day Abraham Walwood and Isobel Dagleich had Marjory.
That day William Wilson and Janet Donald had Adam.
The 16 day George Wilson and Kate Wilson had William.
The 30 day William Wrycht and Christian Tomson had John.
That day Wat Cryste and Janet Watson had Ellen.
That day John Tomson and Ellen Horn had Isobel.
That day Tom Steill and Margaret Inglis had John.
That day William Mubray and Elizabeth Whitson had David.

M.   The 30 day William Gay was married to Janet Andirsone.

FEBRUARY.

B.   The 6 day William Mudie and Marjory Burn had Patrick.
The 13 day John Paton and Christian Nicoll had Gilbert.
The 20 day Tom Andirson and Ellen Peirson had David.
That day William Wilson and Christian Hunnon had Margaret.
That day John Patirsone and Meg Huchie had Arche.
That day Tom Blak and Janet Daingzeill had Thomas.
That day Thomas Blak and Christian Meldrum had Thomas.

M   The 13 William Philp was married to Janet Trumbill.
The 27 day John Wallet was married to Isobel Walkar.

MARCH.

B.   The 6 day John Smart and Margaret Kirk had Barbara.
That day Gilbert Martine and Katherine Gray had Janet.
That day James Logtoun and Margaret Brand had Isobel.
That day Tom Yownge and Marjory Hunnon had Bessie.
That day Andrew Trumbill and Margaret Andirsone had Peter.
That day Andrew Currour and Janet Piers had Andrew.
That day Andrew Wallet and Isobel Chalmer had Janet.
That day Henry Peirsone and Bessie Reid had Margaret.
That day William Angus and Margaret Dewer had Nans.
The 9 day David Warkman and Maige Schortes had Charles.
That day Rob Tomsone and Isobel Donaldsone had Marjory.
The 13 day Patrick Chalmeris and Janet Curre had David.
That day William Steinsone and Nans Bachok had Janet.
The 20 day James Hendirson and Margaret Meldrum had James.
That day Alexander Andirsone and Bessie Steinsone had John.
The 27 day [1569] Henry Jonsone and Bessie Bankis had Adam.

[1] In margin, " fled out of Edinburgh for the pest."

APRIL [1569].

B.   The 3 day John Rae and Margaret Direnoch had Margaret.
   The 6 day Allan Tomson and Margaret Edison had George.
   The 10 day Rob Peiris and Janet Gray had Peter.
   That day John Makkie and Janet Jonson had John.
   The 13 day Pete Galt and Bessie Edison had Harry.
   The 17 day Gilbert Cowstoun and Metie Montheithe had Christian.
   That day John Bwll (Rossyth) and Isobel Watsone had Katherine.
   That day John Kellok and Janet Durie had Elizabeth.
   The 24 day John Gammill and Janet Donaldsone had John.
   That day Adam Robertsone and Kate Bennait had James.
   The 27 day William Black and Margaret Robertsone had David.

M.   The 17 day James Whyt was married to Mause Inglis.

MAY.

B.   The 1 day John Kellok and Bessie Peirson had Isobel.
   That day James Symson and Isobel Hendirsone had Margaret.
   The 15 day David Eson and Annie Wardlaw had Andrew.
   That day Lowrie Weittit and Janet Spens had John.
   That day Robert Kyd and Margaret Reddie had Margaret.
   The 18 day Robert Frisser and Margaret Denistoun had Bastian (a son).
   The 22 day Nicol Donaldson and Kate Wilson had Janet.
   The 25 day James Brown (Ferrie) and Bessie Lwn had Robert.
   That day John Walwood and Grizel Mastirtoun had Gelis.
   The 29 day Tom Peirson and Bessie Wilson had Janet.
   That day Henry Dewer "had a woman chyld born to him of his harlot, Elein
      Dewer, in fornication, baptizit and callit Marjorie."
   That day William Keir and Mase Walkar had Mase (in fornication).

M.   The 1 day John Clerk in the Ferrie was married to Janet Curre.
   David Clerk to Margaret Levinton.
   The 8 day William Huton in Brinteland was married here to Janet Walwood.
   The 29 day David Law was married to Bessie Dewer.

JUNE.

B.   The 5 day John Huton and Janet Paton had John.
   That day John Beveraig and Bags Findlaw had Lowrie (in fornication).
   That day James Tod and Marion Clerk had Katherine (in fornication).
   The 8 day Lowrie Tod and Christian Wilzemson had Adam.
   The 12 day Henry Wilson and Mage Faergus had John.
   The 15 day Robert Davidson and Isobel Bankis had William.
   The 19 day Nicol Dagleich and Bessie Carnis had John.
   That day Andrew Jonsone and Bessie Lidell had Gelis.

M.   The 19 day Alexander Carsan was married to Ellen Cusin.

JULY.

B.   The 3 day Patrick Keir and Gelis Peirson had Thomas.
   That day Henry Harthsyid and Mady Watson had Christian.
   The 10 day William Horn and Janet Philp had Thomas.
   That day Margaret Donaldson "presentit the woman chyld begottin in
      fornication betwix hir and David Busie, he remaining obstinat, whilk
      wes resavit at hir hand aftir hir repentance, baptizit and callit Isobell."
   The 17 day Hector Breidheid and Elizabeth Bruis had Robert.
   That day David Wilson (Barndie) and Katherine Stewart had Janet.
   The 31 day John Watsone and Nans Dewer had George.

M.   The 3 day Adam Sanders was married to Isobel Cuninghame.

The 10 day Andrew Ged was married to Margaret Andirson.
The 17 day John Dagleich was married to Janet Penman.

AUGUST.

B. The 14 day Robert Kellok and Bessie Wallet had Christian.
That day William Schortus and Bessie Cryste had Effie.
That day James Knox and Christian Bruis had Margaret.
That day James Schortus and Annie Schortes had Janet (in fornication).
The 28 day Tom Doncane and Margaret Caven had twins, Rosina and Margaret.
That day George Smyth and Janet Angus had Robert.

M. The 7 day Adam Wilson was married to Christian Lyall.
The 21 day Andrew Wallet was married to Marjory Peirson.

SEPTEMBER.

B. The 4 day David Logtoun and Christian Mudie had Bessie.
That day John Phillen and Janet Patirson had Janet.
The 11 day Henry Keir and Marjory Edison had Patrick.
The 14 day Patrick Durie and Elizabeth Lundyn had Ellen.
The 25 day Cuthbert Wardlaw and Kate Dagleich had Thomas.

M. The 11 day John Tod was married to Janet Litilljone.

OCTOBER.

B. The 2 day John Cuninghame and Kate Wallet had Alexander.
That day John Sanderis and Grizel Hodgs had Margaret.
That day Henry Broun and Bessie Dagleich had James.
The 9 day Peter Trumbill and Janet Horn had Peter.
The 12 day John Wallet and Christian Dagleich had Maws.
The 16 day Rob Inglis and Christian Donaldsone had William.
"The 19 day Wilzem Huton had twa soanis borne to him of his wyf Effie Carkettill, the eldest 7 quarteris ald, for sa lang wes he onbaptizit the father remaining obstinat at last wes now baptizit and callit Richert, the uther callit David."
That day Thomas Huton and Marion Broun had Andrew.
The 26 day John Walker and Margaret Tomson had William.
The 30 day Captain David Murray and Janet Wems had Patrick.

M. The 16 day Patrick Car was married to Isobel Millikin.

NOVEMBER.

B. The 2 day James Kinloch (Carnok) and Ellen Lyndsay had Margaret.
The 6 day George Sanderis and Margaret Durie had William.
The 13 day John Lyndsay and Janet Harlay had Janet (in fornication).
The 20 day William Robertsone and Janet Boswell had Adam.
The 30 day David Sword and Elspet Gibson had Harry.

M. The 6 day William Steidman was married to Isobel Gib.
Andrew Rowan to Bessie Spittell.
The 20 day William Philp was married to Christian Angus.
The 27 day John Hwton was married to Bessie Steinson.

DECEMBER.

B. The 4 day William Wilson and Nans Donat had Ellen.
That day James Paycok and Ellen Whyt had William.
The 11 day Andrew Ged and Margaret Andirson had Janet.
That day Nicol Cant and Kate Kellok had Andrew.
The 18 day William Mikiljone and Bessie Baxter had Gilbert.
That day Tom Broun and Christian Miche had Thomas.

The 25 day Robert Lyndsay "had a woman chyld born to him in fornication of Jonat Kinrois, to whom he had promissit mariage befoir, baptizit and callit Besse."

That day Jok Wallet and Isobel Walker had Lowrie.

M.   The 11 day Lowrie Dempster was married to Janet Peirson.
The 18 day James Garvan was married to Bessie Cryste.

JANUARY [1569-70].

B.   The 1 day Nicol Michell and Janet Norwall had John.
That day Tom Kellok and Christian Martiall had Kæte.
The 8 day Robert Straqwhin and Isobel Warkman had John.
That day William Andirson and Janet Yonger had Andrew.
The 11 day John Fyff and Maig Red had Barbara.
The 15 day John Murie and Kæt Smeton had David.
The 22 day Lowrie Kirk and Margaret Bennet had Janet.
The 29 day George Fleming and Isobel Burn had Christian.
That day Robe Peirson and Janet Broun had Christian.
That day Watte Strang and Ellen Lyall had Margaret.
That day John Steinson and Marjory Trumbill had William.
That day John Hodgs and Christian Dewer had Janet.
That day Robe Andirson and Janet Walkar had Thomas.

M.   The 8 day Michael Stewart was married to Janet Kellok.
The 29 day Robert Angus was married to Margaret Rae.
John Warkman to Bessie Aitkin.

FEBRUARY.

B.   The 5 day John Moris and Isobel Edisone had John.
That day James Dewer and Janet Law had Elspet.
The 8 day Richard Steinson and Margaret Wallet had John.
That day Robe Legait and Janet Andirsone had Patrick.
The 12 day David Fyf and Annie Hodgs had Margaret.
That day Anton Rutherfurd and Masie Færgusson had James.
That day Gilbert Kennedy and Margaret Bredie had William.
The 19 day John Andirson and Janet Ranald had Isobel.
That day John Wrycht and Bessie Broun had Grizel.
The 22 day Robert Patrik and Marion Andirson had Harry.
The 26 day Tom Cumand and Kæt Mudie had Edward.

M.   [*None.*]

MARCH.

B.   The 12 day John Crichtoun and Bessie Mutray had Patrick.
That day John Alison and Janet Cim had Bessie.
The 19 day John Ball and Marjory Doncane had Margaret.
That day John Kellok and Ellen Wilson had James.
That day Lowrie Bonalay and Ellen Andirsone had Isobel.
The 22 day William Cragie and Isobel Andirson had Patrick.
That day John Keir and Isobel Dasone had Katherine.

M.   [*None.*]

APRIL [1570].

B.   The 16 day Michael Tomsone and Margaret Cutbert had David.
That day David Michell and Bete Kellok had Andrew.
The 24 day James Brwis and Marjory Gibbon had Janet.
The 26 day John Aldstoun and Bessie Warkman had Allan.
The 30 day Tom Mudie and Christian Harper had Thomas.

M.   The 9 day Andrew Robertson was married to Marjory Wallet.
The 30 day Mr. John Crysteson was married to Bessie Keir.
Thomas Clwne to Janet Purrok.

MAY.

B. The 3 day Arche Cuninghame and Isobel Sands had Arche.
The 7 day John Andirsone and Kate Huton had Bessie.
That day David Bull and Meg Curry had Margaret.
The 14 day John Mill and Marion Strageith had two children baptized,
Henry and Christian.
That day John Burn and Emmie Cuming had Margaret.
The 17 day Robert Phillen and Janet Couper had Robert.
The 24 day Lowrie Smyth and Margaret Edison had Robert.
The 28 day " Elison Andirson had a man chyld baptizit, whilk sche had born
in fornication to Andro Cowan, baptizit and callit Robert."

M. The 7 day Florie Tomson was married to Bessie Kent.
The 28 day Adam Whyt was married to Bessie Landels.

JUNE.

B. The 11 day Patrick Murray and Marjory Wallet had Janet.
That day William Tomson and Nans Schortes had David.
That day George Barnat and Mege Angus had Peter.
That day William Angus and Marjory Dewer had Peter.
The 18 day John Kar and Annie Sibbet had Robert.
The 25 day Charles Walker and Margaret Reid had Andrew.

M. The 11 day John Law was married to Barbara Stewart.

JULY.

B. The 2 day Robert Wilson and Rosina Ramsay had Isobel.

M. The 9 day John Hill was married to Marion Sword.
The 24 day George Nasmyth was married to Isobel Fergusson.
William Keir to Christian Bull.

AUGUST.

B. The 2 day John Montereif and Bessie Dully had Janet.
The 6 day Robert Harrower and Christian Atkin had Katherine.
The 13 day John Sanderis and Bessie Burn had Thomas.
The 20 day Patrick Durie and Elspet Lundy had William.
That day Riche Potter and Kate Walker had Isobel.
That day Adam Sanderis and Isobel Cuningham had Janet.

M. [*None.*]

SEPTEMBER.

B. The 3 day John Smyth and Mege Kellok had Isobel.
The 13 day Henry Glas and Marion Greig had Ellen.
That day William Burn and Janet Broun had Marjory.
The 17 day John Scirlin and Effie Morphi had Lowrie.
That day William Schortus and Barbara Douglas had Bessie.
That day John Peirson and Mege Watson had David.
The 24 day David Fœrgusson and Isobel Durhame had Janet.
The 27 day Lowrie Steinson and Bessie Mutray had Elspet.

M. The 10 day James Hwi was married to Nans Hog.
The 17 day David Duglas was married to Bessie Cuming.

OCTOBER.

B. The 1 day James Immerrie and Alison Paycok had Duncan.
The 8 day Rob Angus and Margaret Rae had John.
That day Alexander Culros and Isobel Levistoun had Charles.
That day Wille Mudie and Marjory Burne had James.

C

The 11 day Patrick Blakater and Bessie Davidson had William.
The 15 day Henry Reid and Margaret Stobie had Bessie.
That day Henry Sempill and Margaret Goddie had Peter.
That day William Symson and Kete Bennait had William.
That day William Horn and Margaret Stenhus had Peter.
That day William Philp and Christian Angus had George.
That day David Eson and Annie Wardlaw had Effie.
That day James Hardie and Marion Clunie had Janet.
That day Michael Kilgour and Janet Hendirson had David (in fornication).
The 22 day John Inglis and Janet Atkin had Janet.
That day David Fergus and Margaret Trumbill had Margaret
That day James Whyt and Maus Inglis had Isobel.
That day Michael Stewart and Janet Kellok had Emmie.
The 25 day Pete Burn and Bessie Steinson had John.
The 29 day William Moris and Margaret Andirson had Janet.

M. [*None.*]

NOVEMBER.

B. The 5 day John Robertsone and Marjory Steinson had David.
That day James Keir and Nans Brown had Robert.
That day John Potter and Katie Wilson had James.
The 17 day John Broun and Christian Andirson had James.
That day John Greig and Marjory Hutcheon had Effie.
That day Nicol Cryste and Christian Balward had Henry (in fornication).[1]

M. The 12 day Andrew Dugall was married to Christian Clark.
The 19 day Andrew Brand was married to Isobel Cuming.
William Duglas to Janet Tennand.
The 28 day William Davidson was married to Catherine Andirson.

DECEMBER.

B. The 3 day John Elder and Effie Smeton had Lowrie.
The 6 day Alexander Marschall and Gelis Kellok had Marion.
That day William Steinson and Marjory Sibbet had Janet.
The 10 day James Blak and Christian Peirson had George.
That day Andrew Drummond and Janet Patirson had Margaret.
The 13 day John Dagleich and Janet Penman had Ellen.
The 17 day Robert Roxburch (Rossyth) and Janet Michell had Christian.
The 20 day Hector Greig and Janet Ranald had Thomas.
The 27 day James Garvan and Bessie Cryste had Christian.
The 31 day Robert Dewer and Kate Law had Janet.
That day Loure Schortes and Kate Mill had Janet.
That day Henry Finlason and Margaret Sharpe had George.[2]

M. The 10 day John Mubray was married to Christian Paton
Alexander Wilson to Christian Tempilman.
Pete Lawson to Ellen Wilson.
The 24 day Symon Davidson was married to Ellen Nicoll.

JANUARY [1570-71.]

B. The 3 day William Mikiljon and Bessie Baxter had David.
The 14 day Henry Davidsone and Kate Mutray had Patrick.
The 17 day James Burn and Janet Mackie had Janet.
That day Andrew Smyth and Bessie Coustoun had Peter.
That day David Burne and Kate Durie had Effie.
The 21 day James Cusin and Christian Paton had James.
The 28 day James Kid and Mag Roddie (? Reddie) had Patrick.
That day James Smyth and Kete Paycok had Margaret.

M. The 7 day William Jonsone was married to Margaret Stirk.

[1] In margin, " song ewirs."   [2] *Birshan* in margin.

The 14 day John Couper was married to Gelis Wilsone.
The 21 day Robert Marschall was married to Christian Huton.
John Huton to Nans Donald.

FEBRUARY.

B.   The 4 day James Hwt and Annie Hoge had Adam (in fornication before
the marriage).
That day James Whyt and Janet Mudie had Robert.
That day Alexander Cuninghame and Margaret Kemp had Patrick.
That day James Bwist and Janet Huton had John.
The 11 day John Dewer and Kete Angus had Bessie.
That day James Symson and Isobel Hendirson had David.
That day Andrew Wallet and Marjory Peirson had Gelis.
That day Robert Mastirtoun "had a man chyld born to him, aftir his
departur, of his wyf Jonet Ewlie, baptizit and callit Robert."
The 14 day David Murray "the capitane" and Janet Wemis had David.
The 21 day John Bull and Nans Simson had John.

M.   The 4 day Nicol Mackie was married to Katherine Horn.
The 18 day William Wostwood was married to Janet Kellok.
William Horn to Katherine Dewer.
David Michelson to Nans Steinson.
The 25 day Mungo Gray was married to Marion Tomson.
Thomas Elder to Bessie Dewer.

MARCH.

B.   The 4 day Tom Pullour and Meg Wostwater had John.
That day John Stenhus and . . . Duglas had Margaret.
That day Rob Andirson and Nans Millar had Christian.
The 21 William Roxburch and Isobel Andirson had William.
The 25 day [1571] Tom Blak and Christian Meldrum had Andrew.
That day John Kellok and Janet Durie had Janet.
The xviij day [1570] George Nasmyth and Isobel Fergusson had Elizabeth.

M.   [*None.*]

APRIL [1571].

B.   The first, Alexander Scotland and Margaret Hendirson had Richard.
That day Alexander Carsan and Ellen Cusin had John.
That day William Colzear and Margaret Brown had Patrick.
The 8 day William Horn and Janet Philp had William.
The 11 day Gilbert Colzear and Ellen Sanderis had Margaret.
The 15 day William Keir and Annabel Lowrie had Janet.
That day Wille Tomson and Janet Walkar had Marjory.
That day Pete Chalmers and Janet Curre had Alexander.
That day Thomas Marlzeon and Agnes Whyt had Janet.
That day Adam Whyt and Bessie Landels had William.
That day John Spidie and Bessie Keir had William in fornication .
The 18 day Pete Gat and Bessie Edison had Christian.

M.   [*None.*]

MAY.

B.   The 2 day Tom Duglas and Maus Burn had Emilie.
That day Andrew Peirson and Christian Loudian had John.
That day James Speir and Marjory Sibbald had Margaret.
That day William Duglas and Janet Leumand had Bessie.
That day John Murray and Ellen Daingzell had Katherine.
That day John Broun and Margaret Muire had twins, Andrew and Janet.
The 6 day John Brown and Janet Walker had John.
That day Geordi Gray and Margaret Galt had Andrew on fornication .

The 13 day Thomas Hendirsone and Katie Hutson had Robert.
The 16 day.[1]
The 20 day "John Makb.e (aftir his dæth) had a man chyld born to him of his wyf Kate Moyse, baptizit and callit David."
The 23 day Hector Breidheid and Elizabeth Bruis had Bessie.
The 27 day Andrew Wilson and Marion Meldrum had Henry.
The 30 day Robert Paton and Janet Dalgleich had John.

M. [*None.*]

JUNE.

B. The 3 day John Patirsone and Bessie Dangzell had Thomas.
That day Andrew Currour and Janet Peirs had Christian.
The 6 day James Miller and Elspeth Yonger had James (after the father's death).
The 10 day David Paycok and Isobel Cuninghame had Isobel.
That day Tom Sanderis and Margaret Lowri, "his brother's wyff" had Willie (in incest).
The 13 day Andrew Ged and Margaret Andersone had James.
The 24 day John Paton and Christian Nicoll had Margaret.

M. The 17 day Andrew Angus was married to Margaret Horne.

JULY.

B. The 15 day Arche Angus and Bessie Dewer had Andrew.
The 22 day John Steinsone and Janet Paycok had George.
That day John Miller and Nans Craik had Alexander.
The 25 day James Logtown and Margaret Brand had John.
That day Henry Deis and Bessie Arnald had Thomas.

M. The 1 day of July Andrew Smith was married to Christian Dewer.
Robert Wastwod to Margaret Henry.
The 8 day John Tod was married to Janet Bankis.
The 22 day William Kirk was married to Bessie Huntair.
David Anderson was married the 29 day to Margaret Mudie.
William Leich to Isobel Horn.

AUGUST.

B. The 12 day William Gay and Janet Andirsone had Isobel.
That day Tom Hendin and Janet Barklay had Isobel.
The 15 day Lowrie Thomson and Ellen Huton had William.
That day Tom Millar and Janet Keir had Lourence.
The 26 day Arche Cuninghame and Mæge Davidson had John.

M. [*None.*]

SEPTEMBER.

B. The 2 day Andrew Spittal and Katherine Logan had Ellen.
That day Charles Wallange and Margaret Durie had Margaret.
That day Andrew Wallet and Isobel Chalmer had William.
That day "Janet Alison presented a man chyld begotten in fornication betwix hir and Johne Blakater, who wes disobedient to the kirk, thairfoir the chyld wes resavit at hir hand, baptized and callit Jhone."
The 9 day James Cois and Bessie Frothringham (*sic*) had Robert.
That day David Schortus and Janet Andersone had Laurence.
That day John Skirling and Effie Morphie had David.
The 16 day James Hendirson and Margaret Meldrum had John.
That day John Phillen and Janet Patirson had James.
That day John Hill and Marion Sworde had Marjory.
That day Andrew Dugall and Christian Clark had John.
That day Wille Bennat and Christian Inglis had Janet (in fornication).
The 19 day Patrick Durie and Elspet Lundy had Janet.

[1] The rest of the entry left blank.

The 23 day John Hodgs and Christian Dewar had George.
That day David Wilzemson and Janet Harrowar had John.
That day John Rae and Margaret Direnoch had Bessie.
The 26 day Andrew Brand and Isobel Cuning had James.
That day John Law and Barbara Stewart had Andrew.
The 30 day Adam Knox and Janet Doncan had Margaret.
That day John Fyff and Mage Red had Janet.
That day Robert Angus and Margaret Rae had George.

M.   The 9 day Andrew Angus was married to Margaret Dewar.
The 23 day Adam Andirson was married to Ellen Sanderis.

OCTOBER.

B.   The 3 day David Warkman and Maige Schortes had George.
That day Robe Peirson and Elspet Huton had Grizel (in fornication).
The 10 day William Young and Bessie Burne had Bessie.
That day Tom Steill and Margaret Inglis had Robert.
That day John Walkar and Margaret Tomson had John.
The 17 day Edward Andirson and Christian Moyes had Kete.
The 21 day Henry Mill and Kæti Harrowar had Kæte.
That day Tom Cuming and Margaret Baird had Isobel.
The 24 day Robert Kellok and Bessie Wallet had James.
The 28 day Andrew Lytill and Kæte Sibbald had Robert (in fornication).
That day Simon Davidson and Ellen Nicoll had Henry.
That day David Hendirson and Kete Andirson had Kete (in fornication).

M.   The 28 day James Cuning was married to Margaret Brown.
David Tod to Maus Dagleich.
William Huton to Janet Smyth.

NOVEMBER.

B.   The 4 day John Millair and Christian Andirson had William.
That day John Walkair and Isobel Blyth had John.
That day Tom Andirson and Ellen Person had Janet.
That day John Watson and Nans Dewer had Janet.
That day Henry Elder and Margaret Craik had Margaret.
The 7 day Alexander Robeson and Elison Spens had Janet.
The 14 day John Bull and Isobel Watson had Margaret.
The 18 day Andrew Jonson and Bessie Liddell had Janet.

M.   The 11 day Andrew Lytill was married to Kæte Sibbet.
The 18 Henry Reid was married to Margaret Tod.
Robert Peirson to Elizabeth Huton.
The 25 day William Andirson was married to Marjory Bellok (? for Kellok).

DECEMBER.

B.   The 5 day Richard Potter and Kæte Walkar had Henry.
That day Robert Man and Margaret Stark had David.
The 16 day John Potter and Isobel Walkar had Andrew.
That day John Steinstown and Marjory Trumbull had Margaret.
That day David Tod and Kete Watson had James (in fornication).
The 19 day Rob Donaldson and Ketie Huntair had Janet.
The 23 day John Watsone and Janet Davidson had Agnes.
The 26 day David Andirson and Ellen Kelt had Alexander.
That day Willie Keir and Isobel Menteith had James.
The 30 day Andrew Moris and Isobel Edison had Thomas.
That day William Jonson and Margaret Stirk had Elizabeth.

M.   The second day David Andirson was married to Janet Martyn.
The 9 day James Meldrum was married to Katherine Cunninghame.
The 23 day Thomas Sanderis was married to Katherine Trumbill.

JANUARY [1571-52].

B. The 9 day William Wostwod and Janet Kellok had Margaret.
That day John Burne and Emmie Cuming had John.
The 16 day William Eson and Margaret Peirson had Margaret.
The 20 day Walter Strong and Ellen Lyall had William.
That day Laurence Tod and Christian Wilzemson had Gyles.
The 23 day James Mubray and Bessie Denistoun had Margaret.
That day Tom Young and Marjory Hunon had John.
That day John Huton and Nans Donald had Isobel.
That day John Lowrie and Margaret Wrycht had Robert.
The 27 day Adam Robertson and Kete Bennet had Margaret.
That day John Mubray and Christian Paton had Margaret.
The 30 day Robert Bennie and Isobel Andirson had John.

M. The 13 day David Hendirson was married to Kate Andirson.

FEBRUARY.

B. The 3 day David Swenton and Annie Ewin had John.
That day John Wright and Bessie Brown had John.
The 13 day Patrick Mudie and Margaret Beny had John.
That day Tom Wostwod and Effie Moyes had Henry.
The 17 day John Wilzemsone and Alison Atkin had Bessie.
That day Tom Elder and Bessie Dewar had Katherine.
That day Tom Logtoun and Janet Philp had Janet.
That day John Mackie and Margaret Jonsone had Janet.
That day James Paicok and Ellen Whyte had Barbara.
That day Charles Walkar and Margaret Reid had Thomas.
That day James Wostwod and Isobel Pacok had Isobel.
The 24 day John Galrig and Janet Weild had Janet.
That day Robert Dik and Masie Michell had Margaret.
That day John Kellok and Ellen Wilson had Isobel.
That day Patrick Keir and Giles Peirsone had Katherine.
That day Laurence Kirk and Margaret Bennat had Ellen.
That day Patrick Lausone and Ellen Wilsone had John.
The 27 day Robert Phillan and Janet Couper had Janet.
That day John Greige and Maig Hutcheon had John.

M. The 17 day Robert Huton was married to Megie Walkar.
That day William Eson was married to Margaret Callender.

MARCH.

B. The 5 day Robert Wilson and Rosina Ramsay had Marjory.
That day William Wilson and Janet Donald had Andrew.
The 16 day John Andirson and Janet Ranald had Thomas.
That day William Makkie and Katherine Steinson had Isobel.
That day John Walwod and Isobel Walker had Thomas.
That day John Thomson and Alison Horn had Isobel.
The 19 day David Cunnand and Ketie Alison had John.
The 23 day William Tomson and Nans Schortus had John.
That day John Wilsone and Christian Bankis had Isobel.
The 26 day [1572] William Blak and Margaret Robertson had Margaret.
That day John Walwod and Christian Dagleich had Adam.
The 30 day David Burn and Katie Durie had James.
That day Patrick Burne and Margaret Steinson had Marjory.
That day John Sanders and Grizel Hodge had George.

M. [*None.*]

APRIL [1572].

B. The 6 day Robert Legat and Janet Anderson had Janet.
That day Robert Doncane and Annie Donaldsone had John.

That day Andrew Hending and Annie Snawdon had James (in fornication).
The 16 day William Cant and Beatrix Hodgs had Beatrix.
That day Richard Steinson and Margaret Wallet had Janet.
That day John Tod and Janet Bankis had Margaret.
That day James Sibbet and Bessie Brown had William (in fornication).
That day Rob Tomson and Isobel Donaldson had Bessie.
That day John Sanderis and Bessie Burne had Andrew.
That day Robe Smyth (cadger) and Isobel Wilson had Thomas.
The 23 day Peter Trumbull and Janet Horn had William.
That day Michael Stewart and Janet Kellok had Andrew.
The 27 day James Dewar and Janet Law had James.
That day Thomas Smyth and Katherine Chalmer had Gyles.
The 30 day George Fleming and Isobel Burne had Robert.
That day Andrew Angus and Margaret Horn had Peter.
That day Andrew Trumbill and Margaret Andirson had Bessie.
That day David Condie, an Edinburgh man, and Giles Murray had Harry.

M. The 6 day John Smith was married to Janet Strong.
The 13 day Robert Lyndsay and Janet Kinross, "after their repentance
maid for mariing with a papist priest 9 yeir befoir, solempnized and
ratified their mariage of newe befoir the kirk."
The 27 day David Peirson was married to Christian Stirk.
Edward Fothringhame to Christian Clune.

MAY.

B. The 4 day Alexander Reid and Janet Pirnie had Katherine.
The 7 day William Cragie and Isobel Andirsone had John.
That day William Wilsone and Christian Hunnone had Ellen.
The 11 day William Robertson and Janet Boswell had Thomas.
That day Thomas Mudie and Christian Harper had John.
That day William Horn and Catherine Dewer had John.
The 14 day James Simson and Isobel Hendirson had Thomas.
The 21 day John Keir and Isobel Dasone had Grizel.
That day James Garvan and Bessie Chrystie had Janet.
The 28 day Cuthbert Wardlaw and Kate Dagleich had Katherine.
That day Nicol Mackie and Katherine Horn had William.
That day John Kellok and Bessie Peirson had Marjory.
That day John Grant and Janet Wat had Janet.

M. The 18 day Allan Couts was married to Isobel Bodwell.

JUNE.

B. The first day Henry Broun and Bessie Dagleich had John.
That day Thomas Dangzeill and Marjory Dagleich had Katherine.
The 4 day Henry Keir "had a man chyld born to him of his wyf Edison
(*sic*) baptizit and callit Andrew."
The 15 day Robe Dagleich and Kate Russall had Maus.
The 22 day William Mikiljon and Bessie Baxter had James.
The 29 day William Wright and Christian Thomson had David.
That day James Knox and Christian Bruice had John.
That day Wille Mar and Bessie Littill had Christian (in fornication).

M. The 8 day William Trumbull was married to Janet Dewar.
Peter Ewin to Malie Dun.

JULY.

B. The 6 day John Chattu and Janet Martiall had Katherine.
The 13 day Robert Schortes and Christian Duglas had Janet.
That day John Brown and Christian Andirsone had James.
That day Alexander Huton and Christian Nicoll had James (in fornication).
The 20 day John Huton and Janet Paton had Robert.

The 23 day Thomas Cumand and Katie Mudie had Bessie.
That day William Morgan and Janet Dewer had William.
The 27 day John Reid and Marjory Simson had Janet.
That day Andrew Angus and Margaret Dewar had Robert.
That day Will Stirk and Kate Mastirtoun had Janet (in fornication).
The 30 day Laurence Smith and Margaret Ædison had Janet.

M.   The 27 day Archie Cokburne was married to Bessie Paycok.

AUGUST.

B.   The 13 day Robert Davidsone and Isobel Bankis had Thomas.
That day William Simson and Katherine Bennat had Robert.
The 20 day William Kirk and Bessie Huntair had Janet.
The 24 day David Andirsone and Nans Mudie had Nans.
That day John Lyndsay and Marion Chalmer (whom afterwards he married) had Nans (in fornication).
That day David Tod and Mause Dagleisch had Kate.
The 31 day David Murray and Janet Wemis had James.
That day Henry Hartsyd (Rossyth) and Marjory Watsone had Alexander.
That day John Wemis and Janet Huton had David (in fornication).

M.   The 10 day John Trumbull was married to Marjory Cuper.
The 17 day Adam Murray was married to Margaret Law.
Thomas Ædison to Isobel Stenhus.
The 24 day John Lyndsay was married to Marion Chalmer.

SEPTEMBER.

B.   The 3 day John Walwod and Grizel Mastirtoun had Thomas.
The 24 day Richard Walker and Janet Kennedie had Janet.
That day Henry Jhonsone and Bessie Bankis had Katherine.
That day Rob Andirson and Janet Walkar had David.

M.   The 21 day John Stenhus was married to Ellen Horn.

OCTOBER.

B.   The 5 day John Bull and Marjory Doncane had Bessie.
The 8 day Patrick Durie and Elizabeth Lundy had David.
That day Andrew Walwod and Marjory Peirson had William.
The 12 day Adam Andirson and Ellen Sanders had Laurence.
That day Andrew Macmuniche and Kete Clarke had Isobel.
That day Alexander Carsan and Ellen Cousing had Andrew.
The 19 day John Andirsone and Ketie Hutone had Margaret.
The 26 day Andrew Smith and Christian Dewer had Janet.
Tat day Alexander Culrois and Isobel Levistoun had Rosina.

M.   [*None.*]

NOVEMBER.

B.   The 2 day David Miche and Kete Sanders had Janet.
The 9 day John Mill and Marion Strageith had Janet.
The 12 day Arche Cuminghame and Isobel Sandis had William.
The 16 day David Andirsone and Janet Martine had Margaret.
The 19 day John Man and Christian Meldrum had John.
The 23 day Sande Wobstar and Janet Gervais had James (in fornication).
That day Andrew Balfour and Margaret Burges had Richard.

M.   The 23 day Adam Brown was married to Katherine Elder.
John Andirson to Christian Oliphant.
Donald Bein to Bessie Smeton.
Michael Trumbill to Janet Person.
John Crumbie to Effie Huton.
John Davidsone to Kete Kirstell.

DECEMBER.

B.   The 7 day John Dagleich and Janet Penman had James.
The 10 day Wille Tomson and Janet Walkar had Bessie.
The 21 day George Sanders and Margaret Durie had Elspet.
That day Andrew Spittall and Kete Logan had William.
The 24 day Alexander Mastirtoun and Kate Broun had John.
The 31 day Robert Angus and Margaret Rae had Robert.
That day John Trumbill and Maige Couper had William.

M.   The 14 day John Andirsone was married to Katherine Bonalay.
Andrew Alison to Ellen Cumming.
The 28 day George Edison was married to Janet Burne.

JANUARY [1572-73].

B.   The 7 day David Sword and Elspet Gibson had Thomas.
That day James Hendirson of Fordell and Jehan Murray had Barbara.
That day Henry Reid and Margaret Tod had William.
The 18 day John Car and Annie Sibbet had James.
The 21 day David Fergusson, minister, and Isobel Durhame had David.
That day William Christe and Isobel Tempilman had Christian.
That day William Andirson and Janet Yonger had Katherine.
That day David Peirson and Christian Stirk had Peter.
The 25 day Mr. John Crysteson and Bessie Keir had William.
The 28 day David Bredie and .   .   .   .   Crafurd had James.

M.   The 25 day Mark Burgan was married to Janet Currour.

FEBRUARY.

B.   The one day Wille Mar and Janet Car had John (in fornication).
The 8 day James Wostwod and Mans Paycok had Thomas.
That day William Steinson and Marjory Sibbet had David.
The 15 day John Patirsone and Begis Huchie had twins, Janet and Kate.
That day Robert Peirsone and Janet Brown had Janet.
That day John Stenhus and Margaret Duglas had John.
That day Michael Singour and Nans Young had Janet in fornication .
The 22 day Andrew Riche and Effie Cuike had David.
The 25 day Gilbert Kennedy and Margaret Bredie had James.

M. The 1 day Robert Dagleich was married to Janet Harper.
Robert Mudie to Katherine Wilson.
The 8 day James Clerk was married to Margaret Foster.

MARCH.

B.   The 1 day Nicol Michelson and Janet Norwall had Adam.
The 4 day William Keir and Christian Bull had John.
The 11 day William Burne and Janet Broun had . . .
The 15 day Allan Coutis, elder, and Isobel Bodwell had Bessie.
That day William Duglas and Janet Tennand had Janet
That day Laurence Schortus and Katie Mill had Eline.
That day John Browne and Janet Walkar had Margaret.
The 18 day Allan Coutis, younger, and Helen Balfour had Grizel.
The 22 day Robert Lindsay and Janet Kinross had Normand.
The 29 day [1573] George Nasmith and Isobel Ferguson had Harie.
That day John Mudie and Marjory Burne had Andrew.

M.   [*None.*]

APRIL [1573].

B   The 5 day David Pitcarne and Elizabeth (Elzbet) Ogilvy had John.
That day George Bodwell and Nans Sandilands had Katherine.

The 12 day John Watson and Nans Dewer had Nans.
That day John Robertson and Marjory Steinson had Girsell.
That day John Montcreiff and Bessie *sic* had Margaret.
The 19 day William Gay and Janet Andirson had Marjory.
That day William Horn and Janet Philp had Allan.
The 22 day William Schortes and Barbara Duglas had Meg.

M. The 12 day Robert Trumbill was married to Janet Sanders.

MAY.

B. The 6 day James Keir and Nans Broun had Ellen.
The 17 day Robert Straqwhin and Isobel Wakman had George.
That day Adam Sanders and Isobel Cunninghame had George.
The 20 day John Stirk and Margaret Henry had Elzbeth.
The 31 day John Huton and Mage Straqwhin had Robert (in adultery).

M. The 10 day John Steill was married to Christian Parke.
The 17 day Andrew Chrystie was married to Margaret Steward.
The 24 day David Fin was married to Besse Harrowair.
James Wilson to Margaret Kedy.
John Wilson to Elison Bull.
William Bryson to Bessie Dunino.
The 31 day Nicol Hart was married to Besse Hartsyd.

JUNE.

B. The 3 day Michell Horne and Christian Broun had David.
The 7 day John Gannall and Bessie Donaldsone had Andrew.
The 10 day John Dewar and Kcte Angus had Margaret.
The 14 day Edward Fothringhame and Christian Clune had Janet.
The 17 day John Crichtoun and Bessie Mutray had James.
The 21 day John Steinson and Marjory Trumbill had Janet.

M. The 28 day John Sanders was married to Isobel Hendirson.
And James Car was married to Ellen Sanderis.

JULY.

B. The 1 day Andrew Angus and Margaret Dewar had Isobel.
The 8 day John Smyth and Janet Moris had James.
The 12 day John Law and Barbara Stewart had Janet.
That day John Stenhus and Ellen Horne had Robert.
That day Andrew Angus and Margaret Dewer had Margaret.
The 15 day David Fergus and Margaret Trumbill had Margaret.
The 19 day John Skirling and Effie Morphie had Marjory.
The 22 day James Whyt and Nans Inglis had John.
The 26 day Robert Duglas and Beatrix Edisone had David.

M. The 12 day Duncan Mories was married to Bessie Cuninghame.
William Miller to Isobel Cunninghame.
Mark Donat to Margaret Lourie.
The 19 day George Gray ratified his marriage with Margaret Gat unlawfully
done before after they had made their public repentance.
The 26 day Andrew Swenton was married to Janet Normond.

AUGUST.

B. The 19 day John Crombie and Effie Huton had Ellen.
That day Thomas Sanderis and Katherine Trumbull had Janet.
The 23 day Willie Walkar and Bessie Trumbull had Janet.
That day Andrew Dick and Margaret Scot had Christian.
The 26 day James Bwist and Janet Huton had William.
The 30 day John Gauhig and Janet Weild had John.
That day Alexander Cuninghame and Margaret Kemp had James.

M. The 9 day Robert Andirson was married to Christian Hendirson.

SEPTEMBER.

B. The 2 day John Steill and Christian Parke had Marjory (begotten before the marriage).
The 6 day David Paicok and Isobel Cuninghame had John.
The 9 day William Trumbill and Janet Dewair had Janet.
The 20 day William Andirsone and Janet Mudie had Margaret.
That day William Horne and Katherine Dewer had Janet.
That day John Davidsone and Katherine Kustell had Laurence.
The 30 day George Gray and Margaret Galt had Christian.
That day Thomas Young and Marjory Hunnon had John.

M. The 20 day David Horne was married to Bessie Stewart.

OCTOBER.

B. The 4 day John Phillen and Janet Patersone had Marjory.
That day Wille Elder and Christian Morgan had twins, Patrick and Janet (in fornication).
The 7 day Pete Galt and Bessie Edison had Margaret.
The 11 day Andrew Littill (deceased) and Kate Sibald had Alexander.
That day John Warkman and Bessie Atkin had Bessie.
That day John Inglis and Janet Atkin had Isobel.
That day Donald Bein and Bessie Smeton had Bessie.
That day Geordie Edison and Janet Burne had John.
The 18 day Andrew Brand and Isobel Cumming had Andrew.
The 25 day James Cumming and Margaret Broun had Eunnie.

M. [*None.*]

NOVEMBER.

B. The 1 day Gilbert Colzear and Ellen Sanders had Bessie.
That day Donald Sandis and Kate Bell had Adam (in fornication).
The 4 day John Dryisdaill and Margaret Duglas had James.
That day Rob Patrik and Marion Andirson had twins, George and Nans.
That day Richard Potter and Katie Walkar had Isobel.
The 8 day John Dagleich and Kete Loudiane had Thomas (begotten in incestuous adultery).
The 18 day James Harde and Christian Clune had William.
The 25 day Robert Dewar and Catherine Law had John.
That day David Wilzemson and Janet Harrowar had James.
The 29 day John Elder and Effie Smeton had twins, Henry and Bessie.

M. The 15 day Troyelus Lausone was married to Elspet Traill.
The 23 day John Litiljone was married to Bessie Chryste.
The 29 day John Jameson was married to Isobel Winter.

DECEMBER.

B. The 2 day John Reid and Janet Tomson had Margaret.
The 6 day David Hendirsone and Ketie Anderson had James.
The 9 day William Mikiljone and Bessie Baxter had Andrew.
The 13 day Peter Ewin and Mahe Dun had Allan.
That day John Couper and Gillis Wilson had Janet.
That day Simon Davidsone and Ellen Nicoll had Janet.
The 27 day John Tod and Janet Banks had Thomas.
The 30 day Laurence Kirk and Margaret Bennat had Margaret.
That day William Wright and Christian Tomson had Isobel.

M. The 6 day David Dewer was married to Bessie Peirson.
David Smeton to Isobel Cunninghame.
The 13 day Patrick Harper was married to Katherine Bennat
The 27 day John Broun was married to Bessie Wilsoun.

JANUARY [1573-4].

B. The 3 day Arche Angus and Bessie Dewer had Janet.
That day John Rae and Margaret Direnoch had Thomas.
That day Andrew Currour and Janet Piers had Marjory.
That day John Paton and Christian Nicoll had Andrew.
The 10 day John Wemis of Pittincreiff and Girsell Myrton had Janet.
That day Wille Andirsone and Bessie Hodge had Robert.
The 17 day Arche Cokburne and Janet Paycok had Charles.
That day David Bull and Meg Currie had Maus.
The 31 day Rob Kid and Meg Reddie had Thomas.
That day Rob Andirsone and Nans Millair had Robert.
That day John Kellok and Janet Durie had James.

M. The 3 day James Sibbet was married to Elspet Stevin.
The 17 day Archibald Blakwod was married to Bessie Stalkar.

FEBRUARY.

B. The 7 day John Fyffe and Maige Reid had Christian.
That day Patrick Lawsone and Ellen Wilson had Andrew.
That day Archie Cunninghame and Margaret Davidsone had James (in fornication).
The 14 day Thomas Andirsone and Ellen Peirsone had Margaret.
That day James Sibbet and Janet Davidsone had David (in fornication).
That day Henry Browne and Bessie Dagleich had Masie.
The 17 day Robert Kellok and Bessie Walwood had David.
That day William Andirsone and Janet Yonger had Thomas.
That day Andrew Peirsoune and Christian Laudiane had Laurence.
The 21 day Andrew Smith and Christian Dewar had John.
That day William Burne and Marjory Logtoun had Marjory.
That day John Andirsoun and Katie Banalay had Marjory.
That day William Esone and Margaret Callender had William.
That day William Roxburgh and Janet Andirsoun had Bessie.
The 24 day James Sibbet and Bessie Broune had Elizabeth (in fornication).

M. The 14 day Andrew Baxter was married to Elizabeth Durie.
Andrew Mudie to Isobel Logtoun.

MARCH.

B. The 3 day David Bredie and Elizabeth Crafurd had Grizel.
That day Robert Paton and Janet Dagleich had Robert.
That day Robert Wilson and Rosina Ramsay had Ellen.
That day Edward Anderson and Christian Moyes had Grizel.
The 21 day Petie Burne and Margaret Steinson had David.
That day James Murray and Marion Preston had Effie.
That day John Wright and Bessie Brown had Ellen.
That day John Murie and Ketie Smeton had William.
That day Nicoll Hart and Bessie Hartsyd had Robert.
The 24 day Robert Phillane and Janet Couper had John.
The 28 day [1574] William Keir and Annabell Lourie had Andrew.
That day William Utterlie and Kete Pugzeon had Margaret. [Baith (Beath) *in margin.*]

M. [*None.*]

APRIL [1574].

B. The 7 day Richard Walkar and Janet Kennedy had Richard.
That day John Wilson and Alison Bull had Margaret.
The 11 day David Andirson and Margaret Mudie had Margaret.
The 18 day Allan Coutis, elder, and Isobel Bodwell had Andrew.
That day John Hodgs and Christian Dewar had Christian.
That day Thomas Steill and Margaret Inglis had David.

That day David Fyff and Annie Hodgs had Marjory.
That day Annie Watson and Robert Wilson had Janet (in fornication).
The 28 day David Esone and Annie Wardlaw had William.

M.   The 11 day Peter Chrysteson was married to Nans Andirsone.
The 25 day Patrick Blakater of Mylnhills was married to Bessie Burne.
That day Andrew Dik was married to Janet Stirling.

MAY.

B.   The 2 day George Bodwell and Nans Sandelands had Nicolas.
That day Charles Walkar and Margaret Reid had Katherine.
The 9 day James Reddie and Christian Angus had John (in fornication).
The 16 day John Burne and Emmie Cuming had Laurence.
The 19 day Robert Lyndsay and Janet Kinross had Christian.
That day John Huton and Nans Donald had Nans.
That day David Fergusson, minister, and Isobel Durham had John.
The 23 day Duncan Moris and Bessie Cunninghame had Isobel.
That day David Bein and Christian Murdo had Katherine.
The 30 day James Dewar and Janet Law had Andrew.
That day Harry Millair and Christian Strageith had Laurence (in fornication).

M.   The 30 day James Sibbet was married to Margaret Logtoun.

JUNE.

B.   The 6 day John Potter, elder, and Ketie Wilson had David.
The 13 day Alexander Scotland and Margaret Hendirsone had William.
That day William Jonsone and Mege Stirk had Andrew.
The 20 of June Thomas Smyth and Ketie Chalmer had Ketie.
The 30 day John Burn, minister at Inverkeithing, and Bessie Turis had
Isobel.
That day Allan Coutis, younger, and Ellen Balfour had Ellen.

M.   That day (prob. 6th) William Campbell was married to Marjory Watson.
Henry Primrois to Margaret Reidoch.
The 13 day John Dewer was married to Janet Chryste.
Henry Broun to Katherine Henrie.
John Haddan to Isobel Walkar.
The 20 day John Kellok was married to Christian Lychtman.
Arche Peirson to Effie Atkin.

JULY.

B.   The 11 day Henry Sempill and Margaret Goddie had David.
The 14 day John Lourie and Margaret Wrycht had Nans.
The 23 day Andrew Chryste and Margaret Stewart had Gilbert.
The 25 day John Walkar and Margaret Thomsone had David.
That day James Immerie and Alison Paicok had Thomas.
The 28 day Robert Lun and Janet Law had John.

M.   The 11 day Thomas Huton was married to Janet Rae.
Charles Palmair to Bessie Galt.

AUGUST.

B.   The 1 day Robert Andirsone and Christian Wobster had John.
The 4 day Patrick Durie and Elizabeth Lundyn had Patrick.
That day John Chryste and Marjory Dagleich had Alison.
That day George Fleming and Isobel Burne had Elspet.
The 15 day James Burne and Janet Mackie had Patrick.
That day James Atkin and Bessie Malcolme had James.
That day Mark Donald and Margaret Laurie had Ellen.
The 18 day Thomas Logtoun and Janet Philp had George.
The 22 day John Lyndsay and Marjory Chalmer had William.

M. The 8 day Andrew Potter was married to Kete Harrowar.
William Andirson to Bessie Mill.
William Dik to Janet Huton.

SEPTEMBER.

B. [*None.*]

M. The 19 day John Huton was married to Annie Mathesoun.

OCTOBER.

B. The 3 day Henry Mill and Katie Harrowair had Henry.
The 10 day Edward Turnour and Margaret Beveraige had James.
The 17 day David Smeton and Isobel Cunningham had John.
That day Thomas Sanders and Katherine Trumbull had Katherine.
The 24 day John Andirsoone and Janet Ranald had John.
That day Patrick Chalmeris and Janet Curre had Margaret.
That day William Robertsone and Janet Boswell had Eupham.
The 31 day Arche Blaickwood and Bessie Stalker had John.
That day James Paycok and Ellen Whyt had John.

M. The 10 day Adam Currie was married to Margaret Edison.
Andrew Hall to Janet Hendirsoun.

NOVEMBER.

B. The 14 day George Smith and Janet Angus had Marjory.
The 17 day Andrew Spittell and Kate Logane had twins, George and **Patrick**.
The 21 day Wille Wilsoun and Janet Donald had John.
The 24 day Patrick Makarten and Christian Tailzeor had Christian.
The 28 day John Sprewlle and Janet Kanill (? Kavill *or* Karrill) had John.

M. The 28 day Robert Cusing was married to Elison Peirson.

DECEMBER.

B. The 12 day Henry Keir and Marjory Ædisone had Margaret.
That day William Kirk and Bessie Huntair had Isobel.
That day Wille Davidsone and Christian Clune had William (in fornication).
The 15 day Charles Wallange and Margaret Durie had Bessie.
The 19 day John Litiljone and Bessie Chryste had Laurence.
The 26 day Andrew Brand and Isobel Cummyng had Adam.
That day James Atkin and Bessie Malcolme had James.

M. The 12 day Robert Bruis was married to Christian Steinson.

JANUARY [1574-75].

B. The 2 day Richard Hynd and Christian Michie had Bessie.
That day Patrick Mudie and Maige Bennie had Marjory.
The 5 day Andrew Angus and Margaret Horn had Bessie.
The 9 day John Wilson and Christian Banks had Marjory.
That day Robert Mudie and Katie Wilsone had John.
That day Robert Gray and Annie Knox had John. [Beith *in margin*.
The 12 day Archie Cuninghame and Isobel Sandis had James.
That day Cuthbert Wardlaw and Ketie Dagleich had Marjory.
The 16 day Robert Angus and Mage Rae had William.
The 23 day David Andirsone and Janet Martyne had James.

M. The 2 day William Baxter was married to Christian Anderson.
The 9 day Gilbert Colzear was married to Katherine Cryste.
George Trumbill to Maus Andirson.
Laurence Steinson to Bessie Meldrum.
The 16 day James Gilqwham was married to Malie Rae.

FEBRUARY.

B. The 2 day Laurence Walwod and Bessie Andirsoun had Barbara.
That day Wille Dewer and Maggie Cuninghame had Ellen (in fornication).
The 6 day William Young and Bessie Burne had Henry.
That day Albert Bruise and Elspet Wright had Janet.
The 9 day Peter Trumbill and Janet Horne had Ellen.
The 16 day David Dewer and Bessie Peirson had James.
The 20 day David Peirson, deceased, and Christian Stirk had Katherine.

M. The 6 day John Mutray was married to Janet Tomsone.
That day Andrew Inglis was married to Marjory Michell.
The 13 day Patrick Fentone was married to Bessie Durie.

MARCH.

B. The 6 day Thomas Damgzell and Marjory Dagleich had Wille.
That day William Mudie and Marjory Burne had William.
That day Henry Falzeour and Margaret Craik had Janet.
That day Edward Fothringhame and Christian Clun had Margaret.
The 20 day John Hadden and Isobel Walkar had Robert.
That day John Brown and Isobel Wilson had Andrew.
The 23 day Andrew Trumbill and Margaret Andirsone had Robert.
That day William Craigie and Isobel Andirson had Katherine.

M. The 6 day Robert Chalmer, parishioner of Halirudhus, was married to
Janet Edison.

APRIL [1575].

B. The 6 day Andrew Alisoun and Ellen Cuming had Janet.
That day William Christy and Isobel Tempilman had William.
The 10 day Walter Strange and Ellen Lyall had Andrew.
The 13 day Thomas Davidsone and Janet Keir had William.
That day Alexander Mastertoun and Katherine Broun had Christian.
That day William Simsone and Katherine Bennat had Janet.
The 17 day John Robertsone and Marjory Steinsone had Margaret.
That day Allan Coutis, elder, and Isobel Bedwell had John.
The 20 day Thomas Wostwod and Effie Moyes had William.
That day James Meldrum and Katherine Cuninghame had Thomas.
The 24 day John Dagleich and Janet Penman had John.
That day Adam Broun, younger, and Katherine Elder had Adam.
That day Wille Durie and Christian Wright had Janet (in fornication).

M. The 10 day Henry Peirsone was married to Marjory Dewer.
The 17 day John Steinson, younger, was married to Margaret Andirson.

MAY.

B. The 1 day Tom Hendin and Janet Barcklay had David.
That day William Miller and Isobel Cuninghame had William.
The 4 day Thomas Elder and Bessie Dewar had Barbara.
The 6 day James Sibbet and Margaret Logtoun had Henry.
The 8 day John Alisoun and Janet Cim had Margaret.
The 18 day John Wemis of Pittincreiff and Grizel Myrtoun had James.
The 22 day Henrie Durie and Christian Brand had Margaret (in fornication).

M. The 8 day Thomas Couper was married to Margaret Mutray.
The 15 day Arche Cuninghame was married to Janet Dagleich.
The 29 day Matthew Withert (Wicheit?) was married to Margaret Steinson.

JUNE.

B. The 8 day William Blak and Margaret Robertsone had Christian.
The 15 day John Watson and Nans Dewer had Margaret.

The 22 day Thomas Kellok and Christian Martiall had Alexander.[1]
That day John Trumbill and Maige Couper had Margaret.

M. The 5 day Robert Huton was married to Isobel Tomson.
That day William Spittell was married to Christian Nicoll.
The 12 day John Colzear was married to Elizabeth Direnoch.

JULY.

B. The 3 day George Sanderis and Margaret Durie had Margaret.
The 20 day William Mikiljone and Bessie Baxter had Helen.
The 22 day Patrick Durie and Elizabeth Lyndie had Arche.
The 24 day Andrew Clark and Isobel Uterlie had Grizell.
That day Michael Stewart and Janet Kellok had Margaret.
The 27 day John Andirson and Katie Huton had Janet.
That day Georde Nasmyth and Isobel Fergusone had twins, Elspet and Nans.
That day Patrick Keir and Gielis Peirson had twins, Girsell and Marjory.

M. The 3 day John Macklarain was married to Violet Peirsone.
The 24 day William Pratus was married to Margaret Carnie.
The 31 day Andrew Hume was married to Janet Schortus.

AUGUST.

B. The 3 day Michael Horne and Christian Young had Thomas.
That day Pete Blakater and Bessie Davidsone had Gilbert.
The 14 day William Horne and Kete Dewer had Mase.
The 21 day William Schortes and Janet Broun had Christian.

M. The 14 day of August Thomas Kellok was married to Annabell Hendirsone.
The 28 day John Craich was married to Christian Balfour.

SEPTEMBER.

B. The 4 day James Garvan and Bessie Chrystie had Thomas.
That day Robert Bennie and Isobel Andirsone had Isobel.
The 18 day Henry Primrose and Margaret Rydoch had Effie.
That day Henry Dicke and Janet Stirling had John.
That day John Huton and Annie Donaldsone had James.
The 28 day John Crichtoun and Bessie Mutray had Thomas.
That day Adam Currie and Margaret Edison had Janet.

M. The 11 day John Tomsone was married to Elizabeth Wilzemson.
The 25 day Tom Sibbet was married to Nans Wilsone.

OCTOBER.

B. The 2 Alexander Martiall and Gelis Kellok had Kate.
The 5 day John Bull and Marjory Doncan had Christian.
The 16 day Robert Davidsone and Isobel Bankis had Janet.
That day Lourie Bonalay and Helen Anderson had William.
The 23 day James Harrowar and Mage Blyth had Patrick.
The 30 day David Pacok and Isobel Cunningham had George.

M. The 2 day William Eson was married to Alison Wright
The 16 day Gavin Crychtoun was married to Maus Couper.
The 30 day Archibald Mallwill was married to Janet Prestoun.
Thomas Alisone to Christian Dagleich.

NOVEMBER.

B. The 2 day Thomas Huton and Kete Bevaraige had Bessie.
The 6 day John Cunninghame and Keti Walwod had Elspet.
The 9 day James Sibbet and Elspet Stevin had Janet.

[1] " Baith."

That day John Blacater and Mage Murray had Janet (in fornication).
That day John Jousie and Maggie Stenhus had James (in fornication).
The 13 day David Broun and Christian Young had James.
The 20 day John Thomsone and Alisone Horne had John.
The 23 day Thomas Sanders and Kate Gothray had William.
The 27 day William Macky and Margaret Steinson had Margaret.
That day John Andirsone and Ketie Bonalay had Margaret.
The 30 day William Graye and Janet Andirsone had John.
That day James Bwist and Janet Huton had James.

M.   The 6 day Robert Ramsay was married to Christian Bonalay.
The 20 day John Tomson was married to Christian Walwod.
The 27 day John Wilsone was married to Kate Moris.

DECEMBER.

B.   The 4 day James Logtoun and Magge Brand had James.
That day John Tod and Bessie Hardie had Thomas (in fornication).
The 7 day William Keir and Isobel Monthecht (Monteith) had Kete.
That day Thomas Huton and Marion Brown had Janet.

M.   [*None.*]

JANUARY [1575-76].

B.   The 1 day Allan Coutis, younger, and Helen Balfour had Archibald.
That day John Lourie and Margaret Wright had David.
That day Harry Peirsone and Marjory Dewer had Patrick.
That day Adam Sanderis and Elspet Cuninghame had William.
That day Robert Cusing and Alison Peirsone had Nans.
The 8 day Robert Peirsone and Janet Brown had Ellen.
The 15 day John Brown and Janet Bell had John.
The 22 day John Sanders and Bessie Burne had John.

M.   The 1 day Mr. William Coke was married to Agnes Beton.
The 8 day Andrew Moris was married to Bessie Littill.
Robert Wilsone to Janet Henrisone.
The 15 day William Dewer was married to Janet Steinsone.
The 22 day Robert Ramsay was married to Christian Fyff.
The 29 day John Blakater of Milhills was married to Janet Law.

FEBRUARY.

B.   The 5 day William Horne and Janet Philp had John.
That day Matthew Weitheid and Margaret Steinson had John.
The 8 day Gilbert Kennedy and Margaret Bredie had David.
That day Tom Donald and Margaret Montheith had Philip (in fornication).
The 12 day John Tod and Janet Banks had Katherine.
That day David Fyffe and Annie Hodgs had Thomas.
That day John Cassillaw and Janet Stewin had Maus.
The 15 day David Fergussone, minister, and Isobel Durhame had Grizel.
That day Wille Wilsone and Janet Donald had Alexander.
The 22 day David Warkman and Marjory Schortes had Isobel.
The 26 day William Angus and Margaret Dewer had Archibald.
That day William Aesone and Margaret Callendar had John.
That day Wille Walkar and Bessie Trumbill had Laurence.

M.   The 12 day William Wilsone was married to Annie Schortes.
The 19 day John Andirsone was married to Margaret Edisone.

MARCH.

B.   The 4 day George Trumbill and Maus Andirson had Andrew.
" The 7 day Alexander Murray (styled of Abirleidnoch) had a man chyld
borne to him of his wyff, being heir for the tyme, Isobell Ridoch, baptized and callit Wilziame."

D

The 11 day Patrick Galt and Bessie Aedisone had Agnes.
That day Geordi Edisone and Bessie Burne had Ketie.
The 28 day [1576] John Car and Annie Sibbet had Nans.

APRIL [1576].

B.   The 4 day James Cuming and Margaret Brown had Bessie.
The 8 day John Crummie and Effie Huton had Nans.
The 15 day John Kellok and Janet Durie had John.
That day Arche Peirsone and Effie Atkin had William.
The 22 Rob Andirson and Janet Walkar had Robert.
The 25 day Wille Pratus and Margaret Carnie had John.

M.   The 29 day James Dewer was married to Margaret Gib.

MAY.

B.   The 6 day James Peirsone and Nans Philp had Isobel.
That day William Schortes and Barbara Douglas had William.
The 9 day John Colzear, the piper, and Elspet Direnoch had Marion.
The 20 day David Wilzemson and Janet Harrowair had Andrew.
That day Robert Kellok and Marjory Walwod had Ellen.
The 23 day David Sibbet, deceased, and Mage Craik had Marjory (in
    fornication).
The 27 day William Morgain and Janet Dewer had Ellen.
That day John Lawe and Barbara Stewart had Margaret.

M.   The 6 day William Bonalay was married to Janet Peirsone.

JUNE.

B.   The 3 day Robert Andirsone and Christian Henderson had Bessie.
That day Andrew Chryste and Margaret Stewart had David.
That day Richard Walkar and Janet Kennedy had Thomas. .
The 20 day John Stirk and Margaret Henry had Edward.
The 24 day David Pitcairne and Janet Hutcheon had Margaret (in
    fornication).
The 27 day George Bodwell and Nans Sandilandis had Margaret.

M.   The 10 day George Wardlaw was married to Nans Michell.
Henry Peirson to Kete Edison.
The 24 day John Gardiner was married to Ketie Sibbet.

JULY.

B.   The 4 day Patrick Durie and Elizabeth Lundy had Allan.
The 11 day John Paton and Ellen Nicoll had Janet.
That day John Urie and Janet Brown had Gelis.
That day Thomas Kellok and Annabell Hendirson had Janet.
That day Thomas Mudie and Christian Harper had Bessie.
The 18 day John Steinson and Margaret Andirson had John.
The 25 day John Burn, minister in Inverkeithing, and Bessie Turis had
    Rachel.
The 28 day William Burne and Janet Brown had twins, Harry and . . . .
The 29 day John Burne and Emmie Cumming had Janet.
That day Andrew Tempilman and Janet Cuming had James.

M.   The 1 day James Tod was married to Marion Meldrum.
The 8 day John Bellok was married to Christian Murie.
Jerome Bad to Kete Meldrum.
The 22 day William Cumberie was married to Christian Phillip.
William Wilson to Janet Henry.
The 29 day William Andirson was married to Janet Donaldsone.
That day Robert Doncane was married to Janet Peirson.

AUGUST.

B. The 5 day Henry Durie and Margaret Macbeth had George.
That day David Horne and Bessie Stewart had Bessie.
That day John Wilson and Kete Moris had James.
The 8 day James Sibbet and Margaret Logtoun had Janet.
The 12 day Robert Dewar and Kate Law had James.
That day Alexander Carsan and Ellen Cusyng had Christian.
That day James Hutson and Janet Bonalay had Barbara.
The 19 Andrew Mores and Bessie Litill had Margaret.
That day James Hardy and Marion Clune had Nans.
The 26 day Arche Cunninghame and Janet Dagleich had Ellen.
The 29 day Tom Sibbet and Annie Wilson had Marjory.

M. [*None.*]

SEPTEMBER.

B. The 2 day George Hakheid of Pithrren and Isobel Hepburne had Robert.
That day Partrick Lawsone and Ellen Wilsone had Patrick.
The 9 day John Warkman and Bessie Aitkin had Robert.
The 16 day John Walkar and Margaret Tomson had Riche.
That day William Flukair and Bessie Hendirsone had John. [Beith *in margin.*]
That day Henry Brown and Bessie Dagleich had Janet.
The 19 day Robert Paton and Janet Dagleich had Christian.
The 23 day Henry Reid and Margaret Tod had William.
That day David Miche and Kete Sanders had Isobel.
The 30 day Andrew Angus and Bessie Inglis had Bessie.

M. The 2 day David Stenhus was married to Janet Cunninghame.

OCTOBER.

B. The 7 day William Horne and Kate Dewer had Kate.
The 10 day George Fleming and Isobel Burne had William.
The 14 day Laurence Steinvesone (*sic*) and Bessie Meldrum had Kete.
The 21 day Thomas Jamesone and Elizabeth Mubray had Mage (in fornication).
The 31 day Robert Huton and Isobel Tomson had Ellen.

M. The 21 day James Cutbert was married to Bessie Nicoll.

NOVEMBER.

B. The 4 day John Wemis of Pittincreiff and Grizel Myrtoun had Robert.
That day Laurence Kirk and Margaret Bennait had Christian.
The 7 day Peter Blakwood and Marjory Cuming had Arche.
That day John Steill and Christian Parkie had John.
The 11 day Andrew Brand and Isobel Cuming had David.
That day Simon Davidsone and Ellen Nicoll had Thomas.
That day George Bull and Christian Wallais had Mage.
That day John Wilsone and Elison Bull had Marjory.
That day Donald Bane and Bessie Smeton had Kete.
The 18 day William Uterlie and Margaret Pudzeon had Thomas.
That day David Andirsone and Margaret Mudie had Maus.
The 21 day John Smyth and Janet Spittall had Pete.
The 25 day Andrew Wallet and Isobel Chalmer had Isobel.

M. [*None.*]

DECEMBER.

B. The 2 day Robert Lun and Janet Law had James.
The 9 day John Ryoch and Bessie Keir had Donald (in fornication).

That day Alexander Wilsone *alias* Culrois and Isobel Levingtoun had David
That day Wille Michell and Ellen Lawsone had James (in fornication).
The 12 day Mark Donald and Margaret Lowrie had Isobel.
The 16 day Charles Wallange, deceased, and Margaret Durie had Charles.
That day Andrew Jonsone and Bessie Liddaill had Ellen.
The 19 day Robert Wilsone, merchant, and Rosina Ramsay had Margaret
That day Robert Wilsone and Janet Hendirsone had Nans.
The 26 day William Wright and Christian Thomsone had Thomas.
The 30 day Tom Cunnand and Kate Mudie had Peter.

M.   The 2 day William Mutray was married to Marjory Fin.
The 16 day John Makewn was married to Bessie Andirson.
The 30 day James Mochrie was married to Margaret Rodger.
That day William Michell was married to Bessie Brown.

JANUARY [1576-77].

B.   The 2 day Thomas Millair *alias* Davidsone and Janet Keir had Marion.
The 6 day Andrew Alison and Ellen Cuming had Thomas.
That day John Fyff and Keit Reid had Keit.
The 13 day John Thomsone and Christian Wallet had Janet.
That day John Ranald and Janet Proves had John (in fornication).
The 16 day John Andirsone, deceased, and Katie Huton had John.
The 20 day John Gallrik and Janet Weild had John.
That day Thomas Dangzeill and Marjory Dagleich had Nans.
The 27 day John Millair and Nans Oraik had John.

M.   The 6 day Henry Dick was married to Ellen Duglas.
The 20 day Robert Car was married to Effie Abircrombie.
The 27 day Patrick Rowan was married to Gelis Wilson.

FEBRUARY.

B.   The 3 day John Stenhus and Margaret Douglas had Andrew.
That day John Andirsone and Janet Ranald had Margaret
The 10 day James Dewar and Janet Law had Margaret.
That day John Davidsone and Katie Kirstell had Thomas.
The 13 day Adam Robertsone and Keit Bennat had Adam.
The 17 day John Murie and Kate Smeton had Christian.

M.   The 3 day James Boyd was married to Christian Johnston.
The 10 day Robert Simson was married to Marion Smith.
The 17 day Robert Moris was married to Nans Cim.
The 24 day John Smeton was married to Margaret Durye.

MARCH.

B.   The 3 day Adam Reid and Ellen Hwat had George (in fornication).
The 10 day John Reid and Janet Thomson had William.
That day Robert Phillen (parishioner in Beath) and Bessie Walwod **had**
Robert.
That day Gilbert Colzear and Keit Crystie had Janet.
That day William Robertson and Janet Bosswell had Grizel.
That day Wille Thomsone and Janet Mudie had James.
The 13 day William Dewar and Janet Stinsone had Isobel.
The 17 day Andrew Inglis and Maige Michell had Ellen.
That day David Paycok and Isobel Cunninghame had Janet.
That day Henry Peirsone and Keite Edisone had Robert.
That day Edward Andirsone and Janet Dick had Janet.
That day David Hendirsone and Keit Andirsone had Janet.
That day John Dewer and Janet Chrystie had James.
The 20 day John Steinsone and Marjory Trumbill had Robert.
The 24 day Robert Straqwhin and Isobel Warkman had Adam.
That day James Wostwood and Maus Paycok had Bessie.

The 31 day [1577] Duncan Moris and Bessie Cunninghame had Janet.
That day Peter Chrysteson and Nans Andirson had Thomas.

M. [*None*].

APRIL [1577].

B. The 3 day James Garvan and Bessie Chryste had Grizel.
The 7 day Albert Brwis and Bessie Wright had Bessie.
The 10 day Gilcham (*sic*) and Malie Rae had John.
The 17 day David Smeton and Isobel Cunninghame had Janet.
That day Andrew Dewar and Marjory Smeton had twins, Margaret and Nans (in fornication).

M. The 28 day Henry Crawfurd was married to Margaret Prestoun.

MAY.

B. The 5 day Allan Coutis, younger, and Ellen Balfour had George.
That day Adam Whyt and Bessie Landellis had Robert.
The 8 day George Lundyn and Kete Loch had James.
That day William Kirk and Bessie Huntair had Margaret.
That day Christian Angus "had a woman chyld begottin in fornication of David Leslie (obstinat) baptized and called Margaret."
The 19 day William Wilson in Miltoungrein and Christian Hunnon had Isobel.
The 26 day Robert Lyndsay and Janet Kinross had Robert.
That day William Aeson and Alison Wight had Ellen.

M. The 19 day David Henryson was married to Janet Atkin.
That day James Burt was married to Janet Blair.
The 26 day David Trail was married to Alison Doncane.

JUNE.

B. The second day Thomas Couper and Margaret Mutray had Janet.
That day John Hodgs and Christian Dewer had Mage.
The 5 day William Cummerie and Christian Phillip had Janet.
That day Andrew Andersone and Janet Dagleich had Janet (in fornication).
The 21 day William Mikiljon and Bessie Baxter had Marjory.
The 23 day William Keir and Christian Bull had Margaret.
That day Adam Currie and Margaret Edison had David.
That day William Kent, younger, and Effie Miller had Thomas (in fornication).
The 26 day David Dewer and Bessie Peirson had John.
The 30 day Laurence Tod and Christian Williamson had Janet.
That day James Smyth and Kete Paycok had Isobel.
That day Robert Gray and Nans Knox had Bessie.

M. The 24 day George Colzear was married to Janet Bull.
That day Thomas Sword was married to Katherine Burne.
That day David Piers was married to Isobel Immerie.

JULY.

B. The 14 day James Riche and Margaret Andirsone had Janet.
The 24 day George Gray and Margaret Galt had Patrick.
The 28 day George Halkheid and Isobel Hepburn had Patrick. [Pitfirren *in margin.*]
That day John Phillen and Janet Lauson, his harlot, had Marjory (in fornication).

M. [*None*].

AUGUST.

B. The 4 day William Martiall and Ellen Alexander had Margaret.

The 7 day Alexander Mastirtoun and Christian Brown had Thomas.
The 11 day Patrick Makartain and Christian Tailzour had Grizel.
That day David Andirson and Janet Martin had David.
The 14 day John Robertson and Marjory Steinson had Marjory.
The 18 day George Bodwell and Nans Sandilands had James.
That day William Andirsone and Janet Yonger had Robert.
That day James Cutbert and Bessie Nicoll had Bessie.
The 21 day Arche Blackwood and Bessie Stalker had Marjory.
The 25 day William Bonalay and Janet Peirson had Geilis.

M.   The 18 day John Smeton was married to Effie Colzear.

SEPTEMBER.

B.   The 1 day John Cowye and Elspet Andirson had Patrick.
The 15 day Henry Sempill and Magge Goodie had Janet.
The 22 day Peter Trumbull and Janet Horne had Gilbert.
That day Edward Fothringhame and Christian Clune had Thomas.
The 25 day William Chrystie and Isobel Tempilman had Andrew.

M.   [*None*].

OCTOBER.

B.   The 6 day Allan Coutis, elder, and Isobel Bodwell had Isobel.
That day Robert Angus and Margaret Rae had Adam.
That day John Gray and Janet Murray had Magge.
The 9 day Lourie Wallet and Bessie Anderson had William.
That day Laurence Wellis and Isobel Brown had John.
The 13 day John Mutray and Janet Tomson had Janet.
That day Thomas Sanders and Kete Trumbill had Janet.
The 20 day John Hadan and Isobel Walkar had John.
That day James Reddie and Margaret Broun had Katherine (in fornication).

M.   The 6 day (after their repentance made for unlawful marriage previously)
John Gray and Janet Murray ratified their marriage again here.

NOVEMBER.

B.   The 3 day John Wilyemsone and Alison Aitkin had Isobel.
That day William Symsone and Keit Bennait had Bessie.
The 6 day Wille Keir and Annabell Lourie had Elspet.
The 10 day Harry Murray, divorced for adultery from his lawful wife, had a
child by Masie Fergusson, widow of Anthony Rutherfurd, baptized and
called Harry.   He was ordained by the General Assembly to separate
himself from the foresaid Masie until he obtained a decreet of the law-
fulness of his marriage before the judges ordinary.
The 20 day John Reid and Marjory Simson had Ellen.
That day James Keir and Annie Brown had William.
That day Michael Stewart and Janet Kellok had Christian.
The 24 day Harie Peirson and Marjory Dewer had Christian.
The 27 day John Colzear and Isobel Deiranoch had Alexander.
That day Thomas Blaik and Janet Daingzell had William.   [Beith *in
margin*.]
That day David Fin and Bessie Harrowair had John.
The 28 day John Litiljone and Bessie Chryste had John.

M.   The 17 day Thomas Marizeon was married to Grisel Hodgs.
The 24 day Simon Hair was married to Isobel Blak.
John Chryste to Janet Tod.

DECEMBER.

B.   The 4 day James Hendirson of Fordell, "being heir for the tyme," and
Jehan Murray had Elizabeth.

The 8 day Andrew Angus and Margaret Horne had Janet.
The 11 day William Pratus and Margaret Cairnie had William.
That day James Bwist and Janet Huton had Lawrence.
The 15 day Rob Cwising and Alison Peirsoun had William.
That day Nicol Hart and Bessie Hairtsyd had Janet.
That day James Speir and Marjory Sibbet had William.
That day Wille Burne and Ellen Sanders had Adam (in fornication).
The 25 day John Dagleich and Janet Penman had George.
That day Walter Strange and Ellen Lyall had Bessie.
The 29 day William Stenhus and Margaret Elder had David.

M.   The 8 day James Cois was married to Marion Rowan.
Thomas Aeson to Ellen Aedisone.
The 22 day James Gurlay was married to Marjory Colzear.
The 29 day John Huton was married to Kate Huton.

JANUARY [1577-78].

B.   The 1 day Andrew Potter and Kate Harrowair had Richard.
The 5 day Andrew Turnbull and Margaret Andirsoun had Beatrix.
That day James Paycok and Ellen Whyt had Bessie.
That day Alexander Webster and Nans Young had Janet (in fornication).
That day Richard Potter and Kate Walker had James.
The 8 day John Watson and Nans Dewer had Ellen.
The 15 day Henry Glas and Marion Greig had Laurence.
That day David Bredie and Elspet Crawfurd had Robert.
That day William Broun and Janet Bell had Margaret.
That day Riche Hynd, deceased, and Christian Miche had Lourie.
John Henderson and Nans Putie had William.

M.   The 19 day Wille Gay was married to Christian Paton.
That day John Wastwod was married to Nans Litilljone.
The 26 day Laurence Edison was married to Isobel Dagleich.

FEBRUARY.

B.   The 2 day Tom Huton and Janet Rae had Andrew.
The 5 day John Smeton and Margaret Durie had Patrick.
That day George Trumbill and Maus Andirson had Janet.
That day Andrew Dik and Janet Stirling had Patrick.
That day John Urie and Janet Brown had John.
The 12 day John Steinson "had a woman chyld born to him of his wyf"
(rest blank).
That day Robert Andirson and Christian Hendirson had Grizel.
That day Wille Wallet and Mage Hutcheon had Christian (in fornication).
The 19 day Andrew Wallet and Marjory Peirson had Adam.
That day Allan Smeton and Christian Gray had John.
That day James Sibbet and Elspet Stevin had Marjory.
The 23 day John Kellok and Ellen Wilson had Margaret.
That day David Traill and Elison Doncane had Janet.
That day Matthew Weitheit and Margaret Steinson had Margaret.
The 26 day Pattrick Keir and Geilis Peirson had Isobel.

M.   The 9 day James Bwist was married to Elie Cim.
The 23 day Andrew Westwater was married to Nans Sword.

MARCH.

B.   The 2 day Robert Duglas and Beatrix Aedison had Margaret.
That day Peter Mudie and Maige Bennie had Nans.
The 5 day John Galrig and Janet Weild had Ellen.
The 9 day Andrew Brand and Isobel Cuming had Margaret.
That day James Burt and Janet Blair had David.

The 16 day Henry Reid and Mage Tod had William.
That day David Hendirson and Janet Atkin had Robert.
That day Wille Trumbill and Janet Dewer had William.
That day Peter Chrysteson and Nans Andirson had Christian.
The 23 day William Angus and Meg Dewer had James.
The 30 day [1578] Alexander Normand and Janet Rollok had George.

M.   [*None.*]

APRIL.

B.   The second day William Blak and Margaret Robertson had John.
That day Patrick Chalmers and Janet Currie had Nans.
The 6 day Robert Car and Effie Abircrumbie had John.
That day Riche Walkar and Janet Kennedy had Patrick.
The 9 day Michael Horne and Christian Young had Elspet.
The 13 day Andrew Ged and Margaret Andirsone had Janet.
The 16 day John Andirsone "had a man chyld borne to him (after he was
        gane away secretlie in the nycht na man culd tell wheir) of his wyf Kete
        Bonalay, baptized and called David."
That day William Eson and Margaret Callender had Margaret.
The 20 day Archie Peirsone and Effie Atkin had Kætie.
That day Patrick Galt and Madie Edisone had Isobel.
That day Thomas Young and Marjory Hunnon had William.

M.   The 27 day William Wat was married to Bessie Nicoll.

MAY.

B.   The 11 day David Fyf and Annie Hodgs had George.
The 14 day John Lourie and Margaret Wright had Gelis.
The 21 day Robert Donaldson, horner, and Kete Huntair had William.
That day Peter Ewin and Malie Dun had Isobel.

M.   The 4 day David Greig was married to Christian Peirson.

JUNE.

B.   The 4 day Thomas Huton and Marion Brown had Grizel.
That day Lourie Kirk and Margaret Bennait had Isobel.
The 22 day Allan Simsone and Mage Wallet had Robert (in fornication).
That day Thomas Sanders and Kete Gothray had Isobel.
That day Robert Schortois and Janet Brown had Bessie.
The 29 day James Andirsone and Margaret Andirsone had Simon (in
        fornication).

M.   The 25 day Robert Ranald was married to Janet Baudie.
The 22 day Andrew Wardlaw was married to Maus Dagleisch.
The 29 day George Dagleisch was married to Katherine Reddie.
Donald Hutson to Isobel Bennat.
John Makmartyn to Beatrix Wright.
William Colzear to Isobel Sandis.

JULY.

B.   The 9 day Patrick Rowane and Gelis Wilson had Isobel.
The 20 day John Wemis of Pittincreif and Grizel Myrtoun had Patrick.
That day Wille Horne and Kete Dewair had John.
That day John Makmartyne and Beatrix Wright had Robert.
The 27 day William Æson and Alison Wight had Margaret.

M.   The 6 day Walter Andirsone was married to Margaret Kellok.
Alexander Hendirsone to Janet Gib.

AUGUST.

B.   The 3 day William Yownge and Besse Burne had Charles.

That day Thomas Brown and Janet Bellok had Margaret (in fornication).
The 17 day John Andirson and Christian Oliphant had Janet.
That day James Huton and Margaret Taskar had Kete.
That day John Mubray and Christian Paton had William.
The 24 day David Tod and Maus Dagleische had John.
The 27 day John Tomson and Christian Wallet had twins, Thomas and Robert.
The 31 day John Davidson, collier, and Keit Kirstell had Nans.
That day David Hugon and Janet Miller had Elspet.

M.   The 10 day Andrew Andirson was married to Margaret Thomson.
The 17 day John Tyre, younger, was married to Bessie Andirsone.
The 24 day John Mikiljone was married to Margaret Fargus.
That day David Huton was married to Ellen Peirson.

SEPTEMBER.

B.   The 7 day Andrew Watson and Elspet Andirson had Margaret.
That day John Brumsyd and Janet Rowan had Katherine. [Carnok *in margin.*]
The 21 day John Bull and Marjory Doncane had Stewin.
The 28 day Wille Wilson and Janet Donald had Ellen.
That day William Andirson and Bessie Mill had George.

M.   The 14 day Robert Mubray was married to Christian Dulhe.
The 28 day William Fin was married to Margaret Peiris.

OCTOBER.

B.   The 1 day William Mikiljone and Bessie Baxter had Margaret.
That day Harry Millair and Christian Austian had Janet (in fornication).
That day Wille Colzear, younger, and Margaret Gray had Robert (in fornication).
That day James Sibbet and Margaret Logtoun had John.
The 5 day Wille Spittell and Christian Nicolson had Alexander.
That day Robert Kellok and Bessie Wallet had Marjory.
The 8 day Thomas Elder and Bessie Dewer had Edward.

M.   The 12 day Willie Robeson was married to Ketie Michell.
The 26 day William Robeson was married to Bessie Cowan.
Harry Miller to Christian Austiane.
John Huton to Janet Huton.

NOVEMBER.

B.   The 2 day William Kirk and Bessie Huntair had Andrew.
The 5 day George Lundyn and Katherine Loche had Susanna.
That day George Fleming and Isobel Burne had Barbara.
The 9 day William Dewer and Janet Steinson had John.
The 12 day John Law and Barbara Stewart had Peter.
That day John Car and Nans Sibbet had Gilbert.
The 16 day William Gay and Christian Paton had Andrew.
That same day James Logtown and Margaret Brand had Alexander.
The 19 day William Wilson and Janet Henrie had Margaret.
That day Thomas Pillans and Margaret Westwater had Katherine.
That day John Huton and Kete Huton had Isobel.
The 26 day William Murray and Effie Cim had Margaret.
That day James Cuthbert and Bessie Nicoll had Marjory.
The 30 day Thomas Eson and Ellen Acdison had Besse.

M.   [*None.*]

DECEMBER.

B.   The 10 day George Andirson and Bessie Blak had Margaret.

The 14 day Walter Strang and Ellen Lyall had George.
That day Robert Cowie and Margaret Jhonston had David.
The 17 day James Meldrum and Janet Wilson had Grizel.
The 21 day Andrew Swenton and Christian Murray had Margaret (in
    adultery).
The 24 day Robert Lun and Janet Law had Robert.
That day Thomas Kellok and Annabel Henryson had Patrick.
The 31 day Thomas Couper and Margaret Mowtray had William.

M. The 21 day James Sanders was married to Margaret Burn.
The 28 day James Davidsone was married to Besse Piers.

JANUARY [1578-79].

B. The 4 day Charles Walkar and Margaret Reid had Margaret.
The 11 day Allan Couttis, younger, and Ellen Balfour had James.
That day David Finlasoun and Ellen Keveraill had John.
That day Adam Sanderis and Isobel Cuninghame had Margaret.
That day Wille Andirson and Janet Donaldson had Christian.
The 14 day Andrew Chrystie and Margaret Stewart had Peter.
The 18 day James Garvan and Bessie Chrystie had Margaret.
That day Adam Reid and Bessie Currour had George (in fornication).
The 21 day George Bodwell and Nans Sandelands had George.
That day Simon Hair and Isobel Blak had William.
The 28 day William Schortes in Lethenis and Barbara Duglas had John.

M. [*None.*]

FEBRUARY.

B. The 1 day Michael Stewart and Janet Kellok had Henry.
The 8 day John Steinsone and Margaret Andirson had Robert.
That day David Wilzemsone and Janet Harrowair had Margaret.
The 11 day Robert Andirson and Janet Walkar had James.
The 15 day Andrew Alison and Ellen Cuming had Janet.
The 22 day John Balcais in Beath and Christian Burt had John.

M. "That day" (? 1st) John Dik was married to Grizel Elder.
The 22 day Edward Burne was married to Margaret Mudie.
Willie Whyt to Isobel Craig.

MARCH.

B. The 1 day Thomas Mudie and Christian Harper had Edward.
The 8 day Robert Randal and Janet Baudie had Adam.
The 18 day of March Wille Cumbrie and Christian Phillip had Maus.
The 22 day Patrick Makartein and Christian Talzeour had John.
The 29 day [1579] William Burne, deceased, and Janet Brown had Beatrix
That day John Thomsone and Elisone Horne had Margaret.
That day Lowie Steinson and Bessie Meldrum had Bessie.

M. The 1 day John Gotherstoun was married to Bessie Ougre.

APRIL [1579].

B. The 22 day Andrew Wallet in Tod and Marjory Peirson had Isobel.
M. [*None.*]

MAY.

B. The 10 day John Wilson and Keite Moris had Alexander.
That day Adam Curre and Margaret Edison had Margaret.

M. The 3 day John Burn was married to Marjory Andirson.
The 10 day Henry Dewar was married to Marion Huton.
That day William Elder was married to Janet Wardlaw.

JUNE.

B. The 7 day James Brown and Janet Clark had John (in fornication).
The 10 day Tom Law[1] and Isobel Stirk had James (in fornication).

M. The 7 of June John Pottar was married to Janet Crafurd.
The 21 day of June John Blakater was married to Janet Murray.
The 28 day Adam Brown, younger, was married to Margaret Mudie.
That day Alexander Wilson to Janet Cunninghame.

JULY.

B. The first day Michael Horne and Christian Young had James.
The 5 day John Burne and Emmie Cunning had Effie.
That day John Paton and Christian Nicoll had William.
The 12 day George Hakked of Pithrren and Isobel Hapburne had George.
That day Wille Martiall and Elspet Reddie had John (in incest, "twa sisteris").
The 19 day Peter Trumbill and Janet Horne had John.
That day William Cunninghame and Keiti Jonston had David (in fornication)
The 26 day John Steinson and Marion Trumbill had Adam.

M. [*None.*]

AUGUST.

B. The 9 day Andrew Angus and Bessie Inglis had Marion.
The 16 day John Hodgs and Christian Dewer had Margaret.
The 19 day John Steinson and Janet Stenhus had William.
The 23 day George Bull and Christian Wallace had Thomas.
That day Lowre Bonalay and Christian Patrik had John.
That day Robert Symsone and Marion Smith had Janet.

M. The 2 day of August Andrew Stirk was married to Ketie Huton.
The 9 day Nicoll Cant was married to Margaret Cuthert.
The 30 day of August Adam Wallett was married to Keit Kellok.
And Stein Donald to Janet Kellok.

SEPTEMBER.

B. The 9 day James Brown and Janet Bungain had James.
That day James Harrowain and Margaret Blyth had Janet.
The 13 day Simon Davidson and Ellen Nicoll had Isobel.
That day Adam Andirson and Ellen Sanderis had Margaret.
The 16 day Robert Paton and Janet Dagleich had Laurence.
The 27 day John Andirsone and Janet Ranald had William.

M. The 20 day Arche Cunninghame was married to Margaret Bankis.

OCTOBER.

B. The 4 day James Couper and Christian Bening had Grizel.
That day Andrew Moris and Bessie Littill had John.
The 11 day Andrew Inglis and Maige Michell had James.
That day John Wilson and Elison Bull had Robert.
That day William Roberson and Keit Michell had Marion.
The 14 day John Makmartin and Betie Wright had Marjory.
The 18 day Pete Lauson and Ellen Wilson had Alexander.
The 25 day John Kellok and Margaret Donaldson had David.
That day Thomas Huton in Luscour and Ketie Beveraig had Margaret.
That day David Smeton and Isobel Cunninghame had Margaret.
The 28 day Mark Donald and Margaret Lourie had Janet.

M. The 25 day William Jonson was married to Bessie Sanderis.

[1] " 3 relaps."

NOVEMBER.

B.   The 1 day John Tod and Margaret Blakwod had John.
  The 8 day Robert Wilson and Rosina Ramsay had twins, Bessie and Janet.
  The 18 day Robert Mubray and Christian Dillie had John.
  The 22 day John Crummie and Effie Huton had Effie.
  The 25 Robert Wat and Nans Rowan had Ellen.

M.   The 8 day David Dewer was married to Marjory Wardlaw.
  That day James Chrysteson was married to Rachel Preston.
  John Thomson to Bessie Dangzell.
  Walter Traill to Isabel Lyndsay.
  The 29 day William Duglas was married to Elspet Low.
  David Astiane to Marjory Logtoun.

DECEMBER.

B.   The 6 day John Warkman and Bessie Atkin had Margaret.
  That day John Stenhus and Margaret Duglas had Janet.
  The 9 day David Tod and Mawse Dagleisch had Thomas.
  The 16 day James Immerye and Elison Paycok had George.
  That day Rob Kellok and Margaret Kilgour had Thomas (in fornication).
  The 23 day Robert Nicoll and Bessie Straqwhyn had William (in fornication).
  The 27 day Rob Dewer and Nans Mill had Janet.
  That day John Murray and Effie Cim had John.
  That day Andrew Sanders and Ellen Cant had Katherine.
  That day Willie Whyt and Isobel Craig had Isobel.
  That day John Blakater and Janet Murray had John.
  The 30 day John Oraik in Craig Beath and Katherine Dik had John.
  That day Arche Blakwod and Bessie Stalker had Isobel.

M.   The 13 day John Thomson, mason, was married to Janet Smith.
  That day John Steinson was married to Bessie Smith in Fod.

JANUARY [1579-80].

B.   The 3 day Adam Andirson and Janet Martyn had John.
  The 6 day William Burne and Janet Scotland had John.
  The 10 day Robert Andirson and Christian Wobster had James.
  The 24 day John Wilson and Christian Bankis had Robert.
  That day Thom Kellok and Christian Martiall had Robert.
  That day Alexander Wilson and Isobel Levistoun had George.
  That day Willie Walkair and Gelis Portair had Gelis.
  The 27 Thomas Bell and Janet Huton [1] had John (in fornication).
  That day William Wright and Christian Thomson had William.
  The 31 day John Gotherstoun and Bessie Ougre had Isobel.

M.   The 24 of January Alexander Donaldson was married to Christian
  Donaldson.
  The 31 day John Drysdeill was married to Marjory Sibbet.

FEBRUARY.

B.   The . . . day Lourence Kirk and Margaret Bennet had Bessie.
  That day Robert Davidson and Isobel Bankis had Janet.
  James Cuming and Margaret Brown had Margaret.
  John Wallet and Isobel Erskin had William.
  That day William Wilson and Janet Henry had Walter.
  The 14 day Willie Andirson and Bessie Mill had Christian.
  Willie Keir and Christian Bull had Janet.
  That day Adam Whyt and Bessie Landells had Andrew.
  The 24 day David Ferguson, minister, and Isobel Durhame had Isobel.

[1] Relapse.

That day David Dewer and Bessie Peirson had David.
That day George Horne and Kate Schang had Margaret.
The 28 day James Burt and Janet Blair had Janet.
That day Thomas Wallet and Christian Wright had Elspet (in fornication).

M. The 14 day of February Normand Blakater was married to Janet Law.
Patrick Walkar to Christian Wat.
The 21 day Robert Yong married to Margaret Jonson.

MARCH.

B. The 2 day John Robertson and Marjory Steinson had Nans.
That day John Baird and Christian Kinninmonth had Laurence.
The 6 day Wille Brown and Janet Bell had David.
That day Rob Fillen in Beath and Bessie Wallet had Thomas.
That day James Hutson in Dagatie and Janet Bonalay had Kate.
That day Rob Angus and Mage Rae had Marion.
That day Robert Keith and . . . . Kynnaird had Grizel (in fornication).
The 13 day James Sanders and Margaret Burn had Margaret.
That day William Porteus and Isobel Hendirson had Janet.
That day Geordi Colzear and Janet Bull had Robert.
The 16 day Wille Jonson and Meg Stirk had Margaret.
The 23 day William Pratus and Margaret Cairnie had Margaret.
The 27 day [1580] John Wilzemson and Alison Aitkin had Ellen.
That day James Whyt and Maus Inglis had Isobel.
That day James Cutbert and Bessie Nicoll had Janet.
The 30 day Henry Reid and Margaret Tod had Janet.
That day Geordi Edison and Janet Burne had George.

M. The 6 day John Beveraige was married to Margaret Knox.
The 13 day James Dewer was married to Katherine Eson.

APRIL [1580].

B. The 3 day George Durie and Nans Gat had David.
William Chryste and Isobel Tempilman had Margaret.
Robert Kellok and Bessie Wallwod had John.
Edward Anderson and Janet Dik had William.
That day John Stirk and Margaret Henry had Margaret.
The 6 day Andrew Brand and Isobel Cunning had Walter.
That day George Gray and Margaret Gat had William.
The 10 day John Potter and Janet Crawfurd had James.
The 17 day John Mutray and Janet Tomson had John.
That day Wille Walkair and Keiti Wilson had George.
The 24 day John Swan and Effie Smeton had Marjory.
That day Thom Cumand and Katherine Mudie had Katherine.

M. [*None.*]

MAY.

B. The 1 day Albert Bruis and Elspet Wright had Katherine.
That day Henry Paicok and Christian Martyn had Adam (in fornication).
The 4 day Robert Dagleich and Janet Harper had Katherine.
That day James Davidson and Bessie Peirs had James.
The xv. day John Colzear and Elspet Direnoch had John.
That day John Wostwod and Anny Littiljone had John.
That day Thomas Huton and Janet Rae had Janet.
That day William Young and Bessie Burne had Christian.
The 22 day Wille Hodgs and Christian Stirk had Nans (in fornication).
The 25 day John Lowrie and Mage Wrycht had Christian.
The 29 day Thomas Æson and Ellen Edison had John.

M. The 22 day Andrew Andirson was married to Christian Kellok.

JUNE.

B.   The 1 day James Dewer and Janet Law had Robert.
That day Henry Dewer and Marion Huton had Margaret.
That day David Fin and Bessie Harrowar had Alexander.
That day George Lundie, minister, and Katherine Loch had Margaret.
The 8 day James Bruce and Marjory Gibbon had Ellen.
The 12 day John Burne and Marjory Anderson had Margaret.
That day Thom Sanderis and Christian Trumbill had Bessie.
That day John Steill and Christian Parkie had John.
The 26 day Harry Millair and Christian Astian had Margaret.
The 29 day Robert Cusing and Elison Peirson had John.

M.   The 12 day George Sanderis was married to Margaret Burgoyne.
James Mutray to Margaret Logtoun.
James Anderson to Margaret Lyndsay.

JULY.

B.   The 3 day Arche Peirson and Effie Atkin had William.
That day David Traill and Elison Doncan had Margaret.
Wille Æson and Elison Wight had Margaret.
The 17 day John Steinson and Bessie Smyth had Janet.
That day John Watsone and Nans Dewer had Abraham.
The 24 day Andrew Gray and Janet Straqwhin had Margaret.
Andrew Wardlaw and Maus Dagleich had Katherine.
That day Richard Walkar and Janet Kennedy had William.
The 31 day Rob Car and Effie Abircrumbie had Peter.

M.   The 3 day John Huggon was married to Bessie Wilsone.
The 10 day John Chrystie was married to Ellen Waddell.
The 24 day Andrew Andirson was married to Margaret Muir.

AUGUST.

B.   The 14 day Rob Dewer and Isobel Gray had Andrew.
The 17 day Allan Coutis, elder, and Isobel Bodwell had Margaret.
The 21 day Lourence Schortes and Katherine Mill had Henry.
The 28 day William Elder and Janet Wardlaw had Kate.
That day David Andirson and Margaret Melyn had Janet.
The 31 day David Hendirson, cordiner, and Janet Aitkin had David.
That day William Dewer and Janet Steinson had Marjory.

M.   The 14 day Michael Meldrum was married to Margaret Dagleisch.

SEPTEMBER.

B.   The 7 day Laruence Edison and Isobel Dagleich had Margaret.
The 11 day Walter Andirson and Mage Kellok had Gelis.
The 18 day Robert Duglas and Kate Edison had John.
That day William Trumbill and Janet Dewer had Bessie.
That day James Hardie and Marion Clune had David.
The 25 day Edward Fothringhame and Christian Clun had Bessie.
The 28 day Jok Davidson, collier, and Keit Kirstell had John.

M.   [*None.*]

OCTOBER.

B.   The 2 day Andrew Stirk and Katherine Huton had Janet.
That day William Millair and Isobel Cunninghame had John.
That day Adam Wallet and Keit Kellok had Keit.
The 5 day Stevin Donald and Janet Kellok had James.
The 9 day John Haddane and Isobel Walkar had Marjory.
That day Pete Walkar and Christian Wat had Robert.
The 12 day Harry Thomson and Mage Wright had Robert (in fornication).

That day John Boswell and Mags Atkin had Isobel (in fornication).
The 16 day Patrick Gat and Bessie Edison had Charles.
That day Alexander Wilsone and Janet Cunninghame had Ellen.
That day John Litiljone and Bessie Chryste had Adam.
The 30 day John Reid and Janet Thomson had Bessie.
That day Allan Smeton and Christian Gray had Katherine.

M.   The 22 of October George Ædison was married to Margaret Qwanor.

NOVEMBER.

B.   The 6 day David Pitcairn and Grizel Hay had Janet (in fornication).
The 13 day George Hacheid (*sic*) of Pitfirren and Isobel Hepburn had John.
That day Arche Cunninghame and Margaret Banks had Isobel.
That day David Huton and Ellen Peirson had Isobel.
That day Michael Horne and Christian Young had Janet.
The 23 day James Sibbet and Elspet Stevin had David.
The 27 day George Trumbill and Maus Andirsone had William.
That day James Paycok and Ellen Qwhyt had Abraham.
That day Donald Murie and Nans Smyth had Margaret.
The 30 day Harry Peirson and Marjory Dewer had Nans.
That day John Drysdaill and Marjory Sibbet had Effie.
That day Andrew Angus and Margaret Horne had Katherine.

M.   The 6 day John Craik was married to Janet Reid.
The 20 day David Brown was married to Gelis Reid.
The 27 John Wilzemson was married to Maus Jonson.

DECEMBER.

B.   The 4 day John Dewer and Janet Chrystie had Janet.
That day Alexander Haly and Christian Cunninghame had Adam.
The 7 day James Richie and Margaret Anderson had William.
That day James Andersone and Margaret Lyndsay had John (born before
    the time).
The 11 day William Stenhus and Margaret Elder had Robert.
That day Bessie Sanders "had a man chyld baptized whilk sche fathered
    upon Harie Murray, and he refusing to purge himself therof, it being
    given to his aith, it wes counted for his, and called Hewe."
The 14 day William Angus and Meg Dewer had Kate.
The 21 day George Bodwell and Nans Sandelands had Patrick.
The 28 day James Sibbet and Maige Logtoun had Katherine.
That day Simon Hair and Isobel Blak had Margaret.
That day John Sanders and Bessie Burne had Isobel.

M.   The 11 day Henry Hunnon was married to Ellen Angus.

JANUARY [1580-81].

B.   The 4 day John Galrig and Bessie Bull had Janet.
The 8 day William Martiall and Christian Alexander had John.
The 11 day James Meldrum and Janet Wilson had Nicol.
That day David Austie and Marjory Logtoun had Thomas.
That day George Trumbull and Marjory Couper had George.
The 15 day Adam Broun and Margaret Mudie had Peter.
That day David Hugon and Janet Miller had Isobel.
The 22 day Archie Cunningham and Janet Dagleich had Katherine.
That day Adam Robertson and Keit Bennet had Janet.
The 25 day John Rannald and Emmie Michell had Janet.
The 29 day John Anderson and Margaret Aitkin had Marion.

M.   The 1 day Robert Nicoll was married to Ellen Durie.
The 22 day Lourie Walker was married to Marjory Phillen.
The 29 day James Craik was married to Bessie Dagleich.

FEBRUARY.

B. The first day William Robertson and Janet Boswell had David.
The 5 day James Couper and Christian Benning had James.
The 12 day William Æson and Margaret Calendair had Patrick.
The 19 day William Young and Margaret Jonson had John.
That day Robert Cowye and Margaret Jonson had William.
That day John Thomson and Janet Smyth had Margaret.
The 22 Laurence Schortes and Christian Watson had Katherine (in fornication).
The 26 day John Blakater and Janet Murray had James.

M. The 5 day Thomas Bell was married to Janet Hutcheon.

MARCH.

B. The 1 day Andrew Ged and Margaret Anderson had Edward.
That day James Huton and Margaret Taskar had Margaret.
The 15 day John Prestoun and Janet Spens had Janet (in fornication).
That day Robert Wilson and Janet Henderson had Bessie.
The 22 day Robert Dewer and Nans Mill had Andrew.
The 26 day [1581] Charles Walker and Margaret Reid had Margaret.
The 29 day William Walkar and Gelis Poirtar had William.
That day Adam Reid and Bessie Curtour had Walter (in fornication, under promise of marriage).

M. [*None.*]

APRIL [1581].

B. The 9 day John Car and Annie Sibbet had John.
The 12 day Patrick Keir and Gelis Peirson had David.
The 19 day George Fleming and Isobel Burne had James.
The 23 day Robert Lun and Janet Law had John.
That day Robert Man and Margaret Stark had James.
The 26 day Thomas Couper and Margaret Mutray had Bessie.
That day Walter Strange and Ellen Loyall (*sic*) had Janet.
That day Robert Schortes and Janet Brown had Robert.
That day John Galrig and Janet Weild had William.

M. The 2 day Adam Fargie was married to Janet Thomson.
The 23 day James Hiltoun was married to Janet Martiall.

MAY.

B. The 7 day Andrew Alison and Ellen Cuming had James.
That day William Blak and Margaret Robertson had Katherine.
That day William Boswell and Keit Schortes had Robert (in fornication, under promise of marriage, which afterwards was performed in *anno* (*sic*)).
That day David Cuninghame and Janet Mudie had Patrick.
The 17 day John Hendersone, monk, and Nans Poutie had Robert.
That day James Wostwod and Maus Paycok had Nans.
That day Henry Martiall and Katherine Wilson had James (in fornication under promise of marriage).
The 21 day William Horn and Katherine Dewer had Bessie.
The 24 day Andrew Durie and Maige Hucheon had Grizel (in fornication).
The 28 day Wille Cumberie and Christian Philip had Effie.

M. The 7 day George Peirson was married to Effie Phillen.
That day John Clochie was married to Janet Hendirsone.
The 21 day Thomas Westwood was married to Isobel Harrowar.
The 28 day William Crawfurd was married to Ellen Brown.

JUNE.

B.   The 4 day Crispinie Swyne and Margaret Hutcheon had Janet.
The 11 day Thomas Toscheach and Sibbie Dagleich had John (in fornication).
That day James Garvain and Bessie Chrystie had Isobel.
The 14 day William Mikitjon and Bessie Baxter had Janet.
The 21 day John Steinson and Margaret Andirson had William.
The 25 day Peter Chrysteson and Nans Anderson had George.
The 28 day Allan Coutis, younger, and Helen Balfour had Patrick.

M.   The 4 day John Andirson was married to Janet Barklay.
Donald Blak to Janet Landels.
The 11 day Mark Swenton was married to Isobel Spens.
The 18 day Master David Spens, minister at Kirkcaldy, was married to Margaret Fergusson, daughter to the minister here.

JULY.

B.   The 9 day James Dewer and Keit Æson had Katherine.
The 16 day William Currour, Torry, and Bessie Lawe had Marjory.
The 19 day Norman Blakater and Janet Law had Patrick.
The 23 day Adam Currie and Margaret Edison had James.
That day Robert Benie and Isobel Anderson had David.
That day David Peirs and Isobel Immerie had Patrick.
The 26 day John Dagleisch and Janet Penman had Henry.
That day John Lourie and Margaret Wright had William.
The 30 day John Hugon and Bessie Wilson had John.

M.   The 2 day Andrew Millair was married to Ellen Brwis.
The 16 day George Lyon was married to Katherine Burn.

AUGUST.

B.   The 2 day Cuthbert Broun and Margaret Hereis had Robert.
The 6 day Andrew Chryste and Margaret Stewart had William.
The 13 day William Simsone and Katherine Bennet had George.
The 16 day Patrick Rowan and Gelis Wilson had Nans.
The 20 day Henry Simson and Margaret Purroik had Charles.
That day John Chattw and Janet Martiall had Barbara.
The 23 day James Cuthbert and Bessie Nicoll had Ellen.
That day William Burn and Janet Scotland had John.
The 27 day John Beveraige, Beath, and Margaret Knox had Robert.

M.   The 6 day John Clarke, Torry, was married to Janet Fleming.
The 20 day David Keling was married to Janet Edisone.
The 27 day Robert Whyt was married to Marion Lyndsay.

SEPTEMBER.

B.   The 3 day John Davidsone and Keit Kirstell had Isobel.
The 6 day Andrew Brand and Isobel Cuming had William.
The 20 day Michael Stewart and Janet Kellok had John.
The 24 day John Bull, . . . grein, and Marjory Doncane had William.
That day Robert Maistirtoun and Ellen Davidson had Alexander.

M.   The 3 day John Watsone was married to Bessie Jonsone.
The 10 day George Brown was married to Margaret Sanders.

OCTOBER.

B.   The 4 day Andrew Currie and Keit Davidsone had John (in fornication, under promise of marriage).
The 15 day John Chryste and Ellen Woddell had Ellen.

E

That day Gavin Lillie and Elspeth Huton had Gielis (in fornication).

M.   The 22 day Adam Durie was married to Christian Barrie.

NOVEMBER.

B.   The 1 day Robert Andirson and Christian Henderson had Christian.
The 5 day Lourie Walkar and Maige Phillen had Janet.
That day John Bein and Margaret Makgregoir had Patrick.
That day John Thomson and Elison Burgain had John (in fornication).
The 12 day James Reddie and Elison Stirk had John.
The 15 day William Schortes and Barbara Duglass had David.
That day Lourie Kirk and Margaret Bennet had Robert.
The 19 day John Craik and Janet Reid had Geilis.
That day Matthew Weitit and Margaret Steinson had Patrick.
That day Andrew Angus and Bessie Inglis had Katherine.
The 26 day Henry Peirsone and Keit Ædisone had Beatrix.
That day Donald Bein and Bessie Smeton had David.

M.   The 5 day David Cunninghame in Primrois was married to Bessie
Cuming.
That day Robert Browne was married to Katherine Cant.
The 26 day Henry Bennet was married to Grizel Elder.
That day Alexander Lamb was married to Janet Cunninghame.

DECEMBER.

B.   The 3 day John Andirson and Christian Kneland had Margaret.
The 10 day Patrick Lawson and Margaret Wilson had Isobel.
That day Andrew Potter and Katherine Harrower had Janet.
The 24 day Abraham Wallwod and Isobel Rowan had Robert.
That day John Hodgs and Christian Dewer had Marjory.
That day James Cuming and Janet Brown had Isobel.
That day John Law and Katherine Davidson had Margaret (in fornication,
under promise of marriage).
That day Thomas Haistie and Maus Andirson had John.
The 27 day Peter Turnbull and Janet Horn had Bessie.
That day Alexander Wobster and Janet Gib had Katherine.
That day William Thomson and Janet Mudie had Christian.
That day Thomas Walwod and Christian Wright had Andrew (in fornica-
tion).

M.   The 10 day John Huton was married to Nans Craik.
That day John Steill was married to Janet Chrysteson.
The 17 day John Tomson was married to Bessie Steward.
That day Thomas Trumbill was married to Marjory Duglas.

JANUARY [1581-82].

B.   The 7 day John Steinson and Marjory Trumbill had Beatrix.
The 10 day Adam Saunders and Janet Cunninghame had Katherine.
That day Nicoll Hart and Bessie Hartsyd had Christian.
That day David Pitcarne and Grizell Hay had Robert (in fornication, under
promise of marriage).
The 17 day William Murray and Effie Cim had David.
That day James Colzear and Ellen Montheith had Elspet (in fornication).
The 21 day George Halkheid of Pitfirren and Isobel Hepburn had James.
The 24 day Alexander Oswald and Geilis Bull had James (in fornication).
The 28 day George Bull and Christian Wallace had Janet.
That day John Balcais, Beath, and Christian Burt had Robert.

M.   The 7 day Thomas Walwod was married to Isobel Logtoun.
The 14 day John Dagleich was married to Katherine Bankis.
The 21 day David Pitcairn was married to Grizel Hay.

The 28 day William Stewart was married to Effie Weimis.
That day John Law was married to Keit Davidsone.

FEBRUARY.

B.   The 4 day Robert Nicoll and Ellen Durie had Bessie.
That day Thomas Martiall and Margaret Steill had John.
That day William Alexander and Margaret Proves had Margaret (in fornication).
The 11 day James Meldrum and Janet Wilson had Robert.
The 17 day William Uterlie, Beath, and Catherine Pudzeon had Archie.
The 21 day James Davidsone and Bessie Piers had George.
The 25 day Robert Kellok and Bessie Walwood had William.
That day John Potter, younger, and Janet Crawfurd had Alexander.
The 28 day Robert Ranald and Janet Bandye had Isobel.

M.   The 4 day John Huton was married to Margaret Huton.
That day George Campbell was married to Isobel Huton.
The 11 day James Fergusson was married to Ellen Cant.
The 17 day Robert Piers was married to Ellen Landels.
That day Andrew Currie was married to Keit Davidsone.

MARCH.

B.   The 11 day Laurence Steinsone and Bessie Meldrum had William.
That day David Hume and Janet Dalrimpill had Ellen (in fornication).
The 18 day Arche Blaikwod and Bessie Stalker had Margaret.
That day George Colzear and Janet Bull had Margaret.
That day Adam Elder and Janet Æson had David (in fornication).
That day James Kingorn and Catherine Landels had William (in fornication).
That day John Dugall and Janet Paycok had Janet (in fornication).
The 21 day Mark Swenton and Isabel Spens had Margaret.
The 28 day [1582] John Proud and Christian Brand had Janet (under promise of marriage.

M.   The 4 day John Proud was married to Christian Brand.

APRIL [1582].

B.   The 1 day John Andersone and Janet Ranald had Robert.
That day Peter Ewein and Malie Dun had Thomas.
The 4 day John Blakater and Janet Murray had Margaret.
That day Robert Hoge and Janet Andersone had Margaret.
The 8 day Thomas Elder and Bessie Dewar had John.
That day William Stenhus and Margaret Elder had Edward.
That day John Wilsone and Katherine Moris had Barbara.
That day David Gardin of that Ilk and Emelie Jonsone had Janet (in fornication). [Against this entry, but so situated that it may have reference to the previous entry, is the following :—" Gottin in Edinburgh and broght heir be testimoniall."]
"The 11 day Alexander Mastirtoune in Baeth had twa chyldren baptized born to him of his wyff Katerin Broun, the eldest about thre yeir old called Isobell, the yongest twenty oukis old called Jonat ; the occasion of the lang delay of their baptime proceding of his disobedience and contempt of the kirk." [*in the margin*, James Beveraig, without any apparent connection with any entry.]
That day Robert Paton and Janet Dagleich had Alexander.
The 18 day William Pratus and Margaret Cairne had Elspet.
The 22 day Robert Walwod and Janet Davidsone had Kate (in fornication).

M.   The 29 day Adam Wilsone was married to Janet Proves.

MAY.

B.   The 2 day James Logtoun and Margaret Brand had George.
The 6 day Mark Donald and Margaret Lourie had Margaret.
The 9 day Michael Trumbill and Janet Peirson had Janet.
The 13 day Robert Mudie and Bessie Pontoun had Thomas.
That day Andrew Watson and Elspet Andersone had John.
The 20 day John Andirsone and Margaret Ædisone had Walter.
That day Richard Walker and Janet Kennedy had Robert.
The 22 day William Æsone and Alison Wicht had Bessie.
The 27 day Robert Davidsone and Isobel Bankis had George.
The 30 day John Wricht and Barbara Peirson had Janet.

M.   The 27 day Robert Andirsone was married to Christian Trumbill.

JUNE.

B.   The 13 day Andrew Dick and Janet Stirlin had James.
That day John Gibsone and Ellen Maine had James (in fornication).
The 17 John Tod and Margaret Blakwod had Janet.
The 20 day William Keir and Christian Bull had James.
That day Henry Hunnon and Helen Angus had Janet.
That day David Wilzemson and Janet Harrowar had Margaret.
The 23 day Thomas Huton and Katherine Beveraige had Isobel.
That day Andrew Archebald and Janet Schaw had Isobel.

M.   The 17 day John Cusin was married to Margaret Huton.
That day Thomas Andirson was married to Marion Schortes.
And Nicol Kellok to Nans Meldrum.

JULY.

B.   The 1 day John Smeton and Margaret Durie had Janet.
The 4 day Robert Mubray and Christian Dillie had twins, William and Allan.
The 8 day John Huton and Janet Huton had Robert.
The 15 day John Drysdaill and Marjory Sibbet had James.
That day David Smeton and Isobel Cunninghame had Katherine.
The 22 day Henry Reid and Margaret Tod had Robert.
That day Henry Dewar and Marion Huton had Janet.
The 25 day George Lyon and Katherine Burne had Marjory.
The 29 day William Wricht and Christian Thomson had Bessie.

M.   The 1 day John Forfair was married to Janet Wardlaw.
And David Scharpe to Elspet Hugone.
The 8 day James Blaw was married to Christian Schortes.
The 15 day John Robertsone was married to Nans Lourie.
That day John Mullikin was married to Janet Henryson.
The 29 day Thomas Whyt was married to Janet Dagleich.

AUGUST.

B.   The 5 day George Ædison and Margaret Quariour had John.
The 8 day John Wallet, Suther (? for "suter"), and Isobel Erskin had John.
The 12 day Patrick Makarten and Christian Talzeour had Nans.
That day Thomas Huton, miller, and Janet Rae had John.
The 15 day James Mutray in Galrik and Marjory Brwis had John.
The 19 day Mr. John Fairfoull, schoolmaster, and Margaret Prestoun had James.
The 22 day Andrew Alisone and Helen Cuming had Laurence.
The 26 John Stewart and Janet Andirsone had John (in fornication).
The 29 day John Crummie and Effie Huton had James.

That day Andrew Inglis and Marge Michell had Christian.
That day John Watsone, " suter," and Bessie Jonsone had Bessie.

M. [*None.*]

SEPTEMBER.

B. The 2 day Andrew Sanders and Ellen Cant had Clement.
That day Patrick Makmonich and Nans Paton had John.
That day Robert Angus and Margaret Rae had Margaret.
That day Arche Peirson and Effie Aitkin had Nans.
The 5 day Robert Schortes and Janet Broun had James.
The 9 day John Stenhus and Margaret Duglas had John.
That day William Huton and Marion Law had Margaret (in fornication).
That day Simon Davidsone and Ellen Nicoll had Thomas.
The 12 day James Bwist and Elye Cim had David.
That day John Baird and Christian Kinnimonth had Elspet.
That day John Westwood and Annie Litiljone had Janet.
The 16 day William Chryste and Isobel Tempilman had William.
That day John Craik and Katherin Dik had David.
The 23 day Adam Durie and Christian Barrie had William.
That day James Robertsone and Elspet Rob had Janet.
The 30 day James Cuthbert and Bessie Nicoll had James.
That day Alexander Stewin and Janet Sibbald had William.
That day John Kellok and Christian Donaldsone had Robert.

M. The 2 day Thomas Martiall was married to Kate Blaike.

OCTOBER.

B. The 7 day David Cunninghame and Elizabeth Cuming had Emmie.
That day William Douglas, collier, and Janet Tenend had Margaret.
The 10 day Allan Coutis, younger, and Helen Balfour had Robert.
That day John Thomsone, mason, and Bessie Stewart had Patrick.
That day Robert Whyt and Marion Lyndsay had James.
The 14 day Walter Andirsone and Margaret Kellok had John.
That day George Peirsone and Effie Phillen had Gelis.
That day Robert Phillen, Beath, and Bessie Walwood had Geilis.
That day William Martiall and Bessie Donaldsone had Margaret.
The 17 day John Robertsone and Marjory Steinson had William.
That day John Stobie and Marion Atkin had Adam.
That day Harry Millair and Christian Astie had Isobel.
The 19 day Peter Dewar and Janet Doncane had Catherine (in fornication).
The 21 day James Wilzamsone (collier at Kelty, fugitive) and Bessie Brown
    had William (in adultery).
The 28 day William Stewart and Effie Wemis had Margaret.
That day John Thomsone and Janet Smith had John.

M. The 7 day William Richie was married to Ellen Broun.
The 28 Thomas Makgilliehois was married to Janet Lyndsay.

NOVEMBER.

B. The 11 day John Burne and Marjory Andirsone had Marjory.
That day Patrick Walkar and Christian Wat had Patrick.
That day John Mackalzeon and Ellen Ramsay had Thomas.
The 14 day George Bodwell and Nans Sandilands had Nans.
That day Simon Hair and Isobel Blak had William.
The 25 day William Broun and Janet Bell had Janet.
That day John Steill and Janet Chrysteson had Grizel.

M. The 25 day William Doncane was married to Katherine Davidsone.
William Keir to Elspet Kilgour.
And William Nicolsone to Janet Walker.

DECEMBER.

B.   The 2 day Henry Broun, Carnok, and Catherine Henrie had David.
The 5 day William Wallwod and Elspet Alexander had Ellen.
The 12 day John Kellok and Margaret Donaldsone had John.
That day John Colzear, piper, and Elspet Dyrenoch had Margaret.
The 19 day George Durie and Nans Galt had Ellen.
The 30 day William Æson and Margaret Callendair had James.
That day Robert Andirsone and Margaret Gibson had William (in fornication).

M.   The 2 day Andrew Wardlaw was married to Janet Peirson.
The 16 day Patrick Walwod was married to Marjory Spreull.
The 30 day John Loudone was married to Christian Abircrombie.

JANUARY [1582-83].

B.   The 6 day Adam Wilsone and Janet Purves had Laurence.
The 9 day William Durie and Janet Hutcheon had Margaret.
The 13 day John Wricht and Maus Paton had Patrick.
That day Robert Cusine and Elison Peirsone had Margaret.
The 16 day David Astie and Marjory Logtoun had James.
That day Andrew Brand and Isobel Cuming had Bessie.
That day John Inglis and Margaret Edward had Katherine.
The 20 day John Andirsone and Margaret Aitkin had Maus.
That day John Thomsone and Ellen Horne had William.
The 27 day James Murray and Agnes Lyndsay had John.
That day James Andirsone and Margaret Lyndsay had Katherine.
The 30 day David Huton and Ellen Peirson had Janet.

M.   The 6 day Gilbert Andersone was married to Nans Symmervaill.
That day William Durie ratified his marriage here "whilk befoir wes onordourly celebrat with Jonat Hutcheon in ane uthir kirk, they being parochiners heir."
The 27 day William Archibald was married to Janet Davidsone.

FEBRUARY.

B.   The 3 day Andrew Nicolsone and Bessie Reddie had Janet.
That day Crispinie Swyne and Margaret Hutcheson had Elspet.
The 6 day James Sibbald and Elspet Stevin had Marion.
That day John Craik and Janet Reid had Janet.
The 10 day William Elder and Janet Wardlaw had Barbara.
That day John Huton and Nans Oraik had Margaret.
The 17 day Stevin Donald and Janet Kellok had John.
That day John Davidsone and Keit Kirstell had John.
That day William Wilson and Janet Donalson had Henry (in fornication).
The 24 day John Foirfair and Janet Wardlaw had William.
That day George Edisone and Janet Burne had David.
That day James Couper and Christian Bening had Sibilla.
That day Robert Dagleich and Janet Harper had Janet.

M.   The 3 day David Brand was married to Nans Jonsone.
The 10 day John Andirsone was married to Janet Ædison.
Adam Burne to Isobel Stenhus.
Robert Murie to Janet Wemis.
Thomas Loudian to Margaret Angus.

MARCH.

B.   The 3 day James Mudie and Isobel Nicoll had William (in fornication).
The 10 day James Whyt and Maus Inglis had Marjory.
The 13 day Robert Murie and Janet Kellok had Janet (in fornication).

The 17 day John Wricht and Alison Hutson had Ellen.
That day Alexander Lamb and Janet Cunninghame had John.
The 24 day George Wardlaw and Annie Michell had Nicoll.
That day John Gotherstoun and Bessie Ougre had Christian.
The 27 day [1583] James Peirson and Grisel Tomson had Isobel.
The 31 day Robert Yong and Margaret Jonson had Andrew.
That day William Jonson and Margaret Stirk had Thomas.

M. [*None.*]

APRIL [1583].

B. The 3 day Robert Moris and Nans Cime had Alexander.
The 7 day Laurence Schortes and Katherine Mill had twins, Robert and Isobel.
That day William Walkar and Katherine Wilson had Emmie.
That day Adam Walwod and Katherine Kellok had William.
The 14 day David Anderson and Margaret Mudie had Robert.
The 17 day John Huton and Margaret Huton had Bessie.

M. The 7 day John Huton was married to Janet Peirson.
The 21 day Robert Lyndsay was married to Isobel Scotland.

MAY.

B. The first day Adam Sanders and Isobel Cunninghame had John.
That day John Robertson and Nans Lourie had James.
The 5 day Peter Caye and Nans Walker had Robert.
That day Robert Peiris and Ellen Landels had Margaret.
The 8 day William Trumbill and Margaret Sands had Janet.
That day Andrew Currie and Kate Davidsone had Grisel.
The 12 day Edward Burne and Margaret Mudie had John.
The 15 day George Hacheid of Pitfirren and Isobel Hepburn had Margaret.
The 17 day David Pitcarn and Grisel Hay had William.
The 23 day Nicol Kellok and Nans Meldrum had David.
That day Edward Andirsone and Janet Dik had Janet.
That day John Blakater and Janet Murray had John.

M. The 5 day John Astie was married to Katherine Thomson.
The 19 day Master William Walwod was married to Bessie Alexander.
And John Strang to Ellen Rae.
The 26 day Henry Gibson was married to Nans Robertson.
Antone Spens to Marion Reddie.

JUNE.

B. The 2 day John Law and Barbara Stewart had David.
That day William Crawfurd and Ellen Broun had Thomas.
The 5 day Thomas Walwod and Isobel Logtoun had Christian.
The 9 day Andrew Moris and Bessie Littill had Alison.
The 16 day Thomas Couper and Margaret Mutray had John.
That day John Andirsone and Christian Kneland had Christian.
That day Robert Duglas and Beatrix Edison had Elizabeth.
That day James Paycok and Ellen Whyt had Robert.
The 23 day Thomas Mudie and Christian Harper had William.
That day William Wilson and Janet Donald had Katherine.

M. The 2 day James Beveraige was married to Janet Gib.
The 9 day John Allane was married to Margaret Andirson.
John Hutcheson to Margaret Kent.

JULY.

B. The 10 day George Fleming and Isobel Burne had Patrick.
That day David Scharpe and Elspet Hugone had Janet.
The 14 day William Walkar and Geilis Portair had Andrew.

The 17 day John Hugone and Bessie Wilsoune had Christian.
The 24 Robert Lunne and Janet Law had Margaret.
That day David Hendirsone, *alias* Webster, cordiner, and Janet Aitkin had John.
That day James Burt and Janet Blair had James.

M. The 7 day Adam Reid was married to Bessie Currour.
The 14 day William Smith was married to Janet Smith.
The 21 day John Bankis was married to Margaret Donaldson.

AUGUST.

B. The 4 day George Campbell and Isobel Huton had Elizabeth.
The 11 day Robert Dewar and Nans Myln had James.
That day Arche Cuninghame and Janet Dagleich had Marion.
The 25 day Andrew Sanders and Ellen Cant had Margaret.
That day William Riche and Ellen Broun had Steven.
That day Nicol Mackie and Katherine Horne had David.
The 28 day Andrew Chryste and Margaret Stewart had Laurence.

M. The 18 day John Lyndsay was married to Bessie Chalmer.
Andrew Simson to Christian Clune.

SEPTEMBER.

B. The 1 day Nicol Dagleich and Ellen Blakwod had Janet (in fornication, under promise of marriage, which afterwards took place).
The 4 day Laurence Ædisone and Isobel Dagleich had Bessie.
The 22 day John Andirson and Janet Barklay had Adam.
That day William Horne, smith, and Katherine Dewar had Marjory.
The 25 day James Cuming and Margaret Broun had Ellen.
The 29 day John Wright and Barbara Peirsone had David.

M. The 1 day Andrew Walker was married to Nans Wilson.

OCTOBER.

B. The 6 day Robert Durie, fiar of that Ilk, and Margaret Stewart had Eupham.
That day Thomas Trumbull and Marjory Duglas had Laurence.
That day George Trumbull and Maus Andirsone had George.
That day William Galt and Christian Paton had James.
That day John Steinson and Margaret Andirson had Adam.
The 9 day Robert Murie and Janet Weimis had Grizel.
The 13 day John Litilljone and Bessie Chrystie had James.
That day James Harrowair and Margaret Blythe had Thomas.
The 20 day Thomas Martiall and Katherine Blaik had Thomas.
That day John Paton and Ellen Nicoll had Katherine.
That day John Craige and Nans Martiall had Isobel (in fornication).
The 23 day Patrick Rowan and Geilis Wilson had John.
That day Gilbert Andirson and Nans Simmirvaill had Margaret.
The 27 day John Gaulrig and Janet Weild had Margaret.
That day Arche Swan, Beath, and Annabell Lowe had Sara.
The 30 day John Steinsone and Margaret Trumbill had John.

M. The 13 day John Wilsone was married to Isobel Fergus.

NOVEMBER.

B. The 3 day James Sanderis and Margaret Burne had Abraham.
The 10 day William Trumbill and Janet Dewar had Laurence.
That day William Dewar and Janet Steinson had Andrew.
The 17 day John Tod and Margaret Blakwod had Isobel.
That day David Hugon and Janet Millair had Marion.

That day John Hadand and Isobel Walkar had James.
The 20 day Alexander Mastirtoun and Katherine Brown had Alexander.
That day Thomas Whyt and Janet Dagleich had James.
The 24 day Robert Mudie and Bessie Pontoun had Robert.
That day Robert Stenhus and Katherine Horne had John (in fornication).
The 27 day James Cuthbert and Bessie Nicoll had William.

M.   The 10 day David Mudie was married to Elspeth Astie.
The 24 day Laurence Alison was married to Margaret Chrystie.

DECEMBER.

B.   The 8 day William Nicolsone and Janet Walker had Margaret.
That day Andrew Murray, Blackbarony, and Christian Cunninghame had Christian (in fornication).
The 11 day Laurence Kirk and Margaret Bennait had Margaret.
The 22 day John Chrystie and Ellen Woddell had William.
That day Henry Simson and Margaret Purrok had Isobel.
That day John Andirson and Janet Ædison had Bessie.
That day James Fotheringhame and Isobel Thomson had Barbara.

M.   The 22 day David Elder was married to Nans Dewer.
John Tod to Bessie Hardie.
Richard Martine to Ellen Smith.
Murdo Stewart to Margaret Bruis.
The 29 day Thomas Law was married to Katherine Inglis.

JANUARY [1583-84].

B.   The 1 day James Davidsone and Bessie Peiris had Robert.
That day Thomas Westwood and Isobel Harrowair had Thomas.
That day Laurence Walker and Marjory Phillen had John.
The 5 day Laurence Brand, Beath, and Nans Donaldsone had James.
The 15 day John Dewar and Janet Chryste had John.
The 19 day John Potter, younger, and Janet Crawfurd had John.
The 22 day John Proud and Margaret Brand had George.
The 30 day Adam Currie and Margaret Ædison had twins, John and Marjory.

M.   The 5 day Thomas Kellok was married to Bessie Hunnon.
The 19 day Gilbert Erskin was married to Christian Stewart.

FEBRUARY.

B.   The 2 day John Hodgs and Christian Dewer had Grizel.
That day Patrick Walwod and Marjory Spreull had Bessie.
That day Adam Burne and Isobel Stenhous had Margaret.
That day David Elder and Bessie Webster had Adam (in fornication).
The 9 day James Reddie and Alison Stirk had David.
That day John Astie and Catherine Thomson had Janet.
The 12 day James Meldrum and Janet Wilson had Andrew.
That day James Huton and Margaret Tasker had Margaret.
The 16 day Andrew Young and Margaret Fenton had William.
That day John Strang and Ellen Rae had Marjory.
The 23 day David Huton and Ellen Peirson had James.
That day John Rae and Elison Sanderis had Alexander.
That day John Trumbill and Marjory Couper had John.
The 26 day Harry Peirson and Marjory Dewer had Margaret.

M.   The 9 day Thomas Guild had his marriage with Kæti Gryme (*sic*) [? ratified ; there is nothing stated].
Thomas Doncan married to Keti Thomson.
The 16 day William Rae was married to Isobel Spens.
Henry Wilson to Christian Broun.

William Andirsone to Janet Broun.
Thomas Cuninghame to Katherine Jonson.
And Robert Wood to Isobel Potter.

MARCH.

B. The 1 day James Nasmyth and Effie Broun had James.
  That day Wille Murray and Kaetie Douny had Adam (in fornication).
  The 4 day James Dewer and Ketie Æson had Christian.
  The 8 day Adam Durie and Christian Barrie had Effie.
  That day George Lyon and Katherine Burne had Ellen.
  The 11 day John Watson, cordiner, and Bessie Jonsone had James.
  That day Matthew Weitid and Margaret Steinson had William.
  That day Andrew Archibald and Janet Schaw had Margaret.
  The 15 day John Mutray and Janet Tomson had Bessie.
  That day Arche Peirson and Effie Aitkin had Janet.
  That day Adam Andirson and Ellen Sanders had Bessie.
  The 18 day Alexander Wilson and Janet Cunninghame had Margaret.
  The 22 day William Walwod and Elspet Alexander had John.
  That day Robert Nicoll and Ellen Durie had Ellen.
  The 29 day [1584] George Bodwell and Nans Sandelands had Marjory.

M. The 1 day George Cuninghame was married to Janet Henrie.

APRIL [1584].

B. The 5 day Robert Kellok and Bessie Walwood had Effie.
  That day George Bull and Christian Wallace had Christian.
  The 8 day John Steill and Janet Chrystison had Thomas.
  That day John Dagleich and Janet Penman had Margaret.
  The 12 day Arche Cuninghame and Margaret Bankis had Margaret.
  That day John Huton and Janet Peirson had Margaret.
  The 15 day David Cuninghame and Bessie Cuming had Andrew.
  The 22 day John Huton and Janet Huton had John.
  That day David Williamson and Janet Harrowair had Ellen.
  The 26 day Henry Peirson and Isobel Bryce had Janet.

M The 26 day William Flukair was married to Gelis Thomson.

MAY.

B. The 3 day Michael Stewart and Janet Kellok had James.
  That day William Gay and Janet Andirsone had William.
  The 6 day William Durie and Janet Hutcheon had Janet.
  That day William Aitkin and Margaret Gibson had Isobel.
  The 17 day Robert Ranald and Janet Bandie had John.
  That day Thomas Martiall and Margaret Steill had Robert.
  That day John Colzear and Christian Stark had Nans.
  The 20 day Robert Andirson and Christian Hendirson had James.
  That day David Pitcairn and Helen Wallet had Effie (in fornication).
  The 22 David Peiris and Isobel Immerie had Edward.
  The 31 day Robert Andirson and Marion Portair had Patrick.
  That day John Galrig and Bessie Bull had Allan.
  That day David Brand and Nans Jonson had Margaret.
  That day Robert Reddie and Ellen Reddie had Laurence (in fornication).

M. The 17 day Robert Loudian was married to Katherine Walwod.

JUNE.

B. The 3 day Adam Broun, younger, and Margaret Mudie had Adam.
  That day Walter Lyndsay and Janet Porteus had Nans.
  The 7 day John Lyndsay and Janet Chalmer had Patrick.

The 14 day James Beveraig and Janet Gib had James.
The 17 day John Banks and Margaret Donaldson had David.
The 21 day Tom Cuninghame and Kete Jonson had Margaret.
The 24 day John Levistoun and Christian Beveraig had Nans.
The 28 day James Blaw and Christian Schortes had Marjory.

M. The 7 day David Pitcarne was married to Janet Wright.
The 14 day Martin Barklay was married to Kete Peirson.
That day James Inch was married to Janet Hutson.
The 21 day James Cunand was married to Barbara Walwod.
The 28 day William Broun was married to Margaret Burgan.
And Robert Moris to Marjory Edison.

JULY.

B. The 1 day Master John Fairfull and Margaret Prestoun had Isobel.
The 8 day Norman Blakater and Janet Law had James.
That day John Gibson and Nans Blakwod had Effie.
That day Alexander Cuningame and Isobel Challander had John (in fornication).
The 12 day William Kirk and Bessie Huntair had Robert.
That day Charles Walkar and Margaret Reid had Elspet.
The 13 day William Millair and Isobel Cuninghame had Allan.
The 16 day James Mutray and Marjory Bruis had Margaret.
The 22 day John Wilson and Isobel Fargus had David.
The 26 day George Halkheid of Pitfirren and Isobel Hepburne had Andrew.
That day James Michell (Crumbie) and Janet Paycok had James.
The 29 day Nicol Kellok and Nans Meldrum had John.
That day Allan Smetoun and Christian Gray had James.
That day Alexander Hendirsoun, *alias* Webster, and Janet Gib had William.

M. The 5 day Henry Peirson was married to Margaret Kemp.
The 26 day John Waik was married to Janet Broun.

AUGUST.

B. The 2 day David Mudie and Elspit Astie had Marjory.
That day Edward Rowan, Saline, and Janet Bennet had James.
The 9 day Mark Swenton and Isobel Spens had David.
The 12 day Robert Kellok and Margaret Kilgour had Christian (in fornication).
The 16 day Harry Mudie and . . . . had John (in fornication).
The 19 day Michael Horne and Christian Young had Elspet.
The 23 day William Stewart and Effie Wemis had Grizel.
That day William Turnbull and Margaret Sandis had Margaret.
That day William Andersone and Janet Broun had Christian.
The 26 day Abraham Walwod and Isobel Rowan had William.
That day Thomas Couper and Margaret Mutray had Margaret.
The 30 day Andrew Walwod and Marjory Peirsone had John.

M. The 2 day John Dik was married to Katherine Gib.
The 9 day John Cim was married to Katherine Mackie.
The 16 day David Oraik was married to Elspet Bwie.
The 23 day David Peirson was married to Margaret Cuningham.
Edward Duglas to Janet Sanders.
The 30 day John Brand was married to Christian Brand.

SEPTEMBER.

B. The 2 day James Sibbet, maltman, and Margaret Logtoun had David.
The 6 day Henry Gibson and Nans Robertsone had Janet.
The 9 day John Greiwe and Elison Hutson had Stewin.
The 13 day John Smeton and Margaret Durie had James.

That day Andrew Watson and Elspet Andirson had Andrew.
The 20 day John Huton and Nans Oraik had Christian.
The 23 day George Colzear and Janet Bull had Janet.
The 27 day James Hardie and Marion Clune had Christian.

M. The 6 day Allan Walwod was married to Rosina Walker.
The 13 day Gilbert Cunninghame was married to Margaret Sanders.
John Trottair to Janet Walkair.
The 27 day William Bardener was married to Kate Walwod.

OCTOBER.

B. The 4 day William Pratus and Margaret Cairnie had Robert.
That day George Peirson and Effie Phillen had Janet.
The 11 day Alaster Gowisone and Isobel Mutray had William (in fornication, "quho afterwards mariit hir").
The 14 day Henry Hunnon and Ellen Angus had Katherine.
The 21 day Alexander Halie, slater, and Christian Cuninghame had Andrew.
That day William Martiall and Margaret Donaldsone had William.
The 25 day Thomas Guild and Kate Grym had Margaret.
That day Geordie Lyndsay and Bessie Dewair had James (in fornication).
That day Nicol Dagleich and Margaret Donaldsone had John (in fornication).
The 28 day John Drysdaill and Marjory Sibbet had Thomas.
That day Robert Murie and Janet Wemis had John.

M. The 18 day Alexander Gordoun was married to Kate Watson.
Edward Fothringham to Janet Walker.

NOVEMBER.

B. The 8 day Crispinie Swyn and Margaret Hutcheson had James.
That day George Ædison and Janet Burn had Margaret.
The 11 day Andrew Stirk and Katherine Huton had John.
The 14 day Mark Donald and Margaret Lourie had Bessie.
The 15 day John Andirson and Margaret Ædison had Margaret.
That day John Forfair and Janet Wardlaw had Janet.
The 18 day John Lourie and Margaret Wricht had George.
The 22 day Thomas Cant and Margaret Thomson had Janet.
The 25 day William Andirson and Bessie Milln had George.
That day John Huton and Margaret Huton had Janet.
The 29 day Laurence Steinson and Bessie Meldrum had Robert.
That day Henry Dewar and Marion Huton had George.
That day Thomas Lillie and Margaret Cuninghame had Katherine (in fornication).

M. The 8 day William Smyth, reader, was married to Christian Wright.
David Stewart to Isobel Tempilman.
Thomas Crambe to Marion Fargus.
The 15 day John Thomson in Dachie was married here to Janet Robertson.
And John Huton to Margaret Wilson.
The 22 day John Broun, maltman, was married to Christian Mudie.
Peter Welie to Janet Æson.

DECEMBER.

B. The 6 day James Lyndsay, Carnock, and Marjory Bryce had William.
The 9 day Thomas Kellok and Bessie Hunnon had Isobel.
The 13 day John Andirson and Christian Kneilland had John.
That day William Wricht and Christian Thomson had Andrew.
That day John Wilzemson and Alison Aitkin had James.
The 16 day Lourie Alison and Margaret Chrystie had Laurence.

The 18 day Laurence Strang and Janet Darnie had twins, David and
  Laurence.
The 20 day Robert Angus and Margaret Rae had Bessie.
The 22 day David Henryson, cordiner, and Janet Atkin had Marjory.
The 27 day Antone Spens and Marion Reddie had Margaret.

M. The 13 day Patrick Mikiljone was married to Margaret Burne.
John Murray to Nans Wilson.
And Andrew Westwater to Susanna Meik.
The 20 day George Hill was married to Nans Thomson.
The 27 day Henry Turnbull was married to Ellen Mutray.
Robert Cuningham to Nans Andirson.

JANUARY [1584-85].

B. The 3 day Andrew Ged and Margaret Andirson had Andrew.
The 6 day James Cuthbert and Bessie Nicoll had Nans.
The 10 day David Pitcairne and Janet Wright had Isobel.
That day John Oraik (Beath) and Katherine Dik had Alison.
That day George Ædisone and Margaret Qwariour had Henry.
That day John Watsone and Christian Whyt had James (in fornication).
The 17 day William Elder and Janet Wardlaw had Grizel.
The 27 day Robert Paton and Janet Dagleich had Margaret.

M. The 3 day Robert Walwod was married to Bessie Strang.
Abraham Spens to Christian Watsone.
Nicol Dagleich to Ellen Blakwod.
The 10 day William Mutray was married to Bessie Couper.
Robert Thomson to Bessie Stalker.
The 17 day Robert Kellok was married to Margaret Cunningham.
The 24 day Robert Brand was married to Bessie Fyff.

FEBRUARY.

B. The 3 day Donald Bein and Bessie Smeton had Isobel.
That day Richard Martin and Ellen Smith had Bessie.
The 7 day David Finne and Christian Melvill had David.
That day David Elder and Nans Dewer had James.
That day John Walwod and Isobel Erskin had Elspet. (*Suther* in margin;
  for *souter*.)
That day John Law and Katherine Davidson had Janet.
That day Robert Bardiner, Carnok, and Ellen Hall had Margaret.
The 14 day John Murray, Laird of Tullibardine [1] (resident here for the time),
  and Margaret Drummond had Robert.
That day John Warkman and Bessie Aitkin had John.
That day James Couper and Christian Bening had Christian.
The 17 day William Keir and Elspet Gilgour had Bessie.
The 21 day John Burne and Marjory Andirson had Andrew.
That day Simon Davidson, collier, and Ellen Nicoll had Katherine.
That day John Ædison, Carnok, and Katherine Stewart had Elspet.
The 28 day John Andirson and Janet Barklay had James.

M. The 7 day John Moylle was married to Bessie Sanders.
Robert Gray to Marjory Henryson.
The 21 day Robert Frisser was married to Marjory Durie.
Henry Martiall to Katherine Wilson.
The 28 day John Warkman was married to Annie Schortes.
Andrew Creich to Katherine Brand.

MARCH.

B. The 3 day John Astie and Katherine Thomson had Bessie.

---

[1] In margin the words *Duke Atholl*, and a hand and asterisk.

The 7 day John Colzear, piper, and Elspet Direnoch had Andrew.
The 14 day James Sibbald and Elspet Stevin had John.
The 21 day William Walwod and Elspet Alexander had Henry.
That day John Tod, Clune, and Margaret Blaikwod had David.
That day Henry Peirson and Katherine Ædisone had Thomas.
The 24 day George Bodwell and Nans Sandilands had John.
The 28 day (1585) Gilbert Andirson and Nans Summirvaill had Margaret.
That day John Law and Barbara Stewart had Katherine.
That day Robert Peiris, mason, and Ellen Landels had Nans.
That day George Wardlaw and Annie Michell had Cuthbert.
That day Peter Dewer, Carnok, and Katherine Bruce had Nicoll.
The 31 day Andrew Chryste, deceased, and Margaret Stewart had Andrew.
That day Thomas Huton and Katherine Aitkin had Ellen.
That day John Balcais, Beath, and Christian Burt had Henry.

M. [*None.*]

APRIL [1585].

B. The 4 day Henry Wilson and Christian Broun had Janet.
That day Martin Barklay and Katherine Peirson had Bessie.
That day John Mackalzeon and Helen Ramsay had Margaret.
The 7 day Robert Davidson, weaver, and Isobel Bankis had Andrew.
That day Robert Cunninghame of the Gask and Janet Paton had Katherine.
That day John Steinson and Marjory Trumbull had John.
That day Robert Lausone and Bessie Blak had John.
That day Andrew Baxter, Dalgety, and Elspet Durie had William.
The 11 day John Andirson and Margaret Aitkin had Katherine.
The 18 day Thomas Elder and Bessie Dewer had Thomas.
That day William Gay and Christian Paton had John.
The 25 day William Broun and Janet Bell had Christian.
That day William Cuninghame and Ellen Lausone had Isobel (in fornication, under promise of marriage, shortly afterwards performed).
That day "in lyk maner" George Meson and Margaret Davidsone had Janet (in fornication).
The 28 day John Wostwood and Annie Litiljone had Effie.

M. The 18 day David Henrison was married to Grizel Mudi.
Andrew Broun to Christian Oliphant.
The 25 day Robert Young was married to Christian Brechin.
David Henrison to Margaret Knox.

MAY.

B. The 2 day Matthew Weitit and Margaret Steinson had twins, John and Christian.
That day Thomas Huton and Janet Rae had Thomas.
That day Patrick Makurtny and Christian Taylor had Janet.
That day Andrew Tempilman and Janet Cuming had Christian.
That day Robert Moris and Marjory Ædison had Janet.
The 5 day Robert Cousing and Alison Person had Janet.
The 12 day David Smyton and Isobel Cunyngham had George.
That day Andrew Inglis and Marjory Michell had Janet.
The 16 day Walter Anderson and Margaret Kellok had Alexander.
That day John Stirk and Margaret Hendrie had John.
That day Adam Wilson and Janet Priwes had Bessie.
The 19 day Thomas Walwod and Isobel Logtoun had Marjory.
The 23 day James Clun and Isobel Walker had Janet.
That day Andrew Young and Margaret Fenton had Andrew.
The 26 day George Burn and Janet Finlason had Margaret in fornication.
The 30 day John Gibbon, Carnock, and Maus Bryce had William.

M. The 23 day William Cunyngham was married to Helen Lawson.

JUNE.

B. The 9 day William Akin and Meg Gibson had John.

That day John Robertson and Marjory Steinson had Bessie.

The 16 day David Astie and Marjory Logtoun had Janet.

The 20 day Alexander Lamb and Janet Cunyngham had Robert.

The 23 John Lata and Margaret Glas had Janet (in fornication).

The 27 day Alexander Broun and Bessie Foster had Barbara.

M. The 6 day Eustacius Roughe was married to Francisca Van Dune, a Fleming, servant to the Countess of Batinburg, spouse to William Stewart, Colonel, resident here for the time.

The 13 day John Stirling was married to Christian Craik.

JULY.

B. The 4 day William Hodge and Janet Flokart had Archibald.

The 11 day George Cunyngham and Janet Hendry had George.

That day Andrew Matheson and Katherine Angus had Christian (in fornication, under promise of marriage, shortly afterwards performed).

The 14 day Henry Reid and Margaret Tod had Henry.

The 18 day Thomas Marchell and Margaret Steill had Patrick.

That day James Anderson and Margaret Lyndsay had twins, Margaret and Christian.

The 21 day Robert Marchell and Margaret Lawson had David.

The 25 day Duncan Cumrie and Margaret Tomson had Laurence (in fornication).

M. The 4 day Adam Inglis was married to Janet Peiris.

The 11 day James Crystie was married to Janet Phin.

AUGUST.

B. The 4 day James Kinross, lawyer of Edinburgh, resident here " the tym of the pest," and Janet Orak had William.

That day Robert Dalgleische and Janet Harpar had James.

That day William Dowglas, collier, and Janet Tenan had John.

That day John Crummy and Effie Hutton had Elspet.

The 11 day Robert Fillan, Beath, and Bessie Walwod had Margaret.

That day John Stoby and Marion Akin had Janet.

The 18 day David Steward and Isobel Tempilman had Bessie.

The 25 day William Smyth, reader, and Christian Wryght had William.

That day John Rioche and Bessie Keir had John (in fornication).

The 29 day Robert Anderson and Marion Portar had Margaret.

M. The 22 day Andrew Johnson was married to Janet Valleng.

SEPTEMBER.

B. The 13 day John Thomson, mason, and Bessie Stewart had Margaret.

The 19 day William Schortus and Barbara Douglas had Robert.

That day Stevin Donat and Janet Kellok had Philip.

The 22 day Mr. John Farfull, schoolmaster, and Margaret Preston had Norman.

That day Patrick Makmony and Nans Paton had William.

The 26 day . . . . Magilhois (M'Lehose) and Janet Lyndsay had Walter.

The 28 day John Murray and Amy Wilson had Bessie.

The 29 day Edward Burn and Margaret Mudy had John.

That day Adam Walwod and Katherine Kellok had Allan.

That day John Strange, cordiner, and Helen Rae had Bessie.

M. The 5 day Andrew Matheson was married to Katherine Angus.

The 26 day William Craik was married to Alison Burgane.

OCTOBER.

B. The 3 day John Tomson and Janet Smyth had Laurence.
That day Robert Kellok and Christian Donatson had Nans.
The 6 day Patrick Mikiljhone and Margaret Burne had Janet.
That day James Cumin and Margaret Brown had Elspet.
The 10 day Robert Douglas and Beatrix Ædison had Helen.
The 13 day James Robertson and Elspet Rob had Thomas.
The 17 day Abraham Spens and Christian Watson had Janet.
That day Robert Cunyngham and Nans Andirson had Robert.
The 20 day James Meldrum and Janet Wilson had Helen.
That day Robert Young and Margaret Jhonson had Bessie.
The 24 day David Person and Margaret Cunyngham had John.
That day William Walkar and Catherine Donatson had Margaret.
That day Mark Suynton, slater, and Isobel Spens had Isobel.
The 26 day John Gotterstoun and Bessie Ogrie had Janet.
The 31 day Adam Fargus and Christian Dryisdaill had John.
That day Adam Dury and Christian Barry had Nans.
That day John Wrycht and Barbara Person had Beatrix.

M. [*None*].

NOVEMBER.

B. The 7 day John Lyndsay, Carnock, and Bessie Chalmer had Margaret.
That day John Hutton and Magie Wilson had Bessie.
That day Adam Sanders and Isobel Cunyngham had Adam. (Posthumous *in margin.*)
The 14 day Robert Moreis and Nans Cim had Grizel.
The 21 day William Ogrie "had a lad off Cristen Horn baptized and callit Patrick." (Edinburgh *in margin.*)
That day William Trumble and Margaret Sandis had William.
That day Archie Person and Effie Akin had Archie.
The 24 day James Cunnan and Barbara Valwod had Helen.
The 28 day John Greiwe and Bellison Hudson had Elspet.

M. The 7 day Peter Trumble was married to Isobel Car.

DECEMBER.

B. The first day Robert Kellok and Margaret Cunyngham had William.
The 5 day John Wilson and Isobel Fargus had Bessie.
That day William Millar and Isobel Cunyngham had Robert.
The 8 day George Fleming and Isobel Burn had Henry.
The 12 day Henry Trumble and Helen Moutray had Robert.
That day James Blaw and Christian Schortus had Nans.
The 15 day John Watson and Bessie Jhonson had Katherine.
That day Andrew Currie and Keat Davidson had Janet.
The 19 day John Stenhous and Margaret Douglas had Harry.
That day Murdo Stewart and Margaret Bruce had Beatrix.
That day Andrew Alison and Helen Cuming had Emmie.
That day John Craik and Jany Reid had Adam.
The 29 day Andrew Trinche and Janet Schawe had John.

M. The 12 day John Young was married to Nans Andirson.
John Person to Katherine Macky.
The 26 day Andrew Murray was married to Effie Weimes.

JANUARY [1585-86].

B. The 2 day Andrew Brand and Isobel Cuming had Robert.
That day Thomas Trumble and Marjory Douglas had Thomas.
That day George Campell and Isobel Hutton had George.
That day Robert Brand and Bessie Fyff had Margaret.
The 5 day Wille Rae and Isabel Spens had William.

That day William Durie and Janet Hutcheon had Grizel.
That day William Robertson, younger, in Cragdukie, and Nans Tomson
    had John.
The 9 day John Gray and Janet Maye had Bessie.
The 12 day Thomas Quhyt and Janet Dalgleisch had Helen.
The 16 day John Moreis in Coudoun and Bessie Steinson had William.
That day William Colzear, younger, and Elizabeth Lyndsay had James.
The 19 day William Dewar and Janet Steinson had Helen.
The 23 day John Hutton and Christian Wilson had Janet.
The 30 day Mark Donat and Margaret Lourie had George.
That day Laurie Patrik and Isobel Steinson had Marion (in fornication).
That day Thomas Mudy and Christian Harpar had Beatrix.
That day Andrew Archibald and Janet Schaw had Isobel.
That day Robert Mowbray and Christian Dilly had Janet.
That day Nicol Dalgleisch and Ellen Blakwod had Isobel.

M.   The 2 day James Andirson was married to Christian Michie.
The 23 day Allan Mudy was married to Janet Forfair.
The 30 day Henry Stoby was married to Keat Andirson.

FEBRUARY.

B.   The 9 day Rob Tomson and Bessie Stakar had James.
The 13 day George Hakat of Pitfirren and Isobel Hepburn had William.
That day William Mekiljhon and Bessie Baxter had Robert.
That day James Davidson and Bessie Peiris had Adam.
That day John Dewar and Christian Dewer had Keat.
The 20 day William Hutton and Mage Knox had Harry (in fornication).
That day Rob Walwod and Bessie Strang had David.
That day John Anderson and Jeny Ranet had James.
That day James Sanderis and Margaret Andirson had Elspet.
That day James Elison and Katherine Huch had Laury.
The 27 day Rob Quhyt and Marion Lyndsay had Margaret.
That day John Chatton and Janet Marchel had Robert.
That day David Henderson, *alias* Wobster, and Janet Akin had James.

M.   The 6 day Harry Millar was married to Janet Andirson.
William Legat to Margaret Coupar.

MARCH.

B.   The 13 day Robert Nicol and Henry Durie had Alexander.
That day George Colzear and Janet Bull had Christian.
That day John Huggon and Bessie Wilson had Marjory.
That day James Quhyt and Maus Inglis had Thomas.
That day William Douglas, Rossyth, and Elspet Low had William.
The 20 day Robert Mudy and Bessie Pontoun had Peter.
That day John Bankis and Margaret Donaldson had Catrin.
That day William Tomson, Beath, and Janet Mudy had Janet.
The 27 day [1586] John Chrystie and Helen Weddel had Margaret.
That day William Main and Christian Wrycht had James (in fornication,
    3rd or 4th relapse).

M.   [*None*].

APRIL [1586].

B.   The 3 day John Gib and Isobel Lyndsay had Margaret.
That day Andrew Dik and Janet Stirling had Margaret.
The 10 day David Henderson and Grizel Mudy had Margaret.
That day Robert Ramsay and Christian Fyf had Marion.
That day William Steidman and Margaret Schairp had Nans.
The 13 day David Eldar and Nans Dewar had Edward.
That day James Cuthbert and Bessie Nicol had Grizel.

F

The 17 day John Robertson and Nans Laurie had Helen.
That day Archie Cunyngham and Janet Dagleisch had Emmie.
That day James Inche and Janet Hudson had Grizel.
The 24 day George Trumble and Maus Anderson had Helen.
That day Rob Davidson and Isobel Bankis had Robert.

M. The 17 day John Cuthbert was married to Alison Sanders.

MAY.

B. The first day Robert Dewar and Nans Mil had John.
The 8 day David Phin and Christian Melvil had James.
That day John Anderson and Christian Kneilan had Wattir (Walter).
That day John Hutton and Janet Hutton had Marjory.
The 11 day George Bodwell and Nans Sandilands had William.
That day Norman Blakater and Janet Law had Margaret.
That day John Pottar and Janet Crawfurd had Henry.
The 15 day John Galrik and Janet Wyild had Helen.
That day John Acheson and Isobel Crawfurd had Christian (in fornication).
The 22 day James Moutray and Marjory Bruce had Janet.
That day John Davidson and Keat Cristel had Ellen.
The 29 day David Pitcarn and Janet Wrycht had Janet.
That day William Moutray and Bessie Coupar had John.
That day Rob Young and Christian Brechen had Andrew.
That day John Haddon and Isobel Walkar had James.

M. The 1 day James Vallenge was married to Katherine Wilson.
John Coupar to Christian Angus.
The 15 day James Curror was married to Margaret Gibson.
John Lata to Margaret Glass.
The 22 day John Westwod was married to Janet Cunyngham.

JUNE.

B. The 5 day Thomas Coupar and Margaret Moutray had James.
That day Donat Dun and Bessie Bain had Janet.
That day John Wryght and Maus Paton had Janet.
The 8 day Robert Wallis and Grizel Michy had Robert.
The 15 day John Hutton and Margaret Hutton had David.
The 19 day John Walwod and Margaret Bull had John (in fornication).
That day John Kellok and Margaret Donaldson had Margaret.
The 26 day John Steil and Janet Crystie had Effy.
That day Andrew Walwod and Marjory Peirson had Janet.

M. The 5 day William Burn was married to Ellen Wilson.
The 19 day Adam Wat was married to Nans Brown.
And John Clark to Bessie Brand.
The 26 day David Wallis was married to Janet Alison.
And Robert Anderson to Effy Harrower.

JULY.

B. The 3 day Michael Stewart and Janet Kellok had Margaret.
The 10 day Henry Straquhain and Janet More had Thomas.
The 17 day James Baiwerage and Janet Gib had Janet.
That day Robert Cusing and Alison Person had Katherine.
The 20 day William Horn and Katherine Dewar had Margaret.
The 23 day Edward Fothringham and Janet Walkar had a daughter . . . .
The 24 day James Peacok and Ellen Quhyt had William.
The 27 day Adam Inglis and Janet Peiris had Andrew.
The 31 day William Walwod and Elspet Alschunder had William.
That day John Forfar and Janet Wardlaw had James.
That day Philip Mowbray and Jenet Mil had Christian (in fornication).

That day Thomas Brand and Margaret Wilson had Isobel (in fornication).
That day John Smart and Marjory Hutton had Ellen (in fornication).

M. The 9 day John Walwod was married to Marjory Watson.
George Meason to Margaret Davidson.
The 17 day Robert Kellok was married to Janet Chalmers.
Andrew Lauder to Grizel Hutcheon.
The 31 day Andrew Walwod was married to Marion Preston.

AUGUST.

B. The 14 day Thomas Westwod and Isobel Harrower had Isobel.
That day Adam Burn and Isobel Stenhous had John.
That day Andrew Sanders and Helen Cant had Clement.
The 24 day John Broun and Christian Mudy had Robert.

M. The 7 day John Ker was married to Jean Gib.
John Bennet to Katherine Russel.
The 14 day Andrew Smyth was married to Margaret Walwod.
Alexander Gardinar to Catherine Gothray.
John Orok to Christian Brown.
Robert Gardinar to Janet Gardinar.
The 28 day John Bryce was married to Katharine Angus.

SEPTEMBER.

B. The 11 day David Cunyngham and Bessie Cuming had Ellen.
That day John Jhonston and Christian Broun had Robert.
The 18 day William Walkar and Geilis Porter had Marjory.
The 25 day Allan Walwod and Rosina Walkar had David.
That day John Anderson and Janet Ædison had John.

M. The 11 day Robert Ranat was married to Katherine Aikman.

OCTOBER.

B. The 2 day James Sybbald and Margaret Logton had William.
That day Andrew Moreis and Bessie Litill had Bessie.
That day Geordie Ædison and Janet Miller had Thomas.
The 9 day James Murray and Agnes Lyndsay had Patrick.
That day Robert Cunyngham and Nans Anderson had Charles.
The 16 day Edward Douglas and Janet Sanders had Margaret.
That day Edward Anderson and Janet Dik had Robert.
The 19 day Thomas Alison and Christian Dalgleisch had Katherine.
That day John Steinson and Marjory Trumble had Margaret.
The 23 day James Coupar and Christian Binning had Margaret.
The 26 day William Prathus and Margaret Cairny had Jean.
That day Adam Currie and Margaret Ædisone had Grizel.
That day John Dalgleisch and Janet Penman had Janet.

M. The 23 day Patrick Walker was married to Isobel Muir.
The 30 day Philip Moubray was married to Elspet Spittel.
Alexander Galrik to Grizel Steinson.

NOVEMBER.

B. The 2 day Adam Dury and Christian Barrie had Barbara.
The 6 day David Hutton and Helen Peirson had Margaret.
The 8 day Andrew Murray and Effy Weims had Patrick.
The 12 day Alexander Henderson and Janet Gib had Robert.
That day Patrick Fyllour and Nans Kennedy had Margaret (in fornication).
That day John Clatchie and Janet Hendirson had Margaret.
The 20 day David Huggon and Janet Millar had Margaret.

M.   The 12 day John Wittet was married to Alison Wallas.
George Cant to Beatrix Broun.
The 20 day James Cairnis was married to Margaret Davidson.
The 27 day John Menteth was married to Janet Peacok.

DECEMBER.

B.   The 4 day John Lewinston and Christian Bewarage had John.
That day George Mil and Christian Wallas had Ellen.
That day Peter Trumbil and Isobel Ker had Janet.
That day Henry Hunnon and Ellen Angus had Adam.
The 12 day George Dury and Nans Gatt had William.
That day David Smeton and Isobel Cunyngham had Marjory.
The 16 day Robert Cunyngham and Marion Patton had Bessie.
That day Laurence Walkar and Marjory Fillan had Andrew.
The 21 day John Stoby and Marion Aikin had Bessie.
That day William Eldar and Janet Wardlaw had Marjory.
The 25 day Allan Mudy and Janet Forfair had John.
That day William Kent and Margaret Paterson had Janet (in fornication).
The 28 day Robert Schortous and Janet Broun had Thomas.

M.   The 4 day Francis Nepar was married to Margaret Mowbray.
John Dewar to Bessie Walwod.
The 11 day Robert Aikin was married to Elspet Murray.
John Anderson to Bessie Crystie.
Patrick Marschell to Katherine Crystie.
The 18 day John Crawfurd was married to Katherine Robertson.

JANUARY [1586-87].

B.   The first day Henry Broun, Carnock, and Katherine Hendry had Nans.
The 4 day John Gotterston and Bessie Ogry had William.
The 8 day John Hutton and Bessie Wrycht had Bessie.
The 15 day John Boyd and Janet Blair had John (in fornication).
That day Robert Morcis and Maige Ædison had Ellen.
That day George Dury and Janet Lyndsay had Christian (in fornication).
That day Robert Moutray and Margaret Cunyngham had Bessie (in fornication).
The 19 day Allan Wat and Agnes Broun had John.
That day David Peirson and Marion Lambert had Margaret.
That day William Legat and Margaret Cupar had Christian.

M.   The 8 day John Paterson was married to Janet Peirson.
The 15 day John Blakater was married to Janet Dury.
The 22 day Robert Mey was married to Katherine Smart.
Patrick Lermont to Katherine Roger.

FEBRUARY.

B.   The 5 day William Cairny and Katherine Finlason had Andrew (in fornication).
That day David Read and Bessie Duncan had David (in adultery).
The 12 day Henry Trumbil and Helen Moutray had Margaret.
The 19 day Robert Wilson and Janet Henderson had David.
The 22 day William Dury and Janet Hutcheon had George.
The 26 day William Gray and Isobel Gray had David.
That day Martin Barclay and Katherine Peirson had Thomas.
That day Walter Lyndsay and Janet Porteous had Robert.

M.   The 26 day James Kay was married to Janet Dewar.
Andrew Blakie to Elspet Robertson.

MARCH.

B. The 5 day Andrew Matheson and Keat Angus had Janet.

That day John Dryisdail and Marjory Sibbald had John.

The 12 day Nicol Jhonson and Katherine Davidson had Thomas (in fornication).

The 15 day Patrick Mekiljhon and Margaret Burn had William.

The 19 day William Wilson and Janet Gray had Janet (in fornication).

The 22 day Patrick Stewart and Katherine Baram had Bessie.

The 26 day [1587] John Murray and Agnes Wilson (who died in childbirth of other two) had Patrick.

M. [*None.*]

APRIL.

B. The 2 day Robert Angus and Mage Rae had Christian.

John Law that day and Barbara Stewart had Bessie.

That day William Cuninghame and Ellen Lawsone had John.

That day Charles Walkar and Margaret Reid had Sara.

The 5 day Mr. John Fairfull and Margaret Prestoun had David.

The 9 day Henry Peirsone and Katherine Edisone had Janet.

The 12 day William Smyth and Christian Wright had John.

That day Robert Murie and Janet Weymis had Elspet.

That day Henry Dewer and Marion Huton had John.

The 19 day John Astie and Katherine Tomson had Patrick.

That day John Burn and Marjory Anderson had John.

The 23 day Andrew Stirk and Margaret Huton had Margaret.

That day Alexander Oswald and Bessie Stoby had Rosina (in fornication).

That day John Steinson and Margaret Anderson had Margaret.

M. The 2 day Abraham Walwod was married to Barbara Walwood.

The 30 day Walter Swenton was married to Christian Cant.

MAY.

B. The 7 day Thomas Cant and Margaret Tomson had John.

That day David Wallis and Janet Alison had Margaret.

The 14 day John Proud and Christian Brand had twins, Henry and Andrew.

That day John Smeton and Margaret Dury had Thomas.

That day John Horn and Margaret Broun had Margaret.

That day John Fothringham and Isobel Tomson had Bessie.

The 21 day Robert Kid and Margaret Redy had Christian.

That day David Hendirson and Grizel Mudy had Isobel.

That day Patrick Stenhous and Christian Bowman had Margaret.

That day Andrew Angus and Isobel Inglis had John.

The 28 day James Cuming and Margaret Brown had Eupham.

That day George Lyall and Kate Burn had Marjory.

That day Andrew Wat and Elspet Andirson had James.

The 31 day Alexander Mastirtoun and Katherine Broun had Margaret.

M. The 14 day John Watson was married to Christian Kingorn.

The 28 day John Steinsone was married to Elizabeth Huton.

JUNE.

B. The 6 day John Mutray and Janet Tomson had Margaret.

The 11 day John Clark and Bessie Brand had Margaret.

The 12 Lourie Dagleich and Margaret Carrik had Katherine (in fornication).

The 14 day George Peirson and Effie Phillen had David.

That day Harry Peirson and Marjory Dewer had Nans.

The 20 day William Andirson and Margaret Atkin had John.

The 25 day John Gib and Isobel Lyndsay had James.

That day Matthew Hutsone, collier, and Marion Hendrie had Effie.

M. The 18 day Isobel Gardiner was married to James Hobroun (**Hepburn**).
Peter Robertson to Margaret Aitkin.
The 25 day Adam Andirson was married to Christian Thomson.

JULY.

B. The 2 day John Watsone and Bessie Jonsone had Robert.
That day Mark Swenton and Isobel Spens had John.
That day David Tod, merchant, and Maus Dagleich had Janet.
The 5 day Crispinie Swyne and Margaret Hutcheson had Isobel.
The 29 day William Coumbrie and Christian Phillip had Margaret.
That day Lourence Ædison and Isobel Dagleich had Janet.
The 30 day Patrick Walkar and Isobel Muir had Marjory.

M. The 2 day William Sandelandis was married to Keit Wilson *alias* Culrois.
The 9 day Robert Wilson was married to Margaret Scotland.
That day Edward Thomson was married to Elspet Bennie.

AUGUST.

B. The 6 day Laurence Schortes and Katherine Mill had Thomas.
That day Henry Meldrum and Effie Martiall had Laurence (in fornication).
That day Thomas Wilson (*alias* Culrois) and Janet Donaldson had Laurence (in fornication).
The 9 day Laurence Alison and Margaret Chryste had James.
That day Robert Kellok and Nans Meldrum had Margaret.
The 13 day Andrew Inglis and Maige Michell had John.
That day Robert Kellok in Mastirtoun and Janet Chalmer had James.
The 20 day Henry Gibson and Nans Robertson had Beatrix.
The 27 day William Brown and Janet Bell had William.
The 30 day James Meldrum and Janet Wilson had a daughter. . . .

M. The 6 day Adam Bartoun (*or* Bowtoun) was married to Nans Martiall.
John Peirson to Grizel Mastirtoun.
The 20 day Robert Broun was married to Janet Duglas.

SEPTEMBER.

B. The 3 day David Elder and Nans Dewer had Katherine.
That day George Cuninghame and Janet Henrie had Christian.
The 11 day John Andirsone and Bessie Chryste had Janet. "She bair twynnis, and this that was baptized was first born, the second was dead born."
The 17 day Robert Aitkin and Elspet Murray had James.
The 24 day Rob Young and Christian Brechin had James.

M. [*None.*]

OCTOBER.

B. The 1 day John Furd and Elison Nicoll had Robert.
The 8 day Peter Lermonth and Katherine Roger had Bessie.
The 15 day John Gibsone and Annie Blakwod had Ellen.
That day David Scharp and Elspet Ædisone had Ellen.
The 18 day Thomas Walwod and Isobel Logtoun had Thomas.
That day John Wallet at Touchmill and Isobel Erskin had Christian.
The 22 day Robert Lawson and Bessie Blak had Isobel.
That day John Mackalzeon and Ellen Ramsay had James.
That day Lourence Strang and Janet Darin had Nans.
The 25 day John Trumbill and Marjory Couper had Bessie.

M. The 1 day William Walkar was married to Isobel Kellok.
The 8 day David Barkclay was married to Emily Dagleich.

NOVEMBER.

B.   The 1 day Henry Stobie and Keit Andirson had David.
  The 5 day David Hastie and Marjory Logtoun had Margaret.
  That day John Strang and Ellen Rae had John.
  The 8 day Philip Mubray and Elspet Spittell had James.
  The 12 day Andrew Young and Margaret Fentoun had Patrick.
  That day John Andirson and Margaret Ædison had John.
  That day George Ædisone and Margaret Qwariour had Margaret.
  That day Lourie Andirson and Keit Sutar had James (in fornication).
  The 15 day William Rae and Isobel Spens had Walter.
  The 19 day William Mutray and Bessie Couper had Margaret.
  The 22 day Robert Kellok and Margaret Cunninghame had Robert.
  The 26 day John Davidson and Keit Kirstill had Henry.
  That day James Dewer and Keit Æson had John.

M.   The 19 day James Chalmer was married to Margaret Sandis.

DECEMBER.

B.   The 6 day Clement Sanders and Marion Bell had Janet.
  That day James Kinross and Janet Oraik had Lilias.
  That day Robert Ranald and Keit Aikman had William.
  The 10 day James Murray and Nans Lyndsay had George.
  That day Peter Trumbull and Isobel Car had Margaret.
  That day Nicol Hart and Bessie Hartsyde had James.
  That day Simon Davidsone and Ellen Nicol had Janet.
  The 13 day David Stewart and Isobel Tempilman had David.
  That day Alexander Murray, salter, and Maus Wilson had Janet.
  The 17 day Adam Durie and Christian Barrie had John.
  That day John Brand and Christian Brand had Mawse.
  The 31 day John Huton, weaver, and Margaret Wilson had Janet.
  That day Robert Andirson and Marion Portair had Marjory.

M.   The 3 day Lourie Patrik was married to Janet Moris.
  John Ewin to Janet Nicoll.
  The 10 day Robert Peirs was married to Bessie Burn.
  The 17 day Adam Schortes was married to Margaret Miller.
  The 31 day Alexander Creich was married to Grizel Walker.
  That day Thomas Yong was married to Maus Andirson.

JANUARY [1587-88].

B.   The 3 day John Andirson and Christian Kneland had William.
  That day John Thomson and Bessie Stewart had Barbara.
  That day John Mories and Bessie Steinson had David.
  The 14 day Matthew Withed and Margaret Steinson had William.
  That day Alexander Lambe and Janet Cunninghame had James.
  That day Stevin Donald and Janet Kellok had Robert.
  That day John Huton and Christian Wilson had Isobel.
  That day William Sandelandis and Kete Culross *alias* Wilson had George.
  The 21 day Arche Peirson and Effie Aitkin had James.
  That day John Hodgs and Christian Dewar had Bessie.
  That day John Thomson and Janet Smyth had Andrew.
  The 28 day John Montheith and Janet Paycok had Annie.
  That day James Blaw and Christian Schortes had Janet.
  That day David Peirson and Margaret Cunninghame had Robert.
  That day James Sibbet and Elspet Stevin had Margaret.
  That day Robert Young and Margaret Jonson had James.
  That day Adam Fargus and Christian Drysdaill had Margaret.
  The 31 day Adam Bowtoun and Nans Martiall had Robert.

M.   The 14 day John Tomson was married to Maus Bull.
  Thom Dewer to Janet Bonair.

Thome Kellok to Margaret Huton.
The 28 day David Lillie was married to Janet Jhonston.

FEBRUARY.

B.   The 4 day John Wilson and Kæti Moris had John.
That day John Bankis and Margaret Donaldsone had Barbara.
That day Harry Miller and Janet Andirson had Isobel.
That day Rob Tomson and Bessie Stalker had John.
That day John Greif and Bellisant Hutson had Kæte.
The 18 day John Oraik and Christian Brown had Janet.
That day John Dischintoun, deceased, and Marion Andirson ("that cam
      heir to be nurische in Pittirren") had Robert.
That day William Robertson, younger, and Nans Tomson had Janet.
That day Robert Wallange and Katherine Wilson had Katherine.

M.   The 4 day John Wilson was married to Katherine Makarton.
That day Charles Andirson was married to Margaret Imrie.
The 11 day John Walkar was married to Margaret Stewart.
Henry Mudie to Margaret Reid.
John Burn to Marion Montheith.
The 18 day William Elder was married to Katherine Cuninghame.
John Dempstertoun to Christian Dewer.
George Burn to Marjory Bull.
James Bairdi to Margaret Fleming.
Robert Breid to Nans Andirson.
The 25 day James Cois was married to Margaret Donaldson.

MARCH.

B.   The 10 day Adam Broun of Fod and Margaret Mudie had Elspet.
That day William Dewer and Janet Steinson had Grizel.
That day Andrew Johnson and Janet Wallenge had Janet.
The 17 Walter Anderson and Margaret Kellok had Isobel.
That day William Riche and Ellen Brown had Margaret.
That day John Walker and Margaret Tomson had twins, Janet and
      Christian.
That day Robert Andirson and Effie Harrowar had William.
That day James Young and Nans Andirson had Marjory.
That day James Nasmyth and Effie Brown had Marjory.
The 31 day [1588] John Tod and Margaret Blakwod had Janet.
That day Robert Welles and Grizel Miche had Alexander.
That day George Burn and Marjory Bull had Janet.

M.   [*None.*]

APRIL [1588].

B.   The 7 day John Robertson and Marjory Steinson had John.
That day Robert Walwod and Bessie Strang had Grizel.
That day John Wilsone and Isobel Fargus had Sarah.
The 14 day Geordi Abircrumby and Kati Smyth had Effie (in fornication).
The 17 day Lourence Kirk and Margaret Bennet had Marion.
That day Thomas Trumbill and Marjory Duglas had Andrew.
That day Andrew Archibald and Janet Schawe had Janet.

M.   [*None.*]

MAY.

B.   The 5 day George Fleming in Blaklaw and Isobel Burne had George.
That day Thomas Stenhus and Barbara Douglas had John.
That day Robert Moris and Marjory Edison had Margaret.
That day Donald Dun and Margaret Bain had twins, Thomas and Robert.
That day Thom Burrie and Maige Fuird had Bessie (in fornication).

That day Sande Stirk and Bessie Sanders (whom shortly after he married) had Grizel (in fornication).

The 19 day Henry Durie and Margaret Makbeith had a son . . . .

That day Alexander Scotland and Elspet Bryce had Robert.

The 26 day John Crawfurd and Kate Robertson had Janet.

M. The 12 day Bessie Coutis was married to David Brown.

The 19 day Jeremy Esplein was married to Christian Dagleich.

Tom Burn to Keit Stewart.

JUNE.

B. The 2 day Thomas Huton and Marion Broun had Margaret.

That day James Colzear and Margaret Westwod had Christian (in fornication).

The 9 Arche Cunninghame and Margaret Banks had Janet.

The 12 day Andrew Brand and Isobel Cuming had Adam.

The 12 day Andrew Brand and Isobel Cuming had Adam.[1]

The 23 day Wille Walkar and Kete Wilson had Barbara.

M. The 9 day Alexander Stirk was married to Bessie Sanders.

That day William Levistoun was married to Kaeti Finlason.

Robert Hugon to Isobel Eson.

The 30 day John Andirson was married to Keit Proves.

JULY.

B. The 10 day James Cairnis, weaver, and Margaret Davidsone had John.

"The 11 day Wille Huton had a woman chyld born to him of Isobell Broun, whom (fleing the disciplin of his kirk) unlaufully he maried in Saling, yit the bairn presented be faithfull men we baptized and called Marain."

The 14 day Allan Walwod and Rosina Walkar had Bessie.

That day William Flockart and Nans Cois had Beatrix (in fornication under promise of marriage, afterward promised to be performed— seuerti, R : D :).

The 28 day Norman Blakader and Janet Law had Christian.

M. The 21 day James MacKalzeon was married to Isobel Clark.

Henry Paycock to Christian Martein.

John Patirson to Margaret Watson.

AUGUST.

B. The 18 day Robe Brand and Bessie Fyff had Patrick.

That day Abraham Spens and Christian Watson had Beatrix.

That day William Gay and Christian Paton had Marjory.

That day Adam Wallwod and Keit Kellok had Marjory.

That day Edward Tomson and Elspet Bennie had Margaret.

That day Pete Galt and Bessie Edisone had John.

That day Lourence Steinsone and Bessie Meldrum had Laurence.

That day John Carslaw and Maus Blakat had Bessie (in fornication, but under promise of marriage performed the 18 of May *anno* 1589).

That day Peter Dewer and Katherine Bruce had Robert.

The 21 day Robert Paycok and Margaret Broun [2] had John.

The 25 day Alexander Galrig and Grizel Steinson had Margaret.

The 28 day William Wilson and Janet Donald had Robert.

That day Patrick Stenhus and Janet Bowman had Edward.

M. The 4 day Andrew Spreall was married to Margaret Broun.

That day James Tomson was married to Christian Broun.

The 11 day Arche Wostwood was married to Elspet Horn.

SEPTEMBER.

B. The first day Laurence Walkar and Marjory Phillen had Margaret.

---

[1] This entry is repeated in the register.

[2] "Innerkethin, died in the birth."

That day David Horn, miller in . . . st mill, and Nans Gillespik had James.
The 8 day Andrew Alison and Helen Cuming had John.
That day George Campbell and Isobel Huton had Janet.
That day Adam Wat and Nans Brown had Patrick.
The 11 day Robert Nicoll and Helen Durie had Marjory.
The 15 day Andrew Smyth in Fod and Margaret Walwod had William.
That day Robert Stenhus and Katherine Duglas had Helen.
The 22 day Peter Robertson and Margaret Aitkin had Geilis.
The 25 day George Peirson and Effie Phillen had Nans.
The 29 day John Brown and Christian Mudie had Janet.

M.   The 8 day John Wellis was married to Bessie Blak.

OCTOBER.

B.   The 6 day Robert Peiris and Bessie Burne had Janet.
That day James Talzeour and Emmie Ranie had James.
The 20 day John Peirsoun and Grizel Mastirtoun had Margaret.
The 27 day David Pitcairne and Janet Wright had David.

M.   The 13 day James Alisoun was married to Nans Poutie.
The 27 day Robert Wellis was married to Grizel Anderson.
And Andrew Mutray to Margaret Cuninghame.

NOVEMBER.

B.   The 3 day Edward Burne and Margaret Mudie had Thomas.
That day Richard Potter and   had Richard (in fornication, under promise of marriage).
The 6 day Thomas Makilhois and Janet Lyndsay had twins, John and Patrick.
The 10 day Henry Trumbill and Helen Mutray had Alexander.
The 20 day Alexander Mastirtoun and Kate Broun had John.
That day Robe Bread and Nans Andirson had John.
The 24 day John Walkar and Margaret Stewart had John.
That day Adam Andirson and Christian Thomson had Margaret.
That day Alexander Creich and Grizel Walkar had John.

M.   The 3 day Henry Gilqwhain was married to Isobel Wilson.
The 10 day Laurence Huton was married to Bessie Blak.
That day Edward Cowie was married to Bessie Jonson.
The 24 day John Makie was married to Janet Walwod.
John Gotherstoun to Margaret Clerk.

DECEMBER.

B.   The 1 day John Craik, deceased, and Janet Reid had Bessie.
That day Lourie Patrick and Janet Moris had Robert.
The 4 day John Warkman and Bessie Aitkin had James.
That day James Sibbet and Margaret Logtoun had a daughter . . . .
The 8 day Rob Cusing and Allison Peirson had Robert.
That day John Chrystie and Ellen Woddell had Kate.
The 15 day James Chalmeris and Margaret Sandis had James.
That day Thomas Dewer and Janet Bonair had Andrew.
That day James Mutray and Marjory Bruce had Elspet.
That day John Wostwood and Annie Littiljone had Grizel.
The 22 day Mark Donald and Margaret Lourie had Robert.
That day James Cunnand and Barbara Walwod had David.
That day Robert Cunninghame and Nans Andirsone had George.
That day Harry Mudie and Margaret Reid had Bessie.
That day George Colzear and Janet Bull had Bessie.
That day John Ewne and Janet Nicol had Nans.
The 29 day James Anderson, Inverkeithing, and Janet Mudie had David.

M.   The 1 day Andrew Dik was married to Katherine Hendin.
The 15 day John Dewer was married to Janet Couper.
The 22 day James Reid was married to Bessie Lyndsay.
The 29 day Alexander Huton was married to Margaret Walwod.
Matthew Main to Christian Wallace.
James Lyndsay to Janet Schortes.

JANUARY [1588-89].

B.   The 1 day Robert Mersair and Margaret Balrain had Bessie.
The 5 day William Murdo, Ferrie, and Janet Burgain had James.
That day Richard Martin and Ellen Smyth had Marjory.
That day Simon Peirson and Margaret Oraik had Janet.
That day Peter Trumbill and Isobel Car had James.
The 12 day William Pratus and Margaret Cairnie had Effie.
That day Rob Car and Effie Abircrumbie had Bessie.
The 19 day James Murray and Nans Lyndsay had Katherine.
That day James Peirson and Grizel Thomsone had John.
That day Robert Ranald and Katherine Aikman had James.
That day Arch Cuninghame and Janet Dagleish had Janet.

M.   The 19 day George Warkman was married to Beatrix Smyth.

FEBRUARY.

B.   The 2 day George Warkman and Beatrix Smyth had George.
That day David Wellis and Janet Alison had Bessie.
That day Adam Wilson and Janet Proves had Margaret.
The 9 day James Robertson and Elspet Rob had James.
That day David Cunninghame and Bessie Cuming had a (posthumous) child baptized Margaret.
That day David Callendair and Janet Andirson had David (in fornication).
That day David Huton in Pittindine and Janet Peirson had John.
That day John Hugon and Janet Wilson had Bessie.
The 16 day John Andirsone at the Corss and Christian Kneland had George.
That day Robert Ramsay and Christian Fyff had Robert.
That day Andrew Blakwod and Elspet Robertson had Margaret.

M.   The 2 day William Gray was married to Margaret Fargusson.
Thomas Couper to Margaret Law.
The 9 day David Barklay was married to Christian Schortous.
And Riche Potter to Christian Couper.

MARCH.

B.   The 2 day William Elder and Kete Cuninghame had Margaret.
That day James Widdirspune and Janet Gillespie had Beatrix.
The 8 day John Wemis and Grizel Persone had Elizabeth (in fornication).
That day Robert Aitkin and Elspet Murray had Agnes.
The 9 day Robert Mudie and Bessie Ponton had James.
That day John Dagleich and Janet Penman had Janet.
The 16 day Thom Young and Maus Andirson had John.
That day Martyn Barklay and Kate Peirson had Margaret.
That day Andrew Murray and Effie Wemis had James.
That day David Elder and Nans Dewer had John.
The 19 day George Bodwell, deceased, and Nans Sandilands had Ellen.
That day John Stobie and Marion Atkin had Laurence.
The 23 day William Elder and Janet Wardlaw had Edward.
That day John Lochtoun and Mage Gray had Janet (in fornication).
That day John Wright and Maus Huton had William.
The 26 day [1589] Robert Dagleich and Janet Harper had Nicol.
That day George Trumbull and Maus Andirson had Margaret.
The 30 day Adam Schortes and Margaret Miller had William.

That day James Clune and Isobel Walkar had Margaret.
That day James Inche and Janet Hutson had Margaret.
That day John Wilson and Kate Makartoun had Bessie.

M [*None.*]

APRIL [1589].

B. The 6 day James Cuming and Margaret Broun had James.
That day William Smyth and Christian Wricht had Isobel.
That day John Tomson and Maus Bull had Isobel.
That day Thomas Main "had a woman chyld born to him of his harlot in
  fornication baptized and called Margaret."
The 13 day Andrew Sanders and Margaret Cant had John.
That day Michael Anderson and Margaret Immerie had Alison.
The 16 day David Callender and Christian Wilson had Margaret (in fornica-
  tion).
The 20 day John Wostwood and Janet Cunninghame had William.
That day Henry Mutray and Nans Cuninghame had Bessie.
That day James Whyt and Nans Inglis had Marion.
The 23 day John Watsone and Christian Kingorne had James.
The 27 day James Nasmyth and Maus Broun had Ellen.

M. The 6 day James Hall was married to Christian Bell.
The 27 of April Henry Broun was married to Janet Kellok.

MAY.

B. The 4 day Walter Lyndsay and Janet Portous had Gilbert.
The 11 day James Sanders and Margaret Burn had Janet.
The 18 day James Blaw and Christian Schortes had Allan.
The 21 day Wille Wilson and Bessie Peirson had Alexander (in fornication).
The 25 day Andrew Walker, Rossyth, and Marion Peirson had John.
That day Wille Walkar and Gelis Portair had a daughter . . . .
That day James Scotland and Isobel Portair had Margaret.
The 27 day James Kingorn and Effie Murray had David.
The 28 day John Gib and Isobel Lyndsay had John.

M. The 4 day William Tomson was married to Annie Wilson.
The 18 day John Carslaw was married to Mause Blakait.
The 25 day David Greiff was married to Janet Dagleish.
William Boswell to Kete Schortes.

JUNE.

B. The 8 day William Andirson and Bessie Mill had John.
The 13 day John Stirling and Christian Craik had John.
The 15 day Thomas Elder and Bessie Dewer had Ellen.
That day Robert Kellok and Janet Chalmer had Janet.
That day David Stewart and Isabel Tempilman had Patrick.
That day Andrew Archibald and Janet Schew had Marjory.
The 22 day William Andirsone and Janet Brown had John.
The 29 day Robert Edison, Rossyth, and Christian Whyt had Christian.
That day Sande Huton and Margaret Walwod had Philip.

M. The 15 day Thomas Steinson was married to Marjory Thomson.
John Cowyntre to Elspet Yonger.
John Andirson to Bessie Burne.
The 22 day John Blakwod was married to Isobel Witit.
David Bull to Christian Burn.
Watte Law to Janet Haddan.
The 29 day James Robertson was married to Mause Daling.
Robert Westwod to Janet Cunningham.
Harry Bull with Margaret Car.
Laurence Daglesh to Keit Reid.

Adam Schortes to Margaret Brown.
James Wilson to Marion Finlason.

JULY.

B. The 6 day Lourie Andirsone and Maige Couburn had David (in fornication).

That day John Galrig and Janet Weild had David.

The 10 day Robert Cunninghame and Janet Paton had James.

The 13 day William Bute and Janet Eson had James.

That day Nicol Dewer and Isobel Culrois had Margaret (in fornication).

The 15 day Alexander Webster and Janet Gib had Margaret.

The 20 day Alexander Huton and Margaret Wallet had Philip.

That day John Andirson and Janet Ædisone had James.

The 27 day John Smeton and Margaret Durie had John.

M. The 20 day Robert Whyt was married to Keit Keddie.

AUGUST.

B. The 3 day John Forfair and Janet Wardlaw had Isabel.

That day John Jonson and Christian Brown had Bessie.

That day James Davidsone and Bessie Piers had Simon.

The 10 day Patrick Stewart and Katherine Balrain had Margaret.

That day William Leggait and Margaret Couper had Allison.

The 17 day Philip Moubray and Elspet Spittall had Francis.

That day Laurence Huton and Bessie Blak had Christian.

That day Andrew Dik and Kete Hending had John.

The 24 day William Cairin ("relaps") and Keit Finlason had Elspet (in fornication).

The 31 day James Couper and Christian Binning had Janet.

That day James Litilljon and Elspet Wright had William.

That day Andrew Matheson and Keit Angus had Isobel.

That day Mark Swenton and Isobel Spens had Isobel.

M. The 3 day John Davidson was married to Margaret Mastirtoun.

The 17 day James Stewart was married to Janet Miln.

SEPTEMBER.

B. The 7 day Henry Broun and Bessie Dagleich had Henry.

That day William Durie and Janet Hutcheon had Henry.

That day Cuthbert Walkar and Janet Walkar had Isobel.

That day David Knox and Margaret Walkar had Marjory (in fornication).

That day James Wilson and Marion Finlason had Marjory.

The 14 day Harry Miller and Janet Andirson had James.

That day James Alison and Nans Putie had Thomas.

The 21 day William Wilson and Keit Sprewll had Robert.

The 28 day William Mutray and Bessie Couper had Janet.

M. The 7 day John Wardlaw was married to Beatrix Keir.

The 28 day William Martiall was married to Ellen Andirson.

OCTOBER.

B. The 5 day John Neilson and Keit Hewche had Robert.

That day David Henrison and Grizel Mudie had Janet.

The 8 day William Walwod and Elspet Alexander had David.

That day Edward Duglas and Janet Sanders had Thomas.

The 12 day Robert Murray and Isobel Talyeour had Effie.

The 15 day Clement Sanderis and Marion Bell had James.

The 22 day Gawin Duglas and Janet Lochoir had Patrick.

The 26 day John Andirson and Marion Andirson had James.
That day Edward Wricht and Bessie Peirson had Margaret (in fornication).

M. [*None.*]

NOVEMBER.

B.   The 2 day John Andirson and Keit Proves had James.
The 5 day James Wallange and Kete Wilson had Laurence.
The 9 day John Drysdeill and Marjory Sibbet had Alexander.
The 19 day John Andirsone and Margaret Aitkin had James.
The 23 day Robert Huton and Bessie Huton had Effie.
That day John Madir (after his slaughter by Rob Tomson) had a woman
    child born to him (posthumous) of his wife Bessie Steinson, baptized and
    called Margaret.
That day John Strang and Ellen Rae had David.
That day Isaac Watson and Janet Cutbertson had Bessie.

M.   The 2 day Henry Logtoun was married to Janet Clerk.
The 9 day David Andirson was married to Margaret Ædison.
The 23 day James Mudie and Nans Yong were married.
William Simson and Margaret Logtoun.
James Paycok and Janet Barklay.

DECEMBER.

B.   The 7 day John Clark and Bessie Brand had John.
That day Henry Peirson and Katherine Ædison had Margaret.
That day Geordi Abircrumbie ("relaps") and Bessie Alison had William (in
    fornication).
The 17 day Laurence Strang and Janet Darny had John.
That day John Burne and Marjory Andirson had Bessie.
The 21 day Arche Peirson and Effie Aitkin had Alison.
That day James Mersair, Dagati (Dalgety) and Keit Symson had James (in
    fornication).
The 28 day Adam Currie and Margaret Ædison had Helen.
That day John Paton, collier, and Christian Nicoll had James.
That day John Andirsone and Kæte Burne had John.

M.   The 14 day Rob Andirson was married to Isobel Tomson.
The 28 day George Moris was married to Nans Esplein.

JANUARY [1589-90].

B.   The 4 day Thomas Couper and Margaret Law had Patrick.
That day Thom Chrysteson and Bessie Dewer (relapse) had John (in
    fornication.)
That day Allan Mudie and Janet Forfair had James.
The 11 day John Steinsone and Margaret Andersone had John.
That day David Hugon and Janet Millair had Robert.
That day Andrew Andirsone and Christian Kellok had John.
The 25 day Adam Durie and Christian Barrie had Margaret.
That day Peter Robertson and Margaret Aitkin had Peter.
That day John Law and Barbara Stewart had David.
That day John Levistoun and Janet Beveraig had Janet.
That day George Ædison and Janet Weitit had Margaret.
That day John Huton and Christian Wilson had Marion.
That day Alexander Oswald (relapse 3) and Bessie Stobie (relapse 2) had
    John (in fornication).
That day William Bonalay and Janet Hendirson had Robert.
That day John Blakwod and Isobel Weitit had Christian.
The 28 day Thomas Walwod and Isobel Logtoun had David.

M.   The 11 day Tom Philp was married to Ellen Stenhus.
The 18 day William Stenhus was married to Margaret Philp.

FEBRUARY.

B.   The 1 day Henry Hunnon and Ellen Angus had Thomas.
That day George Cuninghame and Janet Henric had Bessie.
That day James Speir and Margaret Peirson had David (in fornication).
The 4 day David Hendirson and Janet Aitkin had Adam.
That day Andrew Stirk and Kate Huton had William.
The 8 day John Gotherstoun and Margaret Clark had John.
That day John Astie and Kate Thomson had Abraham.
That day Andrew Foster and Margaret Bathcat had Isobel (in fornication).
The 15 day Alexander Lambe and Janet Cuninghame had William.
The 22 day Peter Trumbull and Isobel Car had John.
That day Tom Feldie and Ellen Ranaldsone had Laurence.
That day James Abircrumbie and Keit Logton had Elspet (in fornication).

M.   The 15 day Stevin Jameson was married to Margaret Kilgour.
The 22 day George Moris was married to Margaret Kinninmond.
John Huton to Bessie Burt.

MARCH.

B.   The 1 day James Murray and Nans Lyndsay had William.
That day Walter Andirson and Margaret Kellok had Janet.
That day Robert Wellis and Grizel Andirson had John.
That day Robert Mories and Marjory Edisone had William.
That day Alexander Scotland and Elspet Bryce had John.
That day James Meldrum and Janet Wilson had Christian.
That day John Mories and Bessie Steinson had Andrew.
The 8 day Patrick Mikiljone and Margaret Burne had Patrick.
That day Robert Kellok and Margaret Cuninghame had Isobel.
The 15 day Stevin Donald and Janet Kellok had William.
The 18 day John Blakater and Janet Durie had Elspet.
That day William Robertson of Cragduckie, younger, and Nans Thomson had David.
That day Robert Murie and Janet Weymis had Robert.
The 22 day Laurence Alyson and Margaret Christe had John.
That day Robert Angus and Margaret Rae had Robert.
That day James Huton and Margaret Lyndsay had Gawan.
That day James Gibson and Nans Robertson had Nans.

M.   The 1 day William Kent was married to Marjory Mudie.
William Pottair to Marjory Leslie.

APRIL [1590].

B.   The 1 day David Pitcarne and Janet Wright had James.
That day William Rae and Isobel Spens had Alexander.
That day John Wilson, Pitdunnie, and Isobel Fargus had John.
That day John Bankis and Margaret Donaldsone had Janet.
The 5 day Robert Young and Christian Brechin had Janet.
The 8 day Robert Lawson and Bessie Blak had Effie.
The 9 day John Andirson and Christian Kneland had James.
The 12 day William Broun and Margaret Bell had Bessie.
The 19 day Andrew Brand and Isobel Cuming had Janet.
That day John Dewar and Janet Stenhus had Robert.
That day William Dewar and Janet Steinson had William.
The 22 day William Horn and Kate Dewer had Helen.
That day James Hall and Christian Bell had Christian.
The 29 day Henry Dewer and Marion Huton had James.

M.   The 26 day John Walwod was married to Bessie Dewer.

MAY.

B.   The 3 day John Greiff and Bellisant Hutson had John.
     That day John Andirsone and Margaret Ædison had Isobel.
     That day Laurence Andirson and Keit Morgain had Lourie (in fornication).
     That day Thomas Cant and Margaret Tomson had Andrew.
     That day David Astie and Marjory Logtoun had Christian.
     The 6 day David Bull and Christian Burn had John.
     The 13 day Henry Dewer and Marion Huton had John.
     The 17 day John Trumbill and Marjory Couper had Ellen.
     The 24 day Harry Bull and Margaret Car had Marjory.
     The 31 day John Davidsone, Inverkeithing, and Margaret Mastirtoun had John.
     That day John Mackalzeon and Ellen Ramsay had John.

M.   The 3 day James Haistie was married to Christian Walwod.
     The 10 day Nicol Brown was married to Isobel Tomson.
     The 24 day William Watson was married to Janet Paycok.

JUNE.

B.   The 7 day James Sibbet and Elspet Stevin had Elspet.
     That day John Galrig and Bessie Bull had Maus.
     That day Lourie Thomson and Janet Gray had William.
     The 17 day Thomas Trumbull and Marjory Duglas had Keterin.
     The 21 day John Weithed and Elison Wallace had Robert.
     That day Andrew Alison and Ellen Cuming had James.
     The 28 day Robert Brand and Bessie Fyff had Christian.
     That day William Cuninghame and Ellen Lausone had John.

M.   The 7 day William Stewart, crowner, was married to Isobel Hepburn, Lady of Pitfirren, in Halyrudhous kirk by John Duncansone, one of the King's ministers.
     The 21 day William Morgain was married to Christian Burn.
     The 28 day Andrew Bennet was married to Marjory Esplein.
     Alexander Inglis to Isobel Reid.

JULY.

B.   The 12 day Adam Bouton and Nans Martiall had Margaret.
     That day William Tomson and Nans Wilson had Robert.
     That day David Horn and Janet Gillespik had Janet.
     The 19 day John Crawfurd and Catherine Robertson had David.
     The 26 day George Colzear and Janet Bull had Geilis.
     That day Thomas Steinson and Marjory Thomson had Janet.
     The 29 day Harry Peirson and Marjory Dewer had Marjory.

M.   The 12 day William Spens was married to Janet Swentoun.
     The 26 day Thomas Robertson was married to Marjory Donaldson.

AUGUST.

B.   The 9 day John Walwod of Touch and Isobel Erskein had Janet.
     That day Robert Nicoll and Ellen Durie had Marjory.
     The 16 day James Kingorn and Effie Murray had William.
     That day John Young and Nans Andirson had Helen.
     That day William Sandelands and Keit Wilson [1] had Alexander.
     The 30 day James Mubray and Geilis Andirson had Isobel.
     That day Patrick Rutherfurd and Ellen Balrain had Annas.
     That day Richard Potter and Christian Couper had Janet.

M.   The 16 day John Strang was married to Janet Makkie.
     David Esplein to Bessie Law.

                    [1] (Culrois *in margin.*)

James Andirsone to Margaret Steinsen.
George Dun to Margaret Peirson.
Henry Broun to Kete Elder.

SEPTEMBER.

B.   The 2 day John Tomsone and Janet Smith had Janet.
The 6 day John Brown and Christian Mudie had John.
That day William Wright and Janet Corsair had James.
That day Henry Logtoun and Janet Clark had Simon.
The 13 day Andrew Inglis and Maige Michell had Janet.
That day William Simsone and Margaret Logtoun had Andrew.
The 27 day James Cunand and Barbara Walwod had Robert.
That day Thomas Philp and Ellen Stenhus had Janet.
That day Thom Whyt and Janet Dagleich had Janet.
The 30 day Charles Kennedy and Margaret Bairdy had Elspet.

M.   The 20 day Andrew Wellis was married to Bessie Steinsone.

OCTOBER.

B.   The 4 day Thomas Stenhus and Barbara Duglas had Christian.
That day Crispinie Swyne and Margaret Hutcheon had John.
That day Robert Whyt and Katerine Keddie had Christian.
That day John Walker and Margaret Stewart had Margaret.
That day John Mutray and Janet Thomson had Christian.
That day John Thomson ("fat fidler") and Marjory Finlason had Marjory
    (in fornication).
The 18 day Abraham Walwod and Isobel Rowan had Alison.
That day George Burn and Margaret Bull had Christian.
The 21 day George Moris and Nans Esplein had William.
The 28 day James Cairnis and Margaret Davidsone had Isobel.

M.   The 18 day Robert Huton was married to Helen Dagleich.

NOVEMBER.

B.   The first day Andrew Murray and Effie Weimis had William.
That same day Simon Peirson and Margaret Craik had Margaret.
The 8 day Robert Lun and Janet Law had Janet.
That day John Strang and Ellen Rae had Ellen.
That day John Ewin and Janet Nicol had John.
The 15 day John Huton and Margaret Wilson had William.
That day James Howburne and Isobel Gardiner had John.
That day Edward Andirsone and Janet Dik had twins, Massie and Bessie.
The 22 day Robert Bread and Nans Andirsone had Andrew.
That day James Robertsone and Maus Dauling had Isobel.
That day Adam Man and Christian Michell had Bessie (in fornication, under
    promise of marriage).
The 29 day Philip Mubray and Elspet Spittell had Philip.
That day Robert Walwod and Bessie Strang had Isobel.
That day George Moris and Margaret Kinninmonth had Isobel.

M.   The first day William Smith was married to Isobel Macki.
John Laing to Margaret Kar.
The 22 day David Kar was married to Kate Elder.
And William Smart to Margaret Tod.

DECEMBER.

B.   The 20 day Edward Tomson and Elspet Beinie had Bessie.
That day Abraham Spens and Christian Watson had John.
That day Gibbe Huton and Maige Deis had Walter (in fornication).

M.   The 13 day John Mudie was married to Christian Kellok.

JANUARY [1590-91].

B.   The third day David Elder and Nans Dewer had David.
That day John Huton, younger, and Bessie Burt had David.
That day James Chalmer and Margaret Sandis had Patrick.
That day William Martiall, deceased, and Ellen Anderson had Laurence.
That day John Bull, younger, in the Green, and . . . . had David (in
fornication).
That day John Wilson and Bessie Cuninghame had John (in fornication).
That day George Warkman and Beatrix Smith had Janet.
The 17 day Robert Schortes and Janet Brown had John.
That day James Paycok and Helen Whyte had Abraham.
That day Adam Fergus and Christian Drysdaill had Janet.
That day Henry Peirson and Margaret Cuninghame had Henry.
That day Henry Broun and Janet Kellok had Margaret.
That day John Thomson and Margaret Walker had David.
That day Robert Anderson and Effie Harrowair had John.
The 24 day John Mackie and Janet Walwod had William.
That day John Walwod and Effie Boswell had Ellen (in fornication).
That day James Mudie and Nans Young had Thomas.
The 31 day William Elder and Katherine Cuninghame had Robert.
That day James Mairtin and Janet Hay had Andrew.
That day Laurence Strang and Janet Darnie had twins, Madie and Katherine
That day John Smart and Kete Fothringhame, " his harlot," had Robert (in
fornication).

M.   The 24 day Thomas Chrystie was married to Janet Huton.

FEBRUARY.

B.   The 7 day Robert Wilson and Margaret Scotland had Janet.
That day John Chattu and Kate Kellok had William.
That day John Tomson and Bessie Stewart had Christian.
The 14 day Robert Andirson and Kate Thomson had Janet.
That day John Hadand and Elspet Wright had William.
That day John Robertson and Nans Lourie had John.
That day John Chrystie and Ellen Waddell had Margaret.
That day John Nwall and Nans Carslaw had Nans.
The 21 day John Fleming and Isobel Sandis had William.
That day Robert Andirson and Marion Portair had Grizel.
That day Adam Walwod and Katherine Kellok had Barbara.
The 28 day John Andirson and Bessie Chryste had Margaret.
That day John Steill and Janet Chrystesone had Laurence.
That day Wille Watson and Janet Paycok had Nans.
That day John Webster, *alias* Hendirson, and Mause Dagleisch had Janet
(in fornication, under promise of marriage).

M.   The 14 day Thomas Allain was married to Christian Mailer.
Thomas Gibson to Ellen Blak.
George Abircrumbie to Elizabeth Coutis, Inverkeithing.

MARCH.

B.   The 3 day James Inche and Janet Hutsone had James.
The 7 day William Kent and Marjory Mudie had Helen.
That day Laurence Dagleiche and Katherine Reid had Janet.
That day Robert Ramsay and Christian Fyffe had Robert.
The 10 day Thomas Huton and Janet Beveraig had Mause.
The 14 day John Peirson and Grizel Mastintoun had John.
The 17 day Robert Stenhus and Katherine Duglas had Henry.
The 21 day James Huton and Isobel Kid had Janet.
The 28 day [1591] William Stenhus and Margaret Philip had Robert.
That day James Scotland and Isobel Portair had William.

M.   [*None.*]

APRIL [1591].

B. The 4 day Thomas Mikilhois and Janet Lyndsay had Bessie.
The 11 day Allan Walwod and Rosina Walkar had William.
That day William Pottair and Maige Lesslie had John.
The 18 day George Peirson and Effie Phillen had David.
That day Wille Hamilton and Bessie Pillons had Elspet (in fornication).
That day William Walkair and Katherine Wilson had Ellen.
The 21 day John Stobie and Marion Aitkin had Ellen.
The 25 day Andrew Bennait and Marjory Esplein had John.
That day John Coweintrie and Elspet Youngair had Janet.
That day John Huton and Janet Beveraige had Henry.

M. The 11 day . . . . Wilson was married to Margaret Burn.
The 25 day Andrew Potter was married to Bessie Davidson.

MAY.

B. 2, Henry Turnbull and Ellen Mutray had George.
2, Robert Rannald and Keit Aikman had Christian.
2, Arche Cuningham and Janet Dagleich had James.
16, David Huton and Ellen Peirsone had Janet.
16, Andrew Smithe and Margaret Walwod had Christian.
16, Robert Paton and Isobel Keir had David (in fornication).
19, Robert Mersair and Margaret Barrain had Laurence.
19, John Andirson and Marion Anderson had Janet.
19, James Sibbet, Nethirtoun, and Margaret Logtoun had . . . .
23, James Murray and Nans Lyndsay had Jean.
23, David Broun and Bessie Cutis had John.
23, William Legat and Margaret Couper had William.
23, Peter Robertson and Margaret Aitkin had James.
26, William Smyth and Christian Wright had Christian.
30, Alexander Webster, *alias* Henderson, and Janet Gib had Ellen.

M. [*None.*]

JUNE.

B. 2, Laurence Patrik and Janet Mories had twins, Alison and Ellen.
2, James Cuming and Margaret Broun had George.
13, Laurence Walker and Maige Phillain had Barbara.
16, William Durie and Janet Hutcheon had John.
16, Andrew Wellis and Bessie Steinson had Janet.
20, John Law and Barbara Stewart had Janet.
20, Edward Burn and Margaret Mudie had Christian.
20, John Anderson and Janet Anderson had Margaret.
27, James Reid and Bessie Lindsay had Henry.
27, John Craik and Christian Broun had Janet.
27, James Beveraige and Janet Gib had John.
27, John Watson and Bessie Johnson had Margaret.

M. [*None.* N.B.—No marriages appear to be recorded from April to December of this year.]

JULY.

B. 4, John Gib and Isobel Lyndsay had Jean.
4, James Mutray and Margaret Bruce had James.
4, Arche Peirson and Isobel Dik had Adam.
4, Isaac Watson and Janet Cuddie had Gilbert.
11, Wille Spens and Janet Swenton had William.
25, William Pratus and Mage Cairnie had Jean.
25, John Strang and Janet Mackie had Ellen.
25, Alexander Creich and Grizel Walkar had Janet.
25, James Fothringhame and Isobel Walkar had James.

M. [*None.*]

AUGUST.

B. 1, Richard Martein and Ellen Smith had James.
    1, Thomas Wostwod and Grizel Michell had Robert.
    1, Henry Gibson and Nans Robertsone had Elspet.
    8, John Wright and Nans Wilson had Emillie (in fornication).
    8, John Bennait and Margaret Cuthbert had Janet (in fornication).
    11, Edward Wylie and Nans Hodgs had Janet.
    15, William Wilson and Margaret Burn had John.
    15, Nicol Dagleich and Ellen Blaikwod had Catherine.
    22, Robert Young and Christian Brechin had Margaret.
    22, William Moutray and Bessie Couper had Helen.
    22, David Esplein and Bessie Law had Janet.
    22, Edward Laing and Margaret Car had Barbara.
    22, Adam Andirson and Christian Tomson had Janet.
    29, Rob Tomson and Bessie Stalker had Isobel.
    29, Tom Kellok and Margaret Huton had Elspet.

M. [*None.*]

SEPTEMBER.

B. 2, Robert Peirs and Bessie Burn had Margaret.
    2, Robert Huton and Ellen Dagleische had Janet.
    2, Peter Dewar and Katherine Bruce had John.
    2, John Mudie and Christian Kellok had John.
    8, David Pitcairne and Janet Wright had Margaret.
    22, William Stewart, "crounell," and Isobel Hepburn, his lady, had Frederick.
        [Regina *in margin.*]
    22, John Tomson and Marjory Bull had Janet.
    22, John Huton and Margaret Steinson had Elspet.
    29, Robert Cusing and Alison Peirson had Janet.
    29, Robert Kellok and Bessie Chalmer had Margaret.
    29, William Wilson and Margaret Blakater had Janet (in fornication).

M. [*None.*]

OCTOBER.

B. 3, Laurence Huton and Bessie Blak had Ellen.
    6, John Sumervaill and . . . . had Christian (in fornication).
    6, Patrick Freland and Bessie Keir had Thomas (in fornication).
    6, Will Rae and Christian Arthur had William (in fornication).
    6, Thomas Culrois and Marion Donaldson had John.
    20, William Rae and Isobel Spens had Nans.
    27, Robert Car and Effie Abircrumbie had Isobel.
    27, Adam Broun and Marion Mudie had Margaret.
    27, James Couper and Christian Binninge had Marion.

M. [*None.*]

NOVEMBER.

B. 7, Alexander Inglis and Isobel Reid had John.
    7, Richard Pottair and Christian Couper had John.
    7, John Andirson and Margaret Bruce had Janet.

M. [*None.*]

DECEMBER.

B. 5, Thomas Walwod and Isobel Logtoun had Margaret.
    5, John Strange and Ellen Rae had Rosina.
    5, Richard Huton and Bessie Murriell had Effie.
    12, Alexander Galry and Grizel Steinson had Andrew.
    12, James Haistie and Christian Walwod had Robert.
    19, David Hendirson, cordiner, and Janet Aitkin had Robert.
    19, William Walwod and Elspet Alexander had George.
    19, Peter Trumbill and Isobel Car had Henry.

19, David Wellis and Janet Alison had Christian.
19, James Nasmyth and . . . . had William.
22, William Elder and Janet Wardlaw had William.
26, Thomas Brand and Meg Wilson had John (in fornication).

M. [*None.*]

JANUARY [1591-92].

B. 2, William Walkar and Gelis Portair had Marjory.
5, Rob Car and Kete Andirson had Kete (in fornication).
16, Wille Robertson and Kete Richertson had John (in fornication).
16, William Murray and Mage Culrois had John (in fornication). [*On one margin*, Tillibairn ; *on the other*, Athol's predecessor.]
16, William Wilson and Isobel Paycok had Katherine.
16, John Gothirstoun and Margaret Clark had Isobel.
19, Edward Andirsone and Janet Dik had Ellen.
19, Robert Murray and Bessie Talzeour had Janet.
23, George Abircrumbie and Elspet Couts had Andrew.

M. 30, James Tomson was married to Keit Logtoun.

FEBRUARY.

B. 6, John Kellok and Margaret Donaldson had Marjory.
9, Robert Cuninghame and Janet Paton had Isobel.

M. 6, John Culrois was married to Bessie Tomson.

[*The Record is awanting*, February 1591-July 1598.]

" The names of the personis baptisit and thair parentis, of personis
joynit in mariege and the day of the solemnizasioun, fra the
Witsonday in the yeir of God j^m^v^c^ fourescore auchteint yeiris
in the toun and parochin of Dunfermling during the ministerie
of Mr. Jone Fairfull and Mr. Andro Forrester, ministeris
thaire."

JULY.

B. [*None.*]
M. 15, James Kirkland was married to Katherine Milne.

AUGUST.

B. [*None.*]
M. [*None.*]

SEPTEMBER.

B. [*None.*]
M. 30, James Thomsone was married to Helen Strang.

OCTOBER.

B. 21, Nicol Hunter and Marion Huttoun had John.
21, Laurence Morgane and Janet Daglishe had James.
21, Thomas Philip and Helen Stennos has Thomas.
21, Henry Turnebull and Helen Mowbray had Janet.
29, John Burne and Marion Andersone had Robert.
29, James Huttoun, tailor, and Marion Tod had James.
29, William Wilsoun in Cowsieknawis and Isobel Pacok had Isobel.
29, David Andersone in Pitbachlay and Helen Andersone had William.
29, Robert Schairpe at Lessodie mill and Janet Phinlasone had John.

M. 11, Patrick Steinsone was married to Bessie Reid.
21, Adam Curriour was married to Margaret Swintoun.

NOVEMBER.

B. 4, Laurence Huttoun, merchant, and Bessie Blak had Thomas.
    4, Peter Dewar and Janet Murray had Patrick.
   11, Robert Mersar and Margaret Barrone had Laurence.
   11, William Patrik and Janet Strachan had Bessie.
   11, William Makie and Catherine Horne had Alisone.
   15, George Huttoun and Helen Gibsone had Janet.
   15, John Andersone and Janet Andersone had Henry.
   19, William Schorteus and Janet Gib had Jean.

M. 8, Nicol Lermunthe to Janet Inglis.
   26, John Harrower to . . . . Mikill.

DECEMBER.

B. 3, John Young in the Lymekills and Christian Gray had Grizel.
   3, Robert Kellok of Lessodie mill and Margaret Cuninghame had Thomas.
   3, David Blak in Coklaw and . . . . had Thomas.
   19, Henry Dewar and Marion Huttoun had Marion.
   19, Robert Wallis and Grizel Andersone had Andrew.
   19, Thomas Broun, weaver, and Janet Clawie had David.
   19, James Gibsone, miller, and Margaret Patersone had Nicol.
   19, George Abercrumie and Elspet Cuttis had Robert.
   24, Edward Thomsone, merchant, and Marjory Fergeus had Helen.
   24, Patrick Turnbull and Katherine Smithe had Isobel.
   26, John Wolsoun in Pitconachie and Janet Cuninghame had John.
   26, William Smith (deceased), "rider" at Dunfermline, and Christian Wricht had Henry.
   31, Adam Wallat, baker, and Katherine Kellok had Margaret.

M. 10, David Stewart to Janet Sibbethe.
   27, William Cuninghame to Janet Miller.

JANUARY [1598-99].

B. 7, Andrew Cant, weaver in Wester Gellat, and Janet Pacok had James.
   7, Robert Aikin and Elspet Murray had Effie.
   7, Robert Haa and Catherine Wilsone had Catherine (in fornication).
   25, John Andersoun in the Nethertoun and Janet Andersoun had Janet.
   25, John Meldrum and Bessie Wolsoun had Robert.

M. 14, Richard Walker to Isobel Smithe.
   21, David Hoge to Bessie Bredheid.
   25, William Andersone, tailor, to Margaret Bonalay.

FEBRUARY.

B. 4, John Robertsone and Nans Huttoun had Janet.
   4, James Smeytoun and Christian Ealder had James.
   4, John Dow, collier, and Christian Schortous had Thomas.
   4, Richard Law, servitor to William Robertson of Craigduky, and Janet Knox had Janet (in fornication).
   11, Thomas Mudie in Easter Gellett and Bessie Turnebull had Christian.
   11, Alexander Burne, baker, and Helen Hendersone had Peter.
   11, William Spens, tailor, and Janet Swintoun had David.
   11, John Andersone, *alias* Watterlaird, and Katherine Brown had William.
   11, John Mudie and Janet Huttoun had William.
   11, John Gibsone in Lennoxis and Elspet Meik had Andrew.
   11, Andrew Mathesone and Katherine Angous had Bessie.
   18, ... Warkman and Katherine Finlasone had Margaret.
   18, Allan Mudie, weaver, and Janet Forfar had Allan.
   25, Steven Donald, miller at Pitlever mill, and Marjory Sibbatt had Robert.
   25, Thomas Feldie, cordiner, and Helen Ranneldsone had Isobel.

25, Robert Murray in the Lymekillis and Bessie Berdner had Andrew.
28, George Lindsay of Kevill and Elizabeth Lindsay had Isobel.
28, John Fleming of Blaklaw and Bessie Sandis had Patrick.

M. 14, Andrew Kinninmont to Helen Angus.
18, Mr. James Dagleische to Janet Mikilljone.
18, Thomas Mudie, maltman, to Margaret Wolsone.
25, Henry Gib, collier, to Catherine Gray.

MARCH.

B. 4, Robert Rudderfurd and Elspet Gray had Isobel (in fornication).
4, John Strang, cordiner, and Janet Makie had Katherine.
4, John Thomsone, weaver, and Masie Bull had Margaret.
11, William Crawfert in Wester Lusker and Katherine Tod had William.
11, Laurence Andersone, fornicator, parishioner of Crumie, and Bessie Currour had Margaret.
25 (1599), George Andersone in Lymekills and Margaret Quarriour had Marion.

M. [*None.*]

APRIL [1599].

B. 8, William Douglas, son of William Douglas, collier, and Mary Livingstone had John (in fornication).
8, John Kelloche in the Nethertoun and Janet Reid had James.
15, John Mudie in the Gellat and Christian Kellok had Bessie.
15, Harry Gat in the Limekills and Margaret Kyd had George.
15, Andrew Currour in Baithe and Helen Law had Harry.
15. James Reid, merchant, and Bessie Lindsay had Margaret.
22, Andrew Dewar of Wodend of Keltie and Isobel Dik had Marion.
22, Thomas Smithe, collier, and Margaret Patoun had Andrew.
28, John Greif, tenant in Tunigask, and Christian Bennat had Robert.
28, John Dewar in Garwokwod and Isobel Moreis had James.

M. 11, Robert Duthie of Foddis mill was married to Janet Durie, daughter of Henry Durie in the Nethertoun.

MAY.

B. 5, John Balfour in Maistertoun and Christian Lawsone had Christian.
5, John Schorteus in the Colzera and Janet Broun had John.
5, James Sandis in Wester Gellat and Margaret Aitkin had Harry.
5, Robert Moreis and Marion Adisoun had James.
5, John Adisoun, miller, and Betriche (Beatrix) Turnebull had John.
12, Laurence Andersone in Craiglusker and Marjory Cokburne had Betriche (Beatrix).
12, Nicoll Inglis in Pittdinnie and Bessie Cuninghame had Margaret.
12, Andrew Wischart, servant to Gavin Douglas, and Margaret Messoun had Beatrix (in fornication).
12, Thomas Forfar, parishioner of Abernethy, and Elspet Robertson had Dorothy (after a testimonial of his marriage by the minister of that parish).
12, Alexander Cochren and Katherine Bryse had Laurence (in fornication).
19, John Lawsone "besyd the Milburne" and Janet Donald had John.
19, David Persone in Pitdinnie and Margaret Cuninghame had David.
19, Adam Wolsone at the Milburne and Katherine Wolsone had Elspet.
27, David Pacok in Pitcorthie and Janet Chrystie had Margaret.
19, (*Sic*), (the three entries of that date repeated).

M. 2, John Huttoun to Agnes Smithe.
9, Andrew Potter to Janet Burne.
13, Patrick Stennes to Katherine Ealder.
30, Laurence Horne to Janet Wolsone.
30, Florence Broun to Eupham Fillen.

JUNE.

B. 9, James Daglishe in Craiglusker and Christian Cragie had James.
24, Archibald Douglas, merchant, and Janet Phillen had David.
24, Patrick Steinsone, merchant, and Bessie Reid had Bessie.
24, William Cusing and Margaret Robersone had Janet (in fornication).
29, James Mutray in the Galrik hill and Janet Wardlaw had Thomas.

M. 3, Alexander Culross to Christian Forrester.
17, Patrick Davidsone to Margaret Makildowie.
24, Alexander Baxter, parishioner of Dalgety, to Agnes Persone.

JULY.

B. 1, John Mathesoun in the Newra and Marjory Andro had John.
1, James Hamiltoun and Agnes Mirie had Adam (in fornication).
7, George Walker, merchant, and Marjory Cuthbert had James.
11, James Lindsay and Janet Broun had Janet (in adultery ; satisfied the kirk for three months).
13, James Corse in the Galrik hill and Bessie Sandis had William.
14, Robert Wallett and Bessie Strang had David.
14, John Galrik in Sanct Margrattis stone and Agnes Andersone had Janet.
14, James Kellok in Pittrevie and Margaret Chalmer had . . .
20, James Chalmer in Knokhous and Margaret Sandis had Elspet.
28, James Clark and Bessie Tarvett had Isobel.
28, Peter Dewar and Katherine Bruse had Barbara.
28, Andrew Turnebull, younger, in the Brumhall and Bessie Fudie had George.

M. 7, William Douglas to Mary Livingstone.
15, John Abercrumie to Agnes Andersone.

AUGUST.

B. 3, Thomas Steinsone and Marjory Thomsone had Patrick.
3, William Thomsone and Janet Potter had Margaret.
17, James Meldrum and Janet Wilsone had John.
17, William Elder and Katherine Cuninghame had John and William.
17, James Thomsone and . . . . had Helen.
26, William Potter and Margery Leslie had Margaret.

M. 15, James Hamilton to Agnes Mirie.
19, David Germont to Barbara Douglas.

SEPTEMBER.

B. 9, Harry Mudie and Margaret Reid had George.
9, John Harrower and Bessie Makie had Bessie.
15, James Kinesman and Christian Wallat had David (in fornication).
22, David Broune of the Coklaw and Christian Blake had David.
25, Mr. William Melvine, Commendator of Tungland, and Agnes Lindsay had Sophia (Melvill).
25, Alexander Ingilles and Isobel Rid had Margery.

M. 30, George Thomson to Margaret Gatta.

OCTOBER.

B. 3, John Mill and . . . . had twins, John and Margaret.
7, William Cuninghame and Christian Millar had Margaret.
14, John Thomson in the Lymekills and Christian Keir had John.
14, Edward Douglas in Wester Gellat and Marion Kirk had Bessie.
21, William Deas and Janet Garven had Christain.
21, George Bruse in Blairrothie and Margaret Orrok had Janet.
21, George Hutton, merchant, and Bessie Cudbert had Janet.

21, Mr. Andrew Forrester, minister at Dunfermline, and Helen Ramsay had Margaret.

28, Andrew Reid and Margaret Otsoun had Helen.

M. [*None.*]

NOVEMBER.

B. 17, John Calendar, gardener of Pittincreif, and Jean Nicoll had Patrick.

24, William Steinsoun, collier in the Nethertoun, and Marjory Garvie had Christian.

24, Robert Young and Bessie Lugtoun had Alexander.

24, James Ker and Catherine Robertson had Janet.

24, David Douglas and . . . . had John (in fornication).

27, Henry Miller and Catherine Rawane had Helen.

27, Patrick Miller and Isobel Broun had William.

M. 21, John Walker to Bessie Aitken.

21, David Thomsone to Margaret Wricht.

DECEMBER.

B. 2, William Essoun and Christain Anderson had Bessie.

2, James Scotland and Janet Angus had William (in fornication).

12, William Smart and Bessie Mudie (?) had Christian.

16, Thomas Mudie and Margaret Wilsone had James.

16, Patrick Davidson and Margaret Makildowie had William.

19, Mr. James Daglische and Janet Meikiljone had Margaret.

M. 8, Robert Wardlaw to Christian Daglische.

JANUARY [1600].

B. 2, William Broun in the Lymekillis and Margaret Dewar had Grizel.

9, Robert Halkett of Pitfirren and Margaret Murray had Annas.

9, Peter Dewar and Janet Murray had Eupham.

9, William Sandilans and Jellis Smithe had Richard.

12, Robert Andersoun in Craigdukie and Eupham Harrower had James.

12, John Thomsone in the Nethertoun and Emie Kiming had Christian.

12, Gilbert Blair and Elspeth Jonstoun had Janet (in fornication).

19, Richard Potter and Christain Cuper had Marjory.

27, John Young in the Lymekillis and Agnes Andersoun had Christian.

29, Alexander Chalmer in Logie and Marjory Douglas had Agnes.

M. 2, Thomas Cuthie to Christain Blekwod.

26, John Bene to Agnes Blekwod.

29, William Stennes to Margaret Hugoun.

FEBRUARY.

B. 3, Andrew Wallis, cordiner, and Bessie Stensoun had Alexander.

9, Andrew Huttoun, cordiner, and Elspeth Cuninghame had Thomas.

24, Thomas Chrystia and Janet Huttoun had Janet.

24, Thomas Inglis, cordiner, and . . . .[1] had Helen.

24, Thomas Kellok and Maus Angus had Alison (in fornication).

M. 3, William Murie to Katherine Cuninghame.

3, George Cramie to Janet Broun.

6, Mr. Robert Thomson to Christian Clerk.

MARCH.

B. 2, John Walker and Bessie Aithen had Margaret.

9, Walter Makie and Katherine Horne had Margaret.

[1] There are many instances about this period of the omission of the wife's name, through sheer inadvertence.

9, Patrick Galloway and Marjory Currour had Henry (in fornication).
9, Gilbert Murray and Janet Sibbet had Janet.
9, Henry Miller and Margaret Stirk had Jelis.
9, Edward Burne and Margaret Mudie had Margaret.
9, James Murray, younger, wright, and Isobel Laing had Isobel (in forni-
    cation).
9, William Fillen and Marjory Knox had Marjory (in fornication).
16, George Burne and Marjory Bull had Marjory.
26, William Robertsoun and Agnes Thomsoun had Katherine.

M. [*None.*]

APRIL.

B. 3, John Stirk and Marjory Fleming had John.
    6, Patrick Halked and Margaret Duncisoun had Elspeth (in fornication).
    12, George Warkman, tailor, and Beatrix Smithe had Annas.
    12, Andrew Petter and Janet Burne had Margaret.
    12, John Makie in the Coklaw and Janet Wallett had John.
    16, Henry Douglas in the Gellat and Janet Murray had Janet.
    20, John Huttoun, weaver, and Agnes Smithe had John.
    22, David Smitoun in Over Lessodie and . . . . had John.
    26, John Persone in Nether Baithie and Grizel Mestertoun had Harry.
    26, Robert Andersoun, gardener to "my lord of Tungland," and Nanis
        Bredheid had Phredrik.
    26, Robert Pecok and Katherine Tod had Robert.
    26, Charles Andersone in Prumrose and Margaret Mirie had Masie.

M. 6, William Cuninghame to Janet Lugtoun.
    12, Henry Alexander to Margaret Burne.

MAY.

B. 4, Robert Bevereche in Duntruthell and Katherine Murgoun had James.
    4, William Flokhird in Ester Pitcorthie and Marjory Bull had John.
    4, John Nivin and Helen Currie had Janet.
    4, James Sandilens, son-in-law to Agnes Sandilens, and Katherine Both-
        well had Marion (baptised upon a testimonial from the minister of
        Kinnicher).
    11, Stevin Donald in Pitliver Mill and Marjory Sibbethe had Andrew.
    11, Adam Wolsoun and Katherine Wolsoun had John.
    11, Thomas Key and Marjory Steill had John.
    11, Alexander Culross, bellman, and Christian Forrester had James.
    18, Adam Walker in the Windmilhill and Margaret Bryse had Janet.
    18, George Knox and Margaret Forrester had John (in fornication).
    21, David Douglas in the Nethertoun and Margaret Meikiljohne had Jean.
    31, Mr. John Melvill of Kirkcaldie and Elspeth Kilgoure had William (in
        fornication).
    31, William Douglas and Marjory Livingstoun had Robert.
    31, Andrew Lugtoun and Christian Blekwod had Robert (in fornication).

M. 4, Robert Cuninghame to Janet Wolsoun.
    4, Matthew Barten to Janet Johnstone.

JUNE.

B. 15, Andrew Stirk in the Clune and Janet Huttoun had Margaret.
    18, Andrew Caunt in the Pittiemure and Margaret . . . . had Andrew.

M. [*None.*]

JULY.

B. 18, Richard Lermont and Marjory Furd had Eupham.
    23, Elspeth Nesmithe had her daughter Lilias, begotten in fornication with
        James Stewart, baptized.
    26, James Kingorne, clerk, and Eupham Murray had John.

M. 11, John Arnat to Janet Schankis.
    20, Matthew Egger to Margaret Jemisoun.
    28, Andrew Tuichie(?) to Catherine Fyf.

AUGUST.

B. 3, Adam Walwod, baker, and Katherine Kellok had Bessie.
    10, Andrew Allesoun, mason, and Helen Kuving(?) had Margaret.
    13, David Willemsone, weaver, and Bessie Pacok had Bessie.
    20, William Esplein and Margaret Esplein had Margaret.
    24, John Dow and Christian Schortews had Beatrix.

M. [*None.*]

SEPTEMBER.

B. 6, Andrew Kinninmont in the Kolzera and Helen . . . . had John.
    12, David Watsoun, merchant, and Janet Cuthbert had Bessie.
    21, David Hendrisoun and Grizel Mudie had David.
    28, John Young and Christian Gray had Bessie.
    28, John Davidson in the Nethertoun and Katherine Wardlaw had Andrew.

M. [*None.*]

OCTOBER.

B. 7, Allan Walwod, cordiner, and Rosina Walker had Janet.
    21, Patrick Steinsoun, merchant, and Bessie Reid had David.
    21, Robert Douglas in Pitlever and Helen Donald had Robert.
    21, Thomas Patersoun in the Lymekillis and . . . . had Henry and John, twins.
    26, David Ker, sword slipper, and Katherine Ealder had John.
    26, William Watsoun, cordiner, and Janet Pecok had Helen.
    26, Thomas Gray, miller, and Beatrix Boswell had Alison.
    26, David Astien and Marjory Lugtoun had John.

M. [*None.*]

NOVEMBER.

B. 2, Adam Currour in Wester Gellat and Margaret Swintoun had Bessie.
    6, George Lyndsay of Kevill and . . . . Lindsay had James.
    8, Henry Lawsone and Janet Tod had George.
    8, Williame Simsone, collier, and Isobel Lugtoun had Janet.
    11, Andrew Melvill of Garvok, his Majesty's Master of Household, and . . . . Hamilton had Janet.
    18, Thomas Young and . . . . had Francis.
    18, Mr. John Fairfull, minister, and . . . . had Fredrik.
    20, James Huttoun and Marjory Tod had Bessie.
    20, William Andersoun, tailor, and Margaret Bonalay had William.
    25, William Walwod in Baithe and Elspet Alexander had Janet.
    30, John Burne in the Nethertoun and Janet Michell had Janet.

M. 4, Mr. Hew Myldis to Margaret Durie.
    4, David Burne to Margaret Broun.
    18, Andrew Huttoun to Isobel Stalker.
    25, George Lugtoun to Janet Kiming.
    25, George Jonstoun to Isobel Rae.

DECEMBER.

B. 7, Robert Ker, servant to John Mudie in the Gellat, and Bessie Pecok had Bessie (in **fornication**).
    15, William Walwod in Tuche and . . . . Spittell had Andrew.
    18, John Orliance, violer to the Queen's Majesty, and Dorothy Lokie had Fredrik.
    28, George Huttoun, merchant, and Bessie Cuthbert had Barbara.
    28, James Chalmer in Knokhous and Margaret Sandis had Alexander.

M. 2, John Mathesoune, servant to John Gib, married to Bessie Alisoun.
  2, Thomas Bankis to Isobel Tod.
  9, John Feg, parishioner of Cleish, to Janet Inglis.
  16, Thomas Philp to Janet Lindsay.
  23, Robert Currie to Katherine Michelsoun.
  30, Alexander Crystie to Agnes Lawrie.
  30, James Michell to Isobel Rawen.

JANUARY [1601].

B. 5, John Cunninghame in the Syllitoun and Isobel Cuninghame had Robert.
  5, Patrick Turnebull and Katherine Smithe had Andrew.
  11, John Broun in the Nethertoun and Christian Mudie had David.
  13, David Germont and Barbara Douglas had Bessie.
  20, John Wricht and Nanis Wolsoun had John.
  24, Patrick Davidsoun and Margaret Makilroy had Patrick.

M. 13, Robert Peiris to Effie Schortews.

FEBRUARY.

B. 10, Mr. Robert Thomsone and Christian Clerk had Lawrence.
  10, James Cairnis, weaver, and Margaret Davidson had Robert.
  13, The Master of Orknay and Mistress Margaret Stewart had Anna.
  15, William Esoun, weaver, and Christian Andersoun had William.
  15, John Andersoun in Lusker and Marion Andersoun had Andrew.
  15, Robert Murray in the Lymekillis and Margaret Berner had Grizel.
  17, Patrick Rudderfurd and Helen Baran had Janet.
  20, Thomas Greif in Blernebathie and . . . . had Margaret.
  24, David Dewart and Jean Logan had James.

M. 17, John Anderson to Christian Schortews.
  24, Andrew Turnebull to Bessie Futhie.
  24, William Lugtoun to Janet Smitoun.
  24, Adam Diksoun to Elspet Stirk.

MARCH.

B. 1, William Murie in Urchart and Katherine Cuninghame had Alexander.
  1, John Machreche and Janet Fisher had John (in fornication).
  8, William Currour in Keiris Baithe and Helen Law had Bessie.
  8, Thomas Covintrie in Stewertis Baithe and Janet Raw had Bessie.
  15, John Thomsone and Margaret Primrose had Elspet (in fornication).
  17, John Wolsoun in Pitconochie and Janet Cuninghame had Elspet.
  20, John Huttoun, cordiner, and Helen Steinsoun had Barbara.
  22, Patrick Metland and Bessie Row had Alexander.
  22, Andrew Wallis, cordiner, and Bessie Steinsoun had Andrew.
  24, Robert Lawsoun, smith in the Crosfurd, and Bessie Blak had Andrew.
  26, John Mathesoun, servant to John Gib, and Bessie Alisoun had Isobel.

M. [*None.*]

APRIL.

B. 2, Adam Schorteous, flesher, and Margaret Miller had David.
  2, John Burne in the Newraw and Margaret Steinsoun had William.
  2, David Cunninghame in Pitdinnie and . . . . had Robert (in adultery).
  7, John Adisoun in Pittincreif mill and Beatrix Turnbull had Dorothy.
  7, John Nicoll and Elspet Magill had Elspet (in fornication).
  19, Walter Huttoun, weaver, and Margaret Rae had Margaret.
  19, William Cuninghame in the Crosfurd and Janet Lugtoun had Janet.
  28, Patrick Legat, skinner, and Bessie Blak had Bessie.

M. [*None.*]

MAY.

B. 5, Andrew Mure, merchant, and Janet Mertein had Bessie.
   10, Nicol Jonstoun and Isobel Maxwell had Margaret.
   17, William Rudderfurd and . . . . had David (in fornication).
   17, William Walwod in Tod and Isobel Walwod had Margaret.
   24, John Hepburne and Margaret Lindsay had Margaret (in fornication).
   26, William Cairnie and Margaret Robertsoun had Thomas (in fornication).
   31, David Bruce, baker, and Katherine Walwod had Margaret.
   31, Archibald Douglas, merchant, and Janet Phillen had Robert.

M. 12, Charles Wallense to Margaret Dewar.
   12, John Drysdell to Margaret Pecok.
   26, David Douglas to Janet Smitoun.

JUNE.

B. 2, James Reid, merchant, and Bessie Lindsay had Thomas.
   14, George Walker, merchant, and Marjory Cuthbert had George.
   14, Thomas Stennos in Mestertoun and Janet Douglas had Thomas.
   14, George Jonstoun and . . . . had Andrew.
   16, John Andersoun, servant to James Kingorge (*sic*), and Janet Michie had James (in fornication).
   22, Andrew Tuichie, fisher, and Katherine Fyf had David.
   24, Stevin Donald in Pitliver Mill and Margaret Sibett had David.

M. 2, Alexander Lugtoun to Janet Patoun.
   16, John Stewart to Marjory Wolsoun.
   16, Robert Stirk to Agnes Ker.
   29, William Williamsoun, weaver, to Effie Schortews.

JULY.

B. 12, Robert Andersoun, weaver, and Isobel Thomsoune had Robert.
   17, Robert Halkett of Pitfirren and Margaret Murray had Isobel.
   19, David Andersoun in Pitbachlie and Helen Andersoun had Janet.
   21, David Blak in the Coklaw and Helen Dawie had John.
   26, Andrew Inglis, cordiner, and Marjory Michell had John.
   28, John Andersoun, litster, and Bessie Chrystie had Isobel.
   30, James Makie and . . . . had John.

M. 7, William Cusing to Margaret Burn.
    7, William Cuninghame to Helen Brume.
    7, Andrew Adisoun to Janet Walker.
   14, Edward Stirk to Bessie Bull.
   14, Andrew Horne to Katherine Gray.
   21, Mr. Thomas Wardlaw to Katherine Alisoun.

AUGUST.

B. 4, William Wilsoun in the Coifknawis (?) and Isobel Pecok had Agnes.
    9, William Pecok in Mestertoun and Helen Mure had James.
    9, Robert Schairp and Janet Phinlasoun had James.
   31, Thomas Mudie in the Nethertoun and Isobel Wolsoun had John.

M. 11, Laurence Andersoun to Janet Moreis.
   — John Logan to Margaret Gat (?).

SEPTEMBER.

B. 1, Patrick Stewart of Baithe and Katherine Baram had Margaret
    1, Andrew Bennat, baker, and Marjory Esplein had Margaret.
    6, John Wolsoun and Katherine Makkerten had John.
    6, Thomas Mudie and Bessie Turnebull had William.

6, Richard Walker, merchant, and Isobel Smithe had twins, Laurence and Adam.

12, William Flokert in Pitcorthe and Marjory Bull had David.

15, Thomas Gib, servant to the Queen's Majesty, and . . . . . . had Isobel.

20, John Stirk and Marjory Fleming had Robert.

20, Nicol Hunter in Pittincreif and Helen Huttoun had Marion.

20, Patrick Stennop in North Tod and Katherine Ealder had James.

20, Thomas Richie in Baithe and Margaret Andersoun had Elspeth.

20, Laurence Russell in Tuche mill and Bessie Gib had Isobel.

20, George Lugtoun and Janet Kiming (? Kuning) had James.

20, James Dalglische in the Blaklaw and Christian Cragie had James.

20, Harry Bull, cutler, and Margaret Ker had Robert.

21, Andrew Dewer in Keltiewod and Isobel Dik had John.

27, Clement Sanderis in the Cregis and Marion Bell had Eupham.

27, Adam Watt in the Lymekillis and Nanis Brum had Katherine.

M. 2, David Barrie to Janet Wolsoun.

7, Edward Thomsone, merchant, to Janet Burne.

OCTOBER.

B. 4, Robert Turnebull and Janet Herper had Helen.

4, William Crawfert and Katherine Tod had Bessie.

11, George Huttoun, cordiner, and Helen Gibsoun had Bessie.

11, Henry Turnebull, merchant, and Helen Mutray had James.

20, John Burne in the Gellat and Margaret Anderson had Thomas.

25, Robert Wolsoun, tailor, and Margaret Scotland had Christian.

25, Robert Michie, collier, and Janet Davidson had Bessie.

25, John Schortews and Janet Tod had Janet (in fornication).

25, Mr. John Murray, servant to her Majesty, and Margaret Murray had Barbara (in fornication).

M. 3, Harry Young to Christian Keir.

NOVEMBER.

B. 1, James Sandis in the Wester Gellat and Margaret Etkin had Bessie.

1, John Mudie and Marion Baxter had Thomas.

3, Robert Ross, servant to the Queen's Majesty, and Margaret Hutton had Thomas.

10, John Fliming in the Blaklaw and Christian Sandis had James.

15, Thomas Tod and Barbara Ealder had Thomas.

15, James Fischer and Margaret Storie had Margaret (in fornication, producing a testimonial from Mr. Henry Blyth, minister at Holyrood-house, of their satisfaction there).

17, James Bust and Margaret Muirie had Helen (in fornication).

22, Robert Moreis and Marjory Adisoun had James.

24, Thomas . . . and Margaret Moreis had David (in fornication).

26, Henry Dewar of Letheamond and Marion Huttoun had Nanis.

26, John Niven and Helen Currie had Elspet.

26, David Burne, younger, of the East Mill and Margaret Burne had Janet.

26, Patrick Hutchisoun and Katherine Makie had Nanis.

26, William Currour and Margaret Weitheid had Henry.

M. 17, Andrew Currie to Masie Anderson.

24, Gilbert Wricht to Margaret Esoun.

DECEMBER.

B. 6, Robert Peiris, mason, and Helen Schortews had Robert.

6, Adam Anderson in the Nethertoun and Christian Thomson had Marjory.

6, Thomas Andersoun in the Letheamond and Janet Gemlis had Henry.

13, John Andersoun, younger, and Christian Schortews had Margaret.

13, James Allen and Helen Reid had Charles.

13, Andrew Huttoun, cordiner, and Elspet Cuninghame had Elspet.

13, John Lawsoun in the Mirriehill and Janet Donald had Margaret.

13, George Mories in Cawdoun Baithe and Margaret Kinninmont had Margaret.

13, Robert Broun and Bessie Anderson had Elspet (fornicator in the North Ferrie).

13, William Smart, flesher, and Bessie Mudie had William.

27, John Warkman, tailor, and Katherine Phinlasoun had Elspet.

27, Andrew Meine in Pitconochie and Grizel Anderson had Katherine

M. 30, Patrick Lermont to Christian Davidson.

30, Alexander Robertsone to Janet Turnebull.

JANUARY [1602].

B. 3, John Thomsone in the Nethertoun and Emie Kiming had James.

3, John Orlie, violer to her Majesty, and . . . . had Anna.

3, James Broun and Margaret Thomsone had George.

7, William Thomsone and Janet Potter had James.

17, Thomas Walwod, mealmaker, and Effie Kirk had Isobel.

17, Thomas Smithe, collier, and Margaret Patoun had Marjory.

24, Thomas Broun, weaver, and Janet Clevie had Janet.

24, William Lugtoun in the Nethertoun and Janet Smitoun had James.

31, Thomas Bankis in Wester Lusker and Elspet Murie had Margaret.

M. 12, James Kinsman to Christian Walwod.

19, David Strang, cordiner, to Margaret Andersone.

FEBRUARY.

B. 1, Robert Ettkin in the Nethertoun and Elspet Murray had Janet.

1, Robert Anderson, tailor, and Marion Porter had Margaret.

1, John Robertson, mealmaker, and Nans Huttoun had Laurence.

7, Robert Furd in Pittincreif and Marjory Mestertoun had Bessie.

7, John Mill in the Gask and Janet Mill had Isobel.

9, Mr. James Dalgleische, schoolmaster, and Janet Meikiljohn had William.

9, John Strang, cordiner, and Janet Makie had David.

9, Edward Patoun and Agnes Littiljone had Bessie (in adultery).

11, William Steinsoun in the Nethertoun and Janet Gray had William.

11, William Archbald, one of Her Majesty's cooks, and Katherine Mureheid had Christian.

13, Thomas Walker in the Rodis and Bessie Murgoun had William.

15, James Kellok in Pittrevie and Margaret Chalmer had Christian.

15, Andrew Reid (?), miller, and . . . . had Bessie.

15, John Harruer in the Gask and Bessie Makie had Janet.

28, John Fairlie in Pitfirren and Janet Sanderis had John.

28, David Broun in the Coklaw and Christian Blak had Bessie.

M. 9, Robert Phillen to Helen Cuthbert.

MARCH.

B. 9, David Pitcairne and Janet Wricht had Henry.

17, Robert Merser, flesher, and Margaret Baran had James.

19, Wattie Wylie in Tuche and . . . . Blekwod had Barbara.

28, Robert Kellok in Mestertoun and Janet Chalmer had William.

28, David Douglas, "sumtyme spous" to Janet Smitoun, had a manchild born to him, baptised and called David.

28, Henry Meldrum in the Cungeis and Bessie Wolsoun had Henry.

M. [*None.*]

APRIL.

B. 4, Alexander Creiche in the Wester Gellat and Margaret Walker had Bessie.

4, George Bruse in Blerochie and Margaret Orrok had Michael.
6, William Bust and Helen Turnebull had Peter.
6, Daniel Phinlasoun in Pitliver and . . . . had Robert.
11, Robert Mercer in the Craigis and . . . . Carmichell had Robert.
11, John Thomsone in the Lymekillis and Christian Keir had David.
11, Robert Douglas in the Nethertoun and Margaret Andersoun had David.
11, John Dewer in Pitbachlie and Isobel Moreis had Bessie.
11, William Kiming and Bessie Kiming had Katherine.
19, David Persone in Pitdinneis and Margaret Cuninghame had Robert.
19, David Smitoun in Dinduff and Janet Makie had Henry.
19, William Mudie and Margaret Edisoun had Katherine.
19, John Walker in Pitliver and Bessie Etkin had John.
19, Robert Young and Bessie Lugtoun had William.
19, Harry Mudie in the Nethertoun and Margaret Reid had Helen.
19, Adam Phargus and Christian Drysdell had Adam.
27, Thomas Wast, weaver, and Grizel Mitchell had William.
27, Nicol Dalglische in Tinnigask and Helen Blekwod had Robert.
27, William Murie in Urchart and Katherine Cuninghame had Margaret.
27, Henry Gurlay and Christian Murgonum (?) had William (in fornication).
27, Robert Walwod and Bessie Strang had William.

M. 6, Patrick Gurlay to Marjory Currour.
13, James Patter to Bessie Reid.
13, James Wolsoun to Janet Wolsone.
27, John Mudie to Marion Huttoun.
27, The Clerk of Dalgety to Janet Michell.

MAY.

B. 4, George Strachen, servant to his Majesty, and . . . . had George.
4, Charles Vallenge in Midowend and Margaret Dewer had Bessie.
4, Henry Miller in Craiglusker and Margaret Rawen had Agnes.
9, William Spens and Janet Smitoun had George.
9, Patrick Meffen and Barbara Nicoll had James.
14, John Mure and . . . . had Anna.
17, Adam Wolsone in the Millburne and Katherine Wolsoun had Bessie.
17, Nicol Ingles in the Windmilhill and Bessie Cuninghame had Bessie.
17, Robert Kellok and Margaret Cuninghame had James.
20, William Walwod in Tuche and . . . . Spittell had Katherine.
20, James Cous in the Galrikhill and Margaret Bryse[1] had James.
24, Adam Walker in the Windmilhill and Margaret Bryse had Andrew.
24, Andrew Dik in Mestertoun and Isobel Miller had James.
24, John Logan in the Lymekills and Margaret Gatt had Isobel.
31, George Mill and Bessie Burne had Henry (in fornication).
31, John Young in the Lymekills and Elspet Andersoun had William.

M. 4, Patrick Walker to Janet Cuninghame.
25, James Cunnand to Janet Stennos.

JUNE.

B. 1, Thomas Steinsoune in the Newraw and Marjory Thomsone had Janet.
1, George Cuninghame, weaver, and Christian Henrie had Bessie.
3, John Kellok in the Nethertoun and . . . . had Helen.
6, Lawrence Andersoun in the Hiltoun and Bessie Currour had Bessie.
6, Thomas Gray in the Hewchemills and Beatrix Boswell had Andrew.
6, Donald Yawan and Katherine Smithe had Margaret.
6, Andrew Murray in Pitliver and Eupham Wemis had Margaret.
13, James Thomsone in the Nuke and Helen Strang had William.

[1] Deleted.

13, John Knox and Catherine Gib had Walter (in fornication).
16, Alexander Edie in Kevill and . . . . had . . . .
16, David Douglas in the Nethertoun and Margaret Meikiljone had Elizabeth.
24, Laurence Huttoun, merchant, and Bessie Blak had Janet.
27, Adam Schortews, flesher, and Margaret Miller had Marjory.
27, George Warkman, tailor, and Beatrix Smithe had John.
27, John Bankis in Baldrik and . . . . had Clement.

M. 15, David Culros was married to Christian Bull.
15, Edward Bruse to Christian Allen.

JULY.

B. 4, Robert Stirk and Agnes Ker had Christian.
20, Robert Bevrege and . . . . had Janet.
27, Adam Steinsoun, smith, and . . . . had Robert.

M. 13, ... Pecock was married to Margaret Lawthoun (*sic*).
20, John Anderson to Margaret Prettews (? Porttews).
20, Walter Makie to Marion Anderson.
27, George Sanderis to Helen Wolsoun.

AUGUST.

B. 1, Robert Murray in the Lymekills and Janet Sibbett had twins, Robert and Janet.
1, Adam Walwod in Suthe Fod and Isobel Walwod had Christian.
1, Harry Young in the Lymekills and Janet Keir had twins, Grizel and Christian.
1, William Wolsoun in Pitliver and Janet Sprewill had Marjory.
4, Richard Baxter, one of Her Majesty's "allakeis" (lackeys), and Nanis Wod had Bessie.
15, Patrick Galloway, servant to Patrick Stewart of Beath, and Bessie Currour had Patrick.
15, James Busbie and Margaret Douglas had Marion (in fornication).
22, Edward Douglas in Wester Gellett and Marion Kirk had Helen.
22, William Livingstoune in the Lymekills and Margaret Cawie had James.
22, Edward Thomsone, merchant in Dunfermline, and Janet Burne had Janet.
22, James Huttoun in the Coklaw and Marjory Tod had Robert.
22, John Schortews in the Colyeraw and Janet Broun had Helen.
24, Henry Douglas in the Easter Gellett and Jane Murray had Margaret.
24, David Bull, smith, and Christian Burne had Emie.
29, Andrew Currie in Prumrose and Masie Andersone had Adam.

M. 16, William Broun to Bessie Smitoun.
16, Henry Lawthian to Isobel Thomsone.
31, David Schortews to Christian Russell.
31, John Keir to Jellis Burne.

31, Thomas Kirk to Margaret Blair.

SEPTEMBER.

B. 5, David Watsone, merchant, and Janet Cuthbert had James.
5, John Thomsone in the Nethertoun and Masie Bull had John.
5, Archibald Cambell, litster, and . . . . had William (in fornication).
11, Alexander Lugtoun, collier, and Isobel Patoun had Andrew.
14, William Wolsoun, weaver, and Eupham Schortews had Bessie.
23, Mr. Thomas Wardlaw and Katherine Allesoun had Thomas.

M. [*None.*]

OCTOBER.

B.   4, Thomas Chrystie in the Holl and Janet Huttoun had James.
9, John Feg, tailor, and Janet Inglis had William.
9, Alexander Chalmer in Logie and . . . . had Robert.
17, John Young in the Lymekills and Christian Gray had William.
17, Patrick Davidsone, collier, and Margaret Makildowie had Henry.
19, Sir Robert Halkheid of Pitfirren and Margaret Murray had Grizel.
24, William Wolsoun in the Nethertoun and Katherine Blaketure had William.
24, Henry Drummond in Wester Gellat and Margaret Hertsyd had Margaret.
28, Henry Donald, miller in Garvok Mill, and . . . . had Robert.

M.   6, James Kennetie to Margaret Crystie.
19, John Merteine, parishioner of Inverkeithing, to Katherine Cunnen (? Tunne) of Westertoun.
26, Patrick Walwod to Catherine Walwod.

NOVEMBER.

B.   2, James Moreis, one of Her Majesty's servants, and Margaret Murray had Katherine.
4, Mr. James Durie in Wester Gellat and Margaret Mestertoun had John.
8, John Smytoun in the Nethertoun and . . . . had John.
8, Andrew Smithe in Fod and Margaret Mudie had Christian.
8, Gilbert Currie in the Hilltoun and Margaret Esoun had Nanis.
20, John Bull, smith in Nethertoun, and . . . . had Margaret.

M. 18, John Gipsone to Janet Wylie.
22, John Sanderis to Christian Miller.

DECEMBER.

B.   7, John Young in Hollbaldrik (?) and Margaret Persone had Eupham.
12, Adam Man in Turnebullis Baithe and Marion Drysdell had Janet.
12, James Hunter, flesher, and Katherine Law had Janet.
21, John Gib in the Abay and Isobel Lindsay had Elspet.
21, David Ker, swordslipper in Dunfermline, "had ane women chyld borne to him in adulterie by his wyf of Katheren Lyddell, quho efter satisfactioun was baptisit and callit Katheren."
27, Robert Stewert, master of Orkney, "had ane man child borne to him of Mestres Margarat Stewert his wyfe quho depertit of that berne, baptisit and callit Charlis."
28, John Bennat, merchant, and Helen Meikiljone had John.
28, David Murray, cellarman to Her Majesty, and Christian Garvand had William (in fornication).

M. 14, John Ker to Margaret Bull.
14, Thomas Kirk to Margaret Kiming.
14, Laurence Brand to Margaret Trell.
21, John Wolsone to Isobel Kirk.

JANUARY [1603].

B.   2, Walter Huttoun, weaver, and Margaret Rae had Christian.
2, William Broun in Stevenson's Beath and Isobel Dewer had Margaret.
2, David Cuninghame in Prumbrose and Helen Stennos had James.
9, John Dow, collier, and Christian Schortews had William.
11, Robert Andersone in the Nuke and Annie Bredie had Bessie.
11, James Gipsone in Kevill Mill and Margaret Patoun had James.
13, ... Ker, swordslipper in Dunfermline, and Katherine Ealder had Bessie.
16, David Blak in the Coklaw and Helen Daw had . . . .

16, Robert Anderson in Craigdowkie and Eupham Harrower had Robert.
16, Henry Greif in Blarochie and Janet Trell had Henry (in fornication).
29, Robert Smythe in Pitincreif and Margaret Angus had Helen.
29, John Davidsone in Keltihewche and Christian Warkman had James.
29, James Aitkin, servant to Robert Bruce of Baldrik, and Sara Aittkin had John (in fornication).
29, James Bust, baker, and Janet Danzell had Janet.

M. 11, John Glen to Margaret Strange.
25, Alexander Hynniman to Bessie Turnebull.

FEBRUARY.

B. 6, George Jonstoun and Isobel Rae had Margaret.
13, David Strang, cordiner, and Margaret Andersone had Nanis.
20, Robert Kiningame in Wester Syllitoun and Helen Wolsoun had Isobel.
20, Andrew Turnebull, younger, and Isobel Sanderis had . . . . (in fornication).
20, Robert Phillen, merchant, and Helen Cuthbert had Bessie.
20, Thomas Inglis, cordiner, and Margaret Steinsone had Katherine.

M. 11, Thomas Davidsone to Christian Andersone (marked January but probably February).

MARCH.

B. 3, George Sanderis in the Wakmill and Helen Wolsoun had Bessie.
3, John Dewer in the Fulford and Katherine Here (? had James (in fornication) baptised on a testimonial from the minister of Auchtertull.
3, John Gotterstoun, weaver, and Margaret Clerk had Katherine.
7, John Wricht and Agnes Wolsoun had Isobel.
7, Archibald Douglas, merchant, and Janet Phillen had Thomas.
7, Thomas Coventrie and . . . . had Patrick.
13, David Burne, younger, and Margaret Broun had William.
20, John Galrik in the Stene and Nanis Andersoune had David.
20, Harry Balfour in Mestertoun and Christian Lawsone had James.
20, John Greif in Tynnogask and Christian Bennet had William.
20, William Walwod in Nether Baithe and Margaret Alexander had Christian.
24, James Wolsoun and Janet Wolsoun had Bessie (in fornication).
27, Thomas Kirk, baker, and Margaret Kiming had James.
27, Andrew Wallis, cordiner, and Bessie Steinsoun had Isobel.
27, Donald Reoche and Isobel Wolsoun had Janet (in fornication).

M. 7, James Gray to Janet Jonstoun.
7, James Henderson to Christian Flek.

APRIL.

B. 3, William Cuninghame in the Crossfurd and Janet Lugtoun had William.
3, Thomas Mudie in the Nethertoun and Isobel Wolsoun had William.
3, Allan Mudie and Janet Forfar had James.
20, James Hamiltoun, cottar in Westertoun, and Janet Imrie had Helen.
20, John Waker in Cragluskar and Margaret Fotringame had Margaret.
20 (or 29), Sir Andrew Melvill of Garvok, Master of Household to His Majesty, and . . . . Hamilton had Andrew.
24, David Wolsoun in Keltihewche and . . . . had . . . . . in fornication).

M. [*None.*]

MAY.

B. 1, John Makie, beside Lessodie Mill, and Christian Pringill had Janet.
3, John Andersone, younger, litster, and Margaret Prettews had William.
7, Andrew Currour in Keiris Baithe and Helen Law had Robert.
7, James Kingorne, clerk, and Eupham Murray had Alexander.
21, Peter Dewer in Rescobie and Janet Murray had David.
21, Alexander Wolsoun, weaver, and Janet Phinlasoun had Helen.

27, Wiiliam Walwod in Tuche and Marjory Spittell had Patrick.
31, George Abercrombie and Elspet Cuttis had Alexander.

M. 3, John Pirie to Bessie Esoun.
     3, John Peblis to Masie Cumbrie.
     31, John Dougall to Margaret Stewart.

JUNE.

B. 3, Patrick Stewart of Baithe and Katherine Baram had Janet.
     5, William Spere, weaver, and Margaret Bleketure had Andrew.
     5, George Lugtoun in Wichart and Janet Kiming had Helen.
     5, Robert Douglas in Pitliver Mill and Helen Donald had Isobel.
     19, James Dalglische and Christian Cragie had Bessie.
     29, William Watsone, cordiner, and Janet Pecok had Margaret.
     29, Thomas Waker in the Roddis and Bessie Morgone had Helen.

M. 21, Edward Wastwod to Margaret Forfar.
     29, William Cusing to Margaret Burne.
     29, Henry Drummond to Margaret Quhyt.
     29, John Tailzeour to Margaret Donald.

JULY.

B. 5, James Kennetie and Margaret Crystie had Janet.
     10, William Flokert in Easter Pitcorthie and Marjory Bull had Margaret.
     17, James Cunninan in Mestertoun and Margaret Stennos had Thomas.
     17, Patrick Turnbull and Katherine Smythe had Janet.
     17, Robert Murray in the Lymkills and Katherine Berner had William.
     17, John Wolsoun in Easter Pitdinneis and Janet Cuninghame had James.
     18, John Pirie and Bessie Esoun had James.
     18, Gilbert Blair, slater, and . . . . had Isobel.
     18, John Andersoun, *alias* Watter Laird, and Katherine Broun had Katherine.

M. 5, Robert Crumbie (?) to Janet Cuper.
     5, David Richisone to Helen Mintethe.
     19, William Alexander to Bessie Kirk.

AUGUST.

B. 7, Peter Reid and Bessie Angus had John (in fornication).
     14, Henry Lawthian and Isobel Thomsone had Margaret.
     14, Alexander Creiche and Grizel Walker had Marion.
     21, Michael Lessilis (?) and Helen Jonstoun had Anna.
     21, Robert Wardlaw and Marjory Law had Henry.
     21, William Cusing and Margaret Burne had Robert.
     28, Mr. Robert Thomsone in the Nethertoun and Christian Clerk had Bessie.
     30, Andrew Huchesoun, cordiner, and . . . . had Allan.

M. 23, John Miller to Margaret Hoge.

SEPTEMBER.

B. 11, Alexander Hay and Marjory Steill had George.
     18, John Ker, mason, and Margaret Bull had James.
     20, Adam Watt in the Lymekills and Janet Broun had William.

M. [*None.*]

OCTOBER.

B. 16, Edward Stirk, weaver, and Bessie Bull had Helen.
     23, William Angus and Janet Kellok had Janet.
     25, Robert Kellok in Mestertoun and Janet Chalmer, " quho deid of that
          berne," had Barbara.

M. 4, William Steidman to Katherine Wolsone.
     25, William Andersone to Jellis Persone.

NOVEMBER.

B. 6, Patrick Halkheid and Marjory Duncane had Marjory (in fornication).
13, John Sanderis, mealmaker, and Christian Miller had Katherine.
13, John Andersoun in Kistok and Margaret Andersone had Janet.
20, David Barker in Blerothie and Janet Wolsoun had John.
27, Andrew Meine in Wester Pitcorthie and Katherine Cuninghame had Helen.

M. 8, William Kennetie to Margaret Spere.
25, John Chalmer to Elspet Jonstoun.

DECEMBER.

B. 4, James Wolsoun in Galrik hill and Janet Gipsone had Barbara.
4, John Keir in the Grange and Jellis Burne had Thomas.
4, Alexander Lugtoun in the Colzeraw and Janet Patoun had Margaret.
4, Gilbert Cuninghame and Margaret Smythe had Helen.
6, Mr. Andrew Forrester, one of the ministers of Dunfermline, and Helen Ramsay had Alexander.
13, James Kerins, weaver, and Margaret Davidsone had David.
18, David Kellok in Nether Lessodie and Katherine Pringill had Christian.
20, Harry Stewart, son of Patrick Stewert of Bethe, and Katherine Wardlaw had Patrick (in fornication).

M. 1, Patrick Steine to Margaret Drummond.
6, Laurence Patrik to Margaret Reid.
6, Peter Culross to Katherine Inglis.
11, Robert Clerk to Katherine Crystie.
11, John Miller to Margaret Hoge.
20, David Andersone to Bessie Annan.
27, Thomas Bell to Janet Chrystie.

JANUARY [1604].

B. 1, George Walker, merchant, and Marjory Cuthbert had Bessie.
3, William Sandilans and Jellis Smythe had Marjory.
10, William Thomsone, cooper, and Janet Potter had Janet.
17, William Esoun, weaver, and Christian Anderson had Alexander.
22, William Kiming and Bessie Kiming had James.
26, John Pebillis and Masi Cumbrie had Christian.

M. 3, Robert Douglas to Margaret Edisoune.
3, Thomas Paplay to Margaret Moreis.
31, Henry Turnbull to Katherine Cusing.

FEBRUARY.

B. 5, Patrick Stenison, merchant, and Bessie Reid had Janet.
7, James Reid, merchant, and Bessie Lindsay had Isobel.
12, William Steidman in Keltihewche and Katherine Wolsoun had Marion.
14, James Burne in the Coklaw and . . . . had John.
16, Gilbert Alexander and Katherine Hendersoun had Jean (in fornication).
19, James Kellok in Pittrevie and . . . . Chalmer had Robert.
19, John Thomsone in the Nethertoun and Emie Kiming had Helen.
19, Alexander Colvin and Bessie Harrower had Margaret.
19, George Huttoun, merchant, and Bessie Cuthbert had Margaret.
19, Thomas Greif and Margaret Farsythe had Bessie.

M. 14, Florie Anderson to Helen Cuninghame.
14, Charles Richesoun to Janet Bust.
21, Adam Dewer to Christian Wricht.
21, William Turnbull to Bessie Cupere.

MARCH

B. 8, Alexander Hinniman and Bessie Turnebull had Janet.

8, Alexander Edie in Easter Pitdinnie and Nans Philp had Thomas.
13, Robert Lawsone, smith in the Crossfurd, and Bessie Blak had James.
13, James Corse in the Galrikhill and Janet Sandis had Janet.
18, John Dewer in Pitbachlie and Isobel Moreis had Janet.
18, John Makdougall in the Nethertoun and Margaret Stewert had Thomas.

M. [*None.*]

APRIL.

B. 17, David Schortews, tailor, and Christian Russell had Robert.
22, Andrew Currie in Prumrose and Masi Anderson had Margaret.
24, Andrew Tuthie (? Tuchie), fisher, and Katherine Fyf had Agnes.
26, Robert Durie and Christian Messoun had George (in fornication).
29, Robert Merser in the Craigis and Rachel Carmichell had John.
29, Andrew Huttoun, cordiner, and Elspet Cuninghame had Andrew.
29, John Bull, smith in the Nethertoun, and Janet Gipson had Marjory.

M. 10, John Stewert to Bessie Stewert, daughter to Patrick Stewart of Beath.
24, James Clune to Margaret Done (? Dune).

MAY.

B. 1, Mr. James Dalglische, schoolmaster, and Janet Meikiljone had Robert.
6, George Mene in Wester Pitcorthie and . . . . had Robert.
8, Andrew Wallis, cordiner, and Bessie Steinsoun had Andrew.
10, William Mudie in the Easter Gellet, and Janet Turnebull had James.
13, David Cuninghame in Wester Pitdinneis and Helen Stennes had David.
21, Alexander, Lord Fyvie, President, and Mrs. Margaret Leslie had Charles.
21, John Stewert and Marjory Wolsoun had John.

M. 10, Christopher Porterfield to Janet Turnebull.
10, James Bathcat to Bessie Douglas.
16, James Huttoun to Katherine Walwod.
16, Alexander Greg to Margaret Broun.
22, David Pecok to Janet Makie.

JUNE.

B. 3, John Wolsoun and Isobel Kirk had John.
3, Patrick Legat, skinner, and Bessie Balak had James.
9, James Broun and Margaret Thomsone had Peter.
19, Andrew Bennett, baker, and Marjory Esplein had Margaret.
24, John Warkman, tailor, and Katherine Phinlasoun had Margaret.
30, Adam Kirk in the Wester Gellat and Helen Fargie had Edward.

M. 12, John (?) Smetoun to Margaret Anderson.
12, Nicol Wardlaw to Margaret Huttoun.
12, David Walker to Grizel Meldrum.

JULY.

B. 8, Archibald Robertsoun, weaver, and Helen Huttoun had John.
12, Thomas Walwod, at the Eastend of the toun, and Bessie Kirk had William.
12, Patrick Stennos and Margaret Cuninghame had Peter (in fornication).
17, Thomas Gray in the East Mill and Betie Boswell had James.
17, Adam Currour in the Wester Gellat and Margaret Swyntoun had Janet.
19, Sir Andrew Melvill of Garvok and . . . . Hamilton had John.
24, Patrick Steine in the Wester Gellat and . . . . had John.
24, William Andersoun and Margaret Turnbull had James (in fornication).
29, Edward Thomsone, merchant, and Janet Burne had Edward.
31, Mr. John Fairfull, minister, and Margaret Prestoun had Nanis.

M. 3, George Knox to Janet Angus.
26, Nicoll Thomsone to Janet Pecok.
26, William Spere to Grizel Nesmithe.

AUGUST.

B. 5, John Miller in Mestertoun and Margaret Hoge had David.

5, John Huttoun in Lessodie and . . . . had James.

7, David Walker, cooper, and Christian Mar (? Mur) had Patrick (in fornication).

12, William Andersoun in the Lymekills and Jellis Persoun had Grizel.

12, Thomas Bankis in Wester Luscour and Isobel Tod had Thomas.

12, William Cuninghame in the Crossfurd and Janet Lugtoun had Helen.

14, David Bust and Janet Danzell had David.

14, Robert Turnebull, merchant, and Janet Cuper had Margaret.

19, James Kennetie in Craigdoukie and Katherine Spere had Marion.

19, John Young in the Lymekills and Agnes Andersoun had Jellis.

26, William Smart, flesher, and . . . . had twins, James and David.

26, Robert Stirk, maltman, and Agnes Ker had Helen.

26, Thomas Richie and Mary Anderson had James.

28, John Fleming in the Blaklaw and Christian Sandis had Christian.

30, Mr. Thomas Wardlaw and Katherine Alisoun had Henry.

M. 3, Thomas Rob to Christian Merchell.

7, James Hendersoun to Margaret Wolsoun.

7, James Caddell to Betie Persoun.

14, John Wardlaw to Margaret Bad (? Kad).

28, James Scotland to Isobel Dik.

28, Alexander Wolsoun to Elspet Michie.

SEPTEMBER.

B. 2, Thomas Tod and Barbara Ealder had Helen.

11, John Andersoun, younger, litster, and Margaret Prettens had James.

17, John Wolsoun and Katherine Makie had John.

23, Andrew Dewer in Pitbachlie and . . . . had Andrew.

23, Robert Michie, collier, and Janet Davidsone had Robert.

M. [*None.*]

OCTOBER.

B. 2, Thomas Papla and Margaret Moreis had John.

2, William Murgoun in Pittincreif and Janet Scotland had Frederick.

8, William Robertson in Craigdukie and Agnes Thomsone had William.

8, Alan Walwod, cordiner, and Rosina Walker had Isobel.

8, George Huttoun, cordiner, and Helen Gipsoun had Marion.

8, John Schortews in the Colzeraw and Janet Broun had David.

8, Laurence Patrick, tailor, and Margaret Reid had Robert.

10, William Walwod in Tuche and . . . . had David.

10, Alexander Ratra and . . . . had Alexander (in fornication).

12, John Cuninghame, goldsmith in Edinburgh, and Margaret Thornetoun had David.

15, John Harrower in the Gask and Bessie Makie had Andrew.

15, Andrew Horne and Katherine Gray had Alison.

16, John Lawsoun and Janet Donald had John.

21, Robert Wallis and Grizel Andersoun had Robert.

21, James Potter, wright, and Bessie Reid had Bessie.

23, James Huttoun, tailor in the Colzeraw, and Marjory Tod had twins, David and Katherine.

23, John Mathesoun and Margaret Andro had John.

23, John Broun in the Holl and Margaret Smytoun had Helen.

23, Laurence Huttoun, weaver in the Blaklaw, and Eupham Barklaw had Andrew.

23, John Bennie, merchant in Edinburgh, and Elspet Blekwod had George.

23, Laurence Andersoun, collier, and Bessie Currour had James.

23, Stevin Broun and Margaret Fleming had Katherine (in fornication).

30, George Moreis and . . . . had George.

M. 30, George Douglas to Janet Dalglische.

NOVEMBER.

B. 4, William Mudie, mason, and Margaret Edisoun had Marjory.
   4, Walter Huttoun, weaver, and Margaret Rae had Thomas.
   4, James Caddell in the Easter Gellat and Betie Persoun had Margaret.
   4, William Porter in Wester Gellett and Agnes Edie had Marion.
   6, James Thomsone and Helen Strong had John.
   8, George Walker, merchant, and Marjory Cuthbert had Grizel.
  11, Alexander Wolsoun and Elspet Michie had Magnus.
  13, Robert Peiris, mason, and Christian Schortews had Patrick.
  14, James Kinsman and Christian Walwod had William.
  17, John Edisoun at Pittencreif Mill and Betie Turnebull had Robert.
  17, Thomas Mudie and Isobel Wolsoun had Marjory.
  15 (*sic*), Edward Wastwod and Margaret Forfar had Allan.
  27, Robert Young, officer, and Bessie Lugtoun had Marjory.
  27, James Walker and Marjory Phillen had Marjory (in fornication).

M. 6, William Walwod to Bessie Nicol.
  17, John Watt to Elizabeth Douglas.
  27, Robert Russell to Barbara Ealder.
  27, James Cuninghame to Margaret Cuninghame.

DECEMBER.

B. 2, James Gipsoun at Kevill Mill and Margaret Patoun had John.
   5, Alexander Robertsoun and Janet Turnebull had Janet.
   9, Gilbert Murray in Lymekills and Janet Sibbauld had David.
   9, John Davidsone in the Nethertoun and Catherine Wardlaw had Elspet.
   9, Daniel Fleming, dwelling in Pitlevar, and Helen Durumpill had Anna.
   9, John Huttoun, cordiner, *alias* Satine John, and Helen Stevinsone had
      Margaret.
  11, Robert Phillane, merchant, and Helen Cuthbert had James.
  16, William Williamesone, weaver, and Eupham Schortus had John.
  16, Nicol Hunter in Pittincreiff and Marion Huttoun had Catharine.
  18, Adam Walwod, bailie for the time, and Catherine Kellok had David.
  23, Andrew Currour in Baith and Helen Law had twins, David and John.
  23, John Dow, collier, and Christian Shortous had Margaret.
  23, Gilbert Wricht, collier in Pitfurane, and Margaret Aissoun had Janet.
  23, William Buist, baker, and Helen Turnebull had Charles.
  25, John Aittoun, cordiner, and Janet Aliesone had Agnes.
  30, John Broun, maltman in the Nethertoun (deceased), and Christian
      Muddie had John.

M. 11, Thomas Walker, servant to Sir John Prestoun in the Valeyfield, to
      Catherine Haistie.
  18, Robert Murray at Aberdour Mill to Catherine Huttoun.

" The Register of the chyldrene bapteisit and personis maryed in
the Kirk of Dumfermlyne by the ministrie of Messrs. John
Fairfull and Andro Forrester sen the enterie of Mr. Johne
Walker to be lector at the said kirk quhilk wes and beganne the
fyift day of December in the yeir of God j^m vj^c and four yeirs."

JANUARY [1605].

B. 1, Sir Robert Halkheid of Pitfirrane and Mrs. Margaret Murray had
      James.
   1, David Douglas, merchant (deceased), and Margaret Mekiljohne had
      David.
   6, William Turnebull, maltman in the Nethertoun, and Bessie Couper had
      George.
   8, Umphra Henresone and Christian Fentone had Margaret (in fornica-
      tion).   Thereafter he was married to her.

13, John Makie in the Cockley and Maise Angous had Elspet (in fornication).

20, David Strang, cordiner, and Margaret Andersone had Helen

22, Maisie Clark and Robert Tomesone had Robert (in fornication), "and in hir satisfactioun the bairne wes bapteisit being four yeirs of aige."

22, Nicol Johnstone, quarrier (deceased), and Isobel Maxwell had James.

27, Patrick Davidsone, collier, and Margaret Mackaldow had Margaret.

27, Umphra Henresone (relapse) and Margaret Brand had Andrew (in fornication).

M. 22, William Logtoun in the Nethertoun to Janet Dewar.

22, John Mackie in the Cocklay to Elspet Robertsone.

FEBRUARY.

B. 3, Robert Kellok in Lassodie, weaver, and Christian Donald had David.

5, John Galrick in the Stane and Margaret Andersone had John.

10, John Muddie in Gellat and Christian Kellock had Robert.

10, John Finlaysone and Janet Kay had Henry.

10, Walter Murray, tailor, burgess of Edinburgh, "resident heir for the tyme becaus of the plague in the contrey," and Bessie Christie had Bessie.

10, John Miller, "dryster" at Pitliver Mill, and Mayse Currie had James.

10, Henry Meldrome in Cunigeis (?) and Bessie Wilsone had James.

12, Adam Dewar, surgeon, and Christian Wricht had James.

24, Adam Shortus, flesher, and Margaret Miller had Bessie.

M. 5, David Gib in Solisgirthe to Margaret Turnebull.

12, ... rie to Marjory Burn . . . .[1]

12, Umphra He . . . . to Christian Fe . . . .

12, William Wilson to . . . . . Chalmers.

12, John Wricht in [Lyme]kills to Janet Sibbald.

MARCH.

B. 3, Robert Anderson, weaver, and Isobel Tomesone had James.

5, William Crawfuird in Wester Luscour and Catherine Tod had Janet.

10, Edward Burne, mason, and Margaret Muddie had Janet.

10, Thomas Davidsone, collier, and Catherine Andersone had Isobel.

10, Harry Mudie, maltman in the Nethertoun, and Margaret Keid had James.

14, Thomas Steivinsone, servant to the Earl of Mar, and Bessie Wallange had Margaret (in fornication), on a testimonial of her satisfaction from the minister of the Weymis where the deed was committed, though she was delivered in this parish.

14 (?), John Galrick in Kistock and Nanse Annett had Janet.

14 (?), David Sibbald in Lymkills and Janet Key had Helen (in fornication).

19, Andrew Dewar in Keltiewod and Isobel Dick had George.

24, Robert Peirsone in Lymkills and Grisole Gawt had Geils.

24, Henry Crawfuird and Janet Hamiltoun had Isobel.

24, Nicole Anghous and Margaret Bennat had Bessie.

31, William Murrie and Catherine Cuninghame had Marjory.

M. [*None.*]

APRIL.

B. 2, Charles Ritchardsone and Janet Buist had Charles.

2, Thomas Broun and Janet Klavie had Christian.

7, William Walwod and Margaret Alexander had Nans.

7, John Keir in the Grange and Geils Burne had Margaret.

7, Robert Macknabbe, cordiner, and Bessie Spink had William.

7, Robert Russell in Balmule Mill and Janet Keir had David (in fornication).

9, David Walker, cooper, and Grisole Meldome had Janet.

---

[1] Page torn.

9, Robert Merser, flesher, and Margaret . . . . had Christian.
28, William Gray in Lymkills and Margaret . . . . dersone had Margaret.
28, Thomas Key and Marjory Steill had Catherine.
31, George Knox and Janet Anghous had Margaret.

M. 23, Thomas Ad . . . . in Pitadroe Mill to Janet Kell[ok ?].

MAY.

B. 5, Thomas Kirk, baker, and Margaret Cumming had William.
5, David Burne, miller, and Margaret Broun had Janet.
5, John Logane in Lymkills and Margaret Gawt had Catherine.
7, Henry Douglas, maltman, and Jean Murray had Henry.
12, Thomas Christie in the Hole and Janet Huttoun had Andrew.
12, Adam Walwod in Fod and Isobel Walwod had Margaret.
12, William Robertson and Bessie Arnot had John.
14, John Henrisoun, *alias* Seg, and Janet Inglis had Janet.
14, William Phyllane and Mage Knox had John (in fornication).
14, "The 14 day, James Ogilvie, beggar, had ane woman bairne, born to
him of his wyf Marioun Reid, baptised and callit Bessie ; of quhais
mariage he presentit ane testimoniall subscryvit be George Auld,
minister at Fentrie, quha wes minister of the said mariage, quherof
we tuik the copie as fallows, word be word.—To all and sindrie quhom
it effeiris to quhais knawledge this present salto cum, witt that the
bearar heirof James Ogilbie and Marioun Reid, beggaris, hes lauch-
fullie compleitit the band of matrimonie in face of the holy kirk and
in presens of thir witnesses, Andro Calbreithe, James of Barkgenie,
James Grahame of Craigtoun, and we the saidis personis testifies and
affirmis the samyn to be of veritie be this our present testimoniall
wreitin and subscryvit with our handis at the kirk of Fentrie the 2 day
of August the yeir of God jm vc fourscoir nyne yeiris. *Sic subscribitur,*
Mr George Auld, minister of the evangell at Fentrie."
16, George Durie of Craigluscour and Bessie Echlyne had Margaret.
19, John Trotter and Elspet Gray had James (in adultery), baptised after
entering to satisfy the kirk (Robert Young, cautioner for them).
19, Adam Walker, maltman, and Margaret Bryse had Henry.
19, Richard Potter, wright, and Christian Cowper had John.
21, Adam Mane and Marion Drysdell had John.
21, William Brand, collier, and Catherine Proud had twins, John and George
(in fornication).
21, Janet Tyrie "had ane manchyld borne of hir in fornicatioun, the father
being unknawin for the present ; sho alledgit Adame Broun, quhilk
he ever denyit and efter lang tryall of the kirk wer bayth stead in
oppine face of Christis kirk at Dumfermlyne wpun ane Sonday at
preiching, he swoire that he was nocht father and sho swoir he wes
father ; his aythe absolving him for the present the bairne wes
baptisit wpoun hir satisfactioun and callit Johne."
26, John Young in the Lymkills and Christian Gray had Elspet.
28, James Hutton and Cate Walwod had Adam.

M. 9, P . . . . to . . . . .
9, Archibald Nicole to . . . . Hadstoun.
21, Patrick Blair, tailor, to Helen Meldrome.
28, ... to He[llen] . . . .
28, Henry Cubie to . . . . (married at Aberdour " . . . . suspitioun of
pest ").
28, John Key to Mar . . . .

JUNE.

B. 2, Peter Dewar and Janet Murray had Elspet.
4, John Bennat, merchant, "had a manchyld, borne to him (efter his
departure quha perishit wpoun the sea at Tinmouthe) of his wyf
Helene Mekiljohn, baptized and callit Johne."

9, John Tomesone in Lymkills and Christian Keir had Walter.
25, John Moreis in Lymkills and Margaret Watsone had John (in fornication).
25, Andrew Potter and Janet Burne had John.
29, Thomas Keir in Beath and Helen Baxter had Margaret.
29, John Andersone in Hilend and Marion Andersone had Margaret.
29, David Chrystie and Anabell Bairdner had Andrew (in fornication).

M. 11, David . . . . to Ma . . . . Blair.
18, Andrew . . . . to Janet . . . .

JULY.

B. 7, Robert Kinglassie in Koilbuddo and Margaret Clerk had John.
9, Nicol Wardlaw in Blairathie and Bessie Huttoun had Thomas.
9, John Glen and Margaret Stronge had John.
14, Nicol Inglis and Bessie Cumming had . . . .
—[1] David Kerr and Catherine Elder had . . . .
— James Bewerage in Keltieheuche "[had ane] womanchyld gottin in adulterie be him of . . . . [Gib?], now departit, borne four yeirs befoir . . . [brought?] to licht and satisfactioun maid be him, baptized and callit Rosina."
— John Makdougall and Margaret Stewart had Margaret.
— James Kingorne, clerk of the regality of Dunfermline, and Eupham Murray had Patrick.
— Andrew Turnebull, portioner of Grange, and Janet Dougall had Robert (in fornication).
28, Edward Douglas and Marion Kirk had Catherine.

M. 2, John Peirson to Isobel Davidsone.
2, John Wricht to Catherine Patoun.
2, James Merser to Helen Wilsone.
9, Thomas Stevenson, servant to the Earl of . . . . , to . . . .

AUGUST.

B. 4, David Blak in Coklaw and Helen Dowie had Isobel.
4, John Stewart, creelman, and Mage Wilsone had David.
11, Robert Murray in Lymkills and Catherine Bairdner had Helen.
11, John Smetoun, baker, and Margaret Andersone had Robert,
13, William Wilsone and Helen Chalmeris had William.
18, John Mathesone and Bessie Alisone had Anna.
22, Thomas Keir and Isobel Hendine had Margaret.
25, William Walwod, baker, and Bessie Nicole had Adam.
25, John Makie in Windieage and Christian . . . . had . . . .
— . . . . d Thomesone, merchant, and Janet Burne had Helen.
— Henry Greif and Janet . . . . aill had Marion (in fornication).
27, Malcolm Davidsone and Isobel Peirsone had Janet.
27, John Stirk and Marjory Fleming had Janet.

M. 20, William Patoun to Amy Wilsone.
27, Andrew . . . . to Janet . . . . .

SEPTEMBER.

B. 1, Robert Pratus and Barbara Fyiff (whose goodman, John Rowan, was in Poland) had Janet (in adultery).
3, Adam Stevinsone, smith, and Magie Reid had Bessie.
3, Florie Broun and Effie Phillane had Effie.
5, David Dewar of Lassodie and Jean Logane had Isobel.
8, Thomas Coventrie and Janet Row had Catherine.
10, James Hunter, flesher, and Catherine Law had Margaret.

[1] Edge of leaf torn.

17, Andrew Dewar in Pitbachlie and Janet Seagie had Alison.
24, John Bull, smith, and Janet Gibsone had Margaret.
24, John Strang, cordiner, and Janet Mackie had Janet.
28, John Kellok, tailor, and Janet Reid had Bessie.
— James Cunnone in Mastertoun and Janet Sten . . . . had Catherine.
— John Watt in Lymkills and Margaret Gray had Janet (in fornication).

M. [*None.*]

OCTOBER.

B. 1, James Primrois, writer in Edinburgh, and Sarah Colvill had Robert (the plague of pestilence being in the said city, and he and his family here for the present).
6, James Cuninghame in Easter Sillitoun and Isobel Cuninghame had Margaret.
6, Allan Mudie, "*alias* fill and go," weaver, and Janet Forsan had Janet.
8, Patrick Stevinsoun and Bessie Reid had Thomas.
13, William Steidman and Catherine Wilsoun had Margaret.
13, John Melvill, collier, and Catherine Tod had Barbara (in fornication).
13, Peter Turnbull, baker, and Catie Smythe had William.
14, John Wardlaw, fuller, and Margaret Baid had John.
20, William Tomesone, cooper, and Jean Potter had Janet.
27, James Cowstoun and Janet Dalgleische had Bessie (in fornication).
27, George Douglas in Luscour and Janet Dalgleishe had James.

M. 8, William Gray to Margaret Andersoun.
15, Robert Bennat to Isobel Kirk.

NOVEMBER.

B. 3, James Kellok of Pitravie and Margaret Chalmers had Effie.
— John Christie and Bessie Mershell had Elspet.
12, William Cusing and Margaret Burne had Margaret.
19, Patrick Blair and Helen Meldrome had Isobel.
21, Andrew Sanders and Isobel Westwod had Janet.
24, Andrew Huttoun and Elspet Cunninghame had Agnes.
24, William Dick and Margaret Hillock had Catherine.
26, Mr. Thomas Wardlaw and Katherine Alison had Elspet.

M. 5, Robert Stanehous to Nanse Chalmers.
5, Andrew Hutsone to Margaret K . . . .
12, John Stevinsone to Janet Morie (?).
19, Mr. John Drummond to Isobel Gib.
19, David Stevinsone to Margaret Cowper.
21, James Broun to Margaret Douglas.
26, David Sibauld to Margaret Cuninghame.

DECEMBER.

B. 26, "The 26 day ane pure woman tuentie yeiris of aige surnameit Dewar, throuche obstinacie worne out of rememberance be hir parents deceas, remaneit unbaptized, and now humblie begging it for God's caus, wes baptized and callit Bessie."
29, Umphra Henresoun and Christian Fentoun had Patrick.
29, James Wilson and Janet Gibson had John.
29, John Swentoun and Bessie Horne had Elspet.

M. 10, William Pratus to Bessie Cuthbert.
17, James Kairns to Mage Sibauld.
17, John Haistie to Katherine Chalmers.
17, James Reid to Christian Lyndsay.
31, David Henresoun to Bessie Turnebull.

JANUARY [1606].

B. 5, John Burne and Margaret Stevinsone had Andrew.
     7, William Andersoun and Geils Peirsone had John.
     7, David Orrok and Katherine Burne had Margaret (in fornication).
    11, William Lugtoun and Janet Dewar had William.
    11, John Hutsoun and Janet Murie had David (in fornication).
    14, Patrick Blackwoder and Marion Bruce had Normand.
    19, John Anderson, younger, and Margaret Pratus had Margaret.
    21, William Brown, notary, and Grizel Cuthbert had Bessie (in fornication).
    26, Robert Cuninghame and Helen Wilson had Margaret.
    26, Gilbert Blair and Elspet Johnestoun had William.
    28, Mr. Andrew Forrester, minister, and Helen Ramsay had James.
    28, William Walwod and Elspet Spittell had Thomas.

M. — . . . . , baxter, was married to Katherine Wilson.

FEBRUARY.

B. 2, George Johnstoun and Isobel Rae had Janet.
     2, David Peacok and Janet Mackie had Bessie.
     3, Andrew Gaw and Janet Smythe had Laurence.
     4, Henry Wilson and Kate Keir had Robert.
     4, Mr. Robert Tomesoun and Christian Clerk had Margaret.
     4, Edward Stirk and Bessie Bull had Bessie.
     9, Robert Turnebull and Janet Cowper had Janet.
     9, Archibald Tomesoun and Janet Peacok had John.
     9, Gilbert Car and Marion Bardner had Nanse (in fornication).
    18, David Pitcarne and Janet Wricht had James.
    23, John Tomesoun and Emelie Cuming had Alexander.
    25, Rob. Russell and Barbara Elder had Elspet.
    25, James Kinsman and Kirstie Wallwod had John.
    28, James Reid and Bessie Lyndsay had Janet.

M. 11, John Huttone to Kate Huttoun.
    18, David Christie to Annabell . . . . ner.
    18, Cuthbert Wardlaw to Margaret Galrige.
    25, George L . . . . to Bessie Stevinsoun.

MARCH.

B. 1, James Busbie and Margaret Douglas had Margaret.
     1, Henry Gibsoun and Isobel Cunninghame had Janet.
     4, William Cuming and Bessie Cuming had Helen.
     4, John Galrige and Nanse Andersoun had Bessie.
     4, John Mackie in Cocklaw and Elspet Robertson had John.
     9, Andrew Wals and Bessie Stevinsoun had Robert.
     9, John Wilsoun and Janet Cuninghame had John.
    23, Henry Lauthiane and Elspet Tomesone had Christian.
    23, James Gibsoun and Margaret Patoun had Elspet.
    23, John Wilsoun and Isobel Kirk had William.
    23, Andrew Bennat and Mage Espline had Andrew.
    23, John Wat and Margaret Duglas had John.
    23, Alexander Hunnoun and Bessie Turnebull had Elspet.
    25, Mr. Hew Mylls, burgess of St. Andros, " being heir for the present, the
        plague of pestilence being in St. Andros," and Margaret Durie had
        Christian.
    30, George Knox and Janet Knox had Marjory.
    30, Thomas Gray and Betie Bosswell had John.

M. 4, John Makcalzeoun to Janet Knox.
     4, Patrick Peirsoun to Janet Maistertoun.
     4, Andrew Andersoun to Janet Arnott.
    25, Simon Davidson to Janet Nicole.

APRIL.

B.   6, William Burne and Nanse Alexander had Christian.
      6, Alexander Wilsoun and Elspet Michie had Andrew.
      13, David Laurie and Marion Blair had John.
      13, Thomas Mudie and Margaret Wilsoun had Janet.
      20, Andrew Hutsoun and Margaret Knox had Anna.
      20, Robert Douglas and Helen Donald had Edward.
      20, John Key and Janet Fergus had Thomas.
      20, Laurie Clerk and Meg Gib had Margaret.
      24, Adam Dewar and Christian Wricht had Marion.
      27, Andrew Turnebull and Helen Currie had Bessie.
      27, Thomas Inglis and Magie Stevinsone had Thomas.
      27, John Robertson and Nanse Huttoun had John.
      27, Andrew Mure and Janet Martene had Janet.
      27, Sandie Inglis and Isobel Reid had twins, Janet and Bessie.

M.   8, Thomas Watsoun to Nanse Palmer.

MAY.

B.   4, George Walkar, merchant, and Mage Cuthbert had Helen.
      4, "That day my lord Alexander Setoun, Chancelor of Scotland, had a
          woman chyld borne to him of his lady, Dame Grisole Leslie, baptized
          and callit Jeane."
      6, Thomas Marley and Janet Stevinsoun had John (in fornication).
      11, Robert Merser of the Craigs and Rachel Carmichaell had Jean.
      11, William Cowsteoun and Helen Lyndsay had Andrew.
      11, John Cuninghame and Helen Broun had Helen.
      18, John Peirie and Bessie Aissoun had John.
      18, John Walkar and Elspet Cunninghame had Richard (in fornication).
      18, Adam Schortus and Margaret Millar had William.
      20, John Stewart and Bessie Stewart had James.
      27, Thomas Walker and Bessie Murgane had William.

M.   6, Peter Brown to Cirstie Tomesoun.
      13, Gilbert Car (?) to Helen . . . .
      13, Gavin Ramsay to Janet Davidson.
      27, John Anderson, notary, to Christian Christiesoun.

JUNE.

B.   1, Andrew Currie and Mawse Anderson had Helen.
      7, John Sanders and Christian Millar had Margaret.
      10, John Peibls and Mawsie Combrie had Janet.
      10, James Chrichtoun and Margaret Mowbrey had James.
      15, John Kellok and Katherine Huggoun had Barbara (in fornication).
      15, Rob Moreis and Mage Aidieson had Helen.
      29, Archie Douglas and Janet Phillane had James.

M.   3, George Brown to Margaret Bothwell.
      3, David Brown to Margaret Gibsoun.
      3, Donald Makgrois (? Makgrow) to Helen Grieff.
      10, John Meffane to Katherine Smetoun.
      17, John Henresoun to Margaret Symesoun.
      17, David Sempill to Janet Mudie.

JULY.

B.   8, Henry Turnebull and Kate Cusing had Katherine.
      13, James Kingorne and Effie Murray had Thomas.
      13, John Harrower and Bessie Mackie had Katherine.
      20, Patie Galloway and Marjory Currour had James.
      20, Willie Flockard and Mage Bull had William.
      20, James Buist and Janet Danzell had James.

23, David Sempill and Janet Mudie had Helen.
27, Patrick Stevin and Margaret Drummond had David.
27, Adam Huttoun and Alison Douglas had Janet.
27, James Tomesoun, bellman, and Helen Strong had Andrew.

M. 1, Robert Tomesoun to Elspet Mitchell.

AUGUST.

B. 3, Rob. Phillane and Helen Cuthbert had Janet.
9, Daniel Fleming and Janet Darumpill had William.
17, John Stevinsoun and Janet Moreis had Bessie.
17, Michael Meldrome and Janet Renny had Thomas.
17, William Monteithe and Isobel Buchanan had James.
19, James Quhyt and Christian Gray had Helen (in fornication).
31, Willie Sandilands and Geilis Smyth had John.
31, John Huttoun and Kate Huttoun had James.

M. 26, Henry Greif to Janet Traill.
28, John Burne to Jean Murray.

SEPTEMBER.

B. 7, Peter Broun and Kirstie Tomesoun had James.
7, John Wricht and Janet Sibbauld had Marion.
7, William Spens and Janet Swentoun had John.
14, Florie Andersone and Helen Cunninghame had Andrew.
14, John Keir and Geilis Burne had Helen.
14, David Henresoun and Bessie Turnebull had David
14, David Corsbie, "being heir for the tyme, the pest being in Edinburgh his toun of residence," and Bessie Jacksoun had Bessie.
14, John Sibauld and Margaret Robertsoun, "*alias* Quhytskinns," had Helen (in fornication).
21, Ninian Hutsoun and Helen Glenn had Margaret.
23, James Kairnis and Mage Sibauld had Janet.
23, John Wardlaw and Magie Baid had Margaret.
25, James Smetoun and Jean Tod had John.

M. 2, Richard Law to Janet Tomesoun.
9, Thomas Young to Christian Forester.
23, Robert Quhyt to Christian Hunnoun.

OCTOBER.

B. 1, Sir Andrew Melvill of Garvock and Dame Elspet Hamiltoun had William.
5, Patrick Stewart of Bayth and Katherine Barhame had Robert.
5, John Dewar and Isobel Cuninghame had Andrew.
7, John Wricht and Nansie Wilsoun had Patrick.
16, Thomas Elphinstoun and Helen Craig had Alexander.
19, Wattie Huttoun and Magie Rae had Nanse.
19, Andrew Dewar and Janet Sagie had Robert.
21, George Burne and Mage Bull had Robert.
23, Andrew Mekiljohne and Janet Andersoun had Robert.
28, James Merser and Janet Wilsoun had Robert.

M. 7, John Kellok to Christian Pringle.
7, Donald Reoche to Kate Wilsoun.
14, Alexander Armorer to Bessie Aidiesone.
28, Thomas . . . . to Magie Kingorne.

NOVEMBER.

B. 2, David Cunninghame and Helen Stanehous had William.
6, James Reid and Christian Lindsay had William.
9, Patrick Blair and Helen Meldrom had Elspet.
13, Rob Stirk and Nanse Car had Nanse.

23, Alexander Aidie and Janet Philpe had Janet.
23, William Chattow and Kate Kellok had Margaret.
23, Thomas Tod and Barbara Elder had . . . .
23, Patie Turnebull and Kate Smyth had John.
23, Sandie Lugtoun and Janet Patoun had Janet.
23, Robert Douglas and Margaret Andersoun had Mary.
25, Henry Wardlaw of Balmule, Her Majesty's Chamberlain, and Katherine
    Wilsoun had Anna.
25, Thomas Walwod and Bessie Kirk had Janet.

M. 4, David Bauld to Catherine Aidiesone.
20, Willie Ro . . . to Grizel Cuthbert.
27, Andrew Horne to Bessie Anghous.

DECEMBER.

B. 2, Gilbert Car and Helen Inglis had Janet.
  7, Pate Davidson and Magie Doy had Catherine.
  7, Hary Bull and Margaret Car had Margaret.
13, Edward Tomesoun and Janet Burne had John.
13, David Christie and Annabell Bairdner had Janet.
13, Rob. Keir and Isobel Hendin had Helen.
14, Mr. John Fairfull, minister, and Margaret Prestoun had Andrew.
21, Archie Nicole and Margaret Hadsoune had William.
23, Mr. James Dalgleische, schoolmaster, and Janet Meklejohne had
    Elspet.
23, William Turnebull and Margaret Forester had Andrew (in fornication).
23, John Walwod, officer, and Helen Aikin had James (in fornication.)
23, David Broun and Christian Blak had William.
28, Willie Kennedie and Kate Speir had William.
28, Andrew Andersoun and Janet Arnott had John.

M. 18, John Douglas to Rosina Osswald.
27, Edward Stirk to Nanse (?) Lyndesay.
27, William Cunninghame to Janet Alisoun.
30, George Elder (?) to Bessie Lawsoun.

JANUARY [1607].

B. 1, Robert Stanehous and Nanse Chalmers had Thomas.
  1, John Wricht and Kate Patoun had John.
  4, Thomas Mudie and Bessie Turnebull had Andrew.
  6, Mr. Andrew Forrester and Helen Ramsay had John.
  8, James Huttoun and Mage Tod had Andrew.
11, Geordie Mill and Bessie Burne had George.
11, Laurie Patrick and Magie Reid had Thomas.
11, Robie Lawsoun and Bessie Blak had Anna.
18, Henry Hall and Geils Neifine had Margaret.
18, Robert Turnebull and Janet . . . . had George.
20, Peter Dewar and Janet Murray had Robert.
20, Patrick Murray and Marion Sibauld had James (in fornication).

M. 6, Robert Peirsoun to Margaret Peirsoun.
20, William Cunninghame to Bessie Wilsoun.
27, John Walker to Helen Mekiljohne.

FEBRUARY.

B. 1, John Pullour and Effie Wilsoun had George.
  1, David Wilsoun and Isobel Burt had James (in fornication).
  3, James Dewar and Grizel Hay (? Hoy) had James (in fornication).
  3, George Lugtoun and Bessie Stevinsoun had John.
  3, John Bull and Janet . . . . had Janet.
  8, Tom Poplay, deceased, and Magie Moreis had Elspet.
  8, John Workman and Kate Finlaysoun had Nanse.

8, Jamie Potter and Bessie Reid had John.
8, John Smetoun and Magie Anderson had David.
8, Thomas Greiff and Magie Forsythe had Mary.
10, Janet Levingstoun "adulteress, buir a woman bairne to George Diksoun, ane man besyd Monros, caryer of victuall, hir husband Robert Kinloche being past to Flanders 4 or 5 yeiris befoir, baptized and callit Cirstane."
15, Nicol Dewar and Bessie Huttoun had Andrew.
15, David Watsoun and Janet Cuthbert had Janet.
15, Gilbert Aissoun and Magie Aissoun had Bessie.
22, William Robertsoun and Nanse Tomesoun had Grisole.

M. 17, John Andersoun to Janet Reid.
19, Gilbert Stalker to Christian Weitat.

MARCH.

B. 13, James Kois and Bessie Sands had Bessie.
—— David Andersone and Helen Anderson had John.
— Rob Smythe and Magie Angous had Janet.
24, William Pratus and Bessie Cuthbert had Catherine.
29, Ritchie Walker and Isobel Smyth had James.
29, David Law and Cicill Duncan had James (in fornication).
31, Rob Wilsoun in Pitdinnie and Magie Huttoun had . . . . (in fornication).

M. [*None.*]

APRIL.

B. 6, David Walker and Grizel Meldrome had John.
7, Patrick Colzeir and Isobel Cunninghame had William.
7, David Schortus and Cirstie Russell had James.
12, John Schortus and Janet Broun had David.
12, William Mudie and Margaret Aidiesone had William.[1]
14, Geordie Walker and Kate Cambell had George (in fornication).
19, William Hamiltoun and Bessie Pillour had Thomas.
21, John Lawsoun and Janet Donaldsoun had Robert.
21, James Sanders (*alias* Cloutit Clocks) and Elspet Patersoun had Helen (in fornication).
26, William Currour and Margaret Wittat had Catherine.
26, William Turnebull and Bessie Cowper had Margaret.
28, William Cuninghame and Janet Lugtoun had . . . .

M. 16, George Durie to Barbara Barhame.
23, David Clerk to Nanse Mowtrey.
28, Andrew Gaw to Christian Walker.

MAY.

B. 3, Hary Balfour and Christian Lawsoun had Harry.
10, Andrew Touchie and Kate Hill (?) had Alison.
12, William Smart and Bessie Mudie had Robert.
17, John Wastwod and Janet Steill had Catherine.
17, Umphra Henresoun and Christian Fentoun had William.
17, David Sibauld and Annabel Lyndsay had Helen (in fornication).
17, George Fergussoun and Janet Peirsoun had Elspet (in fornication).
21, George Durie of Craigluscour and Bessie Echline had Sophia.
24, Charlie Ritchiesone and Janet Buist had Isobel.
24, John Miller and Margaret Phun had Margaret.
26, Willie Williamsoun and Magie Schortus had Margaret.

M. 26, James Cowsteoun to Janet Dalglesche.

[1] This entry is among the marriages.

JUNE.

B. 7, Patrick Peirsoun and Janet Mastertoun had Janet.
7, Ritchie Law and Janet Tomesone had Marjory.
7, David Car and Kate Elder had Janet.
7, Rob Michie and Janet Davidsone had Andrew.
7, Tom Bankis and Isobel Tod had Isobel.
7, George Chrystie and Effie Jamiesone had Elspet (in fornication).
14, Andrew Hutoun and Elspet Cunninghame had Bessie.
14, William Brown and Grizel Cuthbert had Geils.
23, John Aidiesoun and Betie Turnebull had Andrew.
28, Patie Legat and Bessie Blak had Robert.
28, Laurence Hutoun and Effie Barklay had John.
30, Mr. Thomas Wardlaw and Kate Alisoun had Janet.
30, Charlie Vallange and Magie Dewar had John.
30, Johne Burne and Jean Murray had Janet.

M. 2, William Neilsoun to Catherine Baid.
4, Rob Adame to Magie Douglas.
9, Thomas Tod to Margaret Huttoun.
9, Edmond Alisoun to Effie Crumbie.
16, John Chopman to Geils Walker.
16, George Donald to Margaret Wilsone.
16, James Gray to Janet Wastwode.
23, John Aitoun to Christian Davidsoun.
25, Andrew Mure to Janet Straquhen.
30, Archie Mowtrey to Kate Bardner.

JULY.

B. 5, Andrew Horne and Bessie (?) Angus had James.
5, John Haistie and Kate Chalmers had Robert.
5, David Burne and Margaret Brown had David.
5, William Andersoun and Geils Peirsoun had . . . .
12, John Brown and Magie Smetoun had John.
21, Clement Sanders and Marion Bell had Isobel.
23, Thomas Stevinsoun and Bessie Vallange had Jean.
28, David Quhyt and Magie Durie had William (in fornication).

M. 14, Edward Wastwod to Janet Walker.
21, William Turnebull to Margaret Law.
23, Andrew Currie to Emelie Broun.
28, Patrick Lawsoun to Janet Cunninghame.

AUGUST.

B. 9, William Cusing and Elspet Hutchesoun had Elspet.
9, John Makdougall and Isobel Stewart had Isobel.
18, William Drysdell and Effie Orrock had Janet.
18, Andrew Hutsoun and Magie Knox had John.
25, Tomie Christie and Janet Huttoun had Katharine.
25, Henry Turnebull and Kate Cusing had Henry.
30, Andrew Peacok and Margaret Lauthiane had David.
30, Rob Wells and Grizel Andersoun had Janet.

M. 4, John Trottar to Janet Craik (?).
11, John Simsoun to Janet Mudie.
18, Tom Tomesoun to Magie Moreis.
18, Alexander Aidie to Kirstie Bartrome.
25, William Broun to Catherine Smythe.
25, John Mackmirrie to Bessie Williamsoun.

SEPTEMBER.

B. 6, Laurie Andersoun and Bessie Currour had Isobel.
    8, Patrick Murray of Pardews and Margaret Colvill had Nanse.
   13, George Walker and Mage Cuthbert had George.
   13, Tom Marley and Janet Burne had Janet (in fornication).
   13, John Walker and Margaret Fothringhame had Isobel.
   20, William Aissoun and Christian Anderson had a daughter . . . .
   20, John Anderson, younger, and Margaret Pratus had . . . .
   20, Tom Deis and Magie Kingorne had James.

M. 8, George Walker to Janet Makilhois.
   15, George Tomesone to Janet Cunninghame.

OCTOBER.

B. 11, James Lugtoun and Magie Nasmyth to Janet.
   13, Hary Robertsone and Magie Galrige had Catherine (in fornication).
   13, Thome Broun and Magie Bairdie had Nanse (ir fornication).
   22, Willie Tomeson and Janet Potter had Michael.
   25, Adam Currour and Margaret Swentoun had Andrew.
   25, Robert Moreis and Janet Turnebull had Christian (in fornication).
   25, Finlay Buchannan and Janet Reidie ("tua idiot Hieland bodyis") had James (in fornication).
   29, Andrew Curronr and Helen Law had James.
   29, James Ros, "vagabund, upoun ane testimoniall that he wes laufullie maryit," and Grizel Murray had Bessie.

M. 2, Finlaw Buchanan to Janet Reidie.
   13, Willie Anghous to Nanse Orrock.
   20, Patie Harrower to Christian Peacock.

NOVEMBER.

B. 1, Thom Key and Mage Steill had Thomas.
   1, Rob Peirsoun and Magie Peirsoun had Catherine.
   1, David Ritchiesoun and Helen Monteith had Isobel.
   3, John Young and Christian Gray had Margaret.
   3, Patie Cowper and Effie Baird had Marjory.
   5, John Chopman and Geils Walker had Marjory.
   8, James Bryse and Helen Hutoun had Margaret (in fornication).
   8, Thomas Ritchie and Margaret Andersone had Katherine.
   17, William Pratus, younger, and Helen Andersone had Dorothea (in fornication).
   19, James Primros and Sarah Colvill had Margaret.
   19, John Bachab and Christian Porteous had Thomas (in fornication).
   22, Adam Stobie and Helen Gibboun had Helen.
   -- James Hutoun and Kate Walwod had Isobel.
   -- James Garvie and Magie Cunninghame had Margaret.
   29, John Douglas and Rosina Osswald had Jean.
   29, Michael Leslie and Helen Johnestoun had Bessie.

M. 3, James Litljohne to Helen Schortous.
   10, George Davidson to Christian Bull.
   10, Pate Stanehous to Kate Leitche.
   17, Duncan Talzeour to Margaret Huttoun.
   24, Thomas Blakwod to Christian Dalgleische.

DECEMBER.

B. 1, Rob Adame and Magie Douglas had Elspet.
   5, Geordie Johnestoun and Isobel Rae had Effie.
   13, William Walwod and Margaret Alexander had John.
   13, Thomas Coventrie and Janet Row had Helen.
   20, Rob Quhyt and Kate Hunnon had Helen.

20, Henry Greiff and Janet Traill had Janet.
22, David Dewar and Jean Logane had Barbara.

M. 1, John Hodge to Helen Quhyt.
    15, James Lachland to Bessie Cunninghame.
    22, James Henresone to Christian Knox.
    24, John Small to Magie Huggoun.

JANUARY [1608.]

B. 3, James Kairnis and Mage Sibbald had Margaret.
    3, Adam Stirk and Marion Henresoun had Robert.
    10, John Wastwod and Janet Elder had Bessie.
    12, Adam Dewar and Christian Wricht had Nanse.
    12, John Mackie and Elspet Robertsoun had James.
    13, John Watsone and Margaret Mekiljohne (afterwards married) had John
        (in fornication).
    17, Robert Turnbull and Janet Cowper had Robert.
    17, William Porteous and Nanse Aidie had Alexander.
    10, (*sic*), Mr. James Aittoun and Barbara Hamiltoun had . . . .
    24, Geordie Clerk and Isobel Lawsoun had James.

M. 19, John Car to Margaret Baird.
    29, John Watsoun to Margaret Mekiljohne.

FEBRUARY.

B. 1, Henry Gibsoun and Isobel Cunninghame had Marion.
    1, John Mudie and Christian Kellok had Andrew.
    1, William Cunninghame and Janet Alisoun had Andrew.
    1, William Walwod and Bessie Nicole had Helen.
    7, William Robertsone and Bessie Arnot had Janet.
    7, Nicol Dalgleische and Helen Blackwod had George.
    7, John Stevinsoun and Janet Moreis had Margaret.
    14, Pate Stanehous and Kate Leitche had Thomas.
    21, Alexander Inglis and Isobel Reid had Alexander.
    21, John Kellok and Christian Pringle had Margaret.
    21, John Watsone and Janet Burt had Bessie (in fornication).
    28, John Andersone and Kirstie Christiesoun had Nanse.
    28, Edmond Alisoun and Effie Crumbie had Helen.
    28, John Walker and Helen Mekiljohne had David.

M. 2, John Rowan to Christian Dewar.
    2, Thomas Betsoun to Margaret Beverage.
    2, Willie Bryse to Janet . . . .
    9, ... to . . . .
    9, Peter Law to . . . .
    9, William Mekiljohne to . . . . . Mowtrey.
    9, Walter Phinn to Margaret Wastwode.

MARCH.

B. 6, Robert Andersone and Isobel Tomesoun had Isobel.
    6, James Buist and Janet Danzell had Adam.
    20, John Sanders and Kirstie Miller had Christian.
    20, Rob Cuninghame and Helen Wilson had Andrew.
    27, John Moreis and Margaret Watsoun had Elspet (in fornication).

M. [*None.*]

APRIL.

B. 10, John Tomesoun and Emie Cuming had Robert.
    10, William Aidie and Elspet Bryse had John.
    10, John Peirsoun and Marion Merser had Janet (in fornication).
    14, Andrew Mekiljohne and Janet Andersoun had Bessie.

17, James Mill and Janet Rowan had Isobel.
19, Davie Semple and Janet Mudie had John.
24, James Kellok and Helen Chalmers had Nanse.
24, Andrew Maine and Kate Stevinson had John.
30, Robert Brown and Janet Bell had James.

M. 12, John Stirk to Janet Meldrome.

MAY.

B. 3, Willie Turnebull, smith, and Magie Law had Andrew.
8, John Galrige and Mause Andersone had Helen.
8, Adam Schortus and Magie Miller had Grisole.
8, James Kadell and Betie Peirsoun had Katherine.
12, James Reid and Bessie Lindsay had Robert.
12, Rob Merser, flesher, and Margaret Barhame had Catherine.
15, Willie Buist and Helen Turnebull had Andrew.
15, Thomas Keir and Helen Baxter had Isobel.
15, Hary Mudie and Margaret Reid had Janet.
22, Alexander Hunnieman and Bessie Turnebull had Patrick.
24, Thomas Broun and Janet Klavie had Thomas.
29, Rob Andersoun and Effie Harrower had Nicole.
29, John Trottar and Janet Craik had Margaret.
29, George Donald and Janet (Margaret*) Wilsoun had Janet.

M. 17, David Burne to Margaret Fothringhame.
26, David Wilson to Isobel Burt.
31, David Gray to Elspet Murray.
31, David Betoun to Christian Hog.
31, Robert Colzeir to Bessie Young.

JUNE.

B. 7, James Turnebull, piper, now in Kavill, and Helen Johnestoun had Isobel.
12, George Tomesoun and Janet Cunninghame had Walter.
14, Andrew Gaw and Kirstie Walkar had William.
14, Robie Currie and Kate Makcalzeoun had Margaret.
19, Daniel Fleming and Helen Darumpill had George.
19, Nicol Meldrum and Janet Renny had Margaret.
25, Henry Wilsoun and Kate Keir had Andrew.

M. 14, James Ready to Margaret Sharpe.
14, James Huttoun to Marjory Walwod.
14, John Melvill to Isobel Tod.
28, John Wilson to Nanse Huttoun.

JULY.

B 12, Rob Phillane and . . . . had a son . . . .
12, Rob Stirk and Nanse Car had Margaret.
16, Archie Mowtrey and Kate Bardner had John.
16, James Cansleoun and Janet Dalgleische had William.
16, Rob Russell and Barbara Elder had Robert.
23, Andrew Currie and Mawse Andersoun had Andrew.

M. 5, Thomas Webster to Elspet Greiff.
12, Adam . . . . to . . . .

AUGUST.

B. 5, Andrew Andersone and . . . . had a son . . . .
28, David Walker and Grizel Meldrum had Nanse.
30, James Gib and Bessie Stevin had Isobel (in fornication .

M. 30, William Tomesone in Leith to Catherine Tomesoun.

* Written above.

SEPTEMBER.

B. 11, William Drysdell and Effie Orrock had Bessie.
11, John Keir and Geils Burne had Elspet.
11, Thomas Tod and Barbara Elder had Effie.
13, Gibbie Car and Helen Inglis had James.
13, John Makmirrie and Bessie Williamson had Elspet.
15, William Walwod and Elspet Spittell had Margaret.
18, John Peat and Kate Stewart had Margaret.
18, Edward Douglas and Marion Kirk had Andrew.
18, Edward Tomesoun and Janet Burne had Isobel.
18, James Litljohne and Effie Schorteous had John.
—, (An entry here entirely torn away.)
22, David Christie and Anabeil Bardner had Bessie.
27, Geordie Walker and Janet Mekilhois had Janet.

M. 8, William Mastertoun to Marion Mudie.
13, John Moreis to Margaret Watsoun.

OCTOBER.

B. 9, Hary Stevinsone in Rossyth "the plague of pestilence being in Innerkething his awin paroche kirk," had a man child baptised called
William (wife's name omitted).
23, Wattie Huttoun and Magie Rae had Isobel.
25, William Andersoun in Lymkills and Geils Peirsoun had Geils.
27, Sir Andrew Melvill of Garvock and Dame Elspet Hamiltoun had
Marjory.
30, Andrew Sanders and Isobel Wastwod had John.
30, George Douglas and Janet Dagleishe had George.
30, John Hutoun and Kate Hutoun had Thomas.
30, William Cowsteoun and Helen Lyndsay had Margaret.
30, George Davidsoun and Kirstie Bull had Isobel.

M. 25, James Roxburgh to Christian B . . . ., parishioners of Innerkething
"quha in respect of the plague of pestilence in that toun wer maryit
heir."

NOVEMBER.

B. 1, William Sibauld and Janet Christie had John (in fornication).
8, James Kingorne and Effie Murray had Andrew.
8, Andrew Mure and Janet Straquhenn had Andrew.
8, Umphra Henresone and Christian Fentoun had John.
13, William Flockard and Marjory Bull had Andrew.
13, Adam Walwod in Fod and Christian Walwod had William.
20, Andrew Turnebull in the Grange and Helen Currie had Helen.
27, Henry Meldrome and Bessie Wilsone had William.
29, Mr. James Aitoun and Elspet Hamiltoun had Grisole.
29, Alexander Lockard and Helen Bruse had Helen (in fornication).
29, Robert Stanehous and Nanse Chalmers had Robert.

M. 8, Thomas Burne to Janet Austiane.
8, Abraham Grege to Effie Chrichtoun.
22, James Bryse to Christian Young.
22, James Burne to Janet Young.

DECEMBER.

B. 4, John Kellok and Janet Reid had Margaret.
4, Alexander Lugtoun and Janet Patoun had Margaret.
4, Nicol Wardlaw and Bessie Hutoun had Janet.
11, James Chrichtoun and Margaret Mowbrey had Elspet.
15, David Peirsoun in Wester Pitdinnie and Margaret Andersone had John
(in adultery).

18, Patrick Galloway and Mage Currour had a daughter . . . .
18, William Kennedy and Kate Speir had Margaret.
18, Thomas Wastwod and Grizel Michell had Katherine.
18, Peter Dewar and Janet Murray had a son . . . .
18, Gavin Ramsay and Janet Davidson had Janet.
18, James Hamiltoun and Nanse Imrie had Margaret.
—, Laurence[?] Patrik and Margaret Reid had Helen.
27, Pate Davidsone, collier, and Megie Doy (who died in childbirth) had Harry.

M. 6, James Stevinsone to Margaret Douglas.
20, John Huslope to Janet Lachland.
27, John S . . . . to Margaret Tomesone.
27, Alexander Lockard to Janet Hunnoun.

JANUARY [1609].

B. 11, John Andersone, merchant, and Janet Reid had Bessie.
11, Tom Walwod and . . . . Kirk had Marion.
15, David Broun and Margaret Gibson had Janet.
15, Edward Stirk and Nanse Lindsay had a daughter . . . .
15, John Awstie(?) and Kate Chalmers had Catherine.
17, John Lidell and Nanse Galt had Andrew (in fornication).
24, John Small and Margaret Huggoun had Margaret.
24, Wattie Andersoun and Bessie Cuming had Bessie (in fornication .
29, George Miller and Bessie Lowsoun had John (in fornication).
29, William Cusing and Elspet Hutchiesoun had Catherine.
31, Thomas Stevinsoun and Bessie Wallange had James.

M. 3, Andrew Cunninghame to Margaret Turnebull.
3, Thomas Elder to Nanse Gregge.
22, William Moreis to Bessie Stevin.
22, Thomas Robertsone to Janet Harrower.

FEBRUARY.

B. 2, Andrew Cunninghame in Primros and Janet Ruche had Thomas (in fornication).
4, John Wricht, collier, and Kate Patoun had Robert.
7, William Henresone, cordiner, and Margaret Gray had Catherine (in fornication).
7, David Blak and Helen Dowie had James.
7, John Car and Margaret Bairdie had Margaret.
12, Simon Davidsone and Jean Nicole had Marjory.
12, Adam Wilsone and Katherine Wilsoun had David.
12, George Knox and Janet Angus had Margaret.
19, John Marre, cook, and Janet Gray had William (witnesses, William Murray, William Cuninghame, William Drysdell).
19, Patrick Peirsoun and Janet Mastertoun had Marjory.
19, Thomas Robert and Janet Harrower had John (antenuptial).
19, John Mossman and Catherine Smetoun had John.
21, Mr Andrew Forrester, minister, and Helen Ramsay had Jean.
26, John Miller and Margaret Phun had Andrew.
28, David Sibauld, parishioner of Inverkeithing, and Catherine Anderson had Janet (bap. here because of the pestilence).

M. 7, Robert . . . . to Margaret Huttoun.
14, William Stanehous to Elspet Pirni . . . .
14, George Fergussoun to Janet Peirsone.
21, Gavin Stanehous to Marjory Nicol.

MARCH.

B. 5, Nicol Cowie and Margaret Fentoun had Christian (in fornication).

5, John Key and Margaret Fergie had William.

12, David Peirsone, younger, in Pitdinnie, and Helen . . . . had Robert (in fornication).

14, John Melvill, collier in Bayth, and Isobel Tod, had twins, Patrick and Janet).

19, Patrick Turnebull and Catherine Smyth had Peter.

19, James Gray and Janet Wastwod had Robert.

19. Henry Stevin and Marjory Drummond had Marjory.

26, John Robertsone and Nanse Huttoun had James.

28, Peter Brown in Fod and Christian Tomesoun had William.

28. "That day Robert Murray had a womanchyld borne to him of his wyff Kate Hutoun un[baptized and callit] (deleted) died in cumming to the kirk befoir the sacrament was ministred."

28, Florence Andersoun and Helen Cunninghame had Bessie.

M. [*None.*]

APRIL.

B.   9, John Davidsone and Catherine Wardlaw had Henry.

9, John Smetoun and Magie Anderson had Alexander.

9, Andrew Andersoun and Janet Arnott had Christian.

9, James Wilsoun and Janet Gibsone had Janet.

14, Patrick Andersone and Bessie Roxburghe had John.

16, Thomas Mudie and Bessie Turnebull had John.

16, Andrew Dewar and Effie Waterstoun had Marion (in fornication).

18, Henry Turnebull and Kate Cusing had Alison.

18, Patrick Colzeir and Isobel Cunninghame had George baptised ("upoun our testimoniall").*

22, John Moreis ("departit in ane castin away schipe at Dundie water") and . . . . had a daughter . . . .

22, John Harrower and Bessie Mathie (?Mackie) had twins, John and Janet.

22, John Stirk and Janet Meldrom had John.

22, William Currour and Margaret Weitit had Elspet.

22, Thomas Tomesoun and Margaret Moreis had James.

22, Gilbert Wricht and Margaret Eassoun had Margaret.

25, Mungo Murray and Mrs Margaret Halkheid (befoir thei wer maryit efter thei had satisfied the discipline of the kirk at Balingrie wpoun ane testimoniall from the minister thair to the ministeris of Dunfermling) had James.

30, Andrew Horne, miller, and Bessie Anghous had John.

M. 18, James Henresoun to Janet Dewar.

18, James Nasmythe to Christian Hardie.

MAY.

B.   2, Andrew Touchie and Catherine Fyiff had Geils.

3, William Steidman and Kate Wilsoun had Janet.

7, Rob Michie, collier, and Janet Davidson had Margaret.

7, James Hutoun and Catherine Walwod had Isobel.

11, James Hutoun, tailor, burgess of the burgh, and Marjory Tod had Bessie. Witnesses, James Kingorn, John Warkman, Gilbert Car.

14, William Broun, notary, and Grisole Cuthbert had David.

16, James Cummon in Maistertoun and Janet Stanehous had Nanse. Witnesses, Mark Lunn, Andrew Mitchell, John (?) Stanehous.

16, David Burne, miller, and Margaret Broun had Andrew.

16, Charlie Ritchiesoun and Janet Buist had a daughter . . . .

21, William Turnebull and Bessie Cowper had Janet.

21, George Mill and Bessie Burne had John.

23, Pate Meffwan, collier in Lassodie Heuch, "had twa wemen chyldren borne to him in adulterie, the ane of Issobell Kellok, the other of Kate Proud, baptized and callit, the ane Catharine and the uther Nans.

* Noted in the marriage column.

The said Pate Meffwan efter the first adulterie committit with Issobell
Kellok in the verray tyme that he wes making his repentance for the
same he falls the second tyme in adulterie with Kate Proud."

28, John Dewar in Pitbachlie and Isobel Moreis had Helen.

28, John Christie and Bessie Merschell had John.

M. 23, John Burgane to Alison Orrock.

23, Andrew Neilsone to Marion Steidman.

JUNE.

B. 6, James Cois in Galrighili and Bessie Sandis had Alexander.

6, Willie Murray in Lassodymill, miller, and Mage Kellok had William (in adultery).

6, Andrew Kinninmond and Isobel Makkennoche had Robert (in adultery).

11, Peter Law and Margaret Walker had Barbara.

11, John Andersone, notary, and Christian Christiesone had William.

11, David Watsone and Janet Cuthbert had David.

18, James Oswald and Bessie Cowsteoun had Andrew (in fornication).

25, William Mudie and Margaret Aidieson had John.

25, William Aidie and Elspet Bruse had Margaret.

27, George Lugtoun in Knokes and Bessie Stevinsoun had Annas.

M. 4(?), Alexander Bart . . . . to Isobel . . . .

JULY.

B. 1, William Wilsone and Helen Chalmers had Anna.

9, George Fergussoun and Janet Peirsoun had Alexander.

9, David Broun in Cocklaw and Christian Black had David.

16, John Aidiesone and Beatie Turnebull had Margaret.

16, David Symsone and Barbara Broun had Thomas.

16, John Peirsoun and Janet Tomesoun had Bessie (in fornication).

23, John Stevinsoun and Janet Moreis had John.

23, Wattie Phinne and Magie Wastwod had John.

30, Adam Andersone and Christian Tomesoun had Bessie.

M. 11, James Trottar to Bessie Lowsoun.

11, Peter Sanders to Marion Kirk.

11, Andrew Patoun to Isobel Johnestoun.

18, William Kellok to Margaret Kellok.

25, John Smithe to Effie Burne.

AUGUST.

B. 8, John Andersone, younger, litster, and Margaret Pratus had Janet.

13, David Laurie and Marion Blair had a son . . . .

13, Mr Thomas Wardlaw and Catherine Alisoun had Catherine.

20, Andrew Huttoun and Elspet Cunninghame had Marjory.

22, Thomas Drysdell and Isobel Bruse had John (in fornication).

26, Andrew Buchannan and Bessie Row had Janet.

29, Archie Vylie and Grisole Walwod had Janet (in fornication).

M. 8, William Andersone to Isobel Gilmure.

15, William Henrisoun, cordiner, to . . . . Forsyithe, parishioner of Cleish.

17, Andrew Law, merchant, to Elspet Nasmithe.

29, James Abercrumbie to Mause Burgane.

SEPTEMBER.

B. 3, James Bryse and Christian Young had John.

7, David Burne in Wester Gellat and Margaret Fothringhame had Margaret.

14, John Fleming of Blaklaw and Bessie Sands had John.

17, Edmond Alisone and Effie Crumbie had James.

19, George Halkheid and Helen Brumlie had George (in fornication).
24, Patrick Lawsone and Margaret Cunninghame had Patrick.

M. 19, John Potter to Christian Leggatt.
26, John Williamsone in Pittenweem to Janet Mongomrie.

OCTOBER.

B. 3, Mr. James Dalgleische, schoolmaster. and Janet Mekiljohn had Walter.
8, Geordie Hendine and Bessie Bennat had Adam.
10, John Wardlaw, walker, and Margaret Baid had Andrew.
15 (?), John Hislope and Janet Laichlands had Janet.
15 (?), Nicole Inglische and Bessie Cunninghame had Nanse.
22, John Stevin and Margaret Tomesoun had Bessie.
26, David Maingzies and Margaret Fylour had Jean (in fornication).
29, Thomas Bankis and Isobel Tod had Janet.
29, Archibald Douglas and Janet Phillane had Janet.

M. [*None.*]

NOVEMBER.

B. 5, Thomas Hutoun in Luscour and Margaret Lyndsay had Nanse.
5, William Stanehous and Elspet Pirnie had William.
5, Robert Wilsoun and Margaret Huttoun had Bessie.
7, Gavin Stanehous, maltman, and Marjory Nicole had Helen.
12, James Tomesone, belman, and Helen Strange had Alexander.
12, Robert Quhyt, maltman, and Helen Hunnoun had Helen.
12, James Kairnis and Marjory Sibbauld had a daughter . . . .
22, John Davidsone, collier in Keltieheuch, and Nanse Broun had Nanse.
22, William Neilsoun and Catherine Baid had Catherine.
22, Charles Wallange and Janet Dewar had a daughter, ...
22, John Mudie and Christian Kellok had John.
22, James Sanders and Barbara Wilsone had a son, ... (in fornication).
22, George Turnebull, younger, and Margaret Tomesone had William (in fornication).
26, William Andersoun and Margaret Bonalay (?) had Robert.
26, Andrew Peacok and Margaret Lauthiane had James.
26, William Turnebull and Margaret Law had John
28, William Cunninghame in Crocefuird and Janet Lugtoun had Anna.
28, Patrick Murray and Margaret Colvill had Margaret.

M. 7, Nicol Dewar to Janet Robertsone.
21, John Donaldsone to Christian Broun.
28, Andrew Renny to Bessie Brand.

DECEMBER.

B. 3, Andrew Cunninghame in Primrois and Margaret Turnebull had David.
3, Andrew Sanders and Isobel Westwode had Marjory.
10, Adam Stobie, portioner of Wester Luscour, and Helen Gibbone had John ; witnesses, John Aikin of Burrowane, Robert Broun of Barhill, Mr. John Walkar.
10, John Makbayth and Catherine Wat had Margaret (in fornication).
10, Archibald Nicole and Margaret Hadstoun had Bessie.
10, James Mastertoun and Grisole Stewart had Alexander.
17, William Andersone in Lymkills and Geils Peirsone had William.
17, Alexander Lockard, walker, and Janet Hunmon had John.
17, William Cuninghame, weaver, and Janet Alisone had John.
17, John Burne, younger, in Easter Gellat, and Jean Murray had James.
— Alexander Wilsone in Grange and Elspet . . . . hie had John.
24, James Garvie and Margaret Cunninghame had William.
26, "The 26 day ane noble and potent lord, Alexander, Earle of Dunfermlyne, and heiche Chanceler of Scotland, had ane womanchyld borne to him of his lady, Dame Margarit Hay, baptized and callit Grisole."

31, George Dewar and Catherine Wardlaw had twins, Robert and Janet (in fornication).

31, Andrew Neilsoun and . . . . had Elspet.

M. 5, Allan Galrig to Janet Currie.

5, John Andersone to Janet Meldrome.

5, George Christie to Effie Jamiesoune.

19, Robert . . . . to Geils Bonalay.

JANUARY [1610].

B. 14, Henry Hall and Janet Neiffeine had Patrick.

14, John Huttoun, weaver, and Nanse Smithe had James.

16, Patrick Leggat and Bessie Blak had Christian.

21, James Fargie and Marion Fyiff had Adam.

21, Robert Smythe and Margaret Anghous had Marjory.

21, John Andersone and Janet Henresoun had Marjory.

23, Andrew Turnebull, younger, in Bromehall, and Bessie Futhie had Janet.

28, Robert Douglas and Margaret Douglas had Anna.

M. 2, David Barklay to Christian Murie.

9, James Kellok to Margaret Mudie.

9, John Weitatt to Christian Moreis.

11, Mr. Alexander Lindesay of Canterland was married in one of the kirks of Edinburgh to Jean Murray, sister of Patrick Murray of Pardewis (on a testimonial from our ministers of Dunfermline).

16, Helias Scharpe to Nanse Tomesoun.

23, David Monteithe to Janet Brogge.

30, James Osswald to Bessie Cowsteoun.

FEBRUARY.

B. 4, William Smart and Bessie Mudie had Margaret.

11, John H . . . . and Nanse Smithe had Margaret.

11, James Henresoun and Janet Dewar had James.

11, Thomas Coventrie and Janet Row had Margaret.

11, Thomas Broun and Margaret Bairdie had Thomas.

18, Robert Young and Christian Lugtoun had George.

18, Gilbert Stalker and Christian Weitat had Catherine.

25, James Potter and Bessie Reid had Margaret.

25, John Lawson and Janet Donald had Patrick.

25, Adam Stirk and Marion Henresoun had Henry.

M. 13, ... Maingzies to Margaret Fyler.

13, David Tod to Janet Aidiesoune.

20, Alexander B (?) . . . . to Helen Huttoun.

MARCH.

B. 4, John Makmirrie and Bessie Williamsone had Nanse.

4, James Burne and Janet Young had Catharine.

4, John Sanders and Christian Miller had Christian.

4, James Turnebull, piper, and Helen Johnestoun had Bessie.

4, David Dewar of Lassodie and Jean Logane had Janet.

11, Harry Younge and Helen Keir had Florence (son).

11, Umphra Henresoun and Christian Fentoun had a son, ...

— Patie Harrower and Christian Peacok (?) had Margaret.

13, Andrew Law and Elspet Nasmithe had Janet.

18, John Pullenis and Effie Wilsone had Andrew.

20, John Makkie and Elspet Robertsone had Margaret.

22, David Henresone and Bessie Turnebull had Margaret.

25, John Douglas and Rosina Osswald had Anna.

25, James Mill and Janet Rowane had Henry.

25, Robert Peirsoun and Isobel Galt had Elspet.

M. 13, Thomas . . . . to Margaret Fentoun.
19, James Dewar to Grisole Hoy.

APRIL.

B. 3, Andrew Wilsone and Marjory Fothringhame had Patrick (in fornication).
3, George Tomesoun and Janet Cunninghame had a daughter . . . .
15, Andrew Andersone and Janet Touchie had Margaret.
15, Thomas Deis, cutler, and Magie Kingorne had Henry.
17, Mungo Murray and Mrs. Margaret Halkheid had Robert.
22, William Walwod and Bessie Nicole had Bessie.
22, Thomas Key and Mage Steill had Margaret.

M. 24, John Coventrie to Janet Walwod.
29, Alexander Areskine, master of Fenton, was married to Lady Anna Setoun, eldest daughter of Alexander, Earl of Dunfermline, Chancellor.

MAY.

B. 1, George Walker, merchant, and Marjory Cuthbert had William.
3, John Wilsone and Isobel Kirk had Bessie.
6, James Cadell and Beatrix Peirsone had John.
6, Robert Tomesoun and Elspet Mitchell had Catherine.
13, John Trottar and Janet Craik had Janet.
13, James Fargie, weaver, "had twinnis men chyldren borne to him in fornicatioun of Beatie Watt, the ane died efter birthe without baptisme, and the uther wes baptized and callit George."
15, Thomas Elder, flesher, and Nanse Gregge had Thomas.
20, Adam Huttoun and Alison Douglas had Andrew.
20, John Henresoun, *alias* Fegge, and Janet Inglische had Catherine.
27, James Buist and Janet Dangzell had George.
27, James Gib and Bessie Aissoun had George (in fornication).

M. 22, John Burne to Janet Law.
22, William Hering to Isobel Sim.
22, Nicolas Elmer to Margaret Durie.
22, Thomas Coventrie to Janet Murray.
24, Abraham Gregge to Isobel Cunninghame.
29, ...

JUNE.

B. 3, Andrew Dewar in Pitbachlie and Janet Segie had Peter.
5, Sir Andrew Melvill of Garvock and Dame Elspet Hamiltoun had Isobel.
5, John Watsone, merchant, and Margaret Mekil[johne] had a son.
17, Johne Logane and Margaret Galt had Margaret.
17, William Chattow and Catherine Kellok had Mary.
17, Thomas Christie of the Hoile and Janet Huttoun had Bessie.
24, John Tomesoun and Emelie Cuming had Margaret.
24, Archie Tomesoun and Janet Peacok had Marion.
24, George Christie and Effie Jamesoun had Janet.
24, James Nasmyth and Christian Hardie had Janet.
25, James Kinggorne, clerk of the regality of Dunfermline, and Eupham Murray had Adam.

M. 5, William Rae to Janet Orrock.
5, William Robertsone to Janet Litljohne.
5, Laurence Huttoun to Isobel Davidsone.
26, Thomas Mudie to Margaret Turnebull.
26, James Wilsoun to Janet Walker.

JULY.

B.   1, William Kellok and Margaret Kellok had Margaret.
   1, William Henriesoun, cordiner, and Bessie Forsythe had Catherine.
   10, James Robertsone and Janet Bryse had Marjory (in fornication).
   15, John Schortus and Janet Brown had Janet.
   15, Harry Stevinsoun in Rossyth parish and Helen Wotterlie had John.
   22, Thomas Stevinsoun, servitor to the Earl of Murray, and Bessie Vallange
      had David.
   22, Alexander Lugtoun and Janet Patoun had Helen.
   24, Mr. James Aittoun, portioner of Grenge, and Barbara Hamiltoun had
      James.

M. 10, John Watsone to Janet Kennedie.
   10, David Stronge to Margaret Sibbauld.
   31, James Sanders to Barbara Wilsoun.

AUGUST.

B.   7, Davie Christie and Annabell Bardner had . . . .
   12, John Keir and Geils Burne had John.
   12, Robert Wels and Grisole Andersoun had Bessie.
   12, Andrew Renny and Bessie Brand had Andrew.
   19, Archibald Mowtrey and Catherine Bardner had David.
   19, John Wricht, collier, and Catherine Patoun had Helen.
   19, David Sempill and Janet Mudie had Catherine.
   21, Patrick Cowpar and Elspet Smetoun had Janet (in fornication).
   26, Adam Wilsoun and Catherine Wilsoun had Catherine.
   26, John Potter and Christian Legat had Margaret.
   26, John Tomesoun and Effie Wastwod had Christian (in fornication).
   26, Andrew Gaw and Christian Walker had a son . . . .

M.   7, Florence Burgan to Janet Palmer.
   14, Alexander Gib to Christian Mackie.
   21, John Hutoun to Helen Stanehous.
   21, John Colzeir to Janet Sempill.

SEPTEMBER.

B.   2, Andrew Currie and Mawse Andersone had David.
   2, Nicol Huntar and Marion Hutoun had Christian.
   4, Mr. Andrew Forrester, minister, and Helen Ramsay had Isobel.
   9, William Gray and Margaret Andersone had John.
   9, James Gray and Janet Westwod had Janet.
   9, Robert Merser and Margaret Barhame had Christian.
   13, David Watsone, merchant, and Janet Cuthbert had John.
   16, Henry Greiff and Janet Traill had Catherine.
   16, Jerome Broun and Katherine Dowie had Catherine (in fornication).
   18, Wattie Murray and Alison Tomesone had John (in fornication).
   20, Nicol Dewar and Jennie Robertsone had Marjory.
   25, Andrew Mekiljohne and Janet Anderson had Janet.
   30, Thomas Tod and Barbara Elder had William.

M. 11, Patrick Cowper to Janet Murray.
   25, Gavin Douglas to Marjory Burgane.
   25, John Christie to Janet Tyrie.

OCTOBER.

B.   2, John Gibe to Marjory Shortous (married).[1]
   7, William Murie and Christian Cunninghame had Alexander.
   7, Gavin Ramsay and Janet Davidsone had John.
   14, Thomas Burne, miller, and Janet Austiane had Marjory.

[1] Inserted in the baptism column.

14, Michael Meldrum and Janet Renny had Robert.
14, William Porteous and Nanse Aidie had Sarah.
14, James Litlejohne and Helen Schortous had James.
21, Andrew Hutoun, cordiner, and Elspet Cunninghame had Elspet.
21, James Dewar and Grisole Hay had Catherine.
28, James Hairt and Janet Murie had Margaret (in fornication).

M. 16, John Ros to Helen Huttoun.

NOVEMBER.

B. 4, William Lugtoun and Catherine Dewar had Janet.
6, Janet Lessells "had ane man chyld, borne of hir in fornicatioun to William Stevinsone then aff the countrey as scho gave hir aithe, baptized and callit Williame."
8, William Pratus, elder, and Bessie Cuthbert had Marjory.
11, Laurence Andersone and Bessie Currour had Helen.
— Andrew Currie and Emelie Cuming had Andrew.
— John Watsone and Janet Kennedie had Janet.
— William Drysdell, deceased, and Effie Orrock had Catherine.
25, John Austiane, miller, and Catherine Chalmers had Jone (daughter).
25, Henry Gibsone and Isobel Cunninghame had Bessie.
25, Allan Galrige and Janet Currie had Janet.

M. 6, Andrew Colzeir to Nicolas Abercrumbie.
6, Robert Orrock to Janet Dewar.
20, Thomas . . . . to Grisole Westwode.
20, John Makbayth to Christian Tomesone.
27, Richard Potte to Bessie Tomesone.

DECEMBER.

B. 2, Alexander Bartrome and Isobel Broun had Janet.
4, John Burne in the Nethertoun and Janet Law had a daughter . . . .
9, Robert Cunninghame and Helen Wilsone had William.
9, Robert Bennat tailor, and Geils Banalay had David.
16, Alexander Wilsone and Margaret Donaldsone had Nanse.
23, David Barklay and Christian Murie had Alexander.
23, George Davidsone and Christian Bull had Margaret.
23, Thomas Sands and . . . . had Marjory.
23, (Entry torn away.)
23, James Cowsteoun and Janet Dalgleische had James.
23, William Cusing and Elspet Hutchiesone had Alison.
25, John Andersone, notary, and Christian Christiesone had Robert.
30, Alexander Beane and Margaret Huttoun had John.
30, James Hunter and Catherine Law had a son . . . .

M. 4, George Wallace to Janet Dalgleishe.
11, James Sanderis to Marion Hutoun.
11, Richard Hendine to Margaret Chrichtoun.
11, George Imrie to Margaret Stevinsone.
11, David Hardie to Bessie Potter.
18, Andrew Walwod to Marjory Mudie.
18, John Broun to Christian Neilsone.
27, ... Smythe to Margaret Maistertone.

JANUARY [1611].

B. 1, George Donald and Margaret Wilsone (who died in child birth) had Mark. "This samyn day the barne was baptized and the mother buryit."
13, Laurence Patrik and Margaret Reid had Margaret.
13, John Coventrie and Janet Walwod had Adam.
13, John Rowane and Marion Cunningham had Janet (in fornication).

20, John Brown and Margaret Smetoun had Janet.
20, John Andersone and Janet Meldrome had George.
20, Thomas Keir and Helen Baxter had Harry.
20, Thomas Westwod and Nanse Clerk had Adam (in adultery).
— Richard Cuthbert and Bessie Moreis had a son . . . .
— Andrew Horne and Bessie Anghous had David.
— Abraham Grege and Christian Cunninghame had Margaret.

M.   1, James Hairt to Janet Murrie.
    8, Patrick Robertsone to Jean Edmonstoun.
    29, Andrew Walker to Christian Rowan.
    29, George Ivatt to Janet Gedde(?s).

FEBRUARY.

B.   3, Patrick Galloway and Marjory Currour had Margaret.
    10, David Burne, miller, and Margaret Broun had David.
    10, John Schortus and Marjory Stevinsone had Robert (in fornication, under
        promise of marriage).
    17, John Reanny and Margaret Huttoun had Henry.
    17, Robert Dewar and Janet Moreis had Patrick.
    17, Patrick Dewar and Janet Mathesone had Andrew (in fornication).
    19, Robert Stirk, customer in Dunfermline, and Nanse Car had David.
    19, George Fergussone and Janet Peirsone had David.
    24, William Cowsteone and Helen Lindesay had James.
    24, Adam Currour and Margaret Swentoun had Margaret.
    24, John Kinross and Helen Ross had Bessie.
    24, John Dow and Elspet Beverage had John (in fornication).

M.   [*None.*]

MARCH.

B.   3, Patrick Stevin and Margaret Drummond had Bessie.
    —, ...[1] and Jean Hutoun had Bessie.
    —, Willie Rae and Janet Orrock had John.
    24, Gilbert Car and Helen Inglis had Michael.
    24, Richard Law and Janet Tomesone had Effie.
    26, John Andersone, merchant, and Janet Reid had William.
    26, John Andersone, younger, litster, and Margaret [Pr]atus had John.
    31, Andrew Turnebull, portioner of [Gran]ge? and Helen Currie had
        Andrew.
    31, John Stirk and Janet Meldrome had James.
    31, Andrew Andersone and Janet Arnott had Marion.

M.   [*None.*]

APRIL.

B.   6, Thomas Greif and Margaret Forsyithe had Andrew.
    7, Patrick Stanehous and Catherine Leithe had Elspet.
    7, John Stevinsone and Janet Moreis had Thomas.
    9, Simon Davidsone, collier, and Jean Nicole had John.
    14, Thomas Robertsone and Janet Harrower had David.
    —, Thomas Peirsone and Christian Kant had Margaret.
    —, ... and Grisole Meldrome had Elspet.
    —, Edward Tomesone and Janet Burne had Nanse. Witnesses, Thomas
        Stevinson, John Car, Richard Porter, younger.
    —, Laurence Horne and Jean Wilsone had John.
    —, William Thomesone in Bayth and Helen Watson had Catherine.
    5,[2] Andrew Touche and Catherine Fyiff had Effie.
    7, Willie Buist and Helen Turnebull had a daughter . . . .
    10, Willie Kennedie and Katherine Spear had Jean.
    10, Robert Scotland and Jean Tomesone had James.

[1] The edges of the leaves towards the end of this volume are much mutilated, in
consequence of which there are many defective entries in this year's record.
[2] Here the dating of the month begins over again, but it seems still to be April.

10, Thomas Tod and Margaret Hutoun had Thomas.
10, John Small and Margaret Huggoun had Patrick.
10, Stevin Broun and Margaret Inglische had Robert.
12, Robert Trumbill and Janet Cowper had . . . .
12, Elspet Patersone "had ane manchyld quhilk scho buire in the thrid fall in fornicatioun with ane vagabund fellow nicknameit Clout on the Schulder, baptized and callit . . . ."
—, ... and Kate Cusine had William.
21, Robe Currie, *alias* Lotche, and Kate Makcalzeoun had Bessie.
21, David Care, armourer, and Catherine Elder had George.
23, William Monteithe of Randiefuird and his lady Jean Bruse had Margaret.
28, David Wilsone, collier, and Isobel Burt had Margaret.
28, Henry Wilsone and Katherine Keir had Bessie.

M. 2, William Davidsone to Margaret Mowbrey.
9, William Flockart to Janet Burne.

MAY.

B. 5, Robert Peirsone (deceased) and Margaret Peirsone had Robert. "The bairne was borne about twentie tua dayis within thrie quarters of ane yeir efter the departure of the father."
14, Robert Quhyt and Nanse Hairt had Janet.
14, John Dowie and Margaret Blak had John.
14, Alexander Wilsone in Grange and Elspet Michie had Elspet.
16, William Robertsone, weaver, and Janet Litlejohne had William.
16, James Wilsone in Galrigehill and . . . . had Henry.
19, Peter Brown, portioner of Fode, and Christian Tomesone had Adam.
—, ... and . . . . sone had a son . . . .

M. 14, James Baide in Culros to Ephie Murray.
—, William Keir to Janet Turnebull.
—, John Lawsone to Janet Nasmithe.
28, Patrick Davidsone, collier, to Janet Tomesone.

JUNE.

B. 2, Duncan Cherrie and Janet Fischar had Bessie.

2, Robert Phillane, maltman, and Helen Cuthbert had Isobel.
4, Charles Ritchardsone and Janet Buist had John.
13, Wattie Phune, saltbearer, and Magie Westwod had twins, Margaret and Janet.
16, George Mill in the Knok and Bessie Burne had James.
23, James Cunninghame and Isobel Cunninghame had Archibald.
23, Archibald Douglas and Janet Phillane had Margaret.
23, Wattie Hutoun and Margaret Rae had Bessie.
30, John Hutoun in Pitdinne and Helen Stanehous had Christian.
30, Gilbert Blair, slater, and Elspet Johnestoun had Anna.
30, John Melvill, collier, and Isobel Tod had George.

M. 4, Thomas Mitchell, younger, to Margaret Dick upon a testimonial from the minister of Dalgatie).
4, Alaster Balfour to Catherine Proude.
11, James Makbreck to Catherine Peirsoun.
25, John Tomesone to Christian Tomesone.
25, John Simsone to Bessie Hutoun.
25, Archibald Hoge to Bessie Wilsone.
25, James Stevinsone to Janet Garnocke.

JULY

B. 7, Robert Wilsone in Pitdinnie and Margaret Hutoun had John.
9, John Strange, officer of the burgh, and Janet Mathie had . . . .

14, John Wilsone and Isobel Kirk had Margaret.
14, John Watsone, merchant, and Margaret Mekil . . . . had Janet.
— . . . . and Jean Edmonstoune had a son . . . .
23, Archibald Gray and Catherine Tomesone had David.
30, Clement Sanders and Marion Bell had Marion. Witnesses, Umphra
    Fegge, John Banks (?), David Sibauld.

M. — . . . . to Margaret L. . . . .
— Patrick Young (?) to Helen Nicole.

AUGUST.

B. 4, John Kay and Margaret Fergie had John.
   11, David Andersone in Knokes and Helen Andersone had David.
   12, Sir Robert Halkheid of Pitfirrane and Dame Margaret Murray had
       James.
   18, David Tod and Janet Dalgleische had Margaret.
   20, William Cunninghame in Crocefuird and Janet Lugtoun had Elspet.
   25, William Neilsone and Catherine Baid had William.
   25, David Dewar of Lassodie and Jean Logane had Christian.
   25, Thomas Ritchardsone, tailor, and Helen Reid had Margaret (in fornica-
       tion).

M. 6, J . . . . Walker to Jean Max . . . .
    6, George Levin to Marjory Smyth.
   13, ... Walwode to Margaret Peirsone.

SEPTEMBER.

B. 8, Richard Hendine and Margaret Chrichtoun had Margaret.
   10, Peter Law and Margaret Walkar had Margaret.
   — . . . . and Janet . . . . had . . . .
   — George Walker and Janet Mekilhois had Elspet.
   22, Thomas Mudie in Mastertoun and Margaret Turnebull had Bessie.
   24, George Walker, merchant, and Marjory Cuthbert had Thomas.
   — Harry Stewart of Bayth and Catharine Kirkcaldie had Bessie.
   29, Edward Douglas in Wester Gellat and Marion . . . . k had Effie.
   29, Patrick Peirsone and Janet Maistertoun had Harry.
   29, James Hutoun and Catherine Walwod had Margaret.

M. 10, ... Sanders to Catherine . . . .

OCTOBER.

B. 1, Richard Potter, younger, and Bessie Tomesone had Bessie.
    1, Thomas Stevinsone and Bessie Vallange had Thomas.
    1, David Broun and Margaret Gibsone had Bessie.
    6, James Austiane and Mawse Alexander had Margaret.
    8, Sir Andrew Melvill of Garvock and Dame Elspet Hamiltoun had Harry.
    8, Patrick Turnebull, baker, treasurer of Dunfermline, and Katherine
       Smythe had David.
   — . . . . Maistertoun and Grisole Stewart had a son . . . .
   — . . . . and Margaret Turnebull had Andrew.
   — David Laurie and Marion Blair had Janet.

M. 8, William Dawsoun to Marion Robertsone.

NOVEMBER.

B. 3, Adam Man and Marion Drysdell had Bessie.
    3, William Henresone and Bessie Forsyithe had Andrew.
   — William Walwode and Bessie Nicole had Janet.
    7, John Huslope and Janet Laichlands had Robert.

M. 12, Thomas Walwode to Effie Scott.

K

19, Andrew Beany to Janet Reanny.
26, Peter Sempill to Isobel Gilmure.

DECEMBER.

B. 1, Umphra Henresone and Christian Fentoun had Bessie.
— William Stanehous and Elspet Pirnie had John.
— Gilbert Wricht and Margaret Eassone had John.
— James Turnebull and Helen Johnestoun had Anna.
— . . . . Kellok and Margaret Kellok had a son . . . .
— . . . . and Margaret Stevinson had a daughter . . . .
— . . . . and Bettie Murdoche had a daughter . . . .
— . . . . and Jean Huttoun had Isobel.
— John Walker, tailor, and Barbara Fyff had William (in fornication). "This womanis husband callit Johne Rowan ; it is wncertane quhither he leifit or nocht (being ane long tyme and yit still all (*sic*) aff the contrey) at this tyme, and therefor it wes thocht and suspectit to be adulterie, and their satisfactioun continewit till testimonie and tryall wes had therin till."
20, Andrew Colzier, drummer of the burgh of Dunfermline, and Nicholas Abercrumbie had Margaret.
20, James Crichtoun and Margaret Mowbrey had Margaret.
20, William Smithe in Fode and Margaret Maistertoun had Andrew.
20, John Young and Christian Peirsone had Catharine.
20, James Lugtoun and Margaret Nasmythe had Helen.
22, Robert Peirsone in Lymkills and Isobel Galt had Margaret.
22, Rob Orrock and Jenie Dewar had Janet.
27, Nicol Broun in Lassodie Mill and Mawse Spittall had a daughter . . .

M. 3, Alexander Spittell to Isobel Hiltoun.
22, Bar[tole] Gilmure to Janet B[ull].

[End of First Volume of the Register, pp. 1-286, average size 10½ ins. long by 8 ins. wide.]

DECEMBER [1611].

B. 22, Adam Stevinsone, smith, and Margaret Reid had Laurence.
22, James Gray and Catherine Craigie had Margaret (in fornication).
24, John Wilsone, seaman, and Janet Sanders had George (in fornication).
24, William Broun, notary, and Grisole Cuthbert had Marjory.
31, William Cuninghame, weaver, and Janet Alisone had Bessie.

M. 24, ... Quhyt to Christian Gray.

JANUARY [1612].

B. 1, John Trottar and Janet Craik had John.
1, John Hutoun, smith in Lassodie, and Isobel Gregsone (?) had David.
1, Nicol Dewar and Janet Andersone had Catharine.
1, Gavin Stanehous and Marjory Nicole had Janet.
1, Mr. Andrew Forrester, minister, and Helen Ramsay had Janet.
4, Johne Lawsone, miller, and Janet Nasmyth had James.
19, John Davidsone and Kate Wardlaw had John.
26, Edward Stirk and Nanse Lindsay had Marion.
28, John Scott and Margaret Kirk had Janet (in fornication).
31, John Fleming of Blaklaw and Bessie Sandis had Marion.

M. 7, James Purdie to Isobel Beany.
21, Henry (?) Douglas to Helen Welles (?)
28, J . . . . Robertsone to Margaret Brand.

FEBRUARY.

B. 2, James Henresone and Janet Dewar had Janet.
2, George Knox and Janet Anghous had Marion.

2, Patrick Harrower and Cirstie Peacok had Nanse.

2, William Currour and Margaret Weitat had David.

5, Nicol Wardlaw and Bessie Hutoun had a son . . . .

9, John Potter and Kirstie Leggat had Janet.

9, John Smetoun and Magie Andersone had Grisole.

9, Alaster Balfour and Kate Proud had Robert.

9, Thomas Mitchell and Margaret Dick had Thomas.

9, Adam Stobie and Helen Gibboune had Adam, baptized in the kirk of Carnock.

11, Thomas Hutoun and Margaret Lindsay had Thomas, baptized in Carnock kirk.

13, Geordie Davidsone and Christie Bull had John.

13, Mr. Thomas Wardlaw and Katie Alisone had Isobel.

16, John Walker and Margaret Fothringhame had John.

16, Thom Rodger and Grizel Westwod had . . . .

18, John Stevin and Magie Tomesone had John.

18, John Burne, a young lad, and Bessie Broun had Margaret (in fornication).

23, James Trottar and Bessie Lawsone had William.

23, Geordie Hendine and Bessie Bennat had Helen.

23, ... Abercrumbie and . . . . had Susanna.

27, Mungo Murray and Margaret Halkheid had Nicolas.

M. 4, William Cu . . . . to Bessie Hutoun.

11, Robert Wilson to Christian Sumraell.

16, David Lyndsay of Balcarrois to Sophia Setoun, daughter of Alexander, Earl of Dunfermline.

18, Ar . . . . Hodge to Margaret Walker.

18, Henry Peirsone to Helen Williamesone.

23, Patrick Douglas to Margaret Schortus.

23, Robert Broun to Christian Kidde.

MARCH.

B. 1, Thomas Peirsone and Christian Kant had Bessie.

1, James Sanders and Barbara Wilsone had Andrew.

3, John Galrige and Nanse Andersone had George.

9, William Flockart and Janet Burne had James.

10, John Burgane and Alison Orrock had Janet.

10, Grisole Smithe "had ane womanchyld borne of hir in fornication to James Gib, quha wes at Lundon for the tyme and thairfor not tryit in this sclander, and the bairne wes takine out the hands of Andro Mekiljohne and baptized and callit Nanse."

15, Rob Pringle, collier, and Madge Brand had Janet (in fornication).

15, "That day Davie Simsone, ane wncouthe sowter fallow, had ane womanchyld borne to him of his wyff Barbara Broun, maryit with him in the kirk of Dunfermlyne, baptized and callit Margaret."

22, Adam Walwod in Fod and Isobel Walwod had Catharine.

22, Allan Galrige and Janet Currie had Alexander.

31, James Stevinsone and Janet Garnok had James.

M. [*None.*]

APRIL.

B. 5, William Sanders and Marion Mastertoun had a daughter . . . .

12, Archibald Hodge, collier, and Bessie Wilsone had Allison.

14, John Gib and Marjory Schortus had Margaret.

14, Patie Lawsoun and Margaret Cunninghame had Isobel.

19, David Broun and Christian Blak had Isobel.

19, William Turnebull and Magie Law had Peter.

19, George Moreis and Margaret Kinimond had Henry.

19, John Raithe, "ane litster servand," and Nanse Haddock, "ane woman in Edinburgh," had a manchild (in fornication) called David.

19, Rob Henresone, skinner, and Elspet Baird had Robert (in fornication).

19, Robert Merser, flesher, and Margaret Barhame had Robert.
26, John Lawsone and Janet Donaldsone had Margaret.
28, Patrick Young and Helen Nicole had Andrew.

M. 28, David Peirsone to Bessie Peirsone.

MAY.

B. 3, James Gibsone and Margaret Patoun had Margaret.
    8, John Keir and Geils Burne had Janet.
    8, John Walker, tailor, and Jean Maxwell had Marjory.
    17, Willie Mudie and Magie Daglesche had Margaret.
    26, Jamie Quhyt and Bessie Wilsone had William (in fornication).
    31, Abraham Grege and Isobel Cunninghame had Helen.
    31, John Davidsone and Nanse Broun had Marie.

M. 19, Adam Patoun to Mage Phillane.
    26, Adam Hendine to Margaret Grieve.

JUNE.

B. 7, Nicol Inglis and Bessie Cuninghame had Alexander.
    7, William Walwod, cordiner, and Magie Lyndesay had Elspet.
    7, Edmond Alisone and Effie Crumbie had Andrew.
    7, John Watsone and Margaret Mekiljohne had Nanse.
    9, James Kellok and Margaret Cumming had Robert (in fornication).
    15, Robie Kellok, weaver, and Margaret Rowan had twins, John and Marion.
    22, Adam Wilsone and Catharine Wilsone had Marjory.
    23, Andrew Buchanane and Bessie Row had Christian.
    30, Pate Merschell and Isobel Hiltoun had William (in fornication).

M. 2, Andrew Colzeir, "ane pore pyper," to Helen Bonaly.
    23, William Ratrey to Janet Speir.
    30, John Baid to Bessie Spens.

JULY.

B. 5, William Wilsone and Isobel Peacok had a son . . . .
    5, Andrew Andersone and Janet Touchie had Helen.
    16, William Andersone in Lymkills and Geils Peirsone had David.
    19, Patrick Douglas and Magie Schortus had Janet.
    19, John Wricht and Kate Patoun had Bessie.
    19, Thomas Alexander and Janet Kineland had Margaret.
    23, John Tomesone and Emelie Cuming had Isobel.
    26, George Douglas and Janet Dalgleische had Robert.
    26, Andrew Sanders and Isobel Westwod had Andrew.
    26, John Burne in the Nethertoun and Janet Law had . . . .

M. 7, James Fergussoun to Janet Cunninghame.
    7, William Kirk to Bessie Dalgleische.
    28, Richard Potter to Bessie Leirmonthe.

AUGUST.

B. 1, Rob Quhyt and Kate Hunnon had Isobel.
    2, Willie Keir and Janet Turnebull had twins, Isobel and Bessie.
    4, William Robertsone and Janet Litlejohne had Janet.
    4, James Kinsman and Christian Walwod had Bessie.
    18, Patrick Bothwell and Alison Tomesone had Susanna (in fornication).
    29, Henry Wilsone and Kate Keir had Marjory.
    29, Malcolm Makqueyne and Janet Donkie had Janet.
    29, John Coventrie and Janet Walwod had James.

M. 11, Rob Gray to Elspet Stevinsone.
    25, Matthew Kirkland to Mause Brand.

SEPTEMBER.

B. 6, James Lethome and Isobel Makbaithe had Margaret.
  6, John Douglas and Rosina Osswald had Isobel.
  13, Nicol Dewar and Janet Robertsone had Nanse.
  13, David Christie and Annabell Bairdner had Janet.
  15, Andrew Horne and Bessie Anghous had Robert.
  20, Archibald Gray and Margaret Tomesone had John.
  20, Cuthbert Wardlaw and Margaret Gahige had Bessie.
  20, Bartole Gilmure and Janet Bull had John.
  20, Adam Dewar (deceased) and Christian Wricht had Jean.
  22, John Burne and Jean Murray had Janet.
  27, David Mylne in Pitliver and Mage Mekiljohne had Margaret.
  27, Laurence Patrik and Magie Reid had Henry.
  27, William Gray and Margaret Andersone had Bessie.
  27, Thomas Walwod and Effie Scott had Thomas.

M. 8, John Burne to Margaret Hutoun.

OCTOBER.

B. 4, William Low and Nanse Gibe had Margaret.
  4, Andrew Hutoun and Elspet Cunninghame had Andrew.
  4, John Andersone and Janet Meldrum had Robert.
  6, John Mackie and Elspet Robertsone had Andrew.
  6, George Gray in Turnbull's Beath and Catherine Dowie had Margaret
    (in adultery, the child being over a year old).
  11, James Dewar and Grisole Hoy had Robert.
  16, Willie Williamesone and Effie Schortus had Janet.
  25, John Donaldsone and Helen Stevinsone had Andrew.
  25, David Andersone in Kistok and Margaret Bardner had Janet.
  28, Andrew Ged and Marion Finlay had John (in fornication).

M. 6, David Peacok to Margaret Hodge.

NOVEMBER.

B. 15, Robie Murray and Catharine Bairdner had Patrick.
  17, George Davidsone and Magie Pitcarne had William (in fornication).
  17, Thomas Walwode and Bessie Kirk had Bessie.
  24, Henry Dick and Margaret Douglas had Robert.
  24, John Dewar and Isobel Moreis had Isobel.
  24, Robert Broun and Margaret Kid had Robert.
  24, James Mastertoun and Grisole Stewart had Harry.
  29, George Durie and Barbara Barhame had Marjory.
  29, Archibald Hodge and Margaret Walker had Janet.

M. 3, Robert Aidiesone to Margaret Peirsoune.
  10, James Quhyt to Helen Aikine.
  10, Andrew Young to Elspet Fiurd.
  10, Thomas Moire to Grizel Walwod.
  17, William Lawsone to Margaret Lethome.

DECEMBER.

B. 1, George Walkar, merchant, and Marjory Cuthbert had Bessie.
  4, Robert Halkheid of Pitfirrane and his lady (omitted) had Jean.
  6, John Sanders and Christian Millar had Janet.
  6, Gavin Douglas in the Ferrie "had ane barne baptized and callit Gavin."
  8, William Smart and Bessie Mudie had John.
  11, Edward Tomesone and Janet Burne had David.
  13, Ritchie Scotland and Margaret Blaikwod had Margaret.
  13, James Robertsone and Magie Brand had Elspet.
  13, John Andersone and Christie Christiesone had George.
  13, James Buist and Jenie Dainzell had Robert.

15, James Quhyt and Christian Gray had Janet.
20, Gilbert Stalker and Christian Weitat had Margaret.
20, William Neilsone and Catherine Baid had Laurence.
20, Thomie Ritche and Margaret Andersone had John.
20, John Tomesone and Margaret Douglas had Margaret.
20, Robert Kirk and Barbara Moreson had Janet (in fornication).

M. 1, Robert Balcais to Lucrece Noreis.
1, Laurence Lugtoun to Janet Bennat.
29, Thomas Fermour to Isobel Patoun.

JANUARY [1613].

B. 3, James Hamiltoun and Nanse Imrie had Alexander.
6, John Raithe and Janet Michie had Margaret (in fornication).
10, David Sempill and Janet Mudie had Marjory.
10, William Steidman, collier, and Margaret Wilsone had Alison.
10, Janet Cambell "had ane womanchyld borne and gottin in harlotrie with ane man in Edinburgh callit Haddane baptized and callit Issobell."
12, William Culane and Bessie Hutoun had Isobel.
12, Patrick Murray of Pardewis and Margaret Colvill had James.
17, John Schortus and Janet Broun had Robert.
19, James Cunnon (? Cummon) and Janet Stanehous had Jean.
21, Andrew Cokburne and Margaret Monypenny had Jean.
24, James Oswald and Bessie Cowsteoun had Alexander.
24, William Cusine and Elspet Hutchisoun had William.
26, Patrick Cowper and Janet Murray had Thomas.
26, James Nasmythe and Christian Hardie had Elspet.
26, George Christie and Effie Jamiesone had twins, John and Margaret.
31, Thomas Burne and Janet Austiane had Janet.
31, Robie Bennat and Geils Bonalay had James.
31, George Ewat and Janet Ged had Janet.

M. 12, John Alisone to Marjory Elder.
19, James Sim to Marjory Allane.

FEBRUARY.

B. 7, James Kellok and Margaret Mudie had Robert. Witnesses, Robert Kellok, Robert Mudie.
9, Elspet Douglas "had ane womanchyld borne in incest to Johne Watt hir wmquhill husbands brother sone baptized and callit Jonet."
14, James Burne and Janet Young had John.
21, Robert Scotland and Jean Tomesone had Robert.
21, John Trottar and Janet Craik had John.
21, George Dewar in Lathamond and Jean Hutoun had Marion.
28, John Coilzeir and Janet Sempill had Catherine.
28, Rob Smithe and Margaret Anghous had George.

M. 2, Robert Lambe to Janet Wilsone.
2, Henry Wilsone to Elspet Stevin.
18, Robert Halyday to Marion Steidman.

MARCH.

B. 4, John Andersone and Janet Reid had John.
7, Robert Wilsone and Nanse Simrauell had Marjory.
7, John Miller in Lassodiemill and Alisone Wilsone had Bessie.
9, Michael Chalmers and Effie Gray had Peter.
11, Thomas Key and Marjory Steill had Bessie.
14, James Mill in South Lethame and Janet Rowan had John.
23, Andrew Currie and Mawse Andersone had George.
23, Lawrie Lugtoun and Janet Bennat had Christian.
23, Alexander Bean and Helen Hutoun had Janet.
23, John Anderson, younger, and Margaret Pratus had Margaret

28, John Henresone, tailor (*alias* Fegge) and Janet Inglis had Marjory.
28, David Burne and Margaret Broun had William.
30, Patrick Dewar and Janet Mathesoun had William (in fornication).

M. 6, Robert Walwod to Marion Mitchell.

APRIL.

B. 11, Rob Russell and Barbara Elder had Janet.
11, Thomas Coventrie and Janet Murray had Thomas.
18, John Watsone, "chopeman," and Janet Kennedie had James.
18, Andrew Hutsone and Margaret Knox had Margaret.
18, Robe Tomesone and Elspet Mitchell had Margaret.
20, Andrew Mekiljohne and Janet Andersone had Helen.
25, Thome Bankis and Isobel Tod had David.
25, Duncan Tailyeour and Margaret Hutoun had Margaret.
25, Thome Deis and Magie Kingorne had John.
25, William Ratrey and Janet Speir had Grisole.
25, Gilbert Car and Helen Inglis had Margaret.

M. [*None.*]

MAY.

B. 2, Robert Wilsone and Margaret Hutoun had Robert.
9, Andrew Renny and Bessie Brand had Bessie.
9, Henry Turnebull and Kat Cusine had John.
11, Richard Potter and Bessie Leirmonthe had Margaret.
16, Adam Moyas and Nanse Greif had John.
16, Henry Brock and Margaret Scotland had Bessie (in fornication).
18, John Wardlaw and Margaret Baid had John.
20, "The rycht honorabill Williame Monteithe of Randiefuird had ane womanchyld borne to him of his lady, Jeane Bruse, baptized and callit Jeane."
30, Robert Young and Bessie Lugtoun had John.
30, Thome Sands and Margaret Fenton had Robert.
30, John Watsone and Margaret Mekiljohne had David.

M. 25, James Westwod to Isobel Cunninghame.
25, James Colzeir to Janet Lugtoun.

JUNE.

B. 6, John Stirk and Margaret Wilsone had Bessie.
6, Patrick Young and Helen Nicole had Robert.
8, Andrew Turnebull and Helen Currie had Adam.
10, Mungo Murray and Margaret Halkheid had Catherine.
12, James Litlejohne and Helen Schortous had . . . .
20, John Bairdner and Elspet Ready had Patrick.
20, Pate Harrower and Christie Peacok had John.
22, Robert Cunninghame and Helen Wilsone had Janet.
27, William Cowsteoun and Helen Lyndsay had Edward.
27, Umphra Henresone and Christian Fentoun had Nanse.

M. 8, James Broun to Janet Crawfuird.
15, Mr. William Smyth to Marion Dewar.
29, Henry Mershell to Bessie Turnebull.

JULY.

B. 4, James Hairt and Janet Murie had John.
4, James Cois and Bessie Sands had John.
6, George Fergussoun and Janet Peirsone had twins, George and Helen.
11, Robert Douglas and Helen Donald had Alexander.
11, James Cuninghame and Isobel Cuninghame had John.
11, David Walker and Grisole Meldrum had John.
18, John Stevinsone and Janet Moreis had Effie.

18, Andrew Colzeir and Helen Bonalay had David.
25, Robe Adame and Magie Douglas had Isobel.
27, David Peacok and Magie Peacok had William.

M. 6, Archibald Hunniman to Margaret Wels.
6, John Merschell to Janet Fuird.
6, Robert Peacok to Catherine Stevinsone.
13, James Aissone to Catherine Watsone.

AUGUST.

B. 1, John Ros and Helen Huttoun had James.
8, Robe Stirk and Nansie Car had Catherine.
10, Peter Law and Marge Walker had Janet.
15, Adam Hendine and Margaret Greif had Robert.
15, Andrew Currie (deceased) and Emelie Broun had Margaret.
15, Alexander Straquhen and Catherine Moreis had George.
19, John Simsone and Bessie Hutoun had Robert.
22, Edward Douglas and Janet Phillane had Edward.
24, Mr. Andrew Forrester, minister, and Helen Ramsay had Frederick.
— .... and Helen Wels, his wife, had Robert.
29, John Logane and Margaret Galt had Helen.

M. 3, Henry Orock to Margaret Scotland.

SEPTEMBER.

B. 21, James Kingorne and Effie Murray had Harry.
26, David Watsone and Janet Cuthbert had James.
26, David Barklay and Christian Murie had .... "The bairne wes baptized in Carnock, the minister of Dunfermling being seik."
28, Archibald Bowie and Bessie Tomesone had James (in fornication).

M. [*None.*]

OCTOBER.

B. 3, Thomas Tod and Margaret Hutoun had Margaret.
3, John Walker and Jean Maxwell had Bessie.
17, Michael Meldrum and Janet Renny had Henry.
24, William Gray and Margaret Andersone had Andrew.
24, Henry Baxter and Catherine Wilsone had a son .... (baptized in Balingrie, the minister of Dunfermline being sick).
26, John Broun and .... Smetoun had John.
31, John Andersone and Janet Meassoun had James (in fornication).
31, John Smetoun, younger, and Janet Fuird had Thomas (in fornication).
31, James Potter (?) and Bessie Reid had Isobel.
31, James Phinne and Helen Andersone had Christian (in fornication).

M. 12, John Walker to Margaret Turnebull.
12, David Peirsone to Jean Stanehous.
19, Thomas Huton to Bessie Cuninghame.
26, Thomas Blak to Margaret Law.
26, John Dick to Christian Cusine.

NOVEMBER.

B. 2, Johnie Potter and Christie Legat had Catharine.
7, John Burne and Margaret Hutoun had Thomas.
7, John Walker and Helen Wrycht had Bessie (in fornication).
14, David Scotland and Janet Keir had Catherine (in fornication).
21, Thomas Keir in Beath and Helen Baxter had Robert.
23, David Car and Catherine Elder had Margaret.
28, Robert Balcais and Lucrece Noreis had John.
28, Alexander Bartrome and Isobel Broun had Effie.

M. 2, Robert Kirk to Grisole Andersone.

2, George Smetoun to Margaret Turnebull.
9, Ritchie Bairdner to Margaret Fothringhame.
16, Henry Lugtoun to Nanse Ramsay.
23, George Williamsone to Effie Thomesone.
30, James Roxburghe to Beatie Gibsone.

DECEMBER.

B. 5, James Hutoun and Marjory Walwod had Catherine.
13, Andrew Young and Elspet Fuird had William.
19, Willie Kennedie and Christian Speir had Harry.
19, Thomas Mudie and Margaret Turnebull had Robert.
21, Robert Phillane and Helen Cuthbert had Helen.
28, Thomas Thomsone and Margaret Moreis had William.

M. 7, Clement Sanders to Elspet Sanders.
14, David Watche to Cicile Duncan.
28, Robie Miller to Margaret Mowtrey.

JANUARY [1614].

B. 2, Ritchie Scotland and Margaret Blakwod had Alexander.
9, Andrew Cunninghame and Margaret Turnebull had Elizabeth.
16, John Hutoun and Catherine Quhyt had James.
16, Alexander Honyman and Bessie Turnbull had John.
18, George Walker, merchant, and Marjory Cuthbert had David.
23, John Hutoun and Helen Stanehous had James.
23, John Peirsone and Marion Hutoun had David (in fornication 'under
    promeis of mariage as he and scho bayth confessit").
25, Henry Gibsone and Isobel Cuninghame had a son . . . .
30, Willie Walwod and Bessie Nicole had Effie.

M. 11, John Alisone to Grisole Walwod.
25, Jerome Broun to Margaret Dagleische.

FEBRUARY.

B. 1, Adam Stobie and Helen Giboune had Bessie.
13, Simon Davidson and Jean Nicole had William.
13, Patrick Andersone and Bessie Roxburghe had Patrick.
15, Cuthbert Wardlaw and Margaret Galrige had Isobel.
15, Archie Hodge and Margaret Walker had Margaret.
17, John Reid and Catherine Leslie had William (in fornication .
20, Alexander Nicole and Elspet Smetoun had Helen (in fornication .
22, David Bruse and . . . . . . Tomesone had Patrick.
24, John Alisone and Marjory Elder had . . . . . .
26, James Mastertoun and Grizel Stewart had twins, Catherine and
    Grizel.
27, James Wilsone and Janet Walkar had Janet.
27, James Henresone and Janet Dewar had Margaret.

M. 8, John Andersone to Janet Nicole.
22, Willie Rae to Janet Henresone.
22, Thomas Andersone to Alison Drysdell.
22, Gilbert Turnour to Helen Turnebull.
24, Robert Scotland to Helen Stobie.

MARCH.

B. 3, George Maine and Catherine Stevinsone had Andrew.
5, Patrick Galloway and Marjory Currour had David (who died immedi-
    ately).
8, Alexander Wilsone and Margaret Donaldsone had John.
8, Robert Lambe and Janet Wilsone had Alexander.
9, Mr. Thomas Wardlaw and Catherine Alison had Nanse.

10, James Haistie, "milner," and Mawse Alexander had David.
13, Geordie Mill and Bessie Burne had twins, William and Nanse.
20, John Small and Margaret Huggoun had Janet.
24, James Aissoun and Catherine Watsone had Janet.
29, Robert Currie and Catherine Makcalzeoun had James.

M. [*None.*]

APRIL.

B. 3, William Broun, notary, and Grizel Cuthbert had Helen.
5, Robert Aidiesone and Margaret Peirsone had Andrew.
5, Adam Currour and Margaret Swentoun had John.
7, Robie Turnebull and Janet Cowper had twins, David and George.
10, Robert Halyday, collier, and Marion Steidman had a daughter . . . .
12, William Murie and Catherine Cunninghame had Helen.
12, Andrew Gaw and Christian Walker had John.
23, Will Henresone, cordiner, and Bessie Forsyithe had a daughter . . . .
26, William Kellok in Lassodie and Margaret Kellok had Nanse.
26, James Trottar and Bessie Lawsoune had a son . . . .
26, James Hutoun and Catherine Walwod had Robert.

M. 28, Henry Christie to Bessie Bennat.

MAY.

B. 5, William Turnebull, lorimer, and Margaret Law had David.
8, James Westwod and Isobel Cunninghame had Thomas.
8, Gilbert Turnour and Helen Turnbull had Helen.
10, John Gray and Alison Hutoun had Magdalene (in fornication).
10, Andrew Coilzer and Nicolas Abercrumbie had a daughter . . . .
12, Charles Ritchardsone and Janet Buist had a daughter . . . .

M. [*None.*]

JUNE.

B. 12, David Watche and Cicile Duncane had Isobel.
19, John Wilsone and Janet Drysdell had Christian.
21, Thomas Mitchell, younger, and Margaret Dick had Henry.
26, Mr. William Smythe, schoolmaster, and Marion Dewar had Elspet.
26, Henry Wilsone and Elspet Stevin had Janet.
28, William Walwode in Crocegaits and Margaret Peirson had Thomas.

M. 14, Thomas Mudie to Margaret Mill.
16, Philip Dobie to Bessie Patoun.
21, William Bruse of Earlshall to Agnes Lindesay.
28, William Klyide to Nanse Mill.
30, Thomas Young to Isobel Sanders.

JULY.

B. 3, Patrick Cowper in the Newraw and Janet Murray had Margaret.
5, William Sanders and Marion Maistertoun had John.
10, John Andersone, younger, litster, and Margaret Pratus had Alexander.
17, George Williamsone and Effie Tomesone had a daughter . . . .
31, Florence Andersone and Helen Cunninghame had a son . . . .

M. 5, William Levingstoun, portioner of Falkirk, to Margaret Blaccater.
5, John Corsbie to Margaret Young.
5, John Rowane to Marion Cunninghame.
19, John Forrester to Annabel Lyndsay.
19, Robert Forsyithe to Marion Norie.

AUGUST.

B. 2, Henry Peirsone and Helen Williamsone had Janet.
7, John Walkar, dean of guild, and Margaret Turnbull had Janet.

9, Thomas Hutoun in Luscour and Margaret Lindesay had twins, Marion and Helen.
16, Gawin Stanehous and Marjory Nicole had Thomas.
18, Henry Merschell and Bessie Turnebull had Bessie.
18, Wattie Phinne and Magie Westwod had Isobel.
28, Adam Patoun and Marjory Phillane had Thomas.
30, William Gray in Lethornis and Catherine Donaldsone had Isobel.
30, John Scot, trumpeter, and Magie Oliphant had Janet (in fornication).

M. 9, Andrew Colzier to Maige Quhyt.
30, John Watsone to Marjory Smetoun.

SEPTEMBER.

B. 1, James Lambe and Janet Bairdner had Janet.
4, James Lethome in Hiltoun of Pitfirrane and Isobel Makbayth had William.
6, John Meffwane and Catherine Smetoun had Andrew.
11, Alexander Davidsone and Janet Douglas had Janet.
18, James Bathkatt and Christian Cunninghame had James.
18, Patrick Davidson and Janet Tomesone had John.
18, Geordie Walkar and Janet Makilhois had Thomas.
18, David Strang and Magie Sibbald had Bessie.
25, David Tod and Janet Aidiesone had Christian.
25, Thomas Mudie, weaver, and Effie Baverage had Thomas.
25, Richard Potter and Bessie Thomson had Edward.
25, Thomas Blackie and Magie Law had William.
27, Sir Robert Halket of Pitfirran and Margaret Murray had John.
27, James Dewar and Grizel Hoy had William.

M. 6, James Wyld to Mawse Hutoun.
6, John Finlaesone to Marjory Gay.
20, John Peirsone to Marion Hutoun.

OCTOBER.

B. 2, John Andersone and Janet Meldrum had Marie.
2, Robert Kirk and Grizel Andersone had Marion.
8, George Smetoun and Margaret Turnebull had John (born before the time).
9, William Smithe and Margaret Maistertoun had Isobel.
11, Andrew Reanny and Bessie Brand had Thomas.
11, John Wricht and Janet Sibauld had Janet.
18, Adam Douglas and Helen Hutoun had Bessie.
25, Clement Sanders and Elspet Sanders had John.
25, Andrew Andersone and Janet Touchie had Thomas.
25, John Merschell and Margaret Fuird had Catherine.
26, Mr. Andrew Forrester and Helen Ramsay had George.
27, David Christie and Annabell Bairdner had a son . . . .
30, John Baid and Bessie Spens had Margaret.

M. 4, James Warkman to Helen Williamsone.
25, John Aidiesone to Bessie Wilsone.

NOVEMBER.

B. 1, George Imrie and Margaret Stevinsone had James.
6, William Rae and Janet Orock had Christian.
6, Robert Peacok and Catherine Stevinsone had John.
10, John Allesone and Grizel Walwod had Margaret.
13, William Dawsone and Marion Robertson had Isobel.
13, Henry Schortus and Margaret Donaldsone had Janet.
13, Alexander Balfour and Catherine Proud had Janet.
13, James Gibsone and Margaret Patoun had a son . . . .
13, James Robertson and Margaret Brand had David.

15, Richard Bairdner and Margaret Fothringhame had Janet.
15, Jerome Broun and Margaret Dagleische had Bessie.
15, John Hutoun and Cate Hutoun had Margaret.
17, Patrick Turnebull and Catherine Smyth had Alexander.
17, John Simsone and Bessie Hutoun had William.
22, John Andersone and Janet Nicole had Andrew.
22, Allan Galrige and Janet Currie had John.
22, David Murray and Grizel Moreis had Janet.
22, David Henresone and Bessie Turnbull had Effie.

M. 22, George Meldrum to Marjory Walker.
29, Andrew Walkar to Janet Hutoun.
29, James Feg to Elspet Smetoun.

DECEMBER.

B. 4, Robert Dewar and Janet Moreis had Bessie.
4, Andrew Horne and Bessie Anghous had Margaret.
4, William Culane and Bessie Hutoun had John.
11, Gavin Fyiff and Janet Davidsone had Nanse.
11, George Dewar in Lathamond and Jean Hutoun had Janet.
11, John Bull and Janet Gibsone had Christian.
13, John Tomesone and Emelie Cuming had Marion.
15, James Buist and Jonie Dainzell had John.
18, William Low and Nanse Gib had William.
18, John Wels and Effie Gourlay had Robert (in fornication).
18, George Fergussoun, servitor to the Lord Chancellor, and Janet Peirsone
had John.
20, John Kellok and Christian Pringle had John.
27, Robert Stanehous in Mastertoun and Isobel Cunninghame had a son . . . .
27, Pate Douglas and Magie Schortus had Elspet.
29, George Durie and Bessie Echline had James.

M. 6, John Clerk to Catherine Baid.
6, John Tod to Janet Mackie.
13, James Logie to Marjory Burgane.

JANUARY [1615].

B. 3, Robert Scotland and Helen Scobie had John.
10, James Lugtoun and Margaret Nasmithe had Christian.
15, Thomas Rodger and Grizel Westwod had George.
15, Adam Stevinsone, smith, and Magie Reid had John.
22, David Burne, miller, and Margaret Broun had Robert.

M. 3, William Horne to Helen Andersone.
3, Adam Wilsone to Margaret Cunningham.
3, John Moyas to Margaret Christie.
31, Andrew Mudie to Catherine Greif.

FEBRUARY.

B. 5, Alexander Lockard, walker, and Janet Hunnane had Janet.
5, Henry Dick in Foulfuird and Margaret Douglas had Margaret.
5, James Kellok and Helen Cumming had Andrew (in fornication).
16, Thomas Christie in Beath (deceased) and Catherine Philpe had Thomas
(in fornication).
19, Gilbert Wricht and Margaret Aissoun had Isobel.
19, John Kay and Margaret Fargie had David.
28, David Blak in Cocklaw and Helen Dowie had John.
28, William Mudie and Margaret Aidiesone had Thomas.
28, William Cunninghame in Crocefuird and Janet Lugtoun had Marjory.

M. 7. William Moreis to Janet Young.
14, William Spens to Christian Wallange.

14, John Lawsone to Margaret Wilsone.
21, David Stevinsone to Isobel Christie.
23, Andrew Wricht to Elspet Forrester.

MARCH.

B. 5, Robert Scotland in Wester Craigdakie and Jean Thomson had Isobel.
   5, John Douglas and Rosina Oswald had Robert.
12, John Stirk and Janet Meldrum had George.
19, Andrew Greinehorne and Marjory Wilsone had James.
19, Thomas Robertson and Janet Harrower had Bessie.
19, John Anderson, *alias* Water Laird, and Janet Henresone had Isobel.
19, John Walker, tailor, and Jean Maxwell had Laurence.
23, David Andersone and Margaret Bairdner had Robert.
28, John Makie and Elspeth Robertson had Marjory.

M. 21, John Cuninghame to Marion Aikine.

APRIL.

B. 2, Thomas Broun, servant in Foulefuird, and Janet Sim had Catherine (in
       fornication).
   4, John Coventrie and Janet Walwod had Janet.
   6, David Beatoun, litster, and Isobel Andersone had John.
10, Robert Dewar in Lassodie and Margaret Gib had James.
11, John Small, collier, and Margaret Huggane had Janet.
16, Thomas Moire and Grizel Walwod had Grizel.
16, George Iwatt and Janet Gedde had Patrick.
23, Nicol Huntar and Marion Hutoun had Robert.
25, George Douglas in Craigluscour and Janet Dagleische had Isobel.
25, Andrew Currie and Mause Andersone had James.
27, Thomas Hall and Christian Lambe had Margaret.

M. 11, Andrew Gaw to Margaret Colzeir.
18, John Ramsay to Isobel Walwode.
25, James Crichtoun, brother of Lord Sancheir, to Agnes Gib.
25, Harry Walwod to Helen Kennedie.
25, Robert Drysdell to Grizel Currie.
25, James Ronald to Margaret Mathesone.

MAY.

B. 2, George Hendine and Bessie Bennat had John.
   2, Rob Adame and Magie Douglas had Bessie.
   5, William Curror and Margaret Weitat had John.
   7, John Stevinsone and Janet Moreis had David.
   7, John Forrester and Annabell Lyndsay had Margaret.
   9, John Wricht and Catherine Patoun had John.
   9, Laurie Lugtoun and Janet Bennat had Janet.
11, David Dewar of Lassodie and Jean Logane had John.
14, John Rowane and Marion Cunninghame had . . . . (daughter).
14, Alexander Wilsone and Elspet Michie had Alexander.
14, John Schortus and Janet Bankis had Margaret (in fornication).
14, Robert Barcatt and Christian Aidiesone had Marion.
16, Patrick Lawsone and Margaret Cunninghame had Helen.
18, William Keir and Janet Turnebull had William.
28, Thomas Peirsone and Christian Cant had Bessie.
28, Janet Lessells and James Stevinsone, son of John S. in Knokes, had
       John (in incest).
28, Henry Peirsone and Mawse Gulrige had Henry (in fornication).
28, George Durie and Barbara Barhame had Margaret.

M. 9, George Moreis to Bessie Hutoun.
30, Thomas Nasmith to Bessie Donald.

JUNE.

B. 4, John Lawsone and Janet Nasmyth had Thomas.
       4, William Chattoe and Catherine Kellok had William.
       4, Robert Peirsone and Isobel Galt had Catherine.
       13, Nicol Dewar and Janet Robertsone had Janet.
       25, David Bennie in Urquhart and Bessie Moreis had Alexander.
       27, Robert Murray in Lymkills and Catherine Baird had Alexander.

M. 6, William Lawsone to Effie Waterstoun.
       6, Henry Phinne to Nans Sworde.
       13, Andrew Hutoun, cordiner, to Isobel Wilsone.
       20, Patrick Dewar to Isobell Mastertoun.
       20, John Broun to Elspet Tailyeour.
       27, John Miller to Isobel Miller.

JULY.

B. 2, Malcolm Makqueine and Janet Jonkeine, "bayth Hieland personis,"
          had Patrick.
       2, William Stanehous and Elspet Pirnie had Janet.
       2, Sandy Lugtoun, collier, and Nanse Ramsay had Janet.
       4, Robert Russell and Barbara Elder had John.
       6, Harry Stewart of Baithe and Catherine Kirkcaldie had Margaret.
       7, William Duncane in the Ferrie and Marion Gib had James.
       11, Adam Walwod in Fod and Isobel Walwod had John.
       11, Jamie Huntar, flesher, and Catherine Law had Robert.
       16, William Andersone in Lymkills and Geilie Peirsone had Effie.
       20, David Watsone and Janet Cuthbert had Robert.
       23, Thomas Burne, miller, and Janet Chrstiane had Nanse.
       25, John Peirsone in Pitdinnie and Marion Hutoun had Andrew.
       25, Alexander Hunneman, baker, and Bessie Turnebull had Robert.
       25, Bernard Gib and Helen Hutoun had Nanse (in fornication).
       25, Michael Strange, gardener in Garvock, and Helen Aikine had George.
       26, George Smetoun and Magie Turnebull had George.
       30, John Alisone, mason in the Newra, and Marjory Elder had Andrew.

M. 4, John Crambie to Margaret Crichtoun.
       11, John Makrobie to Margaret Sanders.
       18, Thomas Broun, servant in Foulfuird, to Janet Sim.
       25, Robert Douglas to Margaret Peirsone.
       25, Andrew Andersone to Isobel Kennoquhy.

AUGUST.

B. 6, Robert Quhyt and Catherine Hunnon had John.
       13, George Miller, servant in Pitfirrane, and Helen Makcraiche had John
          (in fornication).
       27, Nicol Wardlaw in Blairaithie and Bessie Hutoun had Margaret.
       31, John Trottar, mealmaker, and Janet Craiche had Bessie.
       31, David Stevinsone and Margaret Cowper had David.

M. 6, Laurence Merser of Melginsh to Sarah Bruse in Baldrige (in the kirk
          of Sauling).
       8, George Donald to Margaret Stevinsone.
       15, Henry Scotland to Catherine Wardlaw.

SEPTEMBER.

B. 3, Robert Michie and Janet Davidsone had James.
       5, Robert Maistertoun of Baithe and Margaret Maistertoun had James.
       10, Thomas Mudie in the Nethertoun and Magie Mill had Harry.
       10, Henry Turnebull and Catherine Cusine had George.
       14, Patrick Murray of Pardowis and Margaret Colvill had Nicolas.

17, William Turnebull and Bessie Cowper had Marjory.
19, James Wardlaw, walker, and Magie Anderson had John (in fornication).
24, George Meldrum and Marjory Walker had Andrew.
24, Archibald Hoge and Margaret Walker had . . . . (son).

M. [*None.*]

OCTOBER.

B. 1, Thomas Nasmithe and Bessie Donald had Margaret.
15, William Gray and Margaret Andersone had Florie.
15, David Drysdell and Isobel Touchie had Andrew.
21, Patrick Bothwell and Barbara Tomesone had twins, Elspet and Margaret (in fornication).
22, Gilbert Turnour and Helen Turnebull had Robert.
22, John Wilsone and Janet Drysdell had Nanse.
24, Peter Law and Margaret Walker had John.
24, Gibbie Car and Helen Inglis had John.
29, James Ronald and Margaret Mathesone had Harry.
29, Alexander Straquhen in Kavillmylne and Catherine Moreis had Robert.
31, Robert Wilsone in Pitdinnie and Margaret Hutoun had . . . . (son).
31, James Wilsone and . . . . had . . . . (son).

M. 15, Harry Balfour of Bolfornocht to Christian Blacater (in the kirk of Carnock).
17, John Broun to Isobel Tomesone.
17, James Beany to Elspet Robertsone.

NOVEMBER.

B. 5, John Moyas and Margaret Christie had . . . . (daughter).
7, Patrick Harrower and Christian Peacok had Janet.
7, Thomas Stevinsone and Bessie Vallange had John.
12, Henry Orock and Margaret Scotland had Margaret.
19, Archibald Hunman and Margaret Wels had Robert.
19, George Cunninghame and Isobel Drysdell had Robert.
21, Thomas Andersone and Alison Drysdell had Janet.
26, Thomas Mudie, weaver, and Effie Beverage had Allan.
28, John Finlasone and Magie Gay had . . . . (son).

M. 7, Andrew Meik to Helen Gibsone.
7, Thomas Cowper to Margaret Robertsone.
21, David Callendar to Margaret Smetoun.
21, Patrick Quhyt to Margaret Phillane.
28, James Dagleishe to Catherine Wardlaw.
28, John Mudie to Catherine Wilsone.
28, John Tomesone to Catherine Wilsone.

DECEMBER.

B. 3, Thomas Tod and Margaret Hutoun had John.
3, John Hastie and Catherine Chalmers had Christian.
3, James Tyrie and Effie Pratus had Bessie (in fornication).
10, Rob Kirk and Grizel Andersone had Margaret.
17, William Walwod, baker, and Bessie Nicole had Catharine.
19, John Walker, merchant, and Margaret Turnebull had . . . . (son).
19, John Andersone and Janet Reid had Robert.
19, John Smetoun and Margaret Andersone had Janet.

M. 5, Thomas Bennat to Grizel Nasmith.
12, Andrew Robertsone to Margaret Young.
12, Laurie Andersone to Margaret Lugtoun.
14, Robert Donaldsone to Helen Hutsone.
28, Andrew Dewar to Margaret Hutoun.

JANUARY [1616].

B.　2, Mr. John Sandilands, advocate in Edinburgh, and Helen Hois had
　　　George (in fornication).
　　7, Thomas Mudie and Margaret Turnebull had Janet.
　　9, Patrick Cowper and Janet Murray had Andrew.
　　9, Andrew Mekiljohne and Janet Andersone had William.
　　12, George Moreis, flesher, and Bessie Hutoun had Janet (died two days
　　　after baptism, being prematurely born).
　　21, Thomas Sands and Margaret Fentoun had Isobel.
　　21, Robert Phillane, maltman, and Helen Cuthbert, had Effie.
　　21, Henry Peirsone and Helen Williamsone had Nanse.
　　24, Mr. Andrew Forrester, minister, and Helen Ramsay had William.
　　30, James Bryse and Christian Young had Helen.
　　30, William Spens and Christian Wallange had Thomas.
　　30, James Hairt and Janet Murie had Robert.
　　30, John Andersone, notary, and Christian Christiesone had twins, David
　　　and Marion.
　　30, Andrew Gaw and Magie Coilyeir had Robert.
　　30, David Watche and Cicile Duncane had twins, James and Patrick.
　　30, John Burne and Jean Murray had Marjory.
　　30, Sandie Beane and . . . . had . . . . (born before the time).
　　30, Robert Murray and Catherine Hutoun had Isobel.

M.　2, John Schortus to Janet Bankis.
　　11, John Davidsone to Marjory Broun.
　　16, Malcolm Cowall to Margaret Bosswell.
　　25, John Mayne (? Magno) to Mawsie Wilsone.

FEBRUARY.

B.　6, William Smart, flesher, and Bessie Mudie had Catherine.
　　6, Henry Donald and Bessie Andersone had Margaret.
　　8, Mr. John Phinne of Quhythill and Margaret Hamiltoun had Margaret.
　　11, John Burne, mason, and Margaret Hutoun had Andrew.
　　11, James Henresone, glazier, and Janet Dewar had James.
　　11, John Lawsone and Margaret Wilson had Isobel.
　　13, David Murray and Grizel Moreis had Elspet.
　　13, John Clerk and Catherine Baid had John.
　　13, Willie Lawsone and Effie Waterstoun had John.
　　15, John Alisone and Grizel Walwod had Catherine.
　　20, Richard Potter, elder, and Bessie Leirmonthe had James.
　　20, John Wricht in Lymkilis and Janet Sibauld had Bessie.
　　25, Charles Ritchiesone and Janet Buist had Janet.
　　28, John Pirhie and Bessie Aissoun had Andrew.

M.　6, James Potter to Marion Walker.
　　20, George Miller to Bessie Lawsone.

MARCH.

B.　3, Robert Peacok and Catherine Stevinsone had Andrew.
　　3, William Rattrey and Janet Speir had Margaret.
　　3, Richard Potter, younger, and Bessie Tomesone had Thomas.
　　11, Ninian Duncane and Margaret Merser had Catharine.
　　11, Thomas Alexander and Janet Kneilands had John.
　　11, Henry Douglas and Helen Wels had Grizel.
　　15, James Chrichtoun, brother german of Lord Sanquhar, and Agnes Gib
　　　had Isobel.
　　17, Andrew Gray and Janet Schortus had Robert (in fornication).
　　17, Mr. William Smyth, schoolmaster, and Marion Dewar had Jean.
　　25, George Andersone and Beatie Stewart had James.

M.　[*None.*]

APRIL.

B. 2, James Mastertoun and Grizel Stewart had Nanse.

4, William Walwod, cordiner, and Magie Lindesay had Bessie.

4, John Andersone, younger, litster, and Margaret Pratus had Margaret.

5, Sir John Henrisone of Fordell and Annas Halkat had Jean.

7, John Watsone and Janet Kennedie had John.

8, Robert Merser, flesher, and Margaret Barhame had Marjory.

9, John Broun, smith, and Margaret Smetoun had Patrick.

14, William Robertsone, weaver in Urquhart, and Janet Litiljohne had Marjory (by testimonial).

16, John Crambie "my Lord Chancelers porter in the Abay of Dunfermling," and Margaret Chrichtoun had Alexander.

18, David Tod and Janet Aidiesone had Janet.

24, John Broun and Elspet Tailyeour had Nanse.

28, James Aissoun and Katherine Watson had Catherine.

30, Henry Phinne and Nanse Sword had Thomas.

M. 29, Alexander Gowie to Bessie Stevinsone.

> *Note.*—"Mr. Robert Roche, minister of Innerkething, wes then minister also of Rossyithe, by annexatioun of Rossythe to Innerkething untill ane competent stipend suld be provydit to minister therat."

MAY.

B. 5, John Donaldson, horner, and Helen Stevinson had Beatrix.

7, James Cunninghame in Sillitoun and Isobel Cunninghame had William.

14, James Dewar and Grizel Hoy had Marie.

19, Andrew Hutoun, cordiner, and Isobel Wilson had David.

21, George Mill and Bessie Burne had Isobel.

22, Robert Wilsone and Christian Simrawell had Janet.

28, Harry Walwod, land officer, and Helen Kennedie had Lilias.

M. 7, Andrew Dewar to Helen Stanehous.

7, Laurence Warkman to Isobel Neifing.

12, David Goodell to Janet Walker.

14, Henry Greine to Christian Peirsone.

14, Andrew Colzeir to Isobel Andersone.

28, James Hamiltoun to Margaret Quhyt.

JUNE.

B. 2, Henry Scotland and Catherine Wardlaw had James.

2, James Cowsteoun and Janet Dagleische had William.

4, Mr. Robert Tomesone and Christian Clerk had Robert.

9, James Wilsone and Janet Walkar had . . . . (daughter).

23, Robert Cunninghame in Urquhart and Helen Wilson had Robert (testimonial from Mr. Robert Roche).

30, William Curror and Margaret Weitat had Elizabeth.

30, Robert Dempster and Jean Givenn (of Edinburgh) had James (in fornication).

30, Cuthbert Wardlaw and Margaret Galrig had Catherine.

M. 25, Thomas Phinne to Barbara Baid.

25, David Ratra to Margaret Gib.

JULY.

B. 2, Robert Stirk, messenger, and Nansie Car had James.

9, John Lawsone, smith, and Janet Donald had Thomas.

19, Robert Lambe and Helen Bairdner had Grizel.

19, David Sempill and Janet Mudie had David.

22, David Laurie and Marion Blair had Margaret.

22, Mr. Thomas Wardlaw, provost, and Catherine Alisone had Margaret.
28, William Orrock and Catherine Maxwell had Catherine.
28, Richard Scotland and Margaret Blakwod had Helen.
28, Thomas Hutoun and Margaret Lindsay had Isobel.
30, Thomas Ritchie in Pitravie and Margaret Andersone had Robert.
30, George Donald, miller, and Margaret Stevinsone had Thomas.

M. 2, William Cadzane to Bessie Hutoun.
23, John Stevinson to Janet Andersone.
30, John Andersone to Helen Kingorne.

AUGUST.

B. 6, John Alisone and Marjory Elder had James ; witnesses, Andrew Alisone and James Alisone, brothers of John and James Alisone, burgh officer.
13, James Makcalzeone, miller, and Margaret Awstiane had James (in fornication) ; witnesses, Alexander Hunieman, baker, Robert Ramsay in Inverkeithing, and John Awstiane, miller.
18, Adam Stobie, portioner of Luscour, and Helen Gibbone had Margaret.

M. 13, Robert Peirsone to Marjory Peirsone.
13, Robert Pringle to Marjory Brand.
27, William Touche to Christian Cuninghame.

Note.—"The 6 day of August 1616 Mr. Johne Murray wes planted minister of Dunfermling."

SEPTEMBER.

B. 1, Thomas Bennatie and Grizel Nasmithe had Isobel.
1, William Mudie and Margaret Aidiesone had Andrew (born 27th August).
1, David Barklay and Christian Murie had John.
8, Andrew Young and Elspet Fuird had Grizel.
8, James Oiswald and Bessie Cowsteoun had John.
8, James Lambe and Janet Bairdner had William.
8, John Hyslope and Janet Laichlands had William.
15, David Stevinsone and Elspet Christie had William.
15, Edmond Alisone and Effie Crambie had John.
15, David Callendar and Margaret Smetoun had Janet.
22, John Merschell, miller in Touch Mill, and Margaret Fuird had William.
22, Thomas Mitchell, younger, and Margaret Dick had Janet.
29, Andrew Turnebull in Grange and Helen Currie had George.
29, Patrick Quhyt and Margaret Phillane had Robert.
29, Alexander Donald and Margaret Dagleische had John.
29, Willie Culane and Bessie Hutoun had Barbara.

M. [*None.*]

OCTOBER.

B. 6, John Dewar in Pitbachlie and Isobel Moreis had Barbara.
6, John Kellok in Lassodymill and Christian Pringle had Elspet.
6, Charles Baid and Helen Young had Andrew.
13, Robert Keir and Isobel Hendine had Margaret.
13, John Peirsone in Wester Pitdinne and Marion Hutoun had John.
13, Thomas Thomesone and Margaret Moreis had Janet.
13, James Trottar and Bessie Lawsoun had William.
16, John Simsone, cordiner, and Bessie Hutoun had Helen.
20, Robert Douglas and Margaret Peirsone had Robert.
27, William Brown in Knokes and Bessie Smetoun had Bessie.
27, George Dewar in Lathamond and Jean Hutoun had Elspet.
27, William Sibauld and Isobel Lindesay had Janet.

M. 24, James Drysdell to Isobel Westwod.
29, John Wilsone to Isobel Wilsone (at Culross kirk).

[*Deleted*, John Wilson having taken fever during the night which hindered his marriage on the morn.]

29, James Wallace to Alison Legat (at Carnock kirk).

NOVEMBER.

B. 3, John Hutoun in Pitdinnie and Helen Stanehous had Margaret.

3, James Litlejohne and Helen Schortus had Catherine.

10, Andrew Horne and Bessie Anghous had Janet.

24, John Birrell and Margaret Colyeir had Jean.

24, John Makmirrie and Bessie Williamesone had Helen.

24, John Andersone and Janet Meldrum had Andrew.

27, Charles Tailyeour and Marion Tod had John.

M. 5 (*sic*), Thomas Davidsone to Rachel Douglas.

3, John Wilson to Isobel Wilsone (in Culross kirk).

7, Williame Thomesone to Janet Mekiljon.

19, George Kinkad to Margaret Thomesone.

19, John Davidsone to Margaret Henresone.

DECEMBER.

B. 1, John Watsone and Marjory Smetoun had Robert.

1, Jerome Broun in Luscour and Margaret Dalgleishe had Robert (baptized at Carnock).

4, James Kinsman and Christian Walwod had Helen.

8, George Miller and Bessie Lawsone had Robert.

8, Adam Hendine and Margaret Greive had Janet.

17, John Thomesone and Emily Cumming had David.

22, Archibald Hoge and Margaret Walker had John.

24, James Quhyt and Helen Hutsone had Thomas.

31, John Schortus and Janet Bankis had William.

31, George Walker, merchant, and Marjory Cuthbert had Catherine.

M. 10, John Bennat to Janet Gregge.

10, William Kennedie to Catherine Huggoun.

17, John Cumming to Janet Workman.

24, James Murray to Margaret Reid.

24, John Wels to Christian Awstiane.

31, John Kynneer (? Kynneel) to Janet Philpe.

JANUARY [161].

B. 12, William Rae and Janet Henresone had Janet.

12, John Thomesone and Catherine Wilson had Margaret.

12, Robert Wilsone and Catherine Meldrum had Geils (in fornication).

19, Andrew Gaw and Margaret Colzeir had Edward.

19, William Walwod of Touche and Agnes Alexander had . . . .

21, Patrick Cowper and Janet Murray had James.

26, James Moyas and Janet Stewart had Andrew.

M. 7, Andrew Gray to Janet Peacok (both of Dalmeny parish, "and having ther brydell on this syid of the water becaus of ther friends on this syid also").

28, Laurie Andersone to Jean Hutoun.

FEBRUARY.

B. 2, John Rowane and Marion Cunninghame had . . . . (son).

2, Andrew Andersone and Janet Touchie had Isobel.

2, John Andersone in Kistock and Janet Nicole had William.

9, William Cusine and Elspet Hutchiesone had Helen.

9, James Hutoun and Catherine Walwod had Janet.

9, Henry Chaipe and Janet Young had William (in fornication).

16, Robert Wilsone and Margaret Hutoun had Helen.

16, Alexander Beane, weaver, and Helen Hutoun had William.
23, James Kellok and Margaret Mudie had John.
23, Robert Scotland in Clune and Helen Stobie had Thomas.
27, James Potter and Marion Walker had James.

M. [*None.*]

MARCH.

B. 9, John Andersone and Janet Reid had Margaret.
9, William Low and Nanse Gib had James.
9, James Hamiltoun and Margaret Quhyt had Thomas.
23, Andrew Colyeir, drummer, and Isobel Andersone had John.
23, Alexander Gowie and Bessie Stevinsone had Jean.
23, James Caddell and Beatie Peirsone had David.
23, David Beatoun, litster, and Isobel Andersone had William.
23, Nicol Dewar and Janet Andersone had Robert.
30, John Walker, merchant, and Margaret Turnebull had Peter.
30, Thomas Walwod and Bessie Kirk had Thomas.

M. [*None.*]

APRIL.

B. 1, George Douglas and Janet Dagleische had . . . . (son baptised in Carnock kirk, too weak to carry to Dunfermline).
6, Thomas Sands and Margaret Fentoun had James.
6, William Thomesone, litster, and Janet Mekiljohne had Bessie.
6, David Car and Catherine Elder had Barbara.
8, David Ratraw and Margaret Gib had . . . . (son).
8, Andrew Currie in Primrois and Mawse Andersone had John.
13, Gilbert Turnour in Pitlivar and Helen Turnbull had Janet.
15, Andrew Cunninghame in Primrois and Margaret Turnebull had Marjory.
20, Robert Pringle, collier in Beath heugh, "ane mere ignorant," and Marjory Brand had Christian.
20, William Henresone, cordiner, and Bessie Forsythe had Catharine.
27, Robert Bakcais and Lucrece Norie had Janet.
29, Alexander Bartrome and Isobel Broun had John.
29, Andrew Walker in the Hule and Janet Hutoun had Margaret.

M. 29, David Broun to Isobel Mayne.

MAY.

B. 6, John Miller and Isobel Miller had Janet.
11, James Wallace and Alison Legat had William.
20, Robert Stanehous and Isobel Cunninghame had Robert.
25, John Andersone, younger, litster, and Helen Kingorne had Walter.

M. 20, John Cunninghame to Margaret Swentoun.

JUNE.

B. 1, Robert Huggone, mealmaker, and Janet Smetoun had Marjory.
8, James Drysdell and Isobel Westwod had John.
22, James Lethome and Isobel Makbayth had Marjory.
22, John Wricht, collier, and Catherine Patoun had Margaret.
22, James Hutoun, baker, and Marjory Walwod had Margaret.
24, John Stevenson of Beath and Janet Moreis had Henry (baptised at Ballingry kirk).
24, William Stanehous in Fod and Elspet Pirnie had Christian.
29, Henry Hardie and Margaret Home had Christian.
29, William Broun, clerk, and Grizel Cuthbert had Margaret.

M. 3, James Moorgan to Isobel Bowman (test. from Aberdour).
10, John Peirsone to Janet Thomesone.
24, John Young to Janet Brown.

24, Walter Rae to Janet Quhyt.
24, John Inglis to Nanse Hutoun.

JULY.

B. 6, William Kellok and Margaret Kellok had Christian.
6, William Horne and Helen Andersone had Thomas.
6, Clement Sanders and Elspet Sanders had Margaret.
6, John Aidiesone, miller, and Beatrix Turnebull had James.
20, Robert Russell, miller, and Barbara Elder had Jean.
20, John Baid, weaver, and Bessie Spens had Thomas.
20, William Sanders and Christian Hutoun had John (in fornication).
20, George Ivatt and Janet Gedde had Margaret.
20, Gavin Stanehous and Marjory Nicole had Isobel.

M. 1, Andrew Turnbull to Catherine Anderson.
1, William Westwod to Margaret Forrester.
1, Thomas Harrower to Margaret Gairdner.
8, William Crawfoord to Janet Moreis.
8, James Hall to Margaret Andersone.
15, John Law to Nicolas Andersone.
15, John Raff to Janet Greive.

AUGUST.

B. 3, John Hutoun and Janet Christie had Bessie (in fornication).
3, Archibald Mowtrey and Catherine Bardner had James.
5, John Harlay and Elspet Maknariche had Isobel.
10, Alexander Davidson and Janet Douglas had Thomas.
10, John Moyas and Margaret Christie had Isobel.
12, David Dewar of Lassodie and Jean Logane had Margaret.
12, William Buist and Helen Turnebull had Margaret.
12, George Walker, cadger, and Janet Hois had Janet.
12, James Buist and Janet Danzell had James.
17, John Walker and Jean Maxwell had Grizel.
19, Robert Peirsone in Nether Beath and Marjory Peirson had Margaret.
26, Robert Currie and Catherine Makcalzeoun had Christian.
31, Patrick Dewar and Isobel Maistertoun had . . . . (daughter).

M. 5, Patrick Bruse to Catherine Dowie.
12, David Cunnon (?) to Elspet Dewar.
12, John Hutoun to Catherine Buchanan.
12, James Kellok to Jean Gibson.
19, James Tosheauch to Janet Burne.

SEPTEMBER.

B. 2, Adam Patoun and Marjory Phillane had John.
2, George Fergussoun, servitour to the Chancellor, and Janet Peirsone had twins, Eupham and Barbara.
2, Patrick Murray and Margaret Colvill had Jean.
7, David Scotland in Gask and Janet Aikine had Bessie.
7, David Peirsone, merchant, and Jean Stanehous had George.
9, James Ronald and Margaret Mathesone had Robert.
9, Henry Scotland and Catherine Wardlaw had Robert.
21, Thomas Rodger and Grizel Westwod had John.
28, Thomas Blakie and Margaret Law had . . . . (daughter) (baptised at Crumbie).

M. 28, Nicol Cornuell to Elspet Duncane (in Crumbie kirk).

OCTOBER.

B. 5, William Murie and Catherine Cunninghame had John.
5, David Peirsone, younger, in Pitdinnie, and Bessie Peirsone had Margaret

5, John Kinloche, miller, and Bessie Sim had Robert.
5, Thomas Phinne, weaver, and Barbara Baid had Christian.
5, James Dagleische and Catherine Wardlaw had Janet.
5, John Alisone, mason, and Marjory Elder had John.
7, Laurence Neilsone and Helen Reid had Janet (in fornication).
12, Florence Andersone and Helen Cunninghame had David.
12, Laurence Workman and Isobel Neifing had Isobel.
12, James Aissoun and Catherine Watsone had Helen.
19, William Walwod in Nether Beath and Margaret Peirsone had **Harry**.
19, George Donald and Margaret Stevinsone had Andrew.
26, Thomas Young and Isobel Sanders had John.
26, George Williamsone and Eupham Thomesone had David.
26, Pate Davidsone, collier, and Janet Thomesone had Henry.
26, Robert Phillane (deceased) and Helen Cuthbert had **Margaret** (posthumous).
28, Mr John Phinne of Quhythill and Margaret Hamilton had John.

M. 7, Mark Kinglassie to Catherine Mudie.

NOVEMBER.

B. 2, Alexander Grege and Catherine Philpe had . . . . (son) in fornication.
2, Robert Murray, miller, and Agnes Tailyeour had Bessie.
2, Willie Moreis and Janet Henresone had William.
4, David Christie and Annabel Bardner had Andrew.
9, John Wels, cordiner, and Christian Awstiane had Robert.
12, William Cagzeoun and Bessie Hutoun had Elizabeth (mother died).
16, George Imrie and Margaret Stevinsone had William.
18, John Logane and Margaret Galt had William.
18, James Westwod and Isobel Cunninghame had Robert.
23, William Duncane and Marion Gib had William.
23, Edward Douglas, younger, in Wester Gellat, and Janet Miller had Thomas (in fornication).
25, Patrick Bruse and Catherine Dowie had Janet.
30, Laurence Andersone and Margaret Lugtoun had Margaret (baptised at Crumbie).
30, Thomas Hall, weaver, and Christian Lambe had Patrick.

M. 25, William Hutoun to Catherine Mill.

DECEMBER.

B. 7, John Davidsone, collier, and Agnes Brown had Christian (baptised at Cleish, "becaus of the farre distance from our kirk, and the evill wether and way").
9, Sir Robert Halkat of Pitfirrane and Dame Margaret Murray had Robert.
14, Peter Law, merchant, and Margaret Walker had Andrew; witnesses, Andrew Law, his brother, Andrew Wricht, and George Walker, merchant.
14, William Culane and Bessie Hutoun had Elizabeth.
21, William Wricht and Jean Cambell had Janet.
28, John Douglas and Rosina Oiswald had James.
30, Adam Douglas and Helen Hutoun had David.
30, James Lugtoun and Margaret Nasmithe had Henry.

M. 2, Alexander Greig to Catherine Philpe.
2, Thomas Clun to Christian Sanders (on test. from Inverkeithing).
23, John Mayne to Janet Walker.
30, Henry Christie to Elspet Balfour.
30, Laurence Stevinsone to Catherine Chattoe.

JANUARY [1618].

B. 4, Henry Orock and Margaret Scotland had Mary.
4, John Wilson and Janet Drysdell had Robert.

4, John Burne, mason, and Margaret Hutoun had John.
4, Henry Turnbull and Catherine Cusine had Patrick.
6, Richard Scotland and Margaret Blakwod had John.
11, John Cunninghame and Margaret Swentoun had John.
11, James Rutherfuird and Rosina Walwod had Bessie (in fornication).
13, Harry Stewart of Beath and Catherine Kirkcaldie had Elspet.
18, Alexander Balfour and Bessie Dewar had Agnes (in fornication).
20, Duncan Tailyeour and Margaret Hutoun had William.
20, James Murray, writer, and Margaret Reid had Bessie.
23, James Potter and Bessie Reid had James.
27, James Wilsone and Janet Walker had Ninian.
27, Andrew Dewar and Helen Stanehous had William.
27, Henry Peirsone and Helen Williamesone had John.
27, Andrew Inglis, younger, and Margaret Duncane had Marjory (in fornication).
27, William Rae and Janet Orock had Isobel.
27, Robert Dewar of Beath and Margaret Gib had John.

M. 6, John Hutoun to Janet Christie.
6, William Philpe to Elspet Lindsay (in Carnock kirk).
20, John Murray to Margaret Blair.
27, Henry Phinne to Catherine Garvie.

FEBRUARY.

B. 1, Robert Douglas and Margaret Peirsone had Henry.
1, Henry Merschell and Bessie Turnbull had William.
1, George Moreis and Bessie Hutoun had Christian.
1, James Hutoun and Marion Mill had Laurence (in fornication).
3, Charles Ritchardsone and Janet Buist had James.
3, Sir John Henresone (deceased) and Annas Halket had James (posthumous).
3, Andrew Touche, fishmonger, and Catherine Fyiff had Janet.
5, Alexander Straquhen and Catherine Duchall had Isobel.
8, William Sanders and Marion Mastertoun had George.
8, James Chrichtoun and Nanse Gib had William.
10, Thomas Huggoun and Margaret Kirk had James (in fornication).
15, John Davidsone and Margaret Henresone had David.
15, Andrew Hutoun and Isobel Wilsone had William.
15, George Cunninghame and Isobel Drysdell had William.
17, Andrew Mekiljohne and Janet Andersone had Alison.
22, Thomas Mudie and Margaret Turnebull had James.
22, Adam Stobie, portioner of Wester Luscour, and Helen Gibbone had Patrick.

M. 3, Alexander Grahame to Effie Levingstoun.
3, Laurence Mill to Margaret Hoy (?)
10, Thomas Dow to Janet Davidson.
10, Thomas Sword to Margaret Brand.
17, Thomas Dewar to Margaret Maistertoun.

MARCH.

B. 3, John Kinnell and Janet Philpe had Harry.
8, James Robertsone and Margaret Brand had John.
8, Archibald Hodge and Margaret Walker had Robert.
15, John Peirsone in Pitdinnie and Marion Hutoun had Robert.
15, John Wels and Catherine Drummond had Grizel.
15, Allan Galrig and Janet Currie had Grizel.
15, James Orock in Foulfuird and Christian Rowan had . . . (son).
15, Laurence Lugtoun and Janet Bennat had . . . (daughter) (baptized at Inverkeithing).
15, Laurence Andersoun and Jean Hutoun had David.

15, John Clerk and Catherine Baid had David.
19, William Thomesone, litster, and Janet Mekiljohne had Janet.
22, Richard Bardner and Margaret Fothringhame had Bessie.
22, John Donaldsone (deceased) and Helen Stevinson had John (posthumous).
22, John Inglis and Nanse Hutoun had Isobel.
22, Thomas Nasmithe and Bessie Donald had Nanse.
22, James Tyrie and Isobel Inglis had Janet (in fornication).
24, Nicol Kellok and Janet Robertsone had Marion.
24, Thomas Harrower and Margaret Gairdner had [James baptised]. The child died after being "inbuikit" before the baptism, "and wes unbaptized."
24, Alexander Honyman and Bessie Turnbull had Bessie.
29, George Meldrum and Marjory Walker had Isobel.
29, John Anderson, notary, and Christian Christiesone had Andrew.

M. 10, Alaster Balfour, collier, to Bessie Dewar.

APRIL.

B. 5, George Hendine and Bessie Bennat had Margaret.
7, Thomas Donaldsone and Margaret Wilsone had Janet.
7, John Small, collier, and Margaret Huggone had Isobel; witnesses, Charles Ritchardson, Andrew Walker, Duncan Tailyour.
7, John Dow, Highlandman, and Margaret Merser had . . . . (daughter) in fornication; witnesses, James Huntar, John Crambie, Nicol Cornwell.
7, David Strang (deceased) and Margaret Sibauld had Helen (posthumous): witnesses, David Strang, cordiner, James Car, William Low.
7, John Lawsone and Janet Nasmithe had Effie; witnesses, Henry Turnbull, William Turnebull, John Hislop.
9, John Lawsoun, "ane vagabond traveling in this paroche," and Marion Thomsone, his wife, had John.
19, James Henresone and Janet Dewar had Marjory; witnesses, John Bennat, Gilbert Blair, William Stanehous.
21, George Walker, merchant, and Marjory Cuthbert had James; witnesses, Mr. James Sibauld, schoolmaster, Andrew Gibbon, James Reid, younger, and James Murray.
26, David Beany and Bessie Moreis had Andrew (on testimonial from minister of Rosyth and Inverkeithing).
28, David Broun in Blaklaw and Isobel Mayne had Margaret; witnesses, William Broun in the Stane, David Burne, Andrew Mayne.
28, Henry Donald and Bessie Andersone had Mark; witnesses, Mark Donald, Adam Wilsone, Patrick Greif.
28, James Stewart, son of Patrick S. of Beath, and Marion Clunie had Harry (in fornication; baptised at desire of kirk session of Edinburgh upon testimonial of satisfaction).
28, David Stewart, brother of said James S., and Janet Mitchell had David (in fornication).
28, David Goodell and Janet Walker had Laurence; witnesses, Laurence Walker, Peter Law, John Walker.

M. 14, Henry Simsone to Bessie Thomsone.
21, William Edward to Janet Douglas.
28, John Kay to Grizel Inglis.

MAY.

B. 3, David Robertson of Easter Craigduckie and Grizel Hutoun had . . . . (daughter); witnesses, George Dewar, Nicol Dewar, Alexander Burne, "the tua last his brethren in law."
5, James Turnebull and Barbara Thomson had Andrew (in fornication); witnesses, Thomas Walker, William Turnbull, George Turnbull, younger.

5, Robert Maistertoun of Beath and Margaret Maistertoun had Bessie ; witnesses, John Anderson, elder, John Anderson, younger, his son, and Mr. James Durie.

5, James Hall and Margaret Andersone had Thomas ; witnesses, William Chatto, Harry Mudie, Thomas Stevenson.

12, Patrick Cowper and Janet Murray had Eupham.

27, David Walker and Grizel Meldrum had Richard.

27, Willie Philpe and Elspet Lindsay had Margaret.

31, Thomas Moir and Grizel Walwod had David ; witnesses, David Strang, cordiner, David Walwod, his brother in law, William Wilson, miller.

31, Thomas Tod and Margaret Hutoun had James ; witnesses, James Reid, younger, Thomas Scotland, Adam Stirk.

31, Patrick Lawsone and Margaret Cunningham had John.

M. 5, James Lambe to Janet Lindsay.

12, John Raithe to Janet Tyrie.

19, Alexander Burne to Isobel Robertson.

JUNE.

B. 2, John Burne, younger, and Jean Murray had . . . . (daughter) ; witnesses, Andrew Currie, Andrew Turnbull, William Mastertoun.

2, William Gray and Margaret Andersone had . . . . (son).

5, William Anderson in Lymkills and Geils Peirsone had Elspet ; witnesses, David Peirsone, George Fergusson, Florence Brown.

7, David Cunnoun in Mastertoun and Elspet Dewar had James.

14, Alexander Grahame and Effie Levingstoun had Catherine ; witnesses, Andrew Turnbull in Bromehall, James Phun and George Aidiesone.

14, John Law and Nicolas Anderson had John ; witnesses, John Davidson, John Anderson, John Culros.

14, Robert Balcas and Lucrece Norie had Marion ; witnesses, Henry Greine, Thomas Dewar, John Dick.

14, James Potter and Marion Walker had Christian ; witnesses, Richard Potter, Andrew Potter, James Hutoun.

21, John Hutoun, smith, and Catherine Buchanan had Isobel.

21, Andrew Greinehorne and Marjory Wilsone had John.

21, John Brown, smith, and Margaret Smetoun had James.

21, Robert Adame and Margaret Douglas had Robert ; witnesses, Robert Stirk, John Mayne, William Thomeson.

30, James Murgane and Elspet Bowman had William ; witnesses, Jerome Broun, Andrew Walker, Thomas Walker.

M. 2, James Lindsay to Nanse Menteithe.

2, Robert Westwod to Janet Garvock.

9, James Miller to Christian Mowtrey.

16, Finlay Moyle to Bessie Stevin.

30, John Spens to Janet Cunningham.

30, John Anderson to Grizel Hoge.

JULY.

B. 2, John Alison and Grizel Walwod had James ; witnesses, James Alison, his brother, David Laurie and John Wels.

3, Laurie Stevenson and Catherine Chatto had Laurence ; witnesses, Patrick Cowper, Adam Stevinson, William Turnbull.

5, Thomas Dewar and Margaret Maistertoun had James ; witnesses, Nicol Wardlaw, James Scotland, Robert Russell.

5, John Cumming and Janet Workman had . . . . (son) ; witnesses, Thomas Mitchell, elder and younger, and David Phillane.

5, John Trottar and Janet Craik had Isobel ; witnesses, James Reid, John Dougall, Adam Lugtoun.

14, John Wricht and Janet Sibauld had Helen ; witnesses, Andrew Turnbull, Andrew Currie, John Levingstoun.

19, Wattie Rae and Janet Quhyt had Christian ; witnesses, William Rae, William Spens, James Potter.

19, James Wilsone and Janet Gibsone had Adam ; witnesses, Adam Mastertoun, James Kellok, James Roxburghe.

28, William Cunninghame and Janet Alisone had Helen ; witnesses, William Turnbull, John Alison, Thomas Mudie.

M. 7, William Dewar to Isobel Clerk.

7, Patrick Mowtrey to Helen Cunninghame.

7, John Tyrie to Helen Schaw.

21, David Burne to Marjory Walker.

AUGUST.

B. 5, David Callendar and Margaret Smetoun had Marjory ; witnesses, David Cunninghame, Andrew Currie, Alexander Lambe.

9, David Watche and Cicile Duncane had Marjory ; witnesses, William Sim, Thomas Horne, James Smetoun.

11, Jean Pratus, daughter to William P., had Jean baptised (presented by James Kingorne), begotten in fornication and father not compearing.

11, Thomas Stevenson and Janet Keir had Janet baptised (presented by Richard Law, being begotten in fornication and father fugitive from discipline).

16, John Wilsone and Janet Tod had Thomas (baptised at Crombie).

18, David Tod and Janet Dagleische had Bessie ; witnesses, Robert Scotland, Richard Templeman.

M. 11, John Anderson to Martha Mastertoun.

11, Patrick Allane to Janet Moreis.

18, Andrew Ferlie to Alison Anderson.

18, Peter Douglas to Christian Smythe.

SEPTEMBER.

B. 6, Adam Walwod and Isobel Walwod had Janet (baptised at Inverkeithing).

6, John Stirk, weaver, and Janet Meldrum had Isobel (baptised at Carnock).

13, Henry Scotland and Catherine Wardlaw had Janet ; witnesses, David Scotland, Robert Anghous, Robert Russell.

13, Robert Kirk and Grizel Andersone had John ; witnesses, Robert Andersone, John Andersone, John Rowane.

13, Robert Stirk, messenger, and Nanse Car had William ; witnesses, Mr. Thomas Wardlaw, Robert Crawfurd, Henry (?) Douglas in Aberdour.

17, John Waldgie, master cook to the Lord Chancellor, and Janet Mowbrey had Grizel ; witnesses, James Gib, George Fergusson, Thomas Drysdell.

20, William Darleine, miller, and Isobel Keltie had Bessie ; witnesses, James Allane and David Burne.

20, William Smithe in Fod and Margaret Mastertoun had William ; witnesses, William Stanehous and William Walwod.

27, James Kellok and Jean Gibsone had Nanse ; witnesses, Nicol Dewar, William Kellok, Henry Gibsone.

M. 8, John Donaldson to Christian Westwod (in Cleish kirk).

29, Archibald Mowtray to Bessie Young.

OCTOBER.

B. 4, Robert Drysdell, weaver, and Grizel Currie had Alexander ; witnesses, Alexander Chalmers, Allan Galrige, George Drysdell.

4, George Mill and Bessie Burne had John ; witnesses, John Gib and James Gib, his son.

4, John Watsone, cordiner, and Marjory Smetoun had Janet ; witnesses, John Simson, David Callendar, Alexander Honyman.

4, William Brown, notary public, and Grizel Cuthbert had Agnes ; witnesses, John Gib. James Chrichton, Mr. Thomas Wardlaw.

4, Henry Douglas and Helen Wels had Archibald ; witnesses, Archibald Douglas, Edward Douglas, Thomas Mitchell, younger.

11, David Drysdell and Isobel Touchie had James ; witnesses. Patrick Anderson, James Sanders, James Anderson.

11, Archibald Mowtrey and Bessie Young had Andrew ; witnesses, William Anderson, Andrew Young in Lymkills, John Stevenson, younger, in Pitlivar.

13, James Cuninghame and Isobel Cuninghame had David ; witnesses, David Cunningham, Robert Cunningham, Adam Wilson.

13, Thomas Robertson and Janet Harrower had Janet ; witnesses, John Turnbull, Walter Tailyeour, William Pillons.

13, Edward Wood, gardner, and Catherine Hill had Margaret ; witnesses, Robert Quhyt and Robert Andersone.

18, Malcolm Makqueine and Janet Jonkeine had . . . . (daughter) ; witnesses, Abraham Grege, Adam Anderson, Harry Mudie.

25, William Dewar and Isobel Clerk had Isobel ; witnesses, David Cunnun, Thomas Mudie.

25, Nicol Broun, collier in Lassodie, and Mawse Spittell had David ; witnesses, David Dewar, Thomas Horne, William Mackie.

25, Robe Quhyt and Catherine Hunnon had Martha ; witnesses, John Anderson, younger, John and Thomas Dow, colliers.

25, George Davidson and Christian Bull had Robert ; witnesses, Archibald Douglas, Robert Anderson, Robert Alison, mason.

25, John Dowie, flesher, and Margaret Henresone had David (baptised at Cleish.)

M. 6, Andrew Inglis to Margaret Duncane.

13, John Gotterstanes to Isobel Mackie.

NOVEMBER.

B. 1, William Turnbull and Bessie Cowper had . . . . (son).

1, William Hutoun and Catherine Mill had John ; witnesses, John Dick, William Kirk, John Cusine.

1, William Turnbull and Margaret Law had Margaret ; witnesses, Patrick Cowper, Peter Law, George Fergusson.

1, Harry Walwod and Helen Kennedy had John ; witnesses, John Walwod, his brother, John Car, John Andersone.

10, Nicol Huntar and Marion Hutoun had Isobel ; witnesses, Andrew Walker, John Banks, Robert Cunninghame.

15, William Spens and Christian Wallange had Henry ; witnesses, Henry Wilson, Henry Turnbull, Henry Meldrum.

15, William Lawsone and Effie Waterstoun had Elspet ; witnesses, William Horne, John Smith, John Clerk.

15, James Lindsay and Nanse Mentethe had John ; witnesses, John Anderson, elder, and Andrew Meiklejohn.

22, Laurie Patrik and Margaret Reid had James ; witnesses, James Reid, John Simsone, Robert Anderson.

29, Gilbert Turnour and Helen Turnbull had Nanse : witnesses, Andrew Stevenson, George Lugtoun, Laurie Anderson.

29, John Baid and Bessie Spens had John ; witnesses, William Stanchous, William Chatto, Mr. John Walker, reader of God's word.

29, Thomas Mudie and Margaret Mill had Margaret.

M. 3, Archibald Boyd to Janet Watsone.

10, John Elder to Bessie Blakwod.

10, Henry Gibsone to Margaret Rentoun.

17, Henry Chaipe to Janet Young.

DECEMBER.

B. 1, James Cunnon in Mastertoun and Janet Stanchous had Isobel ; witnesses, Thomas Ritchie, James Mudie, Robert Kellok, younger.

1, John Hislope and Janet Lachlands had Nanse.

3, Malcolm Kowall, smith, and Margaret Bosswell had Christian ; witnesses, James Hutoun, James Thomesone, Adam Schortus.

6, Jerome Brown in Luscour and Margaret Dagleishe had John (baptised in Carnok).

8, Thomas Mitchell, younger, and Margaret Dick had Margaret ; witnesses, Andrew Mitchell, John Burne, elder.

8, John Lawsone in Crocefuird and Margaret Wilsone had Margaret ; witnesses, George Walker, bailie, David Peirsone in Pitdinnie.

8, David Lambe and Marjory Wilsone had William (in fornication) ; witnesses, James Wilson, William Wilson, her father and her brother, John Car.

20, Henry Simsone aud Bessie Thomesone had Janet ; witnesses, John Thomesone, Duncan Tailyior, John Small.

20, Robert Russell and Barbara Elder had Edward ; witnesses, Edward Elder, David Scotland.

22, John Wardlaw and Margaret Baid had Martha ; witnesses, John Anderson, younger, John Anderson, youngest, Andrew Mekiljohne.

M. 1, John Dougall to Bessie Craik.

29, David Smithe to Alisone Simesone.

JANUARY [1619].

B. 5, John Birrell and Margaret Colyeir had Catherine ; witnesses, Patrick Bothwell, James Cunnon, James Marteine in Inverkeithing.

5, John Crambie and Magie Crichtoun had William.

10, James Hairt and Janet Murie had James ; witnesses, James Kellok, James Cunnon, Thomas Mudie.

12, George Dewar in Lathamond and Jean Hutoun had Margaret ; witnesses, David Dewar of Lassodie, and David Robertson of Craigduckie.

12, John Andersone and Janet Meldrum had Janet.

17, William Ratrae and Janet Speir had Elspet ; witnesses, David Moreis, William Currour, John Keir.

17, John Walker and Margaret Turnbull had Andrew ; witnesses, Andrew Law, Peter Law, his brother, and George Walker.

19, Charles Baid and Helen Young had Margaret ; witnesses, Patrick Andersone, Laurence Anderson.

24, John Stevinsone and Janet Fuird had James (in fornication) ; witnesses, James Primrose, Mr. James Primrose, his son, and James Cois in Galrighill.

24, Andrew Gaw and Margaret Coilyeir had William ; witnesses, David Laurie, John Aidie, James Hutoun.

24, John Anderson, younger, and Helen Kingorne had Jean.

26, David Christie and Annabell Bardner had Helen ; witnesses, John Walker, John Anderson, elder, Peter Law.

31, William Rae and Janet Henresone had James ; witnesses, James Cunnon, James Henresone, John Davidsone.

31, John Levingstoun and Janet Smetoun had Margaret ; witnesses, Harry Young, James Boyle, John Tod.

31, John Greif and Janet Robertsone (a vagabond) had a son Nicol (in fornication).

31, Patrick Mowtrey and Christian Inglis had Christian (in fornication) ; witnesses, John Thomeson, James Miller.

31, John Bull and Janet Gibsone had Adam ; witnesses, Adam Stevenson, Patrick Mowtrey, David Bull.

31, Thomas Phinne and Barbara Baid had Isobel ; witnesses, David Williamson, John Gotterstoun, John Clerk.

M. 12, Andrew Lindsay to Marjory Walker.

19, David Aidieson to Isobel Simsone (testimonial from Inverkeithing).

26, David Dewar to Marion Harrower.

FEBRUARY.

B. 7, William Smart and Bessie Mudie had John ; witnesses, Robert May, John Thomson, Thomas Elder.

7, John Makbethe and Marjory Thomson had John (in adultery) ; witnesses, William and George Turnbull, John Banks.

11, Mr. Thomas Wardlaw and Catherine Alisone had Catherine ; witnesses, John Gib, Mr. James Sibauld.

11, Mr. Robert Thomson, minister, and Christian Clerk had Patrick.

11, John Murray and Margaret Blair had David ; witnesses, John Wricht, Robert Stirk, William Trumbill.

14, William Mackie in Cocklaw and Margaret Betsone had John (baptised in Ballingry) ; witnesses, David Blak, Andrew Baverage, William Sim, " all his nichtbours."

16, Andrew Dewar and Margaret Hutoun had Grizel ; witnesses, David Robertson, Thomas Walwod, Robert Lambe.

23, Archibald Honyman and Margaret Wells had Grizel ; witnesses, George Smetoun, Charles Ritchieson, David Car.

23, James Feg and Elspet Smetoun had Janet ; witnesses, John Culross, John Brown, smith.

23, William Robertson and Janet Litlejohn had Andrew ; witnesses, Andrew Walker and Robert Miller.

28, James Reanald and Margaret Mathesone had Helen ; witnesses, Adam Stevenson and John Car.

28, William Henresone and . . . . had . . . . (left unfinished).

M. 2, John Currie to Grizel Murray

2, Robert Wilson to Bessie Mudie.

MARCH.

B. 2, Robert Peacok and Catherine Stevenson had Barbara ; witnesses, Laurence Stevenson, Gilbert Turner, Abraham Peacok.

2, David Scotland and Janet Aikine had Janet ; witnesses, Nicol Wardlaw, Robert Russell.

2, Laurence Workman and Isobel Neifing had Margaret ; witnesses, David Laurie, Adam Schortus.

7, Robert Wilson and Margaret Hutoun, had John ; witnesses, John Wilson, John Peirsone.

7, James Garvie and Beatie Watt had William ; witnesses, George Walker, George Turnbull, John Rowan.

7, James Andersone and Janet Clerk had Isobel ; witnesses, Patrick Andersone, David Drysdell, Henry Clerk.

7, William Walwod and Margaret Lindsay had Isobel.

7, Henry Malcome and Nanse Knox had John (in fornication) ; witnesses, John Anderson, son of Robert A., " muillmaker," and Peter Law.

9, William Horne and Helen Andersone had Janet ; witnesses, Robert Wels, Andrew Meklejohn.

14, James Wallace and Alison Legat had Patrick ; witnesses, Patrick Cowper, Patrick Legat, John Walker, tailor.

16, John Wels and Christian Austiane had William ; witnesses, William Watsone, Robert Wels, David Car.

16, John Rait and Janet Tyrie had John ; witnesses, John Anderson, elder, and his son, and David Car.

21, James Bryse and Christian Young had Robert ; witnesses, David Sands, Thomas Douglas.

21, Robert Westwod and Janet Garvock had Robert ; witnesses, Archibald Douglas, Henry Turnbull, Robert Mitchell.

21, James Hutoun and Marjory Walwod had James ; witnesses, John Alisone, Adam Walwod.

30, Ninian Duncane and Margaret Merser had James ; witnesses, James and William Duncan, James Peirsone.

30, Edmond Alisone and Effie Crumbie had Elspet; witnesses, Andrew Wricht, William Cusine, Thomas Elder.

M. 2, Mark Swentoun to Janet Burgane (married at Inverkeithing).

9, David Lambe to Marjory Wilson.

APRIL.

B. 4, Andrew Awstiane and Margaret Cumming had David (in fornication); witnesses, Andrew Bennat, John Bennat, David Phillane.

7, Thomas Mudie and Effie Baverage had Janet; witnesses, John Sanders, John Hutoun, John Hyslope.

11, George Drysdell and Bessie Gibsone had Thomas; witnesses, George Gray and David Murray.

11, David Stevinson and Isobel Christie had Henry; witnesses, Henry Turnbull, John Alison.

13, Robert Wyld and Alison Gibson had Harry; witnesses, Harry Stewart, Nicol Dewar.

13, David Watsone and Janet Cuthbert had Grizel; witnesses, Thomas Walker, William Brown, notary, John Walker, tailor.

18, John Kay and Grizel Inglis had Margaret; witnesses, John Fergie, Stevin Fergie, Andrew Wilson.

18, James Lugtoun and Margaret Nasmithe had Elizabeth; witnesses, John Hutoun, John Murray.

18, John Brown and Elspet Taylor had John; witnesses, John Brown, John Miller, James Allane.

18, Thomas Alexander and Janet Kneilands had Isobel; witnesses, John Burne and James Garvie.

18, John Schortus and Janet Bankis had Janet; witnesses, John Bankis, Robert Schortus, John Stirk.

25, Robert Dewar and Janet Moreis had James; witnesses, James and William Maynis.

25, James Henresone, glazier, and Janet Dewar had Peter; witnesses, Charles Ritchardsone, Andrew Porter, Thomas Cowper.

25, Robert Wilsone and Christian Simravell had William; witnesses, William Walwod, John Banks, John Hyslope.

M. 27, James Boyle to Margaret Saverall (in Inverkeithing kirk).

27, David Strang to Bessie Ritchardsone.

MAY.

B. 2, Andrew Turnbull and Helen Currie had William; witnesses, John Turnbull in Bromehall, Laurence Turnbull in Logie, and Andrew Walker in the Hoill.

2, George Smetoun and Margaret Turnebull had Henry; witnesses, Henry Turnbull, David Peirsone, Robert Turnbull in Tunigask.

9, James Lethome and Isobel Makbethe had Bessie; witnesses, Robert Fraser, George Donald, Patrick Greive.

16, Finlay Moyle and Bessie Stevin had James; witnesses, James Reid, Andrew Wricht, Charles Ritchardson.

16, Andrew Robertson and Isobel Edward had Jean (in fornication); witnesses, James Beany, Thomas Cowper, James Allane.

16, Robert Lambe and Elspet Taylor had . . . . (son); witnesses, William Cusine, Thomas Mudie, William Mastertoun.

23, Robert Scotland and Helen Stobie had Robert; witnesses, Robert Turnbull, James Gibbone, David Laurie.

23, John Mayne and Janet Walker had John; witnesses, Mr. John Walker, Patrick Cowper, David Walker.

30, John Kinnell and Janet Philpe had Bessie; witnesses, Thomas Philpe, John Philpe, William Philpe.

30, William Philpe and Elspet Lindesay had George; witnesses, George Lindsay of Kavill, Andrew Murray, Harry Mudie.

M. 11, Thomas Philpe to Bessie Mackie.
   11, Alexander Lambe to Janet Dagleische.
   25, William Cadzen to Margaret Burne.
   25, Andrew Drummond to Beatie Wright (testimonial from Inverkeithing).
   31, Robert Levingston to Jean Bruse (in Carnock kirk).

JUNE.

B. 13, James Baverage, collier, and Margaret Greive had Isobel ; witnesses, Thomas Horne, John Baverage, Robert Dicksone.
   13, Alexander Wilson and Margaret Donaldson had Thomas ; witnesses, John Lawson, Thomas Wilson, Thomas Naesmyth.
   22, Richard Potter and Bessie Leirmonth had Andrew ; witnesses, Andrew Potter, James Kennedie, Thomas Rodger.
   27, Patrick Mowtrey and Helen Cunninghame had John ; witnesses, Adam Stevinson, Andrew Walker, John Davidson.
   27, Thomas Ritchie and Margaret Anderson had Annas ; witnesses, Robert Kellok, John Simsone, David Cunnon.
   29, John Peirsone and Helen Hutoun had John (in fornication) ; witnesses, Archibald Douglas, Gavin Stanehous, Laurence Walker.

M. 8, James Makcrobie to Helen Portour.
   8, William Robertson to Marjory Martene.
   15, James Hutoun to Janet Reid.
   15, Wattie Ritchardson to Janet Traill.
   29, Thomas Wilson to Isobel Cunninghame.
   29, John Kellok to Grizel Inche.
   29, Henry Malcome to Catherine Inglis.

JULY.

B. 6, Andrew Meldrum and Bessie Alexander had Robert ; witnesses, William Robertson, Robert Russell, Robert Anghous.
   13, Thomas Harrower and Margaret Gairdner had William ; witnesses, William Chatto, William Stanehous, Patrick Peirsone.
   13, James Miller and Christian Mowtrey had Janet ; witnesses, Thomas Philpe, John Thomesone, Patrick Mowtrey.
   25, William Broun and Bessie Smetoun had James ; witnesses, James Smetoun, John Car, Thomas Scotland.

M. 6, Robert Logane to Janet Mekiljohne.
   20, Robert Henresone to Janet Car.

AUGUST.

B. 1, Alexander Lambe and Janet Dagleische had John ; witnesses, John Lambe, Jerome Broun, John Alison.
   1, Thomas Burne and Janet Awstiane had David ; witnesses, David Burne, Thomas Walker, Andrew Walker, his son.
   6, Sir Robert Halkat of Pitfirrane and Dame Margaret Murray had Margaret ; witnesses, James Hamilton of Kilbraknonthe and Patrick Murray.
   8, Andrew Currie and Mawse Andersone had Bessie ; witnesses, David Cunningham, John Burne, younger, and Thomas Wilson.
   8, Robert Walwod of Touche and Marion Mitchell had Isobel ; witnesses, Henry Turnbull, William Walwod, William Mastertoun.
   10, John Donaldson and Christian Westwod had Christian ; witnesses, James Livingstone, Thomas Horne, William Sim.
   10, William Mudie, mason, and Margaret Aidiesone had Harry ; witnesses, Harry Mudie, William Mudie, his son, Robert Wilson.
   22, Alexander Beane and Helen Hutoun had Alexander ; witnesses, Thomas Mudie, John Wardlaw, John Gotterstanes.
   29, John Dougall and Bessie Craik had James ; witnesses, James Reid, elder and younger, James Hutoun, Patrick Stevinson, merchant.

M. 10, James Kennedie to Janet Hutoun.
   17, William Sanders to Christian Hutoun.

SEPTEMBER.

B. 5, David Henresone, cordiner, and Bessie Turnebull had Janet ; witnesses,
   John Feg, John Rait, John Inglis.
   7, John Anderson and Martha Maistertoun had Bessie; witnesses, Mr.
   Thomas Wardlaw, James Reid, John Anderson, younger.
   7, John Watson, cordiner, and Marjory Smetoun had Marjory ; witnesses,
   Robert Huggon, John Sanders, William Watsone.
   12, Johne Wilsone and Janet Drysdell had Alexander (baptized at Carnock);
   witnesses, Alexander Drysdell, David Chrystie, Henry Wilsone.
   21, Archibald Boyd and Janet Watson had Janet ; witnesses, John Drysdell,
   William Watson, Laurence Watsone, his son.
   28, James Chrichtoun and Agnes Gib had Jean ; witnesses, Sir Robert
   Halket of Pitfirran, Mr. John Murray, minister in Dunfermline.
M. 21, Thomas Baverage to Christian Smart.
   21, Andrew Robertson to Isobel Edward.
   30, John Peirsone to Bessie Stevenson.

OCTOBER.

B. 3, John Dick and Janet Paterson had Effie (in fornication) ; witnesses,
   Henry Orock, Henry Dick.
   3, Robert Moreis and Bessie Wels had Robert ; witnesses, Robert Wels,
   John Wels.
   5, William Walwod, baker, and Bessie Nicole had Allan ; witnesses,
   Charles Ritchardson, George Davidson, William Chatto.
   5, James Hutoun and Catherine Walwod had Andrew; witnesses, Thomas
   Christie and John Alisone.
   10, John Watson and Janet Kennedy had Bessie ; witnesses, George
   Donald, Patrick Greif, John Brown.
   10, Andrew Young and Elspet Furd had James ; witnesses, James
   Chrichton, James Gib, John Merschell.
   13, Archibald Hoge and Margaret Walker had Eupham ; witnesses,
   Laurence Walker, Florence Brown, Thomas Thomson.
   17, Andrew Lindsay and Marjory Walker had Thomas ; witnesses, Thomas
   Walker, Andrew Walker, Thomas Christie.
   17, John Smetoun and Margaret Anderson had Bessie ; witnesses, William
   Horne, John Alisone, Archibald Honyman.
   17, Cuthbert Wardlaw and Margaret Galrige had John ; witnesses, John
   Wardlaw, William Chatto, William Galrig.
   17, Charles Wilson, smith, and Margaret Johnstone had William ; witnesses, William Walwod, William and Robert Stanehous.
M. 19, James Makconneill to Margaret Blacater.
   26, James Robertson to Isobel Car.

NOVEMBER.

B. 2, Patrick Cowper and Janet Murray had Elspeth ; witnesses, John Anderson, younger, Mr. James Sibauld, schoolmaster, and William Mastertoun.
   2, David Sempill and Janet Mudie had Sarah ; witnesses, Adam Walwod,
   William Smart, John Alisone.
   9, Thomas Thomesone and Margaret Moreis had Margaret ; witnesses,
   Alexander Honyman, David Laurie, Archibald Hoge.
   21, John Cowstoun, Highlandman, and Margaret Jonkine had Marjory.
   21, Florie Broun, burgess in Dunfermline, presented a child begotten in
   fornication by Andrew Ferguson, trumpeter, upon Margaret Horne,
   called George ; witnesses, George Walker, merchant, Gilbert Sanders,
   notary.

21, Patrick Davidsone, collier, and Janet Thomesone had Henry.
23, Peter Law and Margaret Walker had Patrick ; witnesses, Patrick
    Stewart, Harry Stewart his son, Mr. Thomas Wardlaw.
28, Henry Chaipe and Janet Young had John ; witnesses, Mr. John Phune
    of Whythill, John Bruse, John Trumble in Bromehall.
28, Andrew Andersone and Isobel Kennoquhy had Effie ; witnesses, Florie
    Brown, John Hyslope, John James.
28, Thomas Sword and Margaret Brand had Catherine ; witnesses, Patrick
    Trumble, John Anderson, elder, John Burne, younger.
30, Robert Wilsone and Bessie Mudie had Bessie ; witnesses, James Reid,
    Harry Mudie, William Mastertoun.
30, John Aikine and Janet Inglis had John (in fornication) ; witnesses,
    Robert Anghous, James Anghous, John Greive.
30, Andrew Inglis and Margaret Duncane had Bessie ; witnesses, John
    Simsone, William Walwod, Gilbert Car.
30, Mr. John Phune of Quhythill and Margaret Hamiltoun had James ; wit-
    nesses, Sir Robert Halket of Pitfirran, James Stewart of Rosyth.

M. 2, James Wardane to Bessie Stirk.

DECEMBER.

B. 5, Andrew Ferlie and Alisone Anderson had John ; witnesses, Thomas
    Mitchell, Andrew Currie, William Sanders.
    5, Bartholomew Gilmure, weaver, and Janet Bull had Edward ; witnesses,
    Mr. James Durie, James Moyas, John Davidson. Presented by
    Edward Thomson, merchant, in the father's absence.
    5, Mr. James Sibauld, schoolmaster, and Isobel Bowstoun had John ;
    witnesses, William Mentethe of Randiefuird, Patrick Wardlaw of
    Torrie, James Reid, merchant in Dunfermline.
    7, John Anderson, younger, litster, and Helen Kingorne had Eupham ;
    witnesses, William Mentethe of Randifuird, Archibald Douglas.
    7, Willie Sim and Marjory Broun had John ; witnesses, Robert Master-
    toun, George Gray.
    21, Andrew Walker in the Hoill and Janet Hutoun had George ; witnesses,
    George Walker, merchant, George Bothwell, George Turnbull in the
    Grange.
    21, Robert Peirsone of Nether Beath and . . . . Peirsone had Harry ;
    witnesses, David P. and Patrick P., and Adam Walwod of Fod.
    26, James Oiswald and Bessie Cowsteoun had Janet ; witnesses, John Turne-
    bull, George his brother, and John Levingstoun.
    26, George Issatt and Janet Ged had Eupham ; witnesses, Richard Bruse,
    Alexander Lugtoun, Henry Simsone.
    28, William Keltie and Isobel Fergie had Margaret (in fornication) ; wit-
    nesses, John Peirson, Robert Wilson, Patrick Andersone.

M. 14, John Potter to Isobel Inglis.
    21, John Oiswald to Christian Hamilton
    21, James Mitchell to Christian Legatt.
    28, Alexander Drysdell to Bessie Walwod.
    28, John Anderson to Helen Lawsone.

JANUARY [1620].

B. 2, William Cunninghame and Janet Alisone had William ; witnesses, John
    Simsone, William Mudie, John Car.
    4, Andrew Andersone and Janet Touche had Bessie ; witnesses, Henry
    Wricht, Adam Lugtoun, James Anderson.
    4, John Murie and Elspet Anderson had Bessie (in fornication) ; witnesses,
    David Cunninghame, Andrew Currie in Primrose, David Callendar.
    4, John Anderson and Grizel Hoge had William ; witnesses, William
    Walwod, William Betoun, John Rowane.

M

9, James Trottar and Bessie Lawsone had Margaret ; witnesses, Patrick Anderson, John Hutoun, elder and younger, in Pitdinnie.

9, Gilbert Turnour and Helen Turnbull had Thomas ; witnesses, Thomas Mitchell, David Mitchell, Andrew Stevinson.

11, Robert Levingstoun of Baldrig and Jean Bruse had Helen ; witnesses, William Menteith of Randiefuird, George Durie of Craigluscour, James Chrichtoun.

16, John Clerk and Catherine Baid had James ; witnesses, Charles Ritchardson, David Williamson, John Baid.

19, David Walker and Grizel Meldrum had Margaret ; witnesses, Andrew Currie, Peter Law, Michael Meldrum.

19, Mr. Bernard Gib and Margaret Workman had William (in fornication) ; witnesses, William Cullane, William Carnie, Charles Ritchardson, William Brown.

23, William Peirsone and Margaret Young had James (baptised at Cleish) ; witnesses, James Crichton, John Hutoun.

23, David Strang and Bessie Richardson had Bessie ; witnesses, Andrew Hutoun, William Watson, John Simsone.

23, John Hyslope and Janet Laichlands had John ; witnesses, William Mastertoun, John Anderson, notary, John Culros.

23, William Dewar in Mastertoun (deceased), and Isobel Clerk had Elspet (presented by Robert Stanehous) ; witnesses, David Cunnon, James Mudie, Thomas Ritchie.

23, Thomas Brown and Janet Sim (deceased) had James ; witnesses, James Kellok, Adam Man.

25, Patrick Murray of Pardewis and Margaret Colvill had John ; witnesses, Mr. John Murray, minister, William Mentethe of Randiefuird, James Crichton.

30, Robert Douglas and Margaret Peirsone had Janet ; witnesses, John Cunningham, Adam Wilson, David Mitchell.

30, Robert Adame and Margaret Douglas had Andrew ; witnesses, David Laurie, George Davidson, Mr. Andrew Forrester.

M. [*None.*]

FEBRUARY.

B. 1, William Culane and Bessie Hutoun had Geils ; witnesses, James Chrichtoun, James Gib, John Anderson, elder.

8, William Broun, notary, and Grizel Cuthbert had Catherine ; witnesses, Robert Levingstoun, Mr. John Phune, Mr. Thomas Wardlaw.

13, Alexander Davidsone and Janet Douglas had Alexander ; witnesses, Archibald Douglas, James Cunnon, James Kellok.

13, John Miller and Isobel Miller had Isobel ; witnesses, Harry Mudie, and Patrick Stevinson, John Brown.

13, Gavin Stanehous and Marjory Nicole had Marjory ; witnesses, William Broun, James Hutoun, David Watson.

20, James Dagleishe and Catherine Wardlaw had Robert ; witnesses, Adam Stobie, Thomas Hutoun, George Douglas.

20, John Peirson in Pitdinnie and Marion Hutoun had Margaret ; witnesses, David Peirson, John Hutoun, Robert Wilson.

20, Robert Stanehous, portioner of Mastertoun, and Isobel Cunninghame had Gavin ; witnesses, Gavin Stanehous, Andrew Mitchell, Mr. James Ready, reader of Inverkeithing.

20, Alexander Greg and Catherine Philpe had Helen ; witnesses, Thomas Philp, John Kinnell, George Gray.

20, William Cadzem and Margaret Burne had David ; witnesses, David Sands, Thomas Mitchell, Andrew Walker.

20, George Davidson, weaver, presented Thomas Abercrombie's child to baptism, begotten in adultery upon Margaret Kingorne, wife of Thomas Deis, cutler, called George (over half a year old).

27, John Lawson and Janet Donald had Janet ; witnesses, Andrew Stevenson, Alexander Wilson, Henry Donald.

27, William Turnbull and Margaret Law had Barbara : witnesses, George Fergusson, David Peirsone, David Douglas.

27, John Peat and Catherine Stewart had Robert ; witnesses, David Dewar, Thomas Horne, James Smetoun.

M. 15, Andrew Anderson to Margaret Greg.

22, Alexander Benning to Janet Michie.

22, Andrew Hutsone to Janet Gentlewoman.

29, John Dow to Margaret Merser.

MARCH.

B. 5, Laurence Watson, cordiner, and Grizel Wilson had John ; witnesses, Patrick Cowper, William Watson, John Wilson.

12, John Murray and Margaret Blair had Thomas (baptised at Garnock) ; witnesses, Thomas Blakwod, Thomas Stevinson, Thomas Elder.

14, Allan Galrig and Janet Currie had James ; witnesses, James Hutoun, William Wilson, John Mayne.

19, John Inglis and Nanse Hutoun had David : witnesses, David Robertson, Robert Russell, James Anghous.

19, John Oiswald and Christian Hamilton had twins, Margaret and Jean (both died within two hours after baptism).

21, Adam Wylie and Catherine Makclarane had Isobel baptised ; witnesses, John Anderson, elder and younger, and youngest.

26, William Kellok and Margaret Kellok had James ; witnesses, William Mackie, John Horne, James Kellok.

26, Thomas Anderson and Alison Drysdell had Janet ; witnesses, Robert Russell, David Scotland, John Remanous.

26, John Mershell, miller, and Margaret Fuird had Janet ; witnesses, Charles Richardson, John and Robert Chattoe.

26, Henry Peirson and Helen Williamsone had David ; witnesses, William Peirsone, David Peirsone, James Rutherfuird.

26, John Law and Nicolas Andersone had Margaret ; witnesses, Peter Law, Patrick Cowper, Andrew Law.

26, Thomas Blakie and Margaret Law had Elspet ; witnesses, David Laurie, Harry Mudie, James Wardlaw.

M. [*None.*]

APRIL.

B. 9, William Orock and Catherine Maxwell had Margaret ; witnesses, Nicol Wardlaw, David Scotland, Henry Orock.

9, Patrick Harrower and Christian Peacok had Bessie ; witnesses, John Burne, Henry Gibsone, Thomas Peirsone.

9, Thomas Sands and Margaret Fentoun had Janet : witnesses, James Cunnon, Robert Kellok, James Mitchell.

9, William Law and Nanse Gib had Isobel ; witnesses, Robert Cunningham, John Feg, James Scotland.

9, Andrew Colyeir, drummer, and Isobel Andersone had Robert ; witnesses, Robert Anderson, William Rae, James Cowstoun.

9, James Buist and Janet Danzell had Thomas ; witnesses, Mr. Thomas Wardlaw of Logie, Robert Moreis, James Garvie.

11, George Walker and Marjory Cuthbert had Margaret ; witnesses, John Walker, John Anderson, James Kennedie, all burgesses of Dunfermline.

16, James Patoun and Bessie Wilson had Andrew (in fornication) ; witnesses, James Rutherford, Andrew Mitchell, Robert Gillespie.

16, Andrew Cunningham and Margaret Turnbull had Janet ; witnesses, William Brown, Thomas Mitchell, George Turnbull.

18, James Kinsmane and Christian Walwod had Nanse ; witnesses, John Walwod, William Walwod, Adam Stevenson.

18, Florie Anderson and Helen Cunninghame had John ; witnesses, John

Currie, Andrew Murray, John Turnbull in Bromehall. Presented by William Andersone, the father's brother, in the father's absence " at the saill."

23, John Cumming and Janet Workman had John ; witnesses, Alexander Chalmers, John Anderson, youngest, litster, John Turkane.

23, Peter Andersone (deceased, being " smored under a brae ") and Catherine Dewar had Janet (presented by Michael Meldrum) ; witnesses, George Meldrum, John Stirk, John Dewar.

23, John Wels and Catherine Drummond had George : witnesses, George Drummond, Samuel Drummond, William Bell.

30, James Hall and Margaret Anderson had John ; witnesses, Andrew Murray, John Davidson, John Burne.

30, Wattie Phinne and Margaret Westwod had Margaret ; witnesses James Reid, James Murray, David Watsone.

M. 25, Laurence Anderson to Grizel Thomson.

MAY.

B. 16, Robert Henresone and Janet Car had Catherine ; witnesses, James and David Car, and Robert Stirk.

21, Henry Orock and Margaret Scotland had Janet ; witnesses, John Orock, David Scotland, James Scotland.

21, Adam Hendine and Margaret Greive had Christian ; witnesses, John Greive, William Chatto, Patrick Peirsone.

21, Henry Peirsone and Jean Gentlewoman had John (in fornication) ; witnesses, John Peirson, David Peirsone, Robert Wilson, indwellers in Pitdinnie.

21, Laurence Anderson and Margaret Lugtoun had Janet ; witnesses, Patrick Anderson, David Mitchell, James Trottar.

23, David Broun in Blaklaw and Isobel Mayne had Janet ; witnesses, Henry Broun, William Mayne, Thomas Walker of the Rodds.

23, John Raithe and Janet Tyrie had James ; witnesses, Gilbert Car, Patrick Stevenson, Archibald Douglas.

28, Alexander Lugtoun and Nanse Ramsay had Bessie ; witnesses, John Drysdell, Henry Simsone, James Wallace.

M. [*None.*]

JUNE.

B. 9, John Currie and Grizel Murray had Andrew ; witnesses, Andrew Currie, Andrew Turnbull, Andrew Wilson.

10, James Robertson and Isobel Car had twins, Margaret and Grizel ; witnesses, Adam Stevenson, John Car, Robert Alison.

10, Robert Pringle, collier in Beath heugh, and Marjory Brand had Margaret ; witnesses, John Henresone, William Wannan, William Immo (?).

18, Richard Scotland and Margaret Blakwod had Janet ; witnesses, Thomas Scotland and Andrew Blakwod.

18, George Meldrum and Marjory Walker had George ; witnesses, George Walker, John Banks, Andrew Mekiljohne.

21, George Walker, cadger, and Janet Hois had John ; witnesses, George Davidson, Robert Lindsay, David Lawrie.

21, John Dow and Margaret Merser had Catherine ; witnesses, William Smart, David Laurie, David Strang.

23, Mr. Thomas Wardlaw and Catherine Alisone had William ; witnesses, William Mentethe of Randifurd, Robert Levingstoun, James Gib.

27, Robert Dewar and Margaret Gib had David ; witnesses, James Gib, David Cunnon, Thomas Philpe.

27, George Fergusson, servitor to the Chancellor, and Janet Peirson had Jean ; witnesses, Peter Law, Archibald Douglas, Patrick Cowper, Andrew Law, all burgesses of Dunfermline.

M. 13, John Makfarlane to Janet Wilson.

27, George Turnbull to Margaret Thomesone.

27, John Keir to Marjory Douglas.

27, James Mill to Isobel Dewar.

JULY.

B. 9, James Potter, wright, and Bessie Reid had Janet ; witnesses, Henry Turnebull, William Maistertoun, Robert Stevenson.

11, William Robertson and Marjory Martene had William ; witnesses, William Robertson of Craigduckie, John R. and William Betone.

16, John Anderson and Janet Nicole had Patrick ; witnesses, Patrick Andersone, David Drysdell, David Anderson.

16, Thomas Rodger and Grizel Westwod had William ; witnesses, Patrick Stevenson, William Smart, John Dow.

18, James Mitchell and Christian Legat had William ; witnesses, William Legat, William Betone, William Mastertoun.

23, Robert Peirsone and Isobel Galt had Christian ; witnesses, Thomas and David Peirson, Harry Young.

23, Andrew Hutoun and Isobel Wilson had Elspet ; witnesses, Edward Thomson, William Baverage, Laurie Watsone, James Cunningham.

30, John Thomesone and Catherine Wilson had Beatrix ; witnesses, David Douglas, Andrew Burne, John Tod.

30, William Gray and Margaret Andersone had John ; witnesses, John Turnbull, Thomas Donaldson, Harry Young.

30, John Finlasone and Marjory Gaw had Robert ; witnesses, John Davidson, Robert Alison, Charles Richardson.

M. 11, Robert Duncane to Elspet Robertson (in Ballingry kirk).

AUGUST.

B. 6, James Potter and Marion Walker had John ; witnesses, John Anderson, notary, Andrew Potter, wright, James Wallace, merchant.

6, George Williamson and Effie Thomsone had Janet ; witnesses, Richard Law, Charles Richardson, Robert Stevenson.

20, Robert Currie and Catherine Makcalyeoun had William ; witnesses, William Philpe, Thomas Stevenson.

27, John Small, collier, and Margaret Huggone had John ; witnesses, Robert Hugoun, Matthew Baverage, Henry Simsone, John Hugoun.

27, William Walwod and Nanse Alexander had John ; witnesses, John Anderson, younger, Harry Stewart, James Kingorne.

M. 8, Andrew Rowane to Bessie Cunningham.

8, Martin Baquhoir to Janet Bennat (in Aberdour, by testimonial).

15, George Cunningham to Margaret James.

15, George Cunningham to Margaret Maistertoun.

22, William Peirson to Grizel Westwod.

SEPTEMBER.

B. 5, George Donald, miller, and Margaret Stevenson had John ; witnesses, John Bennat, John Lawson, John Stevinson.

5, David Guddell and Janet Walker had Elspet ; witnesses, Robert Aikine, Peter Law, James Hutoun.

10, Robert Westwod and Janet Garvock had Marion ; witnesses, Adam Stevenson, Robert Gray, Abraham Greg.

10, Robert Stanehous in Fod and Catherine Stirk had William (in fornication) ; witnesses, William Stanehous, his father, William Walwod in Nether Beathe, Thomas Philpe.

10, John Alison and Grizel Walwod had Margaret ; witnesses, James Alison, Robert Alison, John Coventrie.

17, Andrew Drummond and Beatie Wryght had Beatrix ; witnesses, James
    Sands, John Bruse, John Wrycht.
17, John Burne and Margaret Hutoun had Janet ; witnesses, Thomas
    Christie, William Mudie, Patrick Cowper.
17, John Walker and Margaret Turnbull had George.
19, David Lambe and Marjory Wilson had Alexander ; witnesses, Alex-
    ander Lambe and James Wilson.
24, Adam Wilson and Margaret Cunninghame had Catherine : witnesses,
    Robert and James Cunningham, Patrick Lawsoun.
24, Henry Turnbull and Catherine Cusine had . . . . (daughter) ; witnesses,
    Thomas Elder, John Anderson, notary, Andrew Turnbull.
26, Thomas Walwod and Bessie Kirk had Edward ; witnesses, Edward
    Douglas, John Hislope, David Lambe.

M. 19, Henry Lugtoun to Jean Tulloch.

OCTOBER.

B. 1, William Anderson and Geils Peirsone had Walter ; witnesses, Andrew
    Currie, Andrew Turnbull, Patrick Anderson.
    3, John Peirson and Bessie Stevenson had Janet ; witnesses, Patrick
    Cowper, Thomas Stevenson, David Peirsone.
    8, John Alisone and Marjory Elder had Margaret ; witnesses, William
    Mudie, Thomas Elder, Henry Wardlaw.
    8, James Garvie and Beatie Wat had Catherine ; witnesses, James Buist,
    Nicol Inglis, Henry Phine.
    8, James Lindsay and Nanse Mentethe had Janet ; witnesses, John Ward-
    law, James Miller, John Huntar in Pittincreiff.
    8, Adam Stobie, portioner of Wester Luscour, and Helen Gibbone had
    Adam (baptised at Carnock); witnesses, Laurence Stobie, Thomas
    Scotland, William Gibbone.
    15, Henry Scotland and Catherine Wardlaw had Margaret : witnesses,
    James Scotland, James Anghous, William Dagleishe.
    15, John Anderson and Helen Lawson had Isobel ; witnesses, John Gotter-
    stoun, William Lawsone, William Brown.
    15, William Philpe and Elspet Lindsay had Robert ; witnesses, John
    Davidson, Andrew Murray, Patrick Cowper, burgesses of Dun-
    fermline.
    17, John Bruse and Agnes Balfour had . . . . (son) baptised at Carnock.
    24, David Watche and Cicile Duncane had Catherine ; witnesses, David
    Blak, William Sim, James Rutherfuird.
    24, John Keir and Marjory Douglas had George ; witnesses, George Gray,
    William Sim, William Curror.
    24, John Walwod and Margaret Schortus had Nans (in fornication).
    29, William Wricht and Jean Cambell had Robert : witnesses, William
    Lawson, Patrick Anderson, Robert Wilson.
    31, Robert Anghous and Christian Drysdell had Isobel (in fornication) ;
    witnesses, Nicol Wardlaw, John Dewar, John Inglis.

M. 17, George Bothwell to Elizabeth Wardlaw.
    17, James Lambe to Helen Yowane (both in Carnock kirk).
    24, William Stevenson to Janet Sibauld.
    24, Adam Stevenson to Margaret Alexander.
    31, William Wilson to Helen Hutsone.
    31, David Hutoun to Elspet Walker.

NOVEMBER.

B. 7, Sir Robert Halkat of Pitfirran and Dame Margaret Murray had Elspet.
    12, Charles Richardson and Janet Buist had Geils ; witnesses, James Gib,
    James Alisone, James (?) Wels.
    21, Robert Mastertoun of Beath and Margaret Mastertoun had Margaret ;
    witnesses, James Harper, Adam Mastertoun.

21, Henry Malcome and Catherine Inglis had William ; witnesses, William Smart, John Thomson, Laurence Watson.

21, Alexander Drysdell and Bessie Walwod had Barbara ; witnesses, Peter Law, Patrick Cowper, John Wels.

21, "Inglische Richard, the fyner of Sir George Bruse irone," and . . . . his wife had George baptized ; witnesses, Sir George Bruse and Thomas Blakwod.

M. 7, John Aikine to Christian Dagleische.

14, James Stevinson to Effie Moreis.

21, David Mitchell to Margaret Currie.

28, James Patoun to Margaret Anderson.

28, David Reid to Margaret Lawson.

28, Oliver Culane to Margaret Smithe.

DECEMBER.

B. 3, Thomas Curror and Helen Brown had Janet ; witnesses, John Stevenson, David Moreis, David Brown.

3, Patrick Dewar and Isobel Mastertoun had Adam ; witnesses, David Dewar of Lassodie, Mr. James Dewar, his eldest son, and Robert Dewar.

3, Henry Simsone and Bessie Thomson had Margaret ; witnesses, Charles Richardson, Duncan Talyeour. Robert Hugoun.

5, James Reid, younger, and Magie Schottus had Isobel ; witnesses, Patrick Stevinson, Harry Mudie, William Mudie, his son.

12, Robert Wilson and Bessie Mudie had Janet ; witnesses, James Reid, younger, James Hutoun, Patrick Stevenson.

12, David Callendar and Margaret Smetoun had John : witnesses, John Simsone, John Smetoun. Robert Hugoun.

12, James Hutoun and Helen Mudie had William (in fornication) ; witnesses, Thomas Mitchell, George Davidson, William Burne.

17, Thomas Nasmithe and Bessie Donald had Bessie ; witnesses, George Donald, Henry Donald, David Mitchell.

17, Robert Lambe and Elspet Tailyeour had James ; witnesses, James Lambe, Gavin Stanehous, William Lambe.

31, John Cunninghame and Margaret Swentoun had David ; witnesses, James Sands, David Sands, Thomas Douglas.

31, John Stirk and Janet Meldrum had Robert ; witnesses, Robert Wels, Richard Banks, John Huntar.

31, James Aissone and Catherine Watson had David ; witnesses, David Laurie, David Miller, William Watson.

M. 12, Gilbert Wryght to Margaret Lessells.

12, James Wilson to Janet Miller.

12, William Wannan to Margaret Davidson.

26, William Mudie to Janet Christie.

JANUARY [1621].

B. 7, James Workman and Helen Williamson had John ; witnesses, William and David Williamson, John Car.

7, John Kinloche and Bessie Sim had Violet ; witnesses, Charles Richardson, John Thomson, Robert Moreis.

9, Andrew Barhame and Margaret Stewart (daughter of Patrick S. of Beath) had James (in fornication), baptized presented by Peter Law : witness, Harry Stewart, her brother.

21, James Lethome and Isobel Makbethe had Janet ; witnesses, John and William Lawson, Adam Mastertoun.

23, James Murgane and Elspet Bowman had James ; witnesses, Adam Stobie, James Bowman, James Lindsay.

23, George Dewar in Lathamound and Jean Hutone had Grizel ; witnesses, James Mill, William Hutone, George Turnbull, son of Robert T. in Tunigask.

23, George Smetoun and Margaret Turnebull had James ; witnesses, James Reid, Henry Turnbull.

28, Thomas Mudie in Mastertoun and Margaret Turnbull had Thomas ; witnesses, Mr. Thomas Wardlaw of Logie, George Walker, James Cunnon.

28, James Wallace and Alison Legat had Janet ; witnesses, James Hutoun, merchant, Gavin Stanehous, David Douglas.

28, David Robertson of Craigduckie and Grizel Hutoun had William ; witnesses, Mr. James Dewar, Thomas Stevenson, George Dewar in Lathamond.

28, Laurence Stevenson and Catherine Chatto had Janet : witnesses, William and Thomas Chatto, Alexander Gowie.

30, George Imrie and Margaret Stevenson had Bessie ; witnesses, John Davidson and his son Robert, and William Wilson.

30, Robert Lindsay of Kavill and Lilias Drummond had David : witnesses, James Stewart of Rossyth, Robert Levingstoun of Baldrige, James Reid in Dunfermline.

M. 16, Gavin Anderson to Margaret Chrystie.

30, William Fuird to Margaret Allane.

FEBRUARY.

B. 4, George Miller and Bessie Lawsone had John ; witnesses, John Lawson, John Concord, Peter Sempill.

4, James Westwod and Isobel Cunningham had James (?) ; witnesses, Andrew Gaw, John Finlason, John Burne, mason.

4, Patrick Allane and Janet Moreis had Patrick ; witnesses, Thomas Stevenson, John Makbethe, Harry Bull.

6, Robert Levingstone of Baldrig and Jean Bruse had twins, John and Jean ; witnesses, William Mentethe of Randifurd, William Levingstone in Falkirk, James Gib.

11, Patrick Lawsone and Margaret Cunningham had Robert; witnesses, Robert Cunninghame, George Donald, Adam Wilson.

11, James Caddell and Beatrix Peirsone had James ; witnesses, John Ferlie, James Drysdell, Laurence Anderson.

11, William Spens and Christian Wallange had Bessie ; witnesses, David Strang, Patrick Legat, James Potter.

18, James Wilson in Galrighill and Janet Gibson had James ; witnesses, Thomas Christie, John Makbethe, William Cois.

18, Robert Balcate and Lucrece Norie had James ; witnesses, James Scotland, James Smetoun, Henry Orock.

18, Patrick Mowtrey and Helen Cunningham had Janet ; witnesses, John Thomsone, Harry Mudie, Adam Stevenson.

18, John Davidson, collier, and Nanse Broun had James ; witnesses, Henry Grein, James Levingstoun, David Broun.

25, John Simsone and Bessie Hutone had James ; witnesses, James Kingorne, Gilbert Sanders, David Lawrie.

25, David Sempill and Janet Mudie had Peter ; witnesses, John Walker, Peter Sempill, John Mudie.

M. 6, David Peirson to Isobel Henresone.

6, John Moreis to Isobel Gotterstone.

13, William Andersone to Catherine Cunningham.

13, John Stirk to Janet Meldrum.

13, Robert Murgane to Janet Wryght.

13, Robert Anghous to Catherine Mowse.

19, Andrew Corsane to Marjory Steill.

MARCH.

B. 4, James Robertson and Margaret Brand had Mary ; witnesses, Patrick Turnbull, John Fleming, John Walker, tailor.

4, David Mitchell and Janet Creiche had Laurence ; witnesses, Thomas Mitchell, Laurence Turnbull, Gilbert Turnour.

4, Laurence Anderson and Grizel Thomsone had Christian ; witnesses, Thomas Peirson, Andrew Roxburgh, James Patoun.

6, Mark Swentone in the Ferry and Janet Burgane had . . . . (son), baptised in the kirk of Inverkeithing "becaus of the lang and foull way."

6, John Boyd and Janet Kellok (adulteress with John Aidie, husband to Janet Neish) had Catherine (in fornication) ; witnesses, Henry Turnbull, Patrick Turnbull, Gavin Stanehous.

10, John Dougall and Bessie Craik had Thomas ; witnesses, John Anderson, younger, Thomas Reid, John Trottar.

11, Patrick Peirsone and Janet Mastertoun had Henry ; witnesses, Henry Wardlaw, John Davidson, Adam Walwod.

11, John Anderson and Janet Meldrum had Marjory ; witnesses, John James, Robert Davidson, James Hepburne.

11, John Burne, younger, in Easter Gellat, and Jean Murray had Andrew ; witnesses, Andrew Currie, Thomas Mitchell, James Rutherford.

13, John Rowane and Marion Cuninghame had Jean ; witness, George Dewar.

18, David Beany and Bessie Moreis had Isobel ; witnesses, Robert Lawson, John Lawson, Adam Wilson.

18, John Levingstoun and Janet Smetoun had Janet ; witnesses, John Levingstoun, Laurence Levingstoun, Robert Levingstoun.

18, John Baid and Bessie Spens had David ; witnesses, Patrick Stevenson, David Williamson, Adam Walwod, portioner of Fod.

22, Harry Stewart of Bayth and Catherine Kirkcaldie had Sarah ; witnesses, James Primrose of Todsmilne, Peter Law, Mr. David Kingorne.

25, Clement Sanders and Elspet Sanders had Clement ; witnesses, Andrew Wilson, John Sanders, Alexander Bell.

25, David Drysdell and Isobel Touchie had William ; witnesses, William Lawson, John Lawson, William Cunningham.

27, John Stevin and Isobel Mann had Robert ; witnesses, Robert Mastertoun, George Drysdell, Andrew Gibson.

M. [*None.*]

APRIL.

B. 1, Thomas Drysdell and Grizel Currie had John ; witnesses, Adam Walwod, William Stanehous, John Stevin.

1, David Cunnon and Elspet Dewar had Nanse ; witnesses, John Logane, Mr. James Dewar, James Kellok.

1, David Scotland and Janet Aikine had Margaret, witnesses, Patrick Cowper, Patrick Thomson, James Dewar.

1, Nicol Blakwod and Margaret Walker had Grizel ; witnesses, James Anderson, Duncan Car (baptised at Saline, by testimonial).

8, William Murie and Catherine Cunningham had Bessie ; witnesses, Alexander Chalmers, William Brown, clerk, Andrew Turnbull.

15, John Douglas and Rosina Oiswald had David ; witnesses, David Williamson, David Douglas, Michael Meldrum.

17, Robert Wilson and Margaret Hutoun had Nanse ; witnesses, John, David, and Henry Peirsone.

22, Robert Clerk and Bessie Hodge had Adam ; witnesses, Adam Walwod, William Stanehous, William Walwod of Beath.

24, Alexander Bartrome and Isobel Brown had David ; witnesses, David Scotland, David Smetone, John Inglis.

M. 12, Thomas Drummond of Drumquhense to Isobel Lindsay (in Carnock kirk).

17, John Turnbull to Janet Tod.

17, William Pillonis to Isobel Douglas.

24, John Marlzone to Effie Wricht.

MAY.

B. 1, James Mill and Isobel Dewar had Isobel ; witnesses, George Dewar, Robert Russell, William Hutone.

1, Richard Bardner and Margaret Fothringhame had John ; witnesses, Edward Douglas, John Bruse, David Sands.

1, David Tod and Janet Aidisone had Thomas ; witnesses, Thomas Blakwod, Thomas Reid, Thomas Scotland.

1, Nicol Rowane and Janet Hugone had Catherine ; witnesses, John Hugoun, William Robertson of Craigduckie, David Robertson, his eldest son.

1, John Lawsone and Janet Nasmithe had Robert ; witnesses, Adam Stevenson, Robert Gray, James Kinsman.

1, Archibald Hoge and Margaret Walker had John.

6, William Sanders and Marion Mastertoun had Janet ; witnesses, Mr. James Durie, John Bankis (?) and James Rutherford.

6, William Cunningham and Janet Alisone had Elspet ; witnesses, John Gotterstane, Laurence Neilson, Alexander Beane.

6, John Trottar and Janet Craik had Thomas ; witnesses, James Hutoun, John Wels, Patrick Stevenson, Thomas Reid.

6, Robert Anderson and Mawse Galrige had John (in fornication) ; witnesses, John Anderson, elder, John Anderson, his son, and John Anderson, younger.

13, John Oiswald and Christian Hamilton had Margaret ; witnesses, John Douglas, James Moyas, William Pulwart.

13, Thomas Sands and Margaret Fentoun had William ; witnesses, George Donald, Laure Stevenson, William Wilson.

15, William Thomesone, litster, presented John Land's child (begotten in fornication with Alison Thomesone, sister of the said William), named William : witnesses, John Anderson, youngest, John Anderson, " servand to the said Johnes father," and Adam Wylie.

20, George Moreis and Bessie Hutone had Bessie : witnesses, William Smart, Robert Merser, Adam Schortus.

20, James Ronald and Margaret Mathesone had Margaret ; witnesses, Adam Stevenson, John Car, John Walker, tailor.

27, Robert Murray and Nanse Tailyeour had William ; witnesses, William Walwod, Duncan Tailyeour, Henry Simsone.

27, William Rae and Janet Orock had James ; witnesses, James Thomson, James Kellok, Wattie Rae.

27, George Turnbull and Margaret Thomson had Bessie ; witnesses, George T. his father, Andrew T. his brother, Harry Mudie.

29, William Drysdell and Bessie Gibson had . . . . (son) ; witnesses, Henry Dick, William Sim, John Kellok.

29, John Peirsone and Marion Hutone had Helen ; witnesses, Patrick Anderson, John Hutone, David Peirson.

M. 1, James Clerk to Janet Car.

8, William Legat to Christian Burne.

15, William Legat to Elspet Quhyte.

29, Thomas Brown to Margaret Walwod.

29, Abraham Peacok to Margaret Young.

JUNE.

B. 5, Harry Walwod and Helen Kennedy had George ; witnesses, George Bothwell, Mr. Thomas Wardlaw, Andrew Wryght.

10, Henry Donald and Bessie Anderson had George ; witnesses, George Donald, David Mitchell, David Peirson.

10, James Kennedy and Janet Hutone had James ; witnesses, Andrew Wrycht, James Hutoun, Robert Aikine.

24, Harry Robertson and Agnes Murra had Margaret ; witnesses, John Orock in Craigbeath, David Brown, Robert Duncan. Baptised in Ballingry.

24, Robert Murgane and Janet Wricht had John; witnesses, William Bruse, John Dow, Robert Anderson, "mailmaker."

24, William Mackie and Margaret Betsone had Janet; witnesses, Robert Duncane, John Stevinson, William Sim.

24, Andrew Gaw and Magie Colyeir had Andrew; witnesses, Andrew Wricht, Edward Thomesone.

29, Andrew Currie and Mawsie Anderson had twins, Elspet and Janet; witnesses, Thomas Mitchell, John Burne, younger, David Cunningham, Florence Broun.

M. 5, David Burne to Janet Elder.
    5, John Ready to Isobel Lawson.
   26, Thomas Whyt to Isobel Kellok.

JULY.

B. 3, Thomas Hall and Christian Lambe had Thomas; witnesses, Thomas Stevenson, Andrew Wricht, Alexander Lambe.

   3, Andrew Mckiljohne and Janet Anderson had Walter; witnesses, John Anderson, younger, litster, Gilbert Sanders, John Anderson, youngest, brother-in-law to the said Andrew.

  10, James Cunningham in the Sillitoun and Isobel Cunningham had Robert; witnesses, Robert Cunninghame, George Donald, Robert Cunningham in the Sillitoun.

  10, Charles Baid and Helen Young had David; witnesses, Richard Bankis, David Burne, David Williamson.

  17, John Davidson and Margaret Henresone had Andrew; witnesses, Andrew Henresone, David Miller, Robert Kellok.

  18, James Chrichtoun and Nanse Gib had Margaret; witnesses, Mr. John Murra, minister, Robert Levingstone of Baldrig, Mr. John Drummond.

  24, Thomas Robertson and Janet Harrower had James; witnesses, James Currie, James Mackrobie, William Pillons.

  24, Alexander Wilson and Elspet Michie had Robert; witnesses, Robert Quhyt, Thomas Walker, Nicol Inglis.

  24, Henry Peirsone and Helen Williamson had William; witnesses, William and Thomas Peirson, Robert Wels.

  24, John Schortus and Janet Bankis had Christian; witnesses, Richard Bankis, John Dow, William Inche.

  29, David Peirsone, younger, and Bessie Peirsone had Bessie; witnesses, David Peirson, Robert Wilson, Andrew Peirson.

  29, James Lambe and Helen Yowane had James; witnesses, Andrew Currie, James Kellok, David Williamson.

  29, George Walker and Marjory Cuthbert had Elspet; witnesses, Robert Aikine, John Turnbull.

  29, George Fergusson and Janet Peirson had William; witnesses, Patrick Cowper, John Anderson, younger.

  29, Henry Douglas and Helen Wels had Janet; witnesses, Robert Wels (who presented the child in father's absence), Archibald Douglas, Charles Richardson.

  31, Thomas Peirsone and Christian Cant had David; witnesses, John Burne, younger, David Douglas, Ninian Mather.

M. 3, John Gray to Alison Martene.
    3, James Mudie to Grizel Lambe.
    3, William Chatto to Bessie Brown.
    3, George Ædisone to Bessie Levingstoun.
   10, Thomas Stevinson to Janet Chalmers.
   10, Andrew Berriehill to Isobel Peirson.
   10, Thomas Blakwod to Isobel Inglis.
   17, William Mudie to Nanse Mackie.
   17, Andrew Hutone to Elspet Gilgour.
   24, William Currour to Janet Mitchell.

24, James Scotland to Effie Harrower.
31, William Cunningham to Helen Stevenson.

AUGUST.

B. 5, James Drysdell and Isobel Westwod had Marjory ; witnesses, James Caddell, John Ferly (? Sorly), John Westwod.
  5, David Peirson and Jean Stanehous had Effie ; witnesses, Robert Stanehous, James Cunnon, Patrick Cowper. Presented by Florence Brown in the father's absence abroad.
  7, Patrick Murray and Margaret Colvill had Colin ; witnesses, Colin, Lord of Kintaill, George Bothwell, William Mentethe of Randiefuird.
  7, Robert Anghous and Elspet Robertson had Isobel (in fornication) ; witnesses, William Robertson of Easter Craigduckie (who presented the child) and . . . . Fairwether, miller.
  9, James Patoun and Margaret Anderson had twins, Elspet and Marjory ; witnesses, Andrew Wricht, George Walker, Thomas Hunnon.
  10, James Kellok in Mastertoun and Margaret Mudie had Nanse (died immediately after baptism).
  12, Finla Moyll and Bessie Stevin had Janet ; witnesses, Thomas Elder, John Dougall, Malcolm Cowall.
  12, James Miller and Isobel Tosche had Christian ; witnesses, David Fairwether, James Gray, Andrew Weymis.
  14, William Brown, notary, and Grizel Cuthbert had David ; witnesses, John Gib, John Walker, bailie, and Alexander Nicole.
  19, Malcolm Makqueine and Janet Jonkeine had Christian ; witnesses, Adam Anderson, John Burne, Robert Keir.
  19, Andrew Drummond and Beatie Wricht had John ; witnesses, Mr. John Drummond, John Bruse, Thomas Blakwod.
  26, Robert Adame and Margaret Douglas had Janet ; witnesses, John Simsone, George Davidson, David Laurie.

M. 21, Edward Peacok to Alison Drysdell.
  28, John Stevinson to Janet Furd.
  28, John Kellok to Janet Matheson.

SEPTEMBER.

B. 1, Malcolm Cowell and Margaret Boswell had twins, William and Harry ; witnesses, Harry Bull, Thomas Blakwod, Andrew Potter, John Dow, collier.
  2, Colin, Lord of Kintaill, and Dame Margaret Setoun, daughter of Alexander, Earl of Dunfermline, Chancellor, had Alexander ; witnesses, the Chancellor, William, Earl of Angus, and John, Earl of Perth.
  4, Thomas Mitchell and Margaret Dick had Andrew ; witnesses, Andrew Currie in Primrose, Andrew Mitchell, Andrew Dick.
  9, James Anghous and Elspet Hereme had James (in fornication) ; witnesses, Mr. James Dewar, John Rowane, Robert Russell. Baptised in Ballingry.
  11, Robert Russell and Barbara Elder had William ; witnesses, Mr. William Wardlaw of Balmule, James Smetoun, James Anghous.
  16, James Bryse and Christian Young had Andrew ; witnesses, Andrew Wricht, Andrew Gibbone, John Currie.
  16, Robert Quhyt and Catherine Hunnone had Janet; witnesses, Adam Stobie, Robert Scotland, John Anderson.
  16, Thomas Hunnone and Janet Edward had Janet ; witnesses, Andrew Mekiljohne, John Edward, Andrew Kinninmond.
  16, William Lawsone and Effie Waterstone had George ; witnesses, Thomas Philpe, George Davidson, Alexander Honyman.
  16, William Philpe of Brieriehill and Elspet Lindsay had Lilias ; witnesses, Robert Lindsay, Mr. Normand Lindsay, David Russell.

18, William Thomesone, litster, and Janet Mekeljohne had William; witnesses, Andrew Mekiljohn, John Anderson, youngest, Patrick Stevenson.

23, John Dowie, flesher, and Margaret Henresone (in Cleish kirk) had James; witnesses, James Levingstoun, Andrew Baverage, James Smetoun.

25, David Hutone and Elspet Walker had John; witnesses, John Simsone, Archibald Boyd, James Aissoun.

25, John Dow and Margaret Merser had Jean; witnesses, David Stewart, Adam Stevenson, Nicol Cornwell.

30, John Merser and Elspet Paterson had . . . . (son); witnesses, Robert Mastertoun, John Scot, John Tod.

30, Robert Wilson and Christian Simravell had Marion; witnesses, James Potter, John Mure, John Creiche.

M. 11, Robert Bruse to Barbara Dewar.

25, John Philpe to Christian Walwod.

25, John Culros to Helen Stevinsone.

25, James Cowstone to Helen Christie.

OCTOBER.

B. 7, David Watson and Janet Cuthbert had Margaret; witnesses, James Hutone, James Alisone, Allan Walwod.

14, James Andersone and Janet Clerk had William; witnesses, William Cunninghame, William Lawson, John Anderson.

14, William Robertson and Marjory Martene had John; witnesses, Henry Robertson, John Gray, William Betone.

14, Andrew Inglis and Margaret Duncane had Nicol: witnesses, Nicol Cornwell, John Simsone, David Laurie.

16, John Anderson, younger, litster, and Helen Kingorne had David; witnesses, William Mentethe of Randifurd, Mr. David Kingorne, George Ferguson, servant to the Chancellor.

21, William Walwod, cordiner, and Margaret Lindsay had William; witnesses, William Philpe, William Watson, George Davidson.

21, Alexander Honyman and Bessie Turnbull had Isobel; witnesses, Patrick Turnbull, John Walker, John Bennat.

23, John Wels and Christian Awstiane had Janet; witnesses, Robert Wels, William Watson, Thomas Stevenson.

23, Peter Law, merchant, and Margaret Walker had David; witnesses, David Stewart, David Dewar of Lassodie, Robert Aikine.

23, William Low and Nanse Gib had Robert; witnesses, Andrew Walker, Duncan Tailyeour.

28, John Aikine and Christian Dagleishe had George; witnesses, John Aikine, George Turnbull, James Dagleishe.

28, David Guddaill and Janet Walker had James; witnesses, James Alisone, James Kennedie, John Bennat.

30, David Stevenson and Isobel Christie had James: witnesses, James Stevenson, Henry Turnbull, John Wilson.

30, John Andirsone, youngest, and Martha Mastertoun had James; witnesses, James Reid, elder, Mr. James Durie, John Anderson, younger.

30, Thomas Burne and Janet Awstiane had John; witnesses, David Burne, William Elder, John Wilson.

M. 16, Andrew Galrig to Isobel Johnstone.

NOVEMBER.

B. 4, William Wilson and Helen Hutsone had Marjory; witnesses, Alexander Chalmers, Laurence Turnbull, Robert Cunningham.

6, Laurence Workman and Isobel Neifing had Janet; witnesses, David Laurie, Robert Merser, Charles Richardson.

6, William Ratra and Janet Speir had Bessie.

8, John Thomson, collier in Keltie, and Effie Finla had Isobel (baptized at Cleish by testimonial).

8, Andrew Mackcraith and Margaret Edward had Amas ; witnesses, William Cuningham, David Drysdell, George Miller. (The woman being delivered at the Crocefuird on her way home from Dunfermline to Aungziefair.)

8, Robert Kirk and Grizel Anderson had James ; witnesses, James Alison, Thomas Blakwod.

13, Gavin Andersone and Margaret Christie had John ; witnesses, Andrew Mekiljohn, John Anderson, elder, John Bennatt.

18, John Lawsone and Margaret Wilson had Effie ; witnesses, Patrick Lawsone, David Peirsone, Henry Peirsone.

18, Laurence Watson and Grizel Wilson had William ; witnesses, William Watson, cordiner, William Thomson, litster, William Gray.

20, Robert Scotland and Helen Stobie had Helen ; witnesses, Patrick and Laurence Stobie, Robert Cunningham.

20, Patrick Cowper and Janet Murray had William ; witnesses, William Brown and James Alison.

20, Mr. Thomas Wardlaw, provost, and Catherine Alison had Geils ; witnesses, John Gib and James Gib.

22, Mr. James Sibauld, schoolmaster, and Isobel Bowstoun, had Janet ; witnesses, William Mentethe of Randiefuird, Mr. Thomas Wardlaw, David Stewart.

25, George Cunningham and Margaret James (*sic*) had George ; witnesses, George Cunningham, the child's grandfather, William Cusine and Alexander Lambe.

M. [*None.*]

DECEMBER.

B. 2, John Wilson and Janet Drysdell had Andrew ; witnesses, Andrew Burne, David Stevenson, William Legat.

2, William Sim and Marjory Broun had James ; witnesses, James Weymis of Carskiburyane, Robert Broun, John Weyms.

2, John Hall and Nanse Musshatt had James (in fornication) ; witnesses, Thomas Walker, John Davidson, James Hall.

4, William Turnbull and Bessie Cowper had William ; witnesses, Robert Davidson, James Mayne, Patrick Allane.

9, Thomas Dow and Janet Davidson had Margaret ; witnesses, Duncan Tailyeour, Henry Simsone, John Mayne.

9, Thomas Dewar and Margaret Mastertoun had Margaret ; witnesses, William Robertson of Craigduckie, David R. his son, and William Mastertoun.

9, James Mitchell and Christian Legat had Margaret ; witnesses, Thomas Mitchell, Patrick Legat, John Crambie.

16, James Feg and Elspet Smetoun had William ; witnesses, John Feg, John Brown, John Fleming.

16, Henry Stirk and Margaret Mather had Jean ; witnesses, David Smythe, John Dow, John Wryght.

23, Gilbert Turnour and Helen Turnbull had David ; witnesses, David Mitchell, George Donald, William Turnour.

30, Walter (? William) Fuird and Margaret Allane had James ; witnesses, James Reid, Andrew Hutoun, James Allane.

M. 11, Patrick Greive to Marjory Burgane.

11, William Patoun to Janet Aidisone.

JANUARY [1622].

B. 1, John Warkman and Nanse Knox had Beatrix (in fornication) ; witnesses, John Cuming and John Feg.

1, Adam Stevinson and Margaret Alexander had John ; witnesses, John Stevenson of Baithe and David Moreis there.

6, Andrew Anderson and Janet Touchie had Elspet ; witnesses, Patrick Anderson in Pitconnochie, Adam Lugtoun and James Anderson.

6, John Valdegae, master cook to the Chancellor, and Janet Mowbrey had Margaret ; witnesses, William Walwod, cordiner (who presented the child), David Laurie, George Davidson.

8, George Bothwell and Elspet Wardlaw had Catherine ; witnesses, James Gib, William Mentethe of Randiefurd, Mr. Thomas Wardlaw.

20, Robert Duncane and Elspet Robertson had Elspet (baptised in Ballingry).

20, Robert Puttullok and Marjory Miller had Elspet ; witnesses, William Philpe, William Walwod, William Cusine.

22, James Baverage and Margaret Greif had Janet ; witnesses, Charles Richardson, David Blak, William Steidman.

22, Alexander Beane and Helen Hutoun had Isobel ; witnesses, William Mudie, John Wardlaw, John Gotterstoun.

22, John Buchannane and Janet Peacok had John ; witnesses, Gilbert Primrois, John Currie, John Chatto.

27, William Cusine, baker, and Elspet Hutchiesone had Elspet ; witnesses, William Mastertoun, William Philpe, James Rutherfuird.

29, Robert Stanehous in Mastertoun and Isobel Cunningham had Robert ; witnesses, Robert Kellok, David Cunnon, Robert Cunningham.

29, John Moreis and Isobel Gotterstone had Isobel ; witnesses, John Gotterstone, Henry Turnbull, George Davidson.

29, John Kellok and Janet Mathesone had James ; witnesses, William Kellok, Thomas Quhyt, Patrick Kellok.

M. 1, Andrew Anderson to Effie Henresone.

15, James Stewart to Margaret Greif.

15, John Ritchie to Grizel Stevenson.

29, William Anderson to Janet Cunningham.

FEBRUARY.

B. 3, Oliver Culane and Margaret Smithe had John ; witnesses, George Meldrum, John Alison, David Williamson.

3, James Buist and Janet Danzell had George ; witnesses, George Davidson, Robert Alisone, John Turnbull.

5, William Legat and Christian Burne had Christian ; witnesses, David Broun, David Black, William Robertson of Craigduckie, Patrick Legat.

5, James Cunnon and Janet Stanehous had William ; witnesses, William Kellok, James Mitchell, William Kent, younger.

10, David Broun in Blaklaw and Isobel Mayne had Isobel ; witnesses, George Mayne, John Brown, Henry Brown.

10, Richard Banks and Janet Lessells had Thomas (in fornication) ; witnesses, John Schortus, Thomas Chrystie, Thomas Banks.

17, Robert Peirsone and Isobel Galt had Isobel ; witnesses, Thomas Peirsone, Andrew Young.

17, Archibald Boyd and Janet Watson had Marion ; witnesses, James Reid, younger, John Simsone, William Walwod.

17, Alexander Drysdell and Bessie Walwod had Grizel ; witnesses, Peter Law, Thomas Blakwod, John Walker, Patrick Cowper.

19, Robert Wilson and Bessie Mudie had Margaret ; witnesses, Patrick Stevinson, James Hutone, Harry Mudie.

19, John Clerk and Catherine Baid had Margaret ; witnesses, Adam Stevenson, William Turnbull.

24, Andrew Meldrum and Bessie Alexander had Bessie ; witnesses, Henry Meldrum, John Alexander, Henry Wilson.

26, John Turnbull and Christian Ewen had George (in fornication) ; witnesses, Thomas Stevenson, Mr. James Primrose, George Turnbull.

26, Archibald Honyman and Margaret Wels had John ; witnesses, Patrick Dewar, John Wels, John Smetoun.

M. 5, John Inglis to Marjory Hutone.
12, Andrew Wilson to Helen Portor.
19, Thomas Schortus to Margaret Mowtrey.
19, Alexander Dron to Nanse Kellok.
26, Thomas Mortoun of Cambo to Dame Annas Halkcat, Lady Fordell.
26, John Young to Margaret Wilson.

MARCH.

B. 4, John Kinnell and Janet Philpe had Janet ; witnesses, Thomas Philpe Robert Peirsone, Robert Walwod.
4, John Stevinsone and Janet Fuird had . . . . (son) ; witnesses, Andrew Stevenson, Laurence Stevenson, Gilbert Turnour.
4, Malcolm Whyt and Helen Balfour had Isobel ; witnesses, James Mayne, William Mayne, John Dewar.
4, William Cunningham and Helen Stevenson had Catherine ; witnesses, William Anderson, James Sands, Robert Cunningham.
4, Thomas Mudie and Effie Baverage had Christian ; witnesses, George Davidson, Thomas Baverage, William Mudie.
4, James Potter and Marion Walker had Margaret ; witnesses, Thomas Schortus, Duncan Tailyeour, James Potter.
17, James Hart and Janet Murie had William ; witnesses, David Cunnon, William Kellok, James Cunnon. (Baptised at Inverkeithing.)
18, John Mayne and Janet Walker had Janet ; witnesses, John Dow, Thomas Dow, David Walker.
18, William Bruse and Rose Snellack had Robert ; witnesses, Robert Levingstone of Baldrige, James Gib and Archibald Douglas.
28, Robert Levingstone and Jean Bruse had Geils ; witnesses, James Gib, William Mentethe of Randifurd, James Shaw of Knokhill.
28, John Spens and Janet Cunningham had John (baptised at Crumbie) ; witnesses, John Peirsone, David Peirson, Robert Wilson.
28, Henry Chaipe and Janet Young had James (baptised at Crumbie) : witnesses, Adam Mastertoun, James Lethome, Henry Young.
28, Laurence Anderson and Jean Hutoun had Robert (baptised at Crumbie) ; witnesses, Robert Hwisone, John and David Anderson.
28, James Matheson and Christian Anderson had Christian (in fornication), baptised at Carnock ; witnesses, Laurence Workman, Robert Anderson, litster, Thomas Bennat.

M. 27, Robert Cant to Helen Robertson.

APRIL.

B. 5, John Watson and Marjory Smetone had James ; witnesses, Robert Hugoun, James Reid, younger.
7, William Anderson and Catherine Cunningham had Margaret ; witnesses, James Sandis, John Cunningham, Adam Wilson.
7, Nicol Dewar and Janet Robertson had Grizel ; witnesses, Robert Mastertoun, Thomas Kellok, Thomas Johnestoun.
7, John Smetone and Margaret Anderson had Catherine ; witnesses, Robert Wels, John Turnbull, Alexander Drysdell.
9, Robert Walwod of Touche and Marion Mitchell had Robert ; witnesses, Robert Kellok, John Anderson, litster, John Anderson, notary.
10, David Strang and Bessie Richardson had David ; witnesses, David Car, David Stevensone, William Walwod.
14, William Orock and Catherine Maxwell had Isobel ; witnesses, John Orock of Craigbayth, Robert Turnbull, John Walker, tailor.
14, James Logie in the Ferry and Marjory Bungane had Nanse ; witnesses, Laurence Lugtoun, John Brown and Florence Thomson.
14, Thomas Blakwod and Isobel Inglis had James ; witnesses, David Dewar of Lassodie, John Inglis, Mr. James Dewar.

23, David Blak, younger in Coklaw, and Marjory Blakwood had David ; witnesses, David Blak, elder, David Brown, John Christie.

23, Edmond Ahsone (deceased) and Effie Crumbie had Robert ; witnesses, William Mudie, Andrew Alisone, John Burne.

23, James Mill and Isobel Dewar had John ; witnesses, John Mill, George and John Dewar.

23, David Walker and Grizel Meldrum had David ; witnesses, Thomas Walker, James Kennedie, John Mayne.

28, David Reid and Margaret Lawsone had James ; witnesses, Adam Stobie, Robert Scotland, James Murgane.

28, Williame Currour and Janet Mitchell had Margaret ; witnesses, Harry Stewart of Bayth, John Stevinson, David Moreis there.

28, Andrew Turnbull, portioner of Grainge, and Helen Curie had Margaret ; witnesses, Thomas Turnebull, George Turnbull, younger, David Mitchell.

28, James Trottar and Bessie Lawsone had James ; witnesses, James Hutone, Andrew Andersone, Walter Tailyeour.

28, John Hadstone and Bessie Bainye had James ; witnesses, Patrick Anderson, James Anderson, Andrew Lessells.

M. [*None.*]

MAY.

B. 5, John Andersone and Grizel Hoge had John ; witnesses, John Anderson, younger, litster, John Dewar, John Horne.

7, Robert Peirsone and Marjory Peirsone had Harry ; witnesses, David Peirsone, elder, Patrick Anderson, William Cunninghame.

7, Henry Malcome and Catherine Inglis had James ; witnesses, Mr. James Sibauld, Peter Law, William Smart.

7, John Berill and Margaret Colzere had William ; witnesses, William Bruce, George Ferguson, William Robertson.

12, John Brown and Margaret Smetoun had William ; witnesses, Andrew Walker, William Philpe, William Brown.

12, William Cadzene and Margaret Burne had Thomas ; witnesses, Thomas Douglas, William Anderson, William Cowsteone.

12, William Mudie and Nans Mackie had John ; witnesses, Thomas Mudie, John Kellok, John Low.

12, John Gray and Alisone Martene had Elspet ; witnesses, James Potter, William Robertson.

15, John Potter and Janet Inglis had William ; witnesses, James Kennedy, Andrew Potter, Robert Stevinson, William Potter.

21, William Chatto and Bessie Broun had Janet ; witnesses, David Burne, James Moyas, William Sanders.

27, David Strang (fugitive) and Helen Meldrum (wife of Gilbert Blair, tailor and fugitive) had Marjory (in adultery) ; presented by Henry Wilsone, burgess ; witnesses, David Strang, Allan Neilsone, David Wallace.

28, David Mitchell and Margaret Currie had Janet ; witnesses, Henry Mekill, Andrew Turnbull, portioner of Grange, and Andrew Currie in Primrose.

28, William Horne and Helen Anderson had Margaret ; witnesses, John Walker, merchant, John Anderson, elder, David Chrystie.

28, George Meldrum and Marjory Walker had Michael ; witnesses, Michael Meldrum, Thomas Walker, John Banks.

28, Charles Wilson and Margaret Johnestone had John ; witnesses, Robert Clerk, Alexander Lugtoun, William Kinie (?).

M. 7, William Dow to Janet Galrige.

28, Andrew Barhame to Margaret Stewart.

28, James Balfour to Elspet Mackie.

JUNE.

B. 2, Robert Douglas and Margaret Peirsone had Margaret ; witnesses, George Donald, Robert Cunningham, Thomas Peirson.

9, David Burne and Janet Elder had Christian ; witnesses, George David-son, Charles Richardson, John Sanders.

9, Laurence Andersone and Margaret Lugtoun had Bessie ; witnesses, George Donald, Henry Donald, James Anderson.

9, John Cumming and Janet Workman had William ; witnesses, Thomas Turnbull, William Thomson, William Wilson.

9, John Anderson and Helen Lawson had Henry ; witnesses, William Brown, Henry Brown, John Gotterstoun.

11, Robert Henresone, skinner, and Janet Car had Agnes ; witnesses, James Alisone, John Bennat and James Cairnis.

11, John Dick and Janet Paterson had Bessie (in fornication) ; witnesses, William Sim, Henry Dick, John Dewar.

23, William Rae and Janet Henresone had Barbara ; witnesses, Robert Kellok, James Mitchell, David Peirsone.

28, John Peirsone and Bessie Stevenson had Margaret ; witnesses, George Ferguson, Patrick Stevenson, David Peirson.

28, William Henresone and Bessie Forsyithe had Janet ; witnesses, Patrick Turnbull, Archibald Douglas, John Simsone.

30, Gavin Stanehous and Marjory Nicole had Robert ; witnesses, William Brown, David Watsone, Henry Hakarstone.

30, John Huntar and Janet Wilsone had Nicol ; witnesses, Michael Mel-drum, Nicol Huntar, James Huntar.

M. 11, Thomas Culros to Helen Anderson.

11, James Kellok to Helen Spens.

18, Andrew Drummond to Bessie Young.

JULY.

B. 2, Robert Lambe and Elspet Tailyeour had Robert ; witnesses, James Mudie, Robert Stevinson, David Lambe.

16, John Currie and Grizel Murray had Margaret ; witnesses, Andrew Turn-bull, elder, William Cunninghame and Thomas Wilson of the Walk-mill of Culros.

21, Patrick Davidson and Janet Thomson had Effie ; witnesses, John Henre-sone, William Wannan and William Wnma (? Winma),

21, John Mure and Isobel Thomson had John (in fornication) ; witnesses, David Williamson, John Thomson, John Feg.

23, John Wricht and Catherine Patone had James ; witnesses, James Mudie, John Wardlaw, John Dougall.

25, William Robertson and Janet Litljohne had Thomas ; witnesses, Thomas Christie, John and Andrew Wricht, Archibald Robertson.

30, Andrew Galrige and Isobel Johnestoun had Janet ; witnesses, William Brown, Henry Brown, Patrick Person.

M. 2, John Scot to Catherine Mackie.

9, James Bruse to Janet Hutone.

AUGUST.

B. 2, George Fergussoun, servant to the deceased Alexander, Earl of Dun-fermline, and Janet Peirsone had James ; witnesses, Peter Law, Andrew Mekiljohne.

3, John Watson and Janet Kennedie had John ; witnesses, John Cuning-hame, George Donald, John Stevinson.

8, Richard Scotland and Margaret Clerk had . . . . (daughter).

9, James Lambe and Helen Yowne had Janet ; witnesses, Robert Lambe, William Mastertoun.

11, Henry Scotland and Catherine Wardlaw had David ; witnesses, David Scotland, Henry Orock, Henry Neifing.

11, Robert Lindsay and Isobel Simsone had Janet ; witnesses, Archibald Hog, William Buist, David Goodaill.

25, Patrick Greive (deceased) and Marjory Burgane in Inverkeithing had
. . . . (son).

M. 20, Thomas Douglas to Elspet Chalmers.
20, Robert Hutone to Janet Kirk (in Cleish kirk).
30, Andrew Murray to Margaret Cunningham.

SEPTEMBER.

B. 8, Thomas Peirsone and Christian Cant had Margaret ; witnesses, Robert
Cant, Ninian Mather, Robert Douglas.
8, John Cowslane, "ane pore Heilandman," and Margaret Jonkeline had
John ; witnesses, John Davidson, John Finlason.
15, Andrew Lindsay and Marjory Walker had Margaret ; witnesses, Andrew
Burne, David Douglas, George Mekiljohne.
19, William Peirsone of Morlatbank and Margaret Young had Grizel ;
witnesses, James Chrichtoun, Robert Levingstoun. (Baptized at
Fossoquhey, because of distance and foul weather.)
22, John Peirsone and Marion Hutone had Bessie ; witnesses, John Hutone,
David Peirsone, Henry Peirson.
22, James Hal and Margaret Anderson had Patrick ; witnesses, Patrick
Stevinsone, John Thomesone, Andrew Murray.
29, Robert Balcate and Elspet Rowane had David ; witnesses, James
Smetone, David Smetone, David Rowane.
29, William Mudie and Janet Christie had Harry ; witnesses, James Reid,
elder, Harry Mudie, Andrew Walker, Thomas Reid, John Anderson,
younger.

M. 2, John Lambert to Isobel Cunningham (in Dollar, on testimonial).
10, John Makbethe to Helen Cumming.
23, John Remannous to Catherine Cunningham (in Saline kirk, by testimonial).

OCTOBER.

B. 2, Stephen Fergie and Christian Wilson had Helen ; witnesses, Adam
Stobie, Nicol Wardlaw, David Reid.
6, David Peirsone and Isobel Henresone had Christian : witnesses, Thomas
Peirsone, Robert Douglas, David Miller.
6, William Walwod and Margaret Peirsone had Bessie ; witnesses, Robert
Peirsone, Robert Dewar, Robert Walwod.
8, Duncan Tailyeour and Margaret Hutone had Janet: witnesses, John
Taylor, Thomas Blakwod, Charles Ritchardson.
8, Andrew Drummond and Bessie Young had Elspet ; witnesses, Andrew
Wricht, bailie, Thomas Blakwod, Laurence Stevenson.
13, William Mudie, mason, and Margaret Aediesone had Thomas ; witnesses, Thomas Blakwod, Thomas Mudie, Thomas Walker in the
Rhoes. (Born 11th.)
13, George Imrie and Margaret Stevenson had Thomas ; witnesses, Thomas
Blakwod, Charles Richardson, John Ritchie.
22, Thomas Moore and Grizel Walwod had William ; witnesses, William
Wilsone, Thomas Stevenson, Patrick Stevenson.
27, James Mudie and Grizel Lambe had Robert ; witnesses, Robert Mudie,
Alexander Lambe, William Lambe.
27, William Culane and Bessie Hutone had James ; witnesses, James
Chrichtoun, James Gib, James Kennedie. (Born 22nd.)

M. 15, Thomas Allane to Elspet Thomesone.
17, Claudius Johnston to Jean Sands.
29, Hew Barklay to Bessie Broun.

NOVEMBER.

B. 3, John Tailyeour, collier, and Isobel Grahame had John ; witnesses, John
Dow, John Wright, Duncan Tailyeour.

10. James Kellok and Margaret Mudie had James : witnesses, David
Cummon, John Watson, Thomas Mudie.

10. James Stewart and Margaret Greive had Janet : witnesses, Alexander
Lugtoun, James Baverage, Andrew Stevinson.

12. William Pittons and Isobel Douglas had Margaret : witnesses, Gilbert
Primros, George Donald, John Lawsone.

15. Alexander Drone and Agnes Kellok had William : witnesses, William
Cairne, Robert Kellok, James Kellok, Thomas Edisone.

17. Robert Bruse and Barbara Dewar had Archibald : witnesses, John
Davidson, Robert Millen, John Dewar.

22. Alexander Honyman and Bessie Turnbull had Grizel : witnesses, Andrew
Gibone, Adam Stevenson, David Burne.

24. Florence Andersone and Helen Cunningham had Andrew : witnesses,
Andrew Turnbull, elder and younger, Andrew Currie.

24. William Broun, clerk, and Grizel Cuthbert had William : witnesses,
James Gib, Hew Barklay, Mr. Thomas Wardlaw of Logie.

28. James Dagleische and Catherine Wardlaw had Helen : witnesses, John
Akin, Nicol Dagleische, John Stanehous in Clinkhill.

M. 20. James Fisher to Janet Kent.

20. Patrick Currour to Margaret Moreis.

DECEMBER.

B 1. Andrew Hutone and Isobel Wilsone had James : witnesses, James Reid,
younger, James Hutone, William Watson.

1. William Philipe and Elspet Lindsay had William : witnesses, Thomas
Stevenson, William Walwod, William Mudie.

5. James Garvie and Bessie Wat had Marion : witnesses, Andrew Turnbull,
William Burst, Thomas Walker of the Rhods.

5. William Paton and Janet Edisone had James : witnesses, James Reid,
James Burst, George Davidson.

8. Henry Turnbull and Catherine Cusine had Christian : witnesses,
William Turnbull, William Masterton, William Cusine.

13. Adam Stirk and Helen Whyte had Janet : witnesses, Andrew Stirk,
Thomas Tod, Thomas Scotland.

15. William Anderson and Janet Cunningham had Helen : witnesses, James
Trottar, William Sanders, William Anderson.

15. Claudius Johnstone and Jean Smith had Margaret begotten before the
marriage : witnesses, William Monteithe of Randiford and John
Anderson, younger, litster.

17. Willie Gray and Margaret Anderson had Rachael : witnesses, Pate
Anderson, Andrew Turnbull in Bromehall.

22. Adam Hendeine and Margaret Greive had James : witnesses, William
Walwod, Andrew Perriehill, James Walwod.

22. Abraham Peacock and Margaret Young had Bessie : witnesses, John
Keir, David Williamson, James Walwod.

22. James Greg and Helen Rankeine had Alexander : witnesses, Alexander
Greg, Patrick Peirsone, Abraham Greg.

24. Henry Simsone and Bessie Thomson had Duncan : witnesses, Duncan
Taliyeour, John Clerk, Matthew Baverage.

26. Laurence Levingstoun and Janet Makraltome had John in fornication :
witnesses, John and Robert Levingston and John Levingstoun in the
Lymkills.

26. Thomas Sword and Margaret Brand had Thomas : witnesses, John
Thomson, John Wrycht, James Millet.

31. Henry Peirsone and Margery Mill had Bessie in fornication : witnesses,
John Peirson and David Peirson, father and brother of the said
Henry.

M. 10 Thomas Cumming to Marion Douglas.

10. John Forret to Elspet Smart.

JANUARY [1623].

B. 5, William Dalgleische and Isobel Makcraiche had Nanse (in fornication) ; witnesses, David Scotland, John Greif, Laurence Turnebull.

5, William Gourley and Bessie Gib had Nanse (in fornication) ; witnesses, David Robertson, John Inglis.

12, David Tod and Janet .Edisone had Elspet ; witnesses, Thomas Tod, John Bankis, Thomas Blakwod.

12, Henry Broun and Elspet Bankis had Bernard ; witnesses, Mr. Bernard Gib ; John Thomesone, John Stirk.

19, James Thomesone and Elspet Davidson had John ; witnesses, Richard Bruse, John Baid, John Merser.

28, James Reid, younger, and Marion Broun had Catherine ; witnesses, John Gib, James Reid, elder, provost, and John Anderson, elder, bailie.

M. 16, William Wilson to Christian Wricht.

21, Michael Gray to Margaret Lessells.

26, Hew Clerk to Janet Makcraiche.

28, David Douglas to Alison Mitchell.

FEBRUARY.

B. 2, John Inglis and Agnes Hutone had George ; witnesses, George Meldrum, Nicol Inglis, John Hutone.

2, Alexander Wilson and Margaret Donaldson had David ; witnesses, David Mitchell, Robert Peacok, Laurence Andersone.

2, John Moyas and Christian Philpe had John ; witnesses, John Broun, William Elder, John Makbethe.

2, William Low and Nanse Gib had John : witnesses, John Feg, Duncan Tailyeour, and John Tailyeour, his son.

9, William Mowbrey and Christian Salmont had Isobel ; witnesses, Mr. James Dewar, apparent of Lassodie, James Henreson, John Remainous.

9, Robert Murgane and Janet Wricht had Thomas ; witnesses, John Dow, John Trottar, James Lugtoun.

9, James Patone and Margaret Anderson had Andrew ; witnesses, John Wryght, Archibald Douglas, James Miller.

14, Mr. James Phinne and Agnes Aittone had Isobel ; witnesses, Mr. John Phinne of Quhythill, Andrew Turnbull in Bromehall, Mr. Harry Makgill, minister of Dunfermline.

16, John Wels and Catherine Drummond had Robert ; witnesses, Robert Wels, Thomas Blakwod, Thomas Eldar.

16, Harry Stewart of Baithe and Catherine Kirkcaldie had Janet ; witnesses, George Bothwell, David Stewart, Patrick Bothwell, Laurence Merser.

20, Richard Blakley and Emelie Par had . . . . (son) ; witnesses, Thomas Stevinsone, Andrew Turnbull, William Bruce.

23, David Henresone and Bessie Turnbull had Helen ; witnesses, John Simsone, Archibald Boyd, James Henresone.

23, Andrew Barhame of Skelpie and Margaret Stewart had Michael ; witnesses, Michael Balfour of Bandone, Harry Stewart of Baithe, David Stewart, his brother.

25, Alexander Lambe and Janet Dagleische had Janet ; witnesses, Alexander Lambe, James Mudie, James Kellok.

M. 4, Peter Sempill to Janet Mathesone.

18, John Anderson to Janet Stevinsone.

18, John Levingstone to Margaret Young.

23, John Watson to Margaret Kellok.

23, George Legat to Margaret Anderson.

27, Edward Douglas to Beatie Douglas.

27, Alexander Nicole to Helen Alexander.

MARCH.

B. 2, Robert Lochtie and Catherine Banks had Janet (in fornication) ; witnesses, John Thomson, John and James Lochtie.

 4, William Cambell and Margaret Broun had William (in fornication) ; witnesses, William Mudie, Harry Bull, and John Bull, his son.

 9, John Walker and Margaret Turnbull had Grizel ; witnesses, Patrick Cowper, William Brown, Mr. James Sibauld.

 11, Thomas Currour and Helen Brown had Henry ; witnesses, John Stevinsone, Henry Hakerstoun, David Moreis.

 23, James Lethome and Isobel Makbethe had John ; witnesses, John and Robert Cunningham, John Lawson.

 23, Andrew Colzeir and Isobel Anderson had Anna ; witnesses, George Durie, George Davidson, David Bull.

 23, John Murray and Margaret Blair had John ; witnesses, Thomas Elder, John Johnestoun, James Miller.

 23, Henry Peirson and Helen Williamson had Sarah ; witnesses, William Turnebull, William Mudie, John Alisone.

 23, John James and Margaret Whyt had Janet ; witnesses, John Davidson, George Cunningham.

 26, George Cunningham and Margaret Maistertoun had James ; witnesses, James Mastertoun, John Gotterstone, Alexander Lambe.

 30, John Aikine and Christian Dagleische had Janet ; witnesses, Robert Turnebull, James Dagleische, John Greive.

 31, Robert Lindsay of Kavill and Lilias Drummond had Margaret ; witnesses, Sir Robert Halkat of Pitfirrane, Robert Levingstone of Baldrig, James Gib, William Philpe of Bririelands.

M. [*None.*]

APRIL.

B. 3, George Ædisone and Bessie Levingstoun (who died in childbirth) had John ; witnesses, Thomas Blakwod, Alexander Ædisone, John Levingstoun.

 6, William Anderson and Geils Peirson had Janet ; witnesses, Archibald Douglas, David Douglas, John Anderson.

 6, John Anderson and Helen Hutoun had Isobel (in fornication) ; witnesses, John Thomson, George Davidson, William Anderson.

 6, David Huttoun and Elspet Walker had James.

 10, Thom Blakie and Margaret Law had John.

 17, Robert Levingstone of Baldrige and Jean Bruse had Robert ; witnesses, William Mentethe of Randifurd, James Schaw of Knokhill, John Henresone of Fordeill.

 20, Thomas Mudie, portioner of Mastertoun, and Margaret Turnebull had Margaret ; witnesses, George Turnbull, James Mudie, William Lambe.

 20, Robert Bruse and Bessie Phin had James ; witnesses, Mr. James Phin, Thomas Thomson, Robert Bruse.

 27, John Alisone, mason, and Marjory Elder had Christian ; witnesses, William Mudie, David Williamson, Robert Russell, William Turnbull.

M. 15, David Bull to Margaret Potter.

 15, Thomas Philpe to Catherine Harrower.

 29, Robert Lochtie to Catherine Bankis (testimonial from Aberdour).

MAY.

B. 4, Robert Moreis and Bessie Wels had Nanse ; witnesses, Mr. James Primrois, James Aikine in Culross. Charles Ritchardsone.

 8, Archibald Hodge and Margarat Walker had James ; witnesses, Mr. James Primrois, John Anderson, younger, John Walwod, officer.

11, Laurence Musgrave and Janet Straquhen had Rose ; witnesses, David Stewart, William Bruse, Robert (?) Blakley, Robert Turneley, younger.

21, William Mackie and Margaret Betsone had Helen ; witnesses, John Gotterstone, David Blak, John Betsone.

M. 20, Andrew Mentethe to Catherine Gardner.

27, Adam Stanchous to Isobel Mill.

27, William Thomesone to Janet Sanders.

JUNE.

B. 8, William Currour and Janet Mitchell had . . . . (daughter) ; witnesses, John Stevinson, Henry Hakstoun, Thomas Currour.

8, James Kennedie and Janet Hutone had Margaret ; witnesses, William Mentethe of Randiefuird, Peter Law, William Brown, notary, John Anderson, younger.

15, George Donald, miller in Nethermill, and Margaret Stevinson had James ; witnesses, James Primrose, James Currie, William Cunningham, David Mitchell.

15, David Goodall, town officer, and Janet Walker had David ; witnesses, Andrew Wricht, Peter Law, John Anderson, youngest.

20, Adam Stobie, portioner of Wester Luscour, and Helen Gibone had Margaret ; witnesses, Nicol Wardlaw, Robert Scotland, Thomas Hutone.

29, James Hart and Janet Murie had Isobel ; witnesses, James Mitchell, Alexander Davidson, Thomas Cunnon.

29, James Stevin and Nanse Agae had Robert ; witnesses, William Law, Robert Patersone, John Patersone.

M. 3, Archibald Glennie to Nanse Aissoun.

17, James Hutone to Margaret Walker.

19, William Lundie of that Ilk to Anna Wardlaw, daughter of Sir Henry W. of Pittreavie.

26, Thomas Christe to Elspet Durie.

JULY.

B. 13, William Kellok and Margaret Kellok had William ; witnesses, Thomas Horne, Henry Dick, Nicol Dewar.

13, David Bull and Margaret Potter had Janet ; witnesses, Harry Bull, cutler, David Stewart, Andrew Potter.

13, John Clerk and Catherine Baid had Duncan ; witnesses, Duncan Tailyeour, John Moreis, John Gotterstone.

20, Laurence Lugtone and Janet Bennat had twins, Robert and John : witnesses, John Brown, Florie Burgane, Edward Brown, Robert Drysdell. (Baptised at Inverkeithing, because of the children's weakness and the far distance from their own parish.)

20, William Chatto and Bessie Brown (died after the birth) had Robert ; witnesses, John Brown, Laurence Stevenson, John Moyas.

27, John Coventrie and Janet Walwod had Elizabeth ; witnesses, William Walwod of Touch, John Sanders, Adam Walwod.

M. 8, John Brown to Beatrix Thomson (in Inverkeithing kirk).

8, William Gray to Janet Car (in Carnock kirk).

10, Adam Car to Janet Crawfuird (in Saline kirk).

15, James Anderson to Janet Donaldson.

15, Henry Meldrum to Bessie Makie.

AUGUST.

B. 3, James Murgane and Elspet Bowman had James ; witnesses, Robert Scotland, James Mudie, Robert Russell.

3, James Lambe and Helen Zowine had William ; witnesses, William Lambe, William Cusine, David Williamson, Thomas Hall.

10, John Small and Margaret Huggone had twins, Thomas and Geils ; witnesses, Duncan Tailyeour, Thomas Reid, Robert Huggone, Henry Simsone.

10, David Robertson of Craigduckie and Grizel Hutone had Janet ; witnesses, Robert Russell, James Scotland, Nicol Dewar.

10, James Kellok and Helen Spens had Janet ; witnesses, Charles Richardson, John Bennat, James Moyas.

10, John Anderson and Helen Kingorne had Isobel.

11, John Scot and Catherine Mackie had Janet ; witnesses, John Gotterstone, Robert Gray, George Cunningham, younger.

20, John Moreis and Isobel Gotterstone had John ; witnesses, David Moreis, John Clerk, John Gotterstanes.

24, William Hutone and Catherine Mill had James ; witnesses, James Hutone in Lethomis, James Mill, James Cusine.

24, David Strang and Bessie Ritchie had Walter ; witnesses, David Stewart, John Simsone, William Walwod.

27, Edward Primrois and Elizabeth Merschell had James ; witnesses, William Mentethe of Randifuird, James Gib, George Bothwell.

M. 10, John Stevin to Margaret Bennat.

SEPTEMBER.

B. 1, John Huntar and Janet Wilsone had John ; witnesses, John Stirk, Alexander Dron, Robert Anderson.

1, Archibald Honyman and Margaret Wels had Alexander ; witnesses, Alexander Honyman, Robert Wels, Patrick Dewer.

4, Robert Peacok and Catherine Stevinsone had George ; witnesses, George Donald, Laurence Anderson, Alexander Wilsone.

8, George Fergussone and Janet Peirsone had Mary ; witnesses, Patrick Cowper, Peter Law.

10, Thomas Tod and Margaret Hutone had Janet : witnesses, James Hutoun, George Davidson, David Tod.

10, Wattie Hutone, collier in Bayth, and Elspet Miller had Isobel ; witnesses, John Henresone, George Ivat, William Imma.

18, Wattie Phune and Margaret Westwod had James ; witnesses, James Hutone, Mr. James Sibald, James Reid, younger, James Kennedie.

21, Laurence Watsone and Grizel Wilsone had Isobel : witnesses, David Stevinson, Robert Alisone, and James Wilson.

26, Patrick Allane and Janet Moreis had David ; witnesses, David Car, Harry Bull, John Bull.

M. 2, John Johnstone to Margaret Cumming.

16, Andrew Kellok to Margaret Stocks.

OCTOBER.

B. 5, Alexander Drysdell and Bessie Walwod had John ; witnesses, Peter Law, Patrick Cowper, John Wricht.

5, Alexander Greg and Catherine Philpe had [Margaret (*deleted*)] ; child booked and in the kirk, but died before baptism ; witnesses, Thomas Philpe, Abraham Greg, James Greg.

12, John Remainous and Catherine Cunninghame had Annas ; witnesses, Robert Russell, David Smetoun, Edward Remainous.

12, Henry Donald and Bessie Anderson had Thomas ; witnesses, George Donald, Thomas Nasmithe, Thomas Donald.

19, John Levingstone and Christian Young had Helen ; witnesses, William Anderson, John Levingstone, Andrew Young.

22, Thomas Mudie, weaver, and Effie Baverage had James ; witnesses, James Mudie, John Mudie, John Moreis.

26, John Baverage, collier in Keltieheuche, and Helen Kellok had Helen (baptised at Cleish) ; witnesses, Henry Baverage, Adam Meldrum, John Adamson.

28, Thomas Rodger and Grizel Westwod had Thomas ; witnesses, John Anderson, Thomas Hunnon, Richard Potter.

M. 26, Mark Suentoun to Marjory Stevinson (in Inverkeithing kirk).

NOVEMBER.

B. 4, William Hereme and Isobel Sim had John ; witnesses, John Gotterstoun, John Kellok, James Levingstoun.

4, Peter Law and Margaret Walker had Harry ; witnesses, Mr. Harry Makgill, minister, Harry Stewart of Baithe, Mr. James Sibauld.

9, John Wilson *alias* Culros and Helen Stevinson had Janet ; witnesses, Patrick Cowper, Adam Stevinson, John Anderson, litster, John Walker, tailor.

12, Mr. Normand Lindsay (out of the country) and Jean Edmunstone had George (in fornication) ; witnesses, Andrew Mekiljohne, George Durie, Archibald Hodge.   Presented by William Walwod, cordiner.

30, David Cunnon and Elspet Dewar had David ; witnesses, David Dewar of Lassodie, Patrick Dewar, Robert Mudic, Thomas Ritchie.

M. 18, David Anderson to Marjory Burgane.

18, John Orock to Christian Walwod.

24, Robert Davidson to Janet Smetoun.

30, John Murra to Bessie Thomesone.

DECEMBER.

B. 10, William Walwod of Touche and Agnes Alexander had James ; witnesses, Alexander Nicole, James Walwod, Robert Walwod.

14, Andrew Rowane in Gask and Bessie Cunningham had Margaret ; witnesses, David Blak, William Robertson, David Blak, younger.

21, Robert Wilsone and Margaret Hutone had David ; witnesses, John and David Peirson.

21, William Wilson and Christian Wricht had Andrew ; witnesses, Andrew Wricht, John Wricht, William Wilson, Patrick Cowper, Walter Ready.

28, Henry Orock and Margaret Scotland had John ; witnesses, John Orock of Craigbayth, Robert Masterton of Bayth, and John Dewie, flesher.

M. 2, William Mayne to Margaret Henriesone.

16, James Stevinsone to Christian Bathcatt.

23, David Burne to Marjory Mudie.

30, John Murie to Elspet Anderson.

JANUARY [1624].

B. 1, David Lambe and Marjory Wilson had James ; witnesses James Wilson, John Gotterstoun, William Lambe.

13, William Wricht and Jean Canbell had a child baptised called . . . .

20, Catherine Mitchell had Janet (in fornication by an unknown man, near Cramonthe) ; presented by her brother James Mitchell ; witnesses, Mr. William Cuninghame, weaver, John Alison, Henry Peirson.

25, Robert More (died in Kirkcaldy) and Marjory Gib, his wife (now at Keltie heugh), had Helen baptised ; witnesses, William Mudie, mason, William Trumble, smith, James Henriesone, glazier.

M. 6, Alexander Young to Bessie Williamson.

13, James Westwood to Elspet Quhyt.

15, Sir James Murra of Tipper Mure, knight, to Anna Melvill, daughter of late Sir Andrew M. of Garvok, knight.

FEBRUARY.

B. 1, Alexander Donaldson, miller, and Margaret Dagleische had Helen (baptised at Crumbie) ; witnesses, Richard Blacklay, George Donald, John Sanders.

1, John Bruse and Nanse Balfour had . . . . (son); witnesses, William Bruse, Andrew Trumble in Bromehall, James Sands in Wester Gellat.

1, John Levingstone and Janet Smetoun had Janet; witnesses, Andrew Trumble, John and George Trumble, his sons.

1, Andrew Ferlie and Alison Anderson had Thomas; witnesses, Thomas Mitchell, Thomas Young, Thomas Imrie.

1, Peter Sempill and Janet Cunninghame had John; witnesses, John Walker, merchant, William Legat.

1, James Chrichtoun and Nanse Gib had Annas; witnesses, John Gib, Mr. John Drummond.

7, John Keir and Marjory Douglas had Helen; witnesses, Henry Hakerstoun, Robert Mastertoun, John Stevinson.

22, John Lawsone and Janet Donald had Sarah; witnesses, Gilbert Primrois, David Mitchell, William Bruse.

22, George Cunningham (deceased) and Margaret James had Nanse; witnesses, Thomas Walker, John Davidson, John Alison.

22, George Burgane in Queensferry and Janet Swentoun had . . . . (daughter) baptised in Inverkeithing.

26, Laurence Anderson and Grizel Thomesone had Margaret; witnesses, Andrew Walcar, David Douglas, Thomas Thomesone.

M. 3, William Potter to Catherine Mowse.

8, John Young to Bessie Richardson.

15, James Allan to Catherine Stewart.

MARCH.

B. 2, Edward Douglas in Wester Gellat and Beatrix Douglas had Edward; witnesses, Henry Douglas, David Douglas, James Sands.

7, Alexander Davidson and Janet Douglas had Margaret; witnesses, Henry Douglas, William Rae, Thomas Running(?).

14, John Hutone and Margaret Seatone (? Patone) had . . . . (daughter); witnesses, David Peirson, elder, and John Peirson, his son.

14, David Douglas in Gellat and Alison Mitchell had Henry; witnesses, Henry Mekill, Thomas Mitchell, Andrew Mitchell.

21, James Garvie and Beatie Watt had Helen; witnesses, Thomas Walker, Andrew Trumbill, Andrew Walker.

23, John Stevinson and Janet Moreis had Catherine; witnesses, David Moreis, William Walwood, Henry Halkirstoun.

26, Thomas Scotland and Christian Wilson had Janet (in fornication); witnesses, Mr. John Walker, reader, John Anderson, younger, litster, son of John A., elder, and David Laurie, gardener.

M. 30, George Walker to Geils Brown.

APRIL.

B. 3, Andrew Mekiljohne and Janet Anderson had twins, Alexander and Marjory; witnesses, John Anderson, elder, and John A., his son, Peter Law, Claudius Johnestoun, Alexander Tullidaff.

4, David Scotland and Janet Aitkine had . . . . (son); witnesses, Mr. William Wardlaw of Balmule, James Scotland, William Robertson of Craigduckie, Robert Anghous.

15, Robert Scotland and Helen Stobie had Bessie; witnesses, Adam Stobie, Nicol Wardlaw, Thomas Tod.

M. (*None.*)

MAY.

B. 9, Robert Balcate and Elspet Rowane had Janet; witnesses, David Blak, John Hutone, John Balcate.

9, Robert Stanehous (deceased) and Isobel Cunningham had Janet; witness, Andrew Mitchell.

23, Thomas Hunone and Janet Edward had . . . . (son); witnesses, Robert Schortus, James Mudy, William Wilson.

23, John Watson, cordiner, and Marjory Smetoun had twins, Janet and Bessie ; witnesses, John Simson, William Watson, Laurence Watson, Archibald Boyd, John Sanders, James Beany, John Smetoun, John Walker.

M. 4, John Dagleische to Janet Orock.
9, George Cadzoche to Christian Brown.
11, James Henresone to Mawse Aitkine.
25, Robert Cunninghame to Janet Donald.
25, David Wyld to Bessie Bankis.

JUNE.

B. 13, Andrew Anderson and Janet Touche had . . . . (son) ; witnesses, James Lethome, James Hutone, William Anderson.

M. 1, Andrew Wilson to Janet Douglas.
3, James Cusine to Barbara Dewar.
8, George Ædisone to Bessie Sands.
8, Alexander Watson to Helen Kilgour.
10, James Anghous to Elspet Wilson.

JULY.

B. 20, Mr. William Wardlaw of Balmule and Christian Foulls had Elizabeth : witnesses, Patrick Wardlaw of Torrie, Sir Henry Wardlaw of Balmule, George Bothwell of the Hauchis, Robert Levingstone of Baldrige.
25, Adam Wilson and Margaret Cunningham had Andrew ; witnesses, Andrew Wilson, Andrew Cunningham, William Anderson.
25, Thomas Stevinson and Janet Chalmers had Nanse ; witnesses, Patrick Cowper, Alexander Chalmers, John Thomesone, Patrick Stevinson, John Wricht.

M. 1, John Alexander to Isobel Dewar.
13, David Bull to Christian Balfour.

AUGUST.

B. 8, Laurie Anderson and Margaret Lugtoun had Helen ; witnesses, Alexander Buchanan, David Mitchell, John Johnstoun.
15, John Vicar, wright in Barrowstoun, and Isabel Dawsone had James ; witnesses, James Reid, provost, George Davidson, David Laurie.
15, William Philpe and Elspet Lindsay had Christian ; witnesses, John Davidson, William Mudie.
26, George Trumble and Margaret Thomsone had . . . . (son) ; witnesses, Andrew Trumble, Andrew Murray, James Garvie.
29, Thomas Douglas and Elspet Chalmers had Alexander ; witnesses, Alexander Chalmers, Thomas Stevinson, Edward Douglas, Andrew Trumble.

M. 3, James Brown to Nanse Mill.
3, Thomas Westwood to Bessie Robertson.
11, John Rowane to Effie Dick.
17, Robert Peacok to Bessie Wricht.
24, Henry Brown to Elspet Bankis.
24, Robert Yowne to Christian Inglis.
24, Thomas Currour to Helen Hutson.

SEPTEMBER.

B. 5, Robert Drysdale and Grizel Currie had Janet ; witnesses, Patrick Peirson, William Walwod, William Watson.
5, John Burne and Margaret Hutone had William ; witnesses, William Mentethe of Randifuird, William Smart.

5, Laurence Stevinson and Catherine Chatto had Janet : witnesses, John Anderson, James Cowstoun, John Culros.

12, William Andersone and Catherine Cunninghame had John : witnesses, John Trumble, Thomas and Edward Douglas.

12, Andrew Kellok and Margaret Stocks had Margaret : witnesses, Henry Myll, John Kellok, James Kellok, John Baverage.

16, Alexander Brown, servant to Mr. John Phun of Quhythill, and Geils Peirson had Henry (in fornication) ; witnesses, Mr. James Brown, Charles Ritchardson.

19, Robert Levingstoun of Baldrige and Jean Bruse had James ; witnesses, Mr. Thomas Wardlaw of Logie, Mr. William Wardlaw of Balmule, George Bothwell of the Hauchs.

22, John Anderson, bailie, and Helen Kingorne had Andrew ; witnesses, Andrew Wricht, Andrew Mekiljohne.

23, John Alisone, wright, and Grizel Walwod had Janet ; witnesses, Robert Alisone, Adam Walwod, John Coventrie.

26, Alexander Buchanane and Nans Gourlay had James ; witnesses, James Currie, William Currie, Laurence Anderson.

26, William Thomson and Janet Sanders had Andrew ; witnesses, Andrew Murray, Andrew Young, William Anderson.

26, John Oiswald and Christian Hamilton had Alexander : witnesses, John Douglas, James Oiswald, Alexander Beane.

26, John Scot and Catherine Mackie had Christian ; witnesses, John Kellok, John Tod, Alexander Lambe.

26, John Lawson and Margaret Wilson had Annas ; witnesses, William Cunningham, Patrick and Andrew Anderson.

28, Henry Douglas and Helen Wels had Thomas : witnesses. Mr. Thomas Wardlaw. Peter Law, Robert Aikine.

M. 7, James Westwod to Nanse Colzein.

OCTOBER.

B. 3, John Murie and Elspet Anderson had Helen ; witnesses, Andrew Currie, Andrew Cunningham, Andrew Perlie.

3, John Anderson, litster, and Janet Stevinson had Adam : witnesses, John Anderson, eldest, Adam Stevinson, John Anderson, youngest.

6, Robert Lindsay of Kavill and Lilias Drummond had Grizel ; witnesses, James Reid, elder, Thomas Drummond, Mr. John Drummond, his son.

10, Andrew Cunningham in Primrois and Margaret Trumble had Thomas ; witnesses, Thomas Wilson, Andrew Trumble in Bromehall, Andrew Wilson in Mylneburn.

10, Andrew Young and Elspet Fuird had Isobel : witnesses, John Young, Harry Young, William Thomson.

10, Mr. James Sibauld and Isobel Bowstoun had Elizabeth ; witnesses, Mr. Andrew Leirmonth, John Echline.

11, Alexander Brown (a stranger craftsman) and Bessie Matheson had James (in fornication) ; witnesses, James Hutoun, John Birrell.

12, Andrew Barhame of Skelpie and Margaret Stewart had Laurence ; witnesses. Peter Law, George Bothwell.

12, Patrick Curror and Margaret Moreis had John ; witnesses, William Curror, John Stevenson, David Moreis.

17, James Stewart and Margaret Greive had Helen ; witnesses. Henry Mill, William Stanehous, Robert Levingstone.

24, Robert Wyld and Alison Gibsone had Christian ; witnesses, Henry Orock, Nicol Dewar, John Henresone, flesher.

27, Robert Quhyt and Catherine Hunon had Thomas ; witnesses, William Anderson, Thomas Davidson, Robert Anderson, all litsters.

31, Thomas Whyt and Isobel Kellok had James ; witnesses, Robert Lindsay, Thomas Ritche, Andrew Hutone, James Ritchie.

31, Robert Andersone and Janet Smith had Margaret ; witnesses, John Anderson, younger. John Anderson, youngest, Patrick Cowper, bailie.

M. 5, John Hugone to Cicile Glenn.

12, James Moutrey to Janet Aittoun.

NOVEMBER.

B. 16, Mr. James Phune of Lymkills and Agnes Aittoun had Christian ; witnesses, John Scot of the Selvege, Harry Phune and Andrew Trumble in Bromehall.

21, Alexander Drysdell, merchant, and Bessie Walwod had Margaret ; witnesses, Andrew Wricht, bailie, Allan Walwod, Robert Alisone, mason, John Walcar, merchant.

25, John Simsone and Bessie Hutoun had John ; witnesses, John Anderson, younger, Gilbert Sanders, William Watson.

28, James Andersone and Janet Donald had William ; witnesses, William Cunningham, William Anderson in Pitconnochie, William Anderson, litster.

30, David Mitchell in Pitlivar and Margaret Currie had James ; witnesses, James Leslie of Pitlivar, James Mitchell, James Currie in Crumbie.

M. 9, William Cunningham to Isobel Walwod.

23, James Anderson to Janet Rutherford.

30, Archibald Nicole to Christian Wilsone.

DECEMBER.

B. 9, Adam Car and Janet Crawfurd had Duncan ; witnesses, Duncan Car, father of the said Adam, Thomas Tod in the Clun, James Murgane in Drumtuthill.

12, Thomas Sivess (in Musselburgh parish) and Isobel Brand had Bessie (in fornication) ; witnesses, John Stevinson of Bayth, David Moreis, younger, John Makqueine.

12, John Walker and Margaret Trumble had Barbara ; witnesses, Patrick Cowper, Peter Law, David Moreis.

21, Henry Hakerstone and Helen Cunningham had Isobel ; witnesses, Andrew Mitchell, John Stevinson of Beath.

26, John Kinloch and Bessie Sim had Bessie ; witnesses, Alexander Honyman, David Car, Charles Baid.

26, William Legat and Christian Burne had William ; witnesses, William Smart, David Blak.

28, William Bruse and Rose Snellok had George ; witnesses, Robert Levingstoun of Baldrig, George Bruse of Carnock, Andrew Trumble in Bromehall.

28, Mr. James Dewar of Lassodie and Elspet Moncreiff had Jean ; witnesses, Mr. William Wardlaw of Balmile, David Robertson of Easter Craigduckie, David Cunnone, portioner of Mastertoun.

28, William Cadzone and Margaret Burne had Andrew ; witnesses, Andrew Cunningham, Andrew Currie, Andrew Lathangie.

M. 14, Thomas Johnstone to Nanse Aittoun.

14, James Matheson to Christie Anderson.

30, David Rutherfurd to Marjory Wilson.

JANUARY [1625].

B. 4, David Blak and Marjory Blakwod had William ; witnesses, William Mackie, William Blak, Henry Dick.

4, Thomas Mitchell in Gellat and Margaret Dick had David ; witnesses, David Mitchell, David Douglas, Henry Douglas, burgess of Dunfermline.

4, William Walwod, cordiner, and Margaret Lindsay had William ; witnesses, William Watson, John Simson, John Bull.

4, Harry Stewart of Beath and Catherine Kirkcaldie had John ; witnesses, John Walker, merchant, James Gib, John Anderson, younger, litster.

6, David Seathe and Christian Hog had Isobel ; witnesses, John Anderson, elder, Andrew Wryght, bailie, and Charles Richardson. "This man wes ane stranger cummit from Edinburgh to exerceis his calling being ane wricht efter the visitatioun of Dunfermlyne with fyre."

"The — day," John Greif and Margaret Thomesone had Robert; witnesses, Robert Trumble in Tunigask, Robert Greif, John Thomson.

Same day, John Thomson and Effie Finlay had Annas (baptised at Cleish) ; witnesses, George Moutrey, mariner, Henry Baverage, John Adamson.

Same day, William Potter and Catherine Mowse had Christian ; witnesses, Thomas Blakwod, Andrew and James Potter.

Same day, David Beany and Bessie Moreis had Jean ; witnesses, James Hutone, merchant, Robert Cunningham in Sillitoun, John Huntar in Pittincreiff.

Same day, Henry Peirsone and Helen Williamson had Robert ; witnesses, Robert Stirk, Robert Wels.

Same day, Patrick Cowper and Janet Murray had Catherine ; witnesses, Mr. Thomas Wardlaw, George Bothwell.

16, John Baid and Bessie Spens had Effie ; witnesses, David Stevinson, Patrick Stevenson, Henry Mill.

18, John Anderson and Martha Mastertoun had Marjory ; witnesses, James Reid, provost, Robert Mastertoun of Beath, Gilbert Sanders, clerk.

23, Robert Wilson and Christian Simraell had John ; witnesses, John Davidson in Fod, John Kellok, David Inche.

23, Robert Russell and Barbara Elder had Henry ; witnesses, Nicol Wardlaw, George Dewar, James Murgane.

23, John Moyas and Christian Philpe had James ; witnesses, James Dewar, David Burne, John Brown.

23, Thomas Sands and Margaret Fentone had Harry ; witnesses, Henry Wardlaw, Thomas Stanehous, Thomas Cunnon.

23, William Mudie and Janet Christie had George ; witnesses, George Bothwell, James Reid, provost, Robert Stirk, Andrew Walker, Thomas Christie, Thomas Stevinson.

23, James Hart (deceased) and Janet Murie had twins, Thomas and Catherine ; witnesses, James Kellok, James Cunnon.

23, Harry Robertson and Nanse Murray had Janet (baptised at Ballingry) ; witnesses, Henry Baverage, James Baverage, John Brown.

30, George Drysdell and Bessie Gibson had Margaret ; witnesses, Robert Mastertoun, John Stevenson, James Mann.

30, Andrew Lindsay and Marjory Walker had Margaret ; witnesses, William Walcar, John Brown.

30, William Mudie, weaver, and Nanse Mackie had Christian ; witnesses, Henry Peirson, John Alison, John Scott.

M. 4, James Garvie to Janet Lochtie.

FEBRUARY.

B. 3, James Kellok of Mastertoun and Margaret Mudie had Elspet ; witnesses, David Cunnon, James Mitchell, Thomas Stanehous.

15, Robert Anghous and Christian Smetone had Catherine ; witnesses, Mr. William Wardlaw, Mr. James Dewar, James Anghous, John Rowane, Robert Russell.

15, Patrick Kingorne and Janet Schortus had Francis (in fornication) ; witnesses, Mr. James Durie, Charles Richardson, and George Moreis.

20, John Anderson and Janet Meldrum had Janet; witnesses, Patrick Murray, John Coventrie, John Meldrum.

20, John Gray and Alison Martene had William ; witnesses, William Robertson, David Robertson, Robert Anghous.

20, John Forret, collier, and Elspet Smart had John ; witnesses, John Henresone, John Allane, Wattie Hutone.

21, Richard Potter and Bessie Thomesone had Peter ; witnesses, Peter Law, Andrew Wricht, Patrick Cowper.

27, Robert Douglas and Margaret Peirsone had John ; witnesses, John Trumble and George Trumble, brothers in Bromehall, and John Lawson, smith.

27, James Reid, younger, and Marion Broun had Henry ; witnesses, James Reid, provost, Mr. Thomas Wardlaw, Patrick Cowper.

M. 1, Robert Tod to Bessie Peirson.

7, John Henresone of Fordell to Margaret Mentethe, daughter of William M. of Randiefurd.

22, Patrick Legat to Effie Lawsone.

22, Andrew Drysdell to Janet Bonalay.

22, James Patone to Isobel Watson.

MARCH.

B. 6, Thomas Paterson and Marion Goodfellow had James (baptised at Cleish) ; witnesses, John Henresone, John Thomson, James Robertson.

6, John Hadstone and Bessie Beany had Janet ; witnesses, William Anderson, Thomas Drylaw, David Awstiane.

6, Laurence Anderson and Grizel Thomson had Alison ; witnesses, Thomas Walker, James Murgane, Thomas Key.

6, Henry Trumble and Catherine Cusine had Thomas ; witnesses, Mr. Thomas Wardlaw, Mr. James Sibald, Andrew Wricht.

6, Thomas Hall and Christian Lambe had Andrew ; witnesses, Andrew Murray, William Wilson, Alexander Young.

6, James Matheson and Christian Anderson had William ; witnesses, John Davidson, William Philpe, Nicole Cornvell.

13, John Spens and Jean Brand had John ; witnesses, Duncan Tailyeour, John Tailyeour, Charles Richardson.

13, John Davidson and Marjory Brown had Margaret ; witnesses, Peter Brown, Patrick Trumble, William Stanehous.

13, James Cusine and Barbara Dewar had . . . . (son) ; witnesses, William Hutoun, John Cusine, Gavin Stanehous.

13, James Potter and Marion Walker had Marjory ; witnesses, Richard Potter, Robert Hugone and Richard Potter (*sic*).

15, Thomas Christie in Urquhart and Elspet Durie had Jean ; witnesses, Mr. James Durie, Andrew Walker, William Mudie.

15, Charles Baid and Helen Young had Christian ; witnesses, John Sanders, Robert Hugone, David Laurie.

22, Andrew Wilson and Janet Douglas had Henry ; witnesses, Henry Wardlaw, Alexander Davidson, John Brown.

22, Archibald Boyd, cordiner, and Janet Watson had William ; witnesses, William Watson, Laurence Watson, John Simson.

27, Alexander Glas and Janet Toward had William ; witnesses, William Cunningham in Crocefurd, William Walwod, William Anderson.

27, John Allane, collier in Beath, and Janet Bowar had James ; witnesses, George Ivat, James Stewart, Andrew Murrie.

27, George Moreis, collier, and Bessie Beany had Mary ; witnesses, George Moreis, John Brumat (?), Duncan Taylor.

31, James Mitchell and Christian Legat had John ; witnesses, John Henresone of Fordall, John Laurie, John Anderson, notary.

M. 1, Robert Anderson to Mawse Galrige.

6, Robert Murgane to Helen Smithe.

APRIL.

B. 3, Thomas Dewar and Margaret Mastertoun had Christian ; witnesses, William and David Robertson, David Scotland.

3, William Forrester and Janet Mackgreetie had John ; witnesses, John Forrester, John Ædison, Thomas Cuming.

3, Thomas Philpe and Catherine Harrower had Bessie ; witnesses, William Walwod of Beath, Harry Stewart of Beath, Robert Peirsone of Beath.

5, Claudius Johnestone and Jean Sands had William ; witnesses, William Mentethe of Randifuird, John Anderson, younger, and Peter Law.

7, Gavin Stanehous and Marjory Nicole had Gavin ; witnesses, Mr. Thomas Wardlaw of Logie, Peter Law, John Anderson, younger.

10, George Meldrum and Marjory Walker had Janet ; witnesses, Andrew Walker, William Walker, Thomas Christie.

10, William Wilson and Christian Wricht had Bessie ; witnesses, Patrick Cowper, Andrew Wricht, John Wricht and William Wilson, father of the said William.

17, Malcolm Makqueine and Janet Jonkein had Catherine ; witnesses, John Davidson in the Nethertown, Robert Davidson, his son, and Robert Miller.

19, Andrew Mentethe and Catherine Gardner had Janet ; witnesses, John Trumble, James Cunninghame, Robert Cunningham.

19, Richard Potter and Bessie Leirmonth had Bessie ; witnesses, Thomas Johnstone, Thomas Rodger, Richard and James Potter, sons of the said Richard.

26, John Hogane and Cicile Glen had Robert ; witnesses, Robert Hugane, David Miller, Henry Miller.

26, John Walker and Jean Maxwell had Harry ; witnesses, Mr. Harry Makgill, Andrew Wrycht.

27, James Kennedie and Janet Hutoun had Charles ; witnesses, James Hutone, John Anderson, younger, Mr. James Durie, George Fergusson, Robert Alisone.

M.   [*None.*]

MAY.

B.   1, James Allane and Catherine Stewart had Margaret ; witnesses, Laurence Patrik, John Oswald, Patrick Allane.

15, John Brown and Margaret Smetone had Margaret ; witnesses, John Brown, William Brown and Henry Brown, his son.

15, Andrew Hall and Margaret Hardie had Thomas ; witnesses, Thomas Mitchell, Thomas Stanehous, Thomas Cunnone.

15, Andrew Trumble, portioner of the Grange, and Helen Currie had Janet ; witnesses, James Currie in Crumbie, Andrew Trumble in Bromehall, James Trumble.

22, John Kellok and Janet Matheson had Margaret ; witnesses, William Kellok, Patrick Kellok, Patrick Whyt.

22, John Dow and Margaret Merser had Laurence ; witnesses, Laurence Merser, David Robertson, David Stewart.

24, William Walwod, baker, and Bessie Nicole had Isobel ; witnesses, Patrick Cowpar, Andrew Wricht, Allan Walwod.

M.   3, James Peirsone to Janet Galrige.

31, Robert Kellok to Catherine Douglas.

31, David Keir to Isobel Smithe.

31, John Currie to Margaret Watsone.

JUNE.

B.   5, David Bull and Christian Balfour had John ; witnesses, John Brown, Henry Wardlaw, James Stanehous.

14, George Donald and Margaret Stevinson had Margaret ; witnesses, David Mitchell, William Bruse, Robert Cunningham in Sillitoun.

14, James Anderson and Janet Clerk had David ; witnesses, David Anderson, William Cunningham, Andrew Lessels.

14, Finlay Moyle and Bessie Stevin had Isobel ; witnesses, Peter Law, Thomas Reid, James Hutone.

17, William Mackie and Margaret Betsone had Isobel ; witnesses, John Betsone, David Blak, George Dewar.

19, James Hamilton, piper, and Helen Maknab had James ; witnesses, John Smart, Andrew Lessells, Andrew Dunmure.

22, Henry Brown and Elspet Banks had John ; witnesses, Laurence Merser, George Davidson, Robert Stirk.

23, John Currie, tailor, and Margaret Watson had Helen ; witnesses, Andrew Trumble in Grange, Andrew Currie, James Mudie.

26, James Lethome and Isobel Makbethe had Isobel ; witnesses, James Cunningham, Patrick Lawson, Thomas Nasmith.

26, George Penman and Marion Dregorn had Margaret ; witnesses, Alexander Penman, Duncan Talyeour, George Moreis.

26, John Ritchie and Grizel Stevenson had John.

28, James Henresone, glazier, and Mayse Aikine had Janet ; witnesses, Thomas Blakwod, James Moyas, Patrick Legat, Malcolm Cowell.

30, Margaret Anderson (vagabond) had a child baptised called . . . , alleged begotten in adultery with George Lindsay of Kavill ; witnesses, George Davidson (presenter of the child) and Andrew Gaw.

M. 7, George Dewar to Isobel Blak.

14, John Wilson to Margaret Brand.

21, James Oiswald to Janet Anderson.

28, Robert Mudie to Christian Lundie.

28, James Mitchell to Isobel Cunningham.

JULY

B. 3, Robert Zowne and Christian Inglis had Catherine ; witnesses, Mr. Thomas Wardlaw of Logie, George Bothwell, Robert Kellok.

10, John Huntar and Janet Wilson had Janet ; witnesses, Andrew Maker, George Meldrum, Michael Meldrum.

10, James Grege and Helen Rankine had Janet ; witnesses, Patrick Peirson, James Anderson, Alexander Greg.

17, John Henresone, flesher in Keltieheugh, and Bessie Anghous had . . . . (son) ; witnesses, Robert Anghous, James Baverage, Robert Trumble in Tunygask. (Baptised at Cleish.)

19, Andrew Galrige and Isobel Johnstone had Andrew ; witnesses, James Garvie, Nicol Inglis, Robert Johnstone.

24, James Westwod and Nans Colzeir had John ; witnesses, John Henresone of Fordall, Robert Alisone and John Burne, masons.

24, William Curror and Janet Mitchell had Christian ; witnesses, David Moreis, John Stevinson, Patrick Curror, Robert Mudie.

M. 19, John Tomesone to Janet Hutone.

AUGUST.

B. 2, William Smithe, portioner of Fod, and Margaret Mastertoun had Catherine ; witnesses, Patrick Trumble, John Davidson, William Mastertoun.

4, Robert Davidson and Janet Smetone had John ; witnesses, John Davidson, his father, John Anderson, younger, litster, and Harry Smetone, his father-in-law.

9, William Dougall and Jean Scot had Janet ; witnesses, George Trumble, James Cunningham, Robert Peacok.

9, John Daglishe and Janet Orock had Catharine ; witnesses, John Wels, Thomas Blackwood, Alexander Lambe.

12, John Bell and Helen Makcraiche had Nanse ; witnesses, Andrew Walker, Alexander Chalmer, Robert Makcraiche. (Begotten in fornication in Rosyth parish, and discipline satisfied at Inverkeithing, and baptised here by request of minister of Inverkeithing.)

13, John Wilson and Janet Drysdell had James ; witnesses, James Reid, younger, James Gib, James Moyas.

16, James Trottar and Bessie Lawsone had Lawrence ; witnesses, Lawrence Anderson in Pitlivar, David Anderson in Kistock, William Sanders in the Hiltoun.

23, Andrew Rowane in Gask and Bessie Cunningham had William ; witnesses, Robert Trumble in Tunygask, and George Trumble his son, and Robert Russell, miller.

23, James Layng and Effie Anderson had Janet; witness, Thomas Walwod.

23, Peter Sempill and Janet Cunningham had Isobel; witnesses, Patrick Legat, Andrew Potter.

28, Lawrence Anderson and Jean Sutone had William; witnesses, Patrick Anderson, William Anderson, his son, John Lawson.

28, Robert Bruce, servant to William Menteith of Randifurd, and Bessie Fine had Margaret; witnesses, William Mentethe of Randifurd, John Bruse, cook, Stevin Mekirt (?).

28, John Ritchie and Christian Lindsay had Elspet; witnesses, Thomas Ritchie, William Walwod of Beath, William Stanehous.

28, James Mowtrey and Janet Aittone had Andrew; witnesses, Andrew Trumble, Andrew Cunningham, Thomas Douglas.

M. 9, David Inglis to Helen Cumming.

SEPTEMBER.

B. 4, William Sanders, tailor, and Christiane Hutone had Nanse; witnesses, Robert Blakatter, James Sanders, and Robert Scotland.

4, Jerome Brown and Catherine May had George (baptised at Carnock); witnesses, George Durie of Craigluscour, Robert May in Culross, James Anderson in Luscour.

11, George Ædison and Bessie Sands had Margaret; witnesses, James Sands, David Sands in Gellat, his son, and William Anderson there.

11, James Hutone in Crocefuird and Margaret Walker had James; witnesses, William Cunningham in Crocefuird, William Saunders in Hiltoun, James Peirson in Pitdinnie.

11, David Broun in Mylnehills and Isobel Mayne had Helen; witnesses, William Wilson in the Mill, Andrew Wilson, his son, William Mayne, Henry Brown.

11, John Birrell and Margaret Colzeir had Janet; witnesses, Adam Masterton, John Walker, merchant, Abraham Greg.

13, John Wels, cordiner, and Christian Austiane had John; witnesses, John Simsone, William Walwod, Gilbert Car.

18, James Andersone and Janet Rutherfurd had William; witnesses, James Trottar, James Peirson, William Anderson.

18, John Clerk and Catherine Baid had Thomas; witnesses, Thomas Phinne, Thomas Huaon, James Lugtoun.

18, John Alisone, mason, and Marjory Elder had Barbara; witnesses, Robert Russell, Thomas Davidson, George Mudie.

18, William Philpe and Elspet Lindsay had Janet; witnesses, Nicol Cornwell, William Wilson, Patrick Stevenson.

20, Andrew Mekiljohne and Janet Anderson had James; witnesses, James Gib, John Walker, Peter Law.

M. 26, Robert Makcraiche to Isabel Donaldson.

OCTOBER.

B. 9, Thomas Alexander and Janet Knelands had Christian; witnesses, William Mudie, John Brown, John Burne.

10, Thomas Cumming in Gellat and Marion Douglas had twins, one dying unbaptised and the other baptised Thomas; witnesses, Thomas Mitchell, Alexander Davidson, Thomas Johnstoun.

11, Archie Hodge and Magie Walker had Helen; witnesses, John Anderson, younger, Robert Stirk, William Kairne (?).

16, William Walwod in Touch and Agnes Alexander had Bessie; witnesses, Mr. James Durie, bailie, John Anderson, elder and younger.

17, James Aissone (in Edinburgh) and Bessie Watson had Geils (in fornication); witnesses, James Hutone, James Kennedy, William Watson, cordiner, presented by Gavin Stanehous.

20, William Lambe and Janet Cunningham had Alexander ; witnesses, Alexander Lambe, James Mudie, David Lambe.

25, William Peirsone in Mortlathank and Margaret Young had William (baptised at Fossoway) ; witnesses, Robert Levingstone in Cruikmylne, Harry Dempstertoun in Dalkeithe.

25, Thomas Curror and Helen Hutsone had David ; witnesses, David Moreis, John Stevenson, Henry Hukstoun.

25, Robert Peirsone in Beath and Marjory Peirson had Robert ; witnesses, Robert Masterton, James Reid, younger, Harry Stewart of Beath.

30, Thomas Cowane and Jean Burnesyd had James ; witnesses, William Masterton, James Kennedy, David Lawrie.

M. 12, David Weymis of Romegay to Christian Wardlaw, daughter of Mr. Thomas Wardlaw of Logie.

NOVEMBER.

B. 6, John Watson and Janet Kennedy had Elspet ; witnesses, Edward and Thomas Douglas, David Sands, William Anderson.

6, Henry Simsone and Bessie Thomson had James ; witnesses, John Brown, George Penman, John Thomson, Duncan Tailyeour.

13, John Burne and Margaret Hutone had Margaret ; witnesses, Robert Alisone, Andrew Walker, George Mudie.

13, James Mudie and Grizel Lambe had James ; witnesses, Robert Mudie, John Davidson, Alexander Lambe.

13, Thomas Moire and Grizel Walwod had Thomas ; witnesses, Thomas Stevinson, William Philpe, James Hill.

13, James Feg and Elspet Smetoun had Henry ; witnesses, John Feg, Thomas Walwod, Henry Wilson.

13, Alexander Young and Bessie Williamson had Margaret ; witnesses, Harry Walwod, Harry Bull, Robert Alisone.

13, Robert Anghous and Christian Drysdell had Robert ; witnesses, Robert Anghous "his master for the tyme," John Currie, Walter Cowbraithe.

15, Thomas Stevinson and Janet Chalmers had Thomas ; witnesses, David Stevenson, elder and younger, Thomas Douglas, Thomas Trumble, Thomas Elder.

22, Nicol Rowane and Janet Hugone had John ; witnesses, David Blak, younger, Henry Dick, younger, William Mackie.

27, Robert Murgane and Helen Smithe had James ; witnesses, James Lugtone, James Patoun, George Moreis.

29, Robert Henresone and Janet Car had Jean ; witnesses, David Stewart, John Anderson, James Hutone, tailor.

29, John Thomson and Janet Hutone had Patrick ; witnesses, Patrick Trumble, Patrick Stevenson, James Hutone.

M. 7, James Hamilton to Jean Sanders.

8, James Stanehous to Margaret Trumble.

15, John Broun to Eupham Simson.

22, William Wastwater to Margaret Clerk.

22, John Chatto to Catherine Mudie.

22, William Inche to Margaret James.

DECEMBER.

B. 2, Andrew Colzeir and Isobel Anderson had George ; witnesses, George Davidson, John Dagleische, Andrew Gaw.

4, Archibald Gleinzie and Agnes Æssone had Nanse ; witnesses, James Lethome, William Sanders, William Lawson.

4, James Mill in Lochend and Isobel Dewar had Helen ; witnesses, John Mill, George Dewar, William Hutone.

4, John Kinimond and Elspet Chalmers had Jean (in fornication); witnesses, Alexander Chalmers, James Gib, George Bothwell.

6, David Bull and Margaret Potter had David ; witnesses, David Car, William Trumble, Robert Anderson.

11, David Peirsone and Isobel Henryson had Elspet; witnesses, James Kellok, David Cunnon, Robert Stanehous.

11, John Dougall and Bessie Craik had David; witnesses, David Stevinson, Thomas Hunnon, James Ronald.

11, Peter Buist and "his woman" had Helen (in fornication); witnesses, Charles Ritchardsone, John Simsone, Archibald Hodge.

13, William Hereme and Isobel Sim had Andrew; witnesses, William Mackie, David Blak, John Kellok.

13, Robert Levingstone of Baldrige and Jean Bruce had William; witnesses, William Mentethe of Randifurd, John Henresone of Fordall, Sir John Gib.

18, Ninian Duncane and Bessie Hutone had Bessie; witnesses, James and William Duncane, Patrick Anderson, John Hutone.

18, William Anderson in Hiltown of Pitfirran and Janet Cunningham had Isobel; witnesses, Patrick Anderson, William Lawson, William Sanders.

18, James Dagleishe and Catherine Wardlaw had Christian; witnesses, Mr. William Wardlaw, George Trumble, James Smetone.

18, Edward Douglas in Gellat and Beatrix Douglas had David; witnesses, David Douglas, David Mitchell, Thomas Mitchell.

18, David Strang and Bessie Ritchie had Christian; witnesses, John Simsone, William Walwod, George Davidson.

27, Robert Peacok and Bessie Wricht had James; witnesses, James Lethome, Adam Wilson, George Donald.

27, Oliver Culane and Margaret Smithe had William; witnesses, William Gray, George Meldrum, John Huntare.

27, Harry Walwod and Helen Kennedy had Harry; witnesses, Mr. Harry Makgill, minister, Mr. Thomas Wardlaw, provost, David Weyms of Rumgay, George Bothwell of Haughs.

M. 13, Laurie Gibone to Margaret Sanders.

20, David Christie to Janet Peacok.

JANUARY [1626].

B. 1, Alexander Spittell and Isobel Hiltone had Marjory; witnesses, David Blak, William Robertson.

1, Alexander Greg and Catherine Philpe had James; witnesses, James Stanehous, James Grege, James Hutoun.

1, Henry Malcome and Catherine Inglis had Annas; witnesses, James Æssoun, John Smith, Henry Smetone.

8, George Cunningham and Margaret Mastertoun had Janet; witnesses, Alexander Lambe, William Keir, Robert Hutone.

15, John Baid and Bessie Spens had Thomas; witnesses, Thomas Stevenson, David Stevenson, elder and younger, William Peirsone.

15, Robert Anderson and Janet Smith had Catherine; witnesses, John Bennat, George Davidson, David Lawrie.

17, Thomas Rodger and Grizel Westwod had Margaret; witnesses, Richard Potter, Thomas Johnestoun, David Stevinson.

22, James Cunningham and Isobel Cunningham had twins, Andrew and Isobel; witnesses, Thomas Wilson, William Anderson, Andrew Cunningham, James Lethome.

29, William Henresone and Bessie Forsyth had Jean; witnesses, James Hamilton, Robert Stirk, John Simsone.

31, Robert Lochtie and Catherine Bankis had John; witnesses, John Bankis, John Stirk, John Schortus.

M. 2, James Dewar to Christian Philpe.

3, Mr. Harry Makgill, minister, to Isobel Lindsay.

3, David Hoge to Marjory Bull.

17, Thomas Davidson to Isobel Anderson.

31, William Potter to Janet Porter.

FEBRUARY.

B. 5, Alexander Lambe and Janet Dagleische had Alexander ; witnesses, Alexander Honyman, Adam Wylie, James Moyas.

7, James Garvie and Janet Garvie had Thomas ; witnesses, James Kellock, David Cunnon, Thomas Cunnon.

12, William Hutone and Catherine Mill had Robert ; witnesses, Robert Wels, James Mill, John Mill.

12, John Potter and Janet Inglis had Janet ; witnesses, Patrick Cowper, William Trumble, John Anderson, litster.

12, James Patoun and Isobel Watson had Margaret ; witnesses, John Watson, James Mudie, Robert Quhyt.

12, John Jamesone and Marion Dick had Lilias ; witnesses, Robert Lindsay, John Makcraiche, James Dick.

16, Henry Douglas, merchant, and Helen Wels had William ; witnesses, William Brown, clerk, David Peirsone, Robert Stirk.

21, John Greif and Margaret Thomson had Helen ; witnesses, Robert Greive, Robert Russell, John Dewar.

21, Wattie Hutone and Elspet Miller had John ; witnesses, John Henresone, George Ivat, William Imma.

21, William Spens and Christian Wallange had William ; witnesses, William Smart, David Strang, John Allisone.

21, Robert Kirk and Grizel Anderson had Thomas ; witnesses, James Moyas, Harry Bull, Thomas Schortus.

21, John Peirsone and Marion Hutone had David ; witnesses, David Peirsone, elder, William Cunningham in Knokes, Robert Cunningham in the Sillitoun.

26, Alexander Davidson and Janet Douglas had Elspet ; witnesses, Henry Wardlaw, Robert Kellock, James Stanehous.

28, John Moreis and Isobel Gotterstoun had Janet ; witnesses, John Walker, bailie, Robert Mudie, Henry Moreis.

M. 21, George Trumble to Isobel Gib.

22, George Mudie to Helen Stirk.

22, John Dagleische to Janet Craik.

23, John Anderson, eldest, to Grizel Lindsay (in Carnock kirk).

MARCH.

B. 3, William Walwod, cordiner, and Margaret Lindsay had James ; witnesses, James Reid, James Hutone, John Simson.

5, John Inglis and Nanse Adame had Helen ; witnesses, George Dewar, David Blak, Maurice Inglis.

5, Adam Stobie of Luscour and Helen Gibbone had William (baptised at Carnock).

12, Andrew Meik and Helen Gibson had Margaret ; witnesses, David Mitchell, Laurence Anderson, Alexander Wilson.

12, Robert Westwod and Janet Garnok had Catherine ; witnesses, John Scot, James Mitchell, Abraham Greg.

14, John Hodge and Effie Brown had Janet ; witnesses, John Crock, John Dick, John Tod.

15, George Ferguson and Janet Peirson had John ; witnesses, Patrick Cowper, John Walker, bailie, Peter Law, dean of guild.

19, David Drysdell and Isobel Touchie had David ; witnesses, David Peirson, Patrick Anderson, William Sanders.

19, David Reid and Margaret Lawson had Janet ; witnesses, Nicol Wardlaw, Patrick Stobie, John Stirk.

19, James Lindsay and Nanse Mentethe had Thomas ; witnesses, Thomas Davidson, Thomas Rodger, John Wilson.

28, Henry Donald and Bessie Anderson had Janet ; witnesses, Robert Cunningham, Charles Lawson, Thomas Wilson.

28, William Robertson and Janet Littlejohn had Jean ; witnesses, James Littlejohn, John Williamson, John Robertson.

28, David Stevinsone and Isobel Christie had Andrew ; witnesses, Patrick Trumble, Andrew Trumble, William Masterton.

28, Thomas Blakwod and Isobel Inglis had Nanse ; witnesses, Robert Anderson, Maurice Inglis, Nicol Inglis.

28, Robert Pittilloche and Marjory Miller had James ; witnesses, James Reid, William Philipe, Thomas Blaikie.

28, James Æssone and Catherine Watson had James ; witnesses, James Anderson, David Miller, Peter Buist.

M. [*None.*]

APRIL.

B. 2, James Anderson and Elspet Christie had Janet ; witnesses, Patrick Peirson, John Christie, David Christie.

2, John Wels, baker, and Catherine Drummond had Nanse ; witnesses, John Bennat, Thomas Elder, John Dagleische.

4, Thomas Davidson, litster, and Isobel Anderson had John : witnesses, John Davidson, his father, Robert Davidson, his brother, John Anderson, younger.

6, Mr. James Sibald, schoolmaster, and Isobel Bowstoun had Margaret : witnesses, David Weymis of Romegay, Mr. Andrew Leirmonth, minister of Saline, Mr. Thomas Melvill, brother of the Laird of Raith.

11, David Robertson of Craigduckie and Grizel Hutone had Henry; witnesses, Mr. William Wardlaw, Mr. James Dewar, George Dewar.

11, James Oiswald and Janet Anderson had George ; witnesses, George Trumble, James Hall, William Anderson.

11, David Cunnon in Mastertoun and Elspet Dewar had Thomas ; witnesses, Thomas Ædisone, Thomas Stanehous, Thomas Cunnon.

11, Wattie Phune and Margaret Westwod had Christian ; witnesses, Charles Richardson, Robert Wels, John Sanders.

16, John Baverage in Keltie and Helen Kellok had Janet ; witnesses, William Mackie, John Betsone, John Adamson. (Baptised at Cleish.)

23, Andrew Drysdell and Janet Bonaley had James ; witnesses, James Ritchie, James Peirsone, David Scotland.

23, James Dewar and Grizel Hoy had David : witnesses, David Dewar of Lassodie, Andrew Rowane in the Gask.

23, John Merschell and Margaret Fuird had John ; witnesses, John Sanders, James Murray, Robert Hugoun, Charles Richardson.

25, John Coventrie and Janet Walwod had Catherine ; witnesses, John Simsone, James Stanehous, James Mitchell.

25, Thomas Johnestone and Agnes Aittone had Harry ; witnesses, William Mastertoun, Harry Mudie, John Johnstone.

26, Richard Scotland and Margaret Clerk had Grizel ; witnesses, William Brown, Robert Wels, Robert Scotland.

M. 25, David Smetoun to Elspet Russell.

25, James Miller to Nanse Moreis.

25, Laurence Hutone to Janet Stevinson.

25, John Robertson to Janet Lindsay.

MAY.

B. 2, William Pillonis and Isobel Douglas had Margaret ; witnesses, David Mitchell, Thomas Douglas, Edward Douglas.

2, Andrew Drummond and Bessie Young had John ; witnesses, Patrick Cowper, James Ritchie, Thomas Ritchie, William Wilson.

4, John Dagleische and Janet Craik had Marjory; witnesses, William Brown, James Hutone, William Walker.

4, Francis Cokburne and Alison Cokburne had twins, Patrick and Alexander ; witnesses, John Anderson, Peter Law, Robert Stirk, Andrew Trumble, portioner of the Grange.

4, Andrew Gaw and Margaret Colzeir had John ; witnesses, John Simsone, Andrew Colzeir, George Davidson.

7, William Robertson and Marjory Martene had Margaret ; witnesses, John Robertson, John Anderson, John Thomson.

14, Archibald Nicole and Christian Wilsone had John ; witnesses, Patrick Anderson, John Anderson, Robert Cunningham.

16, Mr. James Phinne of Lymkills and Agnes Aittone had John ; witnesses, William Mentethe of Randifurd, John Henresone of Fordall, James Stewart of Rossyithe.

21, Adam Hendeme and Margaret Greive had Margaret ; witnesses, William Walwod, Robert Peirson, John Walwod.

21, William Lawsone and Effie Waterstone had James ; witnesses, James Cusine, John Clerk, Patrick Legat.

25, Mr. William Wardlaw of Balmule and Christian Fowls had Janet ; witnesses, Sir Henry Wardlaw of Pitreavie, George Durie of Craigluscour, Sir John Gib of Knok.

28, James Hall and Margaret Anderson had Andrew ; witnesses, Andrew Murray, William Mudie, William Wilson.

31, William Mackie and Margaret Betsone had . . . (daughter ; witnesses, John Betson, John Gotterstone, David Blak. (Baptized at Ballingry.)

M. 2, John Orock to Janet Mastertoun.

2, Robert Drysdell to Marjory Burgan (in Inverkeithing).

9, James Beany to Margaret Honyman.

JUNE.

B. 4, Mark Swentone and Marjory Stevenson had Janet ; witnesses, John Thomson, George Trumble, younger, in Bromehall, and Florie Burgane. (Baptized at Inverkeithing.)

4, Williame Patone and Janet Ædisone had Bessie ; witnesses, John Simson, Laurie Anderson, Peter Buist.

6, Donald Fraser and Margaret Berill had Catherine ; witnesses, John Hutone, Wattie Cowbraithe, Thomas Murray.

11, George Moreis and Bessie Hutone had John ; witnesses, John Simsone, John Bennat, William Smart.

16, Patrick Legat and Effie Lawson had Annas ; witnesses, John Lawson, Patrick Lawson, William Legat.

17, John Robertson and Isobel Hutone had John ; witnesses, Laurie Anderson, Thomas Peirson, Robert Cant.

19, Robert Maistertoun of Baithe, and Margaret Mastertoun had Thomas ; witnesses, David Moreis in Baith, John Harper, John Stevinson, Patrick Dewar.

19, Allan Walwod and Margaret Forrester had Janet (in fornication) ; witness, Charles Richardson.

22, John Henreson of Fordall and Margaret Mentethe had John ; witnesses, Sir John Gib of Knok, William Mentethe of Randifurd, Sir Robert Halkheid of Pitfirran, George Durie of Craigluscour, James Logane of Cowstcoun.

27, James Mitchell in Masterton and Isobel Cunningham had Nanse ; witnesses, Thomas Mitchell in Gellat, Henry Mekill, Henry Hakirstone of Beath.

M. 13, Andrew Elder to Janet Phune.

13, Henry Dick to Bessie Stevinson.

13, William Cambell to Margaret Brown.

13, William Moreis to Elspet Guild.

16, William Straquhen to Elspet Mastertoun.

27, Robert Stevinson to Elspet Davidson.

27, James Anderson to Janet Gray.

JULY.

B. 2, George Trumble and Margaret Thomson had James ; witnesses, James Trumble, James Stanehous, James Brown.

2, John Anderson and Helen Lawson had Andrew; witnesses, Andrew
Curie, Andrew Cunningham, David Key.

2, James Stanehous and Margaret Trumble had Elspet; witnesses, Thomas
Stanehous, David Cunnon, James Kellok.

2, Andrew Barhame of Skelpie and Margaret Stewart had Catherine;
witnesses, Laurence Mercer, George Bothwell, Peter Law.

9, Robert Makcraiche and Isobel Donaldson had Janet; witnesses,
Alexander Chalmers, Andrew Walcar, Thomas Christie, Thomas
Stevinsone.

11, Robert Andersone and Helen Miller had John; witnesses, John
Watsone, Robert Kellok, David Cummon in Mastertoun.

11, James Murgane and Elspet Bowman had Margaret; witnesses, George
Durie, Nicol Wardlaw, William Walcar. (Baptized in Carnok.)

11, John James and Margaret Whyt had Harry; witnesses, David Moreis,
Mr. Harry Makgill, William Cunningham, Robert Cunninghame.

16, Archibald Honymane and Margaret Wels had Maudie; witnesses,
Adam Walwod, James Moyas, James Beamy, Andrew Wilsone.

16, Andrew Hall and Margaret Hardie had Margaret; witnesses, Alexander
Davidsone, Thomas Cuming, Andrew Wilsone, James Fischer.

16, Thomas Tod and Elspet Lyall had Catherine; witnesses, David Tod,
John Lyall, Nicol Wardlaw.

16, Alexander Drysdell and Bessie Walwod had William; witnesses,
William Walwod in Touche, William Broun, notary, Harry Walwod.

23, George Moreis, collier, and Bessie Beany had Thomas; witnesses,
Thomas Hunnon, John Dow, Thomas Dryla.

M. 4, James Mill to Grizel Robertsone.

4, James Mitchell to Christian Thomesone.

4, Thomas Stanehous to Barbara Dewar.

19, John Bull to Janet Phillane.

25, John Finlasone to Janet Bromesyd.

AUGUST.

B. 1, James Man and Isobel Wilsone had John (in fornication); witnesses,
John Stevinsone, David Moreis, Henry Moreis, Henry Dick.

1, Harry Thomson and Nanse Ædisone had Margaret (baptized in
Inverkeithing); witnesses, John Thomson, skipper, and Robert Kellok
in Mastertoun.

3, Richard Blaklaw and Emelie Parhe (*sic*) had Thomas; witnesses,
Thomas Wilson, Andrew Trumble, William Bruse.

3, David Wyld and Bessie Banks had James; witnesses, Thomas Tod,
David Tod.

8, Robert Broun in the Ferrie and Christian Kid had Janet; witnesses,
Laurence Lugtoun, John Burgane, Edward Broun.

8, Andrew Wilsone and Janet Douglas had Robert; witnesses, Robert
Kellok, George Donald, James Kellok.

15, Andrew Cant and Janet Man had Walter (in fornication); witnesses,
Watie Cant, Robert Cant, Thomas Peirsone.

22, John Andersone, litster, and Janet Stevinsone had Margaret; witnesses,
Harry Walwod, William Smart, John Broun.

27, James Andersone and Janet Clerk had David; witnesses, Andrew
Anderson, William Cunningham, John Anderson. (Baptized in
Carnok kirk.)

M. 29, John Bruse to Marjory Law.

SEPTEMBER.

B. 3, William Forrester and Janet Grysie had a daughter . . . .; witnesses,
James Ritchie, John Broun, Patrick Harrowar.

3, John Bull and Janet Phillane had Margaret; witnesses, Patrick
Cowper, Harry Bull, James Hutone, merchant.

— Adam Car and Janet Crawfurd had Janet; witnesses, George Trumble
in Tunigask, John Greif and Robert Greif.

17, John Smart and Margaret Baverage had Helen ; witnesses, John Smart, William Smart, James Drysdell.

24, David Tod and Janet Ædisone had John ; witnesses, James Hutone, George Davidsone, Thomas Tod.

25, George Mudie, mason, and Helen Stirk had Robert ; witnesses, Robert Stirk, elder, Robert Stirk, younger, Robert Wilsone, Harry Mudie.

M. 5, William Smart to Bessie Steinsone.

OCTOBER.

B. 1, Thomas Douglas and Elspet Chalmers had Thomas ; witnesses, Alexander Chalmers, Thomas Stevenson in the Newraw, Robert Kellok, younger, in Mastertoun.

1, James Buist and Janet Danzell had Elspet ; witnesses, Patrick Trumble, Charles Ritchardsone, John Bennat.

1, William Inche and Margaret James had Janet ; witnesses, John James, Thomas Walker, John Stirk.

1, William Cambell and Margaret Broun had Bessie ; witnesses, William Smart, Robert Davidsone, Thomas Baverage.

13, Peter Law and Margaret Walker had James ; witnesses, James Gib, Mr. James Durie, Mr. James Sibauld.

17, Maurice Inglis and Janet Gibsone had twins, Andrew and William (in fornication) ; witnesses, Andrew Walker in Logie, William Anderson in Pitconochie, John Inglis, Patrick Anderson, James Henresone, David Inglis.

17, "Young" John Andersone and Helen Kingorne had Geils ; witnesses, Sir John Gib of the Knok, knight, James Gib, Peter Law.

20, Laurie Andersone and Margaret Lugtoun had Isobel ; witnesses, William Cunningham in Knokes, Richard Blaklaw, Thomas Wilsone.

20, Robert Russell and Barbara Elder had James ; witness, James Smetone.

22, John Levingstone and Christian Young had John ; witnesses, William Anderson, John Wricht, Harry Young.

22, Robert Douglas and Margaret Peirsone had Isobel ; witnesses, Thomas Douglas, Edward Douglas, James Cunninghame.

22, William Kellok and Margaret Kellok had Elspet ; witnesses, Alexander Mastertoun, William Horne, Laurence Anderson.

22, John Walker and Margaret Trumble had James ; witnesses, Mr. James Sibald, Mr. James Durie.

22, James Hamiltoun and Jean Sanders had Catherine ; witnesses, William Mentethe of Randifurd, John Henresone of Fordall.

29, David Hodge and Marjory Bull had Geils ; witnesses, Robert Stirk, John Anderson, notary, Harry Bull.

M. 10, Andrew Wilsone to Catherine Wels.

31, James Henresone to Christian Inglis.

NOVEMBER.

B. 5, James Anderson and Janet Donaldsone had Janet ; witnesses, Robert Wels, Archibald Hodge, John Anderson, notary.

7, John Broun, tailor, and Effie Simsone had Elspet ; witnesses, William Broun, Harry Walwod, Peter Law, John Bennat, John Simsone, cordiner.

7, Andrew Wilsone and Margaret Lessells had Jerome (in fornication) ; witnesses, Jerome Broun, James Murgane, David Murie.

12, David Peirsone, merchant, "absent in his laufull travell for the tyme," and Jean Stanehous had Janet, presented by Patrick Cowper, bailiff ; witnesses, Peter Law, John Anderson, bailiff, Thomas Schortus, John Broun, tailor, Thomas Stanehous.

13, David Weyms of Romegay and Christian Wardlaw had John ; witnesses, Sir John Gib of Knok, Mr. Thomas Wardlaw, provost, George Bothwell of the Haughis.

15, James Kellok and Jean Gibson had John; witnesses, John Kellok, Laurence Anderson, Laurence Walker. "This infant wes giffin upe and registrat *ut supra* by the father of the samyn, and nochttheles on the morne the barne cuming to the kirk to be baptized departit this lyff and receivit nocht the outward seall of baptisme."

15, Robert Lindsay of Kavill and Lilias Drummond had James : witnesses, James Gib, James Reid, James Halkat, young Laird of Pitfirrane.

19, Abrahame Peacok and Margaret Young had James; witnesses, James Stewart, James Pirhie, James Peacok.

21, James Cusine and Barbara Dewar had James; witnesses, John Cusine, Robert Wels, William Hutone.

21, James Kellok and Helen Spens had John; witnesses, John Bennat, John Sanders, John Broun in the Nethertoun.

26, John Hugane and Cicile Glenn had Janet : witnesses, John Davidson in Fod, William Stanehous, Robert Hugane.

26, Harry Robertson (deceased) and Nanse Murray had George, baptised in Balingre kirk; witnesses, James Robertson, John Orock, David Moreis.

26, William Aikine and Janet Clerk had James (in fornication); witnesses, Andrew Mekiljone, David Tod, Robert Miller. "The fault wes committed in the paroche of Culrois, and upon thair request wes baptized in our kirk."

28, Robert Yowne and Christian Inglis had William; witnesses, Andrew Walker, William Kellok in Mastertoun, William Mudie.

M. 7, John Smetoun to Barbara Clerk.
7, Alexander Watsone to Bessie Stevin.
21, Matthew Donaldsone to Janet Young.
29, Laurie Merser to Margaret Dagleische.

DECEMBER.

B. 1, Archibald Hodge and Margaret Walker had Catherine; witnesses, Robert Wels, Harry Walwod, Gilbert Sanders, James Hamiltoun.

6, Robert Stanehous in Fod and Mawse Tailyeour had John (in fornication); witnesses, Patrick Peirsone, William Peirsone, John Hugane.

10, Robert Pringle and Marjory Brand had Isobel; witnesses, George Ivat, Alexander Penman, John Allane.

17, William Andersone in Pitconnochie and Margaret Caddell had Thomas (in fornication); witnesses, William Anderson, William Lawson, James Anderson.

21, Patrick Allane, armourer, and Janet Moreis had Thomas ; witnesses, Thomas Stevinsone, Thomas Walker, Thomas Elder.

24, William Potter and Janet Portour had William ; witnesses, William Potter, William Portour, James Kennedie.

M. 26, David Johnestone to Elspet Gilgour.

JANUARY [1627.]

B. 2, Charles Wilsone, smith in Primrois, and Margaret Johnestoun had Francis ; witnesses, Andrew Cunningham, William Bennat, Francis Wilsone.

2, Thomas Westwod and Bessie Robertson had Elspet ; witnesses, James Fischer, Thomas Bannatie, Robert Westwod.

7, Thomas Peirsone and Christian Kant had Thomas ; witnesses, Robert Cant, Ninian Mather, Laurence Andersone.

7, Walter Christie and Janet Russell had Margaret ; witnesses, David Sands, Harry Sands and Andrew Christie, all in Wester Gellat.

9, Alexander Baine and Helen Hutone had David ; witnesses, David Laurie, George Davidson, John Smetoun.

16, John Keir and Marjory Douglas had Margaret ; witnesses, Charles Richardsone, Henry Hakerstoun, David Moreis.

21, Alexander Nicole and Helen Alexander had Helen ; witnesses, William Broun, James Hutone, William Walwod, Harry Walwod, Patrick Bothwell.

23, George Trumble in Tunigask and Isobel Gib had Janet ; witnesses, Andrew Trumble, John Cusine, James Dagleische.

23, William Wilsone and Christian Wricht had John : witnesses, John Wricht and his son John, Gilbert Primerois, John Broun.

23, David Lambe and Marjory Wilsone had John : witnesses, James Mudie, William Mudie, Alexander Beane, Robert Stevinsone.

23, William Dagleische and Elspet Makcraiche had Robert (in fornication) : witnesses, John Makcraiche, Robert Makcraich, Thomas Christie.

25, Tobiah Muirebeck, servant to the Laird of Fordall, had John (in fornication) by Margaret Workman ; witnesses, Mr. James Sibauld, John Bennat, Gilbert Saunders.

30, William Cairnis and Marjory Burgane had John (in Inverkeithing kirk) : witnesses, John Thomson, Harry Thomson.

30, Thomas Cuming and Marion Douglas had Margaret : witnesses, Thomas Mitchell, Andrew Burne, David Douglas, all in Easter Gellat.

30, Andrew Hutone, slater, and Elspet Kilgour had Laurence ; witnesses, James Hutone, James Kennedie, David Watson, John Alison, mason.

30, Mr. Harry Makgill, minister, and Isobel Lindsay had Isobel ; witnesses, Sir John Gib, Mr. John Drummond, Mr. Robert Roche, Mr. James Sibald.

30, John Scott and Catherine Mackie had Margaret ; witnesses, John Gotterstone, William Mudie, weaver, Andrew Drummond.

M. 30, James Corslaw to Bessie Cowstoun.

FEBRUARY.

B. 6, Adam Wilson and Margaret Cunningham had Helen ; witnesses, William Cunningham, George Donald, John Peirsone.

6, William Anderson and Janet Cunningham had William ; witnesses, William Cunningham, William Lawson, William Anderson.

6, Robert Balcate and Elspet Rowane had John ; witnesses, John Balcate, John Rowane, Andrew Henresone.

6, David Douglas and Alison Mitchell had Janet ; witnesses, Thomas Mitchell, Andrew Burne, Edward Douglas.

6, Laurence Merser and Margaret Dagleische had Geils ; witnesses, Sir John Gib, Mr. John Drummond, James Gib.

9, Laurence Stevinsone and Catherine Chatto had Robert ; witnesses, Robert Stevenson, Robert Gray, Thomas Hunnone.

9, Patrick Cowper and Janet Murray had Normand ; witnesses, Normand Blakater, David Weyms of Romegay, Harry Walwod.

13, William Anderson and Catherine Cunningham had Janet ; witnesses, Andrew Trumble in Bromehall, Robert Cunningham in Sillitoun, Adam Wilsone and Robert Trumble in Tunigask, and Patrick Lawson.

13, John Spens and Janet Cunningham had a son . . . . ; witnesses, Thomas Douglas, Edward Douglas, Andrew Cunningham, Andrew Currie.

13, John Thomesone, flesher, and Janet Hutone had Elspet ; witnesses, Thomas Stevinsone, William Philpe, David Hodge.

18, James Wyld and Mawse Hutone had Thomas ; witnesses, Thomas Hutone, Thomas Melvill, brother of the deceased Laird of Raith, and John Coventrie.

18, William Hareme, "after his departure this lyff about half ane yeir thereafter" had Christian by his wife Isobel Sim ; witnesses, William Mackie, John Gotterstone, David Blak.

18, James Kennedie, wright, and Janet Hutone had Alexander ; witnesses, Alexander Car, Harry Walwod, James Hutone, David Watson, Gavin Stanehous.

20, John Oiswald and Christian Hamiltoun had Margaret ; witnesses, James Cowstoun, John Douglas, David Inglis, William Cowstoun, Oliver Culan.

25, James Lethome and Isobel Makbethe had Robert; witnesses, Robert Cunninghame, John Lawsone in Crocefuird, William Pillonis.

25, James Anderson and Elspet Christie had John; witnesses, John Christie, John Blak, John Moyas, John Davidson.

25, James Pottar and Marion Walker had Thomas; witnesses, Thomas Schortus, Richard Potter, Thomas Cowper.

27, "Cat Car, ane vagabond and inordinat persone, had Janet baptised, "quhilk scho baire to James Thomsone, ane colyeir in Blairnebathie, as scho allegit," presented by Robert Henreson, skinner in Dunfermlyne; witnesses, John Simsone and William Walwod, cordiners.

M. 8, William Paterson to Janet Peirs.

8, James Cowstoun to Grizel Moreis.

27, James Hutone to Mary Dempstertoun.

MARCH.

B. 4, Henry Orolk and Margaret Scotland had Geils; witnesses, James Gib, George Durie of Craigluscour, Thomas Blakwod.

4, Andrew Cunningham in Primrois and Margaret Trumble had Robert; witnesses, Andrew Murray in Lymkills, Adam Currie, James Mayne, John Hog.

4, William Thomesone, tailor, and Janet Sanders had Nanse; witnesses, Mr. James Phinne, portioner of Lymkills, John Levingstone, James Bryce.

11, David Scotland and Janet Aitkine had William; witnesses, Mr. William Wardlaw of Balmuile, Patrick Cowper, John Scotland.

11, William Sanders and Christian Hutone had Robert; witnesses, Nicol Wardlaw, Robert Scotland, Robert Blakwod.

11, Thomas Mitchell in Easter Gellat and Margaret Dick had James; witnesses, Mr. James Sibauld, schoolmaster of Dunfermline, James Mitchell in Mastertoun, David Douglas in Easter Gellat.

11, John Smetoun and Barbara Clerk had Bessie; witnesses, James Anghous, Mr. James Phinne, William Broun in Inverkeithing.

11, John Culros and Helen Stevinson had John; witnesses, Robert Stevinson, William Smart, John Sanders.

11, James Beany and Margaret Honyman had Margaret; witnesses, John Bennat, John Watson, Henry Peirsone.

11, Andrew Ferlie and Alison Anderson had Margaret; witnesses, Andrew Burne, William Burne, Robert Burne.

18, John Broun in the Ferrie and Beatrix Thomson had Edward, baptised in Inverkeithing kirk; witnesses, . . .

18, David Mitchell and Margaret Currie had Margaret; witnesses, William Bruce, John Currie, Thomas Stevenson.

20, John Allisone, wright, and Grizel Walwod had Christian; witnesses, David Weyms of Romegay, Charles Ritchardsone, Robert Alisone, John Clerk.

20, Edward Broun, mariner in the Queinisferrie, and Agnes Saverall had Beatrix (in fornication); witnesses, Andrew Marteine, Helen Scharpe, Harry Cant.

25, Andrew Elder and Janet Phinne had Isobel; witnesses, Mr. James Phinne, portioner of Lymkills, Andrew Trumble in Bromehall, George Ædisone.

25, Thomas Murray, husband to Janet Law in Crail, had Andrew (in adultery) by Janet Pryd; witnesses, David Dewar of Lassodie, Mr. James Dewar, his eldest son, and Donald Fraser.

25, John Inglis and Nanse Hutone had James; witnesses, James Mill, William Hutone, James Henresone.

M. [*None.*]

APRIL.

B. 1, John Bennat in Lassodie and Marion Cunnone had Margaret; witnesses, Robert Anghous, John Kellok, Thomas Schortus.

1, John Walker, cadger in the Clun, and Margaret Dewar had Helen ; witnesses, Robert Scotland, Richard Scotland, John Clerk, cadger, James Wilson in Carnok.

1, Thomas Hunnon and Janet Edward had Isobel ; witnesses, John Anderson, youngest, William Wilson, James Ronald.

1, Laurence Lugtoun and Janet Bennat had Bessie ; witnesses, John Bennat, David Bull, Robert Drysdell.

15, Andrew Mentethe and Catherine Gardner had Margaret ; witnesses, John Tailyeour, John Buchannane, John Lawsone.

15, James Cunnone, younger, and Christian Messwan had Catherine (in fornication) ; witnesses, Thomas Cunnon, William Kent, John Drysdell.

15, Thomas Stanehous and Barbara Dewar had Jean ; witnesses, David Dewar of Lassodie, Robert Kellok, portioner of Mastertoun, James Kellok, his eldest son.

18, John Trumble in Turnourschill (deceased) and Marjory Maistertoun had Margaret ; witnesses, Mr. James Phune, Adam Mastertoun, her father.

22, David Blak, younger in Cocklaw, and Marjory Blakwood had John ; witnesses, George Dewar, David Robertson, John Paterson in Inchgaw.

22, Robert Anghous and Christian Smetone had Isobel ; witnesses, Mr. James Dewar of Nether Lassodie, James Anghous, brother of the said Robert, Peter Law in Dunfermline, David Greine in Pitadro.

22, Gilbert Primrois in the Nethertoun of Dunfermline, and Isobel Gib had James ; witnesses, James Gib, apparent of Knok, James Gib of Pow, James Gib of Lambehill, his son, James Stewart, apparent of Gremsay.

22, William Wannane, collier, and Margaret Davidson had Jean ; witnesses, John Henresone, Robert Pringle, John Allane.

22, John Dowglas, tailor, and Janet Orock had William ; witnesses, William Paterson, Robert Anderson, David Bull, John Laurie.

29, Isobel Ladathis bairn "quhom scho allegit and said Johne Horne wes father to it, gottin in fornicatioun," was baptised and called Janet.

M. 1, Alexander Anderson to Elspet Kellok.

10, John Mylls to Margaret Mackie.

17, Henry Meldrum to Agnes Hardeis in Cleish kirk (on testimonial from our kirk).

17, Mr. Robert Bruce of Wester Kennat to Annas Murray.

24, Henry Beany to Helen Wricht.

MAY.

B. 6, John Thomesone, collier, and Effie Finlay had Janet ; witnesses, James Thomson, Thomas Paterson, William Richardson. (Baptised in Cleish kirk.)

6, Robert Broun and Catherine Forsyithe had William ; witnesses, Andrew Trumble in Bromhall, George Trumble, his son, Thomas Stevinson, David Mitchell.

6, William Orolk and Catherine Maxwell had Helen ; witnesses, John Orolk, David Moyas, Henry Baverage.

6, James Pirhie and Barbara Patone had Janet (in fornication) ; witnesses, James Stewart, William Kennedie, Abraham Peacok.

6, David Bull, cutler, and Margaret Potter had Marjory ; witnesses, John Simsone, John Orolk, John Potter.

20, John Makmoniche and Janet Porteous had Margaret ; witnesses, John Anderson, litster, James Henresone, Robert Alisone.

22, Robert Levingstone of Baldrige and Jean Bruse had Margaret ; witnesses, John Henresone of Fordell, William Mentethe of Randifuird, George Durie of Craigluscour.

22, Wattie Anderson, servant in Baldrige, and Helen Makinlay had Jean ; witnesses, William Patoun, "coilcawer," and John Hog, "the greive of the heughe of Baldrige."

27, James Hamiltoun, piper, and Helen Maknabe had William; witnesses, William Hey, servant to Sir John Gib, Mr. John Walker, reader in Dunfermline, Andrew Walker in Logie.

27, Charles Baid and Helen Young had Helen; witnesses, John Bennat, Laurie Anderson, Charles Tailyeour.

27, James Anderson and Janet Gray had James; witnesses, Patrick Anderson, David Anderson, William Cunningham.

27, Robert Stevenson and Elspet Davidson had Adam; witnesses, Adam Stevenson, Mr. Thomas Wardlaw, Laurie Stevenson.

27, John Kirk and Marion Greg had Thomas; witnesses, Thomas Horne, James Henresone.

29, William Culane, deceased, and Bessie Hutone had Bernard; witnesses Bernard Gib, Sir John Gib of Knok, James Hutone, merchant.

M. 15, Wattie Richardsone to Grizel Hodge.
15, James Man to Isobel Wilsone.
17, James Dick to Isobel Toward.
27, John Workman to Elspet Duncane.
29, John Gibone to Janet Horne.

JUNE.

B. 9, John Scharpe had John, born to him of Janet Workman, whose husband "wes aff the contrie and unknawn quhither deid or allyve"; witnesses, John Workman, Robert Yowane, William Walwod, cordiner.

12, John Vicar and Isobel Dawsone had Helen; witnesses, James Kenedy, Harry Walwod, Archibald Hodge.

13, George Lindsay of Kavill and Jean Mowtrey had Adam (in fornication); presented by Peter Law in Dunfermline because of the father's obstinacy and disobedience to kirk discipline.

17, James Dewar and Christian Philpe had David; witnesses, John Philpe, James Cunnon, younger, James Moyas, David Dewar.

22, Henry Dick and Bessie Stevenson had Bessie; witnesses, John Dick, John Anghous, John Dick in the Hilsyid.

24, John Finlasone and Janet Bromesyd had Janet; witnesses, Thomas Blakwod, Robert Wels, Patrick Legat.

27, Mr. James Dewar of Nether Lassodie and Elspet Moncreiff had Margaret; witnesses, Thomas Stanehous, David Cunnon, Robert Anghous.

M. 5, Mr. Patrick Auchinleck to Elspet Forrester.
12, William Galrige to Helen Broun.
12, John Boyd to Catherine Andersone.
26, . . . Donkiesone to Nanse Douglas.

JULY.

B. 1, John Spens, collier, and Jean Brand had Marion; witnesses, Duncan Tailyeour, George Penman, Henry Simsone.

1, David Anderson and Marjory Burgane had John; witnesses, Helias Sharpe, John Burgane, William Anderson.

8, John Simsone, cordiner, and Bessie Hutone had George; witnesses, John Anderson, younger, Robert Aitkine, Andrew Walcar in Logie.

15, Andrew Rowane in the Gaske and Bessie Cunningham had Bessie; witnesses, David Dewar of Lassodie, William Legat, David Robertson of Craigduckie.

15, James Stewart and Margaret Greiff had Margaret; witnesses, John Henresone, John Mill, Patrick Murray.

17, William Bruce and "Roise Snellok" had David; witnesses, David Bruse, David Mitchell, Francis Cokburne.

24, Henry Moreis aud Isobel Duncane had Margaret (in fornication); witnesses, John Stevenson, David Moreis, Henry Dick in Quhythous.

24, John Clerk and Catherine Baid had James ; witnesses, James Lugtoun, John Baid, John Wilsone.

31, James Hutone, weaver, and Mary Dempstertoun had James ; witnesses, James Kingorne, James Hutone, David Watson.

M. 3, John Sands to Janet Wardlaw.

3, William Suentone to Margaret Lauthiane.

3, Allan Mudie to Bessie Keir.

10, James Clerk to Janet Beany.

AUGUST.

B. 5, James Fischer and Janet Kent had Thomas ; witnesses, James Kellok Thomas Stanehous, Thomas Fischer, David Cunnone.

14, James Mitchell and Christian Thomsone had Marion ; witnesses, William Trumble, smith, Thomas Walwod, James Mitchell, elder.

21, Mungo Cunningham and Marjory Anderson had Helen ; witnesses, Adam Stobie, James Anderson, George Hendeine.

28, John Law and Nicolas Anderson had Janet ; witnesses, David Stewart, Patrick Cowper, Peter Law.

M. 2, George Straquhen to Helen Nicole.

7, John Smithe to Nanse Hog.

9, Robert Dick to Jean Sands.

14, Fergus Kennedie to Janet Durie.

28, William Litljohne to Christian Broun.

SEPTEMBER.

B. 4, Henry Hakerstone and Helen Cunningham had Margaret ; witnesses, Robert Mastertoun, John Orolk, James Mitchell.

4, John Aikine and Christian Dagleische had George ; witnesses, George Trumble in Tunigask, George Douglas, John Greive.

4, John Shortus and Janet Banks had Thomas ; witnesses, Thomas Schortus, John Banks, John Stirk.

4, William Philpe and Elspet Lindsay had Bessie ; witnesses, Harry Mudie, Thomas Stevinsone in the Newraw, Robert Davidson.

4, James Reid and Marion Broun had William ; witnesses, Mr. Thomas Wardlaw of Logie, Peter Law, William Broun, clerk, and Patrick Cowper, " balleif for the tyme."

4, Alexander Young and Bessie Williamson had Alison ; witnesses, Robert Alison, Robert Henresone, Robert Yown.

6, Charles Tailyeour and Marion Tod had Margaret ; witnesses, John Anderson, litster in the Kirkgate, John Sanders, John Wilsone.

9, John Lawson in Crocefuird and Margaret Wilson had Elspet ; witnesses, Patrick Legat, James Anghous, Robert Lindsay.

9, William Anderson in the Lymekills and Geils Peirsone had Margaret ; witnesses, Patrick Cowper, John Anderson, bailies for the time, and Robert Aikine.

9, Henry Broun and Elspet Banks had Margaret ; witnesses, James Cusine, Laurence Merser, John Murray.

12, James Ritchie and Nicolas Sandilands had Bessie (in fornication) ; witnesses, Andrew Burn, James Dewar, James Mayne.

16, Harry Thomsone and Nanse Ædisone had Janet ; witnesses, Robert Kellok, James Kellok, John Broun. (Born 9th, baptised in Inverkeithing kirk.)

16, John Anderson, youngest, litster, and Martha Mastertoun had Grizel ; witnesses, Andrew Walker, Thomas Christie, James Hamiltoun.

23, John Anderson and Janet Meldrum had Helen ; witnesses, John Coventrie, David Broun, Robert Davidson.

23, John Robertson and Isobel Hutone had Elspet ; witnesses, Andrew Burne, William Burne, Thomas Peirsone.

23, Alexander Glas and Janet Toward had . . . ; witnesses, James Patone, Adam Brand, David Anderson.

23, Thomas Baverage and Christian Smart had Andrew ; witnesses, William Smart, Andrew Roxburghe, John Wels.

23, Henry Beany and Helen Wricht had John ; witnesses, John Wricht, Andrew Wricht, John Beany.

30, Thomas Patersone, collier, and Rosina Baverage had Helen, (baptised in Cleish kirk) ; witnesses, John Henresone, John Baverage, John Hill.

30, John Hadstoun and Bessie Beany had Bessie ; witnesses Thomas Johnstone, Patrick Anderson, William Anderson in Pitconnochie.

30, David Maxwell, litster, and Nanse Hamilton had Grizel ; witnesses, John Anderson, elder, William Broun. John Andersoun, youngest, litster.

30, James Mitchell and Christian Legat had Thomas ; witnesses, Thomas Blakwood, James Mitchell, Thomas Schortus, James Potter.

M. 2, John Lindsay to Bessie Peirson.

2, John Hog to Margaret Thomesone.

11, Peter Buist to Isobel Walwod.

13, William Huton to Isobel Wardlaw.

13, John Wels to Margaret Stevinsone.

23, John Sanders to Helen Watsone.

25, John Phune to Margaret Dinn.

OCTOBER.

B. 2. William Smart and Bessie Stevenson had Bessie ; witnesses, John Simsone, Adam Stevenson, John Anderson, litster in the Kirkgate.

7, James Henresone and Christian Inglis had Bessie ; witnesses, Henry Dick, Thomas Horne, John Kellok.

7, Thomas Christie of the Hoill and Elspet Durie had Margaret ; witnesses, Mr. James Durie, John Anderson, younger, David Stevenson.

7, James Mudie and Grizel Lambe had Janet ; witnesses, William Lambe, Patrick Allane, Andrew Broun.

14, John Davidson and Marjory Broun had James ; witness, William Smithe.

14, Laurence Anderson and Grizel Thomson had Beatrix ; witnesses, David Douglas, Edward Douglas, James Murgane.

14, William Anderson in Pitconnochie and Janet Curror had a son . . . . (in fornication) : witnesses, Laurence Anderson, John Wilson, David Hodge.

14, John Watson, cordiner, and Marjory Smetoun had Margaret ; witnesses, John Smetoun, John Sanders, John Simesone.

14, Andrew Barhame of Skelpie and Margaret Stewart had Margaret ; witnesses, James Kingorne, Peter Law, David Stewart.

16, Thomas Rodger, weaver, and Isobel Broun had Christian (in adultery) ; witnesses, George Davidson, James Lindsay, Thomas Davidson.

21, John Allane. collier in Baithe, and Janet Bowar had Bessie ; witnesses, George Ivat, John Henreson, John Penman.

28, William Potter and Catherine Mowse had Andrew ; witnesses, Andrew Potter, John Wricht, William Wilson.

M. 7, John Colzeir to Marjory Corsane.

30, Nicol Inglis to Marjory Law.

NOVEMBER.

B. 6, James Mill and Grizel Robertson had Isobel ; witnesses, William Robertsone of Craigduckie, William Hutone, David Robertson, brother of said Grizel.

11, Thomas Douglas, parishioner of Edinburgh, and Marjory Schortus had Thomas (in fornication), baptised on testimonial declaring the woman's satisfaction to the kirk ; witnesses, Charles Ritchardson, Mr. Patrick Fleck, Laurence Merser.

11, John Dow and Magie Merser had a child baptised called . . .

13, William Mudie and Janet Christie had Thomas ; witnesses, Thomas Reid, Thomas Christie, Thomas Stevenson.

15, George Mudie, mason, and Helen Stirk had Margaret ; witnesses, James Reid, James Hutone, William Mudie.

20, George Ædisone and Bessie Sands had David ; witnesses, David Sands in Gellat, William Anderson, skipper, William Anderson in Gellat.

20, Robert Murgane and Helen Smithe had Andrew ; witnesses, Andrew Walker, Robert Scotland, John Dow, James Lugtoun.

20, John Colzeir and Marjory Corsane had John ; witnesses, John Alison, William Trumble, Henry Peirsone.

25, Thomas Dewar and Margaret Mastertoun had William ; witnesses, William Mastertoun, Robert Russell, Robert Anghous, David Scotland.

25, John Walker, tailor, and Jean Maxwell had Robert ; witnesses, Robert Stirk, Robert Alisone, James Hutone, bailie.

27, Harry Stewart of Baithe and Catherine Kirkcaldie had Patrick ; witnesses, David Stewart, George Bothwell, David Moreis in Bayth.

M. 6, James Hutone to Janet Huntar

DECEMBER.

B. 2, William Forrester and Janet Makgrysie had Nicolas ; witnesses, John Anderson, John Robertson, William Young.

2, James Patone and Isobel Watson had a son . . . ; witnesses, John Watson, tailor, William Watson, cordiner, Adam Brand.

11, John Blair and Grizel Peirson had Andrew ; witnesses, Robert Wels, Andrew Wilson, Andrew Hutone, slater.

11, James Æssone and Catherine Watson had Bessie ; witnesses, John Simsone, David Laurie, Andrew Hutone, cordiner.

11, Henry Balfour and Isobel Mackie had John ; witnesses, William Mackie, William Black, John Gotterstoun.

11, David Peirsone and Isobel Henresone had Catherine ; witnesses, Robert Kellok, Robert Cant, Thomas Stanehous.

16, Allan Mudie and Bessie Keir had Christian ; witnesses, William Æssoun, William Mudie, weaver, William Lambe.

16, Laure Neilsone and Isobel Litljohne had John ; witnesses, John Wels, John Bennat, John Hutone.

16, John Currie and Margaret Watson had Annas ; witnesses, Andrew Currie, Andrew Trumble, Nicol Inglis.

16, James Henresone, glazier, and Mayas Aitkine had John ; witnesses, John Moreisone, James Cusine, Richard Potter, younger.

23, William Cadzone and Margaret Burne had Helen ; witnesses, Andrew Trumble in Bromehall, John Smetoun, John Makcraiche.

23, James Cowstoun and Grizel Moreis had Grizel ; witnesses, William Brown, clerk, Patrick Cowper, James Corslaw.

23, John Anderson and Isobel Allane had Helen ; witnesses, Archibald Boyd, Laurence Stevenson, Thomas Williamson.

24, John Hog and Margaret Thomson had Robert ; witnesses, Robert Levingstoun of Baldrig, Mr. John Walker, Mr. James Thomson, James Kennedie.

27, James Patone and Elspet Dick had John (in fornication) ; witnesses, Henry Hakirstone, John Keir, William Patone.

30, John Kinloche and Bessie Sim had David ; witnesses, David Mitchell, John Merschell, Alexander Wilson.

30, John Bull, cutler, and Janet Phillane had Helen ; witnesses, William Broun, John Anderson, younger, James Phillane.

M. 4, Thomas Smetone to Elspet Anghous (in Cleish kirk).

6, Patrick Stevenson to Christian Mudie.

P

9, George Dewar to Margaret Maistertoun.
23, Robert Scot to Janet Davidson.

JANUARY [1628].

B. 2, William Dougall and Jean Scot had Bessie ; witnesses, Richard
Blaklay, Andrew Mudie, Robert Tailyeour.

8, Richard Blaklay, "irone miller" in Burnemouthe, and Emelie Parre had
a son . . . . ; witnesses, Andrew Trumble in Bromehall, Thomas
Wilson, William Bruse.

8, David Keir and Isobel Smithe had William ; witnesses, Mr. William
Smithe, William Maistertoun, David Walker, John Wricht.

8, Peter Buist and Margaret Cusine had Andrew (in fornication);
witnesses, Andrew Burne, Charles Ritchardson, Hary Walwod,
Archibald Hodge.

13, James Thomson, collier in Blairnebathie, and Marion Gib had Elspet ;
witnesses, John Thomson, James Baverage, John Baverage. Baptised
in Cleish kirk "becaus of the cauld wether and evill way."

13, James Kellok and Jean Gibsone had John ; witnesses, John Kellok,
Michael Chalmers, John Kellok in Hill of Bayth.

15, Pate Davidson and Janet Thomson had Christian ; witnesses, David
Strong, Thomas Baverage, William Annan.

15, Peter Law, bailie, and Margaret Walker had William ; witnesses,
William Mentethe of Randifuird, Mr. Thomas Wardlaw of Logie,
Patrick Cowper, William Broun, clerk.

21, William Robertson and Marjory Martene had Janet ; witnesses, James
Hutone, bailie, Henry Trumble, John Robertson, father of said
William.

22, James Hamilton and Jean Sanders had Margaret ; witnesses, Patrick
Cowper, Robert Aikine, Gilbert Sanders.

27, Henry Meldrum and Agnes Hardeis "in the kirk of Cleische" had
Andrew ; witnesses, Andrew Cokburne of Traittoun, Andrew Henreson
and Andrew Meldrum.

27, Thomas Brigs and Nanse Wricht had William (in fornication);
witnesses, William Cunningham, William Anderson in Pitconnochie,
William Lawsou in Hiltoun of Pitfirrane.

M. 1, John Barklay to Nanse Chalmers.
15, James Hutone to Janet Peirsone.

FEBRUARY.

B. 3, James Cunnon, younger, and Jean Philpe had Catherine ; witnesses,
James Cunnon, elder, Gavin Stanehous, Thomas Cunnon, William
Philpe.

3, Matthew Donaldson and Janet Young had Helen ; witnesses, David
Sanders, William Anderson, Edward Douglas, Thomas Douglas, all
in Wester Gellat.

5, Alexander Beane and Helen Hutone had Christian ; witnesses, William
Lambe, John Gotterstoun, George Davidson.

12, John Kellok and Janet Mathesone had Marjory ; witnesses, Patrick
Kellok, James Mathesone, Thomas Kellok.

12, George Penman and Marion Dreddoun had Janet ; witnesses, William
Walwod, Duncan Tailyeour, John Penman.

12, Andrew Barrehill and Elspet Broun had Margaret ; witnesses, William
Walwod, William Peirsone, John Walwod.

12, Archibald Boyd and Janet Watson had John ; witnesses, John
Sanders, John Simsone, John Walker.

17, Robert Pittilloche and Marjory Miller had Alexander ; witnesses,
Francis Cokburne, Thomas Blakwod, Robert Davidson.

21, James Kellok, portioner of Mastertoun, and Margaret Mudie had
William ; witnesses, James Stanehous, William Kellok, Thomas
Ædisone.

23, James Wallace and Janet Henresone had Marion; witnesses, Gavin Stanehous, James Hutone, Alexander Drysdell.

24, George Donald and Margaret Stevenson had Isobel; witnesses, Andrew Wilson, Andrew Walker, David Mitchell, Thomas Wilson.

24, Thomas Tod and Elspet Lyall had William; witnesses, William Lyall, David Tod, William Maistertoun.

24, James Carslaw and Bessie Cowstoun had Nanse; witnesses, Mr. Thomas Wardlaw of Logie, George Bothuell of the Haughis, James Cowstoun.

24, John Wels and Christian Austiane had Helen; witnesses, John Simsone, William Watson, Harry Bull.

27, Robert Quhyt and Catherine Hunnon had James; witnesses, Laurie Neilsone, James Patone, Thomas Hunnon.

27, James Anderson and Janet Donald had Grizel; witnesses, John Walker, James Kennedie, Thomas Elder.

28, Patrick Stevenson and Christian Mudie had Thomas; witnesses, Thomas Stevenson, Thomas Reid, Patrick Cowper.

M. 5, Robert Hutone to Janet Trumble.
12, James Allett to Isobel Reid.
19, David Spens to Helen Mitchell.
19, John Broun to Janet Hall.
26, George Lindsay of Kavill to Jean Mowtrey.
28, Robert Bull to Margaret Smetoun.

MARCH.

B. 4, David Bull in Mastertoun and Christian Balfour had Christian; witnesses, Robert Mudie, David Bull, Thomas Stainehous.

4, John Broun in the Northferrie and Barbara Thomson had John; witnesses, John Broun, father of the said John, John Chatto, John Broun, spouse to Beatrix Thomson, baptised in Inverkeithing kirk "becaus of the evill wether."

9, Robert Greive and Margaret Douglas had William; witnesses, William Hutone, George Dewar, James Mill.

9, John Kinnell and Janet Philpe had Catherine; witnesses, William Peirsone, James Broun, Michael Chalmers.

13, Mr. James Sibauld, schoolmaster, and Isobel Bowstoun had Geils; witnesses, William Mentethe of Randifuird, Mr. Thomas Wardlaw of Logie, Peter Law, bailie of the burgh.

16, John Gray and Alison Martene had Robert; witnesses, Robert Anghous, William Robertson, David Scotland.

16, Alexander Penman, collier, and Catherine Horne had Robert; witnesses, Duncan Talyeour, George Penman, James Stewart, William Wannan.

16, Peter Sempill and Janet Cunningham had Marjory; witnesses, Andrew Potter, John Potter, James Cusine, Patrick Legat.

18, Henry Simsone (deceased) and Bessie Thomson had Helen; witnesses, John Anderson, John Simsone, John Broun.

30, Robert Anghous and Christian Drysdell had Catherine; witnesses, Nicol Inglis, Robert Anghous, Robert Russell.

30, William Westwod and Janet Quhyt had Margaret (in fornication); witnesses, William Mudie, James Westwod, James Mitchell.

M. [*None.*]

APRIL.

B. 1, Robert Anderson in the Maygat and Janet Smith had Robert; witnesses, Patrick Cowper, James Hutone, bailie, William Anderson.

5, William Galrige and Helen Broun had William; witnesses, Andrew Trumble of Grange, William Broun in Mylnehills, William Inglis in Grange.

6, James Greg and Helen Rankine had William; witnesses, William Stanehous, John Davidson, James Anderson.

6, James Mathesone and Christian Anderson had Elspet; witnesses, William Philpe, Robert Davidson, Thomas Bleckie.

10, John Broun and Effie Semsone had Christian; witnesses, Peter Law, James Hutone, Patrick Cowper, William Broun, James Ronald.

12, John Gotterstone and Isabel Mackie had Margaret; witnesses, George Davidson, William Mackie, William Lambe.

13. Thomas Kingorne and Janet Burne had Effie [in fornication]; witnesses, Mr. Bernard Gib, Laurence Merser, Francis Cokburne. Presented by William Anderson, son of John Anderson, litster, because of the father's absence.

15, Mr. James Phune, portioner of Lymkills, and Agnes Aittoun had Jean; witnesses, Harry Phune, Adam Mastertoun of Grange, Robert Kellok in Mastertoun, William Mentethe of Randifuird.

20, John Peirsone in Pitdinnie and Marion Hutone had James; witnesses, James Peirsone, brother of said John, James Hutone, grieve in Pitfirran, William Cunningham in Knokes.

20, John Hugone and Cicile Glen had John; witnesses, John Westwod, John Small, John Rowane.

20, Thomas Blakwod and Isobel Inglis had a son . . . . ; witnesses, George Meldrum, David Inglis, David Scotland.

20, Robert Dick and Jean Sands had Jean; witnesses, William Mentethe of Randifuird, Harry Stewart of Baithe, Thomas Mitchell, John Anderson, younger.

20, Henry Malcome and Catherine Inglis had Isobel; witnesses, Francis Cokburne, Thomas Walwod, James Feg.

27, John Bruse and Nanse Balfour had Mary; witnesses, Andrew Trumble in Bromehall, Robert Trumble in Tunygask, William Bruse.

27, John Jamesone and Marion Dick had Margaret; witnesses, Robert Lindsay, David Peirson, John Lindsay.

M. 15, James Wallace to Janet Henresone.
22, William Anderson to Nanse Chalmers.

MAY.

B. 4, Alexander Spittell and Isobel Hiltoun had Andrew; witnesses, Andrew Kellok, Robert Wyld, John Broun.

4, John Lawson and Catherine Drysdell had Helen; witnesses, Patrick Lawson, Gilbert Primrois, John Bruse.

4, Peter Ferlie and Elspet Breadfoote had William; witnesses, William Inche, George Meldrum, Michael Meldrum.

4, James Dick and Effie Towart had Robert; witnesses, Robert Levingstone of Baldrige, Robert Lindsay of Kavill, Laurence Anderson.

4, William Lambe and Janet Cunningham had James; witnesses, Gilbert Primrois, David Stevenson, James Mudie.

11, Andrew Hall and Margaret Hardie had Alison; witnesses, Thomas Mitchell, David Douglas, Andrew Burne, Thomas Young.

11, John Huntar and Janet Wilson had Thomas; witnesses, Thomas Christie, Andrew Walker, David Greins.

18, John Mill and Marion Mill had a daughter . . . . (in fornication); baptised in Saline kirk.

20, James Nevinn and Agnes Wilson had Margaret; witnesses, Andrew Burne in Gellat, Walter Cant, Thomas Bull.

20, Andrew Mentethe and Catherine Gardner had Nanse; witnesses, Thomas Nasmithe, James Miller, James Maknabie.

20, Fergus Kennedie and Janet Durie had Jean; witnesses, Sir Robert Halkheid of Pitfirrane, James Gib of the Knok, George Durie of Craigluscour.

20, John Scot and Catherine Mackie had John; witnesses, John Kellok, John Gotterstoun, John Makmirrie.

21, David Hodge and Marjory Bull had James; witnesses, James Gib, Peter Law, John Walker, dean of guild, Robert Scotland.

27, David Cunnone and Elspet Dewar had Robert; witnesses, Robert Kellok, James Stanehous, Robert Mudie.

27, James Buist and Janet Danzell had Janet; witnesses, Charles Ritchardson, Thomas Bennat, Peter Buist.

30, James Cusine and Barbara Dewar had Margaret; witnesses, Adam Walwod, Robert Wels, Gavin Stanehous.

M. [*None.*]

JUNE.

B. 3, Robert Douglas and Margaret Peirson had Andrew; witnesses, Thomas Douglas, Edward Douglas, William Anderson in Wester Gellat.

15, William Mudie and Nanse Mackie had Allan; witnesses, John Kellok, Allan Mudie, Robert Stevenson.

15, Thomas Johnestone and Nanse Aittoun had Isobel; witnesses, Andrew Trumble in Broineball, John Walker, dean of guild, John Anderson, litster.

15, James Phillane and Helen Hutone had Janet (in fornication); witnesses, John Bull, Thomas Schortus, Thomas Davidson.

18, Francis Cokburne and Alison Cokburne had Bessie; witnesses, Patrick Cowper, Thomas Johnestoun, James Hamiltoun.

22, John Ritchie and Grizel Stevenson had a daughter . . . ; witnesses, William Stanehous, John Davidson, William Walwod.

24, Peter Buist and Isobel Walwod had William; witnesses, Patrick Trumble, Charles Richardson, Alexander Honyman.

29, William Sanders and Christian Hutone had Helen; witnesses, Robert Scotland, Patrick Anderson, James Sanders.

29, David Scharpe and Janet Moreisone had John; witnesses, Mr. John Walker, John Law, John Scharpe.

30, William Kellock and Janet Dewar had Thomas (in fornication); witnesses, Thomas Stanehous, Thomas Cummon, Robert Kellok younger.

30, Robert Henresone and Janet Car had Helen; witnesses, Harry Walwod, Archibald Hodge, Henry Peirson.

M. 17, Henry Broun to Beatie Sandis.

17, Thomas Hall to Bessie Portour.

24, Gilbert Johnestoune to Christian Wels.

29, David Murray to Isobel Phune.

JULY.

B. 2, Mark Suentoun in the Northferrie and Marjory Stevenson had a daughter . . . ; witnesses, . . .

6, John Baverage at Keltieheuche and Helen Kellok had Elspet (baptised at Cleish Kirk); witnesses, Robert Mastertoun, John Betsone, William Makie in Coklaw.

6, David Strang and Bessie Ritchie had Helen; witnesses, Patrick Trumble, Thomas Elder, John Simsone.

13, Alexander Drysdell, merchant, and Bessie Walwod had Andrew; witnesses, Andrew Murray, Mr. Patrick Auchinleck, John Simsone, cordiner.

20, Henry Trumble and Catherine Cusine had Henry; witnesses, Andrew Trumble, John Trumble, Robert Hutone.

22, David Christie in Babougie and Janet Peacok had John; witnesses, Robert Wilson, James Anderson. (Baptised here because of Inverkeithing minister's absence.)

27, John Sanders and Helen Watson had Janet; witnesses, William Watson, John Simson, Laurence Merser.

27, Henry Peirson and Helen Williamson had William; witnesses, William Wilson, Robert Stirk, William Keir, William Trumble.

M 8, David Scot to Christian Thomson.

AUGUST.

B. 3, John Gibone and Janet Horne had Margaret (baptised in Carnok kirk) ; witnesses, John Lawson, James Gib, Alexander Gib, David Horne.

4, Robert Alisone and Catherine Row had Jean ; witnesses, William Mentethe of Randifurd, Mr. James Sibald, Mr. Thomas Wardlaw.

10, Edward Douglas and Beatie Douglas had Henry ; witnesses, Thomas Mitchell, Andrew Currie, Henry Douglas.

10, Andrew Murray in Lymkills and Margaret Cunningham had James ; witnesses, Mr. James Phinn, Harry Stewart of Gramsie, Gilbert Primrois.

10, Andrew Colzer and Isobel Anderson had William ; witnesses, Robert Anderson, John Dagleische, William Paterson.

10, John Clerk, merchant, and Annas Portour had William ; witnesses, Robert Wels, David Stevenson, Charles Ritchardson.

10, Andrew Mekiljohne and Janet Anderson (?) had Grizel ; witnesses, William Anderson, Thomas Davidson, Stephen Tyllidaff.

17, George Meldrum and Marjory Walker had William ; witnesses, Laurence Walker, William Walker, merchant, William Walker, son of Thomas Walker in the Rods.

26, Wattie Richardson and Grizel Hodge had John ; witnesses, Robert Walwod, William Walwod, William Betoun.

26, John Bruse and Marjory Law had Barbara ; witnesses, David Stewart, Peter Law, William Trumble.

28, John Levingstoun and Janet Smetoun had Janet ; witnesses, Laurence Merser, John Tod, John Smetoun.

M. 26, Laurence Hutone to Janet Robertson.

26, James Peirsone to Nanse Stevinsone.

26, William Ritchie to Bessie Miller.

SEPTEMBER.

B. 2, David Anderson and Margaret Bairdner had James ; witnesses, William Cunninghame, John Anderson, James Anderson.

2, Robert Stevin and Helen Hyslope had a daughter . . . ; witnesses, William Bruce, Mr. James Phinne, Andrew Trumble in Bromehall.

4, David Smetoun and Elspeth Russell had Christian ; witnesses, Robert Trumble, Robert Huggone, John Cusine.

9, James Mitchell and Christian Thomson had Margaret ; witnesses, William Trumble, Andrew Potter, Alexander Lambe.

11, Mr. Patrick Auchinleck and Elspeth Forrester had Helen ; witnesses, Mr. Thomas Wardlaw of Logie, Mr. Archibald Moncreiff, minister at Dollar, Mr. James Sibauld, schoolmaster of Dunfermline.

21, James Feg and Elspeth Smetoun had Margaret ; witnesses, Francis Cokburne, John Broun, Andrew Broun.

25, Harry Currour and Christian Cuik had David ; witnesses, David Moreis, John Stevinsone, Henry Hakirstoun, all in Baithe.

28, John Hutoune in Pitdinnie and Margaret Patoun had John ; witnesses, John Peirson, John Lindsay, William Lawsoun.

M. 16, Robert Douglas to Margaret Harrower.

16, David Ready to Helen Galrig.

OCTOBER.

B. 5, John Ritchie and Christian Lindsay had John ; witnesses, James Ritchie, William Hutsone, John Hutsone.

5, John Johnestoun and Margaret Eiling (?) had Elspet ; witnesses, William Bruse, Thomas Stevenson, David Mitchell.

5, George Dewar in Lathamond and Margaret Maistertoun had Jean ; witnesses, Robert Maistertoun of Baithe, William Maistertoun, Robert Anghous.

5, William Falkland and Isabel Logane had Geils ; witnesses, William Anderson, John Anderson, Robert Anderson.

12, William Litlejohne and Christian Broun had James ; witnesses, James Mudie, John Watson, Thomas Hunnon.

12, James Garvie and Janet Lochtie had James ; witnesses, James Kellok, James Mitchell, James Dewar, Mr. James Phinn of Lymkills.

14, William Philpe in the Nethertoun and Elspet Lindsay had a daughter, ... ; witnesses, Mr. Laurence Thomesone, John Murray, William Mudie, maltman.

19, Robert Stevenson, smith, and Elspet Davidson had Robert ; witnesses, Robert Davidson, Patrick Cowper, Andrew Murray.

21, John Thomson, flesher, and Janet Hutone had John ; witnesses, Mr. John Walker, John Hog, Thomas Stevenson, John Small.

23, John Hodge and Effie Broun had Catherine ; witnesses, David Moreis, John Stevinson, John Inglis.

26, James Clerk and Janet Beany had Margaret ; witnesses, William Lawson, William Anderson, Andrew Lessells, James Trottar.

26, John Raff and Janet Greive had Isobel ; witnesses, Robert Trumble, John Greive, Robert Greive, all in Tunigask.

26, James Hutone and Janet Peirsone had Andrew ; witnesses, Andrew Hutone, David Cunnon, Thomas Stanehous.

26, Thomas Rodger and Grizel Westwod had Alexander ; witnesses, Alexander Beane, William Æssoun, James Lindsay.

26, John Stevenson and Janet Fuird had William ; witnesses, William Cois, James Peirsone, John Maistertoun.

30, Mr. Harry Makgill, minister, and Isobel Lindsay had Margaret ; witnesses, John Henresone of Fordall, Mr. Frederick Gib, Mr. James Sibauld.

M. 21, James Fairnie to Margaret Hutone.

NOVEMBER.

B. 1, Walter Henresone of Granton and Jean Robertson had Walter (in fornication) ; witnesses, Peter Law, John Henresone, writer in Edinburgh, David Stewart.

1, George Lindsay in Kavill and Jean Mowtrey had George ; witnesses, William Philpe, William Broun, clerk.

2, John Aitkine and Christian Dagleische had Helen ; witnesses, Laurie Stevenson, James Maxwell, James Dagleishe.

2, James Hutone and Margaret Walker had William ; witnesses, William Anderson, John Peirson, William Lawson.

2, David Broun and Isobel Mayne had John ; witnesses, John Mayne, James Mayn, William Walker, James Ritchie.

4, Gavin Stanehous and Marjory Nicole had Thomas ; witnesses, Thomas Stanehous, Thomas Mitchell, William Anderson, litster.

4, William Mackie and Margaret Betsone had Margaret ; witnesses, John Orolk, David Blak, John Kellok.

9, Andrew Kellok and Margaret Stocks had Grizel ; witnesses, Henry Mill, John Kellok, Henry Baverage.

18, John Broun in the Ferrie and Beatrix Thomson had Margaret (baptised in Inverkeithing kirk) ; witnesses, ...

18, Robert Levingstone of Baldrige and Jean Bruse had Patrick ; witnesses, Frederick Gib, William Mentethe of Randiefuird, James Gib.

23, Thomas Henresone, cook, and Helen Cuming had William ; witnesses, David Peirsone, elder, George Gib in Torrieburne, William Mitchell, salter.

23, William Mudie, mason, and Margaret Ædisone had Janet ; witnesses, Patrick Cowper, William Mudie, David Laurie. (Born 22nd about 4 a.m.)

23, Robert Scot and Janet Davidson had William ; witnesses, James Kennedie, James Hutone, merchant, John Dow, grieve of Baldrig.

30, James Lindsay and Nanse Mentethe had Isobel ; witnesses, William Litljohne, Thomas Davidson, William Aissoun.

M. **4**, David Din to Bessie Fergie.

4 Robert Fultoun to Margaret Austiane.

6, James Rutherfuird to Rosina Walwod.

11, George Ivat to Annas Barklay.

11, Andrew Ritchie to Marjory Ædisone.

25, John Penman to Helen Samuell.

DECEMBER.

B. **7**, John Berill and Margaret Colzeire had James ; witnesses, James Gib of Lethome, Mr. James Phinne, portioner of Lymkills, James Walker.

14, James Stewart and Margaret Greive had Effie ; witnesses, John Kellok, Patrick Murray, John Rowane.

16, James Stanehous and Margaret Trumble had Robert ; witnesses, Robert Mudie, Robert Kellok, younger, Robert Stanehous in Dowloche, Robert Trumble in Tunygask.

16, William Spens and Christian Vallange had Nanse ; witnesses, Thomas Baverage, William Smart, William Watsone.

16, James Miller and Nanse Miller had David ; witnesses, David Burne, Robert Hugone, John Sanders.

21, Archibald Glenny and Nanse Æssone had Margaret ; witnesses, William Æssone, John Lindsay, William Cunningham, James Peirsone.

21, Robert Hutone and Janet Trumble had Catherine ; witnesses, William Keir, Henry Trumble, Thomas Schortus.

26, John Burne and Margaret Hutone had Elspet ; witnesses, Robert Alisone, Robert Davidson, William Mudie.

28, John Greive and Margaret Thomson had Margaret ; witnesses, John Raff, William Hutone, Robert Greive.

M. **2**, James Andersone to Isobel Inglis.

9, Matthew Neivene to Margaret Ædie.

23, Andrew Thomson to Janet Flokard.

23, John Quhyt to Nanse Stirk.

30, John Potter to Elspet Walker.

JANUARY [1629].

B. **4**, William Cambell and Margaret Broun had William ; witnesses, William Mudie, William Smart, Robert Davidson.

4, Malcolm Makqueine and Janet Jonkeine had Janet ; witnesses, Robert Davidson, Robert Miller, Robert Logane.

4, John Moreis and Isobel Gotterstone had Andrew ; witnesses, Andrew Moreis, James Henresone, Robert Yowane.

11, Archibald Nicole and Christian Wilsone had William ; witnesses, Patrick Andersone, William Anderson, John Lindsay, William Anderson in the Hiltoun.

11, William Inche and Margaret James had Margaret ; witnesses, Michael Meldrum, John James, George Meldrum.

11, John Anderson, younger, and Helen Kingorne had Grizel ; witnesses, William Mentethe of Randifuird, James Gib, Mr. Patrick Fleck.

18, David Reid and Margaret Lawson had John ; witnesses, John Stobie, John Walker, John Scotland. (Baptised in Carnok kirk.)

18, John Broun and Janet Hall had Christian ; witnesses, William Broun, David Broun, Henry Broun, William Smart.

18, John Fin and Margaret Din had John ; witnesses, James Hutone, John Miller, David Din.

20, David Robertson of Craigduckie and Grizel Hutone had David ; witnesses, David Scotland, George Dewar, James Mill.

25, Nicol Inglis and Marjory Law had Janet; witnesses, Richard Law, Robert Russell, James Mill.

25, John Richard and Christian Blakwod had a son . . . ; witnesses, . . .

25, John Coventrie, miller, and Janet Walwod had Henry; witnesses, John Simsone, Andrew Currie, Robert Kellok, younger.

25, Robert Lindsay of Kavill and Lilias Drummond had Helen; witnesses, Robert Mowtrey of Rescobie, Andrew Walker, James Reid, bailie of Dunfermline.

M. 13, John Dougall to Bessie Thomson.

20, Thomas Walwod to Christian Simraell.

20, Robert Tailyeour to Margaret Young.

27, James Kellok to Bessie Gibsone.

FEBRUARY.

B. 1, William Wilsone and Christian Wricht had William: witnesses, William Wilson, elder, William Mudie, William Philpe.

1, Jerome Broun and Catherine May had Margaret; witnesses, Adam Brand, Adam Car, James Broun.

1, Peter Law and Margaret Walker had David; witnesses, David Stewart, Mr. Patrick Auchinleck, Patrick Cowper.

3, William Hutone and Catherine Mill had Helen; witnesses, George Dewar, Robert Russell, James Mill.

3, James Anderson and Elspet Christie had William; witnesses, William Smithe, William Cunninghame, William Walker.

5, James Simsone and Isobel Weitche had John: witnesses, John Simsone, Harry Walwod, William Watsone.

8, Adam Car and Janet Crawfuird had Sophia; witnesses, James Durie, James Broun, James Car.

8, David Spens and Helen Mitchell had Margaret; witnesses, William Trumble, George Cunningham, John Small.

8, Andrew Burne and Elspet Ritchie had William; witnesses, James, Currie, Andrew Trumble in Bromehall, Andrew Trumble in Grange, William Burne.

8, William Anderson and Catherine Cunningham had Bessie; witnesses, Robert Cunningham, Edward Douglas, Adam Wilsone.

15, John Hill, collier in Keltieheughe, and Margaret Steidman had Andrew; witnesses, Henry Baverage, John Baverage, John Adamesone. (Baptised in Cleish kirk.)

15, John Smetone and Barbara Clerk had Janet; witnesses, Andrew Trumble in Bromehall, George Trumble, his son, John Broun in Inverkeithing.

15, Andrew Johnstone and Catherine Stewart had Margaret; witnesses, David Weymis, John Mill, James Mill, Robert Russell.

15, John Oiswald and Christian Hamilton had James; witnesses, James Gib, James Cowstoun, James Osswald, David Inglis.

15, Thome Reid and Magie Phillane had Bernard (in fornication); witnesses, ...

19, Thomas Stevenson, maltman in the Newra, and Janet Chalmers had Janet; witnesses, Edward Douglas, Thomas Douglas, David Stevenson at the Croce, William Anderson in Pitconnochie.

22, James Moutrey and Margaret Broun had a daughter (in fornication).

22, James Mitchell in Mastertoun and Isobel Cunningham had Thomas; witnesses, Thomas Mitchell, Thomas Stanehous, William Cunningham in Little Fordell, David Mitchell in Pitlivar.

22, Andrew Elder and Janet Phin had Jean; witnesses, William Anderson in Lymkills, David Murra, Andrew Young, Robert Bruse.

22, James Anderson in Knokes and Janet Clerk had William; witnesses, William Cunningham in Knokes, William Anderson and William Cunningham.

24, William Murra and Christian Mudie had Janet; witnesses, Robert Cunningham, George Trumble, Andrew Young.

M. 5, William Kellok to Bessie Trumble.
    12, David Sands in Gellat to Bessie Christie (married in Carnok).
    15, Mr. Bernard Gib to Eupham Abircrumbie.
    17, John Blakwod to Christian Sim.
    17, James Broun to Nanse Gray.

MARCH.

B. 1, Alexander Grege and Catherine Philpe had David; witnesses, David Weymis, John Thomesone, William Hugane.
    1, John Bennat, weavar, and Marion Cunnone had Christian; witnesses, Mr. James Dewar, John Miller, George Hendeine.
    1, John Merschell and Margaret Fwird had Margaret; witnesses, William Cunninghame in Knokes, Andrew Walker in Logie, David Mitchell in Pitlivar.
    1, John Smart and Margaret Baverage had Margaret; witnesses, William Smart, John Smart, Thomas Baverage.
    1, Adam Stobie of Wester Luscour and Helene Gibone had Sophia; witnesses, James Durie, James Wardlaw, Thomas Hutone, John Wilson.
    1, Andrew Drummond and Bessie Young had Patrick; witnesses, Patrick Cowper, Andrew Murra, Patrick Allane.
    3, Alexander Lambe and Janet Dagleische had William; witnesses, William Lambe, James Mitchell, William Cunninghame, John Dagleische.
    3, Robert Hutone and Janet Speir had John (in fornication); witnesses, John Huntar, John Schortus, Thomas Banchrie.
    8, John Livingstone and Christian Young had Bessie; witnesses, John Wricht, Andrew Murray, Andrew Young.
    8, Robert Peirsone and Marjory Peirsone had Nanse; witnesses, William Smithe, William Peirsone, John Walwod.
    8, John Anderson, litster, and Janet Stevenson had James; witnesses, Mr. James Durie, John Walker, dean of guild, James Hamiltone.
    8, James Kellok and Bessie Gibsone had Thomas (in fornication); witnesses, Mr. Thomas Wardlaw, George Bothwell, William Cuninghame.
    15, John Lindsay and Bessie Peirsone had Robert; witnesses, John Lindsay, Patrick Lindsay, Richard Templemen, David Peirsone, Robert Cunninghame.
    15, William Rattray and Janet Westwod had Emelie; witnesses, George Donald, Henry Donald, Richard Blaklay.
    22, David Peirsone and Helen Henresone had Henry; witnesses, Alexander Henresou, Robert Stanehous, Thomas Peirson.
    22, James Murgane and Elspet Bowman had Elspet; witnesses, Thomas Walker, Andrew Walker his son, and William Walker.
    22, Thomas Hall and Bessie Portour had Andrew; witnesses, Andrew Trumble, William Potter, Andrew Cunninghame.
    22, Andrew Drysdell and Janet Bonalay had William; witnesses, William Cunningham, Thomas Ritchie, William Anderson.
    29, James Hutone and Marion Dempstertoun had Marjory; witnesses, William Broun, David Maxwell, John Bruse.

M. [*None.*]

APRIL.

B. 6, John Dagleische and Elspet Hutone in Lethomis had Bessie (in fornication), baptised in Saline kirk: witnesses, John Dick in Hilsyd, James Broun in Halburnis, Robert Dagleische, brother of said John.
    6, James Hamilton and Jean Sanders had Gilbert; witnesses, Gilbert Sanders, Robert Merser of Kirkland of Saline, Mr. Patrick Fleck.

7, Patrick Cowper, bailie, and Janet Murray had Helen ; witnesses, Mr. Patrick Auchinleck, Harry Walwod, John Anderson, younger.

12, John Wels and Catherine Drummond had Effie ; witnesses, Mr. Bernard Gib, David Stevenson, Thomas Baverage.

15, Mr. James Sibauld, minister of Torrie, and Isobel Bowstoun had George ; witnesses, Steven Tyllidaff, Robert Alisone, Mr. John Duncane, minister of Saline.

16, William Aikine and Janet Clerk had John (in fornication) ; witnesses, John Broun, George Moreis, Andrew Smith.

17, Archibald Honyman and Margaret Wels had a daughter . . . . ; witnesses, John Walker, Gilbert Johnstone, James Cusine.

19, James Trottar and Bessie Lawsoun had Simon ; witnesses, William Cunningham, Patrick Anderson, William Sanders.

20, James Kennedie and Janet Hutone had Colin ; witnesses, Charles Ritchardsone, Gavin Stanehous, David Walker, cooper.

26, Thomas Stanehous and Barbara Dewar had Robert ; witnesses, Robert Kellok, younger, Gavin Stanehous, Mr. James Dewar.

M. 7, Andrew Fergussone to Barbara Moreisone.

7, John Whyt to Janet Reid.

12, David Galrige to Margaret Yowane.

28, David Stirk to Janet Smetone.

30, Henry Baverage to Catherine Stewart.

MAY.

B. 3, David Scotland and Janet Aikine had David ; witnesses, David Robertson of Craigduckie, Mr. William Wardlaw of Balmule, James Mill in Lochend.

3, Henry Broun and Beatie Sands had Elizabeth ; witnesses, David Broun, David Sands, William Galrige.

3, John Colzeir and Marjory Corsane had James ; witnesses, James Peirsone, James Westwod, John Baid.

6, Wallie Walwod, cordiner, and Magie Lindsay had John ; witnesses, John Simsone, cordiner, Robert Lindsay of Kavill, David Lawrie, Robert Dick, John Thomesone, George Davidson.

10, John Makmoniche and Janet Porteous had Catherine ; witnesses, Robert Alisone, John Johnestoun, William Cunninghame.

10, James Beany and Margaret Honyman had James ; witnesses, James Gib, John Bennat, William Walker.

11, Robert Makcraiche and Isobel Donaldson had Jean ; witnesses, Thomas Christie, John Smart, Robert Lochtie.

12, William Smart and Bessie Stevenson had William ; witnesses, William Broun, Robert Wels, Robert Stevenson.

17, Thomas Tod and Elspet Lyall had Helen ; witnesses, John Lyall, David Tod, Clement Bankis.

17, Patrick Stevenson and Christian Mudie had Marjory ; witnesses, James Hutoun, merchant, David Burne, Robert Wilsone.

17, William Anderson in Pitconnochie and Nanse Chalmers had Patrick ; witnesses, Patrick Anderson, Thomas Douglas, Andrew Roxbroughe.

17, Laurie Anderson and Margaret Lugtone had William ; witnesses, William Anderson, litster, William Walwod of Touche, Thomas Hunnon.

20, William Patoun and Janet Ædisone had twins, John and William ; witnesses, John Simsone, John Wricht, Peter Buist, Thomas Stevenson, William Anderson, litster.

24, James Anderson and Janet Gray had William ; witnesses, William Cunningham, Patrick Anderson, Adam Wilson.

24, Thome Sands and Margaret Fentoun had William ; witnesses, Mr. William Wardlaw of Balmule, James Stanehous, John Gentleman.

24, James Mill and Grizel Robertson had William ; witnesses, Mr. William Wardlaw, William Robertson, William Hutone.

24, John Dougall and Bessie Craik had John ; witnesses, John Whyt, John Anderson, James Hutone.

24, John Schortus and Janet Bankis had Bessie ; witnesses, Alexander Broun, Clement Bankis, John Schortus.

24, David Murray and Isobel Phinne had John ; witnesses, Andrew Trumble, George Trumble in Bromehall, John Watt.

24, Robert Anghous and Christian Smetoun had William ; witnesses, Mr. William Wardlaw of Bamule, William Robertson, George Dewar, David Scotland.

M. 5, Andrew West to Janet Trumble.

19, Pate Harrower to Janet Man.

26, James Legat to Margaret Stirk.

26, Robert Lendoirs to Isobel Broun.

26, Andrew Broun to Bessie Wilson.

26, John Maklarane to Janet Murie.

26, John Anderson to Margaret Horne.

28, James Donaldsone to Margaret Cunningham.

JUNE.

B. 2, George Trumble in Tynnygask and Isobel Gib had a son . . . . ; witnesses, Andrew Trumble, portioner of Grange, Adam Stobie, portioner of Wester Luscour, George Trumble in Bromehall.

5, John Potter and Janet Inglis had twins, John and Margaret ; witnesses, George Donald, John Anderson, litster, William Cunningham, weaver, William Trumble, lorimer.

7, Laurence Hutone and Janet Robertson had Nanse ; witnesses, James Hutone, merchant, William Robertson of Easter Craigduckie, Alexander Drysdell, merchant.

11, John Makdougall and Bessie Thomson had Margaret ; witnesses, William Mudie, James Hall, Henry Phinne.

14, John Keir and Marjory Douglas had Margaret ; witnesses, Henry Hakerstoun, John Stevinson, David Moreis, all dwelling in " the Baithes."

14, Robert Greive and Margaret Douglas had Catherine ; witnesses, George Dewar, John Aikine, John Greive.

14, Robert Peacok and Bessie Wricht had Margaret ; witnesses, David Mitchell, George Donald, John Merschell.

14, John Spens, collier in Touch, and Jean Brand had Marion ; witnesses, George Penman, Alexander Hird, William Walwod, younger.

14, John Small and Margaret Hugone had George ; witnesses, George Penman, John Hugone, Robert Henresone, skinner, John Clerk.

16, George Burgane in the North Queinisferrie and Janet Swentoun had a daughter . . . . (Baptised in Inverkeithing kirk.)

18, John Bull and Janet Phillane had Marjory ; witnesses, Harry Bull, David Hoge, James Car.

21, William Mudie, weaver, and Nanse Mackie had James ; witnesses, Gavin Stanehous, James Anderson, Robert Stevenson.

28, Alexander Davidson and Janet Douglas had John ; witnesses, Mr. John Wardlaw, John Gentleman, William Kellok.

28, David Blak and Marjory Blakwod had Helen ; witnesses, William Blak, Robert Dowie, Andrew Henresone.

28, James Scharpe and Nanse Richardson, both servants to the Laird of Rumgay, had Nanse (in fornication) ; witnesses, Thomas Reid, Laurie Merser, Gilbert Johnstone.

30, Thomas Blakwod and Margaret Bossuell had James ; witnesses, James Gib of Knok and Mr. Bernard, his brother, Mr. Thomas Wardlaw of Logie, George Bothwell of the Haughes.

M. 4, Sandie Wilsone to Catherine Ritchie.

4, David Welwod to Isobel Blair.

11, Robert Thomesone to Margaret Cusine.
14, Robert Anderson to Bessie Johnestoun.

JULY.

B. 5, Gilbert Johnestone and Christian Wels had Catherine ; witnesses, Mr.
Thomas Wardlaw, William Broun, Robert Wels.

5, Andrew Barhame and Margaret Stewart had Janet ; witnesses, Robert
Livingstone, James Gib, Mr. Bernard Gib.

7, Andrew Galrige and Isobel Johnstone had Robert ; witnesses, James
Trumble, William Inglis, Robert Johnstone.

9, Robert Mowtrey and Lady Annas Erskine had a daughter . . . .

12, Thomas Douglas and Elspet Chalmers had Robert ; witnesses, Robert
Kellok, David Douglas, David Sands.

12, Peter Sempill and Janet Cunningham had William ; witnesses, Steven
Tylliduff, John Anderson, notary, James Moyas.

23, Andrew Lindsay and Marjory Walker had Isobel ; witnesses, John
Brown, James Huntar, George Meldrum.

26, Richard Blaklay and Emelie Par had Andrew ; witnesses, Andrew
Wilsone, Thomas Wilsone, his son, and William Bruce.

26, James Henresone and Mays Aikine had David ; witnesses, David
Mastertoun, glazier, Gilbert Blair, Andrew Potter.

26, John Walker, dean of guild, and Margaret Trumble had Catherine ; witnesses, William Broun, clerk, William Walker and David Walker,
merchants.

28, James Peirsone and Nanse Stevenson had David (baptised in Torrie
kirk) ; witnesses, David Peirsone, John Peirsone, his son, William
Cunningham in Knokes.

M. 7, William Williamsone to Marjory Broun.
26, James Palmer to Catherine Anderson.

AUGUST.

B. 2, James Æssone, cordiner, and Catherine Watson had John ; witnesses,
John Simsone, James Simsone, John Smart.

13, Archibald Hodge and Margaret Walker had Geils ; witnesses, James
Gib, Mr. Bernard Gib, Mr. Patrick Fleck.

16, Mr. Bernard Gib and Effie Abercrombie had Isobel ; witnesses, James
Gib, Sir Robert Halket of Pitfirran, George Bothwell of the Haughes.

17, Thomas Walwod and Christian Simruell had Peter ; witnesses, Peter
Buist, James Mitchell, William Walwod, baker.

18, John Watson, cordiner, and Marjory Smetoun had Robert ; witnesses,
Robert Cunningham in Sillitoun, Lawrie Watson, John Simsone.

18, Francis Cokburne and Alisone Cockburne had William ; witnesses,
William Bruce, George Davidson, John Broun, officer.

23, George Ivatt and Nanse Barklay had William ; witnesses, John Davidson, John Rowane, William Smith in Fod.

23, William Young and Nanse Plane (under promise of marriage) had
Margaret ; witnesses, William Anderson, Andrew Murray, John
Anderson.

23, Andrew Miller and Nanse Gourley had John ; witnesses, John Lindsay,
Robert Lindsay of Kavill.

23, Stevin Tyllidaff and Margaret Row had Grizel ; witnesses, William
Mentethe of Randifurd, James Gib of Lethomis, Mr. Bernard Gib, his
brother.

30, Andrew Trumble in Grange and Helen Currie had John ; witnesses,
John Henresone of Fordell, William Mentethe of Randifurd, William
Kellok.

30, John Buchannane, miller in Kavill, and Janet Peacok, had Nanse ; witnesses, David Mitchell in Pitliver, John Mershell there, Alexander
Wilson.

30, Lawrence Lugtoun and Janet Bennat had Margaret ; witnesses, Harry Cant, Alexander Ædisone, George Davidson.

M. 18, Andrew Drysdell to Margaret Wilson.
25, John Mudie to Janet Rowane.

SEPTEMBER.

B. 6, Lawrie Anderson in Kistock and Jean Hutone had Janet ; witnesses, William Nicole, Patrick Dumbar, Andrew Leslie.
6, William Anderson and Janet Cunningham had Margaret ; witnesses, William Lawson, Patrick Anderson, David Peirsone.
6, Andrew Wilson and Janet Douglas had Robert ; witnesses, Robert Kellok, younger, David Bull in Mastertoun, Thomas Cunnon. "This bairne wes ane of twynnis, and the other died without baptisme."
6, John Gray and Alison Martene had John ; witnesses, John Alisone, William Robertson, Henry Peirsone.
6, William Forrester and Janet Grysie had Robert ; witnesses, George Moreis, collier, William Cowstoun, Robert Murgaine.
13, Thomas Baverage and Christian Smart had Bessie ; witnesses, William Smart, Thomas Elder, John Wels.
20, William Sanders and Christian Hutone had Catherine ; witnesses, William Hutone in Dunduff, John Cusine, Robert Scotland.
20, Robert Quhyt and Catherine Hunnon had Robert ; witnesses, Robert Davidson, John Anderson, litster in the Kirkgate, Peter Law, James Hamilton.
20, Alexander Drysdell, merchant, and Bessie Walwod had Thomas ; witnesses, Mr. Thomas Wardlaw of Logie, John Walker, dean of guild, John Clerk, merchant, William Walker, merchant.

M. 1, William Cois to Margaret Bowman.
20, Adam Stevinsone to Margaret Bull.
29, Thomas Keir to Helen Yowane.

OCTOBER.

B. 4, Andrew Hutone, slater, and Elspet Kilgour had Elspet ; witnesses, Gavin Stanehous, John Workman, Robert Yowane.
4, James Mitchell and Christian Thomson had James ; witnesses, James Reid, Patrick Cowper, Andrew Murray.
18, George Trumble and Margaret Thomson had Helen ; witnesses, Andrew Trumble, Adam Trumble, William Galrige, John Currie.
18, John Inglis and Nanse Hutone had John ; witnesses, John Aikine, Robert Russell, Andrew Rowane in Gask.
18, James Anderson and Janet Miller had Robert ; witnesses, John Stobie, Thomas Stevenson, James Broun. (Baptised in Carnok kirk.)
18, David Douglas and Alison Mitchell had Jean ; witnesses, Andrew Burne, William Burne, David Mitchell.
18, John Clerk and Catherine Baid had Catherine ; witnesses, John Wilsone, James Lugtoun, James Miller.
20, Mr. Thomas Wardlaw of Logie and Catherine Alisone had John ; witnesses, Mr. John Wardlaw, son of Sir Henry Wardlaw of Pitravie, William Hutone of Bellilisk, George Bothwell of the Haughis.
25, Andrew Meldrum and Bessie Alexander had Margaret ; witnesses, William Hutone in Dunduff, John Greive, Robert Russell, Thomas Meldrum.
25, Robert Tailyeour and Margaret Young had Elspet ; witnesses, Harry Young, John Levingstoun, John Anderson, Robert Peirsone.

M. 20, John Huntar to Bessie Wels.
20, William Nicole to Margaret Bardner.
22, John Wilsone to Barbara Kellok.

NOVEMBER.

B. 1, John Penman and Helen Savenell had John ; witnesses, John Allane, collier, Abraham Peacok, George Penman.

1, John Alisone, mason, and Marjory Elder had Elspet ; witnesses, David Smetoun, Robert Russell, William Cunninghame, weaver.

1, George Straquhen, a stranger, and his wife, Helen Nicole (married in Dunfermline kirk) had George ; witnesses, James Hutone, bailie, William Walker, William Mastertoun.

6, Wattie Horne and Christian Young had Catherine (in fornication) ; witnesses, George Davidson, Robert Anderson, William Patersone. (Purpose of marriage intimated.)

11, Edward Douglas and Beatie Douglas had Robert ; witnesses, William Anderson, David Douglas, David Sands.

15, William Potter and Catherine Mowse had William ; witnesses, Alexander Young, David Keir, Edward Stirk.

15, James Patoun and Isobel Watson had Marjory ; witnesses, William Walker, Alexander Drysdell, Adam Brand, Robert Murgane.

17, James Maxwell and Marion Allane had Christian (in fornication) ; witnesses, John Aikine, younger, William Dagleishe, Oliver Culane, John Inglis.

20, John Potter and Elspet Walker had Richard ; witnesses, Richard Potter, John Trumble, Andrew Potter.

22, Alexander Wilson and Margaret Donaldson had Alexander ; witnesses, Alexander Donald, John Lawson, John Wilson in Galrickhill.

22, John Hadstone and Bessie Beany had William ; witnesses, Thomas Johnstone, William Anderson, William Nicole.

22, George Moreis, collier, and Bessie Beany had William ; witnesses, John Hog, Robert Murgane, Thomas Dreddone.

26, William Kellok and Bessie Trumble had Robert ; witnesses, Robert Kellok, Andrew Trumble in Grange, James Kellok.

29, William Anderson in Lymkills and Geils Peirsone had Nanse ; witnesses, Mr. James Phune, Andrew Currie, William Anderson, and William Anderson in Pitconnochie.

29, William Philpe and Elspet Lindsay had a daughter . . . . ; witnesses, William Mudie, Robert Davidson, William Wilson, Patrick Stevenson.

M. 19, Andrew Patoun to Isobel Richardson.

20, Thomas Williamson to Margaret Portour.

24, John Scotland to Marjory Inglis.

24, Thomas Cunnon to Janet Douglas.

DECEMBER.

B. 6, Lawrence Watson, cordiner, and Grizel Wilson had Janet ; witnesses, Mr. Patrick Fleck, Charles Richardson, John Bennat.

6, John Hugane and Cicile Glen had Margaret ; witnesses, William Keir, Robert Hutone, James Westwod, John Small.

18, James Cowstoun and Grizel Moreis had Effie ; witnesses, Thomas Stevenson, James Huntar, Robert Davidson.

22, William Kellok and Margaret Kellok had Thomas ; witnesses, John Kellok, Henry Mill, Henry Stocks, Thomas Kellok.

22, John Dagleishe and Janet Orolk had John ; witnesses, Thomas Blakwod, David Laurie, George Davidson, James Kellok, John Wels.

22, Laurence Anderson and Grizel Thomson had Catherine ; witnesses, Robert Kellok, William Walker in the Rhods, Andrew Patoun.

22, James Peacok and Janet Burgane had David (in fornication) ; witnesses, David Greins, William Peacok, David Scott.

22, David Hoge and Marjory Bull had John ; witnesses, John Anderson, James Hutone, bailies, and John Walker.

24, Thomas Hunnon and Janet Edward had John ; witnesses, John Sanders, John Bruse, Robert Hugoun.

26, James Kellok and Helen Spens had Isobel ; witnesses, John Bennat, Charles Richardson, Thomas Reid.

27, William Falkland and Isobel Logane had Margaret ; witnesses, Mr. James Phinne of Lymkills, Robert Peirsone, Andrew Young.

27, John Dow and Margaret Merser had Elspet ; witnesses, Laurie Merser, Charles Richardson, James Cusine, Robert Wyld.

31, William Gray and Margaret Anderson had Helen ; witnesses, William Anderson in Lymkills, and Robert and John, his sons.

M. 1, Thomas Hutone to Isobel Keir.
8, William Dagleishe to Isobel Sim.
15, Andrew Christie to Helen Currie.
15, Henry Moreis to Isobel Duncane.
22, William Young to Nanse Plaine.
22, James Alexander to Nanse Robertson (in Aberdour kirk).

JANUARY [1630].

B. 3, James Clerk and Janet Beany had Margaret ; witnesses, William Anderson in Pitconnochie, James Peirsone, William Lawson.

3, William Galrige and Helen Broun had James ; witnesses, James Trumble, Henry Broun, George Trumble, John Currie.

3, Thomas Mitchell in Gellat and Margaret Dick had Jean ; witnesses, William Mentethe of Randifuird, John Henresone of Fordall, Robert Dick.

5, George Cunningham and Margaret Mastertoun had Nanse ; witnesses, William Keir, Robert Hutone, John Gotterstoun.

12, Henry Dick and Bessie Stevenson had John ; witnesses, John Stevenson of Bayth, William Mackie in Coklaw, John Dick.

12, John Currie and Margaret Watson had Andrew ; witnesses, Andrew Walker, Andrew Currie, Andrew Trumble, James Anghous.

17, James Cusine, flesher, and Barbara Dewar had Bessie ; witnesses, John Dewar and James Dewar in Pitbauchlie, and John Cusine.

24, John Mackcraiche and Nanse Donaldsone had Thomas (in fornication) ; witnesses, Robert Scotland, Robert Mackcraiche, Thomas Tod, Robert Currie.

31, Hercules Howat and Marjory Setoun had Margaret ; witnesses, David Bull, Gilbert Car, Andrew Potter, Robert Patrik.

M. 5, John Wricht to Bessie Law.
12, Robert Currie to Elspet Mackcraiche.
26, Patrick Lawsone to Margaret Lathangie.

FEBRUARY.

B. 2, James Reid and Marion Broun had Margaret ; witnesses, Mr. Thomas Wardlaw of Logie, Mr. Bernard Gib, John Anderson, younger.

2, David Lambe and Marjory Wilson had Janet ; witnesses, James Mudie, William Keir, Allan Mudie.

9, Thomas Christie of the Hoill and Elspet Durie had Janet ; witnesses, Mr. James Durie, David Sands, Andrew Christie.

9, Andrew Ritchie and Marjory Ædisone (who died in childbed) had John ; witnesses, John Ædisone, Henry Ædisone, John Watt.

11, David Mitchell in Pitlivar and Margaret Currie had Catherine ; witnesses, Andrew Trumble in Bromehall, James Eweine, Andrew Walker in Logie.

12, John Law and Nicolas Anderson had Janet ; the child died within two days after baptism.

14, William Currour and Marion Gardner had Andrew (in fornication) ; witnesses, Henry Hakirstone, William Currour, father of said William, and John Stevenson of Baithe.

14, Alexander Beane and Helen Hutone had Thomas ; witnesses, Robert Dick, Thomas Johnestoun, John Simsone.

14, John Baid and Bessie Spens had Barbara ; witnesses, David Miller Edward Stirk, John Sanders.

14, James Anderson and Janet Donaldson had John ; witnesses, John Walker, "gild," John Anderson, notary, John Anderson, litster in Kirkgate.

14, Heary Smetoun and Margaret Wardlaw had Harry (in fornication) ; witnesses, Mr. Bernard Gib, Laurie Merser, Mr. Patrick Fleck.

21, Patrick Harrower and Janet Mann had David ; witnesses, David Douglas, Robert Douglas, James Mann.

21, Thomas Philpe and Catherine Harrower had Jean ; witnesses, Harry Stewart of Baithe, John Davidson, William Stanehous in Fod.

21, James Thomson, collier, and Marion Gib had John (baptised in Cleish kirk) ; witnesses, John Hill, John Betsone, John Baverage.

21, James Legat and Margaret Stirk had Robert ; witnesses, Robert Stirk, messenger, William Legat, Patrick Legat, Mr. Bernard Gib.

24, Mr. James Dewar of Nether Lassodie and Elspet Moncreiff had David ; witnesses, David Weyms, David Cummon, David Robertson, Thomas Stanehous.

25, Mr. Harry Makgill, minister, and Isobel Lindsay had Robert ; witnesses, Sir Robert Halkat of Pitfirran, William Mentethe of Randiford, and George [Durie] of Craigluscour.

28, James Murgane in Drumtuthill and Christian Wilson had a son . . . . (in adultery) ; witnesses . . . .

28, James Lawson and Janet Smith had Catherine (in fornication) ; witnesses, Alexander Wilson, James Ritchie, Andrew Broun.

M. 4, Harry Richardson to Christian Peacock.

11, James Broun to Helen Stobie.

MARCH.

B. 7, Andrew Broun, smith, and Bessie Wilson had Bessie ; witnesses, Gilbert Primrois, Mr. James Durie, William Wilson.

7, Henry Orolk and Margaret Scotland had David ; witnesses, David Dewar of Lassodie, Mr. James Dewar, his son, and David Moreis of Colden Bayth.

7, Henry Smetoun and Nanse Wricht had William (in fornication) ; witnesses, Archibald Glennie, William Lawson, David Drysdell. Presented by William Mudie.

7, John Boyd (deceased) and Catherine Anderson had George ; witnesses, John Edie, George Johnestoun, William Beatone. Presented by George Davidson, weaver.

7, David Anderson in the Ferrie and Marjory Burgane had a son . . . . (baptized in Inverkeithing kirk).

12, Abraham Peacok and Margaret Young had Catherine ; witnesses, John Wilsone, Allan and William Mudies.

14, Andrew Sorlie and Alison Andersone had Janet ; witnesses, Thomas Mitchell, David Key, Thomas Peirsone.

14, George Mudie, mason, and Helen Stirk had Nanse ; witnesses, Robert Stirk, messenger, Thomas Stevenson, maltman, Archibald Hodge, James Legat.

15, William Currour and Janet Mitchell had twins, John and Janet ; witnesses, Henry Hakirstoun, Henry Moreis, James Arnott, John Kerr, Charles Richardson, Harry Currour.

16, Andrew West and Janet Trumble had Andrew ; witnesses, Andrew Trumble in Grange, Andrew Trumble in Bromehall, Mr. James Phine of Lymkills.

21, James Hutone and Janet Peirsone had Robert ; witnesses, Robert Mastertoun, Robert Peirsone, Robert Mudie, younger.

21, James Wallace and Janet Hendresone had James ; witnesses, James Hutone, William Broun, James Legat.

Q

22, James Dagleische and Catherine Wardlaw had Nicol; witnesses, Nicol Wardlaw, Andrew Trumble, George Trumble.

25, Adam Wilson and Margaret Cunningham had twins, Thomas and Robert; witnesses, Andrew Wilson, Thomas Wilson, William Bruse, James Cunningham, Robert Cunningham, William Anderson.

28, Henry Moreis and Isobel Duncane had John; witnesses, David Moreis, John Stevenson of Baithe, John Walker, merchant in Dunfermline.

28, John Hog and Margaret Thomson had James; witnesses, William Cowstoun, Robert Murgane, Geordie Morcas (?), all colliers in Baldrig heugh.

28, Robert Yowne and Christian Inglis had Nanse; witnesses, William Legat, William Maistertoun, William Mudie, weaver.

M. [*None*].

APRIL.

B. 1, Laurence Stevenson and Catherine Chatto had Margaret; witnesses, Patrick Cowper, Andrew Murray, David Stevenson.

8, John Robertson, weaver, and Janet Lindsay had Archibald; witnesses, Archibald Robertson, Alexander Lambe, David Lambe.

13, Andrew Rowane in Gask and Bessie Cunningham had a daughter . . . . ; witnesses, ...

13, James Hamilton, piper, and Helen Maknabe had David; witnesses, David Laurie, Andrew Thomson, James Fairnie.

13, William Robertson and Marjory Martene had Marjory; witnesses, James Hutone, merchant, . . . Gaw in Stanehous, John Workman.

13, Alexander Young and Bessie Williamson had Catherine; witnesses, John Anderson, litster, William Smart, Henry Peirson.

13, James Hamilton and Jean Sanders had Catherine; witnesses, Robert Merser of Kirkland in Sauling, Peter Law, Thomas Reid.

13, James Palmer and Catherine Anderson had James; witnesses, Robert Merser of Kirkland in Sauling, Robert Anderson in the Maygait, David Laurie.

18, James Rutherfuird and Rosina Walwod had Janet; witnesses, William Walwod, cordiner, James Moyas, Gilbert Johnestoun.

18, David Galrige and Margaret Yowne had Nanse; witnesses, John Galrige, William Galrige, William Mudie.

18, Mr. Patrick Fleck and Elspet Forrester had Nanse; witnesses, Mr. Bernard Gib, Mr. Thomas Wardlaw, Charles Richardson.

19, Andrew Thomson, belman, and Janet Flokard had James; witnesses, Mr. Harry Makgill, minister, Mr. Bernard Gib, John Simsone, George Davidson, weaver.

24, David Cunnone, portioner of Mastertoun, and Elspet Dewar had John; witnesses, John Dewar, brother of David Dewar of Lassodie, John Dewar, son of said David, and Thomas Stanehous, "his nichtbour."

24, Robert Murgane and Helen Smith had Margaret; witnesses, James Lugtoun, James Patone, John Hog.

M. 4, William Hodge to Janet Cant.

MAY.

B. 2, James Donaldson in Easter Pitcorthie and Margaret Cunningham had Robert; witnesses, Robert Cunningham in the Sillitoun, Mark Donald, baker, Andrew Cunningham, her brother.

2, John Culros and Helen Stevenson had William; witnesses, William Broun, clerk, Adam Stevenson, younger, Andrew Murray.

9, Mr. James Ready, schoolmaster, and Barbara Koyle had Andrew; witnesses, William Mentethe of Randifuird, Mr. Thomas Wardlaw of Logie, Andrew Wood, Andrew Walker, Andrew Edisone.

11, James Mitchell and Christian Legat had Christian; witnesses, William Legat, James Legat, James Mitchell in the Newraw.

16, John Blakwod and Christian Sim had James ; witnesses, Adam Car, James Anderson, Andrew Meldrum.

16, John Alisone, wright, and Grizel Walwod had Laurence ; witnesses, John Coventrie, Charles Richardson, Adam Walwod, baker. Gilbert Johnston.

17, John Spens and Janet Cunningham had John ; witnesses, Thomas Douglas, Edward Douglas, William Anderson. Mr. John Walker, reader in Dunfermline.

17, Robert Dick and Jean Sands had William ; witnesses, William Mentethe of Randifuird, Thomas Mitchell, Mr. Bernard Gib.

19, Patrick Cowper and Janet Murray had Isobel : witnesses. . . .

25, John Horne and Mary Weyms had James ; witnesses, Mr. James Dewar, James Lindsay of Dowhill, James Hamilton, David Weymis, " his brother in law."

27, James Kellok in Mastertoun and Margaret Mudie had twins, Janet and Bessie (baptised in Inverkeithing kirk) ; witnesses, Alexander Anderson, Robert Kellok, James Mitchell.

M. 2, Wattie Horne to Christian Young.

25, Edward Broun to Janet Broun (in Inverkeithing kirk).

25, John Makcraiche to Marjory Anderson.

JUNE.

B. 6, James Mitchell and Isobel Cunningham had Margaret ; witnesses, Thomas Mitchell in Gellat. David Mitchell in Pitliver, James Kellok, portioner of Mastertoun.

6, David Keir and Isobel Smithe had Isobel : witnesses, Mr. James Durie, John Walker, merchant, John Bennat, baker.

6, Robert Broun in the Ferrie and Christian Kid had Nanse ; witnesses, Edward Broun, William Kairnis, George Burgane.

13, William Kairnis and Marjory Burgane had Annas ; witnesses, John Broun, Andrew Diksone, and Harry Cant.

13, Robert Anderson and Bessie Johnstone had Isobel : witnesses, Robert Anderson, George Davidson, Thomas Johnstone.

15, Peter Ferlie and Elspet Breidfoote had Margaret ; witnesses, Robert Miller, William Walker, Robert Logane.

20, Allan Mudie and Bessie Keir had Nanse : witnesses, William Mudie, Henry Peirsone, David Lambe.

22, John Cusine and Agnes Fitt had Catherine (baptised in Saline kirk).

27, Thomas Keir and Helen Yowne had John ; witnesses, Robert Yowne, John Coventrie, David Galrige.

27, John Walker and Margaret Dewar had Adam (in Carnok kirk) ; witnesses, Adam Stobie and Thomas Huton. portioners of Luscour, and Thomas Tod in the Clun.

M. 8, Robert Hutone to Annas Cunningham.

8, John Anghous to Margaret Kellok.

10, Robert Lugtoun to Nanse Wilson.

22, Leonard Henresone to Marjory Mudie.

29, John Horne to Marjory Murie.

JULY.

B. 8, David Scott and Christian Thomson had Janet : witnesses. James Hutone, bailie, John Wricht, David Walker.

9, Peter Law and Margaret Walker had Bessie ; witnesses, John Bruse, David Stewart, John Wricht. younger, Mr. Patrick Auchinleck.

11, John Huntar and Janet Wilson had David : witnesses, David Greims, Robert Anghous, George Meldrum.

18, Andrew Berriehill and Elspet Broun had Janet ; witnesses, James Hutone in Baithe, John Gotterstoun and John Sanders. burgesses of Dunfermline.

18, John Broun, officer, and Effie Simsone had Janet; witnesses,- Mr. Patrick Fleck, Patrick Trumble, John Simsone, Thomas Elder.

19, William Bell in Linlithquo and Bessie Christie had Marion (in fornication); witnesses, John Walker, Thomas Schortus, George Mastertoun in Linlithquo.

25, John Scot and Cate Mackie had Nanse; witnesses, John Kellok, John Gotterstoun, William Mudie.

28, Thomas Whyt and Isobel Kellok had Thomas; witnesses, Thomas Kellok, Robert Straquhen, John Buchannane.

M. 13, James Baverage to Janet Steidman (in Dalgety kirk).

AUGUST.

B. 1, John Wilson and Nicolas Sandilands had James (in fornication); witnesses, James Cois, William Cois, Andrew Drysdell.

1, Robert Anghous and Christian Drysdell had Alexander; witnesses. Henry Crawfuird, Robert Russell, Nicol Inglis.

1, Robert Livingstone of Baldrige and his lady, Jean Bruse, had Alexander; witnesses, John Howstoun, William Broun, clerk, Mr. Patrick Makgill.

3, Robert Fultoun and Margaret Awstiane had Robert; witnesses, Robert Aikine, John Burne, Alexander Young.

5, John Robertson and Isobel Hutone had Margaret; witnesses, Andrew Burne, Andrew Roxburghe, James Garvie.

8, John Quhyt and Nanse Stirk had Edward; witnesses, Edward Stirk, George Meldrum, John Stirk.

15, Andrew Christie and Helen Currie had Andrew; witnesses, Andrew Walker in Logie, Andrew Curre in Primrois, Andrew Trumble in Grange, Andrew Merschell, millwright.

17, James Cunnon and Jean Philpe had John; witnesses, John Philpe, James Dewar in Mylnetoun greine, and James Cunnon.

29, Andrew Wilson and Margaret Workman had Elspet (in fornication); witnesses, Andrew Trumble in Grange, John Warkman, Nicol Inglis.

29, Patrick Allane and Janet Moreis had Janet; witnesses, William Mudie, William Wilson, William Walker.

M. 17, Robert Harper to Christian Speir.

17, John Litljohne to Janet Wilsone.

24, Andrew Ritchie to Jean Toscheauche.

24, William Dow to Janet Lugtoun.

29, John Stobie to Helen Trumble.

31, Robert Blakwod to Janet Alexander.

SEPTEMBER.

B. 3, James Ritchie and Helen Makcraiche had Isobel (in fornication); witnesses, William Smart, Thomas Elder, Alexander Wilson.

5, John Anderson and Janet Meldrum had Henry; witnesses, Robert Davidson, Henry Davidson, John Cowentrie.

5, Edward Broun, sailor in the Ferrie, and Janet Broun had a daughter . . . (baptised in Inverkeithing kirk).

12, Thomas Cunnon and Janet Douglas had Janet; witnesses, James Cunnon, David Cunnon in Mastertoun, Robert Kellok there.

12, Robert Anderson and Margaret Witit had Catharine (in fornication); witnesses, John Anderson, Abraham Pacok, James Dick.

13, "Ane vagabund woman, Christane Tannoche (as scho callis hirselff), had ane womanchyld borne of hirselfi and scho alleadgit that Johne Anderson, colzeir in Kistock, had gottin the barne in adulterie with hir that nicht that William Nicole, his nichtbour colzeir, wes maryit, he being drunk and scho getting lodging that nicht in his hous, quhilk he obstinatlie denyit and said he never saw that woman befoir to his knawlege. The bairne in the meane tyme wes baptized and callit

Margaret, and tryall to be prosequtit till God bring it to licht." Witnesses, Gilbert Car, George Davidson, Thomas Elder, Andrew Potter, Andrew Thomson, belman, all burgesses of Dunfermline.

19, James Fischar and Janet Kent had Elspet ; witnesses, David Cunnon, Robert Kellok, Luke Broun, John Gentleman.

19, Robert Clerk and Bessie Hodge had Robert ; witnesses, Andrew Cunningham, Andrew Currie, Robert Cunninghame.

19, Robert Anderson, tailor, and Janet Smithe had Janet ; witnesses, Robert Merser of the Kirkland of Sauling, Andrew Murray, Patrick Cowper.

28, Laurence Walker and Elspet Smart had Margaret ; witnesses, William Mackie, Henry Mill, John Walker.

M. 21, Patrick Kingorne to Margaret Forrester.

OCTOBER.

B. 3, John Wilsone and Barbara Kellok had John ; witnesses. John Kellok, James Hutone, bailie, Thomas Reid.

3, Thomas Hall and Bessie Portour had William ; witnesses, William Wilson, William Cunningham, William Potter.

5, John Wels, cordiner, and Christian Awstiane had William ; witnesses, William Walwod, William Henresone, John Simsone.

6, James Mudie and Grizel Lambe had William ; witnesses, William Lambe, Patrick Stevenson, John Gotterstone.

6, Thomas Williamson and Margaret Portour had Thomas ; witnesses, Andrew Murray, Patrick Cowper, Thomas Schortus.

10, Matthew Donaldson and Janet Young had John ; witnessses, Edward Douglas, William Anderson, David Sands.

10, John Anderson in the Newra and Isobel Allane had Elspet ; witnesses, Laurie Stevenson, Robert Anderson in the Maygate, James Allane.

24, John Horne and Marjory Murie had Elspet ; witnesses, James Anghous, William Anderson in Gellat, David Mitchell.

24, John Peirsone and Marion Hutone had William ; witness, Patrick Anderson.

24, John Glen, miller, and Janet Webster had Andrew ; witnesses, Andrew Trumble, baker, Andrew Thomson, belman, John Sanders, mealmaker.

31, John Lawson and Margaret Wilson had Bessie ; witnesses, John Lindsay, James Peirsone, William Walker, merchant.

31, James Car, mason, and Catherine Simsone had John ; witnesses, George Davidson, Adam Stevenson, John Gotterstoun.

M. 26, John Wilson to Margaret Anderson.

NOVEMBER.

B. 7, John Kirk and Marion Greg had David ; witnesses, Thomas Horne, James Henresone, David Kirk.

7, Thomas Stanehous and Barbara Dewar had David ; witnesses, David Dewar of Lassodie, David Cummon, John Stanehous.

9, Alexander Donaldson and Janet Reid had Bessie ; witnesses, David Mitchell, James Eweine, George Donaldson.

9, Archibald Honyman and Margaret Wels had John ; witnesses, Robert Wels, Henry Peirsone, John Huntar in Culrois.

14, Robert Bossuell and Margaret Craig had Janet ; witnesses, John Anderson, notary, John Workman, William Anderson, litster.

14, Henry Hakirstone of Baithe and Helen Cunningham had David ; witnesses, David Moreis, Alexander Maistertoun, Robert Cunningham in Otterstoun.

16, George Trumble in Bromehall and Dorothy Ædisone had John (in fornication) ; witnesses, John Ædisone, George Trumble in Tinnigask, John Currie in Crambie.

21, William Robertson and Janet Litljohne had Margaret ; witnesses, Andrew Walker, Andrew Christie, John Currie, tailor.

21, James Walwod in Netherbaithe and Marion Greiff had Andrew (in fornication) ; witnesses, John Walwod, John Rowane, James Hutone.

21, Patrick Davidson and Janet Thomson had William ; witnesses, William Smart, Thomas Elder, John Wricht.

23, Gilbert Johnestone and Christian Wels had Elspet ; witnesses, Laurie Merser, John Smetone, John Wricht, carpenter, Thomas Hereis.

23, Robert Primros and Margaret Kinsman had Sarah (in fornication) ; witnesses, William Lambe, James Mudie, John Gotterstoun.

25, James Simsone and Isobel Weitche had James ; witnesses, John Simsone, John Wricht, Harry Walwod, James Hamiltoun.

30, George Ædisone and Bessie Sands had Grizel ; witnesses, William Anderson, David Sands, Andrew Young.

30, William Cambell and Margaret Broun had George ; witnesses, William Mudie and James Car, mason.

M. 21, John Sandelands to Margaret Moreis.

23, John Scharpe to Elspet Sands (in Torrie kirk).

23, Thomas Bryse to Christian Gray.

23, David Elder to Marjory Currour.

DECEMBER.

B. 5, Thomas Hutone and Isobel Keir had Elspet ; witnesses, Thomas Christie, Andrew Walker, John Burne, mason.

5, John Sanders, mealmaker, and Helen Watsone had John ; witnesses, Robert Wels, John Bennat, Thomas Hunon.

12, Robert Currie and Elspet Makcraiche had Robert ; witnesses, Mr. James Durie, Robert Makcraiche, David Blair.

12, "Ane vagabund woman quha said that hir guidman wes ane creilman and gone in Ingland callit Garveis scho had ane man chyld borne of hir and baptized and callit George" : witnesses, David Stevenson, merchant, Mr. James Ready, schoolmaster.

13, David Strange, cordiner, and Bessie Ritchie had Janet ; witnesses, James Hamilton, Andrew Thomson, George Davidson, James Fairnie.

17, John Mudie and Janet Rowane had Catherine ; witnesses, Robert Kellok, elder and younger, and David Cunnon.

19, John Straquhen in Kistock and Isobel Fothringhame had Janet ; witnesses, William Cunningham, Robert Straquhen, James Fothringhame.

19, Harry Richardson and Christian Peacok had Patrick ; witnesses, Patrick Cowper, John Gotterstone, Alexander Lambe.

19, Andrew Hall and Margaret Hardie had Elspet ; witnesses, Thomas Mitchell, David Douglas, Thomas Douglas in Gellat.

26, James Dick and Christian Stirk had John ; witnesses, John Anderson, Abraham Peacok, John Allan.

26, Robert Stevenson, lorimer, and Elspet Davidson had Catherine ; witnesses, Patrick Cowper, Thomas Stevenson, Thomas Hereis.

26, James Anderson in Pitincreiff and Isobel Inglis had William ; witnesses, William Inglis, George Meldrum, John Huntar.

28, William Mudie, maltman, and Janet Christie had Andrew ; witnesses, Andrew Walker, Andrew Christie, George Bothwell, Patrick Stevenson.

28, Archibald Boyd and Janet Watson had Grizel ; witnesses, William Broun, Robert Wels, Laurence Watson.

M. 28, John Neilson to Janet Buist.

28, Thomas Dewar to Isobel Elder.

28, James Hamilton, piper, to Janet Portour.

JANUARY [1631].

B. 2, Andrew Patone and Isobel Ritchardson had Andrew ; witnesses, Andrew Burne, Andrew Roxburghe, David Douglas.

11, John Clerk, merchant, and Annas Portour had John ; witnesses, Mr. Patrick Auchinleck, John Bennat, James Hutone, merchant.

16, Robert Patrik and Elspet Low had Laurence : witnesses, Laurie Merser, William Smart, James Hamilton.

20, John Livingstone and Christian Young had Geils ; witnesses, William Anderson, Thomas Baverage, George Ædisone.

25, William Pillons and Isobel Douglas had George : witnesses, Thomas Mitchell, Robert Cunningham in Sillitoun, George Trumble in Bromehall.

25, James Trumble and Margaret Callendar had George (in fornication) ; witnesses, George Trumble, George Mayne, William Walker in the Rods.

25, George Donald and Margaret Stevenson had Nanse : witnesses, David Mitchell, Thomas Wilson, James Peirsone.

30, John Smetoun and Barbara Clerk had Robert : witnesses, Robert Livingstone of Baldrige, Robert Anghous, Robert Russell.

30, Andrew Burne in Gellat and Elspet Ritchie had Marjory ; witnesses, David Douglas, John Currie in Crumbie, Robert Burne.

M. 2, James Burgan to Nanse Saverall.

17, James Mill to Christian Blacater.

FEBRUARY.

B. 1, David Peirsone in Mastertoun and Helen Henresone had a daughter . . . ; witnesses, John Coventrie, Robert Kellok, Robert Stanehous.

1, David Sands in Gellat and Bessie Christie had Margaret : witnesses, Andrew Walker, William Aikine of Burrwane, John Broun of Barhill.

1, Mr. Bernard Gib and Effie Abercrumbie had Nanse : witnesses, Mr. Harry Makgill, minister, William Mentethe of Randifurd, James Gib of Lethomis, brother of said Mr. Bernard.

9, Thomas Johnestoun and Nanse Aittone had Margaret : witnesses, John Simsone, cordiner, Robert Anderson, tailor, George Trumble in Bromehall.

16, Janet Robertson "ane beggar," had a daughter Janet "quhom scho fatherit on ane Galloway, ane vagabund pyper," presented by Robert Henresone, skinner : witnesses, William Walker, merchant, Andrew Trumble, baker.

20, Robert Balcate and Elspet Rowane had Christian ; witnesses, Robert Rowane, John Inglis, John Quhyt.

20, Patrick Kinninmond of that Ilk and his lady Margaret Bossuell had Mary ; witnesses, Mr. Thomas Wardlaw of Logie, Mr. Bernard Gib, William Broun, clerk.

24, John Anderson, litster, and Helen Kingorne had Mary ; witnesses, Mr. Andrew Melvill, Harry Melvill, Peter Law.

27, William Cagzone and Margaret Burne had Margaret ; witnesses, Thomas Mitchell, Andrew Burne, David Douglas in Gellat.

27, Patrick Lawson and Margaret Lathangie had William ; witnesses, William Cunningham in Knokes, William Anderson in Gellat, William Bruse.

27, Adam Car and Janet Crawfuird had Grizel : witnesses, Robert Greive, George Trumble in Tunigask, Thomas Tod in Clun.

27, David Maxwell and Nanse Hamilton had Barbara : witnesses, William Broun, Robert Stirk, Mr. James Ready, Thomas Hereis.

27, William Philpe and Elspet Lindsay had Elspet : witnesses, Gavin Stanehous, Henry Trumble, John Workman, tailor.

M. 15, Patrick Donaldson to Christian Anderson.

22, George Anderson to Isobel Smetoun (in Cleish kirk.)

MARCH.

B. 4, William Litljohne and Christian Broun had Thomas ; witnesses, James Mudie, Peter Law, Laurence Neilson.

6, Leonard Henresone and Marjory Mudie had William ; witnesses, William Mudie, mason, William Mudie, maltman, David Miller.

13, William Mackie and Margaret Betsone had James ; witnesses, James Betsone, David Blak, Henry Baverage.

13, James Mill and Grizel Robertson had Robert ; witnesses, Robert Russell, Robert Anghous, William Hutone.

13, Andrew Drysdell and Margaret Wilson had Janet ; witnesses, John Wilson, James Murgane, John Litljohne.

13, Patrick Kingorne and Margaret Forrester had James ; witnesses, Mr. Thomas Wardlaw of Logie, George Bothwell, Mr. Bernard Gib.

15, Mr. James Phinne, portioner of Lymkills, and Agnes Aittone had Margaret ; witnesses, Andrew Trumble in Bromehall, George Trumble, his son, William Anderson in Lymkills.

20, Mungo Cunningham and Marjory Anderson had John ; witnesses, Adam Stobie, John Stobie, Nicol Wardlaw in Luscour. (Baptised in Carnok.)

20, James Wyld and Mawse Hutone had Isobel ; witnesses, James Coventrie, Henry Broun, Patrick Murray.

24, John Lawson and Catherine Drysdell had Janet ; witnesses, William Bruse, Thomas Wilson, Robert Cunningham in Sillitoun.

29, George Tailyeour and Margaret Brand had John : witnesses, John Tailyeour, John Brand, George Donald, Robert Tailyeour.

M. [*None.*]

APRIL.

B. 3, Robert Broun and Catherine Forsyth had Robert ; witnesses, Adam Wilson, Robert Anderson in Lymkills, Robert Bruse, son to William Bruse.

9, James Stanehous and Margaret Trumble had Henry ; witnesses, John Gentleman, Robert Kellok, younger, Thomas Hereis.

10, John Davidson and Marjory Broun had Marjory ; witnesses, William Smithe, William Stanehous, William Walker.

12, Robert Douglas and Margaret Peirson had Catherine ; witnesses, Adam Wilson, James Lethome, Patrick Lawsoun.

12, Lawrence Neilson and Isobel Litljohne had Isobel ; witnesses, John Bruse, John Sanders, John Alisone, wright.

12, William Kellok in Mastertoun and Bessie Trumble had James ; witnesses, James Mitchell, Alexander Chalmers, Thomas Ædisone.

17, James Anderson and Elspet Christie had James ; witnesses, James Mitchell, John Coventrie, William Walwod.

17, Gavin Stanehous and Marjory Nicole had John ; witnesses, John Stanehous, brother of said Gavin, John Law, Thomas Stevenson, maltman.

26, John Hodge and Effie Broun had David ; witnesses, John Orolk, John Stevenson, Henry Moreis, all in Baithis.

26, David Smetoun and Elspet Russell had Robert ; witnesses, Robert Russell, George Dewar, Robert Anghous.

28, John Anderson, litster, and Janet Stevenson had Bessie ; witnesses, Mr. James Durie, Mr. James Ready, William Smart.

M. 5, William Curror to Margaret Schort.

12, Robert Barklay to Margaret Henresone (in Cleish Kirk).

27, Robert Merser of the Kirkland of Sauling to Nanse Wardlaw, daughter of Mr. Thomas Wardlaw of Logie.

MAY.

B. 1, John Aikine and Christian Dagleische had Catherine ; witnesses, James Dagleische, George Trumble, Robert Greive.

1, James Hamilton and Jean Sanders had John ; witnesses, John Anderson, younger, litster, Adam Stobie, Robert Stewart.

8, James Kellok and Bessie Gibson had Robert ; witnesses, David Peirson, John Lindsay, William Davidson.

8, Pate Anderson in Pitconnochie presented the bairn "Lorne in adulterie be Margaret Caddell, quhom scho fatherit upon Patrik Archbauld, husband to Marjorie Cunninghame," baptised and called Patrick ; witnesses, George Davidson, weaver, John Wilson, weaver, George Tailyeour.

15, James Mann and Isobel Wilson had Janet ; witnesses, John Orock in Craigbaithe, John Orock, his son, John Stevenson, John Hodge.

15, James Hutone and Janet Peirsone had Janet ; witnesses, James Greg, Harry Peirsone, James Bruse.

17, Henry Douglas and Margaret Keir had Beatrix (in fornication) ; witnesses, David Douglas, Edward Douglas, Thomas Douglas, Andrew Burne.

22, Thomas Stevenson and Janet Chalmers had Marjory ; witnesses, Gavin Stanehous, James Mayne, Robert Stevenson.

22, Robert Makcraiche and Isobel Donaldson had William ; witnesses, William Walwod of Toughe, John Kellok, Andrew Kellok.

22, John Bruse and Marjory Law had Peter ; witnesses, Peter Law, Peter Buist, Laurie Merser.

24, William Wilsone, maltman, and Christian Wricht had Thomas ; witnesses, Robert Aikine, Thomas Stevenson, Thomas Cowper.

M. 24, William Walker to Marjory Broun.

24, John Cunningham to Christian Wilson.

JUNE.

B. 5, George Dewar in Lathamond and Margaret Mastertoun had George ; witnesses, George Trumble in Tunnigask, David Robertson of Easter Craigduckie, Andrew Rowane in Gask.

16, Thomas Davidson, litster, and Isobel Anderson had Thomas ; witnesses, John Anderson, younger, Mr. Patrick Auchinleck, Robert Davidson in the Nethertoun.

19, Robert Murgane and Helen Smith in Cleish kirk had a son . . . . ; witnesses, ... Smart, William Cowstoun.

19, John Horne and Mary Weymis had Marjory ; witnesses, James Weymis of Corskiebyrrane, Mr. James Dewar of Lassodie, James Hamilton in Dunfermline (?), and David Robertson of Craigduckie.

26, William Anderson in Gellat and Catherine Cunningham had Robert ; witnesses, Thomas Wilson, Thomas Douglas, Edward Douglas, Robert Cunningham in Sillitoun.

28, David Weymis and Margaret Clerk had Margaret (in fornication), presented by John Inglis ; witnesses, Nicol Inglis, David Barklay.

M. 7, Patrick Durie to Margaret Wilsone.

7, James Baverage to Janet Rae.

14, George Wardlaw to Jean Kennedy.

16, Robert Tailyeour to Margaret Cunningham.

28, Mr. Michael Weymis, minister of Canongate, to Margaret Durie, daughter of Mr. James Durie in the . . . .

JULY.

B. 11, James Garvie and Janet Lochtie had Christian ; witnesses, Andrew Burne, Robert Burne and William Burne, brothers, in Easter Gellat.

11, Thomas Blakwod and Isobel Inglis had Robert ; witnesses, George Meldrum, John Stirk, John Huntar.

14, David Bull and Margaret Potter had Harry ; witnesses, Mr. Harry Makgill, minister, Harry Bull, Thomas Hereis.

24, John Broun in the Ferrie and Barbara Thomesone had Janet ; witnesses, Laurence Lugtone, John Thomson, John Chatto.

31, Robert Anghous in Balmule and Christian Smetone had James ; witnesses, James Anghous in Crocefuird, James Mill in Lochend, William Templeman in Pitwarre, David Greins.

31, John Stirk and Margaret Wardane had James; witnesses, Nicol Wardlaw, Adam Stobie, James Wardlaw, Thomas Hutone, younger, all in Luscour.

31, James Dewar and Christian Philpe had William; witnesses, William Wilson, James Moyas, Robert Elder.

M. 19, John Forsythe to Margaret Potter.

26, David Gerne (?) to Janet Douglas.

AUGUST.

B. 2, John Richard and Christian Blakwod had George; witnesses, George Durie of Craigluscour, James Broun, John Smetoun, baker.

5, James Hutone, weaver, and Mary Dempstertoun had David; witnesses, David Miller, David Hutone, David Tod.

9, George Trumble in Turnourshill and Helen Grinlay had Andrew; witnesses, Andrew Trumble in Bromehall, his father, Andrew Trumble in Grange, Andrew Burne in Gellat, Andrew West, Andrew Walker in Logie.

9, Thomas More and Grizel Walwod had Janet; witnesses, Thomas Stevenson, Robert Davidson.

12, Patrick Stevenson and Christian Mudie had Bessie; witnesses, Robert Wilson, Andrew Broun, James Mayne.

16, William Anderson and Christian Peirson had William; witnesses, Robert Walwod, William Walwod in Touch, Nicol Anderson.

16, Andrew Mentethe and Catherine Gardner had John; witnesses, John Tailyeour, John Buchanan, Laurence Gibone.

16, Robert Dik and Jean Sands had Patrick; witnesses, Harry Stewart, Thomas Mitchell, John Walker, bailie of Dunfermline, Mr. Bernard Gib.

28, David Blak and Marjory Blakwod had David; witnesses, David Blak, elder, David Broun, Henry Dick in the Coklaw.

28, William Orock and Catherine Maxwell had Catherine; witnesses, David Moreis, John Stevenson, John Orock in Craigbaithe.

28, Andrew Kellock and Margaret Stockis had John; witnesses, John Kellok, John Davidson in Fod, Patrick Murray in Touche.

28, William Hutone and Catherine Mill had Bessie; witnesses, Thomas Christie, James Sanders. John Mill.

28, John Allane, collier in Baithe, and Janet Bowar had Margaret; witnesses, John Penman, William Kennedy, Andrew Lessells.

28, John Potter and Janet Inglis had Elspet; witnesses, Robert Stevenson, Alexander Lambe, John Forsyth.

M. 16, James Simsone to Bessie Walker.

16, David Broun to Janet Dewar.

SEPTEMBER.

B. 11, John Litljohne and Janet Wilson had James; witnesses, James Litljohne, his father, John Wilson in Galrighill, Andrew Drysdell in Drumtuthill.

16, Alexander Drysdell and Bessie Walwod had Isobel; witnesses, John Walker, bailie William Broun, clerk, Gabriel Chrichtone, son of James Chrichtoun of Wester Aydie.

16, David Elder and Marjory Curror had Elspet; witnesses, David Cunnon, Thomas Stanehous, James Stanehous, all in Mastertoun.

18, Robert Henresone, skinner, and Janet Car had John; witnesses, John Walker, bailie, John Anderson, litster in the Kirkgate, John Bennat.

25, John Lindsay in Pitdinne and Bessie Peirsone had Nanse; witnesses, Patrick Anderson, William Anderson, his son, in Pitconnochie, Richard Templeman in Carnok.

29, James Peirsone and Nanse Stevenson had George : witnesses, David Peirson, John Peirson, his son, in Pitdinne, George Donald.

M. [*None.*]

OCTOBER.

B. 2, James Fairnie and Margaret Hutone had Helen : witnesses, John Simsone, Andrew Thomson, belman, David Stewart, cordiner.

9, John Greif and Margaret Thomson had John (baptised in Saline kirk).

5, Andrew Ritchie and Jean Toscheauche had Grizel (baptised in Inverkeithing kirk) ; witnesses, Mr. James Phine, John Ædisone, Andrew Young.

15, Thomas Bryse and Christian Gray had Grizel ; witnesses, Andrew Hill (?), Thomas Andersone (?), William Nicole (?).

15, Andrew Thomson, belman, and Janet Flokard had Harry ; witnesses, Mr. Harry Makgill, minister, John Simsone, Robert Dik. (Born 12th inst.)

23, John Greif in the Stormonthe and Bessie Steill (coming here to visit friends) had Andrew (born in this parish) : witnesses, Andrew Roxburghe, Patrick Anderson (presenter of the child), James Roxburghe, Robert Cant.

23, Robert Pitilloche and Marjory Miller had James ; witnesses, James Reid, bailie, Thomas Blakie, Robert Davidson, maltman.

23, James Miller and Nanse Moreisone had Marjory ; witnesses, John Sanders, David Burne, miller, Charles Baid.

24, James Lindsay, weaver, and Nanse Mentethe had Grizel ; witnesses, Andrew Mekiljone, William Lamb, and Charles Baid.

M. [*None.*]

NOVEMBER.

B. 1, John Coventrie, miller in Garvock Mill, and Janet Walwod had Isobel ; witnesses, Andrew Trumble, baker in Dunfermline, James Anderson in Fod, James Donaldson in Pitcorthie.

6, John Anderson and Janet Meldrum had Isobel : witnesses, Henry Broun, James Coventrie, William Mitchell.

13, William Bruse in Mylneburne and Rose Snellok had twins, James and William ; witnesses, James Eweine, David Mitchell, William Cunninghame, Thomas Wilson.

18, Archibald Hodge and Margaret Walker had William ; witnesses, James Reid, bailie, William Walker, merchant, William Anderson, litster, son of John Anderson in Colzeraw.

30, John Walker, tailor, and Jean Maxwell had William ; witnesses, Robert Dick, William Broun, clerk, Charles Ritchardson.

30, John Anderson, son of William Anderson in Lymkills, and Isobel Moreis had Geils (in fornication) : witnesses, John Lawson, Thomas Anderson, David Murray. (Presented by said John Lawson, the alleged father being out of the country, and the mother having satisfied discipline.)

M. 1, Robert Thomson to Helen Sibald.

8, Patrick Broun to Margaret Mudie.

8, Andrew Muire to Christian Lauthiane.

20, John Bert to Margaret Blair.

22, Andrew Wilson to Elspet Johnstoun.

22, James Walwod to Janet Lugtoun.

25, William Cowstoun to Janet Scharpe.

29, Mark Donald to Marjory Bennat.

DECEMBER.

B. 4, James Beany and Margaret Hunyman had Janet : witnesses, John Bennat, Thomas Hereis, John Watson, cordiner.

13, William Anderson in Pitconnochie and Nanse Chalmers had William : witnesses, William Anderson in Gellat, William Anderson in Lymkills, William Lawsoun.

13, John Jamieson and Marion Dick had John ; witnesses, John Peirsone, John Lindsay, John Wilson, David Peirsone, all indwellers in Pitdinne.

13, Henry Broun and Effie Banks had Nanse; witnesses, Thomas Johnstoun, Thomas Deis, James Deis.

15, David Mitchell in Pitlivar and Margaret Currie had Thomas ; witnesses, Thomas Mitchell in Gellat, Andrew Currie in Primrois, James Eweine in Fodsmylne.

22, John Cusine and Agnes Foote had James (baptized in Dunfermline kirk).

22, Patrick Cowper and Janet Murray had Helen.

27, David Douglas and Helen Ready had Robert ; witnesses, Robert Douglas in Craigis, Adam Ready, William Smithe in Fod.

27, Peter Buist and Isobel Walwod had Thomas ; witnesses, Thomas Walwod, John Bruse, Edward Douglas.

M. 6, Henry Douglas to Margaret Cunningham.
23, Stephen Wentoun to Janet Knielands.

JANUARY [1632].

B. 1, John Broun and Effie Simsone had William ; witnesses, William Broun, William Walker, Mr. William Daw ?.

3, James Anderson and Janet Craik had Janet ; witnesses, James Anghous, James Hutone, Andrew Anderson in Pitfirran.

3, James Murgane and Elspet Bowman had David ; witnesses, David Walker, merchant, Thomas Christie, James Mill.

8, John Gibone and Janet Horne had Isobel : witnesses, Andrew Leslie, James Anderson, John Straquhen.

10, John Schortus and Janet Banks had Clement ; witnesses, Thomas Tod, Malcolm Cowell, Clement Banks, John Stirk.

11, David Sempill presented a child to baptism " borne of his dochter Catharine Sempill, quhilk bairne scho said wes gottin in Ireland be ane unmaryit man callit Hary Wood," baptized Janet ; witnesses, John Walker, bailie, John Anderson, litster, John Anderson, doctor in the grammar school. " The said David Sempill wes actit under the pane of 40 lib. to report ane testimoriall betwixt and 14 day of Februar nixt from the kirk there of the father of the bairne, and bothe parties satisfactioun for their offence acording to the ordour and discipline of the kirk."

15, John Broun and Janet Hall had Margaret ; witnesses, John Broun, Thomas Broun, Henry Broun.

17, Robert Greive and Margaret Douglas had a daughter . . . . ; witnesses, John Mill, John Greive, James Mill in Lochend.

17, Andrew Napeir and Janet Mill had Margaret (in fornication) ; witnesses, Andrew Rowane, James Mill, Robert Russell.

17, Thomas Hereis and Elspet Thomson had Henry ; witnesses, Sir Henry Wardlaw of Pittreavie, Mr. Harry Makgill, minister, David Maxwell, litster.

17, James Gray and Isobel Webster had Janet ; witnesses, John Bennat, Robert Hugane, Thomas Hunnon.

19, James Kennedie and Janet Hutone had William (baptised 22nd) ; witnesses, William Broun, Patrick Trumble, William Walker.

22, James Legat, merchant, and Margaret Stirk had Patrick ; witnesses, Patrick Legat, Robert Stirk, William Legat, William Broun, clerk.

22, Robert Anderson, younger, tailor, and Bessie Johnstone had William ; witnesses, Andrew Thomson, Thomas Johnstone, Robert Anderson.

24, Peter Law and Margaret Walker had Margaret ; witnesses, Sir Robert Halket of Pitfirran, provost, Mr. Bernard Gib, Mr. Thomas Wardlaw of Logie.

31, William Smart, flesher, and Bessie Stevenson had Margaret ; witnesses, Thomas Wilson, Andrew Roxburghe, John Harper in Brunteland.

31, Laurence Merser and Margaret Dalgleish had John.

31, David Robertson [of] Craigduckie and Grizel Hutone had Isobel.

M. 17, Archibald Fergie to Janet Murray.

17, William Wilsone to Margaret Watsone.

24, John Swentoun to Margaret Tailyeour.

31, John L(?) . . . to Catherine Logane.

FEBRUARY.

B. 5, John Oiswald and Christian Hamilton had Rosina ; witnesses, John Douglas, John Finlasoun, David Inglis.

12, Alexander Donald and Janet Reid had Robert ; witnesses, Robert Cunningham, Thomas Wilson, Andrew Walker.

19, Thomas Douglas and Elspet Chalmers had David ; witnesses, David Douglas, David Mitchell, David Sands, all his neighbours.

19, William Inche and Margaret James had John ; witnesses, John Kellok, William Walker, maltman, and George Meldrum.

19, Laurence Watson, cordiner, and Grizel Wilson had Robert ; witnesses, Robert Wels, Robert Stirk, Robert Creiche.

26, James Henresone, glazier, and Mays Aitkine had Harry ; witnesses, William Low, William Trumble, John Kellok, "mailmaker."

28, Thomas Hutone and Isobel Keir had Janet ; witnesses, Andrew Walker, Andrew Christie, Robert Hutone.

29, James Reid and Marion Broun had Jean ; witnesses, Sir Robert Halkat of Pitfirran, Edward Broun in the Ferrietoun, Mr. Bernard Gib.

M. 7, John Laurie to Nanse Grege.

7, John Stirk to Bessie Crawfuird.

9, Mr. William Blakburne to Elspet Johnstone.

26, Henry Russell to Nanse Hutone.

MARCH.

B. 5, Harry Thomesone in the Ferrie and Agnes Edisone had a daughter . . . (baptised in Inverkeithing kirk).

5, Robert Wilson in Milhillis and Bessie Mudie had Thomas ; witnesses, Thomas Steinsone, Robert Wels, John Coventrie, Gilbert Sanders, James Hamiltoun.

7, John Neilson and Janet Buist had Helen ; witnesses, Patrick Trumble, Peter Buist, Robert Neilson in Culrois.

11, Robert Harper and Christian Speir had Barbara ; witnesses, Robert Turner, William Bruse, William Ratrey

11, William Cowstoun and Janet Scharp had Martha ; witnesses, . . . James Isatt, Thomas Baverage.

11, Thomas Walwod and Christian Simraell had Andrew : witnesses, Peter Buist, Andrew Gaw, Andrew Walwod, Andrew Muire.

18, William Colzeir, cottar in Lassodie, and Margaret Kinninmond had David ; witnesses, John Betson, William Mackie, James Kellok.

18, Edward Broun in the Ferrie and Janet Broun had a son . . . (baptised in Inverkeithing kirk).

18, Edward Douglas in Wester Gellat and Beatrix Douglas had Beatrix ; witnesses, Andrew Trumble in Bromehall, George Trumble, his son, and Thomas Mitchell in Gellat.

18, John Makraiche and Marjory Anderson had Margaret ; witnesses, James Cunningham, Robert Currie, Thomas Mitchell.

18, William Galrige and Helen Broun had Helen ; witnesses, Andrew Currie in Primrois, Adam Currie, his son, Andrew Trumble in Grange, Adam Trumble, his son.

25, Thomas Cunnon and Janet Douglas had Robert ; witnesses, Robert Kellok, Robert Douglas, Thomas Stanehous.

25, John Bell and Margaret Blair had George ; witnesses, George Trumble in Turnourhill, Robert Currie, Andrew Wilson.

25, Henry Douglas and Margaret Cunningham had Isobel; witnesses, David Douglas, Thomas Mitchell, Andrew Burne in Gellat, Thomas Wilson in Walkmylne.

25, David Spens and Helen Mitchell had James; witnesses, James Mitchell, James Kellok, James Litljohne.

25, James Dick and Elspet Toward had Helen; witnesses, William Lawson, Robert Pittilloche, John Smetone.

25, Janet Bankis had a son Thomas, borne as she alleged to Andrew Mudie in fornication, presented by David Tod: witnesses, John Bankis, John Walker, John Wyld.

27, John Smart and Margaret Baverage had Thomas; witnesses, Thomas Stevenson, Thomas Baverage. John Smart. father of said John.

M. 30, William Cambell to Mawse Galrige.

APRIL.

B. 7, James Cusine, flesher, and Barbara (? Clara) Dewar had Catherine; witnesses, John Walker, dean of guild, Robert Miller, John Dewar in Pitbachlie.

8, William Curror and Margaret Schort had Christian; witnesses, James Schort, William Curror, elder, John Stevenson of Baith.

8, Henry Broun and Beatrix Sands had Harry; witnesses, John Coventrie, Harry Melvill, John Anderson in Garvok.

15, David Douglas and Alison Mitchell had Alison; witnesses, Thomas Mitchell, Andrew Burne, Edward Douglas, all possessors in the Gellats.

15, John Phune and Margaret Dinn had James; witnesses, James Dewar in Bayth, James Walwod there, Patrick Broun there.

17, John Wels and Catherine Drummond had Janet; witnesses, Patrick Kingorne, John Bennat, baker, John Huntar in Culross.

22, Thomas Cunnon and Marion Douglas had Thomas; witnesses, Thomas Mitchell, elder and younger, and David Douglas, all in Gellat.

24, James Donald and Margaret Cunningham had Elspet: witnesses, Andrew Hutone, Robert Davidson, John Creiche.

29, David Galrige and Margaret Yowane had Margaret: witnesses, George Donald, Andrew Christie, David Mitchell.

M. 10, John Hekfurd to Bessie Thomson.

MAY.

B. 6, William Anderson and Janet Cunningham had William: witnesses, William Cunningham in Knokes, William Lawsone, William Sanders.

9, Mr. James Dewar of Lassodie and Elspet Moncreiff had Isobel: witnesses, David Dewar, his father, and David Robertson of Craigduckie.

13, Laurence Hutone and Janet Robertson had Margaret; witnesses, Thomas Cowper, Robert Davidson, Henry Davidson.

13, George Moreis, collier, and Bessie Beany had James; witnesses, John Bennat, Andrew Mckiljohne, Thomas Baverage.

13, Andrew Broun and Bessie Wilson had Elspet; witnesses, Patrick Stevenson, Robert Wilson. James Cunningham.

20, James Wallace and Janet Henresone had Elspet; witnesses, John Anderson, notary, James Murgane, James Anderson in Fod.

27, Andrew Ritchie and Janet Miller had Robert: witnesses, Robert Russell. Thomas Patone, John Ritchard.

M. 22, James Hut[one] to Isobel Fergus.

22, Thomas Weitche to Margaret Gibson.

22, Thomas Livingstone to Barbara Patone.

JUNE.

B. 3, James Simsone, merchant, and Bessie Walker had George; witnesses, William Broun, clerk, John Walker, Andrew Walker, William Walker, merchant.

10, James Mitchell and Isobel Cunningham had Isobel; witnesses, William Cunningham in Fordell, James Anderson in Fod, David Douglas, John Coventrie.

10. Mr. Bernard Gib and Effie Abercrumbie had Geils; witnesses, Mr. Harry Makgill, minister, Peter Law, John Murray.

10, Andrew Colzeir, drummer, and Isobel Anderson had Bessie; witnesses, John Simsone, William Patersone, Andrew Gaw, George Davidson.

11, Robert Livingstone and Jean Bruse had Harry; witnesses, Mr. Harry Makgill, minister, and William Broun, clerk.

11, George Mudie and Helen Stirk had William; witnesses, William Broun, clerk, William Mudie, maltman, William Maistertoun.

17, Patrick Durie and Margaret Wilson had Robert; witnesses, Robert Kellok, James Kellok, David Cunnon.

17, David Reid and Margaret Lawsone had Margaret; witnesses, James Wardlaw in Luscour, Thomas Scotland, baker, Thomas Hutone, younger.

17, Alexander Beane and Helen Hutone had Jean; witnesses, Robert Dick, Andrew Thomson, John Simsone.

M. 5, Andrew Key to Janet Stevenson.

5, Robert Anghous to Isobel Dewar.

12, John Dewar to Rachel Anderson.

12, David Flokard to Bessie Dewar.

12, Laurence Gray to Bessie Peacok.

12, David Alaster to Nanse Maistertoun.

21, James Kellok to Elspet Darlein.

26, Thomas Burne to Margaret Gibson.

26, James Hamilton, piper, to Isobel Brown.

JULY.

B. 1, Robert Tailyeour and Margaret Cunninghame had James; witnesses, George Donald, John Tailyeour, James Cunningham, Robert Cunningham.

1, Thomas Baverage and Christian Smart had John : witnesses, John Wels, Robert Wels, John Smart.

8, George Wardlaw and Jean Kennedie had Catherine : witnesses, Harry Stewart, Laurie Merser, John Wilson.

8, Malcolm Makqueine and Janet Jonkeine had Margaret ; witnesses, Robert Davidson, Robert Miller, Thomas Blakie.

8, William Robertson and Marjory Marteine had Bessie ; witnesses, Alexander Young, Laurie Hutone, weaver, John Kellok.

12, William Spens and Christian Wallange had Elspet : witnesses, David Stevenson, Patrick Legat, David Spens.

12, James Hutone and Isobel Fergus had twins, Nanse and Helen ; witnesses, David Peirson, William Anderson, William Lawson.

15, George Ivat and Nanse Barklay had Patrick ; witnesses, Patrick Kinninmond of that Ilk, David Maxwell, John Banks.

15, John Dougall and Bessie Thomson had Bessie ; witnesses, James Huntar, James Dewar, Alexander Wilson.

20, David Moreis in Bayth and Janet Lundie had John ; witnesses, Mr. Harry Makgill, minister, Harry Stewart of Bayth, John Walker, merchant.

M. 3, James Car to Isobel Ritchardsone.

3, Andrew Anderson to Margaret Rae.

10, Patrick Walker to Margaret Young.

10, William Mitchell to Janet Nasmithe.

21, Robert Straquhen to Bessie Nicole.

AUGUST.

B. 7, Thomas Peirsone and Christian Cant had Henry; witnesses, David Douglas, Henry Douglas, Andrew Ferlie.

7, James Mitchell and Christian Thomson had Andrew; witnesses, William Trumble, Andrew Trumble, his son, and William Cunningham.

9, Thomas Stanehous, portioner of Mastertoun, and Barbara Dewar had a daughter. . . .; witnesses, Alexander Chalmers, John Dewar, William Kellok in Mastertoun.

9, Andrew Hutone, slater, and Elspet Kilgour had Janet; witnesses, John Workman, David Walwod, James Kinsman.

9, James Palmer and Catherine Anderson had Robert; witnesses, Robert Anderson, George Davidson, David Laurie.

23, Andrew Christie and Helen Currie had Janet; witnesses, Thomas Christie, William Mudie, David Sands.

26, David Cunnon, portioner of Mastertoun, and Elspet Dewar had William : witnesses, William Kellok, Robert Kellok in Mastertoun.

26, John Hutone and Margaret Patone had William; witnesses, William Cunningham in Knokes, William Lawson, William Sanders.

26, John Law and Nicolas Anderson had Thomas; witnesses, Thomas Stevenson, Robert Davidson, William Trumble.

27, John Dow and Margaret Merser had Margaret; witnesses, Laurie Watson, John Anderson, litster.

M. 28, James De[war ?] to Isobel Hutone.

28, Thomas Lessells to Bessie Lawson.

SEPTEMBER.

B. 2, Harry Grege in the Ferrie and Bessie Broun had Alexander (in fornication); witnesses, Alexander Grege, Laurie Lugtoun, John Bennat, baker.

11, John Gotterstone and Isobel Mackie had William ; witnesses, William Mackie, William Cunningham in Knokes, William Æssone, weaver.

11, Robert Thomson and Helen Sibald had William ; witnesses, William Anderson, David Sands, Thomas Douglas, Edward Douglas, all in Wester Gellat.

11, Adam Currie and Helen Galrige had Margaret (in fornication) ; witnesses, James Cunningham, Thomas Mitchell, Adam Trumble.

16, John Penman and Helen Samuell had William ; witnesses, William Penman, George Penman, Andrew Kellok.

23, James Anderson and Janet Gray had John ; witnesses, William Cunningham, Patrick Anderson, John Peirson.

23, David Stewart, cordiner, and Helen Kirkland had Margaret ; witnesses, John Walker, Peter Law, John Simsone.

30, Andrew Wilson and Elspet Johnstone had John; witnesses, Andrew Trumble in Grange, James Johnstone, Nicol Inglis.

30, Gilbert Johnstone and Christian Wels had Robert ; witnesses, Robert Wels, Peter Law, William Walker, merchant, John Broun.

30, David Peirson and Helen Henresone had a daughter . . . ; witnesses, Robert Douglas, Robert Stanehous, Thomas Peirsone.

M. 4, David Mowtrey to Janet Sanders.

11, Robert Anghous to Marion Dewar.

OCTOBER.

B. 2, David Lambe and Marjory Wilson had Grizel : witnesses, James Mudie, John Gotterstone, William Mudie.

7, Archibald Fergie and Janet Murray had William : witnesses, William Anderson, William Murray, Henry Russell.

7, John Wilson and Barbara Kellok had Catherine ; witnesses, James Reid, John Clerk, merchant, John Kellok in Windieage.

12, Mark Donald and Marjory Bennat had John ; witnesses, John Bennat, George Donald, Robert Cunningham in the Sillitoun.

14, Laurie Gray and Bessie Peacok had Margaret ; witnesses, Harry Richardson, James Walwod in Fod, John Davidson there.

14, David Hutone and Janet Kempe had John (in fornication) ; witnesses, William Walwod, cordiner, William Walker, merchant, John Neilsone cordiner.

14, Andrew Drummond and Bessie Young had Elspet ; witnesses, Thomas Stevenson, Andrew Murray, Patrick Cowper.

19, Mr. Matthew Weyms, minister in Canongate, and Margaret Durie had David ; witnesses, Sir Robert Halkat of Pitfirrane, Robert Colvill of Cleishe, Mr. Thomas Cowper, minister of Saline.

21, William Anderson, litster, and Bessie Wilson had a daughter . . . . (in fornication) ; witnesses, William Smart, William Walker, Gavin Stanehous.

23, George Trumble in Turnourshill and Helen Grinlay had Bessie : witnesses, Andrew Trumble, his father, James Leslie of Pitlivar, David Mitchell there, William Bruse.

25, Thomas Stevenson and Janet Chalmers had Elspet : witnesses, John Simsone, Robert Wilson, Thomas Cowper.

28, William Mackie and Margaret Betsone had William ; witnesses, David Blak, John Betson, Patrick Grege. (Baptised in Cleish kirk.)

30, John Lawson, younger, and Catherine Logane had William : witnesses, William Anderson in Lymkills, William Anderson, his son, and John Lawson, elder.

30, John Alisone, wright, and Grizel Walwod had Bessie : witnesses, Alexander Drysdell, Laurie Watson, James Car, mason.

30, John Anderson, litster, and Janet Stevenson had Elspet ; witnesses, Mr. James Ready, Andrew Mekiljohne, Thomas Hereis.

30, George Trumble in Tynnigask and Marjory Mastertoun had John ; witnesses, John Mastertoun, Andrew Trumble, George Dewar.

30, Mr. Patrick Auchinleck and Elspet Forrester had George : witnesses, George Bothwell, James Reid, Mr. James Durie.

M. 16, Jasper Drysdell to Marion Inglis.
30, Andrew Cowstoun to Catherine Wannan.

NOVEMBER.

B. 5, Patrick Kingorne and Margaret Forrester had Helen : witnesses, John Anderson, litster, Mr. Patrick Auchinleck.

6, William Mudie, weaver, and Nanse Mackie had Elspet ; witnesses, James Anderson in Fod, John Gotterstone, James Mudie.

6, John Hekfuird and Bessie Thomesone had Janet ; witnesses, Thomas Davidson, Duncan Tailliour, Andrew Thomson, belman.

8, David Hutone and Margaret Dempstertoun had William ; witnesses, William Walker, merchant, James Hutone, officer, Thomas Davidson.

11, Andrew Elder and Janet Phune had Isobel ; witnesses, Edward Douglas, Thomas Douglas, William Pillonis.

17, Henry Dik and Bessie Stevenson had John ; witnesses, John Stevenson of Baithe, John Kellok, William Mackie.

18, Alexander Greg and Catherine Philpe had Bessie : witnesses, James Greg, Thomas Philpe, James Walwod.

22, William George and Elspet Miller had Catherine ; witnesses, Andrew Miller, Alexander Wilson, Andrew Lindsay.

22, "That day Marioun Greif had ane manchyld borne be hir and as scho affirmed gottin be ane servand fellow callit William Remainous, sone to Johne Remainous in Gask, quhilk bairne he obstinatlie denyit to be the father therof becaus as he said the bairne wes borne ane long tyme to wit the space of ane quarter of ane yeir befoir ever he knew hir and had carnall copulatioun with hir, and the woman affirmeit otherwyse. It come befoir the Presbytrie, and becaus he culd get no other father to the bairne he was ordanit to tak on him to be father therto, as the woman constantlie affirmeit, conforme to the law and ordour of the kirk in sic caces. Nevir [theles] the said George (*sic*) wald nocht present the bairne to baptisme, bot it wes presentit be Andro Thomesone, belman, baptized and callit Andro."

25, Nicol Inglis and Mage Law had Robert ; witnesses. James Mill, Robert Russell, George Meldrum.

25, John Scot and Catherine Makie had Isobel ; witnesses, William Mudie, Allan Mudie, David Scot.

27, William Davidson and . . . . Makcraiche had William (in fornication) ; witnesses, William Anderson in Pitconnochie, William Hutone in Dunduff, William Currie.

M. 20, James Lawson to Bessie Galrige.

27, Andrew Trumble to Barbara Law.

27, Andrew Mentethe to Bessie Fothringham.

DECEMBER.

B. 2, Allan Mudie and Bessie Keir had Bessie ; witnesses, James Mudie, Alexander Young, William Lambe.

2, Robert Mudie in Mastertoun and Christian Lundie had Peter ; witnesses, David Moreis, James Stanehous, James Mudie.

4, David Barklay in Blairuthie and Janet Anderson had Effie ; witnesses, James Weyms of Carskiburrane, John Horne, James Baverage.

4, William Walwod, cordiner, and Magie Lindsay had David ; witnesses, David Lindsay, John Simsone, Archibald Boyd.

4, James Kellok and Margaret Mudie had Margaret ; witnesses, Robert Kellok, Andrew Trumble in Grange, Thomas Ædisone in Pitadro Mill.

11, John Lawsone in Crocefuird and Margaret Wilson had Robert ; witnesses, Patrick Lawson, John Lawson, Adam Wilson.

11, John Ramsay, collier, and Christian Thrislo had Bessie (in fornication) ; witnesses, John Watson, George Moreis, William Dow, all colliers.

11, James Mudie and Nanse Workman had Andrew ; witnesses, Andrew Trumble in Bromehall, George Trumble, his son, and William Smart.

16, James Simsone, cordiner, and Isobel Weitche had William ; witnesses, James Simson, merchant, William Smart, William Anderson, litster.

M. 4, Thomas Makinlay to Janet Paterson (in Cleish kirk).

11, William Anderson to Isobel Russell.

11, James Cunnon to Bessie Garvie.

21, John Baverage to Grizel Westwod.

JANUARY [1633].

B. 1, Thomas Christie of the Hoill and Elspet Durie had Bessie ; witnesses, James Durie, apparent of Craigluscour, Mr. Robert Durie, George Dewar in Lathamond.

8, William Trumble, lorimer, and Helen Rob, his servant, had Christian (in fornication) ; witnesses, John Law, James Mitchell, William Cunningham, weaver.

8, Archibald Boyd and Janet Watson had James ; witnesses, Mr. James Phun, portioner of Lymkills, John Simsone and William Walwod, cordiners.

8, Andrew Mudie and Annas Workman had Margaret (in fornication) ; witnesses, John Workman, James Mudie, William Murray.

13, Mark Wels and Christian Chaipe had Margaret ; witnesses, Henry Dick, David Blak, William Mackie (baptised in Cleish kirk).

13, David Broun and Janet Dewar had John ; witnesses, John Dewar, Andrew Walker, Andrew Christie.

13, James Clerk and Janet Beany had Helen ; witnesses, William Anderson in Pitconnochie, John Peirsone and James Peirsone in Pitdinne.

14, David Blak in the Cocklaw and Marjory Blakwod had James ; witnesses, James Legat, John Betsone, John Kellok.

14, Thomas Hardie and Margaret Mershell had Annas ; witnesses, John Dewar, James Kellok, John Scotland.

14, Andrew Hall and Margaret Hardie had John : witnesses, Patrick Peirsone, John Burne, Robert Miller.

14, Robert Hutone and Janet Trumble had Janet ; witnesses, William Keir, George Cunningham, Robert Gray.

14, Andrew Tempilman and Helen Hutsone had Helen (in fornication) : witnesses, Thomas Tod, Robert Scotland.

22, William Murray and Christian Mudie had Andrew ; witnesses, Andrew Trumble and George Trumble in Bromehall, and Andrew Mudie.

22, Harry Richardson and Christian Peacok had John : witnesses, John Gotterstoun, Allan Mudie, William Cunningham.

22, Thomas Hunnon and Janet Edward had John ; witnesses, John Anderson, litster, Peter Buist, James Reid.

24, John Laurie and Nanse Grege had David ; witnesses, David Laurie, Andrew Clyd, John Bennat, baker.

25, John Stevenson, son of Harry Stevenson in Pettie Muire, and Jean Murray (thrice fallen in fornication) had Janet ; witnesses, William Maine, John Spens, Ninian Mather. The said John Stevenson was often cited before the Session, but never compeared, and is fugitive from discipline.

29, Leonard Henresone and Marjory Mudie had David ; witnesses, David Tod, David Miller, Robert Wilson.

29, Peter Trumble, litster, and Martha Masterton had Isobel (in fornication) ; witnesses, Andrew Trumble, baker, John Gib, Thomas Elder, flesher.

M. 3, Andrew Cunningham to Margaret Ædison.

15, James Mayne to Christian Johnestoun.

29, James Peacok to Janet Burgane.

FEBRUARY.

B. 3, Robert Tailyeour and Margaret Young had John ; witnesses, John Wricht, David Murray, William Anderson, Andrew Young, all in Lymkills.

3, Alexander Young, mason, and Bessie Williamson had William : witnesses, William Mentethe of Randifuird, William Anderson, litster, and William Smart.

12 John Lawson and Catherine Drysdell had Robert ; witnesses, George Donald, Robert Turneley, Robert Drysdell.

David Bull and Margaret Potter had Andrew ; witnesses, Andrew Potter, Andrew Thomson, Andrew Colzeir.

17, William Grinley and Margaret Workman had Andrew (in fornication : witnesses, William Walwod, cordiner, James Buist, Thomas Keir. The child died after registration, but before baptism.

17, James Westwod and Nanse Colzeir had Patrick ; witnesses, Patrick Kininmonthe of that Ilk, James Mitchell, wright, John Colzeir.

17, Mr. James Ready, schoolmaster, and Barbara Kyle had Annas : witnesses, James Henreson, James Reid.

19, James Mill and Grizel Robertson had Nanse ; witnesses, David Robertson of Craigduckie, George Dewar, Thomas Christie in Luscour.

19, Henry Hakirstone of Baithe and Helen Cuningham had Helen : witnesses, Alexander Mastertoun of Baithe, John Orock, John Hodge in Foulfuird.

24, Alexander Nicole and Helen Alexander had Robert : witnesses, Mr. James Durie, William Walwod, David Watsone.

26, James Reid and Marion Broun had James ; witnesses, James Halkat, apparent of Pitfirrane, James Henresone, son of the deceased Sir John Henresone of Fordall, and Mr. James Ready.

28, Robert Andersone and Janet Smithe had Patrick ; witnesses, Patrick Cowper, Andrew Murray, James Hamiltoun.

M. 19, William Garvie to Bessie Walker.

MARCH.

B. 3, John Cunningham and Christian Wilson had a daughter . . . .; witnesses, Robert Cunningham, Andrew Wilson, Andrew Donaldson.

3, Patrick Lawson and Margaret Lathangie had Andrew; witnesses, George Donald, Adam Wilson, Robert Cunningham in the Sillitoun.

3, Robert Murgane and Helen Smithe had John: witnesses, Charles Baid, James Lugtone, James Miller.

6. James Kellok and Elspet Darleine had Elspet: witnesses, James Reid, Mr. Patrick Auchinlek, James Moyas.

10, Robert Peacok and Bessie Wricht had Robert: witnesses, Robert Cunningham in Sillitoun, Thomas Wilson, Robert Wilson.

10, John Moreis and Isobel Gotterston had William: witnesses, William Trumble, Thomas Schortus, Robert Bull.

10, Andrew Wilsone and Janet Douglas had Thomas; witnesses, Thomas Douglas, Edward Douglas, William Pillons.

17, William Rae and Janet Henreson had Thomas; witnesses, Thomas Mitchell, Thomas Bull, Thomas Key.

17. Thomas Hereis and Elspet Thomson had John; witnesses, Mr. John Wardlaw, son of Sir Henry Wardlaw of Pitravie, John Walker, merchant, John Anderson, litster in the Kirkgate.

17, Robert Stevenson and Elspet Davidson had John: witnesses, John Anderson in the Kirkgate, John Anderson in the Colzeraw, Patrick Cowper.

19, Andrew Muire and Christian Lauthiane had Janet; witnesses, John Broun, James Ronald, John Litljohne.

24, John Spens and Janet Cunningham had Thomas: witnesses, Thomas Douglas, James Roxburghe, William Mayne.

26. James Anderson in Fod and Elspet Christie had Isobel: witnesses, Peter Trumble, John Stanehous, James Coventrie.

31, John Hadstone and Bessie Beany had John; witnesses, John Anderson, William Anderson, James Clerk, all in Pitfirrane bounds.

31, John Colzeir and Marjory Corsane had Henry: witnesses, Henry Peirsone, James Peirson, John Mudie.

M. 3, Mark Swentone to Margaret Saverall.

7. Adam Currie to Catherine Christie.

APRIL.

B. 7. John Straquhen and Isobel Fothringhame had Bessie; witnesses, Robert Straquhen, James Fothringhame, Andrew Mentethe.

7. James Oiswald and Janet Anderson had Henry; witnesses, William Anderson, James Hall, John Gentleman.

7, William Wilson and Margaret Watson had William; witnesses, Laurence Watson, John Sanders, John Wilson, father of said William.

12, Alexander Drysdell, merchant, and Bessie Walwod had Nanse; witnesses, Mr. Thomas Wardlaw of Logie, Patrick Cowper, John Walker, merchant.

14, Andrew Anderson in Kistock and Margaret Rae had William; witnesses, William Cunningham in Knokes, William Anderson in Hiltoun, John Anderson.

14, James Mudie and Grizel Lambe had Bessie: witnesses, William Mudie, Allan Mudie, William Eassoun.

14, Patrick Harowar and Janet Man had a son . . . ; witnesses, William Anderson in Gellat, Andrew (Burne?), and Henry Douglas in Gellat.

14, David Flokard and Bessie Dewar had Isobel; witnesses, William Flokard, John Dewar, James Donaldson.

21, James Peirsone and Nanse Stevenson had Margaret ; witnesses, David Peirson, George Donald, Robert Cunningham in Sillitoun.

21, John Horne in Coklay (deceased) and Mary Weyms had a daughter . . . ; witnesses, Mr. James Dewar of Nether Lassodie, Nicol Dewar, David Robertson of Craigduckie.

21, Patrick Walker and Margaret Young had David : witnesses, Mr. Thomas Wardlaw of Logie. Mr. John Walker, reader, David Walker, cooper.

28, George Ædisone and Bessie Sands had Geils ; witnesses, David Sands, William Anderson in Gellat, William Anderson in Lymkills.

28, David Sands and Bessie Christie had Janet : witnesses, Andrew Walker in Logie, William Mudie, maltman, Edward Douglas in Gellat.

28, John Makmirrie and Janet Porteous had David : witnesses, David Bull, Henry Peirson, Andrew Drummond.

M. 23, John Danskin to Helen Watson.

23, James Henreson to Margaret Hereme.

MAY.

B. 4, David Scot and Christian Thomson had Elspet ; witnesses, Mr. John Walker, John Wricht, William Keir, Robert Gray.

5. David Dewar and Dorothea Maxtoun had Janet : witnesses, James Dewar John Philpe, John Dewar, Andrew Wilson.

5, Archibald Glennie and Nanse Aessone had Marjory : witnesses, William Æssoun, James Lethome, William Lawsone.

5, David Douglas and Helen Ready had James ; witnesses, James Mitchell, James Anderson, John Davidson in Fod.

5. John Robertson and Isobel Hutone had Robert ; witnesses. Robert Cunningham in Sillitoun, Thomas Nasmithe, Robert Cant.

5, Thomas Williamson and Margaret Portour had Marjory ; witnesses, William Stanehous, John Stanehous, Thomas Hall.

6, John Hog and Margaret Thomson had Janet ; witnesses. Mr. John Walker, reader in Dunfermline, James Lindsay, Andrew Thomson.

12, George Donald and Margaret Stevenson had Robert : witnesses, Robert Cunningham in Sillitoan, Robert Cunningham in the Stane. Robert Turneley.

12, William Kairnis in the Ferrie and Marjory Burgane had Nanse : witnesses, Florie Burgane, Andrew Ædisone. Harry Thomson.

12, James Dagleische and Catherine Wardlaw had Nanse : witnesses, Robert Merser of Kirkland in Sauling, Thomas Christie in Luscour, Richard Templeman in Bandirin, James Wardlaw.

12, James Farnie and Margaret Hutone had Bessie : witnesses, James Simsone, Thomas Elder, Archibald Boyd.

12, David Smetone and Elspet Russell had Barbara ; witnesses. Robert Russell, James Smetone, William Smart.

12, George Wat and Janet Robertson had John : witnesses, William Anderson. David Murray, John Wat.

17, Abraham Peacok and Margaret Young had Elspet ; witnesses, William Walwod, younger of Touche, William Kennedie, Andrew Kellok.

21. Robert Anghous in Balmulle and Isobel Dewar had George ; witnesses, George Dewar in Lathamond, William Hutone in Dunduff, Robert Anghous in Cleish.

21, John Hoy and Christian Barkley had Nanse ; witnesses, Nicol Inglis, David Dewar of Lassodie, Robert Balcate.

21. Henry Anghous and Christian Drysdell had Henry ; witnesses, Henry Crawfurd, John Henre, Richard Law.

26, Thomas Burne and Helen Gibsone had Isobel : witnesses, Robert Walwod of Touche, John Simsone, cordiner, John Kellok, "mail-maker."

26, David Maxwell, litster, and Agnes Hamilton had William : witnesses, William Walker, merchant, Thomas Hereis, Thomas Davidson, litster. (Born 22nd inst.).

30. John Kinnell in Netherbaithe and Janet Philpe had Thomas : witnesses, Thomas Philpe, John Davidson in Fod, Thomas Baverage, Henry Baverage.

M. [None.]

JUNE.

B 2, John Horne and Marjory Murie had James ; witnesses, James Angous, James Eweine, James Horne.

2, Andrew Burne in Gellat and Elspet Ritchie had John ; witnesses, Andrew Trumble in Grange, John Currie in Crumbie, Edward Douglas.

4, William Saunders and Christian Hutone had a daughter . . . . ; witnesses, William Hutone, John Cusine, Robert Scotland.

4, William Young in Lymkills and Nanse Plaine had Janet ; witnesses, Thomas Donaldson, Watie Horne, William Anderson.

13, William Pullonis and Isobel Douglas had Thomas ; witnesses, Thomas Wilson, Thomas Douglas, Adam Wilson.

14, Andrew Tomesone, belman, and Janet Lockart had Christian ; witnesses, Mr. Harry Makgill, minister, Mr John Walker, reader, John Simsone, cordiner, James Hamilton, George Davidson (?).

23, James Walwod in Netherbayth and Janet Lugtone had William ; witnesses, William Walwod of Touche, James Baverage, Laurence Lugtone in the Ferrie.

23, James Dewar in Pitbachlie and Isobel Hutone had John ; witnesses, John Dewar, John Coventrie, John Burne, mason.

23, Edward Broun, "sealer" in the Ferrie, and Janet Broun had Bessie ; witnesses, Andrew Wod, Robert Broun, Mark Swentoun. (Baptised at Inverkeithing.)

24, John Anderson and Helen Lawson had Bessie ; witnesses, David Sands, William Anderson, Thomas Mitchell in Gellats.

24, John Merschell and Margaret Fwird had Isobel ; witnesses, Thomas Mitchell, William Kellok, Robert Douglas in the Craigis.

24, John Cusine and Nanse Foote had William ; witnesses, William Hutone, William Saunders, William Hutone (*sic*).

24, John Clerk, merchant, and Annas Portour had Thomas ; witnesses, James Reid, Mr. Patrick Auchinleck, Thomas Reid.

24, George Mudie, mason, and Helen Stirk had David ; witnesses, Mr. David Stirk, David Hodge, David Burne.

30, David Galrige and Margaret Yowane had James ; witnesses, James Mayne, James Mitchell, William Mudie, weaver.

M. 4, Thomas Elder, flesher, to Helen Simsone.

6, Robert Lockard to Janet Wels.

11, Thomas Key to Margaret Smart.

13, David Inglis to Helen Lugtone.

25, John Wilson to Elspet Blair.

JULY.

B. 3, Robert Currie and Elspet Mackcraiche had James ; witnesses, Mr. James Durie, James Durie of Craigluscour, James Cowstoun.

7, James Patone and Isobel Watson had James ; witnesses, James Mudie, Thomas Hunnon, Robert Quhyt.

9, Robert Peirsone in Baithe and Marjory Peirson had Patrick ; witnesses, Patrick Peirson, David Peirson, Thomas Elder.

21, Matthew Donaldson and Janet Young had David ; witnesses David Sands, William Anderson, Walter Horne (? Lorne).

25, David Hoge and Marjory Bull had David ; witnesses, John Walcar, merchant, Patrick Kingorne, clerk, Mr. David Stirk.

28, Henry Moreis and Isobel Duncane had Harry ; witnesses, Harry Stewart, David Moreis, John Stevenson, all of Baiths.

28, James Peacok and Janet Burgane had Janet ; witnesses, Laurie Lugtoun, William Kairnis, Andrew Peacok.

M. 9, Thomas Dewar to Janet Peacok.

9, James Simraell to Margaret Mudie.

16, Robert Elder to Margaret Barklay.

16, William Milier to Janet Gibsone.
18, Adam Stevenson to Catherine Feg.

AUGUST.

B. 3, Thomas Cuming and Marion Douglas had Alexander ; witnesses, Thomas Mitchell, David Mitchell, Edward Douglas.

3, John Gray and Alison Martene had Catherine ; witnesses, Henry Trumble, William Robertson, James Peirson.

6, Thomas Beitche and Margaret Gibsone had Catherine : witnesses, John Bennat, baker, Harry Bull.

13, John Peirsone and Marion Hutone had a daughter . . . . ; witnesses, David Peirson, his father, Patrick Anderson in Pitconnochie, William Cunningham in Knokes.

13, Adam Car and Janet Crawfurd had Isobel ; witnesses, Andrew Rowane in the Gask, John Aikine, William Inche.

18, Andrew Cowstoun and Catherine Wannane had Robert ; witnesses, Robert Cunningham in Sillitoun, Robert Wannan, Edward Douglas.

20, James Murgane and Elspet Bowman had Andrew ; witnesses, Nicol Wardlaw, Thomas Christie, William Huttone.

27, David Alaster and Nanse Mastertoun had Janet ; witnesses, David Robertson of Craigduckie, James Mill in Lochend, George Dewar in Lathamond.

27, John Potter and Elspet Walker had Margaret ; witnesses, Patrick Cowper, John Walker, Thomas Schortus, William Trumble.

27, Robert Patrik and Elspet Low had Abraham ; witnesses, Abraham Greg, Mr. Robert Anderson, Henry Patrik.

27, Laurence Anderson, miller, and Margaret Lugton had John ; witnesses, John Anderson, litster, John Sanders, John Baid, Peter Buist.

M. 13, Robert Inglis to Isobel Bruse (in Carnok kirk).

20, Robert Wardlaw to Margaret Johnestone.

20, Thomas Arnott to Elspet Schort.

27, Harry Livingstone to Janet Russell.

27, John Fergus to Nanse Wricht.

SEPTEMBER.

B. 8, John Walker, cadger, and Margaret Dewar had Margaret ; witnesses, Robert Scotland, John Scotland, his son, in the Clun of Pittincreiff, Adam Stobie, portioner of Luscour (baptized in Carnok kirk).

8, James Car, armourer, and Catherine Cairns had Janet (in fornication) ; witnesses, David Bull, Peter Buist, Robert Henresone, Mark Donald.

8, John Muire, porter of the Abbey, and Nanse Scheiphird had Helen ; witnesses, Thomas Elder, Andrew Thomson, William Anderson, litster.

8, John Allane and Janet Bowar had Isobel ; witnesses, George Wardlaw, John Henresone, William Kennedie.

9, Mark Donald, baker, and Marjory Bennat had George : witnesses, Patrick Trumble, baker, George Donald, Andrew Trumble, baker.

15, Thomas Makinlay and Janet Paterson had a son . . . . : witnesses, William Wannan, William Ritchie, Thomas Paterson.

15, John Gentleman and Janet Galrige had John (in fornication) : witnesses, John Coventrie, John Broun, officer in Dunfermline, John Smithe.

15, Thomas Keir and Helen Yowne had Janet ; witnesses, David Burne, Patrick Peirsone, John Keir.

22, Robert Straquhen and Bessie Nicole had William ; witnesses, William Cunningham in Knokes, William Nicole, Robert Straquhen.

29, William Falkland and Isobel Logane had James ; witnesses, James Maknabie, Andrew Young, John Lawson.

29, James Lowsone and Bessie Galrige had Alexander ; witnesses, Alexander Wilsone, William Wilsone and Robert Wilsone, "the father and the tua chyldren."

M. 24, Harry Grege to Bessie Broun.
    24, John Dagleische to Elspet Hutone.
    26, Andrew Anghous to Marjory Mackie.

OCTOBER.

B. 1, John Cambell, gardener in Pitfirrane, and Margaret Robertson had James; witnesses, William Lawson, John Lawson, William Leslie, James Henresone.
    6, James Stewart and Elspet Mayne had Robert; witnesses, Robert Mayne, Robert Mayne, his son, and James Henresone.
    6, Andrew Cunningham and Margaret Ædison had Robert; witnesses, Robert Aikine, Robert Burne and Robert Burne (*sic*).
    10, Robert Dick and Jean Sands had Helen; witnesses, John Walker, dean of guild, Mr. Robert Anderson, musician, John Simsone, cordiner.
    13, Andrew Key and Janet Stevenson had Margaret; witnesses, Thomas Douglas in Gellat, Edward Douglas there, Thomas Key in Rossythe.
    13, Andrew Mentethe in Kavill and Bessie Fothringham had William; witnesses, William Cunningham in Knokes, William Kellok, William Mentethe.
    13, Andrew Ritchie and Jean Toscheauche had Margaret; witnesses, John Wilson, John Hog, James Miller.
    14, Andrew Wels and Christian Awstiane had Thomas; witnesses, Thomas Davidson, Thomas Philpe, John Simsone.
    20, John Broun in the Ferrie and Barbara Thomson had Robert; witnesses, Robert Drysdell, Robert Chatto, Robert Thomson (baptised in Inverkeithing).
    20, Jasper Drysdell and Marion Inglis had John; witnesses, John Chatto, John Thomson, John Lillie. (Baptised in Inverkeithing.)
    20, Sir William Nisbitt of the Dean, knight, and Marjory Schortus had Mary (in fornication); witnesses, James Reid, Mr. Patrick Fleck, bailie, Patrick Kingorne, presented by James Legat.
    22, Patrick Broun and Bessie Mudie had Robert; witnesses, James Stanehous, Robert Mudie, John Hodge in Foulfuird.
    22, Andrew Trumble, baker, and Barbara Law had Patrick; witnesses, Patrick Trumble, John Walker, Peter Law.
    23, David Hutone and Margaret Dempstertoun had Catherine; witnesses, Thomas Davidson, Peter Buist, John Broun, officer.
    25, James Halyday (deceased) and Janet Watson had twins, John and James; witnesses, William Mayne, Andrew Young, William Murray, John Spens. These persons were proclaimed in the kirk of Leith to be married, and before the celebration of their marriage the man died, and the woman brought forth these children, being unmarried.
    27, James Cunnon and Bessie Garvie had James; witnesses, James Garvie, James Cunningham in Pitadro, James Cunnon in Mastertoun.
    29, George Moreis and Bessie Beany had Janet; witnesses, John Bennat, Mark Donald, Thomas Hunnon.
M. 6, George Durie to Margaret Broun.

NOVEMBER.

B. 1, John Broun, tailor in the Nethertoun, and Catherine Imrie (a married woman) had Barbara (in adultery); witnesses, John Brown, David Miller, Henry Davidson.
    3, John Sanders and Helen Watson had Patrick; witnesses, Mr. Patrick Auchinleck, James Reid, John Wels.
    3, Thomas Philpe and Catherine Harrower had Catharine; witnesses, Harry Stewart of Baithe, James Stewart, Henry Moreis.
    3, George Trumble in Tunigask and Marjory Maistertoun had John; witnesses, Adam Maistertoun, John Maistertoun, his son, James Dagleische.
    12, William Anderson in Gellat and Catharine Cunningham had William; witnesses, William Anderson in Lymkills, David Sands, Thomas Douglas, Edward Douglas.

12, James Mayne and Christian Johnstone had Helen ; witnesses, John Coventrie, James Ritchie, John Mayne.

12, James Burgane in the Queinisferrie and Nanse Saverall had a daughter . . . . ; witnesses, George Burgane, Harry Cant. (Baptised in Inverkeithing.)

12, John Heckfurd, collier, and Bessie Thomson had Margaret ; witnesses, Thomas Davidson, litster, Andrew Thomson, belman, William Cowstoun.

12, William Wilsone, maltman in the Nethertoun, and Christian Wricht had Nanse ; witnesses, William Walker, maltman, John Wricht, Robert Wilson.

14, James Hamiltone, piper, and Isobel Broun had Margaret ; witnesses, Andrew Thomson, Andrew Gaw, John Brown, officer.

17, John Litljohne and Janet Wilson had John ; witnesses, John Wilson, William Mudie, weaver, Thomas Schortus.

17, George Cunningham and Margaret Maistertoun had Grizel ; witnesses, James Mudie, William Lambe, William Keir.

19, John Colzeir and Grizel Murray had Margaret (in fornication); witnesses, Andrew Trumble in Bromehill, George Trumble, his son, David Murray, sailor. (The man fugitive from discipline, and the child baptised upon her giving satisfaction.)

19, David Bull and Christian Balfour had Andrew ; witnesses, Andrew Cunningham, James Balfour, Harry Balfour in Mastertoun.

19, Robert Hutone and Nanse Muschat had James (in fornication); witnesses, John Alisone, wright, James Dewar in Pitbauchlie, James Coventrie.

19, Mr. Patrick Auchinleck and Elspet Forrester had Janet ; witnesses, James Reid, bailie, Mr. Bernard Gib, John Bennat, baker.

23, Andrew Colzeir and Isobel Anderson had Janet ; witnesses, Andrew Thomson, William Paterson, George Davidson, Robert Anderson, tailor.

24, William Kellok in Pitravie and Bessie Trumble had Elspet ; witnesses, James Anghous, David Mitchell, Thomas Ædisone.

24, David Peirsone, merchant, and Jean Stanehous had John ; witnesses, John Anderson, litster, John Anderson in Lymkills, Thomas Hereis.

24, John Neilson and Janet Buist had Isobel ; witnesses, Robert Neilson, Patrick Trumble, Peter Buist.

29, Mr. Bernard Gib and Effie Abircrumbie had Annas ; witnesses, James Reid, George Bothwell, Mr. Patrick Auchinleck.

M. 19, Robert Anderson to Margaret Weitit.
  20, John Huntar to Christian Donaldson.

DECEMBER.

B. 10, James Hamilton and Jean Sands had William ; witnesses, William Anderson, Mr. Patrick Auchinleck.

  19, James Cowstone and Grizel Moreis had Patrick ; witnesses, David Inglis, James Corslaw, Robert Elder.

  24, John Lindsay in Pitdinne and Bessie Peirsone had Janet ; witnesses, Patrick Lindsay, John Peirson, William Lawson.

  31, James Man and Isobel Wilson had Adam ; witnesses, William Mackie, John Betsone, David Moreis in Bayth.

M. 8, John Gentleman to Effie Douglas.
  17, James Steinsone to Isobel Clerk.
  17, David Peacok to Barbara Thomson.
  31, Andrew Donaldson to Catherine Huntar.

JANUARY [1634].

B. 7, John Wels and Margaret Stevenson had Harry ; witnesses, John Stevenson of Bayth, Henry Moreis, David Moreis.

10, Henry Wyper and Grizel Workman had twins (in fornication), one dying unbaptised, the other baptised Margaret; witnesses, John Simsone, John Bartleman, Andrew Thomson.

12, Laurence Watson, cordiner, and Grizel Wilson had Patrick; witnesses, Mr. Patrick Auchinleck, Patrick Kingorne, John Bennat.

14, William Hutone and Catherine Mill had Isobel; witnesses, Thomas Christie, James Murgane, Robert Anghous.

19, James Legat and Margaret Stirk had Agnes; witnesses, John Anderson, litster, in the Colzeraw, Patrick Legat, William Legat, his son, George Mudie.

20, John Watson, seaman in Brunteland, and Dorothy Ædisone had Andrew (in fornication); witnesses, Andrew Cunningham, Andrew Trumble, James Reid, bailie.

21, Andrew Cant and Christian Bull had a daughter . . . ; witnesses, Robert Cant, Ninian Mather, William Wod.

21, James Simraell and Margaret Mudie had William; witnesses, William Mudie, mason, William Mudie, maltman, Robert Davidson.

28, James Ritchie and Christian Anderson had Thomas; witnesses, Thomas Ritchie, Alexander Anderson, Andrew Burne.

28, William Mudie, maltman, and Janet Christie had Patrick; witnesses, Patrick Cowper, Patrick Stevenson, Adam Currie in Primrois, James Simraell.

M. 2, Thomas Wylie to Isobel Bruse.

14, John Anderson to Margaret Cadell.

30, James Dewar to Helen Trumble.

31, James Kellok to Nanse Aittone.

FEBRUARY.

B. 2, Andrew Berriehill and Elspet Broun had Catherine; witnesses, Patrick Broun, James Walwod in Nether Baithe, Robert Peirson there.

4, George Trumble in Bromehall and Helen Grinlay had Marion; witnesses, Andrew Trumble in Bromehall, Patrick Grinlay, Andrew Trumble in Grange.

4, John Ramsay, collier, and Isobel Laduthe had William (in fornication); witnesses, William Wannan, Thomas Barklay, Donald Fraser. (Baptised in Cleish.)

4, Thomas Betoun, 'chopeman,' and Helen Anderson had Thomas; witnesses, Thomas Keir, Andrew Mure, John Workman.

9, Harry Greg and Bessie Broun had Janet; witnesses, William Cairnis, John Broun, Florie Greg.

9, John Bruse and Marjory Law had John; witnesses, John Turkan, John Wricht, John Law.

11, Thomas Tod in the Clun and Isobel Templeman had Thomas; witnesses, Mr. Thomas Wardlaw, Thomas Reid, Richard Templeman.

14, William Cowstone, collier, and Janet Scharpe had Janet; witnesses, Thomas Baverage, Thomas Hunnone, Andrew Mekiljohne.

23, William Anderson in Pitconnochie and Nanse Chalmers had Alexander; witnesses, Alexander Chalmers, Thomas Douglas, John Dewar in Kinneder.

23, John Cowie and Isobel Lawson had John (in fornication); witnesses, William Wilson, John Broun.

25, Wattie Horne and Christian Young had Patrick; witnesses, Patrick Cowper, Andrew Murray, William Anderson, litster.

27, Peter Buist and Isobel Walwod had Janet; witnesses, John Bennat, Andrew Trumble, James Walwod, officer.

M. 4, Alexander Greg to Janet Burgane.

20, Robert Anderson to Marjory Anderson.

20, David Scot to Isabel Broun.

MARCH.

B. 11, Patrick Stevenson and Christian Mudie had William; witnesses, William Mudie, maltman, William Anderson, litster, William Wilson, maltman.

16, Andrew Broun and Bessie Wilson had Margaret; witnesses, James Mitchell, James Mayne, David Broun.

18, Robert Tailyeour and Margaret Cunningham had John; witnesses, John Lawson, John Cunningham, John Swentoun. (Baptised in Torrie kirk.)

23, William Anderson and Isobel Russell had Thomas; witnesses, Thomas Stevenson, Thomas Mayne (?), Thomas Burne.

23, Andrew Patone and Isobel Richardson had Robert: witnesses, Robert Burne, William Burne, Andrew Burne in Gellat.

23, David Moreis of Baithe and Janet Lundie had Elspet; witnesses, John Oliphant in Bochlavie, John Stevenson of Baithe, Henry Hakirstone there.

23, William Litljohne and Christian Broun had John: witnesses, Laurie Neilson, John Clerk, cadger, William Peirson.

23, John Bartleman, fuller, and Nanse Fleming had Janet; witnesses, Peter Trumble, David Maxwell, Thomas Davidson, all litsters.

30, William Bruse and Rose Snellok had Isobel; witnesses, Thomas Wilson, George Donald, David Sands in Wester Gellat.

M. 4, James Moyas to Rosina Walwod.

18, John Moreis to Margaret Westwod (in Auchtertule kirk).

APRIL.

B. 6, David Inglis and Helen Lugtoun had Marjory; witnesses, James Cowstone, John Inglis, Nicol Inglis.

7, John Potter, wright, and Marion Clerk had Andrew; witnesses, David Bull, John Bruse, Andrew Potter.

13, John Laurie and Nanse Grege had Margaret: witnesses, Andrew Thomson, Thomas Elder, John Muire.

20, John Livingstone and Christian Young had Christian; witnesses, William Anderson, Thomas Baverage, Andrew Young.

20, John Forsythe and Margaret Potter had Elspet; witnesses, Thomas Stanehous, John Gentleman, Robert Kellok in Mastertoun.

20, Andrew Cunningham in Primrois and Margaret Trumble had William: witnesses, William Cunningham in Knokis, William Wilson, maltman, Adam Currie in Primrois.

20, Andrew Kellok and Margaret Stocks had Andrew; witnesses, John Davidson in Fod, John Kellok, John Baverage in Keltie.

20, John Wilson in Galrikhill and Margaret Anderson had Bessie; witnesses, Andrew Walker in Logie, William Cois and Alexander Cois, brethren.

27, Andrew Ferlie and Alison Anderson had Isobel: witnesses, Thomas Mitchell, Thomas Mitchell, his son, and Thomas Peirsone.

27, William Smart, flesher, and Bessie Stevenson had Adam; witnesses, Adam Stevenson, elder, Thomas Key, Thomas Elder.

M. 13, David Laurie to Effie Gibsone.

22, John Ramsay to Christian Thrislo.

24, Mr. Harry Makgill, minister in Dunfermline, to Margaret Wardlaw, daughter of Mr. Thomas Wardlaw of Logie.

29, Andrew Trumble to Janet Anderson.

MAY.

B. 4, Thomas Dewar and Janet Peacok had Robert; witnesses, David Robertson, Robert Russell, Robert Anghous.

4, Thomas Stanehous, portioner of Mastertoun, and Barbara Dewar had Elspet; witnesses, William Kellok in Pitravie, Thomas Ædisone, younger, in Pitadro mill, John Gentleman in Mastertoun.

6, Robert Levingstone and Isobel Marschell had James; witnesses, Andrew Potter, George Davidson, weaver, John Wilson, weaver.

11, William Inche and Margaret James had William; witnesses, James Reid, bailie, John James, William Cunningham in Knokes.

13, Thomas Hall and Bessie Portour had Thomas; witnesses, Thomas Stevenson, Thomas Cowper, William Portour.

18, James Anderson in Pittincreiff and Isobel Inglis had Isobel; witnesses, David Makbethe, John Stirk, Andrew Inglis.

18, James Reid, bailie, and Marion Broun had Margaret: witness, Mr. Patrick Auchinleck.

20, Robert Henresone, skinner, and Janet Car had Agnes; witnesses, Mr. David Stirk, James Legat, William Mudie, weaver.

25, Andrew Christie and Helen Currie had Elspet; witnesses, Thomas Christie, Thomas Douglas, David Mitchell, William Cois.

M.   [*None.*]

JUNE.

B. 1, John Stirk, weaver in Wester Luscour, and Margaret Wardane had John; witnesses, Adam Stobie, Nicol Wardlaw, John Sands of Longsyd.

1, Robert Elder and Margaret Barklay had Catherine; witnesses, David Burne, James Cowstoun, David Inglis.

8, David Mitchell in Pitlivar and Margaret Currie had Catherine; witnesses, William Kellok in Pitravie, John Currie in Crumbie, Adam Currie in Primrois.

8, David Robertson of Craigduckie Easter and Grizel Hutone had James; witnesses, Mr. James Dewar, Mr. William Wardlaw, James Finlasone in Aberdour.

15, James Donaldson and Margaret Cunningham had Janet; witnesses, Andrew Cunningham in the Stare, David Flockard, Andrew Hutone.

15, John Fergus and Nanse Wricht had Isobel; witnesses, David Peirson, James Peirson, and John Peirsone in Pitdinne.

15, David Wyld and Bessie Bankis had a son . . . .: witnesses, David Tod, James Murgan, Robert Scotland, Thomas Tod.

15, Laurence Merser and Margaret Dagleische had Euphan; witnesses, Robert Merser of the Kirkland in Sauling, John Rowane of Craighous.

22, Archibald Honyman and Margaret Wels had Andrew; witnesses, Andrew Wilson, Patrick Kingorne, James Car, mason.

24, William Curror and Margaret Schort had Helen: witnesses, David Moreis, James Schort, Thomas Arnott.

M. 3, David Robertson to Elspet Bossuell.

3, Archibald Forrest to Bessie Quhyt.

10, John Anderson to Margaret Gibsone.

17, John Broun to Marion Glas.

24, John Broun to Marion Allane.

24, David Stevenson to Catherine Thomesone.

JULY.

B. 4, Robert Anderson and Bessie Johnstone had John; witnesses, ..., Peter Buist, George Davidson.

13, David Blak, younger in Coklaw, and Marjory Blakwod had James; witnesses, James Legat, James Baverage, John Kellok, younger.

13, John Oiswald and Christian Hamilton had John: witnesses, John Anderson, litster, William George, William Pillonis.

15, James Hutone and Mary Dempstertoun had George; witnesses, George Davidson, Patrick Murray, James Simsone.

20, Thomas Arnott and Elspet Schort had James: witnesses, James Schort, James Mitchell, James Bruse.

27, John Danskine and Helen Watson had David; witnesses, David Cunnone, David Peirson, Robert Logane.

27, John Ritchie and Christian Blacatter had Janet; witnesses, Richard Law, Wattie Ritchie, Robert Anghous in Balmule.

29, Thomas Elder, flesher, and Helen Simsone had John; witnesses, John Bennet, William Walker, merchant, James Simsone, shoemaker, Mark Donald, Patrick Peirson.

M. 6, John Dick to Bessie Stevenson.

8, Andrew Wilson to Janet Cunningham.

24, Robert Dewar to Margaret Flokart.

29, William Dagleish to Catherine Wardlaw.

29, John Fyiff to Catherine Hereme.

AUGUST.

B. 3, John Inglis and Nanse Hutone had Catherine; witnesses, William Hutone, William Dagleishe, Robert Russell.

3, Laurence Neilson and Isobel Litljohne had Margaret; witnesses, Patrick Kingorne, James Kennedie, Alexander Beane.

3, John Stanehous and Jean Fentone had Janet; witnesses, John Davidson, William Stanehous, John Blair.

3, John Kirk, "creilman," and Marion Greg had Catherine; witnesses, George Dewar in Lathamond, William Hutone in Dunduff, James Mill in Lochend.

7, James Mitchell and Christian Thomson had James; witnesses, James Mayne, John Huntar, John Potter.

11, James Kennedie, wright, and Janet Hutone had Peter; witnesses, Peter Law, Patrick Trumble, Robert Stirk, Peter Buist.

19, Adam Currie in Primrois and Catherine Christie had Janet; witnesses, Thomas Christie, Thomas Mitchell, William Mudie.

24, John Dougall and Bessie Thomson had Marjory; witnesses, David Burne, Robert Elder, Robert Burne, David Inglis.

27, James Anderson and Janet Clerk had twins, John and Christian; witnesses, Patrick Anderson, William Cunningham, John Lawson, William Lawson.

M. 5, David Broun to Margaret Greg.

7, Robert Meldrum to Christian Smart.

19, Thomas Beinstone to Margaret Horne.

26, George Chopeman to Grizel Glas.

26, David Sim to Margaret Meldrum.

SEPTEMBER.

B. 3, Robert Douglas and Margaret Peirson had James; witnesses, James Leslie, Thomas Mitchell (?), Henry Douglas.

7, James Dick and Margaret Kilgour had Jean; witnesses, John Anderson, Robert Anderson, Harry Young.

7, John Watson, cordiner, and Helen Hutone, "sewster," had John (in fornication); witnesses, John Sanders, Adam Wylie, Robert Anderson in the Maygate.

14, Andrew Smithe and Bessie Weir had James; witnesses, James Kellok in Mastertoun, James Stanehous there, James Feg, burgess of Dunfermline.

16, John Stirk and Bessie Crawfurd had John; witnesses, John Stirk, father of said John, George Meldrum, Henry Crawfurd.

21, Henry Douglas and Margaret Cunningham had David; witnesses, David Douglas, David Mitchell, Edward Douglas.

28, Thomas Lessells and Bessie Lawson had Bessie; witnesses, William Lawson, James Clerk, Patrick Anderson.

29, James Litljohne and Christian Chrichtone had Thomas; witnesses, Thomas Schortus, William Mudie, Allan Mudie.

M. 1, Matthew (?) Banks (?) to . . . [*illegible*].

23, Mr. Robert Anderson to Marion Dewar.
30, William Walker to Margaret Drummond.

OCTOBER.

B.   5, William Walker, maltman, and Marjory Broun had George ; witnesses.
George Walker, merchant in Edinburgh, Andrew Walker in Logie,
James Broun of the Pratus, George Meldrum in Pittincreiff.

12, John Gentleman and Effie Douglas had Elizabeth ; witnesses, Robert
Kellok, David Cunnon in Mastertoun, John Coventrie.

12, David Robertson and Elspet Bossnell had Elizabeth ; witnesses, Mr.
John Wardlaw, Andrew Currie, David Currie.

12, James Anderson and Elspet Christie had John ; witnesses, John
Coventrie, John Christie, John Stanehous.

12, Peter Ferlie and Elspet Breadfute had Janet ; witnesses, William Mudie,
maltman, John Burne, James Muidie.

14, Thomas Mitchell and Bessie Curror had Margaret (in fornication) ;
witnesses, Andrew Currie, Henry Douglas, Thomas Cumming.

21, John Lawson, tailor, and Catherine Logane had John ; witnesses, John
Lawson, John Lawson, his son, John Tailyeour.

23, Robert Mudie, portioner of Mastertoun, and Helen Mudie had Janet ;
witnesses, Andrew Walker in Logie, Andrew Trumble in the Grange,
Davie Cunnon, portioner of Mastertoun, Robert Kellok there.

30, James Miller (?) and . . . had Robert ; witnesses, Robert Burne, John
. . . , Robert Bruse (?), collier. [*Partly illegible.*]

M. 21, James Meldrum to Marjory Feg.
30, John Orolk to Margaret Mackie.

NOVEMBER.

B.   2, Andrew Donaldson and Catherine Huntar had Bessie ; witnesses, David
Sands, John Hunter, James Donaldson.

9, David Broun and Janet Dewar had Janet ; witnesses, George Meldrum,
Andrew Broun, Robert Dewar.

9, Alexander Galrige and Christian Ritchie had Robert (in fornication) ;
witnesses, Robert Tod, Robert Ritchie, Robert Galrige. (The child
died unbaptised before reaching the church).

9, James Thomson and Janet Law had Helen (in fornication) ; witnesses,
John Wels, Henry Moreis, Andrew Berriehill.

9, George Penman, collier in Fordall heugh, and Marjory Wilson, his
coalbearer, had Margaret (in adultery) ; witnesses, Andrew Gaw,
Duncan Tailyeour, David Stevenson. Presented by William Penman,
brother of said George.

13, George Durie in the Nethertoun and Margaret Broun had Margaret ;
witnesses, Sir Robert Halkett of Pitfirran, Robert Colvill of Cleish,
Mr. Matthew Weymis, minister in Canongate.

13, Laurence Steinsone and Catherine Chatto had Elspet ; witnesses, John
Alisone, John Kellok, Thomas Cowper.

20, Andrew Hutone, slater, and Elspet Kilgour had Elspet ; witnesses,
William Mastertoun, James Feg, John Potter.

20, James Simsone, merchant, and Bessie Walker had Marjory ; witnesses,
James Reid, Peter Law, John Walker, Andrew Walker in Logie.

23, David Hoge and Marjory Bull had Margaret ; witnesses, John Walker,
Dean of Guild, William Walker, merchant, James Legat.

23, John Potter and Janet Inglis had Marjory ; witnesses, John Stevenson.
William Mudie, James Mitchell.

23, A vagabond calling himself James Wardlaw presented a child, "gottin
on Janet Ogilbie, quhom he sa nameit and said scho wes his wyff bot
had no testificatioun of ther laufull mariage," baptised Thomas.

26, Thomas Douglas and Elspet Chalmer had Janet ; witnesses, Thomas
Mitchell, Thomas Stevenson, John Gentleman.

26, Patrick Kinninmond and his lady, Margaret Boswell, had John ; witnesses, Sir John Boswell of Balmuto, Sir Robert Halket of Pitfirran, George Bothwell.

30, James Anderson and Janet Gray had Margaret ; witnesses, James Peirson in Pitdinne, William Lawson, James Anghous.

M. 9, William Kent to Isobel Broun.

13, John Watson, cordiner, to Barbara Bruse.

20, Nicol Blakwod to Margaret Murray.

20, John Quhyt to Margaret Kellok.

27, John Bryse to Helen Quhyt.

27, William Inglis to Bessie Cowper.

DECEMBER.

B. 1, Andrew Trumble, lorimer, and Janet Anderson had William ; witnesses, William Trumble, father of said Andrew, William Anderson, litster, Peter Law, bailie.

6, Mr. Harry Makgill, minister, and Margaret Wardlaw had Thomas ; witnesses, Mr. Thomas Wardlaw of Logie, Mr. Bernard Gib, George . . . , Mr. Robert . . .

9, Robert Anderson and Marjory Anderson had Jean ; witnesses, Thomas Christie, James Hall, William Anderson.

14, Robert Greive and Margaret Douglas had Annas ; witnesses, Andrew Rowane, Robert Anghous, David Scotland, Robert Russell, younger.

14, William Cadzone and Margaret Burne had Robert ; witnesses, Robert Burne, William Burne, Andrew Burne, Robert Cusine, Thomas Mitchell.

16, Robert Anderson and Margaret Weitat had John ; witnesses, James Anderson, John Davidson, John Anderson.

18, William Garvie and Bessie Walker had Andrew ; witnesses, Andrew Currie, James Garvie, Thomas Stanehous in Mastertoun.

28, James Moyas and Rosina Walwod had Janet ; witnesses, John Broun, David Walwod, John Moyas.

28, David Douglas and Alison Mitchell had David ; witnesses, Thomas Mitchell, younger, David Mitchell, Andrew Burne.

M. 11, Alexander [Young ?] to . . . [*illegible*].

18, George Stirk to Elspet Walker.

JANUARY [1635].

B. 4, John Davidson in Fod and Marjory Broun had Christian ; witnesses, Peter Broun, James Mitchell, William Stanehous in Fod.

4, John Alisone, wright, and Grizel Walwod had Grizel ; witnesses, James Legat, Laurence Stevenson, Archibald Honyman.

4, John Lawson, smith, and Catherine Drysdell had James ; witnesses, Mark Donald, James Cunningham in the Sillitoun, James Mather.

4, William Mackie and Margaret Betsone had a son . . . : witnesses, John Betsone, David Blak, Patrick Greg.

11, James Kellok, tailor, and Nanse Aittone had Catherine ; witnesses, Thomas Baverage, John Clerk, merchant, James Donald.

11, John Smart and Margaret Baverage had John ; witnesses, John Smart in Over Anziefair, flesher, William Smart, John Smart, younger.

15, Thomas Wylie and Isobel Bruce had Adam ; witnesses, Adam Wylie, James Reid, John Watson.

18, David Flokart and Bessie Dewar had William (baptised in Inverkeithing) ; witnesses, William Flokart, John Dewar, Robert Dewar, James Donaldson.

18, Thomas Curror and Effie Alexander had Janet (baptised in Cleish kirk) ; witnesses, Henry Hakirstone, George Trumble, John Keir, all in Baithe.

25, John Anderson and Margaret Cadell had Margaret ; witnesses, John Lawson, William Cunningham, James Lawson.

25, Mark Donald and Marjory Bennat had Janet ; witnesses, John Bennat, George Donald, John Wricht.

25, Robert Pittilloche and Mage Miller had Robert ; witnesses, Robert Logane, Robert Miller.

M. 8, Richard Gray to Geils Anderson.

25, James Dunkiesone to Isobel Feldie.

FEBRUARY.

B. 1, James Henresone, glazier, and Mays Aikine had Marjory ; witnesses, James Meldrum, James Stewart, James Feg.

1, John Huntar and Christian Donaldson had James ; witnesses, James Donaldson, George Meldrum, James Anderson in Pittencrieff.

8, Andrew Muire, tailor, and Christian Lauthiane had Isobel ; witnesses, John Broun, William Swentoun, James Ronald.

10, David Galrig and Margaret Yowne had Helen : witnesses, Thomas Keir, William Mudie and Allan Mudie, weavers.

14, Harry Anderson, master stabler to the Earl of Dunfermline, and Margaret Colzer had Charles : witnesses, Charles Setoun, Earl of Dunfermline, Mr. Bernard Gib, George Bothwell.

22, John Ramsay, collier, and Christian Thrislo had Janet ; witnesses, Robert Scot, John Watson, collier, Robert Brown, collier.

24, George Tailyeour and Nanse Hutone had Margaret ; witnesses, Robert Tailyeour, Robert Cunningham, Mark Donald, George Donald.

26, Edward Douglas and Beatie Douglas had Jean ; witnesses, Thomas Mitchell, John Gentleman, Robert Kellok, younger, Henry Douglas.

M. 5, Andrew Currie to Helen Stirk.

MARCH.

B. 8, Thomas Blakwod and Isobel Inglis had John ; witnesses, John Huntar, John Stirk, John Inglis.

8, James Simsone, cordiner, and Isobel Weitche had Thomas : witnesses, Thomas Elder, Thomas Cowper, William Smart, William Walker, merchant.

15, James Coventrie and Elspet Robertson had Patrick : witnesses, Patrick Murray, John Coventrie, Adam Coventrie.

15, William Kent and Isobel Broun had Helen ; witnesses, William Gibone in Carnok, William Kellok, Robert Mudie, younger.

15, John Kellok, younger, in Quhythous, and Barbara Abernethie had Nanse (in fornication) ; witnesses, David Blak, Henry Dick, William Kellok.

15, William Galrige and Helen Broun had Bessie ; witnesses, John Galrige, Andrew Trumble, William Inglis in the Grange.

17, James Eweine and Margaret Primrois had Margaret : witnesses, James Reid, Robert Aikine, Henry Davidson.

19, John Law and Magie Keir had a bastard baptised Margaret.

22, Alexander Cois and Nanse Imrie had James : witnesses, Mark . . . , William (?) Cois, John Wilson.

22, John Wilson and Barbara Kellok had William : witnesses, James Reid, Thomas Reid, John Clerk, treasurer of the burgh.

22, William Robertson and Marjory Martene had John ; witnesses, John Burne, mason, John Sandilands, Laurie Stevenson.

M. 12, John Mill to Marjory Dewar (in Cleish kirk).

APRIL.

B. 5, John Buchanan and Janet Peacok had Bessie ; witnesses, Thomas Nasmithe, David Currie, David Drysdell.

5, John Mill and Marjory Dewar had a daughter . . . . (begotten before marriage); witnesses, Henry Mill, Nicol Dewar, Harry Mill.

5, William Anderson and Janet Cunningham had Nanse; witnesses, James Anghous, William Anderson in Pitconnochie, James Hutone.

5, John Stevenson (deceased, buried 30th March ult. and Janet Fuird had Margaret; witnesses, George Donald, Robert Cunningham, John Mershell.

5, William Anderson in Geilat and Catherine Cunningham had Isobel; witnesses, Thomas Wilson, Adam Wilson, David Sands, Robert Cunningham.

7, John Orock and Margaret Mackie had a son . . . . baptised in Cleish kirk).

12, John Makcraiche and Marjory Anderson had Thomas; witnesses, Thomas Mitchell, Robert Currie, Thomas Mitchell, younger.

12, John Anderson and Margaret Gibson had Janet; witnesses, James Mitchell, John Stanehous, James Anderson.

12, James Dewar and Christian Philpe had David; witnesses, David Dewar, James Moyas, William Peirson, John Broun.

12, Allan Mudie and Bessie Keir had William; witnesses, William Mudie, Thomas Keir, William Lambe.

12, Alexander Drysdell, bailie, and Bessie Walwod had Bessie; witnesses, Peter Law, bailie, Mr. Patrick Auchinleck, Patrick Kingorne, clerk, John Clerk, William Walker.

21, Mr. James Dewar of Nether Lassodie and Elspet Moncreiff had Matthew; witnesses, David Robertson of Craigduckie, David Cunnone, portioner of Mastertoun, Thomas Stanehous, portioner there.

21, John Car, weaver, and Bessie Clerk had Janet; witnesses, William Lambe, John Gotterstone, William Mudie, all weavers.

26, Thomas Beinstone and Margaret Horne had Robert; witnesses, John Wels, Thomas Baverage, John Stirk.

M. [*None.*]

MAY.

B. 3, William Pillons and Isobel Douglas had Janet; witnesses, Andrew Wilson, Mark Donald, David Sands.

5, John Craiche, mason, and Janet Gotterstoun (?) had John; witnesses, William Walker, merchant, James Ker (?), John Burne, mason.

10, Edward Kirk, weaver, and Janet Thomson had Robert; witnesses, Robert Kellok, Robert Mudie, John Gentleman, David Cunnon in Mastertoun.

12, David Cunnone, portioner of Mastertoun, and Elspet Dewar had Peter; witnesses, Peter Law, Mr. James Dewar of Lassodie, John Dewar, younger, John Law.

24, Robert Dewar and Margaret Flokart had John; witnesses, John Dewar, James Dewar in Pitbachlie, William Flokart.

24, Thomas Hutone and Isobel Keir had Robert; witnesses, Robert Hutone, Robert Keir, Robert Davidson.

31, James Reid and Marion Broun had Janet; witnesses, John Bennat, William Anderson, Mr. Patrick Auchinleck.

M. 21, William Kirk to Margaret Wode.

26, William Robertson to Isobel Ladathe (?).

28, James Wod to Isobel Anderson.

JUNE.

B. 2, Robert Anghous in Balmule and Isobel Dewar had Janet; witnesses, George Dewar, James Anghous, David Greins, Robert Russell.

7, George Wardlaw and Jean Kennedie had Catherine; witnesses, Harry Stewart of Bayth, George Bothwell, Thomas Philpe.

M. 2, Thomas Bankis to Bessie Barklay.

7, James Robertson to Isobel Wallace.
9, James Cumming to Janet Gibsone.

JULY.

B. 7, Patrick Lawsone, weaver, and Margaret Lathangie had James; witnesses, James Cunninghame in the Sillitoun, Thomas Wilson in the Mylneburne, James Leslie of Pitlivar.

7, Thomas Christie of the Hoile and Elspet Durie had James; witnesses, James Durie of Craigluscour, Mr. James Durie in the Nethertoun of Dunfermline, James Cunningham in Pitadro.

7, John Muire and Nanse Schiphird had Margaret; witnesses, Thomas Cowper, William Anderson, Andrew Thomson, John Laurie.

12, James Mitchell in South Fod and Isobel Cunningham had James; witnesses, James Cunningham in Pitadro, James Anderson in Southfod, Thomas Mitchell, younger, James Coventrie in the Wodmylne.

12, James Meldrum and Marjory Feg had Janet; witnesses, Thomas Schortus, Robert Davidson, John Workman.

12, Laurence Gray and Bessie Peacok had Grizel; witnesses, John Kellok, Andrew Kellok, Archibald Robertson, shepherd.

12, Thomas Curror and Helen Hutsone had Effie: witnesses, Andrew Berrihill, John Stevenson, younger of Baith, David Moreis there.

12, John Wilson and Helen Currie had Margaret; witnesses, Sandie Wilson, Andrew Walker, James Cunninghame in Pitadro.

12, William Mudie, weaver, and Nanse Mackie had Janet: witnesses, John Bennat, John Gotterstone, Andrew Muire.

17, Thomas Baverage and Christian Smart had Janet; witnesses, David Stewart, cordiner, Thomas Elder, John Smart, flesher.

19, Edward Broun in the Ferrie and Janet Broun had Edward; witnesses, Harry Greg, Harry Cant, Charles Watson. (Baptised in Inverkeithing.)

23, William Wilson and Margaret Watson had Laurence; witnesses, Laurie Watson, John Sanders, Archibald Boyd.

26, Andrew Drummond and Bessie Young had Thomas; witnesses, Thomas Cowper, Thomas Ritchie, Robert Dewar.

26, James Walwod in Nether Bayth and Helen Inglis had Isobel; witnesses, William Inglis, Andrew Inglis, his son, Laurence Lugtoun.

26, Robert Thomson and Helen Sibauld had Catherine; witnesses, William Anderson, Thomas Douglas, David Sands, Edward Douglas, all in Gellat.

26, James Hamilton and Jean Sanders had Robert; witnesses, Robert Scotland, Peter Law, William Anderson.

26, Nicol Inglis and Marjory Law had William; witnesses, Robert Anghous, William Hutone, John Inglis.

M. 7, Andrew Williamson to Janet Barker (in Inverkeithing kirk).
12. William Anderson to Margaret Cowper.
14, George Remainous to Catherine Dewar.
14, David Hutsone to Janet Ritchie.
21, Alexander Chalmer to Catherine Walker.
28, James Cowstoun to Janet Blak.

AUGUST.

B. 2, David Reid and Margaret Lawson had Bessie; witnesses, James Wardlaw, Adam Stobie, James Fyiff.

2, John Forsyithe and Margaret Potter had Barbara; witnesses, William Potter, John Potter. Thomas Cunnon.

2, John Broun and Marion Allane had Thomas; witnesses, Henry Sandilands, Robert Murgane, James Wedderstoun, Thomas Jackson.

6, Andrew Betsone and Janet Thomson had Andrew (baptised in Balingrie kirk) ; witnesses, John Betsone, William Mackie, Andrew Betsone.

6, Mr. Patrick Auchinleck and Elspet Forrester had Catherine ; witnesses, James Reid, George Bothwell.

8, Robert Elder and Margaret Barklay had David ; witnesses, David Burne, James Dewar, Andrew Cunningham, Robert Burne.

9, George Stirk and Elspet Walker had John ; witnesses, Mr. John Walker, reader, John Stirk in Pittencreiff, David Walker, cooper, George Meldrum.

14, Robert Meldrum and Christian Smart had Janet ; witnesses, George Meldrum, John Stirk, John Huntar.

14, David Stewart and Helen Kirkland had John ; witnesses, John Sanders, John Tod, Laurie Watson.

14, John Lawsone in Crocefuird and Margaret Wilson had James ; witnesses, James Angous, James Hutone, James Lawson.

18, David Sands and Bessie Christie had Elspet ; witnesses, Thomas Christie, Thomas Douglas, Andrew Walker.

23, Nicol Henresone in Blairnebathie and Isobel Gray had James (in fornication), baptised in Cleish kirk ; witnesses, James Henresone, Henry Meldrum, Andrew Henresone.

23, Andrew Burne in Gellat and Elspet Ritchie had Robert ; witnesses, George Trumble in Bromehall, Thomas Mitchell, younger, Robert Birnie.

25, Patrick Kingorne, clerk of the burgh, and Margaret Forrester had David ; witnesses, Mr. David Kingorne, clerk of regality, James Reid, Gilbert Sanders.

30, Peter Buist, baker, and Isobel Walwod had Andrew ; witnesses, Andrew Trumble, baker, Peter Law, bailie, Edward Douglas in Wester Gellat.

M. 11, Robert Thomson to Elspet Broun (in Cleish kirk).

11, William Walwod to Margaret Wardlaw.

SEPTEMBER.

B. 2, John Wels, baker, and Catherine Drummond had Margaret ; witnesses, Mr. Harry Makgill, minister, Laurie Merser, William Walker, merchant.

3, John Broun, tailor, and Marion Glas had Robert ; witnesses, Robert Aikine, George Durie, John Broun.

5, Patrick Stevenson and Christian Mudie had James ; witnesses, James Mudie, James Simraell, James Mayne.

8, Robert Anderson in the Maygate and Janet Smith had William ; witnesses, William Anderson, William Paterson, John Broun, officer.

13, John Straquhen and Isobel Fothringhame had John ; witnesses, William Cunningham in Knokes, John Walwod, John Wanderstone (*sic*).

20, George Wat and Janet Robertson had Janet ; witnesses, John Wat, John Livingstone, Patrick Wat.

21, John Watson, cordiner, and Barbara Bruse had Margaret ; witnesses, Adam Wylie, Robert Miller, John Smetoun.

21, Alexander Young, mason, and Bessie Williamson had James, witnesses, Gilbert Sanders, William Smart, James Car, mason.

27, James Ritchie and Christian Anderson had Alexander ; witnesses, Alexander Anderson, Robert Anderson, Robert Ritchie.

27, William Young and Nanse Plaine had Christian ; witnesses, William Anderson, John Livingstone, Richard Gray.

27, James Mill and Grizel Robertson had Henry ; witnesses, Henry Wardlaw, David Roberston of Craigduckie, Robert Russell.

27, William Inglis and Bessie Cowper had Patrick ; witnesses, Thomas Cowper, William Anderson, Thomas Schortus, Andrew Inglis.

29, Nicol Blakwod and Margaret Murra had Margaret; witnesses, Alexander Drysdell, William Walker, merchant, George Davidson.

M. 1, John Buchane to Grizel Stevenson.

OCTOBER.

B. 4, George Ædisone and Bessie Sands had Elspet; witnesses, David Sands, John Lawson, tailor, William Anderson in Gellat.

4, Thomas Keir and Helen Yowne had Thomas; witnesses, Andrew Mure, Thomas Burne, William Mudie, weaver.

4. Mr. Robert Anderson, musician, and Marion Dewar had John; witnesses, John Dewar, John Anderson, John Wricht (born 3rd inst.).

4. Patrick Walker, cooper, and Margaret Young had John; witnesses, Mr. John Walker, reader in Dunfermline, John Bennat, baker, Thomas Elder, flesher.

6. Andrew Turnbull, baker, and Barbara Law had Peter; witnesses, Peter Law, Peter Buist, Peter Trumble.

12, Sir James Murray of Tippermuire, knight, and Annas Melvill had Jean; witnesses, William Mentethe of Randifuird, Mr. Bernard Gib, George Bothwell.

20. James Mayne in Pitcorthie and Christian Johnestone had Isobel; witnesses, Patrick Stevenson, David Broun in Clinkhill, Andrew Broun, smith.

20. Laurence Hutone, weaver, and Janet Robertson had Thomas; witnesses, Thomas Cowper, William Anderson, litster, Robert Stevenson, smith.

22. Thomas Cowper in the Newra and Grizel Cumming had Margaret (in fornication); witnesses, William Anderson, litster, Peter Buist, Patrick Stevenson.

25, Gasper Drysdell and Marion Inglis had Robert (baptised in Inverkeithing); witnesses, Laurence Lugton, Robert Drysdell, Robert Inglis in Inverkeithing.

27, George Dewar in Lathamond and Mary Chalmers had Christian; witnesses, Mr. John Chalmers, younger, James Chalmers, his brother, Mr. James Dewar of Lassodie.

M. 6, William Wilson to Elspet Young.

25, John Trumble to Jean Murray.

NOVEMBER.

B. 1. Mark Swentone, sailor in the Ferrie, and Marjory Stevenson had a son . . . . (baptised in Inverkeithing); witnesses, Alexander Greg, Harry Greg, Charles Watson.

3. John Laurie and Nanse Greg had Nanse; witnesses, Andrew Clyd, Andrew Thomson, John Muire.

8. Andrew Broun, smith, and Bessie Wilson had Jean; witnesses, Patrick Stevenson, Robert Wilson in Mylnehills, Robert Tailyeour.

15, Richard Gray, sailor, and Geils Anderson had William; witnesses, William Anderson, grandfather and presenter of the child in the father's absence, Mr. James Phine, Andrew Currie in Primrois.

15, James Hamilton, piper, and Isobel Broun had Andrew; witnesses, Andrew Colzeir, Andrew Gaw, Andrew Thomson.

21, James Wallace, merchant, and Janet Henresone had twins, James and Peter; witnesses, Peter Law, John Walker, merchant, Peter Buist, James Henresone, glazier, James Murgane, James Anderson in Fod.

22, Laurence Watson, cordiner, and Grizel Wilson had Elspet; witnesses, David Maxwell, John Bennat, David Stewart, cordiner.

29, John Phinne in Dewarsbaith and Margaret Dinn had David; witnesses, David Dinn, Henry Baverage, Robert Peirson in Baith.

M. 10, James Kellok to Margaret Broun.

24, James (? John) Baverage to Christian Wilson.

DECEMBER.

B. 1, Andrew Drysdell in Craigluscour and Margaret Wilson had David ;
witnesses, David Scotland, Thomas Crystie, James Murgane.

3, Thomas Davidson, litster, and Isobel Anderson had John ; witnesses,
Robert Davidson, maltman, Robert Scotland in the Clun, Gilbert
Sanders.

4, John Rae and Margaret Miller had David ; witnesses, David Miller,
Robert Miller, John Walker, dean of guild.

6, James Donaldson and Margaret Cunningham had Andrew ; witnesses,
Andrew Cunningham, Andrew Mayne, Andrew Hutone.

6, James Dewar and Isobel Hutone had James ; witnesses, James Cunno,
James Coventrie, James Mayne.

10, James Dagleishe and Catherine Wardlaw had Barbara ; witnesses,
Robert Merser, James Durie, James Wardlaw. (Baptised in Saline
kirk.)

15, Henry Sanderson and Elspet Ramache had Helen ; witnesses, Andrew
Mekiljohne, James Wederstone, Geordie Davidson.

19, David Peirson and Helen Henresone had Bessie ; witnesses, William
Cunningham, servant in Pitravie, Thomas Peirson, Robert Stanehous
in Dowloche.

22, James Simraell and Margaret Mudie had Robert ; witnesses, Robert
Davidson, Robert Wilson, Patrick Stevenson.

25, William Walwod, cordiner, and Margaret Lindsay had Helen ; witnesses,
Mr. Patrick Auchinleck, Thomas Jaksone, James Simsone, cordiner.

28, Andrew Mentethe and Bessie Fothringhame had Isobel ; witnesses,
William Cunningham, James Anghous, Henry Douglas.

28, Thomas Elder, flesher, and Helen Simsone had Nanse ; witnesses,
John Bennat, Mr. Patrick Auchinleck, James Reid, David Mitchell.

M. 1, James Walwod to Catherine Key.

15, Thomas Cunnon to Isobel Dewar.

18, Robert Scharpe to Nanse Kellok.

18, Thomas Jaksone to Helen Walwod.

29, John Broun to Helen Broun.

JANUARY [1636].

B. 3, David Wyld and Bessie Banks had a son, ... : witnesses, ...

3, James Stewart, mealmaker, and Elspet Mayne had twins, Grizel and
Janet ; witnesses, John Kellok, William Smart, George Durie,
William Mitchell.

3, Andrew Currie and Helen Stirk had Margaret ; witnesses, Andrew
Currie in Primrois, Robert Stirk, messenger, David Mitchell,
Thomas Wilson.

8, John Smetoun and Isobel Chopeman had Margaret (in fornication) ;
witnesses, James Eweine, Patrick Stevenson, James Simraell.

8, William Kellok in Pitravie and Bessie Trumble had John ; witnesses,
John Coventrie, John Watsone in Inverkeithing, David Cunnone,
portioner of Mastertoun.

9, Robert Stevenson and Elspet Davidson had Adam ; witnesses, Adam
Stevenson, Robert Davidson.

12, David Moreis of Baithe and Janet Lundie had David ; witnesses,
David Lundie, Mr. David Kingorne, David Hodge in the Foulfuird.

12, Alexander Young and Helen Whyt had Robert ; witnesses, Robert
Quhyt, Robert Young, James Cunningham in Pitadro.

12, John Neilsone and Janet Buist had Patrick ; witnesses, Patrick Trumble,
Peter Buist, James Richardson.

12, David Smetoun and Elspet Russell had David ; witnesses, James
Smetoun, Robert Russell, David Scotland.

18, John Thomson and Janet Huton had Isobel ; witnesses, William Wricht,
Patrick Trumble, David Trumble.

23, Robert Scharpe and Nanse Kellok had Robert (before their marriage) ; witnesses, James Kellok, Robert Kellok, William Kellok.

26, George Donald and Margaret Stevenson had David ; witnesses, David Mitchell in Pitlivar, David Sands in Gellat, David Horne in Culrois.

26, John Makunnoche and Janet Porteus had John ; witnesses, John Baid, John Robertson, John Alisone.

31, John Bryse and Helen Quhyt had Helen ; witnesses, Mr. Patrick Auchinleck, Robert Anderson in Gellat, Patrick Kingorne.

31, John Clerk, merchant, and Annas Portour had Margaret : witnesses. Mr. Patrick Auchinleck, James Reid, Alexander Drysdell.

31, James Cusine and Barbara Dewar (who died after her delivery) had Barbara ; witnesses, . . .

M. 12, John Moreis to Janet Moreis.

19, Thomas Mitchell to Helen Trumble.

26, John Huton to Janet Touchie.

FEBRUARY.

B. 1, John Hog and Margaret Thomson had Margaret ; witnesses, Mr. William Ged, Robert Livingstone, Andrew Thomson.

14, Thomas Dewar and Janet Peacok had David ; witnesses, David Robertson of Craigduckie, David Scotland, David Peacok.

14, Adam Car and Janet Crawfuird had George ; witnesses, William Hutone, David Tod, James Murgane.

14, James Anderson and Janet Miller had Adam ; witnesses, Adam Stobie, Nicol Wardlaw, James Murgane.

16, George Trumble in Bromehall and Helen Grinlay had George ; witnesses, Mr. James Phine, Adam Trumbull in Bromehall, David Mitchell in Pitlivar, Adam Trumble in the Grange, Patrick Grinlay.

21, Andrew Wilson and Janet Douglas had George ; witnesses, George Donald, Adam Wilson, David Mitchell.

21, John Robertson and Isobel Hutone had James ; witnesses, James Cunnon, Robert Cant, Thomas Peirsone.

28, Robert Tailyeour and Margaret Cunningham had Robert ; witnesses, Robert Turneley, Robert Cunningham in Sillitoun, Robert Cunningham in the Stone, Robert Wilson.

28, John (? Robert) Anderson and Margaret Gibson had James ; witnesses, James Mitchell, James Anderson, John Davidson, John Stanehous.

28, Henry Broun and Beatie Sands had Bessie ; witnesses, David Broun, David Sands, William Galrig.

28, James Clerk and Janet Beany had Jean ; witnesses, John Lindsay, William Anderson in Pitconnochie, John Peirson there.

28, Robert Anghous and Christian Drysdell had John ; witnesses, Robert Anghous. David Scotland, David Robertson of Craigduckie.

28, David Ferlie (?) and Nanse Chalmer had Nanse ; witnesses, George Trumble, James Broun, John Christie.

28, James Simsone, merchant, and Bessie Walker had John ; witnesses, Andrew Walker in Logie, Peter Law, William Walker, merchant. William Walker, maltman.

M. 2, John Dewar to Mage Burne.

4, John Wricht to Margaret Lawson.

7, David Waterstone to Margaret Workman.

11, James Primrois to Janet Tailyeour.

14, David Hodge to Catherine Smart.

MARCH.

B. 1, James Mudie, weaver, and Grizel Lambe had Helen ; witnesses, Robert Mudie, younger, Robert Kellok, John Gotterstone.

2, Robert Patrik and Elspet Low had Alexander ; witnesses, Alexander Drysdell, John Clerk, Henry Patrik.

6, Matthew Donaldson, horner, and Janet Young had William ; witnesses, William Anderson in Lymkills, William Anderson in Gellat, Thomas Douglas, David Sands there.

6, Robert Russell and Janet Mill had Bessie (in fornication) ; witnesses, Henry Crawfurd, Harry Blakwod, John Stirk, younger, in Pittincreiff.

6, John Quhyt and Margaret Kellok had John ; witnesses, John Kellok, John Kellok, his son, in the Bray, and William Kellok.

8, David Hutone, tailor, and Margaret Dempstertoun had Peter ; witnesses, Peter Buist, Peter Law, Thomas Davidson.

13, William Scotland and Margaret Robertson had Isobel ; witnesses, Robert Anghous, John Cusine, Adam Bryse.

13, Jean Murray had a son "borne to Johne Trumble quha deceavit the kirk, giffing himself forthe for ane unmaryit man and his wyff living in Falkirk, and upone his culourit and fals dealling and purchasing ane testimoniall from St. Laurence kirk he wes maryit with this Jeane. and the barne baptised and callit George" ; witnesses, Wattie Cant. Ninian Mather.

15, David Dewar in Campsieknowes and Dorothea Makstoun had Catherine ; witnesses, James Dewar, John Galrig, John Dewar.

20, James Peirson and Nanse Stevenson had John ; witnesses, David Peirson, John Peirson, his son, and George Donald.

20. Andrew Cowstoun and Catherine Wannan had Janet ; witnesses, John Coventrie, Robert Wilson, James Cowstoun.

20, John Stanehous and Jean Fentoun had Elspet ; witnesses, William Stanehous, John Davidson, James Mitchell.

20, James Robertson and Isobel Wallace had Henry ; witnesses, Henry Moreis, Henry Baverage, Laurence Hutone, weaver.

20, John Potter and Elspet Walker had Jean ; witnesses, Mr. David Kingorne, William Anderson, Thomas Cowper.

27, Thomas Stanehous and Barbara Dewar had Nanse ; witnesses, John Stanehous, James Kellok, John Gentleman.

M. 8, Andrew Wilson to Margaret Lethome.

APRIL.

B. 3, Henry Beany and Helen Wricht had Andrew ; witnesses. Andrew Wricht, John Beany, William Dougall.

3, James Dewar of Baithe and Helen Trumble had Margaret : witnesses, Peter Law (?), George Trumble, John Dewar.

5, John Litljohne and Janet Wilson had Helen ; witnesses, James Litljohne, Thomas Schortus, John Wilson.

7, James Car, mason (deceased), and Isobel Richardson had James : witnesses, Mr. Patrick Auchinleck, Peter Law, Peter Buist.

10, William Anderson in Pitconnochie and Agnes Chalmers had Thomas.

10, Robert Duncane and Margaret Tod had David (in fornication) ; witnesses, Andrew Wilson, David Tod in Pittincreiff, James Simraell, mason.

12, George Trumble and Marjory Maistertoun had Elspet ; witnesses, Adam Mastertoun of the Grange in Culros, Mr. James Dewar of Lassodie, William Mackie in Coklaw.

16. Andrew Kay and Janet Stevenson had Andrew ; witnesses. Andrew Currie, Thomas Douglas. Thomas Key.

17, William Cairns and Marjory Burgane had Marjory : witnesses, John Watson, Laurie Lugtoun, Harry Greg.

19, Leonard Henresone and Marjory Mudie had Andrew : witnesses, Patrick Stevenson, Andrew Broun, Andrew Mudie.

19, Henry Moreis and Isobel Duncane had Janet ; witnesses, David Moreis, John Stevenson, John Walker, merchant.

30. James Murgane and Elspet Bowman had George ; witnesses. Robert , Scotland, Robert Russell, Nicol Wardlaw.

M. 26, John Stevenson to Marjory Hugone.
   26, Robert Westwod to Margaret Kinsman.

MAY.

B. 8, James Patone and Isobel Watson had William ; witnesses, William
     Walcar, Archibald Boyd, Robert Quhyt.
   15, Harry Grege in the Ferrie and Bessie Broun had John ; witnesses, John
     Broun, Mark Doncane. (Baptised in Inverkeithing.)
   15, John Broun, messenger, and Effie Simsone had Margaret ; witnesses,
     John Cokburne, William Walker, merchant, James Simson.
   15, John Hugane and Cicile Glenn had John ; witnesses, John Workman,
     John Stevenson, Robert Miller.
   31, Andrew Thomesone, belman, and Janet Flokard had Isobel ; witnesses,
     Mr. John Drummond, Mr. John Walker, Mr. Harry Makgill.

M. 3, William Dougall to Janet Phinne.
   3, William Sanders to Catherine Cusine.
   31, John Wilson to Christian Harlay.

JUNE.

B. 12, Henry Broun and Effie Banks had Patrick.
   14, John Smart and Margaret Baverage had William ; witnesses, William
     Smart, Thomas Baverage, Thomas Elder.
   27, James Walwod, officer, and Catherine Key had Helen ; witnesses, Mr.
     David Kingorne, Mr. Bernard Gib, Peter Buist.

M. 7, James Thomson to Isobel Sanders.
   7, John Stevenson to Bessie Allane.
   12, James Trumble to Margaret Callendar.
   14, Laurie Greife to Margaret Vannan.
   14, James Smetoun to Janet Smetoun.
   14, John Leitche to Bessie Lawson.
   21, John Peirson to Janet Mentethe.
   21, James Hutone to Nanse Ogilbie.
   28, William Keir to Margaret Baid.
   28, John Keir to Catherine Dewar.

JULY.

B. 8, John Jamesone and Marion Dick had a daughter . . .
   8, David Bull, cutler, and Margaret Potter had Margaret : witnesses,
     William Walker, William Paterson, Andrew Thomson.
   23, David Broun, weaver, and Janet Dewar had Andrew : witnesses,
     Andrew Trumble, Andrew Dewar, Andrew Broun.
   23, John Car, weaver, and Bessie Clerk had William ; witnesses, William
     Lambe, William Mudie, David Lambe.
   23, James Reid and Marion Broun had Isobel ; witnesses, James Espline,
     Mr. David Kingorne, John Bennat.
   31, Andrew Muire and Christiane Lauthiane had John : witnesses, John
     Broun, William Swentone, John Gotterstone.

M. 5, Thomas Horne to Bessie Rowane.
   5, Adam Coventrie to Bessie Walwod.
   10, James Wilkie to Mage Muire.
   26, Nicol Henresone to Catherine Wels.
   26, James Cusine to Bessie Kinsman.

AUGUST.

B. 2, William Walker, maltman, and Marjory Broun had Andrew ; witnesses,
     Andrew Walker in Logie, James Murgane, Andrew Broun, smith.
   9, John Wilson in Galrighill and Margaret Anderson had a son . . . ;
     witnesses, Andrew Walker in Logie, John Litljohne, William Cois.

16, John Lindsay in Pitdinnie and Bessie Peirson had David ; witnesses, John Peirson, James Wilson, William Lawson.

17, James Kellok, tailor, and Nanse Aittone had Elspet ; witnesses, Mr. Patrick Auchinleck, Patrick Kingorne, David Stewart.

17, Thomas Jaksone and Helen Walwod had James ; witnesses, Sir James Halkat, James Henresone, George Davidson.

19, George Chopeman, weaver, and Grizel Glass had Thomas ; witnesses, Thomas Christie, Andrew Walker, George Meldrum.

29, Robert Murgane and Helen Smith had John ; witnesses, John Watson, Henry Sanderson, Alexander Melvill, all colliers.

M. 16, John Mill to Janet Trumball.

16, James Baverage to Janet Coventrie.

23, James Dunbar to Nanse Richardson.

30, David Currie to Alison Mitchell.

SEPTEMBER.

B. 18, James Trumble and Margaret Callendar had Helen ; witnesses, Thomas Mitchell, younger, Adam Trumble, George Trumble.

18, William Kirk and Margaret Woode had Elspet ; witnesses, David Currie, David Sands, Edward Douglas in Gellat.

20, William George and Elspet Miller had a daughter . . . ; witnesses, George Durie, William Cois, John Wilson.

20, Robert Tailyeour in the Lymkills and Margaret Young had William ; witnesses, William Anderson, William Young, David Murray.

25, David Inglis and Helen Lugton had William ; witnesses, James Lugtoun, William Dow, Robert Burne.

25, Archibald Fergie and Janet Murray had David ; witnesses, David Murray, Robert Thomson, John Wricht.

M. 18, John Steill to Jean Ramsay.

OCTOBER.

B. 2, Robert Young and Margaret Broun had Elspet ; witnesses, Robert Kellok, younger, David Cunnon, Simeon Broun.

6, James Litljohne and Christian Chrichtoun had James, witnesses, James Litljohne, Thomas Schortus, John Warkman, tailor.

7, John Stevenson, smith, and Marjory Hugoun had Adam ; witnesses, Adam Stevenson, Robert Stevenson, Laurence Stevinson.

16, Thomas Hutone and Isobel Keir had Isobel ; witnesses, George Walker in Logie, David Sands in Gellat, Adam Currie in Primrois.

18, James Espleine, servitor to Charles, Earl of Dunfermline, and Margaret Coldene had Alexander ; witnesses, . . .

25, James Mill and Grizel Robertson had Henry ; witnesses, Henry Mill, Thomas Christie, Mr. William Wardlaw.

30, John Broun in the Ferrie and Helen Broun had Janet ; witnesses, Robert Drysdell, Robert Broun, Harry Grege. (Baptised in Inverkeithing.)

30, John Ritchie and Christian Blakwod had Robert ; witnesses, Robert Anghous, James Mill, Robert Russell.

M. 25, John Hasswell to Christian Chaipe.

NOVEMBER.

B. 8, George Durie and Margaret Broun had William ; witnesses, William Merser, Mr. Patrick Auchinleck, William Anderson, Thomas Christie.

20, Alexander Greg and Janet Burgane had Harry ; witnesses, John Burgane, Harry Cant, Harry Greg. (Baptised in Inverkeithing).

20, George Henresone in Fod and Margaret Reid had James ; witnesses, James Mitchell, James Anderson, Andrew Broun, smith in the hospital.

27, Patie Harrower and Janet Mann had Christian ; witnesses, William Anderson, David Currie, Thomas Donaldson.

27, Andrew Flokhart and Isobel Peat had Janet ; witnesses, David Flokhart, John Flokhart, Robert Dewar.

27, Harry Richardson and Christian Peacok had George ; witnesses, John Gotterstone, William Mudie, James Mitchell, wright.

M. 7, Cornelius Johnstone to Catherine Murray.

7, John Flokart to Isobel Peat.

7, Mr. William Makgill, doctor of physic, to Catherine Wardlaw.

27, William Lyall to Elspet Lyall.

29, John Kellok to Isobel Hassuell.

DECEMBER.

B. 4, William Walwod, younger, in Toughe, and Margaret Wardlaw had William ; witnesses, William Walwod, Nicol Wardlaw, Robert Davidson, James Wardlaw.

4, John Kellok and Janet Stirk had William (in fornication) ; witnesses, William Kellok, his father, John Kellok, John Wilson.

11, Pate Makgaw and Bessie Bardner had John (in fornication) ; witnesses, John Lawson, Cornelius Johnstone.

18, Mr. David Kingorne and Jean Lundie had William.

20, Charles, Earl of Dunfermline, and Dame Mary Douglas had Margaret ; witnesses, Lord of Dalkeith and Lord Home.

27, George Tailyeour and Nanse Hutone had Robert ; witnesses, Robert Tailyeour, Robert Cunningham, Robert Turneley, Robert Douglas.

27, Thomas Cunnone in Mastertoun and Isobel Dewar had Helen ; witnesses, James Cunnon, David Flokard, Robert Dewar.

27, William Smart, flesher, and Bessie Stevenson had Christian ; witnesses, Peter Law, David Hodge, Peter Buist.

M. 12, James Flokkart to Margaret Stalker.

12, James Kellok to Marjory Schortus.

19, John Walker to Jean Gowie.

19, Lawrence Walker to Nanse Wischert.

29, William Orolk to Janet Walwod.

JANUARY [1637].

B. 1, James Primrois and Janet Talyeour had John ; witnesses, John Tallier, George Donald, George Tallier.

2, John Cambell, gardener in Pitfirran, and Margaret Robertson had Robert ; witnesses, William Anderson in Pitconnochie, Andrew Mentethe, William Trumble, smith.

8, Andrew Anderson and Margaret Rae had Jean ; witnesses, William Cunningham, John Lindsay, William Nicole.

10, John Wricht and Margaret Lawson had Andrew ; witnesses, John Lawson, Charles Lawson, Henry Wricht.

10, David Robertson and Grizel Hutone had Robert ; witnesses, George Dewar, Robert Anghous, James Mill.

15, Robert Straquhen and Bessie Nicole had John ; witnesses, John Straquhen, John Walwod, John Wanderstone.

15, James Mitchell and Christian Thomson had Janet ; witnesses, Thomas Cowper, David Laurie, David Broun.

19, Thomas Mitchell, younger, in Gellat, and Helen Trumble had twins, Helen, and another stillborn ; witnesses, David Mitchell, David Currie, Andrew Burne.

22, Andrew Wilson in Baldrig and Margaret Lethome had William (baptised in Carnock) ; witnesses, Adam Wilson, William Lethome, William Lawson.

22, John Anderson and Margaret Gibson had Harry; witnesses, Harry
Stewart of Baithe, George Wardlaw, Thomas Philpe. (Baptised in
Inverkeithing.)

24, John Stirk and Bessie Crawfurd had Henry; witnesses, George
Meldrum, Henry Crawford, George Stirk.

25, Mr. Robert Anderson, musician, and Marion Dewar had Robert;
witnesses, Peter Law, John Wricht, Mr. Robert Smyth.

29, John Wilsone and Christian Harla had Helen: witnesses, William
Hutone, John Cusine, James Mill.

M. 1, John Simsone to Margaret Makcartour.

1, William Keir to Christian Peirson.

FEBRUARY.

B. 2, Andrew Christie, miller, and Helen Currie had David : witnesses, David
Mitchell, David Sands, David Currie.

5, James Hutone and Nanse Ogilvie had James; witnesses, James Peirson,
John Lindsay, William Anderson.

5, Andrew Cant and Christian Bull had Elspet : witnesses, Robert Cant,
James Cunnon, William Kirk.

12, John Ædisone, miller, and Isobel Huntar had a son . . . : witnesses,
Robert Tailyeour, Robert Ædisone, Andrew Cunningham, weaver.

26, Andrew Williamson and Janet Barker had Harry ; witnesses, Harry
Thomson, Harry Cant, John Thomesone. (Baptised in Inverkeithing.)

26, James Dick and Margaret Kilgour had William ; witnesses, John Dick,
William Kilgour, James Bruse.

M. 12, Robert Logane to Christian Hutone.

12, Andrew Privous to Janet Stevenson.

12, George Young to Bessie Low.

21, Andrew Chopeman to Barbara Hutone.

23, David Scotland to Elspet Dewar.

MARCH.

B. 6, Andrew Currie and Helen Stirk had Janet ; witnesses, George Donald,
Robert Stirk, Adam Currie.

7, David Hodge and Catherine Smart had Margaret ; witnesses, William
Smart, James Hamilton, James Simsone, merchant.

12, James Walwod and Helen Inglis had Helen : witnesses, James Baverage,
John Walwod, John Inglis.

12, John Wels in Keirsbaith and Margaret Stevenson had a daughter . . . ;
witnesses, John Stevenson, David Moreis, Henry Moreis, all in Baithe.

14, James Anghous in Crocefuird and Janet Gilespie had Margaret :
witnesses, Sir Robert Halkat and Sir James Halkat of Pitfirran, and
Peter Douglas.

17, Archibald Honyman, baker, and Margaret Wels had Janet : witnesses,
John Wels, Nicol Henresone, James Dunbar, tailor.

28, Andrew Chopeman and Barbara Hutone had Janet : witnesses, Andrew
Walcar, William Walker, merchant, Thomas Chrystie in the Hoile.

28, David Robertson and Elspet Bosswell had Bessie ; witnesses, Andrew
Thomson, James Moyas, John Robertson.

M. [*None.*]

APRIL.

B. 2, Mark Donald, baker, and Marjory Bennat had Margaret; witnesses,
James Espline, James Reid, Thomas Scotland.

11, James Mayne and Christian Johnstone had Margaret ; witnesses,
Thomas Cowper, Robert Davidson, John Cunningham.

11, David Stewart, cordiner, and Helen Kirkland had James : witnesses
James Simsone, cordiner, James Kirkland, John Tod in Aberdour.

13, James Bennat and Effie Johnstone had Mark (in fornication); witnesses, Mark Donald, Peter Buist, Adam Wylie.

15, William Mudie, maltman in the Nethertoun, and Janet Christie had Janet; witnesses, Andrew Walcar, James Cunningham, Adam Currie, William Walcar, maltman.

16, Andrew Trumble, baker, and Barbara Law had John; witnesses, John Walcar, bailie, John Wricht, John Bennat.

23, John Walker and Margaret Dewar had a daughter . . . ; witnesses, Robert Scotland, Thomas Hutone, James Wardlaw.

23, John Dewar and Christian Bossuell had Jean; witnesses, Mr. James Dewar of Lassodie, Mr. John Chalmers, younger, George Dewar in Lathamond.

25, John Mayne and Margaret Bennat had Andrew; witnesses, Andrew Mayne, William Mayne, James Mayne.

M. 4, Thomas Hutone to Bessie Stobie (in Carnok kirk).

18, Robert Tait to Janet Car.

30, Adam Stanehous to Christian Broun.

MAY.

B. 1, Laurie Greif and Margaret Wannan had John; witnesses, John Bennat, Peter Buist, Mark Donald.

3, Thomas Christie of the Hoill and Espet Durie had Margaret; witnesses, Andrew Walker, David Sands, William Mudie.

7, James Cusine and Bessie Kinsman had Janet; witnesses, William Hutone, John Cusine, James Mudie.

9, David Mitchell in Pitlivar and Margaret Currie had Sarah; witnesses, James Leslie, elder of Pitlivar, James Leslie, his son, and James Reid.

13, Mr. Harry Makgill, minister, and Margaret Wardlaw had a daughter . . . ; witnesses, John Bennat, Mr. John Walker, Patrick Kingorne, Tobiah Murebeck.

13, Tobiah Murebeck and Christian Cant had Anna; witnesses, Mr. Harry Makgill, John Bennat, Patrick Kingorne, James Espline.

21, Laurence Walker and Nanse Wischett had John; witnesses, John Walker, Peter Law, David Stewart, cordiner.

26, James Simsone, merchant, and Bessie Walker had William; witnesses, Andrew Walker, William Walker, merchant, John Broun, messenger.

28, James Anderson and Elspet Christie had Harry; witnesses, Harry Stewart of Baithe, William Anderson, litster, Peter Walker.

28, James Dunbar and Nanse Richardson had Catherine; witnesses, Patrick Dunbar, James Kellok, Robert Anderson, tailor.

28, John Muire and Nanse Schiphird had Mary; witnesses, James Espline, Thomas Christie, John Cokburne.

M. 28, James Clerk to Nanse Æssone.

JUNE.

B. 2, "Ane woman calling hir self Janet Archbald, maryit as scho deponeit on ane tailyeour in Dundie callit Johne Cokburne, and being poire scho come from hir husband of purpois to gadder woll in the Southland, and fell in into Dunfermlyne with vagabund husies quha wer takin for abuseing the Kingis leagis with outing watterit turnouris or tua penny peices and outit them for 20 penny peices, in the tyme that scho wes in prisone scho being with chyld takis hir travell and bringis furthe ane womanbairne, quhilk wes baptized in the kirk of Dunfermlyne and callit Janet": witnesses, Andrew Thomson, belman, George Davidson and Harry Bull, burgesses of Dunfermline.

4, James Walwod and Catherine Kay had William; witnesses, William Mentethe of Randifurd, Mr. David Kingorne and Patrick Kingorne, "clerkis of burghe and regalitie," and William Ferrie, servitor to the Earl of Dunfermline.

11, George Remainous and Catherine Dewar had Robert ; witnesses, George Dewar, Robert Anghous, John Remainous.

14, William Merser, advocate, indweller in Dunfermline, and Isobel Goatts had Jean ; witnesses, Mr. William Makgill, George Bothwell, Mr. Patrick Auchinleck.

14, Robert Ged of Baldrige and Eupham Orolk had Alexander (born 13th) ; witnesses, Mr. William Makgill, doctor of physic, George Bothwell, James Reid, provost of Dunfermline.

18, Archibald Boyd, cordiner, and Janet Watson had Helen ; witnesses, David Stewart, James Æssone, David Peirson in Douarhill.

25, John Coventrie and Janet Walwod had Margaret ; witnesses, James Watson, William Kellok, John Gentleman.

M. 6, John Inglis to Isobel Trumble.

25, William Forrest to Margaret Galrig.

JULY.

B. 2, James Knox and Helen Wels had Alexander ; witnesses, Alexander Wels, David Dewar of Lassodie, William Dewar.

2, Robert Mudie and Helen Mudie had Thomas ; witnesses, Thomas Stanehous, Thomas Cunnon, John Gentleman, James Kellok, all in Mastertoun.

5, John Wilson and Barbara Kellok had Margaret ; witnesses, John Clerk, merchant, Gilbert Car. Adam Wylie.

5, David Scott and Isobel Broun had Robert ; witnesses, Robert Hutone, James Broun, John Anderson, notary.

9, James Simsone, cordiner, and Isobel Beithe had Robert ; witnesses, David Stewart, George Davidson, Thomas Elder.

11, William Anderson, bailie, and Margaret Cowper had John ; witnesses, John Bennat, John Walker, merchant.

11, Mr. William Ged and Barbara Thomson had John (in fornication) ; witnesses, . . .

18, John Peirson and Janet Mentethe had John ; witnesses, John Bennat, Thomas Elder, David Tod.

23, John Whyt and Margaret Kellok had William ; witnesses, William Kellok, John Kellok, Andrew Rowane.

26, George Dewar in Lathamond and Mary Chalmers had John ; witnesses, Mr. John Chalmers, minister in Auchterderane. John Dewar in Bandrum, John Dewar in Lassodie.

26, Thomas Keir and Helen Yowane had Margaret ; witnesses, John Keir, David Galrige, Robert Yowane.

28, Robert Meldrum and Christian Smart had Elspet ; witnesses, George Meldrum, John Smart, elder, John Smart, younger.

28, Nicol Henresone and Catherine Wels had Robert ; witnesses, John Wels, Archibald Honyman, John Smetoun.

M. 11, William Young to Margaret Peirson.

27, George Dagleische to Catherine Hutone (in Saline kirk).

AUGUST.

B. 2, Thomas Elder, flesher, and Helen Simsone had Thomas ; witnesses, Alexander Moutrey in the Wodend, James Reid, John Bennat, James Espline, David Mitchell.

13, Andrew Cunningham and Margaret Ædisone had Henry ; witnesses, Sir Henry Wardlaw of Pitravie, Andrew Cunningham and Andrew Cunningham in Primrois (*sic*). (Baptised in Torrie kirk.)

15, David Smythe and Alison Simsone had David ; witnesses, John Hekfurd, James Lugtoun, Duncan Tailyeour.

15, James Kellok, tailor, and Marjory Schortus had Margaret ; witnesses, Mr. Patrick Auchinleck, Patrick Kingorne, James Moyas.

15, Cornelius Johnstone and Catherine Murray had Andrew ; witnesses, David Mitchell, Mr. James Phin, John Bennat.

20, David Currie in Gellat and Alison Mitchell had Marjory ; witnesses, Thomas Mitchell, David Mitchell, John Currie.

20, Henry Douglas and Margaret Cunningham had William ; witnesses, William Cunningham, Edward Douglas, Thomas Douglas, Thomas Wilson.

27, William Hutone and Catherine Mill had Christian ; witnesses, James Durie, Mr. William Wardlaw, Robert Angous.

27, Laurence Watson, cordiner, and Grizel Wilson had David ; witnesses, David Watson, David Stewart, David Maxwell.

M. 8, Thomas Young to Janet Hakerstone.

15, Robert Baxter to Bessie Anderson.

SEPTEMBER.

B. 3, William Sanders and Catherine Cusine had James ; witnesses, Sir James Halket, fiar of Pitfirrane, John Cusine, William Hutone.

3, William Mackie and Margaret Betsone had Isobel ; witnesses, Alexander Moutrey, James Betsone, Andrew Mackie.

10, Thomas Gardner and Bessie Stevin had Helen (in fornication) ; witnesses, John Lindsay, John Hutone.

22, Alexander Chalmers, merchant, and Catherine Walker had George (baptised 24th) ; witnesses, Andrew Walker, George Walcar, William Walker, merchants.

22, John Wilson in the Crocegats and Jean Angous (who died in her travail) had Marjory ; witnesses, Henry Baverage, James Broun, Henry Baverage (*sic*).

24, Andrew Donaldson and Catherine Huntar had Helen ; witnesses, Thomas Christie, David Sands, George Meldrum.

24, James Hutone and Mary Dempstertoun had Barbara ; witnesses, Mr. James Ready, Andrew Privous, Adam Wylie.

30, James Reid, provost, and Marion Broun had Mary.

M. 6, Thomas Cowper to Isobel Walwod (in Carnok).

OCTOBER.

B. 1, James Brown and Helen Stobie had Adam ; witnesses, Adam Stobie, Adam Broun, Adam Stanehous, William Walker, William Smithe.

1, James Peirson and Nanse Stevenson had Helen ; witnesses, David Peirson, John Peirson.

1, James Legat and Margaret Stirk had William ; witnesses, William Legat, William Stirk, Patrick Legat.

1, John Alisone, wright, and Grizel Walwod had Isobel ; witnesses, James Baverage, Adam Coventrie, James Dunbar.

1, John Simson and Margaret Makartour had Margaret ; witnesses, Henry Hakstoun, James Anderson, George Trumble.

6, James Durie of Craigluscour and . . . . Durie had Robert ; witnesses, Sir Robert Halkat of Pitfirrane, Sir James, his son, and Robert Merser of the Kirkland in Sauling.

9, Patrick Kingorne and Margaret Forrester had George ; witnesses, George Bothwell, James Durie, Mr. James Redy.

10, George Trumble in Baithe and Marjory Mastertoun had Catherine ; witnesses, Alexander Aitkine, William Walker, merchant, George Trumble in Bromehall.

10, David Cunnon in Mastertoun and Elspet Dewar had Adam ; witnesses, Adam Logane, Peter Law, Robert Kellok in Mastertoun.

15, David Blak and Marjory Blakwod had Alexander (baptised in Cleish) ; witnesses, Alexander Moutrey, John Makie, John Aikine.

15, David Flokard and Bessie Dewar had Margaret ; witnesses, Andrew Thomson, George Davidson, Andrew Cunningham.

15, David Sim and Margaret Meldrum had Elspet ; witnesses, George Meldrum, John Stirk, John Gotterstone.

21, James Baverage and Janet Steidman had John (baptised in Cleish) ; witnesses, William Milne, John Baverage and John Baverage, both in Coklaw.

21, Patrick Broun and Bessie Mudie had Margaret ; witnesses, James Stanehous, James Dewar, Henry Baverage.

21, James Flokart and Margaret Stalker had Janet ; witnesses, David Flokart, Robert Dewar, Andrew Thomson.

24, John Hodge in Foulfuird and Effie Broun had Effie ; witnesses, John Stevenson of Bayth, David Moreis, John Orolk, all in Bayth.

29, William Inglis and Bessie Cowper had Janet ; witnesses, Thomas Cowper, William Anderson, Andrew Trumble in Grange.

M. 16, Walter Cokburne to Janet Peirs.

23, John Davidson to Elspet Walwod.

NOVEMBER.

B. 5, John Lawson and Catherine Logane had Thomas ; witnesses, Thomas Douglas, Thomas Nasmithe, Thomas Lawson.

5, James Hamilton and Jean Lauder had Mary ; witnesses, Adam Stobie, Robert Scotland.

5, John Aikine and Christian Dagleische had Alexander ; witnesses, David Blak, George Trumble, James Dewar in Baithe.

5, John Walker and Jean Gowie had David ; witnesses, Mr. John Walker, Mr. Patrick Auchinleck, John Walker, dean of guild.

7, William Keir and Margaret Baid had Bessie ; witnesses, William Keir, John Baid, William Trumble.

9, George Trumble and Helen Grinlay had Janet ; witnesses, Robert Ged of Baldrig, Mr. William Ged, William Grinlay.

12, James Henresone and Mayas Aikine had John ; witnesses, John Kellok, William Legat, James Feg.

19, Robert Dewar and Margaret Flokart had Andrew ; witnesses, Andrew Thomson, James Mayne, David Flokart.

19, John Ramsay, collier, and Christian Thrislo had Laurence ; witnesses, Laurie Greive, John Hog, John Watson.

19, Robert Logane and Christian Hutone had John ; witnesses, Robert Davidson, Henry Davidson, John Smetone.

21, James Espline, servitor to Charles, Earl of Dunfermline, and Margaret Colden had Mary.

24, James Horne and Janet Ædisone had Isobel (in fornication) ; witnesses, George Meldrum, Andrew Thomson.

25, Henry Sanderson and Elspet Rammache had Marjory ; witnesses, Tobias Murebeck, James Waterstoun, Robert Broun.

26, Adam Currie in Primrois and Catherine Christie had Margaret ; witnesses, David Mitchell, Andrew Walker, James Cunningham.

26, James Miller and Nanse Kirk had Margaret ; witnesses, George Donald, John Tailyeour, Andrew Donald.

26, William Kent and Isobel Broun had William ; witnesses, William Walker, bailie, William Gibon, Adam Stobie.

M. 7, Wattie Ritchie to Bessie Mitchell.

26, Patrick Broun to Nanse Young.

DECEMBER.

B. 3, Thomas Douglas and Elspet Chalmers had Edward ; witnesses, Edward Douglas, Robert Kellok, John Gentleman.

5, Robert Anderson and Margaret Weitat had James ; witnesses, James Anderson, John Anderson, James Mitchell.

10, James Ritchie and Christian Anderson had Robert ; witnesses, Mark Duncan, Robert Ritchie, Robert Anderson.

14, James Sumraell and Margaret Mudie had John ; witnesses, John Chatto, John Duncane, John Laurie, John Smetone.

16, David Maxwell and Nanse Hamilton had Violet ; witnesses, Andrew Mekiljohne, Mr. Patrick Fleck, William Walker, William Anderson.

26, Robert Talyeour and Margaret Cunningham had Isobel ; witnesses, Andrew Trumble, Thomas Cowper, Patrick Stevenson, John Kellok.

27, James Gray and Isobel Broun had John ; witnesses, James Legat, William Legat, John Kellok.

27, George Durie and Margaret Broun had George ; witnesses, George Bothwell, James Reid, Mr. Patrick Auchinleck, Peter Buist.

31, James Mill and Catherine Blacatter had Henry ; witnesses, James Kellok, Thomas Stanehous, Henry Mill.

31, William Inche and Margaret James had Grizel ; witnesses, John Stirk, George Meldrum, Robert Scharpe.

M. 5, James Cumming to Margaret Currie.

21. Henry Patrik to Isobel Mill.

JANUARY [1638].

B. 7, Robert Inglis and Isobel Bruse had Robert : witnesses, Robert Anghous, Robert Russell, David Scotland.

7, Thomas Arnott and Elspet Schort had Thomas ; witnesses, James Schort, Thomas Curror, James Arnott, Thomas Peirson.

7, Thomas Jaksone and Helen Walwod had Robert : witnesses, Sir Robert Halket of Pittirrane, Sir James Halket, Robert Halket.

7, John Fergie and Nanse Wricht had Helen : witnesses, John Lindsay, John Peirson, James Peirson.

11, Robert Tait, master cook in the Abbey, and Janet Car had Charles ; witnesses, Charles, Earl of Dunfermline, Thomas Elder, Andrew Thomson, Thomas Christie, William Ferrie.

14, Thomas Cumming and Marion Douglas had James ; witnesses, James Anderson, George Meldrum, Thomas Beinstone.

16, Robert Anghous and Isobel Dewar had Mary ; witnesses, John Dewar, Robert Dewar, William Robertson.

16, David Sands in Gellat and Bessie Christie had Thomas ; witnesses, Thomas Chrystie, Thomas Douglas, Thomas Wilson.

18, James Hamilton and Isobel Bronn had Isobel : witnesses, Archibald Colyeir, Andrew Colyeir.

24, Thomas Hutone in Luscour and Bessie Stobie had Helen : witnesses, Nicol Wardlaw, Adam Stobie, William Scotland.

24, George Stirk and Elspet Walker had George : witnesses, George Meldrum, John Muire, John Walker.

28, William Mudie, weaver, and Nanse Makie had Nanse ; witnesses, Robert Steinsone, James Anderson, John Bennat.

31, John Davidson and Elspet Walwod had Charles ; witnesses, Patrick Kingorne, William Walker, bailie, Jamie Hamilton.

M. 5, Robert Schortus to Margaret Cunningham (in Carnok kirk).

11, John Cois to Janet Trumble.

23, James Mudie to Bessie Cunningham.

25, James Deis to Catherine Westwod.

30, John Wanderstone to Isobel Leslie.

FEBRUARY.

B. 4, William Anderson and Isobel Russell had Janet ; witnesses, William Mudie, John Burne, William Cowper.

5, William Gahrige and Helen Broun had Margaret ; witnesses, Andrew Trumble, George Trumble, William Inglis.

6, John Anderson and Margaret Cadell had Isobel : witnesses, William Cunningham, Patrick Anderson, John Lawsone.

11, Robert Broun in Leith and Anna Lessells had twins, James and Robert (in fornication); witnesses, James Anghous, James Lawson, John Lawson, John Wanderstone.

13, John Inglis and Janet Kinmond had Isobel (in fornication); witnesses, James Herein, James Cusine.

18, George Ædisone and Bessie Sands had William; witnesses, William Anderson in Gellat, William Anderson in Lymkills, David Sands.

18, Thomas Cowper in the Newra and Isobel Walwod had Patrick; witnesses, Mr. David Kingorne, William Anderson, litster, Patrick Kingorne.

18, David Galrig and Margaret Yowne had Catherine; witnesses, John Gotterstone, William Mudie, weaver, William Lambe.

20, James Dewar in Pitbachlie and Isobel Hutone had Catherine; witnesses, Robert Dewar, Andrew Dewar and Robert Dewar.

20, John Makinlay and Catherine Watterstone had Catherine; witnesses, Alexander Melvill, John Nicole, William Beane.

20, James Trumble and Margaret Callendar had Margaret; witnesses, Andrew Trumble in Grange, William Inglis, Alexander Inglis.

25, Thomas Cunnon and Isobel Dewar had James; witnesses, James Cunnon, James Kellok, James Dewar.

25, John Mill and Marjory Dewar had a daughter . . . .

25, Rob Schortus and Margaret Cunningham had William; witnesses, William Lawson, William Anderson.

25, James Anderson and Isobel Inglis had Alexander; witnesses, Alexander Inglis, George Meldrum, David Makbethe.

M. 8, Henry Phine to Christian Hamilton.
22, William Westwod to Janet Johnston.

MARCH.

B. 5, Henry Moreis and Isobel Duncane had David; witnesses, David Moreis, John Stevenson, Harry Stewart.

5, James Dick and Margaret Kilgour had James; witnesses, John Anderson, John Bruse, James Bruse.

5, John Keir and Catherine Dewar had Isobel; witnesses, David Burn, Robert Burne, Robert Currie.

5, Peter Buist and Isobel Walwod had James; witnesses, James Reid, James Kellok, Edward Douglas.

5, John Skeine and Helen Durie had Anna; witnesses, Sir Robert Halket of Pitfirrane, William Merser, George Bothwell.

9, John Potter and Marion Clerk had Marjory; witnesses, John Potter, John Trumble, John Alisone, wright.

11, John Fentone and Margaret Lessells had Margaret (in fornication); witnesses, Thomas Christie, Robert Mercer, David Spens.

19, William Garvie and Bessie Walkar had Adam; witnesses, Adam Currie, Andrew Currie, James Garvie.

25, William Pillonis and Isobel Douglas had Robert; witnesses, Robert Cunningham, Adam Wilson, Andrew Trumble.

25, James Anderson and Janet Gray had Grizel; witnesses, William Anderson, Thomas Baverage, William Lawson.

25, Robert Anghous in Rescobie and Marion Dewar had Isobel; witnesses, George Dewar, William Huton, Robert Anghous.

26, James Cunnone and Bessie Garvie had Catherine; witnesses, Andrew Currie, Adam Currie, William Garvie.

30, John Broun in the Ferrie and Barbara Thomson had twins, William and Alexander; witnesses, William Cairnis, William Burgane, Harry Cant, Harry Greg, Alexander Greg.

M. 20, Thomas Peirson to Grizel Thomas.
20 Patrick Merschell to Nanse Gray.
27, Andrew Wilson to Bessie Peirson.

T

APRIL.

B. 1, Andrew Kellok and Margaret Stocks had Thomas; witnesses, Nicol Dewar, John Kellok, John Gray.

1, James Deis and Catherine Westwod had William; witnesses, Mr. William Wardlaw, William Smart, Thomas Baverage.

8. Robert Greive and Margaret Douglas had Isobel; witnesses, Thomas Elder, Andrew Rowan, David Scotland.

8, John Adame and Margaret Greg had John; witnesses, John Bennat, baker, Robert Stirk, messenger, James Hamilton.

8, John Wels, baker, and Catherine Drummond had Isobel; witnesses, William Walker, bailie, John Bennat, Thomas Elder.

17, John Murie and Elspet Anderson had Catherine; witnesses, Andrew Cunningham, David Currie, George Trumble.

22, Thomas Dewar and Janet Peacok had Elizabeth; witnesses, William Hutoun, James Mill, Robert Anghous.

24, John Inglis and Isobel Trumble had Janet : witnesses, William Hutone, Robert Anghus, Robert Russell.

24. John Lawson and Catherine Drysdell had Margaret : witnesses, Andrew Currie, David Mitchell, George Donald.

24. Adam Coventrie and Bessie Walwod had Nanse; witnesses, John Coventrie, James Baverage, Patrick Murray.

24. William Murra and Christian Mudie had Helen; witnesses, George Trumble, Thomas Key, Andrew Trumble.

26, John Broun, waterman, and Marion Allane had John; witnesses, Alexander Beane, James Broun, Thomas Fraser.

29, David Peirsone and Helen Henresone had Elizabeth ; witnesses, Thomas Stanehous, John Gentleman, Robert Broun.

29, William Mudie and Janet Johnstone had Janet : witnesses, John Trumble, John Litljohn, Robert Wels.

M. 8, Thomas Gardner to Bessie Peacok.

24, Thomas Davidson to Janet Walker.

MAY.

B. 8, Andrew Trumble, lorimer, and Janet Anderson had John ; witnesses, John Wricht, John Bruse, John Trumble, lorimer.

20, William Penman and Cicile Achesone had Margaret ; witnesses, James Anderson, William Nicole, William Anderson.

20. James Anderson and Janet Clerk had James : witnesses, James Hutone, John Car, William Cunningham.

22, John Wels and Margaret Stevenson had Alexander ; witnesses, David Moreis, John Stevenson, Robert Maistertoun.

M. 22, John Walwod to Mary Anderson.

24, William Lethome to Janet Wilson.

24, William Mudie to Margaret Phillane.

27, Gilbert Makcraiche to Margaret Mudie.

JUNE.

B. 10, John Straquhen and Isobel Fothringhame had Margaret ; witnesses, Robert Straquhen, William Straquhen, Andrew Mentethe, miller.

10, William Anderson in Gellat and Catherine Cunningham had David ; witnesses, David Mitchell, David Sands, Thomas Douglas.

12. John Cusine and Nanse Foote had Nanse : witnesses, William Hutone, John Sands, George Dewar.

24. Archibald Cunningham and Isobel Broun had Janet (in fornication); witnesses, George Davidson, James Mayne, Robert Cunningham in Sillitoun.

24. John Watson, cordiner, and Barbara Bruce had Robert ; witnesses, Robert Miller, James Simsone, cordiner, David Stewart.

M. 3, John Young to Margaret Adamson.
12, Andrew Speir to Nanse Hardie.
12, Thomas Bennat to Catherine Riddoche.
12, James Imrie to Margaret Wardlaw.
26, Thomas Fraser to Margaret Henreson.

JULY.

B. 1, David Dewar and Dorothea Maxtone had Marjory ; witnesses, William Mudie, maltman, James Dewar, Andrew Broun.
3, Patrick Makgrow and Bessie Bairdner had Grizel (in fornication) ; witnesses, David Anderson, John Anderson, Andrew Thomson.
6, Robert Baxter and Bessie Anderson had Robert ; witnesses, James Reid, William Walker, Mr. David Kingorne.
8, Wattie Richardsone and Bessie Mitchell had Marion ; witnesses, James Mitchell, Laurie Neilson, William Trumble.
8, John Kellok and Isobel Hasswell had Margaret ; witnesses, James Kellok, "John Kellok and John Kellok, the father and the sone."
15, Andrew Burne and Elspet Ritchie had Thomas ; witnesses, Thomas Ritchie, Thomas Mitchell, Robert Burne.
15, John Lawson in Crocefuird and Margaret Wilson had John ; witnesses, John Peirsone, John Lindsay, John Wilson.
15, James Cusine and Bessie Kinsman had John ; witnesses, John Cusine, John Hutone, William Hutone.
19, James Kellok, portioner of Mastertoun, and Margaret Mudie had Nanse ; witnesses, James Cunnon, John Gentleman and James Mudie.
22, Thomas Beinstone and Margaret Horne had Christian ; witnesses, John Stirk, George Stirk, George Meldrum.
22, "Thomas Tod in the Clun ane fourtene dayis befoir this day declaired that he had ane barne baptized in Carnok kirk, baptized and callit Thomas."
27, James Wilkie and Marjory Mure had James ; witnesses, James Mudie, weaver, William Legat, Robert Steinsone.
29, William Anderson and Janet Cunningham had James ; witnesses, James Anghous, James Hutone, James Hutone, grieve in Pitfirrane.
29, James Patone and Isobel Watson had Janet ; witnesses, Robert Quhyt, James Mudie, James Waterstone.

M. 3, John Kellok to Mary Weyms.
10, Henry Meldrum to Geils Chatto.
17, Robert Wels to Janet Wylie.
17, Robert Broun to Nanse Saverell.
31, John Meldrum to Christian Blakwod.

AUGUST.

B. 5, Patrick Merschell and Nanse Gray had John ; witnesses, John Lawson, William Lawson, John Leitche.
8, David Hutone and Margaret Dempster had Christian ; witnesses, Thomas Davidson, James Hutone, Andrew Privous.
13, William Wilsone, cordiner, and Margaret Watson had John ; witnesses, John Wilson, James Simsone, cordiner, Archibald Boyd.
13, Andrew Flokart and Isobel Peat had Margaret ; witnesses, Thomas Cowper, David Flokart, Andrew Mayne.
14, William Mackie and Margaret Betsone had a son . . . . (baptised in Balingrie kirk).
17, Patrick Stevenson and Christian Mudie had Janet ; witnesses, Thomas Cowper, Robert Davidson, John Coventrie.
17, Laurie Steinsone and Catherine Chatto had Elspet ; witnesses, Andrew Privous, Robert Steinsone, Thomas Cowper.
17, Laurie Greive and Margaret Wannan had Marion ; witnesses, James Reid, John Robertson, Charles Baid.

21, William Mudie, maltman, and Janet Christie had Janet; witnesses, Andrew Walker, Mr. George Walker, Thomas Cowper, Thomas Reid.

21, John Potter and Janet Inglis had Margaret; witnesses, Robert Steinsone, James Mitchell, Harry Richardson.

23, John Stevinson and Bessie Allane had Andrew; witnesses, Andrew Lessells, William Anderson, James Anderson.

M. 7, John Dewar to Effie Robertson.

12, John Wilson to Elspet Dinn (in Sauling kirk).

21, William Straquhen to Elspet Grahame (in Cleish kirk).

SEPTEMBER.

B. 2, Alexander Greg and Janet Burgane had Robert; witnesses, Robert Burgane, Robert Broun, Laurie Lugtone.

7, Sir James Halkat of Pitfirrane and Dame Margaret Montgomrie, his lady, had Mary; witnesses, Charles, Earl of Dunfermline, Robert Colvill of Cleish, William Mentethe of Randifurd.

9, Andrew Patone and Isobel Richardson had William; witnesses, William Burne, Robert Burne, Andrew Burne.

9, John Colzeir and Marjory Corsane had Mawse; witnesses, William Cambell, James Broun, Nicol Henresone.

12, Andrew Currie and Helen Stirk had Helen; witnesses, David Mitchell, Thomas Wilson, George Donald, Andrew Currie.

12, James Miller and Nanse Miller had Geils; witnesses, Robert Broun, Alexander Beane, James Imrie. The child died "that day scho wes baptized and borne."

21, Nicol Blakwod and Margaret Murray had Christian; witnesses, William Walker, bailie of Dunfermline, Andrew Walker in Logie, John Wricht, younger.

25, George Wardlaw and Jean Kennedie had Patrick; witnesses, Harry Stewart of Baithe, John Anderson, Thomas Philpe.

30, Gasper Drysdell and Marion Inglis had James (in Inverkeithing kirk); witnesses, Robert Drysdell, James Peacok, Harry Greg in the Ferrie.

30, John Walwod and Mary Anderson had Isobel; witnesses, William Cunningham, John Gotterstone, James Walwod.

30, William Young and Nanse Plaine had Janet; witnesses, William Anderson, Andrew Young, William Cant, "all duelland in Lymkills for the tyme."

M. 4, Robert Schortus to Margaret Baid.

18, John Leckie to Janet Nicole.

OCTOBER.

B. 2, James Donald and Margaret Cunningham had Margaret; witnesses, Mr. Henry Wardlaw of Pitravie, Andrew Cunningham, David Flockart.

5, James Durie of Craigluscour and Christian Durie had Harry; witnesses, Mr. Harry Makgill, Mr. William Oliphant, Mr. William Merschell.

7, Robert Anderson and Marjory Anderson had Janet; witnesses, David Moreis, John Hodge, John Orock.

14, Henry Patrik and Isobel Mill had Catherine; witnesses, William Hutone, Robert Patrik, James Mill.

14, Laurie Wels and . . . Broun had John; witnesses, John Hasswell, John Kellok, elder, John Kellok, younger.

16, William Watson in the Ferrie and Janet Scotland had James; witnesses, David Greinis, Laurie Lugtoun, Robert Watson.

16, David Smetone and Elspet Russell had Elizabeth; witnesses, Robert Anghous, Robert Russell, David Scotland.

16, Mr. Robert Anderson and Marion Dewar had Margaret ; witnesses,
James Espline, John Dewar, Mr. Robert Smithe, John Bennat,
Mr. Harry Makgill, minister.
19, Patrick Lawson and Margaret Lathangie had David ; witnesses,
William Cunningham in Knokes, David Mitchell, David Anderson
in Lymkills, Archibald Cunningham in Sillitoun, Robert Cunningham
there.
21, Gilbert Makcraiche and Margaret Mudie had Bessie : witnesses,
Andrew Mayne, Harry Ritchardson, John Makcraiche.
21, Robert Dewar, tailor, and Janet Baverage had Margaret (in fornication);
witnesses, James Espline, Thomas Jaksone, William Walwod, officer
of the burgh.
26, John Makmirrie and Janet Porteous had James ; witnesses, James
Mayne, John Robertson, weaver, Alexander Lambe.
28, Adam Thomson and Margaret Galloway had Eupham (in fornication) ;
witnesses, Henry Moreis, John Hakstone, James Thomson.
29, John Nicole, collier, and Janet Hutschone had Thomas ; witnesses,
Thomas Jackson, James Waterstone, Alexander Melvill.
30, John Broun, tailor, and Marion Glas had Janet ; witnesses, William
Smart, Robert Davidson, John Broun, "theaker of houssis."

M. 16, Robert Dewar to Helen Keir.

NOVEMBER.

B.   2, John Wanderstone and Isobel Leslie had Margaret ; witnesses, William
Cunningham in Knokis, John Lawson in Crocefuird. William
Anderson in Pitconnochie.
8, David Trumble, baker, and Margaret Schortus had Isobel (in fornication) ; witnesses, Peter Buist, Mark Donald, William Anderson,
litster.
18, Thomas Mitchell, younger, and Helen Trumble had Margaret ;
witnesses, Thomas Mitchell, elder, David Mitchell, James Mitchell.
18, James Mitchell, wright, and Christian Thomson had Christian ;
witnesses, David Laurie, Andrew Trumble, smith, John Cunningham,
weaver.
20, John Smart and Margaret Baverage had John; witnesses, William
Smart, Thomas Elder, Robert Davidson.
20, Mr. William Wardlaw of Balmule and Christian Fouls had Catherine ;
witnesses, . . .
25, James Hutone and Nanse Ogilwie had Helen ; witnesses, William
Anderson, James Anderson, James Lawson.
25, William Anderson in Pitconnochie and Nanse Chalmers had Elspet ;
witnesses, James Anghous, Andrew Roxburgh, Thomas Douglas,
Henry Douglas.
27, Andrew Williamson and Janet Barker had Christian (baptised in
Inverkeithing) ; witnesses, David Williamson, David Greinis, Laurie
Lugtoun.
27, Andrew Chopeman and Barbara Hutone had Bessie ; witnesses,
George Trumble, David Sands, Robert Cunningham.
29, John Hog and Margaret Thomson had Jane ; witnesses, Robert
Livingstone, Mr. David Kingorne, Patrick Kingorne.
29, James Mudie, maltman, and Bessie Cunningham had Marjory: witnesses,
George Bothwell, David Burne, Robert Burne.
30, John Wilson and Christian Harla had twins, Margaret and Isobel ;
witnesses, George Dewar, William Hutone, David Scotland, William
Sanders.

M. 2, William Thomson, collier, to Helen Wricht.
13, Robert Schortus to Elspet Inche.
18, Patrick Dunbar to Geils Miller.
20, John Broun to Rachel Bleckie.

20, Andrew Currie to Margaret Douglas.
30, Robert Stanehous to Helen Rankin.

DECEMBER.

B. 2, Andrew Johnstone and Catherine Stewart had George ; witnesses,
George Dewar in Lathamond, William Hutone, James Mill.
2, Patrick Broun and Nanse Young had Margaret ; witnesses, Andrew
Broun, David Broun, James Brown, James Anderson in Fod.
2, Robert Elder and Margaret Barklay had John ; witnesses, David Elder,
Andrew Christie, John Huntar.
9, William Young and Margaret Peirson had William ; witnesses, William
Anderson, elder and younger, Andrew Young, all in Lymkills.
10, James Dunbar and Nanse Richardson had Janet ; witnesses, John
Bennat, James Richardson, Thomas Burne, mason.
12, Wattie Horne and Christian Young had James ; witnesses, James
Espline, James Hamilton, Walter Cokburn.
12, Robert Patrik and Elspet Low had Margaret ; witnesses, James
Esplin, William Ferrie, James Patrik.
16, James Baverage and Janet Coventrie had Helen ; witnesses, James
Mitchell, James Broun, James Anderson.
18, William Scotland and Margaret Robertson had David ; witnesses, David
Scotland, James Mill, Robert Anghous.
22, Andrew Christie and Helen Currie had Thomas ; witnesses, Thomas
Christie of the Hoile, Thomas Mitchell, elder, in Gellat, Thomas
Burne there.
23, Patrick Walker and Margaret Young had Catherine ; witnesses, James
Mudie, John Bennat, Thomas Elder.
29, Marjory Callendar had a daughter " borne of hir to ane man in Ireland
callit Jhone Delape (as scho affirmit) " begotten in fornication, and
baptised called Jean ; witnesses, James Trumble (who presented the
child), John Smart, flesher, James Rae, Andrew Thomson, belman.
30, William Blak and Marjory Blakwod had Henry ; witnesses, Alexander
Moutrey, John Henresone, Henry Mill.
30, John Forbus, " beggar and criple," and his wife Isobel Bennat had Mary

M. 18, William Davidson to Isobel Drysdell.
18, James Cunnon to Bessie Trumble.

JANUARY [1639].

B. 1, John Baverage and Helen Kellok had James ; witnesses, James
Baverage, John Gray.
13, John Cois and Janet Trumble had Janet ; witnesses, Robert Davidson,
Thomas Cowper, William Cois.
13, Patrick Broun in Bayth and Bessie Mudie had James ; witnesses, James
Stanehous. John Hodge, Robert Broun.
18, James Dik and Elspet Toward had Elspet ; witnesses, Thomas Christie,
Andrew Walker, David Lindsay in Kavill.
23, James Richardson and Bessie Adame had James (in fornication) ;
witnesses, James Dunbar, Thomas Burne, William Anderson.
27, Edward Broun in the Ferrie and Janet Broun had a daughter . . . . .
baptised in Inverkeithing .
27, George Henresone and Margaret Reid had Catherine ; witnesses, Harry
Stewart of Bayth, James Mitchell, James Balfour.
29, George Chopeman and Grizel Glas had Andrew ; witnesses, Andrew
Walker, Thomas Christie, George Meldrum.
29, Harry Richardson and Sarah Stewart had twins, Archibald and William;
witnesses, John Wricht, William Anderson, David Sandis, Gilbert
Alexander, Archibald Richardson, James Lindsay.
29, George Trumble of Nether Sillitone and Janet May had Nanse (in
adultery) ; witnesses, William Lambe, John Smithe, James Peirsone.
29, William Merser, advocate, and Isobel Gaits had James ; witnesses, Sir

James Halcat. James Chrichtoun of Wester Aidie, William Mentethe of Randifurd.

M. 1, William Anderson to Helen Makbethe.

6, James Dewar to Bessie Sibald.

24, James Currie to Elspet Walker.

25, John Wentone to Margaret Raithe.

29, Patrick Bruse to Isobel Orolk.

29, William Cois to Janet Burne.

29, Troyalus Hutone to Bessie Stevin.

30, Thomas Cowper to Christian Law.

FEBRUARY.

B. 1, Andrew Wilson and Bessie Peirson had Alison ; witnesses, David Currie, John Wilson, David Peirson, Robert Cant.

1, James Hutone, weaver, and Mary Dempster had Janet ; witnesses, Peter Low, Andrew Trumble, baker, Andrew Privous.

3, Thomas Baverage and Christian Smart had Andrew ; witnesses, John Wels, William Smart, Thomas Elder.

5, John Foote and Lucrece Kirk had William ; witnesses, William Walker, merchant, David Bull, cutler, Mark Donald.

12, Robert Murgane and Helen Smith had Janet ; witnesses, Andrew Walker, Mr. George Walker, his son, John Kinloche, Henry Sanders, James Waterston.

12, Nanse Adame, daughter of Robert Adame, had George baptised, "quhilk scho fatheret on Thomas Mitchell in Gellat, quhilk he constantlie denyit." Presented by George Davidson, weaver.

14, James Stewart, mealmaker, and Elspet Mayne had Grizel ; witnesses, John Kellok, Robert Mayne, James Mayne.

17, Andrew Broun and Bessie Wilson had a daughter . . . . ; witnesses, James Simraell, John Broun, Robert Tailyeour.

22, William Anderson, litster, and Margaret Cowper had Catherine, witnesses, Gilbert Sanders, Robert Kellok in Mastertoun, Mr. Patrick Auchinleck.

24, "Effie Papla brocht furthe ane manchyld, gottin as scho said be ane fellow callit Malcome Mun, quha wes aff the contrie, baptised and callit James ; and the woman hir self departit this lyff."

26, James Kellok, tailor, and Marjory Schortus had Helen ; witnesses, James Reid, James Schaw, Mr. Patrick Auchinleck.

26, Robert Tailyeour and Margaret Cunningham had Margaret ; witnesses, James Espline, James Donaldson, John Mayne.

27, Robert Tait and Janet Car had William ; witnesses, William Ferrie, William Walker, John Muire, Andrew Thomson.

M. 19, Thomas Burne to Isabel Richardson.

28, Mr. Samuel Row, minister, to Margaret Cokburne (in Torry kirk).

MARCH.

B. 3, James Dewar and Helen Trumble had Janet ; witnesses, George Trumble, John Dewar, James Broun.

3, James Primrois and Janet Tailyeour had Margaret ; witnesses, John Tailzeour, George Tailzeour, Robert Tailyeour.

3, John Wentone and Margaret Raithe had Elspet ; witnesses, Henry Sanders, Peter Buist, David Tod, Andrew Wilson.

3, Thomas Christie, servitor to the Earl of Dunfermline, and Grizel Schortus had James (in fornication) ; witnesses, James Kellok, Mark Home, James Hamilton.

10, Thomas Elder, flesher, and Helen Simsone had Anna ; witnesses, John Bennat, Peter Walker, William Ferrie.

15, Thomas Bennat and Catherine Riddoche had Janet ; witnesses, Thomas Davidson, Wattie Cokburn, Andrew Privous.

17, Andrew Berriehill and Elspet Broun had James ; witnesses, James Dewar, James Berriehill, James Walwod.

17, Robert Broun and Nanse Saverall had William; witnesses, Harry Cant, William Henresone, son of the Laird of Fordell, and William Cairnis.

19, John Kellok and Mary Weyms had John; witnesses, John Kellok, John Dewar, John Kellok in Lassodie mill.

19, John Westwod and Janet Keir had Marion; witnesses, Robert Anghous, David Scotland, William Mudie, maltman.

24, David Reid and Margaret Lawson had Catherine; witnesses, William Hutone, Adam Stobie, James Wardlaw.

26, Allan Mudie and Bessie Keir had Allan; witnesses, John Workman, John Gotterstone, John Sandilands.

26, Thomas Jackson and Helen Nicole had Margaret.

31, John (? James) Litljohne and Janet Wilson had Margaret; witnesses, James Henresone, John Broun, Andrew Wilson.

31, Leonard Henresone and Marjory Mudie had Barbara; witnesses, Robert Davidson, Henry Davidson, James Simraell.

31, Andrew Trumble, baker, and Barbara Law had George; witnesses, George Trumble, Andrew Thomson, Patrick Law.

31, Andrew Currie and Margaret Douglas had Alison; witnesses, Thomas Mitchell, David Currie, Andrew Burne.

M. 21, William Lawson to Margaret Trottar.

APRIL.

B. 5, Andrew Colzeir, drummer, and Isobel Anderson had David; witnesses, David Laurie, Andrew Thomson, belman, George Davidson.

9, William Smart, flesher, and Bessie Stevenson had Thomas; witnesses, Thomas Wilson in the mill, ... Burne, Peter Law, Thomas Elder.

9, James Imrie and Margaret Wardlaw had Margaret; witnesses, James Mudie, William Lambe, John Gotterstoun.

9, William Walwod and Margaret Wardlaw had James; witnesses, James Wardlaw, James Mitchel, John Coventrie.

14, Patrick Bruse and Isobel Orolk had Bessie; witnesses, David Christie, James Dewar, Andrew Berriehill.

14, John Makcraiche and Mage Anderson had Janet; witnesses, Thomas Mitchell, James Wardlaw, David Currie.

16, James Cunnon and Bessie Trumble had Henry; witnesses, Sir Henry Wardlaw of Pitravie, John Dewar in Lassodie, Robert Kellok, younger.

21, Thomas Gardner and Bessie Peacok had Janet; witnesses, John Kellok, Harry Richardson, David Peacok.

26, John Imrie and Isobel Fermour had Margaret; witnesses, John Henre, Alexander Mastertoun, and John Dewar, younger.

30, James Anghous and Janet Gilespie had Robert; witnesses, Robert Anghous, Henry Douglas, George Donald.

30, John Watson, a wandering beggar, married in Fossoquhy kirk, and Isobel Williamsone had Janet; witnesses, David Tod, Andrew Wilson.

M. 12, Andrew Moreis to Margaret Low.

23, David Russell to Janet Stanehous.

30, Thomas Wedell to Isobel Liddell (in Aberdour kirk).

MAY.

B. 3, John Ædisone and Isobel Huntar had Mary; witnesses, Peter Law, William Patone, Andrew Lindsay.

3, Andrew Speir and Nanse Hardie had David; witnesses, David Cunnon, David Peirsone, James Fischar.

3, Charles, Earl of Dunfermline, and Dame Mary Douglas had Grizel; witnesses, Sir James Halkat of Pitfirran, "James Henresone (*sic*) and Robert Halkat, bretheren to the said Sir James."

5, Robert Dewar and Margaret Flokart had Margaret; witnesses, Thomas Cunnon, William Flokart, George Davidson.

5, William Sanders and Catherine Cusine had William ; witnesses, William Hutone, John Cusine, James Sanders.

5, Andrew Drummond and Bessie Young had Robert ; witnesses, Robert Steinsone, Laurence Steinsone, Robert Elder.

5, George Trumble in Bromehall and Helen Grinlay had Helen ; witnesses, Andrew Trumble in Grange, William Walker, merchant, David Mitchell.

5, Robert Wels and Janet Wylie had Janet ; witnesses, William Smart, James Legat, William Mudie, maltman.

5, David Wyld and Bessie Banks had Marion ; witnesses, Robert Anghous, Adam Stobie, Andrew Meldrum.

7, James Murgane and Elspet Bowman had Robert ; witnesses, Robert Scotland, Robert Russell, James Dagleishe.

10, Robert Thomson and Helen Sibald had Margaret ; witnesses, Thomas Douglas, Edward Douglas, David Sands.

10, James Cunnon and Jean Philpe had Janet ; witnesses, James Cunnon, Thomas Cunnon, John Gentleman.

10, Mark Duncane in Inverkeithing and Margaret Douglas had Peter ; witnesses, Peter Douglas, Thomas Ritchie, James Ritchie in Blaklaw.

10, John Fraser, a poor wandering beggar, and Margaret Barclay had Jean. Their marriage in Auchterderran kirk is certified by Mr. John Chalmers, minister there.

10, Andrew Robertson and Janet Morum had Jean ; testimonial of their marriage in Dundee kirk.

12, James Walwod and Helen Inglis had Andrew ; witnesses, Andrew Smith, Andrew Inglis, William Walwod.

14, William Lethome and Janet Wilson had twins, James and Adam ; witnesses, Thomas Wilson, Robert Cunningham, William Anderson, William Lawson, Andrew Wilson, Robert Douglas.

19, John Meldrum and Christian Blacater had Margaret ; witnesses, James Mill, Robert Russell, Edward Russell.

19, John Wilson and Helen Currie had Jean ; witnesses, Andrew Walcar, Thomas Christie, John Wilson.

19, George Trumble and Marjory Maistertoun had Jean ; witnesses, Andrew Trumble, George Trumble in Bromehall, Alexander Aikine, James Dewar of Bayth.

19, Thomas Wilson and Mary Fergusson had Andrew ; witnesses, John Miller, Andrew Cunningham, David Wilson.

21, George Wat and Janet Robertson had Isobel ; witnesses, William Anderson, David Murray, William Young.

28, William Bowie and Mays Boner had William ; witnesses, William Lambe, William Trumble, Henry Peirsone.

30, Thomas Davidson and Janet Walcar had Margaret ; witnesses, Sir Henry Wardlaw of Pitravie, William Anderson, litster, Peter Law.

M. 5, Henry Douglas to Christian Wilson.

JUNE.

B. 2, Nicol Inglis and Mage Law had Henry ; witnesses, Mr. William Wardlaw of Bamule, William Hutone, Robert Russell.

7, John Angous and Marion Reidie had Andrew ; witnesses, Robert Angous in Rescobie, Andrew Rowane in Gask, David Smetone.

7, John Car and Bessie Clerk had Bessie ; witnesses, Robert Henresone, George Clerk, John Baid.

9, Janet Grege, parishioner of Beath, "delyverit in William Mackie's barne ane barne whome scho fatherit on ane dead man callit Johne Aikine," baptised Annabel ; witnesses, Andrew Thomson, Mr. John Walker, reader.

11, John Stirk and Bessie Crawford had Janet ; witnesses, John Stirk, elder, Andrew Meldrum, George Stirk.

11, Robert Stevenson and Elspet Davidson had Henry ; witnesses, Robert Davidson, Henry Davidson, Andrew Privous.

16, James Mill and Grizel Robertson had Henry ; witnesses, David Laurie, Thomas Christie, Henry Wardlaw.

23, Thomas Fraser and Margaret Henresone had John ; witnesses, John Wricht, Patrick Trumble, Peter Law.

23, Robert Ged of Badrig and Eupham Orock, his lady, had James ; witnesses, James Espline, James Reid, provost. James Robertson of Weltoun of Kingorne Wester.

25, John Dewar in Lassodie and Christian Bosswell had David ; witnesses, Mr. John Chalmers, Mr. William Wardlaw, David Cunnon.

M. 4, John Trottar to Janet Sanders.

4, Harry Blakwod to Bessie Broun.

11, James Chalmer to Elspet Broun.

23, James Danskine to Annas Hamilton.

25, John Cadell to Bessie Stevenson.

JULY.

B. 7, William Walker, maltman, and Marjory Broun had Bessie ; witnesses, Laurence Walker, Adam Stanehouse, David Keir.

7, John Mure in the Abay and Nanse Schiphird had William ; witnesses, William Ferrie, James Espline, James Hamilton.

9, Adam Coventrie and Bessie Walwod had John ; witnesses, John Coventrie, James Baverage, Patrick Murray.

14, Thomas Cunnon and Isobel Dewar had David ; witnesses, David Cunnon, David Flokard, David Broun.

14, David Broun and Janet Dewar had Helen ; witnesses, James Dewar in Pitbachlie, George Anderson, Adam Trumble.

16, Andrew Flokard and Isobel Peat had William ; witnesses, David Flokard, William Flokard, Robert Dewar.

16, Robert Scharpe and Nanse Kellok had Janet ; witnesses, James Kellok, Robert Kellok, Robert Kellok, younger.

21, Robert Westwod and Margaret Kinsman had Nanse ; witnesses, William Horne, Harry Richardson, John Potter.

23, Thomas Christie of the Hoile and Elspet Durie had Anna ; witnesses, Sir Alexander Clerk of Pittincreiff, Mr. Alexander Clerk, his son, and Thomas Douglas.

23, David Hodge and Catherine Smart had Janet ; witnesses, James Simsone, John Workman, James Feg.

26, Tobiah Murbeck and Christian Cant had Elspet ; witnesses, Mr. Harry Makgill, minister, Sir Alexander Clerk of Pittincreiff, James Reid, provost.

28, Robert Broun and Nanse Clerk had William ; witnesses, Thomas Christie, William Mudie, James Dewar.

M. 2, George Anderson to Helen Dewar.

16, John Henre to Catherine Aikin.

16, Mr. William Livingston to Nanse Lindsay.

23, James Moutrey to Margaret Broun.

25, John Rowane to Margaret Stewart.

AUGUST.

B. 3, David Ferlie and Nanse Chalmers had James ; witnesses, James Broun in Fod, James Baverage, younger, James Walwod.

6, James Drysdell and Geils Bryse had Helen ; witnesses, William Lawson, James Hutone, John Hutone.

6, Florie Greg and Effie Patie had James (baptised in Inverkeithing) ; witnesses, John Thomson, Harry Greg, James Patie.

9, Patrick Kinnimouthe and Margaret Grahame had Janet ; witnesses, Patrick Peirsone, Andrew Watson.

10, Mr. Harry Makgill, minister of Dunfermline, and Margaret Wardlaw
   had Christian ; witnesses, Mr. William Wardlaw, William Hutone,
   Mr. William Makgill, doctor of physic.

13, James Hutsone and Catherine Pullons had Thomas ; witnesses, Thomas
   Mitchell, elder and younger, and Thomas Wilson in Crumbie.

13, Andrew Cunningham (deceased) and Margaret Ædisone had Janet :
   witnesses, Robert Kellok, George Trumble in Bromehall, Robert
   Burne.   Presented by John Ædisone, the mother's brother.

16, George Tailyeour and Nanse Hutone had Andrew ; witnesses, David
   Mitchell, Andrew Trumble in Bromehall, Andrew Donald.

18, John Cambell, gardener of Pitfirrane, and Margaret Robertson had
   Mary ; witnesses, David Lindsay, David Bull, Andrew Mentethe.

18, John Lawson and Catherine Logane had Bessie ; witnesses, David
   Sands, George Trumble, Robert Anderson in Lymkills.

20, David Scotland in Craigduckie and Elspet Dewar had George ; witnesses,
   George Dewar, Robert Anghous, Robert Russell.

25, Alexander Chalmer and Catherine Walker had John ; witnesses, John
   Walker, Peter Law, William Walker.

M. 13, Andrew Meldrum to Nanse Young.
   13, Robert Russell to Margaret Dewar.
   13, Robert Wardlaw to Margaret Hutone.
   20, William Beans to Nanse Blakwod.
   20, James Fyiff to Janet Law
   25, John Mudie to Bessie Wardlaw.
   29, William Menteth of Randiefurd to Anna Prestoun, daughter of Sir John
   Preston of Valeyfeild.

SEPTEMBER.

B. 1, John Skeine, burgess of Dunfermline, and Helen Durie had James :
   witnesses, Sir Robert Halkat of Pitfirran, Sir James Halkat, his son,
   Mr. Alexander Clerk, fiar of Pittincreiff.

8, James Litljohne and Christian Chrichtone had Helen : witnesses, James
   Litljohne, William Lambe, William Mudie, all weavers.

10, Robert Schortus, collier, and Margaret Baid had Charles : witnesses,
   Charles Baid, James Lindsay, John Hog.

13, Robert Russell and Janet Christie had Elspet (in fornication) ; witnesses,
   Edward Russell, John Workman, John Potter.

16, Robert Logane and Christian Hutone had Robert ; witnesses, Robert
   Davidson, Wattie Cokburne.

18, James Walwod, land officer, and Catherine Key had Harry ; witnesses,
   Mr. Harry Makgill, William Walcar, merchant, Patrick Kingorne,
   Peter Buist.

22, John Blakwod and Margaret Inglis had Marjory : witnesses, William
   Anderson, William Nicole, Andrew Leslie.

22, William George and Elspet Miller had John : witnesses, William Mudie.
   William Walker, John Miller.

22, John Anderson and Margaret Gibson had Isobel : witnesses. Harry
   Stewart of Baithe, James Mitchell, George Wardlaw.

22, Thomas Blakwod and Isobel Inglis had Isobel : witnesses. George
   Meldrum, Robert Scharpe, John Inglis.

26, Sir James Halkat of Pitfirrane and Dame Margaret Montgumrie had
   Charles ; witnesses, Charles, Earl of Dunfermline, William Mentethe
   of Randifurd, Robert Colvill of Cleishe.

29, William Keir and Margaret Baid had John ; witnesses. John Baid, John
   Trumble, William Mudie.

30, Jasper Drysdell and Marion Inglis had Janet : witnesses, Robert Broun,
   younger, Harry Cant, James Peacok.

M. 10, George Scot to Helen Mekiljohne.
   10, John Kingorne to Bessie Talyeour.

OCTOBER.

B. 6, John Dewar and Marjory Robertson had Andrew; witnesses, Andrew Walker, Andrew Trumble, Thomas Christie.

6, John Laurie and Nanse Greg had Margaret; witnesses, David Laurie, John Mure, James Simraell.

8, Thomas Hutone and Isobel Keir had James; witnesses, James Ritchie, Robert Dewar, James Dewar in Pitbachlie.

20, Robert Willie and Margaret Key had Isobel; witnesses, Thomas Wilson, George Donald, Robert Turneley.

20, John Gilmure and Catherine Blak had David (in fornication); witnesses, David Scotland, David Bull, Robert Anghous.

20, James Legat, bailie, and Margaret Stirk had Bessie; witnesses, Alexander Drysdell, bailie, Wattie Coburne, Andrew Currie.

22, John Potter, wright, and Elspet Walker had Walter; witnesses, Walter Cokburne, Andrew Privous, John Hamilton.

22, Laurence Walker, cordiner, and Nanse Wischatt had Margaret; witnesses, Peter Walcar, Peter Buist, Andrew Trumble, baker.

23, John Bastardfeild, servitor to the Earl of Dunfermline, and Isobel Chopeman had Thomas (in fornication); witnesses, Mr. Patrick Auchinleck, William Anderson, litster, James Simsone, merchant. George Chopeman, brother of Isobel, presented the child.

25, William Mudie and Janet Johnestone had Bessie; witnesses, John Trumble, James Henresone, John Hamiltoun.

27, Robert Henresone and Janet Car had Margaret; witnesses, Peter Law, provost, James Legat, bailie, Andrew Privous, litster.

29, James Lawsone and Bessie Galrige had Henry; witnesses, Robert Davidson, William Cunningham, Henry Douglas.

M. 8, James Hodge to Christian Leslie (in Cleish kirk).

8, John Dothane to Mage Wilson.

20, John Dagleische to Bessie Mekiljohne.

22, Thomas Trumble to Catherine Baid.

22, James Smart to Helen Hoge.

NOVEMBER.

B. 3, John Huntar and Christian Donaldson had Elspet; witnesses, Thomas Christie, Andrew Christie, James Mitchell, wright.

3, George Stirk and Elspet Walker had Anna; witnesses, Sir Alexander Clerk of Pittincreiff, Mr. Alexander Clerk, his eldest son, and Robert Stirk.

5, John Lindsay and Bessie Peirson had John; witnesses, Patrick Lindsay, Richard Templeman, William Sands.

6, Mr. Alexander Clerk, laird of Pittincreiff, and Anna Winrahame, his lady, had Alexander; witnesses, Sir Alexander Clerk, laird of Pittincreiff, his father, Sir Robert Halkat of Pitfirran, and Sir James Halkat, his eldest son and heir.

10, John Forsyithe and Margaret Potter had Robert; witnesses, Robert Kellok, Robert Wardlaw, Robert Kellok, son of James Kellok.

10, John Broun, smith, and Rachel Bleckie had Margaret; witnesses, Thomas Bleckie, David Broun, William Bleckie.

10, David Robertson and Catherine Scot had Andrew; witnesses, Robert Cunningham, Andrew Donald, Alexander Donald.

12, George Young and Bessie Low had Nanse; witnesses, William Smart, William Lambe, William Mudie.

16, Mr Samuel Row, minister, and Margaret Cokburne had Mary; witnesses, William Mentethe of Randifurd, James Reid, Peter Law, provost.

18, John Mayne in Pitcorthie and Margaret Bennat had Margaret; witnesses, David Broun, Patrick Steinson, David Flokard.

19, John Clerk (deceased) and Annas Portour had Bessie (posthumous); witnesses, Mr. Patrick Auchinleck, William Walcar, merchant, Thomas Elder, flesher.

24, John Bryse and Helen Quhyt had James; witnesses, James Bryse, William Anderson, David Sands.

24, William Mudie and Margaret Phillane had William ; witnesses, William Mudie, Henry Douglas, John Cois.

24, James Hamilton, piper, and Isobel Broun had James ; witnesses, James Hamilton, James Farne, James Buist.

24, Nicol Henresone and Catherine Wels had Janet ; witnesses, John Wels, Archibald Honyman, David Stewart.

24, Andrew Drysdell and Margaret Wilson had Christian ; witnesses, James Durie, James Wardlaw, James Horne.

29, Andrew Wilson and Margaret Lethome had Barbara : witnesses, Adam Wilson, Thomas Wilson, William Lethome.

29, Thomas Mitchell, younger, in Gellat, and Helen Trumble had Thomas ; witnesses, Thomas Mitchell, elder, David Mitchell, Andrew Trumble, portioner of Grange.

M. 5, Andrew Cuningham to Janet Wilson.
   10, James Schort to Bessie Lindsay.
   12, James Broun to Janet Cant.
   19, John Cunningham to Nanse Lathangie.
   24, James Dog to Effie Touche.

DECEMBER.

B. 1, John Simson and Margaret Mackartnie had John; witnesses, John Hakstone, John Hasswell, John Stevenson.

   3, William Hutone in Dinduff and Catherine Mill had Janet; witnesses, Walter Cokburne, Thomas Mitchell, John Hutone in Lethoms.

   3, James Durie of Craigluscour and Christian Durie had Margaret ; witnesses, Sir Robert Halkat of Pitfirrane, Robert Colvill of Cleische, Mr. William Ged.

   6, James Simraell and Margaret Mudie had Margaret ; witnesses, William Anderson in Pitconnochie, Mark Donald, Robert Burne.

   8, James Simsone, cordiner, and Isobel Veitche had Helen ; witnesses, Thomas Elder, flesher, David Stewart, cordiner, Mark Donald, baker.

   10, Henry Beany and Helen Wricht had Christian ; witnesses, Andrew Wricht, Thomas Donaldson, William Rae.

   12, Robert Schortus and Elspet Inche had James ; witnesses, James Kellok, tailor, James Smeton, James Reid. Born 9th instant.

   17, Andrew Cant and Christian Bull had Grizel ; witnesses, William Kirk, Andrew Wilson, Thomas Peirson.

   17, John Cusine and Nanse Foote had Robert ; witnesses, John Hutone, George Dewar, Robert Merser.

   22, David Gilmure and Helen Bruce had Bessie ; witnesses, Adam Stobie, Thomas Hutoun, James Wardlaw.

   22, James Gray and Isobel Broun had Grizel ; witnesses, David Broun, John Broun, John Kellok.

   22, James Baverage and Janet Steidman had Helen ; witnesses, John Gray, John Baverage, James Hodge.

   29, John Cadell and Bessie Stevenson had Helen ; witnesses, David Peirson, James Stanehous, Robert Kellok.

   29, John Baverage and Helen Kellok had Grizel ; witnesses, John Gray, James Baverage, William Makie. (Baptised in Cleish kirk.)

   29, James Cumming and Margaret Currie had Thomas ; witnesses, Thomas Mitchell, Andrew Burne, David Currie.

   29, Thomas Cowper and Isobel Walwod had Isobel ; witnesses, Peter Law, Robert Stevenson, Peter Buist.

   30, David Broun and Isobel Mayne had Margaret ; witnesses, Robert Tailyeour, Andrew Mayne, George Currie.

31, Robert Hutone and Janet Trumble had Bessie ; witnesses, James Mudie, maltman, James Mudie, weaver, William Lambe.

M. 3, Thomas Baverage to Janet Tod.
　3, James Stocks to Grizel Broun.

JANUARY [1640].

B. 10, John Adame and Margaret Greg had Mary : witnesses, John Bennat, James Hamiltoun, William Smart.
　12, Thomas Trumble and Catherine Baid had Margaret : witnesses, James Stanehous, Robert Burne, James Miller.
　14, John Greive and Isobel Trumble had William ; witnesses, William Hutone, Robert Russell, James Dagleische.
　14, James Simsone, merchant, and Bessie Walker had Andrew; witnesses, Andrew Walker, " knycht," William Walker, merchant, and Laurence Walker.
　16, William Ged and Janet Hutone had James (in fornication) ; witnesses, James Waterstone, Gilbert Johnstone, James Wallace, merchant.
　19, Henry Douglas and Christian Wilson had Janet ; witnesses, Tobiah Murbeck, James Cunnone in Pitravie, Robert Kellok, son of James Kellok in Mastertoun.
　24, James Espline and Margaret Colden had Grizel : witnesses, Peter Law, James Reid, John Bennat.
　28, Robert Anghous in Craigduckie and Isobel Dewar had Christian ; witnesses, Mr. William Wardlaw, John Dewar in Lassodie, David Greins, Robert Dewar in Lathamond.
　28, John Cunningham and Nanse Lathangie had Janet ; witnesses, George Mayne, James Mayne, Andrew Cunningham.
　31, William Anderson and Helen Makbeth had Marjory ; witnesses, William Nicole, John Anderson, William Lethome. The woman died in bringing forth twins, whereof the one was dead born.

M. 14, Robert Anderson to Nanse Barklay.
　14, James Rae to Bessie Strang.
　14, William Straquhen to Janet Allane.
　21, John Kinloch to Nanse Tailyeour.

FEBRUARY.

B. 2, Andrew Anderson and Margaret Rae had John : witnesses, William Anderson in Pitconnochie, James Anderson, William Nicole.
　4, Robert Angous and Marion Dewar had James ; witnesses, George Dewar, Alexander Moutrey, James Moutrey of Rescobie.
　4, James Walwod and Elspet Christie had Helen : witnesses, Henry Davidson, James Broun, James Baverage.
　4, William Mudie, weaver, and Nanse Mackie had William : witnesses, William Lambe, William Keir, George Young.
　4, Andrew Moreis, litster, and Margaret Low had Thomas : witnesses, Andrew Privous, Walter Cokburne, Adam Wylie.
　9, John Whyt and Margaret Kellok had Robert ; witnesses, John Kellok in the Thornetoun, John Kellok in the Brae, John Kellok in Lassodie-mill.
　11, Gavin Ædisone and Janet Hyslope had James (in fornication): witnesses, Andrew Broun, smith, John Fyiff, James Fyiff.
　11, William Lawson and Margaret Trottar had John ; witnesses, John Dagleische, John Clerk, John Trottar.
　14, Robert Patrik and Elspet Low had Annas ; witnesses, William Ferrie, John Davidson, Henry Patrik.
　16, Patrick Broun and Nanse Young had Elspet : witnesses, Robert Bull, David Broun, Andrew Broun.
　16, John Ramsay, collier, and Christian Thrislo had Nanse (in Auchterderran kirk) ; witnesses, James Wilson, William Hodge, Patrick Peirs.

21, Robert Baxter and Bessie Anderson had Samuel; witnesses, William Menteith of Randifurd, William Walker, merchant, John Bastardfeild.

22, David Maxwell and Nanse Hamilton had George; witnesses, George Durie, George Dewar, George Davidson.

23, James Broun of Fod and Helen Stobie had Margaret; witnesses, William Smith, Andrew Smith, Adam Stanehous.

23, David Cunnon, portioner of Mastertoun, and Elspet Dewar had George; witnesses, James Kellok, Robert Kellok and Thomas Stanehous, all in Mastertoun. Baptised in kirk of Inverkeithing.

23, James Mudie, weaver, and Grizel Lambe had John; witnesses, John Gotterstoun, James Mudie, David Galrig.

M. 11, Charles Wilson to Helen Broun.

25, Thomas Lawson to Catherine Merschell.

MARCH.

B. 1, James Peirsone and Nanse Stevenson had Andrew; witnesses, Andrew Donald, Andrew Peirsone, William Lawson.

3, David Sim and Margaret Meldrum had Janet; witnesses, John Sim, Thomas Meldrum, John Gotterstone.

5, David Young and Janet Gardner, "tua vagabundis unmaryit," had a child baptised (by Mr. Harry Makgill our minister) called Margaret.

6, John Stevenson, smith, and Marjory Hugane had Janet; witnesses, Robert Stevenson, Andrew Pruvoss, David Hodge

8, Troylus Hutone and Bessie Stevin had John; witnesses, James Wardlaw, John Lindsay, James Hutone.

8, John Kellok and Isobel Hassuell had John; witnesses, John Kellok younger and elder, and David Blak, all in Lassodie bray.

8, David Russell and Janet Stanehous had William; witnesses, Mr. William Wardlaw of Balmule, Robert Russell, David Smetoun.

8, Henry Douglas and Margaret Cunningham had Margaret; witnesses Sir Robert Halkat of Pitfirran, David Lindsay of Kavill, Andrew Cunningham in the Stane.

8, Patrick Stevenson and Christian Mudie had Margaret; witnesses, Robert Tailyeour, James Simrell, John Mayne in Pitcorthie.

8, Robert Broun, mariner in the Ferrie, and Janet Broun had a daughter . . . (baptised in Inverkeithing kirk).

8, Wattie Horne and Christian Young had Walter; witnesses, Walter Cokburne, James Espline, James Hamilton.

13, James Ritchie and Christian Anderson had Margaret; witnesses, Robert Anderson in Donibirsle, David Ready, John Anderson in Inverkeithing

15, John Lawson and Catherine Drysdell had Adam; witnesses, John Merschell, Robert Cunningham, Adam Wilson.

15, Robert Straquhen and Bessie Nicole had Robert; witnesses, Robert Straquhen in Pittincreiff, John Straquhen and William Straquhen, brothers of the said Robert.

18, David Hutone and Margaret Dempstertoun had Thomas; witnesses, Thomas Davidson, James Kellok, Thomas Elder.

19, Mr. Robert Anderson, musician, and Marion Dewar had James; witnesses, James Espleine, Mr. Robert Smith, John Bennat, baker.

22, John Wilson in Galrighill and Margaret Anderson had Thomas; witnesses, Thomas Christie, Mr. George Walker, John Litljohne.

22, "That day ane vagabund woman callit Margaret Andesone (hir guidman as scho reportit callit Johne Henresone wes slane at the Brig of Die with the cannon being ane noncoventare (*sic*)) wes in this paroche delyverit of ane chyld," baptised William; witnesses, David Sands, Edward Douglas, William Anderson in Gellat.

29, John Mill and Isobel Harlay had Elspet (in fornication); witnesses, Robert Anghous, Robert Russell, Andrew Dewar.

29, James Reid and Marion Broun had Annas ; witnesses, William Mentethe of Randifurd, Mr. Alexander Clerk of Pittincreiff, Robert Ged of Baldrig.

29, James Henresone, glazier, and Mayse Aikine had William ; witnesses, William Legat, William Trumble, John Litljohne.

29, George Anderson and Helen Dewar had John ; witnesses, Andrew Trumble in the Grange. John Anderson in the Chapell, Robert Dewar in Pitbachlie.

31, William Kent and Isobel Broun had Elizabeth ; witnesses, David Hodge, David Trumble, baker. Henry Davidson.

M. [*None.*]

APRIL.

B. 4, Henry Meldrum and Geils Chatto had Elspet ; witnesses, Laurence Steinsone, George Meldrum, Alexander Melvill.

4, Robert Greive and Margaret Douglas had Bessie ; witnesses, John Scotland in Craigduckie, Edward Russell, George Greive.

14, Harry Blakwod and Bessie Broun had Marjory ; witnesses, David Blak, David Smetoun, John Broun.

14, David Sands in Gellat and Bessie Christie had William ; witnesses, William Aikine, William Mudie, William Anderson.

14, David Currie in Gellat and Alison Mitchell had Alexander ; witnesses, Robert Ged of Baldrig, Mr. William Ged, his son, Alexander Napier.

14, Thomas Durie, "ane criple wandering beggar," had a child baptised (presented by Robert Anderson, tailor), called James.

19, Thomas Stanehous and Barbara Dewar had Janet ; witnesses, John Dewar, James Cunnon, John Stanehous.

—— James Tailyeour and Marion Burgane had a son . . . (in fornication) ; witnesses, . . .

25, James Hamilton and Jean Sanders had Charles ; witnesses, Mr. William Oliphant, James Espline, William Merser.

26, Andrew Meldrum and Nanse Young had Jean ; witnesses, William Walker, merchant, William Ferrie, Thomas Douglas.

26, Laurence Watson, cordiner, and Grizel Wilson had Margaret ; witnesses, Patrick Kingorne, John Bennat, Mark Donald.

26, Henry Steinson and Marion Dewar had Janet (in fornication) ; witnesses, James Mill, Andrew Key, David Steinson.

28, James Dewar and Isobel Hutone had Elspet ; witnesses, Robert Wardlaw, David Flokart, George Anderson.

M. 5, John Buist to Bessie Horne.

14, James Richardson to Nanse Coventrie.

14. Andrew Robertson to Margaret Potter.

MAY.

B. 1, John Henre and Catherine Aikine had James ; witnesses, Wattie Cokburne, James Coburne, John Laurie.

1, Alexander Young and Helen Quhyt had Alexander ; witnesses, Robert Quhyt, David Stewart, James Patoun.

1, Mr. William Ged, fiar of Baldrig, and Nanse Cant had James (in fornication) ; witnesses, Peter Buist, James Ged, John Wricht.

3, John Faulds and Janet Clow had Mary ; witnesses, William Lawson, James Clerk, William Sanders.

3, David Alaster and Nanse Maistertone had John ; witnesses, James Mill, John Hutone, John Greive.

3, John Mill and Marjory Dewar had Marjory ; witnesses, David Blak, John Kellok, Thomas Barklay.

3. James Flokart and Margaret Stalker had Isobel ; witnesses, David Flokart, William Flokart, Robert Dewar.

8, John Potter and Marion Clerk had David; witnesses, David Bull, John Walker, David Keir.

10, James Clerk and Nanse Æssone had William; witnesses, William Lawson, William Anderson, James Anderson.

10, Robert Russell and Margaret Dewar had Christian; witnesses, Henry Wardlaw, George Wardlaw, George Dewar.

13, James Meldrum and Marjory Henresone had Elspet; witnesses, John Walker, James Feg, David Hodge.

17, George Remaynous and Catherine Dewar had Mary; witnesses, George Dewar, Robert Anghous, David Scotland.

17, George Scot, litster, and Helen Mekiljohne had Walter; witnesses, Walter Cokburne, Andrew Privous, John Hamilton.

17, James Deis and Catherine Westwod had Mark; witnesses, Mark Donald, David Hodge, James Westwod.

26, Henry Patrik and Isobel Mill had Margaret; witnesses, Robert Patrik, David Broun, James Kellok, tailor, James Mill.

M. 5, Henry Dick to Helen Mackie [their consignation money distributed, because of the long interval between proclamation and marriage, and they gave each on their marriage day but 2d. to the poor].

26, Andrew Tailyeour to Bessie Currie.

JUNE.

B. 2, John Murie and Elspet Anderson had Janet; witnesses, George Curie, James Currie, Henry Mitchell.

7, Andrew Walker, traveller, and Margaret Young had Nanse; witnesses, James Peirsone, Patrick Merschell, John Fergus.

7, John Mudie and Bessie Wardlaw had Elspet; witnesses, James Kellok, Thomas Stanehous, Robert Kellok in Mastertoun.

7, David Galrige and Margaret Yowane had David; witnesses, William Lambe, William Mudie, James Mudie.

9, James Fyiff and Janet Law had Thomas; witnesses, William Legat, James Mill, David Trumble.

10, Mr. James Gray and Elspet Halkat had Robert; witnesses, Sir Robert Halkat of Pitfirran, Sir James Halkat, his eldest son, and James Coburne.

13, Charles, Earl of Dunfermline, and his lady, Mary Douglas, had Charles; witness, Archibald, Lord Argyll.

14, Thomas Elder, flesher, and Helen Simsone had Bessie; witnesses, Edward Elder, John Bennat, Walter Cokburne.

14, John Watson, cordiner, and Barbara Bruce had William; witnesses, William Walker, merchant, George Durie, John Bruse.

21, John Anderson and Margaret Cadell had Helen; witnesses, David Peirson in Mastertoun, John Cadell, William Cunningham.

21, Robert Inglis and Isobel Bruce had Henry; witnesses, Henry Wardlaw, Robert Russell, Edward Russell, dwelling in Balmule.

23, Alexander Talyeour and Christian Huiesone had James; witnesses, James Waterstone, Tobiah Murebeck, John Hector.

M. 22, Robert Broun to Catherine Peacok, in Inverkeithing.

22, Peter Walker to Effie Ged.

30, Thomas Wilson to Elspeth Wilson.

JULY.

B. 5, James Kellok and Bessie Gibson had Margaret; witnesses, John Peirson, elder and younger, in Pitdunnies, and Thomas Kellok.

5, John Fyff and Catherine Hearing had Catherine; witnesses, Harry Stewart of Baith, David Fyff, his father, and William Dalgleish.

5, George Dewar in Lathamond and Mary Chalmers had James born (baptised 14th); witnesses, Mr. William Wardlaw of Balmule, Henry Wardlaw, his son, John Hutton of North Lethims.

U

12, James Douglas and Christian Watson had John (in fornication);
  witnesses, John Douglas, John Watson, Henry Douglas.

12, Peter Buist and Isobel Walwode had Robert; witnesses, Robert Ged
  of Baldrig, Robert Kellok in Mastertoun, John Wellis, baker.

14, Patrick Lawson in the Craigs and Margaret Lathangie had Adam;
  witnesses, Adam Wilson, William Lathangie, John Cunningham.

14, John Straquhan and Isobel Fothringhame had Annas; witnesses,
  George Meldrum, John Stirk, Mr. Alexander Clerk, fiar of Pittencrieff.

21, John Dalgleish and Bessie Meikiljohne had Janet; witnesses, Andrew
  Meikiljohne, Walter Cokburne, George Scot

21, Robert Anderson and Nans Barclay had Isobel; witnesses, Thomas
  Davidson, litster, Patrick Peirsone, Henry Baverage.

21, John Smart and Margaret Baverage had Nanse; witnesses, James
  Esplin, William Ferry, Thomas Baverage.

26, Robert Angus and Christian Drysdaill had William; witnesses, David
  Scotland, John Huttoun, John Ingils.

26, John Stevenson and Bessie Allane had Thomas; witnesses, William
  Anderson, Thomas Leslie, James Anderson.

28, John Walker, cooper, and Jean Gowie had John; witnesses, Mr. John
  Walker, William Walker, merchant, William Legat, flesher.

28, John Neilsone and Janet Buist had Isobel; witnesses, Patrick Turnbull,
  baker, David Turnbull, his son, and Peter Buist.

29, Mr. Harry M'Gill, minister, and Margaret Wardlaw had William born
  (baptised 30th); witnesses, Doctor William M'Gill, doctor of physic,
  his brother, Mr. William Wardlaw of Balmooll, William Walker,
  merchant. Mr. William Marshall, minister at Saline, officiated.

M. 12, Robert Backais to Barbara Sandilands.

12, James Steill to Janet Wilson.

AUGUST.

B. 2, James Cousing and Bessie Kinsman had Anna; witnesses, William
  Walwoode, portioner of Touch, Thomas Elder, William Legat.

9, David Elder and Jean Duff had John; witnesses, John Skein, John
  Adiesone, Robert Elder.

12, James Dumbar and Nanse Richardson had Margaret; witnesses, Peter
  Law, provost, George Bothwell, David Huttoun, tailor.

16, Peter Walker and Eupham Ged had John; witnesses, Sir Robert
  Halket of Pitfirran, Robert Ged of Baldrig, his father-in-law, Peter
  Law, provost, John Walker, merchant, his father.

(*Here the writing changes, and there is the following note on the
  margin:*—"At this time Mr. Robert Anderson enterit to be lector at
  the kirk of Dunfermline and keeper and wreitter of the Baptisme,
  mariag and dead, and clerk to the Session.")

25, David Steward, cordiner, and Helen Kirkland had William; witnesses,
  William Smert, Thomas Elder, Thomas Baverage.

31, James Mudie and Bessie Cunynghame had George; witnesses, George
  Bothwell, James Mitchell, James Broun.

31, Robert Wardlaw and Margaret Huttoun had Henry; witnesses, Sir
  Henry Wardlaw of Pitreavie, James Kellok, James Dewar.

31, William Coventrie and Christian Drysdaill had Christian; witnesses,
  Robert Walwood, Andrew Smyth, James Broun.

M. 4, James Prymrois, writer in Edinburgh, to Sarah Leslie, daughter of
  James Leslie of Pitliver (on testimonial from the kirk of Edinburgh).

SEPTEMBER.

B. 1, John Skene and Helen Durie had Grizel; witnesses, Sir Robert Halkett
  of Pitfirran, Peter Law, provost, James Reid, Patrick Kingorn.

2, James Imbrie and Margaret Wardlaw had James; witnesses, James
  Wardlaw, fiar of Luscour, James Wardlaw in Mylneburne, John Bad.

2, Robert Schortus and Margaret Cunningham had Anna ; witnesses, Mr. Alexander Clerk of Pittencrieff, Tobias Murebek, George Davidson.

2, Adam Currie and Katherine Chrystie had Andrew born (baptised 8th) ; witnesses, Andrew Currie, Andrew Walker, Thomas Mitchell.

4, Robert Wallis, baker, and Janet Wely had Robert born (baptised 8th) ; witnesses, John Wallis, Robert Stirk, James Moyes.

5, William Young in Lymekilles and Margaret Peirsoun had James (baptised 8th) ; witnesses, William and Robert Anderson, James Young.

5, David Flockard in Easter Pitcorthie and Bessie Dewar had Henry (baptised 8th) ; witnesses, Henry Wardlaw, James Kellok in Maister-toun, Andrew Thomson.

5, John Fraser in Halkerstouns Baith and Margaret Barclay had John (baptised 8th) ; witnesses, John Halkerstoun, John Haswell, John Simsoun.

12, John Broun in North Queensferry and Barbara Thomson had Edward (baptised in Inverkeithing) ; witnesses, Edward Broun, George Burgan, Florence Burgan.

12, James Dick in Stewards Baithe and Margaret Kilgoure had Harry ; witnesses, John Anderson, George Wardlaw, Thomas Philp.

13, John Pirrhie and Elspet Esat had Bessie ; witnesses, Harry Steward, Alexander Esat, William Owisonn.

13, Henry Moreis and Isobel Duncan had Isobel ; witnesses, John Stevin-soun, Thomas Stevinsoun, John Warkman.

20, Walter Richie and Bessie Mitchell had James ; witnesses, James Mitchell at the Well, James Westwood, James Mitchell.

20, Patrick Small, collier in Touche, and Elspet Thomson had David ; witnesses, David Lainge, William Laing, John Huggoun.

20, Andrew Cunynghame in the St. Margaret stane and Janet Wilsoun had Isobel ; witnesses, Thomas Willsoun, Mark Donald, William Cunynghame.

20, Patrick Thomesoun, one of the colliers at Crocegaittes, and Agnes Balke had Helen ; witnesses, Henry Baverage, James Baverage, David Campbell.

20, Laurence Huttoun and Janet Robertson had Elspet ; witnesses, Robert Stevenson, Laurence Stevenson, John Warkman.

29, John Anderson and Margaret Gibson had John ; witnesses, James Mitchell, John Stanehous, Harry Steward.

M. 8, William Anderson to Margaret Kirk.

OCTOBER.

B. 3, Thomas Davidson, litster, and Janet Walker had Katherine ; witnesses, Robert Stevenson, Henry Davidson, Gilbert Sanderis, Peter Law, provost.

3, William Cose and Janet Burne had Beatrix ; witnesses, Edward Douglas, George Donald, Mr. George Walker.

3, James Trumble in Grange and Margaret Callendar had Janet ; wit-nesses, Adam and George Trumble, James Mudie.

13, George Trumble in Brumhall and Helen Greinlay had William ; witnesses, William Walker, William Anderson, Thomas Wilson, Andrew Currie, William Greinlaw.

14, Robert Taitt and Janet Ker had Helen ; witnesses, James Legat, Gilbert Ker, Thomas Elder.

21, Margaret Annas had a daughter "borne be hir in fornication to ane John Mortoun, tailyour in Edinburgh, for whome Jeane Mowtrie, Ladie Cavill, mother to the said Margarett Annas, is cautioner under the paine of 40 li. that she shall produce the said John Mortoun, and that he shall fullie satisfie the kirk," baptised called Margaret, pre-sented by David Hutoun, tailor ; witnesses, Thomas Davidson, bailie, William Walwood, officer.

27, Robert Dewar in Maistertouns Baithe and Helen Keir had Katherine ; witnesses, Alexander Aitkine, Robert Dewar, John Keir.

29, John Arnot, servitor to Mr. William Olyphant, and Isobel Veatche had William ; witnesses, Mr. William Olyphant, William Walker, James Simson, merchant.

31, William Letheme in Craigs and Janet Willsoue had Margaret ; witnesses, Robert Cunynghame, Robert Wilson, Archibald Cunynghame.

M. 13, James Spense to Janet Allane.

15, William Wardlaw of Logie to Margaret Weymes (in Dairsie kirk).

22, John Sibbald to Janet Bull.

28, David Murie to Katherine Wardlaw.

NOVEMBER.

B. 3, William Wilson, cordiner, and Margaret Watson had Helen ; witnesses, James Simson, David Stewart, James Fairny.

7, Sir James Halkett of Pitfirran, knight, and Dame Margaret Montgumrie, his lady, had Robert ; witnesses, Sir Robert Colvill of Cleeshe, Sir John Prestoun of Valyefeild, Sir Robert Halkett of Pitfirrane, William Menteithe of Randifuird, Mr. James Gray, James Gib.

7, John Kellok in Over Lassodie and Mary Weymes had John ; witnesses, John Dewar, John Kellok, his father, and John Kellok in Lassodie mill.

7, John Colzeare and Agnes Bird had Margaret ; witnesses, James Kellok, Robert Anderson, William Walwood.

10, John Walwood and Effie Kinloche had Isobel (in fornication) ; witnesses, William Cunynghame, Henry Douglas, John Gotterstoun.

10, Mr. John Hodge, doctor in the grammar school, and Margaret Scott had Christian ; witnesses, Harry Steward, Mr. James Readdie, Patrick Kingorne.

17, John Halyburtoun, a poor beggar, and Elspet Weddell had John ; witnesses, Robert Angus in Craigdukie, Andrew Thomson, " etc., and the said John is ordanit to be removit out of this paroche and to get a testimoniall of his laufull mariage and honestie."

21, Thomas Lawsone in Mirriehill and Katherine Marshell had Margaret ; witnesses, David Mitchell, George Donald, Thomas Wilson.

21, James Cunnand, tenant in Pitreavie, and Bessie Trumble had John ; witnesses, Mr. John Wardlaw of Ebtoun, John Dewar in Lassodie, William Walker, merchant.

29, James Mitchell at the Well and Christian Thomesoun had David ; witnesses, David Laurie, John Bad, John Alison, mason.

29, William Mackye in Coklaw and Margaret Betsoun had Helen ; witnesses, David Betsoun of Cardoun, John Betsoun in Clunecraige. Baptised in Cleish kirk " becaus of deepe winter weather."

M. 3, Andrew Mudie to Anna Ritchie.

24, Robert Anderson to Helen Hutson.

24, Robert Cusine to Helen Hutsheoun.

DECEMBER.

B. 5, Robert Dewar in Pitbachlie and Margaret Flokart had Isobel ; witnesses, Andrew Thomson, Andrew Cunynghame, John Mayne.

5, James Thomesone and Agnes Kellok had Elspet (in fornication) ; witnesses, John Kellok, elder and younger in Lassodie bray, and John Fyff in Keirs Baith.

11, James Strang and Janet Watt had Margaret (in fornication) ; witnesses, Gilbert Ker, William Young, Walter Anderson.

13, Alexander Nicoll and Helen Alexander had Robert ; witnesses, Peter Law, William Walker, James Donaldson.

15, James Currie and Elspet Walker had James ; witnesses, James Hall,

Robert Currie. Presented by the said Robert Currie, "becaus the
father of the bairne was with the camp."

15, Thomas Dewar and Janet Peacok had Henry ; witnesses, Robert
Angus, David Scotland, Robert Russell, Henry Wardlaw, fiar of
Balmull.

20, Andrew Chrystie and Helen Currie had George ; witnesses, Mr. George
Walker, George Currie, George Trumble.

27, James Donaldson in Easter Pitcorthie and Margaret Cunynghame had
Isobel ; witnesses, James Dewar, William Cunningham, James Mayne.

27, William Pullouns in Broomehall and Isobel Douglas had Edward ;
witnesses, Edward Douglas, Adam Wilson, Andrew Donald.

27, Adam Coventrie and Bessie Walwood had Janet ; witnesses, John
Coventrie, James Richardsoun, James Coventrie.

29, Harry Greg in the Ferrie and Bessie Broun had . . . . ; witnesses,
Alexander Greg, his brother, and Laurence Lugtoun.

M. 1, Thomas Walwood to Katharine Wilson (in Aberdour kirk).
    6, John Davidson to Katherine Kirk.
    8, John Edisoun to Margaret Mitchell.
    13, Robert Kellok to Agnes Greenes.
    15, Andrew Smythe to Katherine Douglas (in Inverkeithing kirk).
    22, Robert Willsone to Marjory Lethem.
    27, John M'Baithe to Janet Stirk.

JANUARY [1641].

B. 1, Andrew Wilsoun in Pittiemure and Bessie Peirsoun had Grizel ; witnesses, David Currie, Thomas Peirson, Ringane Mather.

    1, Andrew Donaldson in Wester Gellett and Katherine Hunter had
Margaret ; witnesses, Thomas Chrystie, David Sandis, Edward
Dowglas.

    2, James Spense and Janet Allane had Elspet ; witnesses, John Heckfoord,
John Allane, John Watsone.

    2, William Edie and Janet Mule had Katherine ; witnesses, David Myllar,
Richard Hamiltoun, Alexander Tailyour, James Waterstoun.

    7, Janet Burne had Jean baptised, presented by Thomas Burne : witnesses,
William Mudie, John Broun, John Burne. The child was half a year
old before it was baptised, "becaus she wantit a testimoniall fra the
minister of Inshe of hir satisfactioun for hir fault, and not surelie
knowne with quhom she got the bairne" ; so the said John Burne, her
brother, is cautioner that a testimonial will be got from Mr. John Dick,
minister of Inshe, before Whitsunday, under 40 li. of penalty.

    17, John Speare in Caudanbaithe and Katherine Ballantyne had Janet ;
witnesses, John Hodge, John Wallis, Henry Moreis.

    17, James Huttoun in Hiltoun of Pitfirrane and Agnes Ogilbie had William ;
witnesses, William Anderson, William Sanderis, John Wrycht.

    17, John Bust and Bessie Horne had Alexander ; witnesses, Mr. Alexander
Clerk of Pittincreeff, Peter Buist, John Bennett.

    17, William Nicoll, creelman in the Newraw, and Isobel Chalmeris had
Helen ; witnesses, Andrew Flokard, Robert Cant, Andrew Drummond.

    19, Thomas Beinstoun and Margaret Horne had Janet ; witnesses, John
Stirk, elder and younger, George Meldrum.

    19, James Durie of Craigluscour and Christian Durie had John ; witnesses,
Sir Robert Halkett of Pitfirran, James Gib, George Bothwell, Walter
Cokburne, Patrick Kingorne.

    24, Thomas Wilson in Grange and Elspet Wilson had Elspet ; witnesses,
Andrew Trumble, John Wilson, Andrew Mayne.

    26, Thomas Huttoun and Isobel Keir had Janet ; witnesses, James Richie,
James Dewar, John Burne.

    30, John Fargus in Easter Pitdinny and Agnes Wright had Agnes ; wit-
nesses, John Lindesay, John Peirsoun, William Anderson.

31, Andrew Broune and Bessie Wilson had Andrew ; witnesses, Andrew Currie, Andrew Walker, Andrew Thomson.

M. 24, John Allane to Christian Dow.

FEBRUARY.

B. 1, Robert Tailyour and Margaret Cunynghame had Robert ; witnesses, Robert Cunynghame, Andrew Cunynghame, Andrew Trumble.

7, George Wardlaw and Jean Kennedye had Harry ; witnesses, Harry Stewart, Thomas Philp, John Anderson.

9, Henry Dick in Over Lassodie and Helen Mackie had Margaret ; witnesses, Alexander Mowtrey, David Blak, John Kellok.

10, James Hoburne (absent with the army at Newcastle) and Grizel Shortus had Janet (in fornication), presented by James Kellok, tailor, who is cautioner that the father shall satisfy the kirk ; witnesses, Thomas Shortus, James Coburne, William Smert.

12, Gilbert M'Craiche (absent with the army at Newcastle) and Margaret Mudie had twins, Robert and William, presented by William Mudie and Robert Currie in the Nethertoun ; witnesses, James Simrell, Henry Peirson, Andrew Mudie, Andrew Thomson, Leonard Henrisoun, Andrew Colzeare.

13, Thomas Chrystie in Legattisbrig and Elizabeth Durie had Marion ; witnesses, Mr. Alexander Clerk of Pittincreeff, John Skene, James Anderson. "The bairne deceist unbaptized."

13, William Walwood in Southfod and Isobel Chrystie had James ; witnesses, James Mitchell in Fod, James Broun in Northfod, William Cunynghame in Knokus.

15, John Lawson in Crocefuird and Margaret Wilson had William ; witnesses, William Cunningham, William Lawsone, William Anderson.

15, Robert Walwood in Touche and Bessie Walwood had Abraham (in fornication) ; witnesses, William Walwood in Southfod, James Walwood in Netherbaith, John Walwood in Keirsbayth.

23, William Keir and Margaret Bad had John ; witnesses, John Bad, William Keir, John Ker.

24, William Bowie (absent with the camp at Newcastle) and Maise Bonar had James, presented by William Lambe ; witnesses, James Mudie, James Duncansone, James Moyes.

27, Thomas Douglas in Gellet and Bessie Murie had Edward (in fornication) ; witnesses, Andrew Currie in Prymros, William M'Break, Edward Douglas.

M. [*None.*]

MARCH.

B. 2, David Dewar in Meidowhead and Dorothy Maxwell had William ; witnesses, Andrew Wilson, James Dewar, William George.

4, William Blaiky in the Nethertoun and Annas Liddell had Thomas ; witnesses, Thomas Blaiky, George Liddell, William Liddell, Walter Coburne.

6, Thomas Horne in Over Lassody and Bessie Rowane had Mary ; witnesses, William and Thomas Horne, Nicol Dewar.

6, William Baverage and Margaret Jhonstoune had William (in fornication) ; witnesses, William Smert, William Baverage, Andrew and Thomas Baverage.

7, Thomas Burne and Isobel Richardson had Janet ; witnesses, Mr. James Reddie, Peter Law, William Smert.

7, John Broun (absent at the camp with the army) and Marion Allane had Marjory ; witnesses, Robert Burne, "etc."

14, John Wilson in Craigdukie and Christian Harlaw had David ; witnesses, David Scotland, Robert Russell, James Mylne.

14, James Steward, mealmaker, and Elspet Mayne had John ; witnesses, John Kellok, James Henrisone, William Lainge.

18, James Dewar in Baith and Helen Trumble had John ; witnesses, John Dewar, Peter Law, James Baverage.

20, Mr. Henry Smythe, minister at Culross, and Marjory Sandis had Margaret ; witnesses, John Bennett, Thomas Elder, John Wrycht, younger, Mr. Robert Anderson.

21, David Blak in Coklaw and Marjory Blaikwod had David ; witnesses, Alexander and James Baverage, James Gray.

23, John M'Mirrie and Janet Porteous had Janet ; witnesses, John Cunyngham, Andrew Drummond, Peter Fairley.

23, William Strawquhen in Kistok and Janet Allane had Andrew ; witnesses, Robert Strawchen, John Strawquhen, Andrew Leslie.

26, Archibald Boyd and Janet Watson had David ; witnesses, David Stewart, Laurence Watson, Gilbert Ker.

27, William Menteith of Randifuird and Anna Prestoun had Charles ; witnesses, Sir Robert Halkett and Sir James Halkett of Pitfirran, knights, Sir John Preston of Valiefeeld, Sir Henry Wardlaw of Pitreavie, James Gib, Mr. Alexander Clerk of Pittincreeff, Mr. Robert Preston, Mr. William Wardlaw.

28, John Broun, tailor in the Nethertoune, and Marion Glasse had Christian ; witnesses, William Smert, Henry Davidson, James Simrell.

28, John Halkstoune in Halkistounes baith and Geills Peacok had Agnes (in fornication) ; witnesses, John Haswell, John Simsoun, Andrew Berriehill.

30, John Westwood in the Nethertoun and Janet Keir had Janet ; witnesses, John Skeine, Robert Burne, Thomas Keir.

30, William Young in Lymekilles and Agnes Plaine had John ; witnesses, William Anderson, John Donaldson, David Anderson.

31, James Hutsoun in Easter Gellett and Katherine Pillones had Margaret : witnesses, Thomas Mitchell, William Pillones, Andrew Wilsone.

M. 14, John Halkstoun to Margaret Peirsoun.

APRIL.

B. 1, Alexander Jamiesoun "a vagabound tinklar," and his wife . . . had Thomas ; witnesses, David Bull, John Bruce, Henry Malcolme.

2, James Simsoun, merchant, and Bessie Walker had James ; witnesses, James Reid, Archibald Hamilton, Mr. George Walker.

3, David Sandis in Wester Gellett and Bessie Chrystie had John ; witnesses, John Broun in Barrhill, William Aitkin in Borrowyn, George Trumble.

11, Andrew Meldrum, weaver in Pittincreff, and Agnes Young had Alexander ; witnesses, David Walkar, James Simsoun, John Stirk.

11, John Wanderstoun, servant to the Laird of Pitfirran, and Isobel Leslie had Mary ; witnesses, William Cunynghame, William Anderson in Pitconnochie, Henry Dowglas in Cavill.

18, Andrew Pattoun in Pittiemure and Isobel Richardsoun had Margaret : witnesses, Ninian Mather, Walter Cant, Andrew Roxburgh.

18, Andrew Burne in Gellet and Elspet Ritchie had Alexander ; witnesses, James Ritchie, Adam Trumble, Alexander Naper.

20, Thomas Fraser and Margaret Henrisoun had Robert ; witnesses, John Watsoun, Robert Henrisoun, William Henrisoun.

25, Robert Broun in the Nethertoun and Agnes Clark had John ; witnesses, William Walker, John Broun, William Wilsone.

25, Andrew Speare in Mastertoun and Agnes Hardie had Isobel ; witnesses, Thomas Hardie, James Mudie, Thomas Bennett.

25, Andrew Adamesoun in Crocegaittes and Janet Baverage had James ; witnesses, James Baverage in Baithe, James Baverage in Keltiebeuche, James Broun in Fod, James Richardsoun in Dunfermline.

25, George Stirk and Elspet Walker had Alexander; witnesses, Mr. Alexander Clerk of Pittincreeff, Mr. John Walker, Thomas Chrystie in Hole.

25, James Reid and Marion Broun had Janet; witnesses, James Gib, Mr. William Olyphant, Alexander Mowtrey, Tutor of Rescobie.

27, William Wilsone in the Nethertoun and Christian Wright had Anna ; witnesses, Alexander Naper, William Mercer, John Wrycht, younger, David Stewart.

27, Robert Cusine in Easter Gellet and Helen Hutsoun had William ; witnesses, David Currie, Andrew Burne, David Hodge, William Burne.

27, John Hamilton, collier at Touch heuche, and Isobel Nisbet had Elspet ; witnesses, Henry Sanders, Alexander Hird, Richard Hamilton.

27, Charles Wilson in Mastertoun and Helen Broun had John ; witnesses, James Mudie, James Mylne, John Wilson.

M. 1, John Fyff to Isobel Broun (in Saline kirk).
13, Thomas Wilson to Margaret Dick.

MAY.

B. 4. William Anderson in Wester Gellett and Katherine Cunynghame had Helen ; witnesses, George Trumble, Andrew Currie, John Scotland.

7, Harry Richardson (absent with the army at Newcastle) and Sarah Steward had Isobel, presented by Archibald Richardson : witnesses, Gilbert Jhonstoun, James Wallace, Thomas Davidson, bailie.

9, John Spense in Pittiemure and Janet Cunynghame had John ; witnesses, Edward Dowglas, Robert Cunynghame, John Watson.

9, John Stirk in Wester Luscour and Margaret Wardane had Elizabeth (baptised in Carnock) ; witnesses, Nicol Wardlaw, James Wardlaw, James Wilson.

9, Richard Hamilton, collier in Baithe, and Elspet Falconer had Patrick (baptised here on testimonial from Clackmannan "quherin he before remanit ") ; witnesses, William Edie, John Hamilton, Alexander Hird.

17, John Mudie in Maistertoun and Bessie Wardlaw had twins, Robert and Jean ; witnesses, Robert Kellok, Robert Wardlaw, James Mylne, James Stanehous, John Wardlaw, Henry Douglas.

17, John Wright in Kistok and Margaret Lawson had Margaret : witnesses, William Cunynghame, Patrick Anderson, William Anderson.

19, Mr. William Olyphant, chamberlain to the Earl of Dunfermline, and Grizel Echline had William : witnesses, John Henrison of Fordell, William Menteith of Randifuird, Mr. William Wardlaw of Balmull.

22, Andrew Chapman in Wester Gellett and Barbara Huttoun had Robert ; witnesses, Robert Cunynghame in Sillietoun, William Anderson in Wester Gellet, John Wilson in Galrighill.

22, John Meldrum in Holebaldrig and Christian Blaccatter had Katherine ; witnesses, James Mylne, Robert Russell, John Huttoun.

24, John Thomson in Keltieheuche and Effie Finlaw had twins, William and John ; witnesses, Henry Barclay, John and James Baverage, James Thomson and James Davidson.

25, James Richardson and Agnes Coventrie had Janet ; witnesses, John Coventrie, James Baverage, James Coventrie.

25, Alexander Mowtrey, tutor of Rescoby, and Isobel Drummond had George ; witnesses, George Barclay, John Dewar, William M'Kye, David Blak.

29, James Baverage in Nether Baith and Janet Coventrie had Janet ; witnesses, John Coventrie, James Mitchell in Fod, James Richardson.

29, William Anderson in Hiltoun of Pitfirran and Janet Cunyngham had John ; witnesses, John Lindesay, John Wrycht, William Sanderis.

29, John Ker, weaver, and Bessie Clerk had James ; witnesses, Gilbert Ker, Robert Stevenson, James Mudie.

M. 16, James Kedglie to Margaret Broun.

JUNE.

B. 1, John M'Baithe in Pitconnochie and Janet Stirk had Margaret : witnesses, Thomas Chrystie, Andrew Walker, John Stirk.

4, William Smert, flesher, and Bessie Stevenson had Janet : witnesses, Alexander Drysdaill, Andrew Purves, Peter Buist.

6, James Mylne in Maistertoun and Katherine Blaccatter had James ; witnesses, James Cunnon, James Mudie, David Peirson.

13, John Stirk, weaver in Pittincreeff, and Bessie Crawford had Alexander ; witnesses, Sir Alexander Clerk, provost of Edinburgh, Mr. Alexander Clerk of Pittincreeff, his son, and Robert Stirk, messenger.

13, Andrew Trumble, baker, and Barbara Law had Peter ; witnesses, Peter Law, Peter Buist, David Scotland.

15, George Trumble in Sillietoun and Marjory Maistertoun had Helen ; witnesses, William Walker, David Mitchell, George Trumble in Broomhall.

17, John Dagleeshe, tailor, and Bessie Miklejohne had Walter : witnesses, Walter Dalgleeshe, Walter Coburne, James Kellok.

20, Helen Henden had Bessie (born about six weeks ago in fornication to Robert Scotland in Clune) : witnesses, James Wardlaw, Mungo Cunynghame, David Reid.   Presented by George Henden. her father, because the father denies the child, though otherwise proved to be his.

22, Mark Donald, baker, and Marjory Bennett had Margaret ; witnesses, John Bennett, Walter Coburne, Andrew Purves.

26, William Anderson in Pitconnochie and Agnes Chalmer had Robert ; witnesses, William Anderson in Lymekilles, Robert Anderson his son, Thomas Douglas in Urquhart.

26, William Dick in Pittincreeff and Elizabeth Mathieson had Alexander ; witnesses, Mr. Alexander Clerk of Pittincreeff, Thomas Chrystie, Tobias Murbek.

29, James Ewine (absent with the army at Newcastle) and Margaret Prymrose had James ; presented by Peter Law ; witnesses, William Mercer, Henry Davidson, Andrew Trumble in Grange, Andrew Mudie.

M. 1, Gilbert Alexander to Janet Couper.

17, Andrew Kirk to Marjory Callender.

22, Robert Burne to Janet Cunynghame.

24, Sir Thomas Ker of Kavers to Grizel Halkett, lawful daughter of Sir Robert Halkett of Pitfirran.

JULY.

B. 1, George Watt, sailor in Lymekilles, and Janet Robertson had William ; witnesses, William Anderson and his son William, both sailors in Lymekills, and William Young there.

1, Alexander Chalmers, merchant, and Katherine Walker had William ; witnesses, William Walker, James Simsoun, William Ferrie.

3, John Cose and Janet Trumble had Isobel ; witnesses, John Wilson in Galrighill, Henry Davidson, John Inglis.

3, Andrew Trumble, smith, and Janet Anderson had James : witnesses, John Wrycht, Robert Stevenson, David Anderson.

12, Andrew Currie and Helen Stirk had Agnes ; witnesses, James Reid, David Mitchell, Thomas Wilson.

17, Andrew Robertson, weaver, and Margaret Potter had Janet ; witnesses, William Smert, Andrew Purves, John Robertson.

18, Andrew Moreis, litster, and Margaret Lowe had Janet ; witnesses, Walter Coburne, Andrew Purves, Adam Welye.

31, Thomas Fyff and Helen Fyff (who died two days after delivery) had
    Eupham ; witnesses, David Fyff, Thomas Fyff, William Dalgleeshe.
31, George Wallis and Christian White had George (in fornication) ; wit-
    nesses, Thomas Baverage, John Smetoun, George Young.

M. 6, James Mather to Eupham Anderson.
   13, Thomas Horne to Janet Watson.
   19, William Wattis to Elspet Chattow.
   20, Andrew Wardlaw to Helen Burley.
   20, George Spens to Marjory Anderson.
   20, John Donaldson to Grizel Mather (testimonial from Inverkeithing).
   22, John Keir to Bessie Walker.

AUGUST.

B. 1, John Cunningham in St. Margaret stane and Agnes Lathangie had
      William ; witnesses, William Cunningham in Knokous, William
      Lathangie and William Cunningham in Blair of Carnok, and William
      Anderson in Gellett.
    8, George Edisoun in Lymekilles and Bessie Sandis had George ; witnesses,
      George Watt, John Trotter, David Anderson.
   10, Henry Beany in Lymekills and Helen Wright had James ; witnesses,
      William Anderson, Robert Anderson his son, and James Young, all in
      Lymekills.
   10, James Peacok in the North Ferrie and Janet Burgan had Laurence ;
      witnesses, Laury Lugtoun, Robert Broun, Andrew Williamson, Robert
      Drysdaill.
   10, George Young, weaver, and Bessie Lowe had William ; witnesses,
      William Lowe, James Legatt, Robert Stevenson.
   10, John Moore, porter, and Agnes Shipheard had Charles ; witnesses,
      Walter Coburne, Andrew Thomson, John Baxter, George Davidson,
      "and the bairne young Lord Charles."
   10, James Fairny, cordiner, and Margaret Huttoun had Janet ; witnesses,
      Andrew Thomson, David Laurie. David Stewart, William Walwood.
   19, David Scotland in Wester Craigdukie and Elspet Dewar had John ;
      witnesses, John Dewar in Lassodie, John Scotland, John Huttoun in
      Dunduff.
   22, John Alisone, barrowman, and Katherine Duncan had Bessie ; witnesses,
      John Burne, Thomas Burne, John Ker.
   29, James Kedglie, collier in Crocegaittes, and Margaret Broun had Janet ;
      witnesses, Patrick Kedglie, Andrew Edisoun, Henry Baverage.
   29, Gilbert Cumming, collier in Touche, and Janet Tasker had Gilbert ; wit-
      nesses, James Wedderstoun, Alexander Hird, William Walwood.
   30, Robert Logan in the Nethertoun and Christian Huttoun had William ;
      witnesses, William Blaiky, Henry Davidson, David Broun.
   30, Andrew Menteith, miller in Cavill, and Bessie Fothringhame had David ;
      witnesses, David Lindesay, David Mitchell, Henry Dowglas.
   30, Robert Stevenson, smith, and Elspet Davidson had Andrew ; witnesses,
      Andrew Purves, Edward Elder, James Ritchie, Adam Anderson.
   30, David Inglis, collier, and Helen Lugtoun had Isobel ; witnesses, Tobias
      Murbek, James Wedderstoun, John Hector, John Walker.

M. 4, James Ritchie to Margaret Dewar (in Aberdour kirk).
   10, Mark Donald to Eupham Beany.
   17, Robert Strachan to Annas Warkman.
   24, James Pugill to Margaret Dick (in Bingrie kirk at our request).

SEPTEMBER.

B. 2, Thomas Wilson in Pitliver and Margaret Dick had Thomas ; witnesses,
      Thomas Mitchell, David Mitchell, John Wilson.

6, John Littiljohne, weaver, and Janet Wilson had twins, Janet and Christian ; witnesses, James Littlejohn, elder and younger, William Legatt, flesher, John Wilson, Henry Wilson, James Wilson in Galrighill.

9, Alexander Hunter, flesher, and Janet Burne had Jean (in fornication), presented by Thomas Couper ; witnesses, William Mercer, William Mudie, Andrew Turnbull, John Bruce.

12, Robert Balcaice in Brae of Lassodie and Barbara Peacok had David ; witnesses, David Smetoun in Blarathie, David Rowan, David Scotland.

15, Thomas Tod in Clune and Isobel Templeman had James ; witnesses, James Wardlaw, Thomas Davidson, James Murgan, Nicol Wardlaw.

18, John Lawson in Lymekilles and Katherine Logan had Charles : witnesses, Patrick Lawsoun in the Craigs, George Donald and Robert Anderson in Lymekills.

18, William Anderson in Kistok of Pitfirran and Margaret Kirk had John ; witnesses, John Kirk, William Cunningham, William Anderson.

18, Henry Patrik, tailor, and Isobel Mylne had James ; witnesses, James Mylne in Mastertoun, James Mylne in Lochend, John Huttoun in Dunduff.

21, James Prymrois in Ridcraig of Mylneburne and Janet Tailyeour had Bessie ; witnesses, Robert Cunningham in Sillietoun, John Tailyeour, George Tailyeour.

24, David Smetoun in Blarathie and Elspet Russell had Edward ; witnesses, Edward Elder, Edward Russell, Edward Remanes.

24, John Robertson in Pittiemure and Isobel Hutoun had Harry ; witnesses, Thomas Cay, Robert Cant, Andrew Wilson.

28, John Adame, footman to my Lord Dunfermline, and Margaret Greg had John (baptised in Edinburgh at our request).

29, George Scott, litster, and Helen Miklejohn had Janet : witnesses, Andrew Miklejohn, Andrew Purves, Walter Coburne.

M. 16, John Broun to Agnes Mylne.

21, John Hamilton to Bessie Anderson.

23, James Littlejohn to Effie Keir.

OCTOBER.

B. 3, William Penman and Cicell Atchesoune had William ; witnesses, William Cunningham in Knokus, William Nicoll in Kistok, Andrew Leslie there.

8, William Mudie and Margaret Phillan had John ; witnesses, John Bennett, John Cose, Robert Burne.

10, James Dewar in Pitbachlie and Isobel Huttoun had Isobel : witnesses, James Huttoun, Thomas Huttoun, Alexander Wardlaw.

10, Robert Willy in the Yron mylne, smith there, and Margaret Kay had Margaret ; witnesses, Thomas Wilson, Andrew Donald, Robert Cunningham.

10, William Currie in the Rodds and Bessie Drysdaill had Bessie ; witnesses, Andrew Walker in Logie, John Currie in Crombie, Mr. George Walker.

17, John Walwood in Garvokwood and Mary Anderson had William ; witnesses, William Cunningham in Knokus, Robert Walwood " in the said wood," and his brother James Walwood.

17, Robert Schortus, collier, and Margaret Bad had Helen : witnesses, Tobias Murebek, Charles Bad, John Heckfoord.

24, David Donaldson and Mause Bryce had James (in fornication) baptised in Carnock at our request ; witnesses, James Donaldson, his brother, James Bryce, James Dewar.

24, John Dewar in the Hole and Marjory Robertson had George ; witnesses, Robert Dewar, Mr. George Walker, John Wilson.

26, David Hodge and Katherine Smert had John ; witnesses, John Wrycht, John Warkman, James Meldrum.

26, Andrew Meldrum, weaver, and Agnes Davidson had William (in adultery); witnesses, William Inche and Henry Meldrum, weavers. Presented by George Stirk, weaver.

M. 3, Thomas Whyte to Agnes Imbrie.
17, John Morton to Margaret Hannan.

NOVEMBER.

B. 5, John Peirson in the Nethirtoun and Janet Menteith had Patrick ; witnesses, Patrick Peirson in Urquhart, George Meldrum and James Anderson in Pittencrieff.

7, James Baverage and Janet Steidman had Elspet ; witnesses, William M'Kye, John Gray, David Blak.

9, William Walker in the Nethirtoun and Marjory Broun had John ; witnesses, John Walker, Adam Stanehous, John Broun.

14, Robert Wilson in Pitliver and Marjory Letheme had Margaret; witnesses, David Mitchell, Thomas Wilson, William Letheme.

14, Harry Blaikwood in Blarathie and Bessie Broun had David ; witnesses, David Blak, David Scotland, David Broun.

18, Thomas Mitchell, younger, tenant in Rossyth, and Helen Trumble had Margaret (baptised here because of the absence of Mr. Walter Bruce, minister of Inverkeithing) ; witnesses, Alexander Steward, Andrew Currie, David Mitchell.

21, John Wilson in the Holl and Helen Currie had Helen ; witnesses, Thomas Chrystie, Andrew Walker, Mr. George Walker, his son.

21, Henry Dowglas and Christian Wilson had Elspet ; witnesses, Thomas Dowglas, Edward Dowglas, James Mitchell.

21, Thomas Elder and Helen Simson had Thomas ; witnesses, John Bennett, Andrew Purves, Walter Coburne, William Walker.

21, William George in the Nethirtoun and Elspet Myllar had Marjory ; witnesses, Andrew Wilson, David Peacok, Thomas Dowglas.

21, Laurence Greive, miller at the Wood mylne, and Margaret Wannan had John ; witnesses, John Robertson, John Bennet, David Hunter.

23, David Russell, tenant in Balmull, and Janet Stanehous had Henry ; witnesses, Robert Russell, his brother, Henry Wardlaw, fiar of Balmull, David Smetoun.

24, James Kellok, tailor, and Marjory Schortus had William ; witnesses, Robert Stevenson, smith, William Smert, flesher, John Dalgleeshe, tailor.

28, James Angus, tenant in Meidowend, and Janet Gillaspie had Beatrix ; witnesses, David Dowglas, Andrew Walker, Adam Bryce.

M. 2, Gavin Edison to Janet Hislop.
4, Thomas Spens to Bessie Arthour.
23, Patrick Wright to Janet Huttoun.
23, John Donald to Margaret Burne.
23, William Currie to Helen Donaldson.
23, James Lawsone to Jean Hog.
30, David Dowglas to Elspet Dewar.

DECEMBER.

B. 3, Tobias Murebek and Christian Cant had Tobias ; witnesses, Mr. Alexander Clerk of Pittencrieff, James Reid, provost, Mr. Harry Makgill, minister.

5, William Inglis in Grange and Bessie Cuper had Bessie ; witnesses, Thomas Cuper, Alexander Inglis, Adam Trumble.

5, Thomas Trumble in the Colzeraw and Katherine Bad had Charles ; witnesses, James Myllar, Charles Bad, John Edison.

7, Andrew Smythe in North Fod and Katherine Dowglas had Katherine ; witnesses, Peter Dowglas, Mark Sprewell, Andrew Turnbull.

7, James Spense, collier, and Janet Allane had twins, James and Janet ; witnesses, John Heckfoord, John Watson, James Watson, David Myllar, John Allane, elder, John Allane, younger.

7, William Beane, weaver, and Agnes Blaikwood had Margaret ; witnesses, Alexander Beane, his father, Thomas Davidson, litster, Nicol Blaikwood.

12, John Phin in Masterton's Baithe and Margaret Din had Katherine ; witnesses, Alexander Aikine of Masterton's Baith, Robert Dewar, John Stevenson, elder, in Stevenson's Baith.

14, John Colzeare, tailor, and Agnes Burt had James ; witnesses, James Espline, Andrew Colzeare, Andrew Thomson, James Kellok, Robert Anderson, younger, tailor.

14, David Trumble and Margaret Schortus had Janet (in fornication) ; witnesses, John Neilson, John Donald, James Anderson.

19, William Pullwort in Wester Gellet and Isobel Dowglas had Helen ; witnesses, David Sandis, Robert Cunningham in Sillietoun, John Tailyeour in Mylneburn.

19, David Cambell, collier in Netherbaith, and Margaret Tailyeour had David ; witnesses, Henry Baverage in Netherbaith, James Baverage, his son, Andrew Berriehill.

19, John Colzeare and Marjory Cassin had John ; witnesses, John Birrell, John Dow, John Peirson.

23, John Fitt and Lucres Kirk had Janet ; witnesses, Andrew Purves, Mark Donald, David Bull.

28, Mr. Robert Anderson and Marion Dewar had Christian ; witnesses, Mr. William Wardlaw of Balmull, Walter Dalgleeshe, John Bennett.

28, Andrew Mudie in the Nethirtoun and Anna Ritchie had Margaret ; witnesses, Thomas and James Ritchie in Blaklaw, William Mudie in Nethertoun.

30, John Fyff in Lassodie and Isobel Broun had Elspet ; witnesses, John Dewar in Lassodie, Robert Broun in Meidowheid of Sawlin, John Syme in Quhythous.

M. 7, Alexander Smetoun to Grizel Wallis.

7, Alexander Galrig to Katherine Potter.

14, Thomas Cant to Isobel Wely.

21, Andrew Donald to Bessie Currie.

JANUARY [1642].

B. 5, William Mudie, maltman in the Nethertoun, and Janet Chrystie had William ; witnesses, William Mercer, William Walker, Mr. George Walker.

6, James Hamilton and Jean Sanderis had Margaret ; witnesses, James Reid, provost, Patrick Kingorne, Walter Coburne, Andrew Purves. Presented by James Espline.

9, John Broun, smith, and Rachel Blaikye had Henry ; witnesses, Sir Henry Wardlaw of Pitreavie, James Kellok, Thomas Stanehous.

9, James Walwood in Nether Baith and Helen Inglis had Christian ; witnesses, William Walwood in Southfode, Andrew Smyth in Northfode, Thomas Walwood in Crocegaittis.

9, John Strachan in Pittencrieff and Isobel Fotheringhame had twins, Andrew and Marion ; witnesses, Mr. Alexander Clerk of Pittencrieff, Andrew Menteith in Cavill, Robert Strachan, George Meldrum, Robert Sharpe, John Stirk.

16, Archibald Gray, piper in Pitdinny, and Janet Cellers had Bessie ; witnesses, John Lindesay, James Peirsone, John Leitche.

21, Alexander Frenche, gardener in Pinkie, and Grizel More had James (in fornication), presented by Thomas More, her father ; witnesses, James Moyes, Robert Wells, David More. The child was baptised on a testimonial of the mother's satisfaction at Aberdour.

31, Robert Russell, miller at Balmull mill, and Margaret Dewar had Barbara ; witnesses, Henry and George Wardlaw, sons of Mr. William Wardlaw of Balmull, William Wardlaw of Logie.

M. 4, Thomas Fyff to Helen Baverage (in Ballingrie kirk).
5, Andrew Maine to Janet Cunningham.
5, Captain James Frenche to Janet Stanehous.
25, William Bowman to Margaret Hearine.
25, Thomas Broun to Agnes Kellok.
27, William Walker to Margaret Trumble.
30, James Sanderis to Janet Peacok.
30, Robert Forrest to Janet Malcolme.

FEBRUARY.

B. 6, John Stevenson in Kistok of Pitfirran and Bessie Allane had John ; witnesses, James Anderson, James Clerk, Thomas Leslie.
6, James Kingorne in Lymekilles and Margaret Kirk had twins, Helen and Bessie ; witnesses, Andrew and George Trumble in Broomhall, Robert Anderson in Lymekilles.
6, Robert Burne, miller at Pittencrieff mill, and Janet Cunningham had David ; witnesses, William Mercer, Andrew Walker, Thomas Dowglas.
6, David Murie in Grange and Katherine Wardlaw had William ; witnesses, John Murie, John Mudie, William Murie, his father.
8, Thomas Cuper and Isobel Walwood had Robert ; witnesses, Peter Law, Robert Stevenson, Robert Walwood.
13, John Keir, miller, and Bessie Walker had Helen ; witnesses, Thomas Keir, Thomas and Robert Burne.
15, James Mylne in Lochend and Grizel Robertson had Robert ; witnesses, Robert Russell, Robert Angus in Rescobie, Robert Broun, servitor to Mr. William Wardlaw of Balmull.
20, Patrick Broun in the Hill of Baithe and Bessie Mudie had Janet ; witnesses, James Stanehous, John Hodge, Robert Mudie.
20, Andrew Kellok, miller at Lassodie mill, and Margaret Stocks had Helen ; witnesses, John Gray, John Baverage, John Kellok
22, John Inglis in Mossyde and Isobel Trumble had Helen ; witnesses, David Moreis, John Haswell, John Simson.
27, William Inche, weaver in Pittencrieff, and Margaret James had Marion ; witnesses, Mr. Alexander Clerk of Pittencrieff, James Reid, Andrew Walker.
28, Thomas, Earl of Kellie, and Eupham Anderson had Hew (in fornication), presented by Mr. Hew Wallace, servitor to the said Earl ; witnesses, Harry Steward of Baithe, James Gib of Carribber, James Reid, provost.

M. 15, John Rowane to Isobel Rowane.
15, William Tailyeour to Annas Dowglas.
24, Edward Russell to Isobel Dewar.
24, John Fygg to Isobel Phin.

MARCH.

B. 2, Robert Anderson in Baithe and Helen Hutsone had twins, Janet and Marjory ; witnesses, James Baverage, John and George Anderson, Patrick Steward, John Meldrum, Thomas Currour.
5, Henry Peirson in Pitdinny and Katherine Currie had Helen (in fornication) ; witnesses, John Lindsay, John Peirson, John Wilson.
6, William Sanderis in Hiltoun of Pitfirran and Katherine Cusine had John ; witnesses, John Cusine in Lethems, John Hutton in Dunduff, John Sanderis in Inzevair.

6, Andrew Cowstoun in Wester Gellett and Katherine Wannan had Edward ; witnesses, Edward Dowglas, William Anderson, Edward Cowstoun, his brother.

6, John Buist in Pittincreiff and Bessie Horne had James ; witnesses, Robert Sharpe, James Richardson, Robert Stirk.

8, Adam Currie in Prymrois and Katherine Chrystie had Bessie ; witnesses, James Cunnand, David Currie, Thomas Chrystie.

8, James Anderson and Janet Robertson had Robert (in fornication) ; witnesses, Andrew Miklejohn, Mr. Robert Anderson, John Hamilton, David Trumble. Presented by said John Hamilton.

13, Andrew Flockard in Baldrig and Isobel Pet had Christian ; witnesses, Robert Ged of Baldrig, Andrew Wilson, David Flokard, his brother.

13, John Neilson, cordiner, and Janet Buist had Robert ; witnesses, Patrick Trumble, Andrew Trumble, Robert Neilson, his father.

20, William Walwood in Southfode and Isobel Chrystie had Isobel ; witnesses, Andrew Smythe in Northfode, David Hunter in Woodmylne, John Stenhous in Southfode.

23, James Simrell, mason, and Margaret Mudy had Christian ; witnesses, Andrew Thomson, Walter Coburne, James Ritchie.

24, James Patton and Jean Tosheoke had John (in fornication) ; witnesses, Mark and John Donald, John Edisone, James Patton.

27, Nicol Inglis in Drumtuthell and Marjory Law had Margaret ; witnesses, James Murgane, William Murgane, James Mylne in Lochend.

27, James Imbrie, weaver, and Margaret Wardlaw had John ; witnesses, Robert Stevenson, John Gotterstoun, John Wardlaw.

27, John Watson, cordiner, and Barbara Bruce had William ; witnesses, William Walwood, cordiner, James Simson, cordiner, James Fairny, cordiner.

29, David Peirson in Doverhill and Helen Henderson had Janet ; witnesses, Robert Cant, James Cunnand, William Henderson.

29, David Mitchell in Pitliver and Margaret Currie had Andrew ; witnesses, David Lindsay, Thomas Wilson, Andrew Currie.

M. 11, William Orrok to Jean Murrey.

11, William Imbrie to Janet Fegg

15, William Logan to Agnes Watson.

29, Alexander Beane to Christian Simson.

APRIL.

B. 2, John Broun, gardener, and Agnes Gillies had Elspet ; witnesses, William Smert, David Stewart, Thomas Baverage.

2, John Angus in Rescobie and Marion Reidie had Marion ; witnesses, Robert Angus, Robert Greive, William Rowane.

2, Thomas Baverage and Janet Tod had Bessie ; witnesses, William Smert, Thomas Elder, Thomas Baverage.

2, Robert Short in Pitconnoquhy and Agnes Donaldson had Bessie (in fornication) ; witnesses, Patrick, William and James Anderson in Pitconnoquhie.

2, David Robertson in Mylneburne and Katherine Scott had Janet ; witnesses, George Trumble, George Donald, Robert Robertson.

2, John Stanehous in Southfode and Janet Cunningham had Isobel ; witnesses, Thomas Mitchell, James Cunningham, Thomas Stanehous.

2, William Wilson, cordiner, and Margaret Watson had David ; witnesses, David Steward, Laurence Watson, Archibald Boyd.

2, James Durie of Craigluscour and Christian Durie had Grizel ; witnesses, Doctor William Makgill, Walter and James Coburne.

5, Robert Tailyeour, miller at the East mill, and Margaret Cunningham had William ; witnesses, Mr. William Olyphant, Andrew Cunningham in St. Margaret stane, and James Donaldson in Pitcorthie.

10, James Hamilton, piper, and Isobel Broun had John ; witnesses, John Hog, Robert Anderson, James Fairny.

10, Thomas Cunnand, tailor in Mastertoun, and Isobel Dewar had Agnes ; witnesses, Robert Dewar, James Stanehous, George Anderson.

10, Thomas Huton in Wester Luscour and Bessie Stobie had Thomas (baptised in Carnock) : witnesses, Nicol Wardlaw, Adam Stobie, Patrick Lindesay.

10, George Chapman, weaver in Wester Sillietoun, and Janet Gryssie had William ; witnesses, William Walker, bailie, George Trumble in Broomehall, George Meldrum in Pittincreiff.

17, William Hodge in Keltieheuche and Grizel Davidson had a son . . . (baptised in Ballingrie).

17, John Davidson, servitor to the Earl of Dunfermline, and Katherine Kirk had John ; witnesses, Thomas Davidson, George Davidson, William Walwood.

17, Thomas Horne, wright, and Janet Watson had William ; witnesses, William Horne, his father, William Walker, bailie, David Watson.

24, Troyollus Hutton in Wester Pitdinny and Bessie Stevin had James ; witnesses, John Lindsay, John Peirson, James Hutton.

24, John Nicoll, collier, and Janet Hutcheon had Marjory ; witnesses, Tobias Murebek, James Waterstoun, James Broun.

24, Patrick Durie in Wester Luscour and Margaret Wilson had William ; witnesses, William Murgane, James Wardlaw, Thomas Huttoun.

26, Patrick Stevenson and Christian Mudie had Grizel ; witnesses, James Mudy, Henry Davidson, Patrick Allane, younger.

28, Patrick Broun in Northfode and Agnes Young had Janet ; witnesses, James Mitchell, John Stanehous, James Anderson.

30, John Whyte in Lassodie and Margaret Kellok had Margaret ; witnesses, John Kellok in the Thornetoun, Thomas Horne there, John Kellok in Lassodie mill.

M. 12, Robert Cant to Christian Peirson.

24, Patrick Rowland (? Rowane) to Katherine Dowglas.

26, John Hutton to Bessie Hutton (in Saline kirk).

26, Mr. William Ged to Annas Steward (in Inverkeithing kirk).

28, James Anderson to Agnes Dewar.

MAY.

B. 8, Adam Car in Dunduff and Janet Crawfurd had Bessie ; witnesses, George Dewar in Lathalmont, Robert Angus in Rescobie, William Dalgleeshe in Tunygask.

8, Robert Thomson in Wester Gellet and Helen Sibbald had Beatrix ; witnesses, James Mayne in Pitcorthie, William Anderson in Wester Gellet, Gilbert Car, armourer in Dunfermline.

8, Andrew Chrystie in Mirryhill and Helen Currie had Margaret ; witnesses, David Mitchell, George Donald, Andrew Donald.

8, David Broun, weaver in Grange, and Janet Dewar had Margaret ; witnesses, David Flokard, Thomas Cunnan, John Brown.

10, John Watson in Wester Baldrig and Isobel Williamson had Isobel ; witnesses, Andrew Wilson, Andrew Flockard, Thomas Baverage.

10, David Hutton, tailor, and Margaret Dempstertoun had Margaret ; witnesses, William Walker, bailie, Thomas Davidson, James Hutton.

15, James Hodge in Keltieheuch and Christian Leslie had Archibald (baptised in Ballingrie) ; witnesses, James Baverage, John Baverage, William Hodge.

18, Andrew Cant in Pittiemure and Christian Bull had Andrew ; witnesses, Robert Cant, Andrew Cant, David Bull in Hiltoun of Rossyth.

18, Thomas Davidson and Janet Walker had Elspet ; witnesses, Peter Law, William Walker, Edward Elder.

22, James Anderson in North Fode and Elspet Chrystie had David ; witnesses, David Chrystie in Rossyth, David Reddye in Babugie, and David Russell in Balmull.

VOLUME 44.

PART CXXIX.

DECEMBER 1935.

SCOTTISH RECORD SOCIETY.

PARISH REGISTER OF DUNFERMLINE

1561-1700

(MARCH 1653—NOVEMBER 1663)

EDINBURGH :

PRINTED FOR THE SOCIETY BY J. SKINNER & COMPANY, LTD.

1935.

INDICES AND CALENDARS OF RECORDS

ISSUED BY

The Scottish Record Society.

+•+

A few unbound Copies of the following completed Volumes are still on hand, and will be supplied to Subscribers *only :—*

Indexes to the Registers of Testaments of the following Commissariots—

1.	Edinburgh, . .	1514–1600.	308 pp.	*Out of print.*	
2.	Do. . .	1601–1700.	448 pp.	· Do.	
3	Do. . .	1701–1800.	300 pp.	Do.	
4.	Inverness, . .	1630–1800.	35 pp.	Do.	
5.	Hamilton and Campsie,	1564–1800.	89 pp.	Do.	
6.	Aberdeen, . .	1715–1800.	72 pp.	Do.	
7.	Glasgow, . .	1547–1800.	553 pp.	Do.	
8.	St. Andrews, .	1549–1800.	426 pp.	Do.	
9.	Argyle, . .	1674–1800.	48 pp.	Price	3s.
10.	Caithness, . .	1661–1664.	7 pp.	„	1s.
11.	The Isles, . .	1661–1800.	10 pp.	„	1s.
12.	Peebles, . .	1681–1691.	13 pp.	„	1s.
13	Brechin, . .	1576–1800.	147 pp.	„	9s.
14.	Dumfries, . .	1624–1800.	96 pp.	„	6s.
15.	Dunblane, . .	1539–1800.	181 pp.	„	10s.
16.	Dunkeld, . .	1682–1800.	58 pp.	„ 3s. 6d.	
17.	Kirkcudbright,	1663–1800.	32 pp.	„ 2s. 6d.	
18.	Lauder, . .	1561–1800.	62 pp.	„	4s.
19.	Lanark, . .	1595–1800.	124 pp.	„	7s.
20.	Moray, . .	1684–1800.	33 pp.	„ 2s. 6d.	
21.	Orkney and Zetland,	1611–1684.	81 pp.	„	6s.
22.	(Parts XXVI & XXVII), Stirling, . .	1607–1800.	180 pp.	„	10s.
23.	Wigtown, . .	1700–1800.	17 pp.	„	2s.
24.	Miscellaneous Executry Papers, . .	1481–1740.	8 pp.	„	1s.

Also Indexes to following have been issued—

25. Holyrood Burial Register, 1706–1900. Price 5s.
26. Greyfriars Burial Register, 1656–1700.
   (Presented by the Trustees of Sir William Fraser, K.C.B.)
27. (Parts XXIX to XXXIV inclusive), Edinburgh
   Marriage Register, 1595–1700. Price 32s. 6d.
28. Edinburgh Apprentice Register, 1583–1666. „ 10s. 6d.
29. (Parts XXXVI to XXXIX inclusive), Protocol
   Book of Gavin Ros, 1512-1532. 278 pp. Price 20s.
30. Register of Baptisms, Chapel of Birnie and
   Tillydesk, 1763-1801. 16 pp. „ 2s.
31. Index to Genealogies, &c., Lyon Office. 58 pp. „ 6s.
32 Restalrig Burial Register, 1728–1854. Price 5s.
33. Argyllshire Inventories, 1693–1702. „ 3s.
34. Consistorial Processes and Decreets, 1658-
   1800. Price 10s. 6d.
35. (Parts XLII, XLIII, XLV, XLVI and XLVIII),
   Edinburgh Marriage Register, 1701-1750. „ 32s. 6d.
36. Calendars to Charter Chests of Earls of Wigton
   and Dundonald, 1666. Price 10s.

[*Continued on page 3 of Cover.*

37. Protocol Book of Sir Alexander Gaw.   Price   5s.
38. Parish Register of Durness, 1764-1814.   ,,   6s.
39. Protocol Book of Sir William Corbet, 1529-55.   ,,   3s.
40. Parish Register of Torphichen, 1673-1714.   ,,   2s.
41. Parish Register of Kilbarchan, 1649-1772. 140 pp.   ,,   10s.
42. Scrymgeour Inventory, 1611. 70 pp.   ,,   6s.
43. Protocol Book of Gilbert Grote.   ,,   9s.
44. (Parts LIV, LXVI, LXX and LXXI), Parish Register of Dunfermline, 1561-1700. (Not completed.)   ,,   21s.
45. (Parts L, LI, LIV, LV, LVI, LIX, LXII and LXX), Parish Register of Melrose, 1642-1820.   ,,   25s.
46. (Parts LIV, LV, LX, LXI, LXIV, LXV and LXVIII), Canongate Marriage Register, 1564-1800.   ,,   40s.
47. Monumental Inscriptions in St. Cuthbert's.   ,,   10s.
48. Canisbay Parish Register, 1652-1666.   ,,   2s.
49. Register of Episcopal Church, St. Andrews, 1722-87.   ,,   2s.
50. Parish Lists of Wigtownshire and Minniegaff, 1684.   ,,   7s.
51. Monumental Inscriptions in St. Cuthbert's (Newer Portion). 101 pp.   ,,   10s.
52. (Parts LXXVI, LXXVIII, LXXXIII and LXXXVII), Protocol Books of Dominus Thomas Johnsoun.   ,,   15s.
53. (Parts LXXIX to LXXXI, LXXXIV to LXXXVI and LXXXVIII to XCII inclusive), Edinburgh Marriage Register, 1751-1800.   ,,   42s.
54. Inventory of Lamont Papers, 1231-1897.
    (Presented by Sir Norman Lamont, Bart.)
55. (Parts LXXIV, LXXV and LXXVII, CVII and CXIII), Calendar of Writs in Yester House. 437 pp.   ,,   42s.
56. (Parts XCIII to XCVIII inclusive), Burgesses and Guild Brethren Roll of Glasgow, 1573-1750. 477 pp.   ,,   63s.
57. (Parts C and CVI), Protocol Books of James Foulis, 1546-1553, and Nicol Thounis, 1559-1564. Price 10s. 6d.
58. Family Papers of the Hunters of Hunterston.
    (Presented by Lieut.-General Sir Aylmer Hunter-Weston.)
59. (Parts CI to CV inclusive and CIX), Roll of Edinburgh Burgesses, 1406-1700. 546 pp. Price 52s. 6d.
60. Register of Edinburgh Apprentices, 1666-1700. 101 pp.   ,,   10s. 6d.
61. Register of Edinburgh Apprentices, 1701-1755. 98 pp.   ,,   10s. 6d.
62. (Parts CXII, CXIV and CXV), Roll of Edinburgh Burgesses, 1701-1760. 240 pp.   ,,   21s.
63. (Parts CVIII and CXI), Protocol Book of Sir John Cristisone. 146 pp.   ,,   10s. 6d.
64. Protocol Book of John Foular, 1500-1503. 265 pp. *Out of print.*
    (Presented by the City of Edinburgh.)
65. Protocol Book of Sir Robert Rollok, 1534-1552. 79 pp.   Price 10s. 6d.
66. Burgesses and Guild Brethren Roll of Glasgow, 1751-1846.   *In the Press.*
67. Inventory of Pitfirrane Writs, 1230-1794. 77 pp. Price 10s. 6d.
68. (Parts CXXIV and CXXV), Roll of Edinburgh Burgesses, 1761-1841. 183 pp.   ,,   15s.

27, William Blaiky and Christane Hutton had Jonet ; witnesses, Henrie Davidson, Andro Maine, Johne Law.

27, Michael Meldrum and Margaret Walker had Mariorie ; witnesses, Andro and William Meldrums, James Broun.

27, Thomas Howie and Jonet Cunynghame had Marion ; witnesses, Robert Hutton, David German, Johne Cunynghame.

29, James Durie of Craigluscour and Christane Durie had Marie ; witnesses, Williame Mercer, Mr. James Gray, James Gib, and Laurence Mercer, presenter of the childe.

29, Johne Wilson and Margaret Peacok had Bessie ; witnesses, Eduard Dowglas, elder, David Bell, and Andro Wilson, presenter of the childe.

29, James Arkie and Bathia Demptertoun had Jeane ; witnesses, James Gray, Robert Mudie, William Kirk.

M. 3, Johne Blaikwood to Grisell Alshunder in the kirk of Torrie.

31, Andro Trumble to Jeane Crawfoord in the kirk of Kinneill.

APRIL.

B. 1, Archibald Gray and Jonet Sellers had Isobell ; witnesses, James Mudie, William Cose, Thomas Davidson.

2, James Lawson and Jeane Hog had Margaret ; witnesses, James Greinhorne, Johne Manderstoun, Johne Lawson.

2, William Keir and Margaret Bad had Margaret ; witnesses, Johne Bad, Johne Duncanson, Andro Hall.

2, William Peirson and Isobell Walwood had Helene ; witnesses, Henrie and Robert Peirsons and Johne Thomson.

2, David Maistertoun and Margaret Primros had Alexander ; witnesses, Andro Wilsons, elder and younger, Andro Drysdaill.

7, Andro Maine and Jonet Cunynghame had Johne ; witnesses, Henrie Davidson, Johne and William Cunynghames, and Johne Mayne, presenter of the childe.

7, Johne Thomeson and Margaret Goodaill had Isobell ; witnesses, Michael Meldrum, James Broune, and George Stirk, presenter of the childe.

10, David Trumble and Christane Legat had Patrick ; witnesses, Peter Law, William Legat, Johne Wright.

12, James Stanehous and Elspet Kellok had Jonet ; witnesses, Robert Sharp, Thomas Stanehous, Robert Kellok.

12, James Hutsoun and Bathia Hendersoun had Margaret ; witnesses, James Stanehous, Henrie Peirson, James Paterson.

12, Johne Westwood and Jonet Keir had Christane ; witnesses, James Mylne, Johne Greeve and William Purves.

21, David Cunynghame and Margaret Paton had Isobell ; witnesses, Patrik Peirson, William Purves, William Weittit. The childe was presented to baptisme by Johne Cunynghame, brother to the said David, becaus of his ignorance.

22, William Anderson and Margaret Anderson had Agnes ; witnesses, James and Andro Andersons, Alexander Wilson.

22, Robert Dewar and Helene Keir had James ; witnesses, James Dewars, elder and younger, George Mudie.

29, William Camron and Bessie Kinnell had Anna ; witnesses, George Bothwell, Robert Stevinson, William Reid.

29, John Snaden and Jonet Mihie had Patrik ; witnesses, Patrik Steward of Baith, James Spens, William Drylay.

M. 4, Johne Hunter to Agnes Tailyeour.

12, Alexander Duff to Jonet Philp.

14, Thomas Pullouns to Margaret Bairdner in the kirk of Torry.

19, Andro Speare to Elspet Mathesoun.

26, James Scott, appeirand of Spenserfeild, to Anna Napeir in the kirk of Crawmount.

28, William Mudie to Elspet Mudie.

MAY.

B. 3, Andro Kirk and Isobell Coventrie had William ; witnesses, Thomas Elder, William Legat, William Smert.

3, Robert Dewar and Margaret Andro had James ; witnesses, James Espline, James Kellok, David Murray.

6, Johne Couper and Jonet Birrell had James ; witnesses, Johne and James Birrells, David Duncanson.

10, David Bad and Jonet Anderson had James ; witnesses, James Reid, provest, James Murray, George Mudie.

17, Johne Fairlie and Mariorie Burn had Thomas ; witnesses, Thomas Mitchells, elder and younger, and Andro Mitchell.

17, David Thomeson and Jonet Peirson had Barbara ; witnesses, David German, Johne Eadie and Patrik Stevinson.

17, Robert Allett and Magdalene Chirneside had Agnes ; witnesses, Johne Stirk, George Stirk, James Anderson.

19, David Anderson and Isobell Anderson had Johne ; witnesses, Johne Mackie, Henrie Mitchell, James Anderson.

22, James Kellok and Isobell Watson had Margaret ; witnesses, Johne Colyeour, Robert Adam, Johne Kellok.

31, William Baverage and Isobell Templeman had Robert ; witnesses, Robert Sharp, Johne and George Stirks.

M. 3, Andro Menteith to Isobell Portour.

17, Johne Tod to Jonet Menteith.

26, Andro Adam to Jeane Philp in the kirk of Baith upon a testimoniall of request to the minister there.

31, William Hadstoun to Annabelle Blaikett.

JUNE.

B. 2, Johne Hunter and Margaret Burn had Isobell ; witnesses, Robert Tailyeour, Johne Burn, Patrik Hall.

3, Johne Kirkland and Agnes Fitt had Jeane ; witnesses, Alexander Chalmers, David Steward, Andro Kirk.

5, James Weyld and Isobell Creiche had Helene ; witnesses, Johne Weyld, James Dewar, Andro Anderson.

5, Andro Scotland and Margaret Moreis had Elspet ; witnesses, William Walker. William Smert, Thomas Baverage.

12, Johne Walwood and Katherine Coventrie had William ; witnesses, Mr. William Oliphant, minister, William Walwood, James Richardson.

14, Johne Litiljohne and Marie Greenes had Bessie ; witnesses, Andro Wilson, William Mudie, James Henderson.

16, Umqle Williame Wardlaw of Logie and Jeane Ker had Grissell ; witnesses, James Gib, George Bothwell, George Wardlaw, and Henrie Wardlaw of Balmull, presenter of the childe to baptisme.

16, Andro Cowe and Ewphame Law (in fornication) had Robert ; witnesses, Robert Russell, David Thomson, and Robert Greeve, presenter of the childe.

17, Andro Mitchell and Margaret Mitchell had Margaret ; witnesses, Mr. George Walker, James Mitchell, Thomas Dowglas.

19, Johne Watson and Barbara Bruce had twinnes baptised and called the ane Margaret and the uther Katherine ; witnesses, James Simson, Johne Duncanson, Thomas Cant.

30, James Kinloche and Bessie Stevinson had Margaret ; witnesses, George Trumble, Henrie Peirson, Robert Heart.

M. 2, William Nicoll to Helene Mylne.

6, Johne M'Kenlaw to Margaret Mudie.

9, Sir Henrie Wardlaw to Margaret Henderson, sister to the Laird of Fordell, in the kirk of Baith.

10, James Hutton to Christane Livings[ton] in the kirk of Cleishe.

14, John Moyes to Bessie Reddie.
14, David Burley to Jonet Anderson.
23, Archibald Marr to Barbara Bruce in the kirk of Carnok.

JULY.

B. 3, Abraham Giro and Grissell Anderson had Margaret ; witnesses, James
       Espline, William Walker, Robert Baxter.
    5, Thomas Cunnan and Isobell Dewar had Margaret ; witnesses, Patrik
       Rowan, James Donaldson, Robert Dewar.
    5, Alexander Dunsyre and Agnes Thomson had James ; witnesses, Tobias
       Murebek, James Watson, James Baverage.
   12, Robert Hutton and Jonet Sanders had William ; witnesses, William
       Hutton, Johne Duncanson, Johne Hamiltoune.
   12, David Russell and Jonet Stanehous had Robert : witnesses, Henrie
       Wardlaw of Balmull, Robert and Edward Russells.
   12, Johne Neilson and Jonet Buist had Williame ; witnesses, William
       Legatt, Andro Trumble, Peter Buist.
   17, Robert Hogane and Bessie Potter had Johne ; witnesses, Johne Hogan,
       Johne Potter, Patrik Wright.
   17, William Spenss and Margaret Inglis had William ; witnesses, Thomas
       Elder, William Smert, Thomas Spenss.
   24, Robert Colyeare and Christane Burt had Robert ; witnesses, Johne Law,
       Andro and Johne Colyears.
   24, George Chapman and Margaret Clerk had Johne ; witnesses, Johne
       Watson, Adam Brand, David Peacok.
   24, Johne Murie and Katherine Kingorne had James ; witnesses, George
       Trumble, James Kingorne, Thomas Dowglass.
   28, Robert Halkett and Jean Hadden had Robert ; witnesses, Robert, Lord
       Colvill, Sir Robert Halkett of Pitfirrane, Robert Dempster of Pitliver.
   28, Johne Walwood and Marie Anderson had Katherine ; witnesses, Johne
       Colyeare, presenter of the childe (becaus of the parent his scandalous
       life in drunknes, &c., for the which he was publictlie declared un-
       worthie of the benefits of the kirk), Robert Anderson and Andro
       Anderson also witnesses.
   31, James Buchannan and Jonet Fotheringham had James ; witnesses,
       Johne and James Donalds and Johne Lawson.

M. 12, Robert Cunynghame to Margaret Burn.
   12, James Donald to Marjorie Lethem in the kirk of Torrie.
   19, Mark Cunnane to Jonet Thomeson in the kirk of Abirdour.
   22, James Birrell to Marion Johnestoun.
   26, William Walwood to Jonet Law.

AUGUST.

B. 7, Johne Wardlaw and Isobell Moreis had Henrie ; witnesses, Sir Henrie
       Wardlaw of Pitreavie, William Purves, William Mudie and Johne
       Ker.
   12, Patrik Anderson and Jonet Dowglas had Alison ; witnesses, William
       Anderson in Pitconnoquhy, Thomas Mitchell, and Henrie Dowglas in
       Easter Gellet.
   12, Duncan Young and Helene Smert had Margaret ; witnesses, James
       Simson, Peter Walker, Andro and Adam Andersones.
   14, Johne Boyd and Issobell Veitche had Jonet ; witnesses, Archibald and
       James Boyds, James Simson, and William Boyd, presenter of the
       childe.
   14, James Moreis and Issobell Hutton had James ; witnesses, Johne Park,
       Johne Anderson, William Hall.
   16, Alexander Wilson and Elspet Russell had Margaret ; witnesses, James
       Simson, Thomas Drysdaill, William Anderson.
   18, Johne Wilson and Bessie Hardie had Andro ; Andro Anderson, Andro
       Mayne, Andro Currie.

21, Johne Millar and Helene Adamson had James ; witnesses, David Bad, Thomas Trumble, Andro Donaldson.

23, Robert Anderson and Katherine Smythe had Henrie ; witnesses, Henrie Davidson, Johne Colyear, Robert Mudie.

28, David Robertson and Katherine Scott had Grissell ; witnesses, Adam Wilson, George Pullons, Manse Malcolm.

28, Patrik Hall and Jeane Purves had William ; witnesses, William Purves, Andro Hall, George Mudie.

30, William Anderson and Jonet Finla had Johne ; witnesses, William Anderson in Pitconnoquhy, Johne Anderson in Innerkething and David German.

M. 4, James Littiljohne to Margaret Anderson in the kirk of Sawlin.

11, David Henderson to Bessie Henderson.

25, James Dewar to Margaret Burn.

SEPTEMBER.

B. 6, James Mitchell and Margaret Mercer had Katherine ; witnesses, Robert Dempster of Pitliver, David Lindsay of Cavill and Thomas Mitchell, elder.

6, Johne Thomson and Jonet Walwood had Christane ; witnesses, William and Mr. Thomas Walkers, Alexander Chalmers.

6, Peter Russell and Jonet Reid had Patrik ; witnesses, Patrik Steward of Baith, Robert and Edward Russells, James Anderson.

11, Robert Greive and Margaret Dowglas had Christane ; witnesses, Robert Angus in Rescobie, William Rowan in Gask, and Robert Russell in Balmull mylne.

12, Henrie Dowglas and Katherine Brand had Alison ; witnesses, Thomas Dowglas, David Dowglas, Adame Brand, younger.

12, Archibald Hamiltoun and Agnes Broun had William ; witnesses, William Walker. late provest, presenter of the childe, Mr. Thomas Walker, schoolmaster, and Alexander Chalmers, merchand.

13, Andro Wardlaw and Helene Burley had Jonet ; witnesses, James Anderson, Johne Burley, Johne Wardlaw.

18, Umquhile James Dewar and Alison Hall had twinnes baptised and called the ane James and the uther Margaret ; witnesses, James Dewar in Holl and James Dewar in Pitbachlie, presenters of the children, Andro Hall, Robert Dewar and Henrie Davidson.

18, David Thomson and Isobell Moreis had Johne ; witnesses, Johne Halieburton of Garvok, Andro Mayne, Andro Mudie.

M. 8, George Buist to Issobell Mylls in the kirk of Tulliebol[e].

OCTOBER.

B. 4, Adam Trumble and Jonet Mitchell had Helene ; witnesses, Andro Trumble in Grange, George Trumble in Broomhall, and William Walker, late provest.

11, Johne Reid and Jonet Boyd had Marioun ; witnesses, Johne Duncanson, William Boyd, Robert Huttoun.

11, James Legat and Margaret Stirk had Christane ; witnesses, William Legat, David Trumble, William Smert.

16, William Dowglas and Mariorie Stevinsone had Jonet ; witnesses, David German, George Walls and Thomas Stevinson.

18, William Dewar and Issobell Fyff had James ; witnesses, James Dewar, Adame Brand, David Dewar, James Moyes.

25, Andro Wilson and Bessie Peirson had Bessie ; witnesses, Johne Dewar, Alexander Garlik, Patrik Roxbrughe.

27, David Scotland and Elspet Dewar had Christane ; witnesses, Henrie Wardlaw of Balmull, William Rowane of Gask, and Robert Stevinson, smith.

M. 20, William Mackay to Agnes Sharp.

21, Laurence Alison to Bessie Portus.

NOVEMBER.

B. 1, William Alexander and Katherine Smert had Margaret; witnesses, Johne Watson, Johne Smert and George Walls.

6, William Strachane and Jonet Allane had Grissell; witnesses, Henrie Mitchell, Robert and Johne Strachans.

8, Robert M'Greggour and Katherine Vass had William; witnesses, William Walker, William Kent, William Chalmers.

13, David Chrystie and Jonet Marshell had James; witnesses, Robert Russell, James Mylne, David Scotland.

13, Johne Eilsone and Margaret Edisone had Katherine; witnesses, James Mudie, litster, Andro Cunynghame, Johne Edison.

15, Johne Smith and Margaret Davidson had Bessie; witnesses, Johne Goold, Patrik Allane, Henrie Peirson.

15, Adame Wilson and Agnes Nasmythe had Adam; witnesses, Thomas Wilson [*a blank left here*].

17, James Wilson and Jonet Dick had Charles; witnesses, Sir Robert Halket of Pitfirrane, Knyt, Charles Halkett his oye (= grandson), William Wilson, Edward Rutherfoord, James Legatt.

17, Robert Philp and Isobell Cunynghame had Isobell; witnesses, Johne Cunynghame, Johne Stirk, younger, and James Anderson.

20, James Anderson and Helene Miklejohne had Adam; witnesses, Adam Anderson, Andro Purves, Andro Miklejohne.

22, William Robertson and Elizebeth Hutton had Grissell; witnesses, David Robertson, David Scotland, Robert Russell.

22, James Buist and Margaret Hardie had George; witnesses, Peter Buist, James Richardson, James Eason.

24, Robert Dowglas and Elspet Peirson had James; witnesses, Andro Wilson, James Dowglas, Johne Lawson.

24, David Marshell and Annas Malcome had Henrie; witnesses, Henrie Malcome, Robert and James Marshells.

24, James Donaldson and Helene Henden had Jeane; witnesses, William Hutton, James Fyff, Johne Greeve, younger.

27, Johne M'Gee and Christane Moreis had Agnes; witnesses, William Walker, Thomas Elder, William Smert.

27, Thomas Falconer and Isobell Kinloch had Jonet; witnesses, Johne Burley, Johne Walwood, Johne Kinloche.

29, James Peacok and Christane Alison had Patrik; witnesses, Patrik Steward of Baith, Edward Russell, Abram Peacok.

29, Andro Chrystie and Mariorie Stevinson had Patrik; witnesses, Patrik Stevinson, George Mudie, Adam Currie.

29, Umqule Donald Peirie and Grissell Anderson had Donald; witnesses, Robert Mercer in Sawline, William Smert, Adam Anderson, and James Malcome, presenter of the childe.

29, David Hodge and Christane Coventrie had Margaret; witnesses, William Smert, James Richardson, Johne Heart.

M. 3, Johne Williamson to Margaret Roxbrughe, they having produced testimonialls of their proclamation, viz. he from Kettell and she from Innerkething.

DECEMBER.

B. 1, David Duncanson and Margaret Patton had James; witnesses, Johne and James Duncansons and James Patton.

4, George Young and Bessie Lowe had Elspet; witnesses, Robert Stevinson, William Mudie, James Legat, William Smert.

6, David Steward and Helene Kirkland had Charles; witnesses, William Smert, Laurence Watson and James Richardson.

8, William Scotland and Isobell Robertson had William; witnesses, William Smert, William Rowan, David Scotland.

13, James Fyff and Margaret Marshell had Jonet; witnesses, James Mylne, William Hutton, Robert Angus.

20, James Trotter and Elspet Young had Helene ; witnesses, Johne Mackie, William Nicoll and James Anderson.

20, William Wilson and Bessie Wilson had Johne ; witnesses, Johne Wright, Johne Stirk, elder, and James Anderson.

25, Thomas Dowglas and Bessie Murie had Katherine ; witnesses, Edward Dowglas, David Currie, Henrie Dowglas.

25, James Stevinson and Margaret Anderson had Agnes ; witnesses, William Anderson, William Stevinson, James Hutton.

M. 6, Johne Grame to Margaret Edison in the kirk of Innerkething upon a testimoniall from this kirk.

6, Robert Currie to Margaret Inche.

13, Andro Murdoch to Katherine Davidson.

22, William Nicolson to Elizebeth Moncreiff in the kirk of Kinross upon a testimoniall to the minister.

23, David M'Braik to Jonet Rutherfoord.

27, Johne Henryson to Marion Forbes.

30, William Gottersto[n] to Christane Strang.

JANUARY [1654].

B. 3, William Cose and Jonet Burn had Edward ; witnesses, Edward Dowglas, Henrie Dowglas, David Currie.

5, James Malcome and Christane Phin had William ; witnesses, William Mudies, elder and younger, William Smert.

5, William Tailyeour and Annas Dowglas had William ; witnesses, William Mudies, elder and younger, and David Trumble.

9, Umqle Johne Bennet, baxter, and Katherine Walker had Euphame ; witnesses, Peter Law, Thomas Davidson, and Peter Walker, presenter of the childe.

10, Peter Chalmers and Margaret Wannan had Marie ; witnesses, Tobias Murebek, James Watson, Alexander Dunsyre.

17, Andro Adam and Jeane Philp had Katherine ; witnesses, Patrik Steward of Baith, William Marshell, Laurence Mercer.

17, Laurence Anderson and Jonet M'Birny had Elspet ; witnesses, George Trumble, Robert Donald, David Astie.

17, Johne Clowe and Beatrix Bennet had James ; witnesses, James Reid, provest, James Simson, James Legat, James Richardson.

19, George Trumble and Margaret Mudie had Johne ; witnesses, Robert Mudie, Johne Trumble, James Balfour.

22, Umqle Andro Anderson and Margaret Keltie had Margaret ; witnesses, William Anderson in Pitconnoquhy, Robert Scotland, William Nicoll, and William Anderson, presenter of the childe.

29, James Makgill and Katherine Broun had James ; witnesses, James Gib, William Walker, James Broun.

30, Andro Robertson and Margaret Potter had Jonet ; witnesses, Robert Stevinson, William Smert, Andro Purves.

M. 10, Mr. Williame Hutson to Joan Din.

24, Andro Fairlie to Isobell Richardson.

24, Harie Peirson to Jonet Stevinson in the kirk off Abirdour.

FEBRUARY.

B. 5, The ryt honorable William Haliday of Tullybole and his Ladie Isobell Rollok had Margaret ; witnesses, Sir Henrie Wardlaw of Pitreavie, Henrie Wardlaw of Balmull, and William Walker, late provest.

7, Johne Penman and Bessie Craig had Helene ; witnesses, Patrik Kedglie, William Cook, William Penman.

7, Robert Chisley and Bessie Greg (in fornication) had ane womanchilde, baptised (upon cautioun for satisfying the discipline of the kirk) and callit Katherine ; witnesses, David Russell, his cautioner, Thomas Philp, and Johne Marshell, presenter of the childe.

12, Henrie Elder, tounclerk, and Elizebeth Elder had Harie ; witnesses, Sir Henry Wardlaw of Pitreavie, Henrie Wardlaw of Balmull, and Thomas Elder, baillie.

13, Alexander Duff and Jonet Philp had Alexander ; witnesses, Andro Mayne, Johne Cunynghame, Johne Stirk, younger.

13, Johne Stevinson and Bessie Allan had Margaret ; witnesses, William Penman, William Strachane, James Anderson.

16, William Young and Margaret Peirson had Margaret ; witnesses, William, Robert, and Adame Andersons.

19, William Walker had ane womanchilde (borne of his wyf Margaret Trumble (the 14 day) baptised and called Margaret ; witnesses, Mr. William Oliphant, minister, Mr. Thomas Walker, Adame Trumble.

19, William Mudie and Elspet Mudie had William ; witnesses, James Mudie, William Mudie, Robert Stirk.

19, Adam Brand and Jeane Ballantyn had Katherine ; witnesses, Henrie Dowglas, Johne Cunynghame, Thomas Howie.

19, James Hutton and Agnes Ogilvie had David ; witnesses, James Drysdaill, William Anderson, James Stevinson.

21, David Anderson and Margaret Blak had Elspet ; witnesses, James Anderson in Fode, William Anderson in Lymekills, and William M'Braik.

26, Robert Stirk and Jonet Mudie had William ; witnesses, James and William Mudies and Johne Stirk.

26, Johne Scott and Jonet Potter had Jonet ; witnesses, James Legat, Robert Stevinson, William Smert.

28, Eduard Dowglas and Jonet Anderson had Jeane ; witnesses, William Anderson, David German, Peter Buist.

28, William Broun and Agnes Smyllum had Harie ; witnesses, Sir Harie Wardlaw of Pitreavie, James Simson, Andro Purves, Johne Thomeson.

M.   7. Robert Bonar to Jonet Horne.

7, Johne Cumyn to Christane Hutton.

23, Adame Clerk to Margaret Sands, he having producit his testimoniall from Culross.

MARCH.

B.   5. Johne Donald and Helene Reddie had Andro ; witnesses, Andro and James Donalds and Thomas Elder.

7, William Lethem and Jonet Wilson had Johne ; witnesses, Johne Lawson, Johne Lethem, Johne Anderson.

9, James Anderson and Isobell Gibbon had William ; witnesses, James Anderson, William Nicoll, Johne Manderstoun.

[Blank] day, Alexander Scotland and Mariorie Whyt had Helene ; witnesses, William Mudie, William Lamb, Andro Robertson.

12, Johne Watson and Helene Nicoll had Johne ; witnesses, Mr. Thomas Walker, James Huton, Laurence Watson.

12, Henrie Anderson and Jonet Sanders had Andro ; witnesses, Andro Mayne, Andro Mudie, Patrik Stevinson.

12, Johne M'Kenlaw and Margaret Mudie had William ; witnesses, William Trumble, William Mudie, Patrik Stevinson.

14, Thomas Pullouns and Margaret Bairdner had Alexander ; witnesses, Johne Bairdner, Andro Donald, Alexander Gib.

21, David Lindsay of Cavill and Katherine Malloche had Alexander ; witnesses, James Reid, Mr. Alexander Malloche and David Mitchell.

21, James Purves and Agnes Spens had Johne ; witnesses, Johne Mackie, William Spens, Patrik Hall, and William Purves, presenter of the childe, the parent being absent.

21, Johne Peirson and Jonet Stevinson had William ; witnesses, William Walker, William Smert, William Dowglas.

26, Thomas Couper and Isobell Walwood had Jeane ; witnesses, Robert Walwood, Henrie Davidsoun, James Allan.

26, Robert Bull, culteller, and Isobell Meldrum had Harie; witnesses, David Bull, Harie Elder, John Eadie, Robert Hutton.

26, William Hunter and Margaret Snaden had Helene; witnesses, James Barrowman, William Cook and Johne Penman.

28, Johne Robertson and Margaret Broun had Johne; witnesses, Johne Cose, William Purves, Johne Wilson, and Andro Donaldson, presenter of the childe, the parent being absent.

30, William Walker and Mariorie Broun had Peter; witnesses, Peter Law, Peter Walker and Mr. George Walker.

M. [*None.*]

APRIL.

B. 2, Laurence Stevinson and Bessie Moore had David; witnesses, David, Robert and Andro Donalds and James Peirson.

2, Adame Clerk and Margaret Hutson had Margaret; witnesses, Robert and William Walwoods and Archibald Robertson.

9, Johne Donaldson and Grissell Mather had Katherine; witnesses, David Mitchell, Henrie Dowglas, Johne Chrystie.

9, Archibald Robertson and Marion Hutsoun had Jeane; witnesses, William Smert, Johne Duncanson, Robert Shortus.

9, Alexander Innes and Margaret Thomeson had Helene; witnesses, Adam Anderson, Robert M'Greggour, and Robert Thomeson, presenter of the childe.

13, Johne Kingorne and Bessie Tailyeour had Robert; witnesses, James Legat, Johne Colyeare, James Kingorne, and Robert Mudie, presenter of the childe becaus of the parent his ignorance and scandalous life in drunknes, for the which he was publictlie declaired unworthie of the benefeets of the kirk.

13, Andro Speare and Elspet Matheson had Robert; witnesses, Robert Kellok, Robert Mudie, Robert Stanehous.

16, James Mudie and Bessie Paton had Bessie; witnesses, Robert Mudie, Johne Hamiltoun, Thomas Davidson.

16, Johne Walwood and Elspet Coventrie had David; witnesses, David Hodge, James Legat, James Richardson and David Waterstoun.

23, Henrie Mitchell and Grissell Lindsay had Jonet; witnesses, David Lindsay of Cavill, Thomas Mitchell and Mr. George Walker.

30, Thomas Elder and Isobell Simson had Margaret; witnesses, Andro Purves, baillie, Harie Elder, clerk, and James Simson.

30, John Mackie and Margaret Elder had William; witnesses, Robert Halket, Henrie Wardlaw of Balmull and William Walker, late provest.

30, Thomas Baverage and Christane Robertson (in fornication) had William; witnesses, Laurence Watson, David Stewart, William Baverage, and William Smert, presenter of the childe.

M. 6, James Anderson to Agnes Drysdaill.

6, Thomas Williamson to Bessie Mayne.

MAY.

B. 7, Adam Anderson and Katherine Gibbon had Elizabeth; witnesses, Andro Purves, Robert Stevinson, James Anderson.

7, James Birrell and Marion Johnestoun had Margaret; witnesses, Andro Mayne, Johne Birrell, Johne Couper.

11, Thomas Mitchell and Margaret Mudie had James; witnesses, James Legat, James Mudie and James Mitchell.

11, Thomas Trumble and Katherine Bad had Bessie; witnesses, James Simson, James Mudie, litster, and Johne Burley.

18, Andro Trumble hade ane womanchilde (borne to him of his wyf Jeane Crawfoord the 8 day) baptised and called Helene; witnesses, George Trumble, William Walker, Mr. William Crawfoord and Thomas Dowglas.

21, Edward Rutherfoord and Margaret Græme had Robert; witnesses, Mr. Robert Anderson, Robert Sharp, William Mercer and Robert Græme.

21, Mr. Thomas Walker and Agnes Gibbon had Katherine; witnesses, Williame Walker, Mr. George Walker, Adam Anderson, Harie Mitchell.

25, Andro Annan and Isobell Hunnan had Jonet; witnesses, Johne Hamiltoun, James Anderson and Johne Lilburn.

25, Robert Kirk and Jonet Currour had Thomas; witnesses, Johne Stanehous, Robert Mudie, Thomas Philp.

25, Alexander Arnot and Jonet Gray had Bessie; witnesses, James Gray, Thomas Gairner, David Peacok, and James Legat, presenter of the childe because of the parent his ignorance.

30, Andro Cunynghame and Mariorie Burne had Katherine; witnesses, Henrie Dowglas, Adam and David Curries.

30, Johne Harrower and Bessie Hall had Katherine; witnesses, Robert Cunynghame, Alexander Gib, William Lethem.

M. 11, Harie Robertson to Grissell Rober[tson].
18, Thomas Conquergood to Beatrix Thomson.
23, James Dewar to Marion Fisher.
23, James Smeall to Grissell Bryce.
30, James Bryce to Katherine Bruce in the kirk of Carnok.

JUNE.

B. 2, The 2 day James Mercer of Clavedge had ane manchilde borne to him of Jeane Mercer in fornication under promise of mariage baptised and called William; witnesses, Alexander Mercer of Kinnaird, Captain William Leslie, Walter Dalgleesh, clerk, and William Mercer, advocat, father to the said Jeane, presenter of the childe.

4, Thomas Hoburne and Bessie Duk had James; witnesses, James Cusine, James Wilson, James Halkett.

4, Alexander Reid and Jonet Johnestoun had Margaret; witnesses, William Hutton, William Anderson, William Primros.

6, James Mudie and Bessie Cunynghame had Bessie; witnesses, Robert Wilson, David Bad, Andro Chrystie.

6, Patrik Allane and Margaret Alison had Jonet; witnesses, Johne Stevinson, David Trumble, David Bull.

18, Johne Kirkland and Agnes Fitt had Helene; witnesses, William Mudie, Johne Walwood, Gawin Edison.

M. 8, Johne Anderson to Margaret Anderson.
13, Johne Lawson to Agnes Sanders.
22, William Potter to Jeane Elder.
22, Thomas Forfar to Jonet Smetoun in the kirk of Innerkething.
29, Donald M'Neill to Margaret M'Nab.

[Just above the second marriage, which occurs at the head of a page, there are inserted the words "Mariage 1654 Aprile 1654." "Aprile" is perhaps a mistake for "June."]

JULY.

B. 4, Johne Park and Katherine Alison had Katherine; witnesses, Harie Elder, Edward Russell, Adam Curry.

9, William Prymos and Jeane Rowane had David; witnesses, David Lindsay of Cavill, George Lindsay and Andro Menteith.

9, Archibald M'Craith had ane manchilde borne to him of his wyf Jonet Cellers (wha depairtit this lyf eftir her Delyverie), the childe was baptised and called James; witnesses, Robert Anderson, Johne Dalgleish, and James Mudie, maltman, presenter of the childe.

11, Robert Eadie and Christane Mitchell had Issobell; witnesses, Johne and Andro Maynes, David Flockhart, William Cunynghame.

11, Johne Burne and Christane Heriott had George; witnesses, Mr. George Walker, George Mudie, Andro Burn.

11, Andro Hall and Agnes Kinsman had Agnes; witnesses, Robert Stevinson, Johne Bad, Peter Buist.

16, Robert Walwood and Jeane Livingstoun had Elspet; witnesses, Mr. George Walker, William Walker, Thomas Couper.

18, Johne Marshell and Helene Greg had Bessie; witnesses, Patrik Steward of Baith, George Wardlaw, Thomas Philp.

20, Robert Barclay and Agnes Cunnan had Robert; witnesses, Robert Mudie, Robert Stanehous and Robert Heart.

20, Thomas Spens and Jonet Harrower had Margaret; witnesses, Robert Colyear, Johne Drumond and William Spens.

27, Patrik Steward of Baith had ane manchilde (borne to him of his wyf Marion Bruce the 17 day about 10 hours at evin) baptised and called Harie; witnesses, Harie Wardlaw of Balmull, James Gib, and James Mowtrey off Rescobie and George Bothwell.

28, Donald Steward and Jeane Mercer had Mariorie; witnesses, Thomas Elder, William Smert, William M'Kay, and Andro Kirk, presenter of the childe.

M. 6, Alexander Lowson to Margaret Keltie.

13, David Haigie to Margaret Rainy.

AUGUST.

B. 6, Johne Chrystie and Barbara Rae had Michaell; witnesses, David and William Bells and George Chapman.

6, Alexander Smetoun and Grissell Walls had Margaret; witnesses, Thomas Elder, George Walls, David Steward.

8, Johne ffyg and Margaret Simson had Katherine; witnesses, James Fyg, Thomas Elder, William Smert.

11, William Broun and Elspet Hendirson had Robert; witnesses, Robert Mudie, Robert Kellok, Robert Stanehous.

11, Thomas Broun and Agnes Kellok had Elspet; witnesses, William Mudies, elder and younger, Robert Stirk, and James Mudies, elder and younger.

13, Neill Neish and Grissell M'Comes had Jeane; witnesses, Thomas Couper, Johne Potter, James Anderson, Johne Clowe.

20, William Cunynghame and Jonet Greins had Robert; witnesses, William Wilson, George Mudy, William Purves.

20, Robert Jak and Jonet Hall had Alison; witnesses, Andro Hall, Robert Mayne, David Thomeson.

27, Johne Moreis and Elspet Dewar had Agnes; witnesses, Alexander Beane, elder, Thomas Elder, James Hutton, elder, webster.

29, William Mackay and Agnes Sharp had Thomas; witnesses, Thomas Elder, Thomas Burn, William Smert, Thomas Baverage, Andro Kirk.

M. 8, James Murgane to Isobell Alexander.

10, Richard Harrower to Annas Ramsay.

15, William Trumble to Jeane Dowglas.

17, Johne Stanehous to Margaret Gibson.

24, William Murgan to Agnes Dalgleish in the kirk of Sawline.

24, Andro Cowe to Margaret Orrok in the kirk of Baith upon testimoniall from this kirk.

SEPTEMBER.

B. 3, Johne Græme and Katherine Peirson had Johne; witnesses, William Youngs, elder and younger, William Makbrek.

5, James Watson in fornication of Margaret Tailyeour had Johne; witnesses, Johne Hector, Johne Marshell, Johne Snadun.

10, James Boyd and Bessie Baverage had Christane; witnesses, Thomas Baverage, William Smert, Archibald Boyd.

10, David Burley and Jonet Anderson had Jonet ; witnesses, Johne Burley, William Anderson, Johne Manderstoun.

17, George Walls and Margaret Smert had Helene ; witnesses, Duncan Young, William Dowglas, William Smert.

17, Johne Manderstoun and Isobell Leslie had Jonet ; witnesses, William Anderson, Robert Scotland, Alexander Reid.

17, David M'Brek and Jonet Rutherfoord had Margaret ; witnesses, William M'Brek, Eduard Rutherfoord, Thomas More.

17, Johne Græme and Margaret Edison had Johne ; witnesses, George Trumble, Johne Edison, Andro Cunynghame.

21, David Fairlie and Jonet Simson had Henrie ; witnesses, Henrie Coventrie, James and Henrie Baverages.

24, Johne Potter and Elspet Mullion had Jonet ; witnesses, Johne Hamiltoun, Johne Clowe, Patrik Wright.

24, William Baverage and Isobell Broun had Margaret ; witnesses, Thomas Baverage, William Smert, and Laurence Watson.

M. 29, Henrie Peirson to Christane Watt in the kirk of Kingorne upon a testimoniall from this kirk.

OCTOBER.

B. 2, William Hutton and Jeane Chrystie had Helene ; witnesses, Robert Angus, James Mylne and Robert Russell.

3, James Cumyn and Margaret Currie had Katherine ; witnesses, Thomas and Andro Mitchell, David Currie, Henrie Dowglas.

3, Johne Weire and Katherine Walwood had Jonet ; witnesses, Johne Thomson, David Hodge, Johne Wright.

8, Harie James and Agnes Blaikwood had Andro ; witnesses, Andro Mayne, James Mayn, James Anderson, younger, Johne Hamiltoun.

10, Robert Adam and Margaret Drysdaill had Thomas ; witnesses, Thomas Drysdaill, Johne Hird, James Anderson. The childe was born the 4 day of this moneth about 11 hours beforenoon.

12, George Anderson and Jonet Fotheringhame had Issobell ; witnesses, Johne Dewar, Robert Anderson, Thomas Fotheringhame.

15, David Makbaith and Bessie Robertson had David ; witnesses, David Currie, Andro Wilson and Thomas Dowglas.

22, James Browne and Helene Thomeson had George ; witnesses, George Bothwell, George Walls, Johne Thomeson.

22, Robert Currie and Margaret Inche had Robert ; witnesses, Robert Currie, William Inche and Thomas Stevinson.

22, William Anderson and Elspet Anderson had David ; witnesses, David Burley, David Anderson and James Drysdaill.

24, Johne Hamiltoun and Bessie Anderson had James ; witnesses, James Anderson, elder, and James Anderson, younger, litsters, and James Mudie, also litster.

24, Johne Dewar and Alison Anderson had Andro ; witnesses, Edward Dowglas, Andro Wilson, Henrie Wilson.

29, William Gotterstoun and Christane Strang had William ; witnesses, Johne Gotterstoun, William Mudie, elder, and William Mudie, younger.

30, William Dowe and Margaret Cunynghame had Bessie ; witnesses, Robert Shortus, James Watson, William Cook.

M. 5, Johne Roy to Jonet Pitilloch.

19, Johne Carmichell to Katherine Wright upon a testimoniall from the kirk of Torrie.

NOVEMBER.

B. 5, Johne Anderson and Margaret Makmirrie had James ; witnesses, Johne Hamiltoun, James Anderson, elder, James Mudie.

5, Laurence Stevinson and Euphame Dick had Jonet ; witnesses, Adam Anderson, Eduard Russell, Thomas Couper.

5, Robert Pitilloch and Jonet Spindie had Johne; witnesses, Johne Roy, Johne Stirk, elder, Michael Meldrum.

5, Johne Small had ane manchilde borne to him of Isobell Reid in fornication, baptised (upon a testimoniall from Edinburgh where the sin was committed) and called James; witnesses, James Reid, provest, James Murray, and James Kellok, presenter of the childe.

19, Henrie Stevinson and Isobell Dowglas had Jonet; witnesses, Edward, Robert, and James Dowglas's.

19, Andro Scotland and Margaret Moreis had Elspet; witnesses, William Marshell, William Walker, Thomas Elder.

21, Patrik Rowane and Jeane Stanehous had Nicoll; witnesses, Robert Mudie, Nicoll Rowane, James Donaldson.

21, Alexander Fairlie and Margaret Miller had Margaret; witnesses, James Kingorne, Johne Murie, William Rae.

21, Johne Buist and Bessie Horne had Elspett; witnesses, James Buist, George Broun, Eduard Russell.

21, Johne Hobsone ane inglish soldier of Captaine Rodgers company had ane manchilde borne to him of his wyf Anna Hobsone, baptised and called William; witnesses, William Seill, Arthure Layne, Eduard Rutherfoord.

26, Robert Mudie and Agnes Moyes had Jeane; witnesses, Robert Walwood, Williame Walwood, James Gray.

28, James Reid, provest, and Margaret Wardlaw had Jonet; witnesses, Henrie Wardlaw of Pitreavie, George Bothwell, George Wardlaw, James Mudie.

28, Robert Tailyeour and Isobell Hunter had Johne; witnesses, James Allan, Johne Mayne, Johne Hunter.

28, James Mylne and Jonet Myllar had George; witnesses, George Dewar, Robert Angus and Johne Broun.

M. 9, James Peacok to Christane Glenn upon a testimoniall from the kirk of Dalgatie.

9, Johne Scott to Jonet Allan.

10, William Hall to Margaret Brand.

21, Johne Livingstoun to Marion Hay in the kirk of Carridin upon a testimoniall from this kirk.

21, Thomas Thomeson to Margaret Anderson.

21, Patrik Johnestoun to Jeane Dick.

30, Robert Raff to Jonet Robertson.

30, Williame Glass to Isobell Williamson.

DECEMBER.

B. 5, William Rowan and Margaret Allan had Margaret; witnesses, James Allan, Henrie Davidson and Thomas Elder.

5, James Buchannan and Jonet Fotheringhame had Margaret; witnesses, James Donald, William Stevinson, David Austie.

7, Patrik Hunter and Jonet Gray had Robert; witnesses, Laurence Gray, Thomas Gairdner, Johne Marshell.

7, David Cunynghame and Elspett Fitt had Elspet; witnesses, Patrik Hall, Andro Burn, Johne Burne.

8, Robert Bonar and Jonet Horne had Jonet; witnesses, Thomas Horne, Patrik Wright, James Legatt.

10, Johne Hutton and Jonet Howie had Jonet; witnesses, Thomas Howie, William Mudie and David Elder.

12, James Durie and Christane Durie had Arthure; witnesses [*blank here*].

17, Peter Walker and Euphame Ged had Andro; witnesses, Robert Ged of Baldrig, Mr. Andro Walker, minister at Auchtertool, and William Walker, late provest.

17, Henrie Meldrum and Jonet Inche had George; witnesses, George Walls, George Stirk and William Inche.

19, Johne Dewar and Margaret Brand had James ; witnesses, James Durie, William Murgane, William Hutton.

21, David Bell and Katherine Maltman had Johne ; witnesses, Henrie Davidson, Johne and James Maynes.

22, David Currour and Margaret Burt had James ; witnesses, James Dewar, James Baverage, Harie Peirson.

26, Johne Walker and Jean Gowane had Margaret ; witnesses, James Legat, William Legat, George Stirk.

26, Allaster Buchannan and Isobell Colyeare had George ; witnesses, David Scotland, Robert Russell, William Robertson.

26, Manse Malcome and Jonet M'Lenochan had Katherine ; witnesses, David Bad, James Daes, Thomas Bennett.

28, Andro Cunynghame and Margaret Trumble had Elizabeth ; witnesses, Henrie Wardlaw of Pitreavie, George Trumble, Andro Mayne.

28, Lawrence Trotter and Jeane Burt had Johne ; witnesses, Johne Mackie, Johne Stevinson, James Clerk.

M. 1, John Mitchell to Elspet Baxter.

7, William Lawson to Agnes Norie in the kirk of Torrie upon a testimoniall from this kirk.

21, William Murgan to Bessie Bryce in the said kirk of Torrie, also upon a testimoniall.

26, William Gray to Elspet Anderson.

26, Cudbert Thomeson ane inglish soldier to Katherine Wilson.

28, Edward Overwhite ane inglish soldier to Grissell Dick.

JANUARY [1655].

B. 2, Henrie Trumble and Bessie Pet had Jeane ; witnesses, George and Andro Trumbles and Mr. George Walker.

2, Duncan Ogilvie and Bessie Wardlaw had Johne ; witnesses, William and Thomas Marshells and James Mowtrey.

2, Archibald Marshell and Jeane Leitche had Marion ; witnesses, Johne Marshell, Thomas Gairdner, Thomas Philp.

2, Thomas Penny had ane manchilde borne to him of Elspet Alison in fornication baptised and called Patrik ; witnesses, Robert and David Russells, and Patrik Allane, presenter of the childe.

7, James Anderson and Agnes Drysdaill had James ; witnesses, Thomas Drysdaill, Robert Adam and Johne Hird, Johne Hamiltoun and Mr. Robert Anderson.

9. James Dewar and Margaret Burn had James ; witnesses, Peter Law, Harie Law, Johne Dewar.

9, Robert Wardlaw and Margaret Hutton had Patrik ; witnesses, Patrik Wright, James Dewar, James Donaldson.

9, James Moyes and Elspet Blaiky had Jonet ; witnesses, Andro Mayne, Andro Mudie, Henrie Davidson.

14, Robert Dewar and Margaret Andro had Annas ; witnesses, Mr. James Phinn, David Murray, James Kellok.

14, Johne White and Jonet Burley had Johne ; witnesses, Johne Wright, Robert Huttoun, James Anderson, elder, Harie Law.

16, Johne Burley and Christane Culros had James ; witnesses, James Anderson, younger, James Mudie, Andro Wardlaw.

23, James Lawson and Jeane Hog had James ; witnesses, Johne Lawson, William Primros, Johne Manderstoun.

25, James White had ane womanchilde borne to him of Rebecca Clowe in fornication baptised and callit Jonet ; witnesses, Robert Adam, David Hodge, and Robert Eadie, presenter of the childe.

25, James Wilkie had ane womanchilde borne to him of Margaret Dowe in adulterie baptised and called Margaret ; witnesses, Johne Penman, Johne Thomeson, and William Dowe, presenter of the childe.

28, Andro Hutton and Isobell Walwood had Jonet ; witnesses, David Hutton, James Hutton, baillie, and James Hutton, younger, weaver.

M. 2, James Scotland to Jonet Angus.
　　2, Johne Lindesay to Jonet Duncan in the kirk of Kinrosse by a testimoniall from this kirk.
　　4, Andro Wardlaw to Isobell Murray.
　　5, Archibald M'Craich, pyper, to Mariorie Small.
　　10, Robert Walwood to Jonet Ged in the kirk of Bruntiland.
　　16, Robert Willy to Bessie Wilson.
　　23, Andro Garlik to Mariorie Williamsone.

FEBRUARY.

B. 6, Johne Eadie and Margaret Phillane had Jonet; witnesses, David German, James Huton, James Simson.
　　6, Robert Russell and Margaret Dewar had Elizabeth; witnesses, David Scotland, Henrie Elder and Eduard Russell.
　　6, Johne Ritchie and Jonet Garlik had Andro; witnesses, Andro Flokart, James Allane, James Balfour.
　　8, James Mack and Marion Blaiky had Elspet; witnesses, Andro Mudie, Thomas Stevinson, Robert Eadie, and Robert Currie, younger, presenter of the childe because of the parent his ignorance.
　　11, James White and Isobell Harla had Isobell; witnesses, Robert Stevinson, George Young, Johne Wilson.
　　12, William Lamb and Jonet Lamb had Jonet; witnesses, William Mudies, elder and younger, Robert Stirk.
　　13, James Broune and Jonet Whitefoord had Margaret; witnesses, David Mitchell, William Lethem, Thomas Wilson.
　　13, Alexander Garlik and Katherine Potter had Margaret; witnesses, James Legat, William M'Brek, Harie Dowe.
　　15, Harie Robertson and Grissell Robertson had David; witnesses, Robert Cunyngham, Johne Harrower, David Robertsone.
　　20, David Trumble had ane manchilde (born to him of his wyf Jeane Zule the 4 day) baptised and called Johne; witnesses, Andro Trumble, Johne Donald and Johne Neilson.
　　20, David Fyff and Jonet Hakistoun had David; witnesses, David Andro and James Fyffs.
　　23, Johne Stanehous and Jonet Cunynghame had James; witnesses, James Mitchell, James Wardlaw and James Browne.
　　25, William Boyd and Marion Wallace had Marion; witnesses, Johne Duncanson, David Steward and Laurence Watson.
　　25, Michell Gillium and Isobell Stevinson had James; witnesses, James Donaldson, James Killoch and Robert Wardlaw.
　　25, James Wilkie and Katherine Kirk had David; witnesses, David Peirson, Robert Currour, and David Fairlie, presenter of the childe because of the said James his adulterie comitted with Margaret Dowe ffor the which he hes not satisfied as yit.
　　27, James Mitchell and Margaret Mercer had David; witnesses, David Lindsay of Cavill, David Mitchell, David Currie.
　　27, John Arkie and Elspet Watson had Mariorie; witnesses, Andro Cunynghame, David Bull, Andro Mayne.

M. 8, James Jameson to Mariorie Dowe.

MARCH.

B. 8, Henrie Davidson and Jonet Allane had Elizabeth; witnesses, Sir Henrie Wardlaw of Pitreavie, Thomas Davidson and Robert Stevinson.
　　13, Andro Menteith and Isobell Portour had Alexander; witnesses, David Lindsay of Cavill, James Lawson, and Alexander Reid, presenter of the childe becaus of the parent his scandalous life in drunknes and swearing, &c.
　　15, Thomas Conquergood and Beatrix Thomeson had Margaret; witnesses, Thomas Thomeson, Henrie and Andro Wilsons.

20, Johne Wilson and Margaret Peacok had William ; witnesses, William Cose, James Peirson, Johne Litiljohne.

20, Thomas Cant and Isobel Wely had Margaret ; witnesses, Thomas Wely, William Boyd, Robert Cant, James Mudie.

20, Alexander Beane and Christane Simson had Agnes ; witnesses, Alexander Beane, elder, James Anderson, elder, Johne Hamiltoun.

20, Robert Honyman and Jonet Peirson had Margaret ; witnesses, Johne Thomson, Johne Eilson, James Simson.

22, William Cunnan and Elspet Hutson had Elspet ; witnesses, Thomas Stanehous, David and Thomas Cunnans.

22, Duncan Clerk and Margaret Horne had Margaret ; witnesses, Eduard Russell, Johne Bad, Johne Clerk.

25, Andro Murgane and Katherine Brughe had Robert ; witnesses, Robert Murgane, James Daes and James Huttoun.

25, David Dowglas and Marion Duff had Elspet ; witnesses, Adam Currie, Andro Cunynghame, David Elder.

27, William Garvie and Jonet Anderson had David ; witnesses, David Browne, David Williamson, Alexander Inglis.

M. 8, Eduard Crowder ane inglish soldier to Marion Mitchell.

29, Johne Dowgall to Margaret Eilson.

APRIL.

B. 3, William Robertson and Elizabeth Huton had Jeane ; witnesses, David Dewar of Lassodie, Robert Huton in Bellielisk, James Legat.

5, James Hutson and Bathia Henderson had James ; witnesses, James Cunnan, James Paterson and James Balfour.

8, James Browne and Jonet Meldrum had Mariorie ; witnesses, Patrik Anderson, William Meldrum and James Anderson.

8, Robert Currour and Grissell Wallace had Helene ; witnesses, James Baverage, James Dewar, Thomas Currour.

9, Johne Walwood and Katherine Coventrie had Henrie ; witnesses, Henrie Coventrie, James Richardson, Andro Kirk.

10, George Pullons and Margaret Cumyn had David ; witnesses, David Currie, Andro Mitchell, and David German, presenter of the childe.

10, James Anderson and Christane Young had Andro ; witnesses, Andro Smythe, Andro Adam, James Anderson.

10, Robert Bryce and Helene Anderson had James ; witnesses, Andro Forrester, William Anderson, Johne Lawson.

12, James Wilson and Jonet Dick had James ; witnesses, James Halket, James Legat, James Mudie.

15, William Purdie and Margaret Dowe had Isobell ; witnesses, William Smert, Andro Kirk, James Malcome.

15, William Kirk and Agnes Adam had Margaret ; witnesses, Robert Adam, James Gray and Robert Mudie.

17, Johne Westwood and Jonet Keir had William ; witnesses, William Cusine, William Wilson and William Purves.

17, William Cook and Isobell Anderson had William ; witnesses, Andro Wilson, Thomas Hoburne and Patrik Kedglie.

20, Alexander Dunsyre and Agnes Thomeson had Agnes ; witnesses, Thomas Hoburne, William Cook and William Hunter.

24, William Peirson and Isobell Walwood had Jonet ; witnesses, Henrie Peirson, Johne Thomeson, Robert Peirson.

24, Robert Shortus and Margaret Bad had Katherine ; witnesses, Thomas Trumble, James Mudie, David Bad.

24, Archibald Buchannan and Christane Pattone had Andro ; witnesses, James Steward, Andro and Archibald Robertsones.

24, Donald Robertsone and Bessie Peacok (in fornication) had Harie ; witnesses, George Wardlaw, Thomas Gairdner, and James Peacok, presenter of the childe.

27, Henrie Coventrie and Isobell Donald had Agnes; witnesses, James Baverage, Andro Donald and James Richardson.

29, David Murie and Katherine Wardlaw had Helene; witnesses, Johne Wardlaw, David Elder and James Bruce.

30, William Nicoll and Helene Mylne had Margaret; witnesses, Johne Mackie, James Mylne, Robert Scotland.

M. 3, Robert Smetoun to Margaret Dick.

10, James Dansken to Margaret Stab.

12, Jerome Cowie to Margaret Smert.

24, James Simson to Helene Mitchell.

MAY.

B. 1, William Anderson and Jonet Finla had Geilles; witnesses, Edward Dowglas, Johne Anderson, and William Gray, presenter of the childe.

3, James Anderson and Issobell Gibbone had William; witnesses, James Anderson, elder, Johne Macky, William Anderson.

6, Thomas Williamson and Bessie Mayne had George; witnesses, Johne Stirk, elder, George Stirk and Andro Garlik.

8, Patrik Broune and Agnes Young had Johne; witnesses, Johne Stanehous, Johne Broun in Fode and Johne Broune in Grange.

8, Johne Gibson and Margaret Miller (in fornication) had Johne; witnesses, Patrik Stevinson, William Wilsons, elder and younger.

10, Robert M'Greggour and Katherine Vass had Agnes; witnesses, Johne Colyeare, Thomas Elder, Robert Stevinson.

15, Thomas Howie and Jonet Cunynghame had Thomas; witnesses, David German, Patrik and Thomas Stevinsones.

15, Johne Hunter and Margaret Burne had Jonet; witnesses, Andro Mayne, Andro Mudie, Andro Burne.

20, David Haigie and Margaret Rainy had James; witnesses, James Lowson, Alexander Lowson, William Strachan and Patrik Anderson.

22, William Keir and Margaret Bad had Jonet; witnesses, William Walwood, Robert Hutton, Johne Wardlaw.

24, William Strachan and Jonet Allan had James; witnesses, Johne and Robert Strachans and James Anderson, younger, in Kistok.

27, Johne Clerk and Margaret Aikin had Andro; witnesses, Johne Hamiltoun, Andro Hamiltoun his sone, Andro Wardlaw, Andro Hannan.

27, Johne Roy and Jonet Pitilloche had Johne; witnesses, Patrik Stevinson, Robert Willy, David Thomeson.

29, Johne Lawson and Agnes Sanders had William; witnesses, Johne Lawson, William Lawson, William Sanders.

29, James Mudie and Bessie Patoun had Robert; witnesses, Robert Mudie, Robert Stanehous, Johne Hamiltoun.

29, David Maistertoun and Margaret Primros had Andro; witnesses, Andro Wilson, Richard Maistertoun, David Allaster.

M. 17, Patrik Anderson to Bessie Mudie.

29, William Mercer to Jonet Donald.

JUNE.

B. 7, Johne Penman and Bessie Craig had Marioun; witnesses, Robert Walwood, Robert Shortus and James Watson.

7, Johne Stevinson and Katherine Kirk (in fornication) had Katherine; witnesses, William Smert, William Mudie, and George Young, presenter of the childe.

12, James Aikie and Bathia Dempstertoun had Robert; witnesses, Robert Mudie, George Wardlaw, Duncan Ogilvie.

17, Robert Heart and Jonet Hendene had Robert; witnesses, Robert Stanehous, Robert Hendene and Robert Barclay.

17, James Bryce and Katherine Bruce had Margaret; witnesses, James Allane, Henrie Davidson, Eduard Russell.

17, Henrie Wilson and Margaret Lindsay had Jonet ; witnesses, Johne Andersone, Thomas Thomson, Johne Dewar.

17, James Smeall and Grissell Bryce had Margaret ; witnesses, Johne Mackie, James Anderson, William Nicoll.

17, Johne Broun and Margaret Naper in fornication had ane womanchilde baptised (in the kirk of Sawline upon a testimoniall to the minister there) and called Margaret ; witnesses, William Walwood, Johne Goold, Johne and William Cusines.

24, Johne Anderson and Margaret Anderson had Jonet ; witnesses, William Andersoun, George Trumble, Eduard Dowglas, younger.

24, Mark Cunnan and Jonet Thomeson had Alexander ; witnesses, James and Thomas Cunnans, Robert Barclay.

26, David Bad and Jonet Anderson had Johne ; witnesses, Johne Anderson, Johne Cunynghame, Thomas Trumble.

28, David Thomeson and Jonet Peirson had David ; witnesses, Robert Russell, David Scotland, David German.

M. 5, Alexander Anderson to Jonet Chrystie.

5, James Watson to Bessie Cook.

7, James Fisher to Christane Russell.

12, William Anderson to Elspet Anderson.

12, Johne Dewar to Jonet Peirson.

14, Robert Drysdaill to Alison Dowglas.

21, William Penman to Lilias Kedglie.

26, Laurence Walker to Jeane Rae.

28, William Lawson to Elspet Chrystie.

JULY.

B. 1, David Trumble and Christane Legat had James ; witnesses, Peter Law, William and James Legatts.

1, James Malcome and Christane Phin had James ; witnesses, James Richardson, James Wilson, David Steward.

1, James Hew and Jonet Anderson had Katherine ; witnesses, Andro Cunynghame, David Dowglas, James Cunnan.

5, Umqule William Cunynghame and Rachel Chrystie had Margaret ; witnesses, Andro Mayne, James Donaldson, and Andro Cunynghame, presenter of the childe.

8, James Marshell and Bessie Strang had James ; witnesses, James Mudie, Andro Huton, William Gotterstoun.

10, Robert Huton and Jonet Sanders had Patrik : witnesses, James Mudie, Andro Anderson, Johne Duncanson and Patrik Sanders.

15, William Mudie and Elspet Mudie had James ; witnesses, James Mudie, Robert Stirk, Patrik Anderson.

17, William Murgan and Agnes Dalgleeshe had Elspet ; witnesses, James Durie, James Wardlaw and James Murgan.

17, Johne Livingstoun and Jonet Wood had Robert ; witnesses, Robert Walwood, Patrik Livingstoun, James Watson.

17, William Greens an inglish soldier of Captaine Rodgers' companie had ane manchilde borne to him of his wife Elizabeth Lie baptised and called Robert ; witnesses, Robert Haddene, Andro Bowthe, and Thomas Elder, baillie.

24, John Wardlaw and Isobell Moreis had William ; witnesses, George Chapman, William Garlik, Patrik Hunter.

24, Jone Lawson and Bessie Walwood had Bessie ; witnesses, James Mudie, James Marshell and William Gotterstoun.

29, William Bowman and Margaret Hearine had William ; witnesses, James Wardlaw, William Murgane, Johne Dewar.

29, David Robertson and Jonet Wilson had Katherine ; witnesses, Johne Bad, William Lamb, Robert Hutton.

31, Johne Litiljohne and Marie Greens had Elspet ; witnesses, William Legat, Williame Alexander, Henrie Trumble.

2 D

M. 3, William M'Craich to Bessie Anderson.

5, James Futhie to Helene Auchinlek.

10, Donald Buchannan to Margaret Turnour in the kirk of Torrie upon a testimoniall from this kirk.

17, Johne Hadstoun to Issobell Pringle.

19, Alexander White to Grissell Weyld.

26, Johne Harla to Jonet Rainy.

AUGUST.

B. 5, James Dewar and Marion Fisher had Agnes ; witnesses, Robert Mudie, William Walwood, James Fisher.

5, James Hutton and Christane Livingstoune had Margaret ; witnesses, James Huton, David Huttone, Peter Walker.

5, Umqle Eduard Chesters and Jeane Touchie had Eduard ; witnesses, George and Andro Trumbles, Andro Cunynghame and Eduard Dowglas, elder, presenter of the childe.

9, David Anderson and Isobell Anderson had William ; witnesses, Johne Mackie, James Anderson, William Nicoll.

12, James Bountorn and Agnes Lawrie had Agnes ; witnesses, Johne Lawrie, Johne Thomeson, Adam Anderson, Peter Buist.

12, Johne Drumond and Bessie Wardlaw had Jeane ; witnesses, Robert Stevinson, Robert Colyeare, Johne Anderson.

12, James Murgane and Issobell Alexander had Robert ; witnesses, Robert and Andro Murgans and Johne Alexander.

16, Johne Scarlet and Issobell Bairdner had Grissell ; witnesses, Laurence Watson, James Mitchell, Johne Anderson, and John Alexander, presenter of the childe becaus of the parent his scandalous life in drunknes, &c.

19, William Baverage and Isobell Templeman had Bessie ; witnesses, Johne Stirk, younger, Robert Marshell, Henrie Meldrum.

21, William Penman and Lilias Kedglie had ane manchild eight weeks or thereby after their mariage, baptised (upon cation that they shall satisfie the discipline of the kirk) and called Patrik ; witnesses, Patrik Kedglie, presenter of the child, Andro Wilson and Thomas Hoburne.

26, Johne Mitchell and Elspet Baxter had Bessie ; witnesses, George Walls, James Mitchell, Johne Thomeson, James Buist.

M. 7, David Inglis to Jonet Cowie.

9, Thomas Coline to Jonet Scotland.

16, George Trumble to Margaret Kellok.

21, Johne Browne to Margaret Naper.

21, Johne Aikin to Elspet Spens.

30, David Hutton to Issobell Lindsay.

SEPTEMBER.

B. 2, William Hall and Margaret Brand had Harie ; witnesses, Sir Harie Wardlaw of Pitreavie, Thomas Hall, elder, and Robert Colyear.

2, William Robertson, colyear, and Jonet Watson had James ; witnesses, James Legat, presenter of the childe becaus of the parents' ignorance, David Scotland and William Robertsone in Craigdoukies.

6, Robert Shortus and Katherine Hutsoun had Anna ; witnesses, Robert Adam, Johne Stevinson, William Mudie, younger.

9, James Rae and Bessie Strang had Elspet ; witnesses, Johne Park, James Moreis, David Cairnes.

9, William Gray and Helene Haddene had James ; witnesses, James Gray, James and Robert Brounes.

11, Robert Raff and Jonet Robertson had Elspet ; witnesses, Robert Russell, William Robertson, David Scotland.

11, James Jameson and Mariorie Dowe had Margaret ; witnesses, William Smert, James Richardson, Thomas Baverage.

11, Johne Watson and Isobell Williamson had Johne ; witnesses, Andro Wilson, Johne Wilson, Johne Lethem.

16, Robert Walwood and Jeane Livingstone had Marion ; witnesses, Johne Haliburtoun, Patrik Livingstone, William Walker, Mr. George Walker.

16, Thomas Pullons and Margaret Bairdner had Jonet ; witnesses, Johne and William Andersons, Johne Bairdner.

30, Johne Moore and Isobell Flewcar had James ; witnesses, James Fleemyne, James Bountorne, Johne Thomeson.

30, Alshunder Wilson and Elspet Russell had Agnes ; witnesses, Patrik Wright, Robert Willy, William Wilson.

M. 6, Johne Trumble to Katherine Mitchell.

11, George Gat to Helene Gray.

11, George Brand to Agnes Elder.

18, Thomas Hall to Jonet Chalmers.

27, William Watson, ane inglish soldier, to Jonet Watson.

OCTOBER.

B. 2, David Russell and Jonet Stanehous had Barbara : witnesses, Sir Henrie Wardlaw of Balmull, Pitreavie [*so it is written*], Robert Russell and Eduard Russell.

4, James Baverage and Jonet Coventrie had William ; witnesses, William Smert, Johne Duncanson and James Richardson.

4, David Chrystie and Jonet Marshell had Robert ; witnesses, David Scotland, Robert Russell, Johne Chrystie.

7, Andro Anderson had ane womanchilde (borne to him of his wife Margaret Kennedie the 1 day) baptised and called Elizebeth ; witnesses, Sir Henrie Wardlaw of Pitreavie, Robert Walwood, James Anderson, James Mudie.

9, Andro Kirk and Issobell Coventrie had James ; witnesses, Thomas Elder, William Smert, James Richardson.

9, Andro Garlik and Marjorie Williamson had Margaret ; witnesses, David Broun, Thomas Williamson, William Inglis.

11, James Mylne and Grissell Robertson had Jeane ; witnesses, William Huton, George Dewar, William Smert.

14, James Richardson and Agnes Coventrie had Thomas ; witnesses, Thomas Burn, Peter Buist, Johne Thomson.

16, Eduard Rutherfoord and Margaret Græm had Geilles ; witnesses, Robert Græm, James Anderson, Johne Duncans.

21, Johne Scot and Jonet Allane had Patrik ; witnesses, Patrik Allane, elder and younger, Patrik Livingstone.

21, That day Thomas Hall had ane manchilde borne to him of his wyf Jonet Chalmers a moneth or thereby after their marriage, baptised (upon cation that they shall satisfie the discipline of the kirk for their fornication) and called William ; witnesses, David Trumble, Thomas Hall, elder, and William Hall, the cautioner and presenter of the childe.

23, Abram Giro and Grissell Andersone had Jonet ; witnesses, William Walker, Robert Baxter and James Anderson, younger.

23, Johne Murie and Katherine Kingorne had Johne ; witnesses, Johne Kingorne, Adam Murie, Thomas Douglas.

28, Robert Anderson and Katherine Smythe had Andro ; witnesses, Andro Smythe, Eduard Russell, Henrie Davidson.

30, David Hendirson and Bessie Hendirson had Margaret ; witnesses, Leonard Hendirson, William Hendirson, Andro Mudie, Andro Mitchell, Andro Mitchell.

M. 18, James Balfour to Marion Bruce in the kirk of Auchtertooll, upon ane testimoniall from this kirk.

NOVEMBER.

B. 1, James Kay and Beatrix Brand had William ; witnesses, William Smert, presenter of the childe becaus of the parent his ignorance, William Wilson and William Garvie.

4, Adam Anderson and Katherine Gibbone had Margaret ; witnesses, Andro Purves, Robert Stevinson, James Anderson.

11, William Potter and Jeane Elder had Katherine ; witnesses, David Murray, Johne Potter, elder, Johne Potter, younger.

11, Johne Broun and Elspet Stirk (in fornication) had (baptised upon cation for their satisfying the discipline of the kirk) and called Margaret ; witnesses, Patrik Kedglie, William Hunter, and Andro Wilson, elder, presenter of the childe and cautioner.

15, Alexander Lowson and Margaret Keltie had James ; witnesses, James Lowson, James Hadstoun and James Anderson.

18, Robert Bull and Issobel Meldrum had Issobell ; witnesses, William Walker, Thomas Elder, James Anderson, Robert Hutton.

20, Andro Mitchell and Margaret Mitchell had Jonet ; witnesses, Mr. George Walker, Henrie Mitchell, Adam Trumble.

25, James Kellok and Issobell Watson had Johne ; witnesses, Johne Duncanson, Robert Adam, Johne Watson.

27, William Currie and Helene Donaldson had William ; witnesses, Robert Currie, William Wilson, Andro Wilson.

27, James Sands and Bessie Touchie had Thomas ; witnesses, David Bell, George Chapman, William Cose.

27, Alexander Duff and Jonet Philp had Katherine ; witnesses, James Anderson, Johne Stirk, Andro Mayne.

M. 1, Robert Adam to Katherine Stevinson.

13, William Purves to Issobell Broun.

15, William Gilkrist to Jonet Drysdaill.

20, Thomas Heart to Katherine Marshell in the kirk of Sawline upon a testimoniall from this kirk.

23, Thomas Mitchell to Marion Trumble.

27, William Smyth to Elspet Mayne.

29, William Anderson to Katherine Wardlaw.

29, William Meldrum to Eupham Stewart.

DECEMBER.

B. 2, William Wilson and Bessie Wilson had Thomas ; witnesses, William and Thomas Wilsons, Johne and Patrik Wrights.

6, James Scotland and Jonet Angus had Elizabeth ; witnesses, David Scotland, Robert Angus, Robert Russell.

9, Alexander Scotland and Mariorie White had Elspet ; witnesses, William Lamb, William Mudies, elder and younger.

11, Andro Cowe and Margaret Orrok had Katherine ; witnesses, William Walwood, James Dewar, Johne Moyes.

13, James Clerk and Margaret Anderson (in fornication) had ane manchilde baptised (upon cation for their satisfaction of the discipline of the kirk) and called James ; witnesses, Patrik Anderson, James Lowson, and David Haigie, cationer and presenter of the childe.

16, Harie Elder and Elizabeth Elder had Margaret ; witnesses, Sir Henrie Wardlaw of Pitreavie, Peter Walker, provest, and Thomas Elder.

16, Michael Meldrum and Margaret Walker had George ; witnesses, George Stirk, George Currie, Andro Meldrum.

18, Henrie Stevinson and Issobell Dowglas had Eduard ; witnesses, Eduard Dowglas, younger, Robert Dowglas, William Lethem.

18, Johne Stanehous and Margaret Gibson had Helene ; witnesses, Robert Stanehous, George Wardlaw, Thomas Philp.

20, Harie Richardson and Sara Steward had Harie ; witnesses, Leonard Henrieson, Johne Ewin, Johne Miller.

20, James Murgane and Jonet Inglis (in fornication) had ane womanchilde baptised (upon cation for satisfying the discipline of the
kirk) and called William [*sic*]; witnesses, Johne Berriehill, Johne
Duncanson, cationer, and William Bowman, presenter of the
childe.

23, Andro Trumble had ane womanchilde (borne to him of his wyf Jeane
Crawfoord the 13 day) baptised and called Margaret; witnesses,
William Walker, George Trumble, Mr. William Crawfoord, Mr.
George Walker.

23, Henrie Anderson and Jonet Sanders had William; witnesses, William
Gotterstoun, William Makcraithe, William Lawson.

25, Johne Reid and Jonet Boyd had Johne; witnesses, Johne Duncanson,
William and James Boyds.

25, Alexander Innes and Margaret Thomeson had Bessie; witnesses, James
Simson, William Harla, Thomas Hoburne.

27, William Trotter and Isobell Anderson had Issobell; witnesses, William
Anderson, Patrik Anderson, James Lawson.

30, Umquhile James Reid, provest, and Margaret Wardlaw had Elizabeth;
witnesses, Sir Henrie Wardlaw of Pitreavie, George Bothwell, and
David Lindsay of Cavill, presenter of the childe.

30, William Alexander and Katherine Smert had Annas; witnesses,
William Smert, George Walls, Andro Robertsone.

30, George Gatt and Helene Gray about a quarter of a yeir after their
marriage had ane manchilde borne and baptised (upon cation for
their satisfaction of the discipline of the kirk for their fornication)
and called William; witnesses, Johne Anderson, David Anderson
and Adam Anderson, cationers, and William Gray, presenter of the
childe.

M. 4, Johne Baverage to Jonet Blaikwood in the kirk of Tullieboll upon a
testimoniall from this kirk.

13, James Lindsay to Helene Currie.

JANUARY [1656].

B. 1, Andro Hannan and Issobell Hunnan had Johne; witnesses, James
Anderson, Johne Hamiltoun, Johne Lymburne.

1, William Anderson and Margaret Kirk had Margaret; witnesses,
William Strachan, James Anderson, Patrik Anderson.

1, Robert Smetone and Margaret Dick had Sara; witnesses, Henrie
Mitchell, Robert Scotland, Andro Meldrum.

1, Robert Pet had ane womanchilde borne to him of Bessie Philp (in
fornication) baptised (upon a cation for their satisfaction of the
discipline of the kirk) and called Katherine; witnesses, Andro
Flokart and Robert Dewar, cationers, Andro Adam, Henrie Gray,
and Thomas Philp, presenter of the childe.

6, David M'Baith and Bessie Robertson had Johne; witnesses, Johne
M'Baith, Andro Wilson, Andro Fairlie.

8, John Clowe and Beatrix Bennet had Johne; witnesses, Peter Walker,
provest, Andro Anderson, baillie, Johne Thomesone.

10, David Donaldson and Mase Bryce had Robert; witnesses, Robert
Mudie, elder, Robert Mudie, younger, and James Donaldson.

13, Andro Speare and Elspet Matheson had Henrie; witnesses, Sir Henrie
Wardlaw of Pitreavie and Henrie Wardlaw, his sone, and Henrie
Peirson.

15, William Lawson and Agnes Norie had Johne; witnesses, Johne Lawson,
elder and younger, Johne Norie.

20, James Makgill and Katherine Broun had Helene; witnesses, William
Walker, William Kent, James Broun.

20, David Marshell and Annas Malcome had Robert; witnesses, Robert
Marshell, Robert Sharp, Robert Strachane.

20, William Cunynghame and Jonet Greens had Agnes ; witnesses, Patrik and Thomas Stevinsons, William Lason.

27, Richard Harrower and Annas Ramsay had Robert ; witnesses, Robert Mudie, Robert Haliburton, Johne Buist.

M. 3, William Anderson to Christane Mitchell.

3, Robert Lawson to Jonet Drysdaill in the kirk of Torrie.

15, James Hunter to Jonet Clowe in the kirk of Torrie.

24, Robert Pet to Bessie Philp.

FEBRUARY.

B 3, George Mayne and Christane Millar had Christane ; witnesses, Robert Mayne, Andro Chapman, Johne Dewar.

5, James Brand and Margaret Forfar had Jonet ; witnesses, William and Allan Mudies and Johne Strachane.

7, Eduard Dowglas and Jonet Anderson had Beatrix ; witnesses, Eduard Dowglas, elder, Thomas Dowglas and William Anderson.

7, James Short and Bessie Walwood had Harie ; witnesses, James Baverage, Harie Walwood and George Wardlaw.

10, William Dewar and Issobell Fyff had David ; witnesses, Adam Brand, James Dewar, Andro Fyff.

11, Mr. George Walker and Jonet Mitchell had Katherine (being a twinn, the uther died) ; witnesses, Mr. Johne Weems, Johne Mackie, Andro Mitchell.

12, Johne Watson and Helene Nicoll had Thomas : witnesses, Mr. Thomas Walker, Thomas Horne, William Broun.

12, Robert Bonar and Jonet Horne had Robert ; witnesses, Thomas Horne, Robert Stevinson, James Legat.

12, William Camrone and Bessie Kinnell had Williame ; witnesses, William Legat, Johne Duncanson, Lawrence Watson and Peter Buist.

12, Andro Mayne and Jonet Cunynghame had Helene ; witnesses, Robert Tailyeour, James Donaldson, James Allane.

12, Cudbert Thomson and Katherine Wilson had Barbara ; witnesses, Johne Wilson, George Curry, Johne Thomson.

14, William Walker had ane manchilde (borne to him of his wyf Margaret Trumble the 5 day) baptised and called Thomas ; witnesses, Mr. Thomas Walker, James Cunnan and Johne Trumble.

14, Henrie Dowglas and Katherine Brand had Jonet ; witnesses, David Currie, Adam Brand, William Trumble.

17, Robert Hogan and Bessie Potter had Robert ; witnesses, Johne Hogan, Johne Potter, Patrik Wright.

17. James Harrower and Eupham Lambert had Jonet ; witnesses, Robert Cunynghame, William M'Brek, Adam Wilson.

19, James Mercer of Clavedge and Jeane Mercer had Marie ; witnesses, George Bothwell, Walter Dalgleish, Duncan Young.

19, David Lindsay of Cavill and Katherine Wallace had David ; witnesses, James Dempster, fier of Pitliver, David Mitchell, Mr. George Walker.

19, Johne Huttone and Jonet Howie had Johne ; witnesses, Johne Cunynghame, Thomas Howie, William Mudie.

19, James Buchannane and Jonet Fotheringhame had Johne ; witnesses, Johne Lason, Henrie Coventrie, James Donald.

19, Lawrence Goodaill and Jeane Coburne had Annas ; witnesses, David Jerman, David Trumble, William Mudie.

24, William Anderson and Margarat Anderson had Jonet ; witnesses, Andro Anderson, Mr. Robert Anderson and Patrik Wright.

24, William Tailyeour and Annas Dowglas had Margaret ; witnesses, William Mudie, David Trumble, Andro Robertsone.

24, Robert Broun and Jonet Russell had William ; witnesses, James Gray, Johne Gray, David Browne.

28, James Broune and Jonet Whitefoord had Bessie ; witnesses, David Lindsay of Cavill, David Mitchell, William Lethem.

28, James Brughe and Jonet Fyg had Issobell; witnesses, James Fyg, Johne Fyg, William Mudie.

28, Johne Graves ane inglish soldier had ane manchilde borne to him of Bessie Garlik (in fornication) baptised and called Johne; witnesses, Andro Mayne, Robert Eadie, and William Garlik her father, presenter of the childe and her cationer.

M. 5, James Clerk to Elspet Scotland upon ane testimoniall fra Carnok.

19, James Millar to Jonet Dick.

25, Robert Lord Colvill to Eupham Mortoun, dochter to the Laird of Camno, in the kirk of Carnok by Mr. William Oliphant, minister of Dunfermline.

MARCH.

B. 2, Johne Anderson and Margaret M'Mirrie had Johne; witnesses, Johne Hamiltoun, James Anderson and Alexander Anderson.

2, Johne Ker and Katherine Dewar had Jonet; witnesses, Gilbert Car, James Murray, David Bull.

2, Laurence Walker and Jeane Rae had Jonet; witnesses, David Steward, David Jerman, William Smert.

9, Johne Moreis and Elspet Dewar had James; witnesses, James Anderson, elder, James Huton, William Scotland.

9, Johne Wardlaw and Jonet Lawson had Jonet; witnesses, Peter Walker, provest, William Keir, Johne Bad.

10, Peter Walker, provest, and Euphame Ged had Helene: witnesses, Mr. Andro Walker, minister at Auchtertooll, his brother, William Walker, late provest, James Mudie.

11, Umquhile David Cunynghame and Margaret Paton had Agnes; witnesses, Thomas Howie, Robert Philp, William Mudie, and Johne Cunynghame, presenter of the childe.

13, Andro Chrystie and Mariorie Stevinson had Andro; witnesses, Patrik Stevinson, Adam and Andro Curries.

13, Thomas Hoburne and Bessie Dick had Charles; witnesses, Andro Wilson, James Wilson, James Cusine.

16, James Watson and Bessie Cook had Bessie; witnesses, Robert Walwood, Robert Shortus, William Drylay.

16, James Weyld and Issobell Creich had Johne; witnesses, James Baverage, Johne Weyld, James Dewar.

23, Robert Currie and Margaret Inche had William; witnesses, William Inche, Robert Currie, elder, and William M'Craiche.

23, Johne Wallace and Margaret Broune had Agnes; witnesses, Adam Wilson, Robert Cunynghame, David Robertson.

24, Henrie Mitchell and Grissell Lindsay had Marie; witnesses, Charles Halket, David Lindsay, Thomas Mitchell, elder, and John Mackie.

25, Robert Dowglas and Elspet Peirson had Helene; witnesses, Robert Cunynghame, Andro Wilson, Johne Lawson.

27, Thomas Thomeson and Margaret Anderson had Katherine; witnesses, William and Johne Andersons, Robert Cunynghame.

30, Patrik Wright and Jonet Huton had William; witnesses, James Dewar, James Richardson, Johne Thomson.

30, Johne Marshell and Helene Greg had William; witnesses, William Marshell, Thomas Philp, Andro Adam.

M. 11, Johne Sandiela[nds] to Jeane Drysdaill.

13, Johne Lindsay to Elspet Reid.

APRIL.

B. 1, William Hadstoun and Annabel Blaiket had Bessie; witnesses, David Lindsay of Cavill, Henrie Mitchell, James Hadstoun.

6, Johne Dewar and Jonet Peirson had Johne; witnesses, Johne Anderson, Johne Chrystie, Johne Broune.

6, Johne Peirson and Jonet Stevinson had Johne; witnesses, David Jerman, Johne Thomeson, Henrie Peirson.

8, Patrik Johnestoun and Jeane Dick had James; witnesses, James Baverage, Johne Stanehous, Harie Anderson.

8, David Anderson and Margaret Blak had Andro; witnesses, Robert and Andro Andersons, Johne Chrystie.

8, Andro Wilson and Bessie Peirson had Mariorie; witnesses, David Currie, Henrie Dowglas, Johne Dewar.

10, Patrick Mayne and Helene Dick (in fornication) had baptised (upon cation for their satisfying of the discipline of the kirk) ane manchilde called Robert; witnesses, Robert Russell, David Thomeson and James Buist, cationer and presenter of the childe.

13, Patrik Anderson and Bessie Mudie had James; witnesses, James Mudie, elder, William Anderson, Alexander Anderson.

13, Johne Dowgall and Margaret Eilson had Margaret; witnesses, Andro Anderson, Andro Cunynghame, Johne Eilson.

14, Robert Stirk and Jonet Mudie had Elspet; witnesses, James Mudie, William Mudie, George Stirk.

15, Lawrence Anderson and Jonet M'Birny had Marie; witnesses, Robert Donald, Robert Lugtoun, Robert Chattow.

15, Andro Adam and Jeane Philp had Jonet; witnesses, Thomas Philp, Duncan Ogilvie, William Anderson.

15, Robert Kirk and Jonet Currour had Jonet; witnesses, Johne Stanehous, Eduard Russell, Thomas Currour.

17, Jerome Cowie and Margaret Smert had William; witnesses, William Smert, Peter Buist, Adam Anderson.

17, That day Katherine Bowie hade ane womanchilde borne of her baptised (after advyce sought of the presbiterie here upon the humble desire of William Bowie father of the said Katherine he promising all requisite dewtie to the childe and presenting the same this day) and called Margaret, The childe being now a year old and more, The occasion of this delay is, Becaus after much tryall it is not certainlie knowen who is the father of the child She affirming ane inglishman called Perpoynt whome she maried in England and is now dead to be the father of it, bot could not prove this, Therefore it is suspect that the childe is unlawfullie begotten she having lived scandalouslie before and fallin divers tymes in fornication and not givin evidence of her repentance for the same And for the present fugitive out of the countrey with ane inglish man called Moyes Baiker, with whom also she fell in fornication before.

20, James Broun and Helene Thomson had Johne; witnesses, Johne Thomson, Robert Hutton, Robert Russell.

20, Andro Scotland and Margaret Moreis had Johne; witnesses, William Walker, Johne Haliburtoun, Johne Mackie.

22, Alexander Reid and Jonet Johnstoun had Andro; witnesses, Andro Johnstoun, George Stirk, Johne Reid.

24, Johne Mackie and Margaret Elder had Henrie; witnesses, Sir Henrie Wardlaw of Pitreavie, Henrie Elder, Thomas Dowglas.

27, Alexander Anderson and Jonet Chrystie had William; witnesses, William and Patrik Andersons, Johne Chrystie.

27, Johne Hadstoun and Issobell Pringle had James; witnesses, William Nicoll, James Hadstoun, James Anderson.

29, James Birrell and Marion Johnestoun had Johne; witnesses, Johne Birrell, Johne Litiljohne, William Mudie.

M. 17, Mr. Johne Ramsay, minister at Ketle, to Annas Steward, ladie of Baldrig, in the kirk of Baith by Mr. Robert Kay, minister of Dunfermline.

25, Mr. David Beton to Christan Wardlaw in the kirk of Baith by Mr. William Oliphant, minister of Dunfermline.

29, Patrik Mayne to Helene Dick.

29, William Primros to Jonet Johnestoun in Carnok upon a testimonial from this kirk.

MAY.

B. 4, James Anderson and Agnes Drysdaill had Bessie : witnesses, Mr.
Robert Anderson, Thomas Drysdaill, Johne Hamiltoun.

6, David Hodge and Christane Coventrie had David ; witnesses, Johne
Thomeson, James Richardson, Johne Heart.

8, Johne Donald and Helene Reddie had David ; witnesses, Mr. David
Reddie, William Mercer, Robert Donald.

11, Johne Park and Katherine Alison had Harie ; witnesses, Harie Elder,
David Trumble, Patrik Allane.

13, James Mitchell and Margaret Mercer had Margaret ; witnesses, David
Lindsay, Thomas Mitchell, David Mitchell, Thomas Elder.

13, James Steill and Jonet Stevinson had Jonet ; witnesses, William Rowan,
Robert Russell, Robert Greeve.

15, Adam Trumble and Jonet Mitchell had William ; witnesses, Mr. William
Oliphant, minister, William Walker and William Trumble.

19, William Mercer and Jonet Donald had Thomas ; witnesses, Thomas
Elder, Johne Donald, Adam Anderson.

20, William Lethem and Jonet Wilson had twinnes baptised and called the
ane James and the uther Thomas ; witnesses, James Donald, Robert
Donald, Thomas Wilson, Thomas Thomeson.

22, James Anderson and Issobell Gibbon had Jonet ; witnesses, James
Anderson, elder, William Nicoll, Johne Manderstoun.

22, James Peacok and Christane Alison had Abram ; witnesses, Abram
Peacok, George Wardlaw, James Short.

25, Mr. Thomas Walker and Agnes Gibbon had Margaret ; witnesses,
William Walker, Peter Walker, Adam Anderson.

25, James Buist and Margaret Hardie had Robert ; witnesses, Robert
Halket, Peter Buist, James Richardson.

M. 9, Alexander Mercer of Kinnaird to Elizabeth Hendirson, sister to the
Laird of Fordell, in the kirk of Dalgatie.

27, Patrick M'Inness to Jonet Ker in the kirk of Sawline.

JUNE.

B. 1, Thomas Colen and Jonet Scotland had David ; witnesses, David Scotland, William Robertson, Robert Russell.

3, Johne Fyg and Margaret Simson had Bessie ; witnesses, James Fyg,
James Brugh, Patrik Legat.

5, Robert Halket and Jeane Hadden had Johne ; witnesses, Mr. George
Walker, Johne Mackie, James Miller.

22, George Trumble and Margaret Kellok had Margaret ; witnesses, William
Walker, James Cunnan, Robert Kellok.

22, Johne Kirkland and Agnes fñt had Elspet ; witnesses, David Steward,
William Smert, Robert Yowane.

26, Johne Harrower and Bessie Hall had Bessie ; witnesses, Robert
Cunynghame, Alexander Gib, William Lethem.

26, Johne Aikin and Elspet Spens had James ; witnesses, Johne Potter,
James Dumbar, Robert Patrik.

29, James Mudie and Bessie Paton had Thomas ; witnesses, Thomas
Trumble, James Mudie, Alexander Beane.

29, Robert Anderson and Margaret Cullen hade twinnes baptised and
called the ane Johne and the uther Jonet : witnesses, George Anderson, Johne Cullen, Alexander Young, William Cusine.

M. 5, Johne Makfarlan to Christane Chrystie.

5, Andro Mudie to Issobell Mudie in the kirk of Fossowhy, he having
gotten a testimoniall to the minister there, she being one of that
paroche.

10, Robert Chisley to Bessie Greg.

12, Johne Creiche to Issobell Douglas.

17, Johne Stevinson to Margaret Dick in the kirk of Ballingrie.
24, Johne Greive to Jonet Walls in the kirk of Baith.
26, Johne Wilson to Margaret Watson.

JULY.

B. 1, Duncan Young and Helene Smert had Thomas ; witnesses, William Smert, James Simson, George Walls.
 6, David Duncanson and Margaret Paton had Johne ; witnesses, Johne Duncanson, James Duncanson, William Mudie, elder.
13, Robert Dewar and Margaret Andro had Margaret ; witnesses, David Murray, Johne Dalgleish, Mr. Johne Phinn.
17, Johne Currie and Bessie Livingstoun had ane womanchilde borne to them in fornication baptised and called Christian ; witnesses, George Trumble, Andro Donald, and William Lawson, presenter of the childe.
20, Johne Trumble had ane manchilde (borne to him of his wyf Katherine Mitchell the 17 day) baptised and called David ; witnesses, David Mitchell, William Walker, Adam Trumble.
22, James Fisher and Christane Russell had Issobell ; witnesses, Johne Stanehous, James Anderson and Eduard Russell.
22, David Burley and Jonet Anderson had Issobell ; witnesses, Johne Faulds, James Hutton, William Anderson.
22, Johne Stevinson and Bessie Allane had Johne ; witnesses, William Strachane, James Anderson, Laurence Trotter.
24, Thomas Drysdaill had ane womanchilde borne to him of Marion Russell in fornication (they being relapsed therein) baptised and called Agnes ; witnesses, Robert Hutton, Peter Buist, and James Richardson, presenter of the childe.
27, William Dowglas and Mariorie Stevinsone had Helene ; witnesses, David Jerman, Thomas Stevinson, Patrik Stevinsone.
27, Johne Burley and Christane Culross had David ; witnesses, David Bad, David Burley, James Mudie.
29, William Hunter and Margaret Snaddon had Robert; witnesses, Robert Russell, David Thomson, William Drylay.

M. 8, Patrik Legat to Issobell Stevinson in the kirk of Bruntiland.
 8, Andro Hutson to Helene Galrik.
10, William Thomson to Margaret Lauthiane.
11, Duncan Campbel to Christan Dalgleish.
17, David Thomson to Agnes Peirson.
22, James Allane to Jonet Moreis.

AUGUST.

B. 5, Johne Hamiltoun and Bessie Anderson had William ; witnesses, James Andersons, elder and younger, and Alexander Anderson.
 7, Johne Rogers and Margaret Rogers had Johne ; witnesses, Sir James Halket of Pitfirrane, Sir Henrie Wardlaw of Pitreavie, presenter of the childe, and Peter Walker, provest.
 7, Patrik Walker and Eupham Phillane had Helene ; witnesses, William Walker, provest, Mr. Thomas Walker, and Alexander Beane, elder, presenter of the childe becaus of the parent his scandalous life in drunknes.
14, Andro Flokart and Issobell Pet had Mariorie ; witnesses, Andro Cunynghame, David Flokart, Adam Murie.
19, William Lawson and Elspet Chrystie had Margaret ; witnesses, Andro Chrystie, Johne Lawson, Johne Cunynghame.
19, Johne Eilson and Jonet Buist had Jonet ; witnesses, Peter Buist, William Legat, Andro Trumble.
19, David Dowglas and Marion Duff had Jeane ; witnesses, Andro Naper, Andro Cunynghame, David Elder.

21, Peter Russell and Jonet Reid had Jeane; witnesses, Robert Russell, Eduard Russell, George Wardlaw.

21, William M'Craiche and Bessie Anderson had Margaret; witnesses, Johne Anderson, Henrie Anderson and Johne Greive.

24, Patrik Allane and Margaret Alison had Johne; witnesses, Johne Stevinson, Johne Scott, Johne Parke.

M. 5, Robert Currie to Margaret Garlik.

7, William Broun to Jonet Anderson in the kirk of Tulliallan upon a testimoniall from this kirk.

14, Andro Wilson to Issobell Lethem.

21, Johne Watson to Katherine M'Mirry.

21, Johne Wardlaw to Margaret Moreis.

22, David Beton to Anna Wardlaw in the kirk of Baith by Mr. William Oliphant, minister off Dunfermline.

22, Johne Gray to Margaret Law.

26, James Thomeson to Katherine Walker in the kirk of Auchertooll.

SEPTEMBER.

B. 7, William Gilkrist and Jonet Drysdaill had Jeane; witnesses, Adam Wilson, Johne Dewar, Johne Sandielands.

7, Thomas Heart and Katherine Marshell had Jonet; witnesses, Robert Philp, Johne Currie, Andro Johnstoun.

11, Johne Potter and Elspet Mullion had Johne; witnesses, Johne Mullione, Johne Clow, Patrik Wright.

14, William Gray and Elspet Anderson had Jonet; witnesses, George Trumble, William Anderson, Adame Anderson.

21, James Kinloch and Bessie Stevinson had Elspet; witnesses, George Trumble, Robert Heart, Michael Gillium.

23, Peter Hay, fier of Naughtoun, and his ladie Dame Margaret Hendersone had George; witnesses, Johne Hendersone off Fordell, Robert Dempster of Pitliver and Alexander Mercer off Kinnaird.

28, Thomas Mitchell and Marion Trumble had Helene; witnesses, Mr. George Walker, Thomas Douglas, David Mitchell.

28, James Stevinsone and Margaret Andersone had Jonet; witnesses, James Andersone, James Drysdaill, William Andersone.

28, Andro Wardlaw and Issobell Murray had James; witnesses, James Andersone, James Imbrie, Johne Burley.

29, Mr. Thomas Mackgill had ane womanchilde borne to him of Jonet Nicoll (in fornication) baptised and called Helene; witnesses, James Broun, presenter of the childe, James Mackgill and Jerome Cowie.

M. 5, Patrik Sanders to Anna Elder.

29, Johne Broun to Elspet Stirk.

OCTOBER.

B. 5, Andro Hall and Agnes Kinsman had Elspet; witnesses, Johne Stevinson, William Mudie, William Gotterstoun.

5, George Chapman and Margaret Clerk had Margaret; witnesses, William Trumble, Andro Chapman and David Bull.

9, David Bell and Katherine Maltman had Henrie; witnesses, Henrie Davidson, Andro Mayne, James Allane.

12, David Trumble and Christane Legat had Jonet; witnesses, William and James Legats, Patrik Anderson.

14, Thomas Cunnan and Issobell Dewar had Bessie; witnesses, William Flokart, James Dewar and Johne Broune.

28, William Anderson in Lymekilles and Jonet Finla had Jonet; witnesses, David Jerman, Edward Douglas, younger, and Johne Andersone in Westir Gellet.

28, Andro Cunynghame and Margaret Trumble had Harie; witnesses, Sir Henrie Wardlaw of Pitreavie, knyt, George Trumble, Andro Mayne.

28, Robert Colyeare and Christane Burt had Johne; witnesses, Andro and Johne Colyears and Johne Law.

28, Johne Walwood and Elspet Coventrie had Andro; witnesses, Andro Smith, James Legat, James Richardson.

28, William Anderson and Elspet Anderson had James; witnesses, Henrie Davidsone, James Allane, Laurie Stevinsone.

30, Robert Drysdaill and Alison Douglas had Johne; witnesses, David Currie, Henrie Douglas, Johne Drysdaill.

M. 2, Robert Richie to Margaret Davidsone in the kirk of Torr[ie] upon a testimoniall from this kirk.

21, Laurence Walls to Margaret Greive.

23, James Mudie to Grissell Espline.

28, James Peirson to Margaret Peacok.

NOVEMBER.

B. 2, Eduard Rutherfoord and Margaret Græm had Magdalene; witnesses, Robert Græm, Robert Sharp, James Anderson.

2, Robert Adam and Katherine Stevinson had Elspet; witnesses, Robert Stevinson, Andro and Adam Andersons.

2, Adam Anderson and Katherine Gibbone had Grissell; witnesses, Andro Purves, Robert Stevinson, Robert Adam.

2, William Mudie and Elspet Mudie had James; witnesses, James Mudie, baillie, his brother, Robert Stirk, William Mudie.

2, William Meldrum and Euphame Steward had George; witnesses, George Stirk, Andro Meldrum, Michael Meldrum.

2, William Baverage and Issobell Broun had Thomas; witnesses, Thomas Baverage, William Smert, George Walls.

2, George Young and Bessie Lowe had Margaret; witnesses, Robert Stevinson, William Smert, Johne Stevinsoun.

9, George Walls and Margaret Smert had James; witnesses, James Mudie, baillie, James Richardson, William Smert.

9, Patrik Hall and Jeane Purves had Margaret; witnesses, James and Andro Halls, William Purves.

9, Robert Honymane and Jonet Peirson had Robert; witnesses, David Jerman, baillie, James Broun, Jerome Cowy.

11, William Anderson and Christane Mitchell had Issobell; witnesses, William, James and Patrik Legatts.

13, William Gotterstoun and Christane Strang had Johne; witnesses, Johne Mackie, Robert Stirk, Henrie Anderson.

13, James Fyff and Margaret Marshell had Jeane; witnesses, William Hutton, Robert Angus, Johne Greive.

13, Johne Scarlet and Issobell Bairdner had Christane; witnesses, Patrik Hunter, James Mitchell, William Hall.

20, Robert Mudie and Agnes Moyes had Johne; witnesses, Johne Haliburtoun, Robert Walwood, Johne Moyes.

20, George Andersone and Jonet Fotheringhame had Margaret; witnesses, Johne Dewar, James Stanehous, Robert Anderson.

20, James Trotter and Elspet Young had William; witnesses, Johne Mackie, William Nicoll, Laurence Trotter.

25, William Mackay and Agnes Sharp had James; witnesses, James Dumbar, James Richardson, Andro Kirk.

25, Archibald M'Craith and Mariorie Small had Margaret; witnesses, Johne Thomeson, James Fairny, Robert Anderson.

M. 6, Robert Angus to Marion Buchannan.

25, Thomas Beane to Katherine Walker.

25, William Watt to Jonet Roy.

DECEMBER.

B. 2, William Boyd and Marion Wallace had Katherine; witnesses, Laurence Watson, David Steward, Johne Duncanson.

2, James Boyd and Bessie Baverage had William; witnesses, Laurence Watson, William Smeit, Thomas Baverage.

2, William Broun and Elspet Hendersone had Alexander; witnesses, Alexander Henderson, James Donaldson, James Hutson.

4, Sir James Halket of Pitfirrane and dame Anna Murray had Elizabeth; witnesses, Robert Lord Colvill, Robert Dempster of Pitliver, Robert Halket and [*blank space here*].

7, Johne Scot and Jonet Allane had Johne; witnesses, Johne Hamiltoun, James Anderson, younger, and Patrik Allan.

7, Johne Roy and Jonet Pitilloch had Annas; witnesses, David Flokart, Eduard Russell and Robert Andersone.

9, James Clerk and Elspet Scotland had Helene; witnesses, Johne Currie, Johne Broun, James Lindsay.

11, William Smythe and Elspet Mayne had Elspet; witnesses, David Lindsay of Cavill, George Lindsay and Eduard Dowglas, younger.

16, Johne Lindsay and Elspet Reid had Jonet; witnesses, James Lindsay, Harie James, James Imrie.

21, Johne Scot and Bessie Cochrane had Bessie; witnesses, Robert Sharp, Johne Stirk, David Marshell.

23, Eduard Crowder ane inglish soldier and Marion Mitchell had Bessie; witnesses, James and Thomas Mitchells and Johne Thomeson.

28, James Anderson and Helen Miklejohne had Jonet; witnesses, Andro Purves, Adam and Andro Andersons.

28, David Robertson and Katherine Scot had Adam; witnesses, Adam Wilson, Harie Robertson, Mark Donald.

30, James Balfour and Marion Bruce had Agnes; witnesses, William Walker, provest, David Jerman, baillie, and Robert Walwood of Touche.

30, Johne Manderstoun and Issobell Leslie had James; witnesses, William Anderson in Pitconnoquhie, Robert Scotland, William Lason.

30, Robert Lawson and Jonet Drysdaill had Jonet; witnesses, David Lindsay, Henrie Mitchell, James Lason.

30, Johne Brand and Jeane Dewar had Marie; witnesses, David Scotland, Johne Dewar, and Robert Russell, presenter of the childe.

M. 2, James Marshel[l] to Jonet Lethem.

4, Andro Cunynghame to Kather[*blank*] [*blank*]kie in the kirk of Glendovane upon a testimoniall from this kirk.

9, Johne Sim to Margaret Hutton.

9, Thomas Forsythe to Bessie Simson in the kirk of Innerkething.

16, James Angus to Helene Cunynghame in the kirk of Carnok.

16, William Inche and Jonet Marshell.

18, Johne Wilson to Katherine Philp.

23, James Trumble to Jonet Drysdaill.

23, James Lamb to Agnes Davidson.

30, Johne Weyld to Agnes Cunynghame.

JANUARY [1657].

B. 1, Robert Gregour and Katherine Vasse had Jonet; witnesses, David Jerman, James Miller, Johne Baverage.

4, William Hall and Margaret Brand had Margaret; witnesses, Thomas Hall, Johne Anderson, Johne Drumond.

13, William Nicoll and Helene Mylne had Margaret; witnesses, Johne Mackie, James Mylne, Johne Mylne.

13, Johne Donaldson and Grissell Mather had Helene; witnesses, Thomas Douglas, Henrie Douglas, Ninian Mather.

13, James Bryce and Katherine Bruce had Adam ; witnesses, Adam Bryce, Johne Dewar and Johne Johnstoun.

13, Johne Clerk and Margaret Aikin had Bessie ; witnesses, Johne Hamiltoun, Johne Bad, Duncan Clerk, Johne Lawson.

15, Thomas Weddell and Issobell Liddell had twinns, Grissell and William ; witnesses, William Liddell and William Blaiky, presenter of the childrene, and James Mudie, Johne Mure and James Fleemyne.

15, Umquhile Josias Tod ane inglish soldier had ane manchilde borne to him of Helene Buist baptised upon her humble desire and called James ; witnesses, James, cationer and undertaker for the honest education of the childe and performance of all requisite dewtie thereto, and presenter of the childe this day, also Peter Buist, James Richardson, and Johne Donald being witnesses. The childe being now about two yeires old and a half. The occasion of the delay of the baptisme of the child is becaus of its said parents' disordorlie mariage.

15, Johne Drumond and Katherine Raiburne had Kathrine ; witnesses, John Car, presenter of the childe, Johne Clow and Johne Burley.

18, David Cunynghame and Elspet Fitt had twinnes, David and George ; witnesses, David Bad, Johne Kirkland, George Mudie, Johne Simrell.

20, David Austie and Margaret Andersone had Katherine ; witnesses, David Lindsay of Cavill, Mr. Alexander Malloch, William Primros.

20, Johne Hunter and Margaret Burn had Christane ; witnesses, Andro Mayne, John and Andro Burnes.

27, William Cose and Jonet Burn had Jonet ; witnesses, David Currie, Henrie Dowglas, James Peirson.

27, Thomas Mitchell and Margaret Mudie had Margaret ; witnesses, James Legat, William Keir, Johne Bad.

29, Johne Chrystie and Barbara Rae had Euphame ; witnesses, William Trumble, William and David Henriesones.

29, James Weemes and Jonet Easone had Katherine ; witnesses, David Steward, William Boyd, Johne Reid.

29. Johne Couper and Jonet Birrell had Margaret ; witnesses, James Kellok, William Boyd, Johne Birrell.

M. 6, Johne Cose to Agnes Cunyngham.

6, Robert Durie to Katherine Chatto.

20, James Harrower to Marion Gay in the kirk of Innerkething.

22, Patrik Drumond to Annas Hardie.

29, Johne Browne to Margaret Wilson.

30, Andro Potter to Jonet Paton.

30, Thomas Law to Margaret Russell.

FEBRUARY.

B. 3, William Strachane and Jonet Allane had Robert ; witnesses, Johne and Robert Strachans and James Andersone.

5, Johne Wilson and Margaret Watson ane half yeir or thereby eftir thair mariage had ane womanchilde baptised (upon cation for thair obedience to the discipline of the kirk for thair fornication) and called Issobell ; witnesses, John Watson her father, cationer and presenter of the childe, Johne Currie and Andro Johnestoun.

5, William Penman and Lilias Kedglie had William ; witnesses, David Trumble, Patrik Kedglie, Andro Wilson.

10, David Huttoun and Issobell Lindsay had Agnes ; witnesses, Johne Peirsone, James Huttoun, James Mudie.

16, James Miller and Jonet Dick had Margaret ; witnesses, Mr. George Walker, Johne Stevinson, Johne Colyear.

23, Thomas Elder and Issobell Simson had twinnes, James and Issobell ; witnesses to the manchilde, Mr. William Olyphant, minister, James

Mudie, baillie, James Simson in Pitkinny ; witnesses to the woman-childe, Henrie Elder, elerk, William Mercer, Patrik Sanders and George Brand.

24, Archibald Buchannane and Christane Patoun had Christane; witnesses, Andro Murgane, William Hunter, Johne Snadene.

M. 2, Andro Walwood to Helene Buist.
3, Robert Sharpe to Elizabeth Porteous in Edinburghe.
5, William Wilson to Katherine Lowson.

MARCH.

B. 1, Johne Lawson and Agnes Sanders had Katherine ; witnesses, Johne and William Lawsons and William Sanders.

5, James Lawson and Jeane Hog had Euphame ; witnesses, William Lason, Johne Manderstoun, William Primros.

5, Laurence Trotter and Jeane Burt had Jonet ; witnesses, Patrik and James Andersons, James Trotter.

8, James Wilson and Jonet Dick had Anna ; witnesses, Charles Halket, James Mudie, James Legat.

8, Johne Walwood and Katherine Coventrie had Johne ; witnesses, Robert Walwood of Touche, Johne Thomson, Allan Mitchell.

8, Robert Durie and Katherine Chatto eight weiks or thairby eftir thair mariage had ane womanchilde baptised (upon cation for thair obedi-ence to the discipline of the kirk for thair fornication) and called Margaret ; witnesses, Robert Chatto, cationer and presenter of the childe, Patrik Durie, Johne Chatto, Laurence Anderson.

8, William Thomeson and Margaret Lauthiane had Agnes ; witnesses, James Baverage, Johne Stanehous, Johne Bell.

10, Andro Cunynghame and Mariorie Burne had Peter ; witnesses, Peter Hay of Naughtoun, Thomas Cunyngham and Adam Currie.

10, Alexander Dunsyre and Agnes Thomeson had Margaret ; witnesses, Johne Mackie, William Nicoll, James Anderson.

15, Duncan Ogilvie and Bessie Wardlaw had Katherine ; witnesses, James Balfour of Baith, Robert Walwood of Touche and James Richardson.

19, William Turnbull and Jean Dowglas had William ; witnesses, William Walker, provest, presenter of the childe (the parent being sick), Adam Turnbull, Henrie Dowglas.

19, Robert Philp and Issobell Cunynghame had Helene ; witnesses, Johne Cunynghame, Johne Lethem, Johne Currie.

22, Andro Mudie and Issobell Mudie had Robert ; witnesses, Robert Mudie in Mastertoun, Robert Mudie in Touche, and Robert Burne in Gellett.

22, Harie James and Agnes Blaiket had Harie ; witnesses, James Andersone, younger, George Stirk and Alexander Beane, elder.

22, Duncan Clerk and Margaret Horne had Johne ; witnesses, Johne Clerk, Johne Bad, Thomas Horne.

22, Robert Ritchie and Margaret Davidson had ane womanchilde ane quarter of a yeir and some more eftir thair mariage baptised (upon catioun for thair obedience to the discipline of the kirk for thair fornicatioun) and called Margaret ; witnesses, Johne Wilsone, cationer and presenter of the childe, Thomas Baverage and Laurence Stevin-son, elder.

24, William Rowane and Margaret Allane had Andro ; witnesses, David Scotland, Robert Russell, Henrie Davidsone.

24, Johne Sandielands and Jeane Drysdaill had Johne ; witnesses, William Mudie, James Drysdaill, William Gilchrist.

29, William Peirson and Issobell Walwood had Bessie ; witnesses, Henrie Peirsone, Johne Thomsone, Robert Peirsone.

29, Robert Chisley and Bessie Greg had Anna ; witnesses, Robert Mudie in Touche, Robert Stevinsone, Andro Hall.

29, William Purdie and Margaret Dowe had Jonet; witnesses, James
     Cusine, Andro Kirk, Robert M'Greggour.

31, Robert Tailyeour and Issobell Hunter had twinnes, Robert and
     George; witnesses, Peter Walker, James Legat, Robert Mudie,
     William Legat.

M.   5, Andro Currie to Agnes Greinlay.

17, Johne Lason to Kathrin[e] Hendrie in the kirk of Torrie.

24, Thomas Wilson to Elspet Stevinson.

APRIL.

B.   2, Andro Chrystie and Mariorie Stevinsone had Thomas; witnesses,
     Patrik Stevinsone, Thomas Stevinson, Adam Currie.

5, Johne Stevinson and Margaret Dick had Robert; witnesses, Robert
     Stevinsone, Robert Adam, William Mudie.

7, Andro Huttoun and Issobell Walwood had Grissell : witnesses, James
     Huttoun, elder, James Huttoun, younger, and Robert Andersone.

9, Henrie Wilsone and Margaret Lindsay had David ; witnesses, Eduard
     and David Douglass and Johne Dewar.

12, Robert Shortus and Margaret Bad had Margaret ; witnesses, Robert
     Walwood, David Bad, Thomas Trumble.

14, Patrik Legat and Issobell Stevinsone had James ; witnesses, William
     and James Legats, William Mudie.

14, James Jamesone and Mariorie Dowe had Margaret ; witnesses, William
     Smert, Thomas Baverage, James Richardsone.

19, James Dewar and Marion Fisher had James ; witnesses, Robert Mudie,
     Eduard Russell, James Fisher.

20, James Malcome and Christan Phinn had Issobell ; witnesses, Henrie
     Malcome, John Fyg and David Marshell, presenter of the childe.

28, Henrie Coventrie and Issobell Donald had James ; witnesses, James
     Baverage, James Richardson, James Donald.

28, Johne Kingorne and Bessie Tailyeour had Agnes ; witnesses, Johne
     Stanehous, Johne Donald, Thomas Elder.

28, James Allane and Jonet Moreis had Bessie ; witnesses, Robert Wal-
     wood, Johne Livingstoun, James Watsone.

M.   7, Johne Mylne to Agnes Anderson in the kirk of Tullyallane.

10, Robert Blaw to Jonet Dowglas.

14, William Anderson to Issobell Anderson.

MAY.

B.   3, Robert Walwood and Jonet Ged had Katherine ; witnesses, George
     Bothwell, Peter Walker, William Walker, David Jerman, James
     Mudie, Andro Anderson, Johne Thomson. [*Here is legibly added,
     though scored out*]—Upon wch day the bells of the kirk were begun to
     be couped, being new stocked and hung.

3, David Bad and Jonet Andersone had Katherine ; witnesses, William
     Andersone, Johne Burley, Thomas Trumble.

3, Alexander Beane and Christane Simson had Johne ; witnesses, James
     Anderson, elder, Johne Hamiltoun, Alexander Anderson.

5, David Andersone and Issobell Anderson had James ; witnesses, Johne
     Mackie, James Anderson, Robert Scotland.

10, Henrie Trumble and Bessie Pet had Jonet ; witnesses, James Simson,
     Robert Huton, George Curry.

21, Andro Hutson and Helene Galrik had James ; witnesses, James Hutson,
     presenter of the childe, William Galrik, David Broun.

24, David Thomson and Agnes Peirsone had Robert ; witnesses, Johne and
     Robert Haliburtouns, Henrie Davidsone.

26, Thomas Douglas and Bessie Murie had Jonet ; witnesses, Eduard
     Dowglas, Henrie Douglas [*sic*], David Currie.

28, Manse Malcome and Jonet M'Lenochene had Thomas ; witnesses, Thomas Bennet, David Bad and Thomas Trumble.

31, William Scotland and Issobell Robertson had Elspet ; witnesses, David Scotland, William Robertson, Robert Russell.

M. 12, Robert Stanehous to Bessie Huttoun.

19, Johne Hunter to Jonet Murgane.

21, George Hall to Margaret Douglas.

21, William Ivatt to Jeane Anderson.

21, Robert Duncan to Bessie Cunynghame.

28, James Burnet and Katherine Angus.

JUNE.

B. 4, Alshunder Wilsone and Elspett Russell had Anna ; witnesses, William Wilsons, elder and younger, and Johne Wilsone.

7, James Dewar and Margaret Burne had Harie ; witnesses, Harie Law, John Dewar, Thomas Howie.

7, Johne Wardlaw and Margaret Moreis had Jeane ; witnesses, William Potter, William Inglis, Patrik Hunter.

7, Johne Andersone and Margaret M'Mirrie had Jonet ; witnesses, Johne Hamiltoun, James Anderson, elder, and Johne Watsone.

9, Andro Kirk and Issobel Coventrie had Johne ; witnesses, William Smert, William Legat, Thomas Burne.

9, Johne Gray and Margaret Law had Margaret ; witnesses, Johne Law, Johne Gray, Robert Colyear.

9, David Mooriesone and Elspet Williamsone in fornication (they being relapsed therein) had Margaret baptised upon cation for thair satis- faction of the discipline of the kirk ; witnesses, George Bothwell, William Smert, Andro Currie, with James Broun and William Glasse, tuo cationers.   The said William presented the childe.

11, Johne Dewar and Margaret Brand had Agnes ; witnesses, James Wardlaw, William Hutton, Johne Greeve.

14, Patrik Sanders and Anna Elder had Margaret ; witnesses, Johne Mackie, Harie Elder, Johne Duncansone.

14, Johne Baverage and Jonet Blaiket had Christane ; witnesses, Thomas Baverage, William Smert, William Baverage.

16, Andro Wilsone and Issobell Lethem had Margaret ; witnesses, Robert Cunynghame, Andro Wilsone, Johne Andersone.

16, Robert Currour and Grissell Wallace had Johne ; witnesses, James Baverage, Thomas Currour, James Dewar.

21, Johne Smythe and Margaret Davidsone had Helene ; witnesses, Patrik Allane, David Trumble, Henrie Peirsone.

21, William Robertsone and Christane Bowie had William ; witnesses, William Bowie, David Elder, Johne Græm.

30, Robert Logane and Bessie Potter had George ; witnesses, George Walls, Johne Potter, Laurence Watson.

30, James Mylne and Jonet Millar had Marie ; witnesses, George Dewar Robert Angus, William Huttone.

M. 11, Thomas Stevinson to Alison Dowglas.

18, Andro Rowe to Marie Lambe.

23, William Cusine to Margaret White in the kirk of Kinross.

25, William Huton to Jeane Ker in Kirklistoun.

25, Johne Thomesone to Katherine Harrow[er ?].

25, Johne Reid to Margaret Garlik.

30, Thomas Drysdail[l] to Katherine Seton in the kirk of Bruntiland.

JULY.

B. 5, James Marshell and Bessie Strang had Bessie ; witnesses, William Gotterstoun, Andro Anderson, Laurence Alisone.

5, James White and Issobell Harla had George ; witnesses, Robert Stevinsone, Johne Wilsone, George Young.

9, John Burn and Christane Heriot had Margaret ; witnesses, William Legat, George Mudie, Thomas Burne.

16, James Huton and Christane Livingstoun had Issobell ; witnesses, Peter Walker, James Livingstoun, and James Huton, elder.

16, Robert Jak and Jonet Hall had Jonet ; witnesses. Andro Wilson, Andro Hall, Robert Mayne.

16, Johne Broun and Elspet Stirk had Helene ; witnesses, William Hunter, Andro Murgane, Johne Currie, and Andro Wilson, presenter of the childe.

23, Archbald Robertsone and Marion Hutsone had David ; witnesses, David Steward, William Smert, Laurence Watsone.

23, Johne Watsone and Katherine M'Mirry had Margaret : witnesses, Johne Hamiltoun, George Chapmane, Johne Andersone.

25, James Bountorne hade ane manchilde (borne to him of his wyf Agnes Laurie the 20 day about 2 hours in the morning) baptised and called Johne ; witnesses, Johne Laurie, Robert Hutone, Johne Thomson.

25, Thomas Williamsone and Bessie Mayne had Jonet ; witnesses, George Stirk, Johne Smyth, Andro Garlik.

M. 7, Robert Lethem to Helen Scotland in the kirk of Sawline.

9, Johne Simrell to Bessie Stevinson.

9, Patrik Walker to Bessie Marshell.

14, Andro Trumble to Sara Dick.

14, Laurence Trott[er] to Jeane Hector.

AUGUST.

B. 2, David Haigie and Margaret Rainy had Marie ; witnesses, Johne Mackie, James Lowson, James Trotter.

6, Duncan Young and Helene Smert had Helene ; witnesses, George Walls, presenter of the childe, William Smert, Peter Buist, Alexander Smetoun.

9, James Mudie and Grissell Espline the 2 day being a Sonday about 9 hours at even, had Margaret ; witnesses, James Mudie, elder, William Walker, provest, Andro Anderson, deane of gild.

9, Robert Huton and Jonet Sanders had Helene ; witnesses, James Mudie, baillie, Andro Anderson, William Huttone.

9, James Peirsone and Margaret Peacok had James ; witnesses, William Cose, James Sands and James Wilson.

9, James Smeall and Grissell Bryce had Daniel ; witnesses, James Andersons, elder and younger, and William Nicoll.

16, Patrik Anderson and Bessie Mudie had William ; witnesses, William Anderson, James Mudies, elder and younger.

16, Johne Dowgall and Margaret Eilson had Issobell ; witnesses, William Mudie, David Trumble, Johne Eilson.

16, Andro Murgane and Katherine Brughe had Grissell ; witnesses, Robert Murgane, James Hutton, James Daes.

20, David Steward and Helene Kirkland had Katherine ; witnesses, Laurence Watson, William Smert, William Boyd.

20, Johne Litiljohne and Marie Greens had Johne ; witnesses, Patrik Legat, Johne Dewar, Johne Hendirson.

23, Thomas Hoburne and Bessie Dick had James ; witnesses, William Lasone, William Hutton and Robert Adam.

23, Johne Græm and Margaret Edison had Issobell ; witnesses, Andro Cunynghame, Andro Donaldson, Alexander Duff.

27, William Robertson and Elizabeth Huttone had David ; witnesses, David Dewar of Lassodie, David Robertson, David Scotland.

30, James Makgill and Katherine Broun had Margaret ; witnesses, William Walker, David Jernian, James Broun.

M. 6, Thomas Sands to Issobell Weyld.

11, Johne Broun to Margaret Kay in the kirk of Innerkething.

11, Walter Sim to Jonet Anderson in the kirk of Bait[h].

13, Johne Gray to Jonet Lindsay.
20, James Blak to Bessie Rowane.
27, William Garvie to Alison Hall.

SEPTEMBER.

B. 3, William Andersone and Katherine Wardlaw had Harie ; witnesses,
George Wardlaw, Duncan Ogilvie, James Anderson.

17, James Murgane and Isobell Alexander had William ; witnesses, Robert
Murgane, William Smert, Andro Murgane.

20, Johne Anderson and Margaret Andersone had Geilles ; witnesses,
William Andersons, elder and younger, and George Trumble.

20, David Duncansone and Margaret Patone had David ; witnesses, Johne
and James Duncansons and William Mudie.

21, James Lamb and Agnes Davidsone had William ; witnesses, William
Mudie, Robert Stirk, William Gotterstoun.

27, William Huton and Jeane Chrystie had James ; witnesses, James Mylne,
Robert Huton, James Cusine.

27, William Primros and Jonet Johnestoun had Johne ; witnesses, David
Lindsay, Johne Johnestoun and Andro Johnestoun.

27, Johne Glasse and Issobell Tosbeok had Margaret ; witnesses, David
and James Mitchell, Johne Broun.

M. 22, William Harla to Jonet M'Gregour.

OCTOBER.

B. 4, William Inche and Jonet Marshell had James ; witnesses, William
Inche, elder, James Marshell, Henric Meldrum.

4, Andro Burn and Issobell Ker had Jonet ; witnesses, George Mudie,
Patrik Hall, Andro Mayne.

4, Thomas Beane and Katherine Walker had Alexander ; witnesses,
Alexander Beane, Harie James, Patrik Walker.

4, Robert Currie and Margaret Inche had Harie ; witnesses, Harie James,
Robert Currie, Johne Law.

4, Patrik M'Innes and Jonet Ker had Johne ; witnesses, George Dewar,
Johne Dewar, William Hutton.

8, Thomas Howie and Jonet Cunynghame had Johne ; witnesses, Johne
Cunynghame, Andro Chrystie, David Bad.

8, James Lindsay and Helene Currie had Christane ; witnesses, Andro
Wilson, Johne Currie, Robert Lethem.

8, Robert Pet and Bessie Philp had Issobell ; witnesses, Andro Flokart,
Thomas Hendirson, Thomas Philp.

8, Alexander Arnot and Jonet Gray had Archibald ; witnesses, William
Robertsone, David Scotland, Thomas Colen.

11, Johne Mitchell and Elspet Baxter had James ; witnesses, George Walls,
Patrik Anderson, James Broun.

12, William Purves and Issobell Broun had twinnes, David and Andro :
witnesses, David Broun, Andro Mayne, George Broun, Patrik Hall.

15, James Futhie and Helen Auchinlek had James ; witnesses, James
Hendirsone, George Trumble, James Richardsone.

22, Johne White and Jonet Burley had Issobell ; witnesses, Alexander
Beane, elder, Andro Harman, Johne Hunnan.

29, David Hendirson and Bessie Hendirsone had Leonard ; witnesses,
Leonard Hendirsone, Robert Burne, Andro Mitchell.

29, James Rae and Bessie Strang had William ; witnesses, James Moreis,
William Andersone, David Cairnes.

M. 8, Alexander Williamsone to Elspet Innes.

15, Johne Bafour to Jonet Watson.

22, David Dewar to Margaret Thomeson.

29, Johne Burnet to Margaret Trotter.

NOVEMBER.

B. 3, Andro Andersone and Margaret Kennedie had Johne ; witnesses, Sir Henrie Wardlaw of Pitreavie, James Anderson, James Mudie.

3, James Mitchell and Margaret Mercer had Agnes ; witnesses, Thomas and Andro Mitchells, Johne Turnbull.

3, Andro Potter and Jonet Patone had Marion ; witnesses, Peter Walker, Patrik Sanders and Johne Potter.

3, James Watsone and Bessie Cook had James ; witnesses, George Wardlaw, Duncan Ogilvie, Robert Shortus.

3, Patrik Johnstoun and Jeane Dick had Margaret ; witnesses, James Baverage, Harie Andersone, James Weyld.

9, Andro Mitchell and Margaret Mitchell had Katherine ; witnesses, David Lindsay of Cavill, Mr. George Walker, Johne Turnbull.

15, Robert Walwood and Jeane Livingstoun had Jeane ; witnesses, James Bafour, Robert Haliburtoun and William Walwood.

19, Alexander Reddie and Rachel Chrystie (in fornicatione) had ane man-childe baptised (upon cation for thair obedience to and satisfaction of the discipline of the kirk) and called Alexander ; witnesses, Alexander Andersone, cationer and presenter of the childe, Johne Chrystie, David Flokard.

19, William Lasone and Agnes Norie had William ; witnesses, William Logane, William Andersone, William Gray.

22, Johne Clow and Beatrix Bennet had Elizabeth ; witnesses, Harie Elder, William Smert, Johne Thomsone.

22, James Greinhorne and Margaret Sanders had Anna ; witnesses, Thomas Hoburn, James Lason, Johne Manderstoun.

22, Johne Broun and Margaret Wilsone had Johne ; witnesses, Johne Broun, Robert Wilsone, William Smert.

M. 19, Daniel Bryce to Helene Clerk.

19, Andro Salmond to Helen Fairny.

19, George Crafoord to Helene Knagane.

26, Johne Henden to Margaret Turnour in the kirk off Saline.

DECEMBER.

B. 1, William Baverage and Issobell Templeman had William ; witnesses, Johne Stirk, Henrie and Andro Meldrums.

1, Alexander Fairlie and Margaret Myllar had William ; witnesses, William Walwood, Robert Mudie, Eduard Russell.

3, Adam Turnbull and Jonet Mitchell had Johne ; witnesses, Johne Turnbull, James Cunnan, James Mitchell.

6, Johne Sim and Margaret Hutton had James ; witnesses, James Corslaw, James Buist, Archibald Sim.

10, Johne Miller and Helene Adamson had Jonet ; witnesses, David Bad, Thomas Turnbull, Harie Richardson.

17, Johne Dewar and Alison Andersone had Elspet ; witnesses, Eduard Dowglas, Andro Wilson, Harie Cant.

20, Patrik Hunter and Jonet Gray had Grissell ; witnesses, Thomas Gairner, Robert Anderson, Walter Smert.

27, James Anderson and Agnes Drysdaill had Alexander; witnesses, Andro Andersone, baillie, Thomas Drysdaill, Robert Adam.

27, Laurence Walls and Margaret Greive had Jonet ; witnesses, Johne Greive, elder and younger, William M'Craithe.

31, William Bowman and Margaret Hearine had Agnes ; witnesses, Johne Dewar, James Stanehous, William Dalgleish.

M. 3, Robert Lason to Margaret Coventrie.

3, Adam Murie to Agnes Richie.

8, Patrik Græm to Rachel Blaik in the kirk of Baith upon a testimoniall of requeist to Mr. Harie Smythe, minister there.

10, Robert White to Margaret Brown.

15, Johne Græm to Margaret Bannaty[ne].
15, Robert B   to Grissell Anders[one].
17, Robert Donald to Helene Baverage.

JANUARY [1658].

B. 3, Johne Weyld and Agnes Cunynghame had Jonet; witnesses, Harie James, George Stirk, Andro Anderson.

3, James Trumble and Jonet Drysdaill had Margaret; witnesses, Adam Trumble, David Browne, James Trumble.

3, Laurence Walker and Jeane Rae had Johne; witnesses, David Steward, Nicoll Hendirson, Johne Duncanson.

5, Johne Cose and Agnes Cunynghame had William; witnesses, William Wilson, Johne Cunynghame, and William Cose, presenter of the childe.

10, David Thomesone and Jonet Peirsone had Bessie; witnesses, David Jermane, Johne Peirsone and William Douglas.

10, William Potter and Jeane Elder had David; witnesses, David Murray, Laurence Stevinson, elder, and Johne Reid.

14, Thomas Thomesone and Margaret Andersone had William; witnesses, William and Johne Andersons and Robert Cunynghame.

14, David Chrystie and Jonet Marshell had Eupham; witnesses, David Scotland, Robert Russell, James Fyff.

17, William Walker, provest, had ane womanchilde borne to him of his wyf Margaret Turnbull upon the 9 Januar 1658, and baptised and called Catherin upon the 17 day; witnesses, Andro Andersone and Mr. George Walker, baillies, and Johne Turnbull.

24, Alexander Smeton and Grissell Walls had George; witnesses, George Walls, William Douglas, Duncan Young.

28, David Russell and Jonet Stanehous had David; witnesses, Sir Henrie Wardlaw of Pitreavie, Robert and Eduard Russells.

28, James Broun and Jonet Whitefoord had Johne; witnesses, David Mitchell, Thomas and Andro Wilsons.

28, James Wilkie and Katherine Kirk had William; witnesses, William Alexander, William Chalmers, and Archibald Robertson, presenter of the childe.

31, Thomas Cant and Issobell Wely had Thomas; witnesses, Johne Peirson, Thomas Wely, James Mudie, William Douglas.

31, Andro Speare and Elspet Mathesone had George; witnesses, Peter Hay of Naughtoun, George Trumble, James Bafour.

M. 7, David Mayne to Margaret Peirson.

12, Alexander Reddie to Rachel Chrystie.

14, Thomas Rae to Helen Lason.

14, Mr. Robert Kay, minister, to Jonet Browne in the Kirk of Dysert.

21, Simon Robertson to Anna Skein in the kirk of Auchtertool.

FEBRUARY.

B. 2, James Mudie and Bessie Patone had Margaret; witnesses, Johne Hamiltoun, Thomas Trumble, Alexander Anderson.

2, William Anderson had ane womanchilde, being twinn (the uther died), borne to him of his wyf Issobel Anderson baptised and called Issobell; witnesses, James Anderson, Alexander and William Ingliss.

7, William Hadstoun and Annabel Blaiket had James; witnesses, David Lindsay of Cavill, Henrie Mitchell, James Hadstoun.

8, Mr. George Walker and Jonet Mitchell had George; witnesses, William and Peter Walker and Andro Anderson.

9, David Anderson and Margaret Blak had Margaret; witnesses, Johne Anderson, William M'Brek and William Anderson.

9, Andro Hannane and Isobell Hunnan had Bessie; witnesses, Johne Hamiltoun, Harie Law, Johne Hunnan.

11, James Mercer of Clavedge and Jeane Mercer had James ; witnesses, Peter Hay of Naughtoun, Duncan Campbell, Laurence Mercer.

14, James Bafour and Marion Bruce had Harie ; witnesses, Sir Henrie Wardlaw of Pitreavie, James Moutrey of Rescobie, and Peter Walker, late provest.

14, Johne Donald and Helene Reddie had Issobell ; witnesses, Robert and James Donalds and Henrie Coventrie.

14, William Anderson and Elspet Andersone had William ; witnesses, Henrie Davidson, Thomas Stevinson and William Anderson.

18, Thomas Colen and Jonet Scotland had James ; witnesses, James Legat, James Blak, William Robertson.

23, George Hall and Margaret Dowglas had Beatrix ; witnesses, Eduard Douglass, elder and younger, and David Douglas.

28, Thomas Stevinson and Alison Douglas had Thomas ; witnesses, Patrik and Thomas Stevinsones, Henrie and Mr. David Douglass and David Currie.

28, James Burnet and Katherine Angus had Elspet ; witnesses, George Dewar, David Scotland, William Robertson.

M. 4, Robert Burn to Jonet Sharp.

11, James Wilson to Christane Phinn.

16, Andro Cowe to Margaret Harrower.

MARCH.

B. 1, Jerome Cowie and Margaret Smert had Adam ; witnesses, William Smert, Adam Anderson, Peter Buist.

4, William Wilson and Katherine Lowson had James ; witnesses, James Kellok, James Boyd, James Lowson, William Wilson.

4, James Buchannan and Jonet Fotheringhame had Henrie ; witnesses, Henrie Coventrie, Johne Lason, James Donald.

4, Johne Hadstone and Issobell Pringle had Christane ; witnesses, James Hadstone, William Nicoll, William Anderson.

7, James Boyd and Bessie Baverage had Jonet ; witnesses, Laurence Watson, Thomas Baverage and William Boyd.

7, Johne Wilson and Katherine Philp had Thomas ; witnesses, Thomas Wilson, Andro Wilson, Johne Currie.

7, Archibald Gray and Mariorie Small had Patrik ; witnesses, Robert Sharp, Robert Hogane, Patrik Small.

9, Laurence Anderson and Jonet M'Birny had Robert ; witnesses, Adam Wilson, David Robertson, Andro Donald.

9, William Lason and Elspet Chrystie had Johne ; witnesses, Johne Cunynghame, Johne Lason, Andro Chrystie.

11, Johne Sandielands and Jeane Drysdaill had Marie ; witnesses, James Drysdaill, Harie Richardson, William Mudie.

14, Mark Cunnan and Jonet Thomeson had James ; witnesses, James Cunnan, James Mylne and Thomas Cunnan.

14, James Broun and Jonet Meldrum had William ; witnesses, William Meldrum, Johne Broun, George Stirk.

14, James Brughe and Jonet Fyg had Margaret ; witnesses, James Fyg, Johne Fyg, William Mudie.

18, Patrik Drummond and Annas Hardie had Harie ; witnesses, Sir Henre Wardlaw of Pitreavie, Johne Drummond, William Broun, and James Buist, presenter of the childe.

21, Johne Stanehous and Jonet Cunynghame had Thomas ; witnesses, Thomas Stanehous, Robert Stanehouss, elder and younger.

21, James Hew and Jonet Anderson had Helene ; witnesses, Adam Currie, Andro Cunynghame, James Thomson.

21, Alexander Scotland and Mariorie White had Eupham ; witnesses, James Broun, Robert Stanehous, William Mudie.

21, Abram Giro and Grissell Anderson had William ; witnesses, William Walker, provest, Johne Mackie, Johne Duncanson.

21, Patrik Anderson and Barbara Turnbull had Patrik ; witnesses, David
    Turnbull, William Anderson, William Nicoll.
21, William Anderson and Elspet Anderson had Elspett ; witnesses, David
    Burley, David Anderson, William Walker.
21, Johne Drummond and Bessie Wardlaw had George ; witnesses, Robert
    Stevinsone, David Jerman, George Wardlaw.
23, William Lethem and Jonet Wilson had twinnes, Issobell and Helene ;
    witnesses, Robert Cunynghame, Robert and James Donalds, James
    Broun, Johne Harrower.
28, Robert Dewar and Margaret Andro had Robert ; witnesses, James
    Simson, Johne Dalgleish, Johne Reid.
28, Andro Mudie and Issobell Mudie had William ; witnesses, William
    Smert, William Hendirson, Andro Mayn.
28, Alexander Reid and Jonet Johnstoun had George ; witnesses, George
    Stirk, Johne Lawrie, William Prymrose.
M. 11, William Legat to Helen Kent.

APRIL.

B. 1, Alexander Lowson and Margaret Keltie had William ; witnesses,
       William Wilson, William Nicoll, James Lowson.
    1, Robert Cowstoune and Euphame Scot had Katherine ; witnesses, Andro
       Cunynghame, Johne Anderson, James Hutsone.
    4, Eduard Rutherfoord and Margaret Græm had twins, Frances and Helen ;
       witnesses, James Anderson, Robert Græm, Robert Russell, Andro
       Wilson.
    4, William Beany and Helene Donaldson had Katherine ; witnesses, James
       Boyd, William Wilson, Johne Cunynghame.
    5, Henrie Dowglas and Katherine Brand had David ; witnesses, David
       Mitchell, David Currie, Mr. David Dowglas.
   11, James Sands and Bessie Touchie had James ; witnesses, James Peirson,
       George Chapman, Thomas Stevinson.
   13, Johne Manderstoun and Issobell Leslie had Jeane ; witnesses, Henrie
       Mitchell, Robert Scotland and William Anderson.
   13, Robert Kirk and Jonet Currour had Euphame ; witnesses, Johne
       Stanehous, James Anderson, Thomas Philp.
   13, Johne Hendirsone and Jonet Hendirsone had Nanse ; witnesses, Robert
       Mudie, Johne Moyes, William Walwood
   15, Patrik Rowane and Jeane Stanehous had Margaret ; witnesses, Peter
       Hay of Naughton, Robert Smetone, Johne Watson.
   15, James Buist and Margaret Hardie had Margaret ; witnesses, Peter
       Buist, James Richardson, George Bothwell.
   18, Johne Willoks and Margaret Broun had Alexander ; witnesses, Alexander
       Gib, Adam Wilson, David Robertson.
   25, Alexander Anderson and Jonet Chrystie had Jonet ; witnesses, William
       and Patrik Andersons, Johne Chrystie.
   25, William Huttone and Jeane Ker had James ; witnesses, William Lason,
       James Greinhorne, Thomas Hoburn.
   25, William Keir and Margaret Bad had William ; witnesses, William
       Walwood, Johne Wardlaw, James Imrie.
   25, Robert Stirk and Jonet Mudie had Grissell ; witnesses, James Mudie,
       George Stirk, Johne Stirk.
   27, Robert Lethem and Helen Scotland had Johne ; witnesses, William
       Lethem, Johne Lethem, Andro Wilson, Thomas Scotland.
M. 15, Johne Marshell to Margaret Anderson.

MAY.

B. 2, Alexander Innes and Margaret Thomeson had Agnes ; witnesses, Johne
       Lawrie, James Bountorne, Johne Thomson.
    4, Robert Dowglas and Elspet Peirson had Henrie ; witnesses, Johne
       Lason, Henrie Peirson, William Lethem.

6, Robert Bryce and Helen Anderson had Andro; witnesses, Andro Currie, Andro Foster, Andro Johneston.

9, Andro Scotland and Margaret Moreis had James; witnesses, William Walker, Johne Mackie, James Broun.

10, Johne Turnbull and Katherine Mitchell had William; witnesses, William Walker, provest, Mr. William Oliphant, minister, and William Turnbull.

16, Umqle William Anderson and Jonet Finla had Margaret; witnesses, David Jerman, George Turnbull, Eduard Dowglas.

16, James Kellok and Issobell Watson had Helen; witnesses, Johne Duncanson, James Legat, David Steward.

16, David Marshell and Annas Malcome had Christian; witnesses, Robert Sharp, Walter Horne, Johne Thomson.

20, George Turnbull and Margaret Kellok had Elspet; witnesses, James Cunnan, Patrik Rowan and William Cunnan.

20, Duncan M'ellop and Jonet Mayne had Johne; witnesses, Johne Anderson, Eduard Dowglas and Johne Donaldson.

23, Thomas Sands and Issobell Weyld had Elspet; witnesses, Robert Anderson, Eduard Russell, Andro Anderson.

23, Johne Reid and Jonet Boyd had Helene; witnesses, David Jerman, William Boyd and James Boyd.

23, Johne Peirson and Jonet Stevinsone had David; witnesses, David Jerman, David Thomson, David Hutton.

25, Johne Harrower and Bessie Hall had Johne; witnesses, Robert Cunynghame, William Lethem, Andro Wilson.

25, Henrie Mitchell and Grissell Lindsay had Anna; witnesses, Sir James Halket of Pitfirran, David Lindsay of Cavill, Thomas and Andro Mitchells.

25, Alexander Duff and Jonet Philp had James; witnesses, Andro Mayne, Johne Cunynghame, Johne Stirk.

31, Umqle David Hodge and Christan Coventrie had Nanse; witnesses, James Baverage, presenter of the childe, James Richardson, and Henrie Coventrie.

M. 4, Andro Johnstoun to Margaret Bruce.

7, James Ffyg to Nanse Dalgleish.

18, James Mitchell to Agnes Nicolson in Bruntiland.

JUNE.

B. 3, Johne Stevinson and Margaret Dick had Adam; witnesses, Adam Anderson, Robert Stevinson, Robert Adam.

6, Walter Sim and Jonet Anderson had Margaret; witnesses, Robert Anderson, Thomas Gairner, Patrik Hunter.

6, Johne Walker and Jeane Goweans had Elspet; witnesses, James Legat, Johne Potter, George Stirk.

6, Johne Simrell and Bessie Stevinson had Christane; witnesses, Andro Mudie, William Swintoun, Thomas Stevinson.

6, Johne Hutson and Jeane Edison (in fornication) had Harie; witnesses, Harie Rowane, William Turnbull, Johne Wrytte.

8, Johne Murie and Katherine Kingorne had Adam; witnesses, Adam Murie, Johne Kingorne, John Peirie.

13, Robert Anderson and Katherine Smyth had William; witnesses, Henrie Davidson, Andro Smyth and William Walwood.

13, Robert Ritchie and Margaret Davidson had Johne; witnesses, Robert Stevinson, Thomas Couper, Johne Meldrum.

13, William Alexander and Katherine Smert had Elspet; witnesses, Johne Potter, Johne Litlejohne, Johne Watson.

15, Robert Bonar and Jonet Horne had Thomas; witnesses, Thomas Horne, James Legat, Robert Stevinson.

20, Robert Fisher and Margaret Adam (in fornication) had Margaret; witnesses, George Stirk, James Legat, David Bell.

20, Thomas Falconer and Issobell Kinloch had Adam; witnesses, Adam
    and James Andersons, Johne Thomson.
20, James Moyes and Elspet Blaiky had James; witnesses, James Dewar,
    William Blaiky, Johne Cunynghame.
22, Sir James Halket of Pitfirrane and his Ladie, Dame Anna Murray, had
        Harie; witnesses, Robert Lord Colvill, Sir Harie Wardlaw of Pit-
        reavie, Sir George Preston off Valleyfield and [*space left here*]
24, William Purdie and Margaret Dowe had Bessie; witnesses, William
    Smert, James Cusine, Andro Kirk.
24, Johne Broun and Margaret Kay had David; witnesses, David Flokart,
    David Broun, Andro Kay.
25, Sir Harie Wardlaw of Pitreavie and his Ladie, Dame Elizabeth
        Wardlaw, had Elizabeth; witnesses, George Wardlaw, James Mudie,
        Andro Wardlaw of Killearnie, and Andro Anderson.
27, Andro Walwood and Helene Buist had Mariorie; witnesses, William
    Dowglas, presenter of the childe, Peter Buist, James Mudie.
29, Gilbert Hamiltoun and Helen Cork had Margaret: witnesses, Andro
    Cunynghame, James Mayne, Alexander Inglis.

M. 1, Robert Nimmo to Agnes Thomson in the kirk of Torry.
    3, Robert Shortus to Bessie Strachane.
    10, James M'Yowane to Margaret Wilson.
    15, Johne Strachan to Katherine Mather.
    17, Harie Moreis to Elspet Tailyeour.
    24, Duncan M'Allum to Helen Turnbull.
    25, Richard Watt[e] the inglish drumc[r] to Margaret Law.
    29, Johne Hutson to Jeane Edison.

JULY.

B. 1, Johne Scarlet and Issobell Bairdner had Elizabeth; witnesses, Henrie
        Elder, James Simson, William Anderson.
    4, James Donaldson and Helene Henden had Margaret; witnesses, Johne
        Greive, Johne Dewar, James Stanehous.
    6, William Gray and Helen Haddane had Marione; witnesses, James
        Baverage, Johne Stanehous, Andro Smyth.
    10, Robert Sharp and Elizabeth Porteous had Robert; witnesses, Johne
        Thomson, Johne Laurie, James Bountorne.
    10, Johne Lason and Bessie Walwood had James; witnesses, James Mudie,
        Robert Colyear, William Gotterstoun.
    12, Patrik Sanders and Anna Elder had Johne; witnesses, Johne Duncan-
        son, Johne Mackie, Harie Elder.
    12, Andro Rowe and Marie Lamb had Marion; witnesses, James Mudie,
        Mr. George Walker, Robert Stirk.
    13, Eduard Dowglas and Jonet Andersone had Eduard; witnesses, Eduard
        Dowglas, elder, Johne Andersone, William Gray.
    13, Johne Livingstone and Jonet Wood had Jonet; witnesses, Robert
        Walwood, Patrick Livingstone, George Wardlaw.
    18, Johne Chrystie and Barbara Rae had Jonet; witnesses, Thomas
        Stevinson, Thomas Rae, David Hendirson.
    18, William Tailyeour and Annas Dowglas had Johne; witnesses, William
        David Turnbull, Johne Tailyeour.
    18, David Robertson and Jonet Wilson had Margaret; witnesses, Johne
        Heart, Johne Wardlaw, James Imrie.

M. 2, David Peacok to Margaret M'Craich.
    2, Johne Moreis to Margaret Burnet.
    6, Johne Barker to Issobell Clerk.
    8, James Anderson to Barbara Russell.
    8, David Haddane to Marion Bryce.
    8, Robert Pullons to Jonet Eduard in Torrieburne.
    20, Johne Dalgleish to Margaret Sandilands.
    29, Laurence Thomson to Eupham Mather.

AUGUST.

B. 1, Johne Lason and Katherine Henrie had Jonet; witnesses, Johne, William and Patrik Lasons.

1, Andro Salmond and Helen Fairny had James; witnesses, James Mudie, Thomas Elder, James Fairny.

10, William Gilkrist and Jonet Drysdaill had Christane; witnesses, William Anderson, James Wilson, James Murie.

26, Johne Potter and Elspet Mullion had Harie; witnesses, Sir Harie Wardlaw of Pitreavie and Harie, his sone, James Legat, Johne Hamiltoun.

29, William Strachane and Jonet Allane had Jonet; witnesses, Johne Strachane, Robert Strachane, Johne Anderson, younger.

29, Andro Wilson and Bessie Peirsone had David; witnesses, David Currie, David Kay, Patrik Roxbrughe.

29, Robert Duncan and Bessie Cunynghame had Peter; witnesses, Johne Anderson, David Cunynghame, William Lethem.

31, William Garvie and Alison Hall had Andro; witnesses, Andro Hall, Andro Garlik, Alexander Inglis.

M. 5, Johne Ker to Jonet Myllar.

10, George Chalmers to Margaret Walker.

12, Johne Goold to Elspet Cunynghame.

12, George Car to Jonet Duncan.

12, Harie Richardson to Elspet Gray.

17, George Wilson to Helen M'Baith in Innerkething.

26, David Bafour to Elizabeth Bafour in Culros.

26, James Marshell to Helen Faulds.

SEPTEMBER.

B. 5, James Baverage and Jonet Coventrie had Issobell; witnesses, James Dewar, David Peirson, Robert Stanehous.

5, Laurence Trottor and Jeane Hector had Laurence; witnesses, James Anderson, James Trotter, James Hadstoun.

7, Cudbert Thomson and Katherine Wilsone had Margaret; witnesses, Alexander Innes, Johne Clerk, Robert Baxter.

9, William Camron and Bessie Kinnell had George; witnesses, Robert Stevinson, Johne Duncanson, George Currie.

12, Andro Garlik and Mariorie Williamson had Thomas; witnesses, Thomas Williamson, George Stirk, David Broun.

14, Peter Hay off Naughtoun and his Ladie, Dame Margaret Hendirson, had Marie; witnesses, Johne Hendirson of Fordell, Thomas Bruce of Blairhall and James Mercer of Clavedge.

16, Johne Drumond and Katherine Raiburn had Johne; witnesses, Johne Turnbull, Johne Clow, Johne Heart.

19, James Marshell and Elspet Moreis had Jonet; witnesses, Johne Thomson, Eduard Dowglas, William Smyth.

21, Johne Fyg and Margaret Simson had James: witnesses, James Fyg, James Brughe, Johne Potter.

26, Adam Murie and Nanse Richie had Johne; witnesses, Johne Thomson, Johne Murie, Johne Richie.

26, David Donaldson and Mase Bryce had William; witnesses, William Primros, Henrie Peirson, Robert Wardlaw.

30, Adam Anderson and Katherin Gibbon had Katherine; witnesses, Robert Stevinson, James Anderson, James Gibbon.

M. 2, George Watson to Margaret Dowe.

14, James Browne to Margaret George.

OCTOBER.

B. 3, William Robertson and Christan Bowie had Christane; witnesses, William Bowie, Andro Donaldson, David Elder.

3, Johne Watson and Katherine M'Mirry had Johne; witnesses, Johne Hamiltoun, Johne Currie, Johne Lethem.

3, David Dewar and Margaret Thomeson had Johne; witnesses, James Dewar, Johne Dewar, Adam Brand.

3, Johne Hunter and Margaret Burn had Marie; witnesses, Andro Mayne, Andro Mudie, Robert Tailyeour.

10, Samuel Denholme and Bessie Alison had Jonet; witnesses, William Walker, Peter Walker, Mr. George Walker.

10, James Lamb and Agnes Davidson had Marie; witnesses, Robert Stirk, William Gotterstoun, James Mudie, elder.

21, Andro M'Kenla and Elspet Gib had Margaret, witnesses, Robert Russell, William Purdie, Patrik Kedglie.

21, Robert Bowie and Grissell Anderson had Margaret; witnesses, Robert Russell, William Purdie, Johne Smythe.

24, William Anderson and Margaret Kirk had Robert; witnesses, Patrick Anderson, Johne Kirk, Laurence Trotter.

28, David Burley and Jonet Anderson had Jonet; witnesses, William Anderson, William Hutton, Johne Faulds.

31, David Dowglas and Marion Duff had Elspet; witnesses, Adam Currie, Andro Cunynghame, David Elder.

31, Johne Moreis and Elspet Dewar had William; witnesses, William Smert, James Huton, Alexander Beane, younger.

M. 7, David Kairnes to Jonet Finlason.

14, Alexander Gibson to Christan Robertson.

14, David Walker to Katherin Fergison in the kirk of Kinross.

28, William Strachan to Margaret Marshell.

NOVEMBER.

B. 7, Harie Elder and Elizabeth Elder had Anna; witnesses, Sir Henrie Wardlaw of Pitreavie, Thomas Elder, Johne Mackie, Patrik Sanders.

7, Robert Donald and Helen Belfrage had Jonet; witnesses, James Belfrage, Andro, Johne and James Donalds.

7, William Anderson and Christane Mitchell had Robert; witnesses, Robert Walwood, William and Patrick Legatts.

9, Robert Smeton and Margaret Dick had Henrie; witnesses, Henrie Mitchell, Robert Scotland, Johne Smeton.

9, James Peacok and Christane Alison had James; witnesses, James Bafour, James Anderson, James Short.

9, David Murie and Katherine Wardlaw had George; witnesses, George Turnbull, Johne Wardlaw, William Mudy.

11, Patrik Græm and Rachel Blaik had Duncan; witnesses, James Baverage, Johne Blaik, William Blaik.

11, George Buist and Issobell Mylls had Robert; witnesses, Johne Buist, James Buist, Peter Buist, Johne Thomson.

14, James Allan and Jonet Moreis had William; witnesses, William Drylay, Robert Shortus, William Smert.

14, James Mudie and Bessie Cunynghame had Annas; witnesses, Thomas Cunynghame, Thomas Howie, George Currie.

18, James Futhie and Helen Auchinlek had twins, Hew and George; witnesses, George Currie, Johne Duncanson, James Richardson, Patrik Law.

18, Robert Gregour and Katherine Vasse had James; witnesses, James Skinner, James Colyear, James Simson.

23, Andro Cunynghame and Katherine Kid had Margaret; witnesses, William Rowan, William Robertson, David Russell.

25, Donald M'Neill and Margaret M'Nab had Margaret; witnesses, Robert Mudie, James Moyes and Johne Moyes.

28, James Brand and Margaret Forfar had James; witnesses, William Mudie, Adam Brand, James Mudie, elder.

28, Johne Kirkland and Nanse Fitt had George; witnesses, George Chalmers, William Smert, David Steward.

28, Laurence Goodaill and Jeane Coburne had Agnes; witnesses, David Jerman, Johne Thomson, Andro Turnbull.

28, William Broun and Elspet Henderson had Margaret; witnesses, David Broun, Johne Broun, James Mayne.

M. 4, James Watson to Jonet Norie in the kirk of Torrie.

9, Johne Henderson to Margaret Watson.

11, Johne Weire to Eupham Kingorn.

23, James Arthure to Jonet Fairlie.

23, James Lamb to Margaret Smert.

DECEMBER.

B. 2, Robert Burn and Jonet Sharp had Mariorie; witnesses, David Currie, Henrie Dowglas, Robert Burn, elder.

2, William Gray and Elspet Anderson had Margaret; witnesses, Adam Anderson, presenter of the childe, James Anderson, Robert Stevinson.

9, Johne Hamilton and Bessie Anderson had Alexander; witnesses, Alexander Anderson, Robert Huton, James Anderson.

12, Thomas Forfar and Jonet Smeton had Thomas; witnesses, Thomas Mitchell, Johne Stirk, James Anderson.

14, Robert Lason and Jonet Drysdaill had James; witnesses, Robert and James Lasons and William Anderson.

23, William Penman and Lillias Kedglie had Henrie; witnesses, Patrik Kedglie, David Turnbull, Robert Russell.

26, Harie James and Agnes Blaiket had Johne; witnesses, Johne Hamiltoun, James Anderson, younger, and Johne Anderson, his sone.

26, James Broun and Helene Thomeson had Helene; witnesses, William Legat, James Maxwell, Robert Hutton.

28, Robert Hoy and Bessie Allane had Bessie; witnesses, Andro Wilson, Johne Wilson, Johne Browne.

30, James Malcome and Christane Phin had Annas; witnesses, David Marshell, Johne Bafour and Nicoll Hendirson.

M. 2, Abram Patrik to Marion Boyd.

2, William Maitland to Mariorie Myllar.

14, Johne Alexander to Margaret Westwood.

16, William Currie to Margaret Mayne.

16, James Donaldson to Margaret Blaike[t].

21, Alexander Dunsyre to Katherine Brughe.

23, James Eason to Jean Peacok in Carnok.

23, Patrik Mayne to Christan Paton.

30, George Ewine to Elspet Potter.

JANUARY [1659].

B. 2, William Gotterstoun and Christane Strang had Johne; witnesses, William Mudie, Robert Stirk, James Marshell.

2, Robert Walwood and Jonet Ged had Hew; witnesses, Sir Henrie Wardlaw of Pitreavie, William and Peter Walkers, Hew Vernor, Johne Ged, Johne Thomson.

2, Johne Watson and Helen Nicoll had William; witnesses, William Walker, William Broun, James Hutton.

4, Andro Adam and Jeane Philp had Andro; witnesses, Thomas Philp, Harie Rowane, James Short.

6, Robert Lason and Margaret Coventrie had Katherine; witnesses, Johne Lason, Henry Coventrie, Johne Thomeson.

6, William Ivatt and Jeane Anderson had William; witnesses, Adam Anderson, Johne Wright, Harie Elder.

9, William Legat and Helen Kent had William; witnesses, William Kent, James Legat, Peter Walker.

9, Johne Hutton and Jonet Howie had Jonet; witnesses, Thomas Howie, William Robertson, David Elder.

11, Johne Burley and Christan Culros had Thomas ; witnesses, Thomas
   Turnbull, Thomas Burley, Johne Clowe.
16, Johne Robieson and Grissell Marshell had George ; witnesses, Mr.
   George Walker, George Walls, George Stirk.
23, Adam Turnbull and Jonet Mitchell had Adam ; witnesses, Adam Currie,
   Andro Mitchell, Henrie Dowglas.
23, Robert Bull and Issobell Meldrum had David ; witnesses, David
   Jerman, David Bull, David Thomson, William Bell.
25, Thomas Heart and Katherine Marshell had Kathrine ; witnesses, Robert
   Philp, Johne Lethem, Andro Johnstone, Johne Dalgleish.
30, Robert Colyear and Christane Burt had Agnes ; witnesses, Johne
   Colyear, Johne Law, Robert Sharp.
30, William Hunter and Margaret Snaddon had David ; witnesses, Johne
   Currie, Alexander Dunsyre, William Menteith.

M. 11, Johne Cusine to Issobell Hutton.
   18, Thomas Anderson to Agnes Yowane.
   25, Johne Dowgall to Margaret Young.
   27, Frances Stevinson to Margaret Dowglas.

FEBRUARY.

B. 6, William Dowglas and Mariorie Stevinson had Thomas ; witnesses,
      Thomas Stevinson, David Jerman, George Walls.
   10, Duncan Campbell and Christane Dalgleish had Robert ; witnesses, Sir
       Henrie Wardlaw of Pitreavie, Peter Hay of Naughtoun. James Clerk
       of Pittincreiff, James Mercer of Clavedge.
   10, Johne Gray and Margaret Law had Johne ; witnesses, Johne Law,
       Thomas Law, Johne Gray, Johne Stevinson.
   10, William Broun and Jonet Anderson had Bessie ; witnesses, William
       and Johne Andersones, Johne Dewar, Johne Cumyn.
   13, James Mitchell and Margaret Mercer had Sara ; witnesses, David
       Mitchell, David Lindsay, Thomas Wilson.
   13, Andro Hall and Agnes Kinsman had Issobell ; witnesses, Peter Buist,
       Johne Cusine, James Duncanson.
   15, William Mackay and Agnes Sharp had Issobell ; witnesses, Johne
       Potter, James Dumbar, James Richardson.
   15, David Lindsay of Cavill and Katherine Malloche had Hew ; witnesses,
       Sir James Halkett of Pittirran, Hew M'Gill and James Mudie.
   20, William Smyth and Elspet Mayne had Johne ; witnesses, David
       Lindsay of Cavill, Eduard Dowglas, Johne Mayne.
   27, Johne Lason and Agnes Sanders had Elizabeth ; witnesses, William
       Sanders, Johne Lason, William M'Brek.

M. 22, Johne Hunnan to Katherine Yowane.

MARCH.

B. 3, George Chapman and Margaret Clerk had Andro ; witnesses, William
      Turnbull, David Peacok, Andro Chapman.
   3, Johne Marshell and Margaret Anderson had Patrik ; witnesses, Robert
      Scotland, James Lowson, David Haigie.
   Andro Anderson had ane manchilde berne to him of his wyf Margaret
      Kennedie upon the 26 of Febr. last, and baptized and called Henrie
      upon the 6 day of Marche instant ; witnesses, Sir Henry Wardlaw of
      Pitreavie, William Walker, late provest, and James Anderson, elder.
   6, David Turnbull and Christan Legat had David ; witnesses, William
      Legat, Patrik Law, William Walwood.
   6, Johne Dewar and Jonet Peirson had David ; witnesses, David Thomson,
      Johne Anderson, Johne Dewar.
   8, James Dansken and Margaret Stob had Christane ; witnesses, James
      Simson, Johne Dalgleish, and Alexander Beane, younger, presenter
      of the childe.

13, Johne Mackie, chamerlane, and Margaret Elder had ane manchilde borne to him of his wyf Margaret Elder upon the 9 day of Marche 1659 about four hours in the morning, and baptised and called Johne upon the 13 day ; witnesses, Sir James Halket of Pitfirran, Sir Henrie Wardlaw of Pitreavie, and William Walker, late provest.

15, William Dewar and Issobell Fyff had William ; witnesses, William Wilson, Andro Wilson, William Mudie.

17, Johne Græm and Katherin Peirson had Andro ; witnesses, Johne Lason, David Anderson, and William Lason, presenter of the childe.

17, Andro Weddell, an inglish soldier, and Grissell Fleemyne had Johne ; witnesses, James Fleemyne, Alexander Anderson, Johne Peirson.

20, James Richardson and Agnes Coventrie had Christane ; witnesses, Peter Buist, Thomas Drysdaill, Johne Thomson.

20, Johne Baverage and Jonet Blaiket had Thomas ; witnesses, Thomas Baverage, William Smert, William Baverage.

22, Johne Strachane and Katherine Mather had Helene ; witnesses, Robert Shortus, Johne Strachane, William Mudie.

22, William Currie and Helen Donaldson had Patrik ; witnesses, Andro Currie, Patrik Hunter, George Mudie.

24, James Anderson and Issobell Gibbone had James ; witnesses, James and William Andersons and Johne Manderstoun.

24, Robert Shortus and Bessie Strachane had James ; witnesses, James Clerk of Pittincreiff, James Mudie, Johne Stirk and Johne Strachane.

27, Thomas Elder and Issobell Simson had Elizabeth ; witnesses, Sir Henrie Wardlaw of Pitreavie, Peter Hay of Naughtoun, George Wardlaw, Peter Walker.

27, William Peirson and Issobell Walwood had Johne ; witnesses, Henrie Peirson, Robert Peirson, Johne Thomson.

27, Eduard Overwhite and Grissell Dick had Elizabeth ; witnesses, Thomas Hoburne, James Wilson and James Anderson.

27, Johne Reid and Margaret Garlik had Johne ; witnesses, David Turnbull, Henrie Peirson, Thomas Hall.

29, James Clerk and Elspet Scotland had Margaret ; witnesses, Robert Scotland, Johne Currie, Johne Broun.

M. 3, Henrie Peirson to Helen Wilson.

3, Robert Barclay to Jonet Hutton.

10, David Bell to Jonet Walker.

15, Johne Edison to Margaret Falkland.

APRIL.

B. 3, William Purves and Issobell Broun had George ; witnesses, David Broun, George Broun, Patrick Hall.

3, William Boyd and Marion Wallace had Margaret ; witnesses, Laurence Watson, Johne Reid, William Wilson.

3, Alexander Fairlie and Margaret Myllar had Thomas ; witnesses, Johne Burn, Andro Burn, Johne Simrell, Thomas Stevinson.

3, William Meldrum and Eupham Steward had Katherine ; witnesses, Adam Anderson, James Broun, Michal Meldrum.

3, Harie Moreis and Elspet Tailyeour had William ; witnesses, William Walker, William Mercer and George Chalmers.

10, Johne Walwood and Katherine Coventrie had James ; witnesses, James Baverage, James Richardson and Henrie Coventrie.

10, Richard Watts and Margaret Law had Patrik ; witnesses, Patrik Law, William Walwood, David Turnbull.

14, James Gib and Elspet Maxwell had Margaret ; witnesses, William Dewar, William Rowane, Robert Angus.

17, Johne Barker and Issobell Clerk had Bessie ; witnesses, William Mudie, James Imrie, James Cusine.

17, George Mayne and Christane Myllar had David ; witnesses, George Turnbull, James Bafour, David Mayne.

17, William Hall and Margaret Brand had Elizabeth ; witnesses, Sir Henrie Wardlaw of Pitreavie, Thomas Hall, Thomas Williamson.

19, Johne Wardlaw and Margaret Moreis had Elspet ; witnesses, Harie Moreis, William Inglis, William Wilson.

21, Robert Stirk and Jonet Mudie had George ; witnesses, George Stirk, elder and younger, and James Mudie.

21, William Nicoll and Helen Mylne had Johne ; witnesses, Johne Mackie, Johne Mylne, Robert Scotland.

21, Alexander Lowson and Margaret Keltie had Bessie ; witnesses James Lowson, James Anderson, James Hadstoun.

24, Johne Lindsay and Elspet Reid had Agnes ; witnesses, James Lindsay, Johne Lindsay, James Anderson.

24, James Short and Bessie Walwood had Christane ; witnesses, James Bafour, Robert Walwood, James Baverage.

24, James Jamesone and Mariorie Dowe had William ; witnesses, William Broun, William Smert and James Legat.

24, Rodger Cræm, ane inglish soldier, and Margaret Campbell (in fornication) had Margaret ; witnesses, Thomas Frissell, presenter of the childe, Johne Thomson, Johne Watson, Johne Dalgleish.

26, Henrie Stevinsone and Issobell Dowglas had David ; witnesses, Eduard Dowglas, David Dowglas, Robert Dowglas.

28, Johne Ker and Jonet Myllar had James ; witnesses, James Legat, James Ker, Thomas Horne.

M. 4, William Hunter to Margaret Cunynghame.

7, James Murgane to Jonet Inglis.

21, Patrick Walker to Elspet Blaiket in the kirk of Baith.

MAY.

B. 1, David Mayne and Margaret Peirson had twins, Helen and Issobell ; witnesses, James Cunnan, James Bafour, Henrie Peirsone, Andro Spear.

1, William M'Craiche and Bessie Anderson had Jeane ; witnesses, William Hutton, Robert Hutton, Laurence Walls.

1, Andro Hutton and Issobell Walwood had Helen ; witnesses, James Hutton, David Hutton, Henrie Mitchell.

3, Johne Gray and Jonet Lindsay had Jonet ; witnesses, Johne Barker, Patrik Broun, James Lindsay.

5, William Rowan and Margaret Allane had Jonet ; witnesses, Henrie Davidsone, Peter Buist, Thomas Baverage.

8, David Haddane and Marion Bryce had Agnes ; witnesses, James Cunnan, George Turnbull, Patrik Rowan.

10, Robert Pitillo and Jonet Spinide had George ; witnesses, George Stirk, Andro Donaldsone, Johne Roy.

10, Rodger Cræm, ane inglish soldier, and Bessie Short (in fornication) had James ; witnesses, Johne Potter, presenter of the childe, and James Huttone.

12, Thomas Drysdaill and Katherine Seton had Bessie ; witnesses, William Walker, late provost, James Anderson, elder.

15, James Arkie and Bathia Dempstertoun had George ; witnesses, James Anderson, Johne Goold, George Wardlaw.

15, Patrik Allane and Margaret Alisone had Katherine ; witnesses, Robert Stevinson, Johne Stevinson, David Turnbull.

22, James Fisher and Christane Russell had Margaret ; witnesses, Andro Wilson, Johne Lethem, Robert Lethem.

22, Thomas Stevinsone and Alison Dowglas had David ; witnesses, David Jerman, Henrie Dowglas, David Currie.

22, Johne Goold and Elspet Cunynghame had Johne ; witnesses, William Mudie, Robert Stevinson, Johne Haliburton.

24, William Inche and Jonet Maxwell had Jonet ; witnesses, William Inche, elder, James Marshell and Eduard Sharp.

26, James Murgane and Jonet Inglis had Johne ; witnesses, Johne Currie, Andro Wilson, William Bowman.

29, William Thomeson and Margaret Lauthian had Johne; witnesses, Johne Græm, Johne Lauthian, William Kirk.

29, Johne Dalgleish and Margaret Sandielands had Elizabeth ; witnesses, Johne Thomson, William Smert, Johne Hamiltoun.

31, Johne Harla and Jonet Rainy had Margaret ; witnesses, Johne Mackie, Harie Elder, Johne Stevinson.

M. 10, Cornelius Robie to Margaret Walker.

26, William Clerk to Margaret Primros.

26, Johne Ritchie to Margaret Conquergo[od].

17, Andro Lindsay to Christan Cowston. [This should have been insert before the 26] (*this note is in edge*).

JUNE.

B. 2, Johne Andersone and Margaret Andersone had Margaret ; witnesses, William Andersone, George Turnbull, Eduard Dowglas, David Jerman.

2, Daniel Bryce and Helen Clerk had Christan ; witnesses, James Anderson, William Lason, James Hadstoun.

5, David Bad and Jonet Anderson had David ; witnesses, George Walls, Johne Anderson, Robert Shortus.

7, James Peirson and Margaret Peacok had Johne ; witnesses, William Cose, Henrie Wilson, David Elder.

9, Johne Turnbull and Katherine Mitchell had Andro ; witnesses, Mr. George Walker, Adam Turnbull, Robert Hutton.

12, Alexander Gibson and Christan Robertson had Alexander ; witnesses, James Legat, James Buist, Patrick Walker.

12, Andro Chrystie and Mariorie Stevinson had Christan ; witnesses, Adam Currie, Andro Currie, Thomas Stevinson.

14, James Lamb and Margaret Smert had Johne : witnesses, David Jermane, Andro Rowe, Robert Stirk.

19, Patrik Rowan and Jeane Stanehous had Robert ; witnesses, Robert Mudie, George Turnbull, Robert Stanehous.

19, Patrick Andersone and Bessie Mudie had Robert witnesses, James Mudie, William Anderson, Robert Stirk.

19, William Mercer and Jonet Donald had Grissell ; witnesses, James Mudie, Thomas Elder, Adam Anderson.

19, Thomas Law and Margaret Russell had Margaret ; witnesses, Johne Law, David Turnbull, Thomas Stevinson.

23, James Browne and Margaret George had Andro ; witnesses, Andro Smyth, Robert Stanehous, younger, Andro Russell.

23, Duncan M'Allum and Helen Turnbull had Jonet ; witnesses, Adam Brand, David Peacok, Adam Turnbull.

26, James Mackgill and Katherin Broun had William witnesses, Mr. William Oliphant, minister, James Mudie and George Stirk.

26, James Weyld and Issobell Creiche had Issobell ; witnesses, Johne Weyld, Thomas Sands, Johne Dewar.

M. 2, Robert M'Craigh to Issobell Anderson.

2, Johne Don to Margaret Anderson.

7, William Blaikie to Margaret Hendene in the kirk of Innerkething.

9, James Dewar to Jonet Hunter in the kirk of Kirkaldie.

30, James Mayne to Margaret Dewar.

30, Henrie Lowson to Grissell Anderson.

JULY.

B. 3, Andro Turnbull and Sara Dick had Grissell ; witnesses, Henrie Mitchell, David Lindsay of Cavill and Robert Smeton.

3, William Primros and Jonet Johnestone had William ; witnesses, David Lindsay of Cavill, William and James Lasons.

3, Duncan Clerk and Margaret Horne had Jonet ; witnesses, Thomas Horne, Robert Bonar, Johne Wardlaw.

11, James Anderson and Christane Young had Harie ; witnesses, Wilham Marshell, James Anderson.

14, Johne Chrystie and Barbara Rae had William ; witnesses, William Rae, Thomas Stevinson, George Chapman.

16, David Kairns and Jonet Finlason had Charles ; witnesses, Charles Wardlaw, William and James Legats, David Turnbull.

16, Johne Aikin and Elspet Spens had Johne ; witnesses, William Mudie, Robert Bonar, William Potter.

24, Robert Huton and Jonet Sanders had Margaret ; witnesses, Peter Walker, provest, James Mudie and Johne Duncanson.

24, Johne Honyman and Bessie Mudie (in fornication) had Margaret ; witnesses, William and Allan Mudies and George Walls.

31, Henrie Coventrie and Issobell Donald had Johne ; witnesses, Johne Lason, Johne Donald, Johne Thomson.

31, James Marshell and Helen Faulds had Jonet ; witnesses, David Lindsay, William Lason, William Hutton.

M. 5, Robert Stanehous to Issobell Broun.

5, Johne M'Kie to Helen Pope in the kirk of Torrie.

21, James Hunter to Katherine Sanders in the kirk of Torrie.

21, William Flokart to Marion Mitchell in the kirk of Baith.

21, James Gibbon to Mariorie Currie.

21, Johne Dyks to Christan Reddy.

AUGUST.

B. 7, Umqle George Car and Jonet Duncane had Jonet ; witnesses, Robert Russell, David Russell, William Huton and Adam Car, presenter of the childe.

11, Johne Marshell and Helen Greg had Johne ; witnesses, James and Johne Dewar, James Baverage, Harie Rowan.

11, Gilbert Young, ane inglish soldier, and Margaret Simrell (in fornication) had Johne ; witnesses, George Mudie, William Henderson, Johne Simrell, and Andro Mudie, presenter of the childe.

14, Arthure Robertson and Margaret Harvie had Elizabeth ; witnesses, Peter Walker, Johne Turnbull and Robert Hutton and Robert Walwood.

18, Jerome Cowie and Margaret Smert had James ; witnesses, William Walker, William Smert, James Anderson, younger.

21, David Peacok and Margaret M'Craich had Margaret ; witnesses, Peter Hay of Naughtoun, William Turnbull, Adam Brand.

21, Johne Græm and Margaret Bannatyn had Christan ; witnesses, George Wardlaw, William Kirk, Robert Bannatyn.

21, James Watson and Bessie Cook had Jonet ; witnesses, Robert Walwood, Harie Moreis, George Wardlaw.

21, James Marshell and Bessie Strang had Grissell ; witnesses, James Mudie, William Gotterston, William Inch.

25, Peter Hay of Naughtoun and his Ladie, Dame Margaret Hendirson, had Margaret ; witnesses, Johne Hendirson of ffordell, Thomas Bruce of Blairhall, Charles Menteith of Randifoord, and Robert Dempster of Pitliver.

25, David Huton and Issobell Lindsay had James ; witnesses, James Lindsay, James Huton, Andro Huton.

28, George Chalmers and Margaret Walker had Alexander ; witnesses, William and Mr. Thomas Walkers and Peter Walker.

28, Abram Giro and Grissell Anderson had Anna ; witnesses, William Walker, Mr. Hew Montgomerie, and James Anderson, younger.

30, James Buchannan and Jonet Fotheringhame had Issobell ; witnesses, Robert Cunynghame, Henrie Coventrie, Johne Lason.

M. 5, William Thomson to Margaret Hendirson in the kirk of Dalgat[y].
    5, Alexander Hammell to Annas Legat.
    11, James Falkland to Jonet Anderson in Carnok.
    11, Robert Stevinsone to Margaret Phillan.
    16, William Anderson to Bessie Hendirson in Muckart.
    18, Thomas Stevinson to Bessie Sands in Carnok.
    18, Mr. Hew Montgomerie to Anna Colden in Kinross.
    25, Johne Allane to Jonet Finla.

SEPTEMBER.

B. 4, Laurence Stevinson and Eupham Dick had Katherine ; witnesses, Johne
    Stevinson, Laurence Stevinson, Johne Peirson.
    6, William Wilson and Katherine Lowson had William ; witnesses,
    William Wilson, elder, William Boyd, Laurence Watson.
    11, Thomas Howie and Jonet Cunynghame had Margaret ; witnesses,
    James Mudie, Andro Cunyngham, Thomas Elder.
    18, Andro Potter and Jonet Paton had Jonet ; witnesses, Johne Potters,
    elder and younger, Patrik Sanders.
    18, Patrik Sanders and Anna Elder had Robert ; witnesses, Johne Duncan-
    son, Robert Huton, Harie Elder.
    25, David Anderson had ane womanchilde and Issobell Anderson had
    Margaret ; witnesses, Robert Scotland, Henrie Mitchell and David
    Burley, presenter of the childe.
    25, Robert Currie and Margaret Inche had Agnes ; witnesses, William
    Inche, Henrie Meldrum, James Fyg.
    27, Johne Donaldson and Grissell Mather had Johne ; witnesses, Johne
    Sanders, Johne Chrystie and Ninian Mather.
    29, William Anderson and Katherine Wardlaw had George ; witnesses,
    George Wardlaw, James Anderson, elder and young.
M. 1, Joseph Harwood to Nanse Hunnan.
    6, Thomas Cochran to Jonet Stevinson.
    8, Alexander Tailyeour to Katherin Malco[m].
    22, Harie Blak to Nanse Peirson.

OCTOBER.

B. 2, Thomas Colen and Jonet Scotland had Margaret ; witnesses, William
    Robertson, David Scotland, Robert Russell.
    2, Andro Wilson and Bessie Peirson had Johne ; witnesses, Johne Dewar,
    Johne Donaldson, Johne Fairlie.
    2, James Boyd and Bessie Baverage had James ; witnesses, Thomas
    Baverage, William Smert, Laurence Watson.
    9, Johne Broun and Margaret Kay had Andro ; witnesses, Andro Kay,
    David Broun, Andro Broun.
    9, James Lindsay and Helene Currie had Andro ; witnesses, Andro
    Wilson, Henrie Broun, Johne Lethem.
    9, William Strachan and Margaret Marshell had Robert ; witnesses,
    Robert Strachan, James Marshell, David Marshell.
    9, Henrie Davidson and Jonet Allan had Margaret ; witnesses, Sir Henrie
    Wardlaw of Pitreavie, Robert Stevinson and Andro Mayne.
    9, William Currie and Margaret Mayne had James ; witnesses, James
    Mayne, David Currie, Henrie Dowglas.
    13, Andro Mitchell and Margaret Mitchell had Christan ; witnesses,
    Alexander Bruce of Broomehall, David Mitchell and Mr. George
    Walker.
    16, Patrick Drumond and Annas Hardie had Helene ; witnesses, James
    Cunnan, George Turnbull, James Buist.
    16, Andro Rowe and Marie Lamb had Grissell ; witnesses, James Mudie,
    Mr. George Walker, Robert Stirk.
    23, Johne Hendirson and Margaret Watson had Grissell ; witnesses,
    Laurence Watson, Thomas Horne, James Hendirson.

23, George Wilson and Helen M'Baith had Marie; witnesses, George Chapman, Johne Chrystie, William Turnbull.

27, Andro Mawer and Jeane Wannan had Andro; witnesses, Andro Murdo, Robert Russell, Andro Cowe.

30, James Moyes and Katherine Broun had Bessie; witnesses, Robert Mudie, Johne Moyes, David Chrystie.

30, Alexander Dunsyre and Katherine Brugh had Katherine; witnesses, William Smert, David Thomson, George Swintone.

30, Thomas Anderson and Nanse Yowan had William; witnesses, William Anderson, Robert Yowane and Johne Hunnan.

M. 11, William Gray to Jonet Wright in the kirk of Innerkething.

11, Johne Honyman to Bessie Mudie.

21, William Donaldson to Issobell Malcom.

27, Johne Chrystie to Christian Hendirson in the kirk off Abercorne.

27, Johne M'Crew to Katherin M'Queen.

NOVEMBER.

B. 3, Johne Moreis and Margaret Burnet had Elspet; witnesses, David Lindsay, William Moreis, Andro Turnbull.

3, Thomas Sands and Katherine Cumyne (in fornication) had Beatrix; witnesses, Johne Dewar, presenter of the childe and cationer for the said Thomas his satisfaction of the discipline of the kirk, Johne Anderson and Eduard Dowglas, younger.

6, James Wilson and Jonet Dick had Elizabeth; witnesses, Johne Haliburton, James Legat, William Mercer.

6, Johne Cusine and Issobell Huton had Bessie; witnesses, William Hutton, Robert Hutton, James Cusine.

6, Johne Hunnan and Katherin Yowan had Jonet; witnesses, Robert Yowan, Andro Hannan, William Mudie.

8, Johne Stanehous and Jonet Cunynghame had Nanse; witnesses, James Wardlaw, Thomas Stanehous, Robert Stevinson.

8, Johne Weir and Eupham Kingorne had George; witnesses, Peter Hay of Naughton and George Hay, his sone, Robert Walwood and Johne Thomson.

13, William Baverage and Issobell Brown had Issobell; witnesses, William Smert, Thomas Baverage, George Wall.

13, Robert Chisley and Bessie Greg had Robert; witnesses, Robert Mudie, Allan Mudie, Andro Hall.

13, Patrik Legat and Issobell Stevinson had Bessie; witnesses, James Legat, Adam Stevinson, William Mudie.

13, Manse Malcom and Jonet M'Lenochen had James; witnesses, Thomas Howie, James Daes, David Bad.

20, Andro Cunynghame and Margaret Turnbull had Bessie; witnesses, Sir Henrie Wardlaw of Pitreavie, George Turnbull, Andro Mayne.

20, Robert Shortus and Margaret Bad had Robert; witnesses, Robert Walwood, David Bad, Thomas Elder.

20, Robert Tailyeour and Issobell Hunter had Margaret; witnesses, Henrie Davidson, Andro Mayne, Johne Bad.

22, Thomas Mitchell and Margaret Mudie had Robert; witnesses, James Legat, Mr. Robert Anderson, Andro Currie.

22, James Broun and Jonet Whitefoord had Jonet; witnesses, David Lindsay of Cavill, Henrie Mitchell, Robert Scotland.

22, Johne Wilson and Margaret Watson had Jonet; witnesses, Andro Wilson, Johne Currie, Henrie Broun.

27, David Greive and Katherine Cunnan had James; witnesses, James Cunnan, James Bafour, Robert Barclay.

27, David Cunynghame and Elspet Fitt had Bessie; witnesses, Johne Kirkland, Thomas Howie, Patrik Hall.

29, David Anstie and Margaret Anderson had Sara: witnesses, David Mitchell, James Mitchell, Johne Cumyn.

M. 1, William Hendirson to Mariorie Broun in the kirk of Torrie.

3, Johne Anderon to Margaret Mayne.

15, James Paterson to Margaret Bowe.

24, Andro Moreis to Elspet Horne.

DECEMBER.

B. 4, Adam Anderson and Katherine Gibbon had Elizabeth; witnesses, Robert Stevinson, James Anderson, James Gibbon.

8, William Garvie and Alison Hall had Robert; witnesses, Robert Jak, Andro Garlik, Adam Turnbull.

11, William Anderson and Issobell Anderson had Anna; witnesses, James Anderson, Johne Stirk, William Trotter.

11, David Walker and Katherine Fergison had Issobell; witnesses, Johne Walker, William Legat, George Stirk.

11, Andro Kirk and Issobell Coventrie had Andro; witnesses, William Smert, William Baverage, Johne Clowe.

11, Alexander Innes and Margaret Thomson had Christan; witnesses, Thomas Baverage, William Broun, Gawin Edison.

13, Johne Hill and Marion Spens had Johne; witnesses, Johne Livingstone, James Watson, Robert Shortus.

15, James Futhie and Helen Auchinlek had James; witnesses, James Broun, Alexander Anderson, and James Richardson, presenter of the childe.

18, James Mudie and Grissell Espline had James; witnesses, Sir James Halket of Pitfirrane, James Clerk off Pittincrieff and James Mudie, eldest.

18, William Walker, late provest, and Margaret Turnbull had Johne; witnesses, Johne Turnbull, Mr. Thomas Walker, Mr. George Walker.

18, Patrik Johnstone and Jeane Dick had Harie; witnesses, Harie Rowan, Robert Anderson, Walter Sim.

25, George Watson and Margaret Dowe had George; witnesses, George Wardlaw, James Watson, Robert Shortus.

25, Patrik M'Innes and Jonet Ker had George; witnesses, Robert Angus, George Angus, James Angus.

25, Johne Sandielands and Jeane Drysdaill had Elspet; witnesses, Harie Richardson, Duncan Clerk, William Gilkrist.

25, James Eason and Jeane Peacok had Margaret; witnesses, Peter Walker, Robert Walwood, George Chalmers.

27, Eduard Crowder, ane inglish soldier, and Marion Mitchell had William; witnesses, Alexander Innes, presenter of the childe, and William Anderson and James Rae.

29, George Ewin and Elspet Potter had Johne; witnesses, David Duncanson, James Imrie, Andro Robertson.

M. 1, James Durham to Geills Livingston.

1, James Robertson to Marion Greive.

1, Archibald Ayton to Marie Hamilton.

8, Harie Broun to Jonet Wyber.

8, David Drysdaill to Elspet Wilson.

13, Johne Alshunder to Margaret Spens.

15, Johne Conquer to Issobell Peacok.

22, Thomas Cant to Alison Wilson.

JANUARY [1660].

B. 1, Archibald Robertson and Marion Hutson had Margaret; witnesses, William Smert, David Steward, Laurence Watson.

3, Robert Donald and Helene Baverage had Margaret; witnesses, James Baverage, Andro and James Donalds.

5, Johne Creiche and Issobell Dowglas had Andro; witnesses, Henrie Dowglas, James Broun, Eduard Dowglas.

8, James Bafour and Marion Bruce had Issobell; witnesses, William
  Walker, David Jerman, Robert Walwood.

8, James Murray and Jeane George had James; witnesses, James Clerk
  of Pittincreiff, David Lindsay of Cavill, James Legat.

8, William Anderson and Margaret Anderson had Marion; witnesses, Mr.
  Robert Anderson, Arthure Robertson, Johne Weire.

8, Patrik Hall and Jean Purves had David; witnesses, David Purves,
  William Broun, Andro Hall.

8, Johne Anderson and Margaret M'Mirrie had Nanse; witnesses, Johne
  Hamilton, James Anderson, Patrik Law.

10, Richard Hendene and Issobell Horne had Margaret; witnesses, Johne
  Greives, elder and younger, and Laurence Walls.

15, George Walls and Margaret Smert had Nanse; witnesses, William
  Smert, William Dowglas, Archibald Honyman.

15, Thomas Williamson and Bessie Mayne had Margaret; witnesses,
  George Stink, John Laurie, Johne Smyth.

15, James Peacok and Christan Alison had Johne; witnesses, Johne Park,
  Eduard Russell, George Wardlaw.

15, Harie Fairfax, ane inglish soldier, and Jonet Hoburn (in fornication)
  had Charles; witnesses, George Chalmers, Patrik Law, and James
  Richardson, presenter of the childe.

26, Thomas Donald and Nicolas Bairdner had Andro; witnesses, Andro
  and James Donalds and Robert Cunynghame.

26, Johne Hunter and Jonet Murgane had James; witnesses, William
  Smert, Robert Russell, David Scotland.

29, Johne Dowgall and Margaret Eilson had Johne; witnesses, Johne
  Eilson, Johne Dalgleish, Johne Kirkland.

29, Richard Harrower and Annas Ramsay had Alexander; witnesses,
  Robert Haliburton, Johne Kingorne, Johne Gray.

29, Andrew Wardlaw and Issobell Murray had William; witnesses, James
  Anderson, William Dowglas, William Harla.

31, Andro Wilson and Issobell Lethem had Jonet; witnesses, Robert
  Cunynghame, William Lethem, Andro Wilson.

31, Alexander Arnot and Jonet Gray had William; witnesses, William
  Robertson, Thomas Colen, William Scotland.

M. 5, Andro Broun to Margaret Stevinson.
  12, Ninian Mather to Katherine Thomson.
  31, Johne Fyg to Margaret Paterson.

FEBRUARY.

B. 2, William Robertson and Elizabeth Huttone had Issobell; witnesses,
  David Dewar of Lassodie, David Robertson, David Scotland.

2, George Hall and Margaret Dowglas had Robert; witnesses, Eduard
  Dowglas, David Dowglas, Henrie Wilson.

5, Johne Hutson and Jeane Edison had Bessie; witnesses, Harie Rowan,
  Johne Wright, Johne Marshell.

10, Sir James Halket of Pitfirran and his Ladie, Dame Anna Murray, had
  Robert; witnesses, Robert, Lord Colvill, Sir Harie Wardlaw of
  Pitreavie, Sir George Preston of Valleyfield.

12, James Birnet and Katherine Angus had George; witnesses, David
  Scotland, William Robertson, Robert Russell.

12, Johne Weyld and Nanse Cunynghame had Nanse; witnesses, Henrie
  Meldrum, Johne Heart, Jerome Cowie.

12, Patrik Græm and Rachel Blaik had Jonet; witnesses, Johne Blaik,
  William Blaik, James Baverage.

21, Johne Allan and Jonet Ramsay had Barbara; witnesses, Andro Wilson,
  Johne Wilson, Robert Hog.

26, William Anderson and Elspet Anderson had Margaret; witnesses,
  Robert Stevinson, Laurence Stevinson, Henrie Davidson.

27, Thomas Rea and Helen Lason had Margaret ; witnesses, David Currie, Henrie Dowglas, Johne Moreis.

28, William Clerk and Margaret Primros had William ; witnesses, William Lason, Robert Scotland, David Lindsay.

28, David Maistertoun and Margaret Primros had Margaret ; witnesses, Andro Wilson, Richard Maistertoun, David Allaster.

M. 2, David Græm to Issobell Keir.

9, James Cunnan to Elspet Kirk.

10, James Skinner to Margaret Bull.

16, Thomas Cullen to Margaret Mayne.

16, Johne Moreis to Nanse Lason.

MARCH.

B. 4, Peter Walker and Eupham Ged had Harie ; witnesses, Sir Harie Wardlaw of Pitreavie, Johne Hendirson of Fordell, James Clerk of Pittincreiff.

4, Patrik Walker and Elspet Blaiket had Johne ; witnesses, Johne Hendirson of Fordell, Peter Walker, James Mudie.

4, Andro Cunynghame and Mariorie Burn had Margaret ; witnesses, Johne Cunynghame, Thomas Howie, Adam Currie.

4, James Steill and Jonet Stevinson had James ; witnesses, William Rowan, Robert Greive, Andro Cunynghame.

6, William Hadston and Annabel Blaiket had Margaret ; witnesses, David Lindsay of Cavill, James Broun, William Primros.

11, Johne Stevinson and Margaret Dick had James ; witnesses, Robert Stevinson, James Anderson, William Mudie.

11, Robert Angus and Marion Buchannan had Johne ; witnesses, Johne Dewar, William Angus, James Angus.

18, James Anderson and Barbara Russell had Robert ; witnesses, Robert Walwood, James Anderson. Eduard Russell.

18, James Kinloch and Bessie Stevinson had Jonet ; witnesses, Johne Mudie, Patrik Drumond, George Turnbull.

18, Thomas Heart and Katherine Marshell had Helen ; witnesses, Robert Philp, Johne Currie, Johne Lethem.

18, Johne Clerk and Margaret Bains had Bessie ; witnesses, Robert Tailyeour, William Mudie, Johne Couper.

18, David Young and Margaret Drysdaill had James ; witnesses, Johne Chrystie, Johne Roy and Robert Broun.

25, Alexander Duff and Jonet Philp had James ; witnesses, James Mudie, Patrik Anderson, David Elder.

25, James Buist and Margaret Hardie had Bathia ; witnesses, Johne Hendirson of Fordell, James Mudie, Peter Buist.

M. 6, Johne Reid to Margaret Forbes.

APRIL.

B. 1, James Fyff and Margaret Marshell had George ; witnesses, George Chalmers, Robert Angus, William Huton.

1, Robert Pet and Bessie Philp had Jonet ; witnesses, Henrie Davidson, Eduard Russell, Robert Anderson.

8, David Anderson and Margaret Blak had Helene ; witnesses, Walter Anderson, George Gatt, William M'Brek.

8, Walter Sim and Jonet Anderson had Marion ; witnesses, Thomas Gairner, James Bafour, Robert Anderson.

8, David Duncanson and Margaret Paton had Johne ; witnesses, Johne Hunnan, Johne and James Duncansons.

8, Abram Patrik and Marion Boyd had Robert ; witnesses, Robert Patrik, Robert Huton, Laurence Watson.

8, James Stevinsone and Margaret Anderson had Margaret ; witnesses, William Anderson, James Anderson, James Huton.

12, Johne Henrieson, Laird of ñordell, and his ladie, Margaret Hamiltoñe
    had Johne ; witnesses, Thomas Bruce of Blairhall, Johne Scot of
    Spensirfeild, Robert Dempster of Pitliver, Peter Hay of Naughton.
15, Johne Drumond and Bessie Wardlaw had Katherine ; witnesses,
    Robert Stevinson, Johne Stevinson, Robert Colyear, George Walls.
15, Andro Scotland and Margaret Moreis had Margaret ; witnesses,
    William Walker, Johne Turnbull, William Smert.
24, Thomas Dowglas and Bessie Murie had David ; witnesses, Eduard
    Dowglas, David Dowglas, Adam Murie.
26, Alexander Reddie and Rachel Chrystie had David ; witnesses, David
    Flokart, Johne Chrystie, elder and younger, and Alexander Anderson,
    presenter of the childe.
29, Alexander Beane and Christane Simson had Jonet ; witnesses, Johne
    Hamiliton, Alexander Anderson, James Hutton.

M. 5, James Dowglas to Jonet Mudie.
   26, Johne Cunynghame to Elspet Cant.
   26, Johne Blelloks to Elspet Robertson.
   26, William Cunyng[hame] to Margaret Gotterstoun.

MAY.

B. 1, Robert Burn and Jonet Sharp had Anna ; witnesses, Henrie Dowglas,
    Andro Mitchell, David Currie.
   6, Andro Flokhart and Issobell Pet had Bessie ; witnesses, Adam Turn-
    bull, David Flokart, William Flokart.
   6, Robert Lason and Jonet Drysdaill had Margaret ; witnesses, William
    Lason, James Lason and William Anderson.
   6, Johne Dyks and Christan Reddie had Marion ; witnesses, Robert
    Walwood, Harie Moreis, Johne Moyes.
  10, Thomas Hoburne and Bessie Dick had Christan ; witnesses, Eduard
    Overwhite, Robert Lethem, William Wilson.
    James Bountorne hade ane manchild borne to him of his wyf Nanse
    Lawrie upon the 6 day betwixt 6 and 7 hours at nyt. Baptized and
    called James upon the 13 day ; witnesses, Johne Lawrie, Robert
    Huton, Harie Elder.
  13, Adam Turnbull and Jonet Mitchell had Margaret ; witnesses, Peter
    Hay of Naughton, William Walker, Andro Mitchell.
  13, Thomas Thomeson and Margaret Anderson had Jonet ; witnesses,
    William and Johne Andersons, David Bad.
  20, David Chrystie and Jonet Marshell had Nanse ; witnesses, Robert
    Mudie, David Scotland, James Moyes.
  20, Johne Wardlaw and Margaret Moreis had Patrik ; witnesses, Patrik
    Hunter, Patrik Inglis, Harie Moreis.
  20, George Turnbull and Margaret Kellok had Nanse ; witnesses, James
    Cunnan, Robert Kellok, Robert Stanehous.
  20, Eduard Rutherfoord and Margaret Græm had Charles ; witnesses
    Charles Grehm, James Anderson, George Currie.
  20, David M'Baith and Bessie Robertson had James ; witnesses, Andro
    Cunyhame in Stane, Andro Cunynghame in Prymros, and George
    Wilson in Gatesyd.
  24, David Haigie and Margaret Rainy had David ; witnesses, Johne
    Mackie, Henrie Mitchell, William Hutton.
  27, William Lason and Elspet Chrystie had William ; witnesses, Andro
    Mayne, William Lethem, Thomas Howie.
  27, Laurence Walls and Margaret Grieve had twins, Johne and Christan ;
    witnesses, Johne Greive, elder and younger, Johne Haswell, William
    Hutton.

M. 8, George Turnbull to Jonet Cowie.
   31, Adam Currie to Geills Anderson.
   31, James Dowglas to Marie Faulds.
   31, John Myllar to Eupham M'Nere.

JUNE.

B. 3, Mr. Thomas Walker and Nanss Gibbon had Nanss; witnesses, William Walker, Mr. George Walker, Adam Anderson.

3, Eduard Dowglas and Jonet Anderson had Margaret; witnesses, Eduard Dowglas, Henrie Dowglas, David Jerman.

3, James Moyes and Elspet Blaiky had Rachel; witnesses, William Hendirson, David Dewar, Johne Cunynghame.

5, James Lyell and Margaret Cowie had George; witnesses, David Anderson, William M'Brek, George Gatt.

10, Andro Mudie and Issobell Mudie had Helen; witnesses, Robert Hendirson, George Mudie, Andro Mayne.

10, William Blaiky and Margaret Henden had Henrie; witnesses, Sir Henrie Wardlaw of Pitreavie, Henrie Davidson, Johne Chrystie.

17, William Huton and Jeane Chrystie had Margaret; witnesses, Robert Huton, Robert Russell, David Scotland.

24, Johne Mackie and Helene Pope had Margaret; witnesses, Johne Mackie, elder, Johne Wilson, Johne Baverage.

M. 14, Andro Wilson to Grissell Dewar in the kirk of Baith.

14, Harie Anderson to Elspet Stanehous.

28, James Litlejohne to Margaret White.

28, William Fergison to Margaret Mitchell.

28, James Huton to Elizabeth Eadie in the kirk of Carno[k].

JULY.

B 1, David Lindsay and Katherine Malloche had Anna; witnesses, Robert Dempster of Pitliver, Hew Mackgill, James Mudie, David Mitchell.

1, Henrie Mitchell and Grissell Lindsay had Alison; witnesses, Mr. George Walker, David Currie, Henrie Dowglas.

1, William Legat and Helen Kent had James; witnesses, James Legat, James M'Gill, James Simson.

1, James Huton and Christan Livingston had James; witnesses, Peter Walker, William Smert, James Huton, elder.

1, Johne Broun and Margaret Wilson had Robert; witnesses, James Mudie, James Wilson, James Anderson.

3, Robert Dewar and Margaret Andro had Issobell; witnesses, David Murray, Andro Johnston, Johne Moore.

8, William Gray and Jonet Wright had Elspet; witnesses, Andro Donaldson, Andro Cunynghame, David Elder.

12, James Trotter and Elspet Young had Elspet; witnesses, William Nicoll, James Anderson, Laurence Trotter.

15, Thomas Stevinson and Bessie Sands had Margaret; witnesses, Thomas Stevinson, James Mudie, Andro Chrystie.

15, William Turnbull and Jeane Dowglas had Alison; witnesses, Mr. David Douglas, David Currie, Johne Turnbull.

15, David Marshell and Annas Malcom had Johne; witnesses, Johne Thomson, Johne Dalgleish, Johne Cunynghame.

24, Johne Eadison and Margaret Falkland had James; witnesses, James Falkland, William Lason, Johne Lason.

26, Robert Heart and Jonet Henden had Jonet; witnesses, William Blaiky, Robert Barclay, William Cunnan.

26, Johne Hunter and Margaret Burn had David; witnesses, Andro Mayne, Robert Tailyeour, Patrik Hall.

26, Johne Clerk and Margaret Aikin had Marie; witnesses, Archibald Aiton, Johne Hamilton, Alexander Anderson.

27, Johne Anderson and Margaret Mayne had Jonet; witnesses, James Anderson, Johne Mayne, William Anderson.

M. 6, Jerome Cowie to Helen Smert.

10, Johne Steward to Bessie Lugton.

17, David Cunynghame to Jonet Kirk.

17, William Smert to Christan Coventrie.
19, Charles Græm to Issobell Harla.
26, Johne Broun to Jonet Gray in Carnok.

AUGUST.

B. 5, Robert Sharp and Elizabeth Porteous had Harie; witnesses, Sir Harie
Wardlaw of Pitreavie, James Mudie, Harie Elder.

7, Johne Glasse and Issobell Tosheoche had Andro; witnesses, Henrie
Davidson, Eduard Russell, Robert Anderson.

7, Andro Workman and Elspet Ewin had Alexander; witnesses, Johne
Haliburton of Garvok, Robert and Mr. Alexander Haliburtons, his
sones, and Mr. George Walker.

12, Thomas Drysdaill and Katherine Seton had Katherine; witnesses,
William Walker, late provest, Johne Turnbull, Deane of Gild, James
Anderson, elder, litster.

12, Joseph Harwood and Nans Hunnan had Jonet; witnesses, Johne
Hunane, presenter of the childe, Johne Hamilton, Alexander
Bone.

14, Robert Stanehous and Bessie Huton had Jonet; witnesses, Robert
Stanehous in Maistertoun, Johne Cusine, James Brown, Robert Huton.

19, Andro Spear and Elspet Matheson had Andro; witnesses, James
Cunnan, Robert Wardlaw, Johne Mudie.

19, Johne Dowgall and Margaret Young had William; witnesses, William
Mudie, William Meldrum, Johne Stirk.

19, Johne Simrell and Bessie Stevinson had James; witnesses, James
Mudie, Andro Mudie, Thomas Stevinson, James Simrell.

19, Johne Honyman and Bessie Mudie had Nanss; witnesses, George
Walls, William Mudie, Allan Mudie.

23, William Reid and Grissell Kirk had Issobell; witnesses, James Mudie,
maltman, presenter of the childe, James Wilson, Thomas Tod, Peter
Buist.

26, William Donaldson and Issobell Malcom had William; witnesses,
William Walker, William Mercer, William Gotterston.

26, Alexander Hammell and Annas Legat had Margaret; witnesses,
William Legat, James Legat, James Makgill.

M. 7, Thomas Hutson to Elspet Austie.
23, Johne Peirson to Elspet Duff.
28, Robert Fisher to Margaret Adam.
30, David Fairgie to Jonet Coventry.

SEPTEMBER.

B. 2, Samuel Denholme and Bessie Alison had Robert; witnesses, Peter
Walker, William Walker, David Jerman.

2, James Alexander and Bessie Spens had Issobell; witnesses, Patrik
Legat, James Hendirson, Johne Watson.

2, James Mayne and Margaret Dewar had Andro; witnesses, Andro
Mayne, David Flokart, Johne Mayne.

2, Johne Wanderston and Issobell Leslie had Johne; witnesses, Johne
Mackie, William Huton, Henrie Mitchell.

9, Henrie Dowglas and Katherine Brand had Margaret; witnesses, David
Mitchell, Andro Mitchell, David Currie.

9, James Turnbull and Jonet Drysdaill had David; witnesses, David
Drysdaill, David Peacok, Duncan M'Allum.

16, James Robertson and Marion Grieve had Henrie; witnesses, David
Lindsay, Henrie Mitchell, James Broun.

16, William Maitlane and Mariorie Myllar had Thomas; witnesses, Thomas
Elder, Eduard Overwhite, Johne Burley.

16, Johne Ritchie and Margaret Conquergood had Thomas; witnesses,
Thomas Conquergood, Andro Mayne, Adam Murie.

23, Robert Walwood and Jonet Ged had Margaret; witnesses, Sir Henrie Wardlaw of Pitreavie, George Wardlaw, Peter Walker, William Walker, Robert and William Walwoods.

23, Archibald Aiton and Marie Hamilton had Katherin; witnesses, James Anderson, elder and younger, Harie Elder.

23, William Purdie and Margaret Dowe had William; witnesses, William Smert, Johne Colyear, Johne Belfrage.

23, Robert Ritchie and Margaret Davidson had Thomas; witnesses, Thomas Horne, Laurence Stevinson, Johne Eilson.

24, William Potter and Jeane Elder had William; witnesses, David Murray, Robert Colyear, William Boyd.

30, James Falkland and Jonet Anderson had Issobell; witnesses, George Turnbull, Johne Lason, William Lason.

30, James Fyg and Nans Dalgleish had William; witnesses, George Turnbull, William Smert, William Dalgleish.

30, Johne Aikin and Elspet Spens had William; witnesses, William Mudie, David Turnbull, Johne Potter.

M. 11, Johne Currie to Helen Livingston in Carnok.

27, Andro Hannan to Grissell Boyd.

OCTOBER.

B. 7, James Broun and Jonet Meldrum had Jonet; witnesses, James Makgill, Henrie Meldrum, Andro Broun.

7, Johne Burn and Christan Heriot had Jonet; witnesses, Andro Burn, Patrik Hall, George Mudie.

11, Henrie Wilson and Margaret Lindsay had Nanss; witnesses, Eduard Dowglas, James Peirson, Johne Dewar.

14, Andro Broun and Margaret Stevinson had David; witnesses, David Broun, David Flokhart and Johne Broun.

14, James Hew and Jonet Anderson had James; witnesses, Adam Currie, Robert Anderson, William Fargie.

14, Robert Philp and Issobell Cunynghame had Christan; witnesses, Johne Cunynghame, Andro Wilson, Johne Lethem.

21, George Gatt and Helen Gray had Margaret; witnesses, William Young, David Murray, David Anderson.

21, James Brughe and Jonet Fyg had William; witnesses, William Walker, provest. James Fyg, William Mudie.

21, Johne M'Grew and Katherine M'Queen had George; witnesses, Peter Walker, George Chalmers, William Keir.

28, Johne Potter and Elspet Mullion had Elspet; witnesses, Johne Haliburton of Garvok, Robert and Mr. Alexander Haliburtons, James Legat.

28, James Smyllum and Grissell Bryce had Robert; witnesses, William Nicoll, Robert Donald, James Anderson.

M. 4, Robert Dowglas to Jonet Eizet.

12, Thomas Spens to Jonet Culros.

16, Johne Weir to Jonet Hamilton.

25, Johne Turnbull to Anna Linton in the kirk of Logie.

NOVEMBER.

B. 4, Johne Dewar and Alison Anderson had Jonet; witnesses, Eduard Dowglas, Andro Wilson, Henrie Wilson.

4, Thomas Stevinson and Alison Dowglas had Henrie; witnesses, Henrie Dowglas, David Currie, William Dowglas.

6, David Bell and Jonet Walker had Geilles; witnesses, Andro Mayne, Andro Mudie, Henrie Davidson.

6, Robert Dowglas and Elspet Peirson had Christan; witnesses, Robert Cant, James Dowglas, Andro Wilson.

8, Mr. George Walker and Jonet Mitchell had Katherine; witnesses, David Lindsay of Cavill, Johne Turnbull, Johne Mackie.

11, Laurence Anderson and Jonet M'Birny had Nanss; witnesses, Robert Cunynghame, James Anderson, William Inglis, Andro Donald.

11, Thomas Beane and Katherine Walker had Helen; witnesses. Alexander Beane, elder, Patrik Walker, Thomas Davidson.

18, William Gray and Elspet Anderson had Elspet; witnesses, James Anderson, presenter of the childe, Adam Anderson and David Anderson.

18, William Keir and Margaret Bad had Helen; witnesses, Johne Duncanson, Andro Hall, Alexander Beane, elder.

18, Robert Shortus and Katherine Hutson had William; witnesses, William Walker, William Smert, William Broun.

22, Johne Drummond and Katherine Reaburn had Helen; witnesses, William Walker, provest, David Jerman, Johne Turnbull.

25, Johne Hadston and Issobell Pringle had Issobell; witnesses, James Hadston, James Anderson, William Anderson.

M. 1, Robert Barclay to Jonet Richieson.
1, William Reid to Jeane Fotheringhame.
16, James Wilson to Jonet Hirdman.
20, Johne Pullous to Margaret Inglis.
20, Gilbert Young to Margaret Simrell.
22, James Hakston to Katherine Yewin.
29, Johne Smyth to Jonet Stirk.
29, David Robertson to Margaret Robertson.

DECEMBER.

B. 2, Andro Moreis and Elspet Horne had Harie; witnesses, William Walwood, Eduard Russell, James Anderson.

4, Laurence Thomson and Eupham Mather had Laurence; witnesses,

9, Alexander Anderson and Jonet Chrystie had Agnes; witnesses, William Anderson, Patrik Anderson, Johne Chrystie.

9, Harie Moreis and Elspet Tailyeour had Robert; witnesses, Robert Walwood, William Walker, William Mercer.

13, Adam Anderson and Katherine Gibbon had Agnes; witnesses, Mr. Thomas Walker, James Gibbon, James Anderson.

13, Johne Dewar and Margaret Brand had Margaret; witnesses, James Wardlaw, William Huton, James Donaldson.

13, Johne Arkie and Elspet Watson had Bessie; witnesses, Johne Harrower, James Arkie, George Lindsay.

16, Andro Garlik and Mariorie Williamson had Bessie; witnesses, Johne Broun, Thomas Williamson, Alexander Inglis.

16, Alexander Wilson and Elspet Russell had Issobell; witnesses, James Duncanson, Johne Wilson, James Wilson.

23, Patrik Hunter and Jonet Gray had Johne; witnesses, Johne Dewar, James Baverage, Thomas Gairner.

23, David Drysdaill and Elspet Wilson had Thomas; witnesses, Thomas Wilson, Eduard Rutherfoord, Andro Wilson.

27, Johne Willoks and Margaret Broun had Margaret; witnesses, Andro Donald, Robert Cunynghame, Adam Wilson.

30, David Burley and Jonet Anderson had Helen; witnesses, William Anderson, James Huton, James Drysdaill.

M. , Johne Richard[son] to Jonet Strang.
20, Robert Peirson to Elspet Mudie.
20, James Anderson to Margaret Strachan.

JANUARY [1661.]

B. 10, William Gotterston and Christan Strang had twins, the one David and the other Robert; witnesses, David Colvill, Robert Stirk, James Marshell, William Mudie, James Mudie and Robert Peirson.

10, William Ross and Elspet Dempstirtoun (in fornication) had James; witnesses, Johne Weir, David Peacok, and James Bontorne, presenter of the childe.

13, Thomas Anderson and Agnes Yowan had Christan; witnesses, Robert Yowan, William Anderson, Patrik Hall.

13, William Hendirson and Mariorie Broun had Jonet; witnesses, Andro Mayne, Andro Mudie, Johne Broun.

15, Andro Kirk and Issobell Coventrie had Robert; witnesses, Robert Walwood, Robert Lason, Henrie Coventrie.

20, Johne Walker and Jeane Gowans had James; witnesses, James Legat, George Stirk, Johne Wright.

20, Johne Alexander and Margaret Spens had Johne; witnesses, William Mudie, Johne Duncanson, Robert Peirson.

20, James Marshell and Elspet Moreis had Elspet; witnesses, Johne Moreis, Eduard Dowglas, Donald Buchannan.

22, Johne Watson and Helen Nicoll had Laurence; witnesses, William Walker, Mr. Thomas Walker, Laurence Watson.

24, Robert Shortus and Bessie Strachan had Johne; witnesses, Johne Cunynghame, Johne Strachane, Johne Smyth.

27, James Durhame and Geills Livingston had Johne; witnesses, Johne, James and David Duncansons, William Keir.

27, Andro Peacok and Katherine Walker had Robert; witnesses, Robert Donald, Robert Cunynghame, Robert Lason, Henry Coventrie.

31, William Anderson and Elspet Anderson had Issobell; witnesses, David Burley, David Anderson, William Walker.

M. 1, William Smert to Eupham Walls.

17, Robert Steward to Jonet Broun.

FEBRUARY.

B. 3, Thomas Rosse and Christan Robertson had Elspet; witnesses, Andro Mayne, Johne Simrell, Andro Burn.

5, James Marshell and Helen Faulds had William; witnesses, David Lindsay, William Lason, William Huton.

7, Robert Anderson and Katherine Smyth had Katherine; witnesses, Henrie Davidson, Eduard Russell, Andro Smyth.

10, William Ivat and Jeane Anderson had Robert; witnesses, Robert Anderson, Adam Anderson, Harie Elder, Johne Wright.

14, William Lason and Nanss Norie had Jonet; witnesses, Johne Lason, Johne Norie, James Smyth.

17, Patrik Anderson and Bessie Mudie had Patrik; witnesses, William Anderson, James Mudie, Robert Kirk.

17, James Paterson and Margaret Bowe had Margaret; witnesses, Henrie Mitchell, Robert Scotland, James Mitchell.

17, William Cunynghame and Elspet Walker had Marion; witnesses, George Chalmers, Jerome Cowie, Thomas Horne.

19, Robert Stevinson and Margaret Phillaue had Elizabeth; witnesses, William Walker, Adam Anderson, Harie Elder.

24, William Robertson and Christan Bowie had Mariorie; witnesses, Thomas Howie, Andro Turnbull, Johne Huton.

26, Robert Lason and Margaret Coventrie had Johne; witnesses, Johne Lason, Johne Harrower, Johne Thomson.

26, Thomas Sands and Issobell Weyld had Margaret; witnesses, Johne Weyld, Andro Anderson, Eduard Russell.

28, Thomas Elder and Issobell Simson had Harie; witnesses, Sir Harie Wardlaw of Pitreavie, Peter Hay of Naughton, Harie Wardlaw, fiar

of Pitreavie, Patrik Sanders, William Broun, Harie Elder and Johne
Mackie.

28, Patrik Sanders and Anna Elder had Harie ; witnesses, Sir Harie
Wardlaw of Pitreavie, Thomas Elder, Johne Duncanson, Harie Elder,
Robert Huton, Johne Mackie.

28, Johne Barker and Issobell Clerk had James ; witnesses, James Imrie,
David Duncanson, Robert Bonar.

M. 5, James Paterson to Issobell Fergus.
26, Alexander Walls to Bessie Huton.
27, Robert Baird to Margaret Walwood.

MARCH.

B. 3, William Cunnan and Elspet Hutson had James ; witnesses, James
Cunnan, James Stevinson, James Hutson.

3, James Murgan and Issobell Alshunder had Issobell ; witnesses, Robert,
Walwood, William Smert, Johne Alshunder.

3, Johne Belloks and Elspet Robertson had Jonet ; witnesses, Robert
Burn, Andro Wilson, Thomas Dowglas.

3, William Hall and Margaret Brand had Harie ; witnesses, Sir Harie
Wardlaw of Pitreavie, Robert Colyear, David Cunynghame.

7, William Penman and Lilias Kedglie had Margaret ; witnesses, David
Turnbull, Andro Wilson, Patrik Kedglie.

10, Johne Hamilton and Bessie Anderson had Charles ; witnesses, Mr.
Hew Montgomerie, James Anderson, Robert Huton.

10, Johne Donald and Helen Reddie had Jonet ; witnesses, Andro Donald,
James Donald, Robert Donald.

10, Johne Wilson and Katherine Philp had Margarett ; witnesses, Andro
Wilson, Thomas Philp, Thomas Wilson.

12, Johne Cunynghame and Elspet Cant had Johne ; witnesses, George
Walls, Johne Creich, Johne Lason.

12, Johne Myllar and Euphame M'Nere had David ; witnesses, David
Erskene, Lord Cardross, George Turnbull, David Robertson and
Johne Pedge.

17, Robert Stirk and Jonet Mudie had Margaret ; witnesses, James Mudie,
George Stirk, William Gotterstone.

17, Robert M'Gregor and Katherine Vasse had Johne ; witnesses, Johne
Colyear, Johne Baverage, Johne Reid.

19, Robert Mather and Jonet Beany (in fornication) had James ; witnesses,
Robert Honyman, presenter of the child, Archibald and Alexander
Honymans.

21, William Primros and Jonet Johnston had Peter ; witnesses, David
Lindsay of Cavill, Henrie Mitchell, Robert Scotland.

21, James Dowglas and Marie Faulds had Jonet ; witnesses, Johne Faulds,
Henrie Dowglas, Eduard Dowglas.

21, James Murgan and Jonet Inglis had James ; witnesses, James Donaldson, Johne Dewar, Johne Greive.

24, Johne Gray and Margaret Law had Elspet ; witnesses, Robert Colyear,
Johne Stevinson, Thomas Law.

24, Robert Fisher and Margaret Adam had Helene ; witnesses, George
Turnbull, George Walls, George Stirk.

28, Johne Mackie and Margaret Elder had Anna ; witnesses, Robert,
Huton, Patrik Sanders, Harie Elder.

28, William Huton and Jeane Ker had Marie ; witnesses, Mr. James Huton,
James Marshell, Henrie Mitchell.

28, George Wilson and Helene M'Baith had David ; witnesses, George
Chapman, David Jerman, William Turnbull.

28, James Cunnan and Elspet Kirk had Katherine ; witnesses, Henrie
Dowglas, David Currie, Robert Drysdaill.

31, William Dowglas and Mariorie Stevinson had Elspet ; witnesses,
Thomas Stevinson, David German, George Walls.

31, Robert Cowston and Eupham Scott had Jonet; witnesses, James
Broun, James Robertson, William Hadston.

31, James Mylne and Jonet Myllar had Johne; witnesses, Robert Angus,
Johne Dewar, William Rowan.

M. 5, Archibald M'Crait[h] to Geills Walker.

14, Johne Watson to Jonet Couper.

APRIL.

B. 7, James Mitchell and Margaret Mercer had Jonet; witnesses, Adam
Turnbull, Andro Mitchell, William Wilson.

7, Jerome Cowie and Helen Smert had Helen; witnesses, Adam Anderson,
William Smert, Johne Thomson.

7, William M'Craith and Bessie Anderson had William; witnesses,
William Huton, James Imrie, Henrie Anderson.

14, William Inch and Jonet Marshell had Margaret: witnesses, William
Inch, elder, George Walls, Henrie Meldrum.

14, Robert Duncan and Bessie Cunynghame had Issobell; witnesses,
Johne Anderson, William Lethem, Robert Cunynghame.

14, Alexander Scotland and Mariorie White had Johne; witnesses, William
Mudie, Johne Stanehous, James Broun.

21, William Purves and Issobell Broun had David; witnesses, David
Broun, Patrik Hall, George Brown.

21, James Allane and Jonet Moreis had Patrik; witnesses, Patrik Moreis,
Robert Shortus, Johne Livingston, James Murgane.

23, James Eason and Jeane Peacok had James; witnesses, Peter Walker,
Mr. Thomas Walker, Robert Walwood.

25, Johne Lason and Nanss Sanders had Johne; witnesses, Johne Lason,
Robert Lason, William Lason.

28, Johne Ker and Jonet Myllar had Johne; witnesses, Thomas Horne,
Johne Don, James Legat.

28, Johne Clow and Beatrix Bennet had William; witnesses, William
Smert, William Belfrage, William Harla.

28, Johne Belfrage [*torn away*] laiket (prob. Blaiket) [*torn away*] age.

M. 9, Thomas Burley to Jonet Hodge.

11, Johne Clerk to Anna Primros.

16, George Scotlan[d] to Christan Russell.

18, William Daike[rs] to Christan Traill.

23, Robert Thomson to Elspet Dewar.

MAY.

B. 5, James Kellok and Issobell Watson had James; witnesses, James
Kinynmont of that ilk, Robert Huton, James Legat.

5, Laurence Walker and Jeane Rea had Helene; witnesses, Laurence
Watson, Johne Duncanson, George Walls.

5, Duncan M'Allum and Helen Turnbull had Adam; witnesses, Adam
Turnbull, Adam Brand, William Turnbull.

14, Thomas Hutson and Elspet Austie had Margaret; witnesses, David
Mitchell, David Austie, Henrie Coventrie.

16, Robert Drysdaill and Alison Dowglas had Katherine; witnesses,
Henrie Dowglas, James Dowglas, Johne Drysdaill.

19, Charles Grem and Issobell Harla had Harie; witnesses, Sir Harie
Wardlaw of Pitreavie, Adam Anderson, William Harla.

19, Johne Huton and Jonet Howie had David; witnesses, David Bad,
David Marshell, David Cunynghame.

21, William Rowan and Margaret Allan had Margaret; witnesees, Henrie
Davidson, Thomas Baveridge, Johne Rowan.

21, Robert Bowie and Grissell Anderson had Elspet; witnesses, Johne
Donald, George Walls, James Mudie.

26, Johne Anderson and Margaret Anderson had William ; witnesses, William Anderson, Walter Anderson, George Turnbull.

26, James Sands and Bessie Touchie had Issobell ; witnesses, Johne Creich, William Cose, Robert Hunter.

30, Harie Anderson and Elspet Stanehous had Jeane ; witnesses, Johne Stanehous, Johne Anderson, Andro Smyth.

M. 16, James Bryce to Jonet Allaster.

JUNE.

B. 2, Andro Hannan and Grissell Boyd had Anna ; witnesses, Patrik Sanders, Johne Hamilton, Johne Hunnan.

6, James Peirson and Margaret Peacok had Jonet ; witnesses [*torn away till at foot of page*] [Turn] [bull ?], James Wilson.

16, Robert Peirson and Elspet Mudie had Nanss ; witnesses, William Mudie, Henrie Peirson, William Gotterstoun.

15, Johne Sim and Margaret Huton had Jonet ; witnesses, James Mudie, maltman, Johne Buist, Johne Dowgall.

20, Henrie Peirson and Helen Wilson had Margaret ; witnesses, William Lethem, Andro Wilson, William Hendirson.

20, Johne Strachan and Katherine Mather had Johne ; witnesses, Johne Duncanson, Johne Strachane, Robert Shortus.

23, James Mudie hade ane womanchilde borne to him of his wyf Grissell Espline upon the 15 day about 2 efternoone, baptised on the 23 day and called Margaret ; witnesses, Sir Henrie Wardlaw of Pitreavie, James Clerk of Pittincreiff, James Mudie, elder.

23, George Anderson and Jonet Rutherfoord had Margarett ; witnesses, Eduart Rutherfoord, Andro Wilson, William Wilson.

23, William Strachan and Margaret Marshell had William ; witnesses, William Nicoll, Robert Strachan, James Marshell.

27, Andro Currie and Nanss Greinlay had Johne ; witnesses, George Turnbull, William M'Brek, Andro Johnstoun.

27, George Dunsyre and Jonet Scot had George ; witnesses, George Swinton, George Wardlaw, William Drylay.

27, William Strachan and Jonet Allane had Robert ; witnesses, George Stirk, Robert Stirk.

30, James Anderson and Nanss Drysdaill had James ; witnesses, Thomas Drysdaill, Johne Hamilton, Johne Wright.

M. 4, James Fyff to Katherin Eduar[d] in the kirk of Dalgatie.

4, James Wilson to Margaret M'Brek.

6, Peter Currour to Barbara Hendirson.

11, Robert Anderson and Katherine Cunan.

28, William Mercer to Elspet Kellok.

JULY.

B. 4, Johne Marshell and Helen Greg had Nanss ; witnesses, Robert Mudie, James Dewar, Thomas Philp.

4, Johne Weir and Jonet Hamilton had Johne ; witnesses, Johne Turnbull, David Jerman, Johne Thomson.

7, Laurence Goodaill and Jeane Coburn had Laurence ; witnesses, Robert Dowglas, David Jerman, Alexander Anderson.

11, David Peacok and Margaret M'Craith had Marie ; witnesses, Peter Hay of Naughton, James Huton, William Turnbull.

11, Christopher Brian, ane inglish soldier, and Elspet Matheson in adulterie had Elspet ; witnesses, Andro Turnbull, Robert Bull, and William Wilson, presenter of the childe.

14, Robert Hogan and Bessie Potter had David ; witnesses, David Steward, Laurence Watson, Johne Potter.

16, Johne Burley and Christan Culros had Charles ; witnesses, Charles Turnbull, James Anderson, Harie James.

21, Johne Donn and Margaret Anderson had Jonet; witnesses, Robert Anderson, Johne Thomson, Johne Ker.

21, Henrie Mitchell and Grissell Lindsay had David; witnesses, David Lindsay of Cavill, David Mitchell, Andro Mitchell, David Currie.

21, Johne Kirkland and Nanss Fitt had William; witnesses, William Legat, William Smert, David Steward.

23, James Boyd and Bessie Belfrage had Johne; witnesses, Johne Duncanson, Laurence Watson, Thomas Belfrage.

28, Thomas Drysdaill and Katherine Seton had Anna; witnesses, William Walker, provest, Johne Turnbull, James Anderson.

28, James Anderson and Barbara Russell had Elspet; witnesses, Eduard Russell, William Anderson, Johne Anderson.

28, Daniel Bryce and Helen Clerk had Margaret; witnesses, William Anderson, William Lason, James Anderson.

M. 16, David Chrystie to Issobell Mayne.

18, William Dowglas to Margaret Huton.

18, Adam Breadie to Jonet Meldrum.

25, James Lason to Issobell Robertson.

AUGUST.

B. 4, Harie James and Nanss Blaiket had Thomas; witnesses, Thomas Elder, William Broun, Johne Thomson.

4, Laurence Trotter and Jeane Hector had Andro; witnesses, James Hadston, James Anderson, James Trotter.

15, George Chalmers and Margaret Walker had Eupham; witnesses, Peter Walker, William Walker, Mr. Thomas Walker.

19, William Peirson and Issobell Walwood had William; witnesses, Henrie Peirson, Johne Thomson, Johne Peirson.

22, David Watson and Eupham Walls (in fornication) had George; witnesses, James Kellok, presenter of the childe, George Walls, Patrik [Sa]nders. This childe was 9 weiks old or thereby before he was baptised.

M. 15, William Flokart to Issobell Mayne.

20, Robert Callend[ar] to Helen Beatie.

27, Johne Dalgleish to Katherine Smyth.

29, Walter Potter to Jeane Buchannan.

29, Robert Currie to Jonet Cunynghame.

SEPTEMBER.

B. 1, James Bountorne and Nanss Lawrie had James; witnesses, James Clerk of Pittincreiff, Johne Lawrie, Robert Huton

1, David Thomson and Jonet Peirson had William; witnesses, David Jerman, William Broun, Johne Peirson.

1, David Duncanson and Margaret Paton had William; witnesses, Johne Duncanson, James Duncanson, William Mudie.

1, James Brand and Margaret Forfar had Adam; witnesses, Adam Brand, William Mudie, Robert Peirson.

1, John Moreis and Margaret Birnet had James; witnesses, David Lindsay, James Browne, James Marshell.

1, Henrie Brian and Annas Dick had Jonet; witnesses, James Anderson, Edwart Overwhite, Archibald Aiton.

8, William Fergison and Margaret Mitchell had Andro; witnesses, Thomas and Andro Mitchells, David Currie.

8, Johne Richardson and Jonet Strang had Jonet; witnesses, William Gotterston, Robert Sharp, Charles Græm.

15, William Reid and Jean Fotheringhame had Margaret; witnesses, James Donald, Robert Cunynghame, Johne Harrower.

15, Johne Turnbull and Anna Linton had George; witnesses, George Turnbull, William Walker.

15, Johne Chrystie and Christan Hendirson had Henrie ; witnesses, Sir Henrie Wardlaw of Pitreavie, Johne Chrystie, Johne Hendirson.

15, Robert Bonar and Jonet Horne had Helene ; witnesses, Thomas Horne, William Legat, Duncan Clerk.

15, Walter Smyth and Annas Deas had Marion ; witnesses, James Baverage, David Peirson, Johne Dewar.

22, William Currie and Margaret Mayne had Harie ; witnesses, Sir Harie Wardlaw of Pitreavie, James Mayn, David Currie.

22, David Kairnes and Jonet Finlason had Helen ; witnesses, James Legat, Robert Thomson, Patrik Legat.

24, Johne Turnbull and Katherine Mitchell had Margaret ; witnesses, David Mitchell, William Walker, provest, and Mr. George Walker.

29, David Robertson and Margaret Robertson had David ; witnesses, Robert Burn, Eduart Dowglas, Henrie Wilson.

M. 3, Harie Broun to Margaret Kingorne.
3, Adam Stevinson to Bessie Peirie.
12, Henrie Dowglas to Issobel Angus.
12, George Watt to Jonet Cubrughe in Falkirk.

OCTOBER.

B. 6, Robert Lethem and Helen Scotland had William ; witnesses, William Lethem, Johne Lethem, Andro Wilson.

6, George Gatt and Helen Gray had George ; witnesses, David Anderson, presenter of the childe, Walter Anderson, William M'Brek.

6, George Walls and Margaret Smert had Margaret; witnesses, William Smert, David Steward, Alexander Smeton.

13, Johne Steward and Bessie Lugton had Margaret ; witnesses, David Mitchell, James Mitchell, Robert Lugton.

13, William Meldrum and Eupham Steward had Margaret ; witnesses, Adam Anderson, George Stirk, Michael Meldrum.

15, Mr. Hew Montgomrie had ane manchilde borne to him of his wyf Anna Colden upon the 5 day at xi hours at nyt. Baptized and called Robert on the 15 day ; witnesses, Peter Hay of Naughton, James Clerk of Pittincreiff, William Walker, provest, Harie Elder, clerk.

20, Robert Walwood and Jeane Livingstone had Robert ; witnesses, Robert Haliburton, Robert Walwood, Johne M'Ky.

20, James Wilson and Jonet Hirdman had James ; witnesses, Johne and James Duncansons, Alexander Wilson.

20, Gilbert Young and Margaret Simrell had Jonet ; witnesses, Andro Mayne, Andro Mudie, William Hendirson.

22, Andro Walwood and Helen Buist had Jonet ; witnesses, David Turnbull, Peter Buist, David Robertson.

27, Thomas Pullons and Margaret Bairdner had George ; witnesses, George Turnbull, Johne Anderson, Robert Bonar.

27, Johne Reid and Jonet Boyd had Robert ; witnesses, Patrik Sanders, Johne Duncanson, James Boyd, Robert Stevinson.

29, Robert Bryce and Helen Anderson had James ; witnesses, William Anderson, Walter Anderson, Andro Foster.

M. 24, Johne King to Margaret Trotter.
29, William Strachan to Helen Walker.

NOVEMBER.

B. 3, Mr. Thomas Walker, schoolmaister, and Nanss Gibbon had William; witnesses, William Walker, Mr. George Walker, Adam Anderson.

3, Robert Steward and Jonet Broun had Issobell ; witnesses, George Broun, Andro Mayne, William Purves.

10, Johne Dick and Jonet Aikin had Katherine ; witnesses, Robert Anderson, Walter Sim, Johne Henrie.

2 G

10, Andro Chrystie and Margaret Græm (in fornication) had David ; witnesses, David Marshell, presenter of the childe, David Chrystie, and David Bad.

10, William Boyd and Marion Wallace had Grissell ; witnesses, James Boyd, presenter of the childe, Andro Hannan, William Wilson.

12, Johne Reid and Margaret Forbes had Robert ; witnesses, Johne Park, James Mitchell, Harie Richardson, James Bruce.

17, James Watson and Bessie Cook had Robert ; witnesses, Robert Walwood, Harie Moreis, James Blak.

17, Alexander Innes and Margaret Thomson had Beatrix ; witnesses, Robert Thomson, Johne Thomson, Johne Wright.

24, Thomas Stevinson and Bessie Sands had Patrik ; witnesses, Thomas Stevinson, James Mudie, Andro Chrystie.

24, David Cunnynghame and Jonet Kirk had Thomas ; witnesses, Thomas Howie, Thomas Drysdaill, Thomas Mitchell.

24, Archibald M'Craith and Geills Walker had Robert ; witnesses, James Legat, Robert Will, Robert Anderson.

28, Peter Hay of Naughton and his Ladie, Dame Margaret Hendirson, on the 22 day being a fryday about 3 hours in the morning, had Johne, Baptised on the said 28 day being the thursday therefir ; witnesses, Johne Hendirson of ffordell, William and James Hendirsons, his breether, and Johne Scot of Spenssrfeild.

M. 7, Henrie Watson to Nans Duncan in Clakmannan.

14, Johne Lennox to Nans Beany.

28, Andro Moreis to Nans Mihie in Auchterderan.

28, Laurence Wilson to Helen Anderson.

28, David Blellok to Margaret Westwater.

28, James Sim to Nans Lason.

28, Johne Spens to Issobell Walls.

DECEMBER.

B. 1, Johne Broun and Margaret Kay had Jonet ; witnesses, David Broun, Andro Kay, Andro Broun.

1, William Wilson and Katherin Lowson had Laurence ; witnesses, Laurence Watson, Laurence Wilson, Andro Turnbull.

3, Harie Blak and Nans Peirson had Margaret ; witnesses, William Robertson, William Scotland, Thomas Colen.

5, Andro Stevinson and Christane Haigie had Johne ; witnesses, Johne Stevinson, David Haigie, William Strachane.

5, James Lyell and Margaret Cowie had William ; witnesses, William M'Brek, William Young, David Anderson

8, Johne Livingston and Jonet Wood had Jeane ; witnesses, Robert Walwood, Harie Moreis, James Black.

8, Johne M'Kenla and Jonet Reoch had David ; witnesses, Harie Moreis, James Watson, George Watson.

8, Johne Dalgleish and Margaret Sandielands had Robert ; witnesses, Robert Stanehous, Johne Thomson, Patrik Hall.

8, James Makgill and Katherin Broun had Thomas ; witnesses, Mr. Thomas M'gill, William Legat, James Duncanson.

12, Henrie Lowson and Grissell Anderson had Margarett ; witnesses, James Andersons, elder and younger, James Lowson.

15, James Brugh and Jonet Fyg had Elizabeth ; witnesses, Harie Elder, James Fyg, Johne Clow.

22, Johne Anderson and Margaret Mayne had Johne ; witnesses, Johne Mayne, Johne Chrystie, William Anderson, Johne Stanehous.

22, James Skinner and Margaret Bull had Barbara ; witnesses, Peter Walker, Arthur Robertson, Johne Potter, James Legat.

22, Thomas Howie and Jonet Cunynghame had William ; witnesses, William Walker, William Lason, William Cunynghame.

24, James Broun and Jonet Whitefoord had Elspet ; witnesses, Henrie Mitchell, Robert Scotland, William Lethem.

29, David Donaldson and Helen Donaldson had Margaret; witnesses, Johne Chrystie, James and Andrew Donaldsons.

29, Johne Chrystie and Barbara Rae had Eupham; witnesses, George Chapman, George Swinton, Johne Watson.

29, William Anderson and Bessie Hendirson had Katherine; witnesses, William Anderson, Alexander Anderson, Robert Scotland.

M. 5, Alexander Cumyn to Jonet Steward.

10, William Mylne to Grissell Alexander.

26, Henrie Mylne to Elizabeth Peirson.

JANUARY [1662.]

B. 5, Thomas Stevinson and Alison Dowglas had Alison; witnesses, Henrie Dowglas, Thomas Stevinson, Johne Stevinson.

5, James Lindsay and Helen Currie had William; witnesses, Andro Wilson, Henrie Broun, Johne Lethem.

5, Johne Wilson and Margaret Watson had Jonet; witnesses, Andro Wilson, Johne Wilson, William Wilson.

14, William Gilkrist and Jonet Drysdaill had Margaret; witnesses, Johne Anderson, Johne Dewar, James Wilson.

19, Andro Mitchell and Margaret Mitchell had David; witnesses, David Mitchell, Mr. David Dowglas, David Currie.

19, Johne Stevinson and Margaret Dick had Helen; witnesses, Robert Stevinson, William Mudie, Adam Anderson.

19, Thomas Colen and Jonet Scotland had Elspet; witnesses, William Robertson, George Scotland, William Scotland.

21, David Austie and Margaret Anderson had David; witnesses, David Mitchell, Robert Lugton, James Mitchell.

21, Johne Dewar and Katherine Dow had Marion, baptized in the kirk of Baith; witnesses, James Dewar, David Dewar, Robert Mudie.

26, Johne Lindsay and Elspet Reid had Margaret; witnesses, James Lindsay, Harie Philp, James Imrie.

26, Andro Moreis and Elspet Horne had Nans; witnesses, Eduard Russell, Johne Goold, Andro Moreis.

26, William Broun and Elspet Hendirson had Bessie; witnesses, James Hendirson, David Broun, James Broun.

28, William Lethem and Jonet Wilson had William; witnesses, William Wilson, Thomas Wilson, James Lason.

30, Henrie Coventrie and Issobell Donald had Robert; witnesses, Rober Walwood, Robert Cunynghame, Robert Donald.

M. 7, Johne Sim to Issobell Car.

7, Johne M'Leish to Margaret Hutson.

14, William Alexander to Bessie Eadie in Carnok.

16, William Wilson to Sara Mitchell.

23, Johne Gibbon to Elspet Hirdman.

FEBRUARY.

B. 2, Johne Gray and Jonet Lindsay had Elizabeth; witnesses, Johne Haliburton, James Lindsay, Patrik Broun.

9, Patrik Drumond and Annas Hardie had Elspet; witnesses, George Turnbull, Johne Drummond, James Buist.

16, James Angus and Helen Cunynghame had Marie; witnesses, William Huton, Robert Angus, William Cunynghame.

16, Johne Hunnan and Katherine Yowan had Johne; witnesses, Johne Hamilton, Johne Greive, Andro Hannan.

20, Andro Mawer and Jeane Wannan had James; witnesses, Robert Russell, Andro Murdo, Thomas Horne.

M. 6, Andro Chrystie to Margaret Creich in Carnok.

11, Robert Smeton to Nans Moyes.

11, Robert Fyff to Bessie Hendirson.

20, Johne Smyth to Isobell Eadie in Carnok.

27, Thomas Falconer to Elspet Walker.

MARCH.

B. 2, Johne Græm and Margaret Bannatyn had Jeane ; witnesses, George Wardlaw, William Kirk, James Tod.

9, Patrik M'Innes and Jonet Car had Patrik ; witnesses, William Huton, James Fyff, William M'Craith.

9, James Buist and Margaret Hardie had Johne ; witnesses, Johne Hendirson of Fordell, James Richardson, Peter Buist.

13, Robert Huton and Jonet Sanders had Harie ; witnesses, Sir Harie Wardlaw of Pitreavie, Harie Elder, Patrik Sanders.

13, David Haigen and Margaret Rainy had Robert ; witnesses, Robert Scotland, William Huton, James Anderson.

16, Patrik Hall and Jeane Purves had Issobell ; witnesses, William Purves, Andro Hall, George Mudie.

16, James Couper and Helen Chalmers had Katherine ; witnesses, James Belfrage, Johne Dewar, David Peirson.

20, William Cusine and Christane Dewar (in fornication) had Johne ; witnesses, Johne Cusine, Johne Dewar, Robert Huton.

23, Thomas Thomeson and Margaret Anderson had Johne ; witnesses, Johne Anderson, Robert Cunynghame, David Bad.

30, David Bad and Jonet Anderson had Johne ; witnesses, Johne Anderson, Johne Cunynghame, Andro Chrystie.

M. 6, David Thomson to Helen Johnston.

27, Harie Philp to Jonet Toward.

APRIL.

B. 1, James Paterson and Issobell Fergus had Johne ; witnesses, Henrie Mitchell, Robert Scotland, William Anderson.

3, James Donaldson and Margaret Blaiket had Johne ; witnesses, William Anderson, James Crafoord, Johne Donaldson.

3, James Wilson and Margaret Makbrek had William ; witnesses, William M'Brek, David Anderson, Andro Currie.

6, Richard Harrower and Annas Ramsay had Elizabeth ; witnesses, Robert Haliburton, Johne Buist, George Broun.

6, James Marshell and Elspet Moreis had Nans ; witnesses, William Purves, William Currie, Johne Westwood.

6, George Hall and Margaret Dowglas had Robert ; witnesses, Eduard Dowglas, David Dowglas, Johne Anderson.

6, Jerome Cowie and Helene Smert had Jerome ; witnesses, William Smert, Adam Anderson, Peter Buist.

6, Peter Currour and Barbara Hendirson had Andro ; witnesses, Andro Mayn, Andro Mudie, James Stevinson.

6, Duncan M'Ellop and Jonet Mayne had Margaret, baptized in the kirk of Saline upon a testimonial from this kirk ; witnesses, James Donaldson, Andro Donaldson, James Littlejohn.

13, William Mercer and Elspet Kellok had James ; witnesses, James Cunnan, Robert Kellok, Adam Anderson.

13, George Scotland and Christan Russell had Margaret ; witnesses, David Scotland, Robert Russell, Robert Angus.

13, James Marshell and Bessie Strang had Christan ; witnesses, William Gotterston, Johne Thomson, William Inche.

15, William Huton and Jeane Chrystie had William ; witnesses, Robert Huton, Robert Russell, Robert Angus.

17, Adam Breadie and Jonet Meldrum had Johne ; witnesses, Johne Chrystie, James Cunnan Johne Clow.

22, James Anderson and Christan Young had Robert ; witnesses, Robert Mudie, Thomas Williamson, William Anderson.

22, Johne Stanehous and Jonet Cunynghame had Johne ; witnesses, Thomas Stanehous, Johne Hendirson, Johne Anderson.

22, Robert Lason and Margaret Coventrie had Jonet ; witnesses, David Jerman, James Belfrage, James Richardson.

22, William Chalmers and Margaret Wannan had Jeane; witnesses, Thomas Horne, Andro Mawer, James Watson.

27, Johne Lason and Katherine Henrie had Margarett; witnesses, William and James Lasons, Andro Wilson.

27, Robert Stirk and Jonet Mudie had Grissell; witnesses, Johne and George Stirks, William Gotterstoun.

27, Andro Potter and Jonet Paton had Anna; witnesses, Johne Potter, William Potter, Patrik Sanders.

M. 3, Johne Fotheringhame to Marion Whitefoord.

3, Robert Dewar to Issobell Alshunder.

15, Robert Baxter to Bessie Chapman.

15, William Drylay to Jonet Allan.

MAY.

B. 1, Umquhile David Lindsay of Cavill and Katherine Malloch had Robert; witnesses, Robert, Lord Colvill, Sir James Halket, presenter of the childe, and Johne Mackie.

1, Robert Donald and Helen Belfrage had Issobell; witnesses, Andro Donald, James Donald and Henrie Coventrie.

4, Johne Watson and Jonet Couper had Barbara; witnesses, Thomas Couper, George Chapman, Andro Wilson.

4, Patrik Rowan and Jeane Stanehous had Barbara; witnesses, Johne Stanehous, Robert Barclay, James Balfour.

4, William Anderson and Issobell Anderson had James; witnesses, James Clerk of Pittincreiff, James Anderson, Alexander Inglis.

4, Johne Pullons and Margaret Inglis had Johne; witnesses, James Mudie, David Thomson, Johne Reid.

4, Patrik Anderson and Barbara Turnbull had Jonet; witnesses, David Turnbull, William Anderson, William Walwood.

4, Robert Hog and Bessie Allan had Robert; witnesses, Johne Allan, Johne Broun, Johne Currie.

6, Thomas Cant and Issobell Wely had William; witnesses, William Broun, William Dowglas, Johne Peirson, James Mudie.

8, David Marshell and Annas Malcome had Elspet; witnesses, Johne Cunynghame, William Lason, Andro Chrystie.

11, William Broun and Jonet Anderson had Katherine; witnesses, Johne Anderson, Walter Anderson, Eduard Dowglas.

11, George Chapman and Margaret Clerk had Jonet; witnesses, Peter Hay of Naughton, William Drummond, Andro Chapman.

11, James Anderson and Margaret Strachan had Jonet; witnesses, William Anderson, William Strachan, William Lason.

11, Mans Malcolme and Jonet M'lenochen had Issobell; witnesses, Thomas Howie, Johne Huton, Johne Hunnan.

18, David Chrystie and Jonet Marshell had Elspet; witnesses, William Robertson, David Scotland, Robert Russell.

18, James Wilson and Jonet Dick had Jonet; witnesses, John Haliburton, James Legat, James Mudie.

18, Walter Potter and Jeane Buchanan had James; witnesses, Sir James Halket of Pitfirran, John M'Ky, Johne Potter, Mr. George Walker.

18, James Lamb and Margaret Smert had Robert; witnesses, Robert Stirk, David Jerman, Andro Mayne.

18, Alexander Reid and Jonet Johneston had twins, Grissel and Jonet; witnesses, David Jerman, James Mudie, David Reid, Johne Thomson, George Stirk.

20, Euphame Hamilton, sometyme a servant in Dunfermline, having brought forth a child in the paroche of Largo the 8 of Marche last, which she confest was begottin heir in fornication with William Anderson, tailyeour, and having givin one James Craig, indweller in Dunfermline, suretie that she should mak publict satisfaction qhen she shall be requyred, The said James presented the childe, which was baptized the 20 day of May instant and called James.

25, Robert Walwood and Jonet Ged had Jeane; witnesses, Peter Walker, William Walker, Johne Ged, James Mudie.

M. 1, William Cusine to Christan Dewar.

8, William Stew[ard] to Marie Drumond in the kirk of Dumeny.

27, Alexander Young to Margaret Callender.

29, Robert Myllar to Jonet Wood.

29, David Burley to Marie Wanderstoun.

31, Robert Dowy to Janet Tod in Kingorne.

JUNE.

B. 1, John Anderson and Margaret Anderson had Johne; witnesses, Adam Currie, Eduart Dowglas, elder, and Eduart Dowglas, younger.

1, William Douglas and Margaret Huton had Jonet; witnesses, James Anderson, Peter Buist, Johne Thomson.

1, William Garvie and Alison Hall had Jonet; witnesses, Johne Broun, Andro Garlik, Alexander Inglis.

1, Johne Walwood and Elspet Coventrie had Henrie; witnesses, James Legat, Robert Walwood, Henrie Coventrie.

5, Robert Pet and Bessie Philp had twinnes, Johne and Robert; witnesses, Eduart Russell, Patrik Broun, George Broun.

5, William Lason and Elspet Chrystie had Andro; witnesses, Andro Lason, Andro Chrystie, Andro Mayne.

8, Andro Rowe and Marie Lambe had Jonet; witnesses, James Mudie, Mr. George Walker, Robert Stirk.

8, Johne Goold and Elspet Cunynghame had James; witnesses, James Mudie, William Walwood, James Anderson.

8, David Fairgie and Jonet Coventrie had Christane; witnesses, Robert and William Walwoods and William Coventrie.

10, William Robertson and Elizabeth Huton had Margaret; witnesses, David Dewar of Lassodie, George Scotland, Robert Robertson.

12, William Walker hade ane womanchilde borne to him of his wyf Margaret Turnbull on the 3 day, and baptized the 12 day and called Anna; witnesses, Sir James Halkett of Pitfirran, Johne Hendirson of ffordell, and Mr. Thomas Walker.

12, David Dewar and Margaret Thomsone had Robert; witnesses, Robert Burn, David Peacok, James Dewar.

22, William Turnbull and Jeane Dowglas had David; witnesses, David Currie, Mr. David Dowglas, Henrie Dowglas.

22. Thomas Williamsone and Bessie Mayne had Thomas; witnesses, Andro Garlik, James Broun and Johne Lawrie.

22, James Huton and Christan Livingstone had Jonet; witnesses, Peter Walker, Robert Walwood and James Huton.

22, David Bell and Jonet Walker had Johne; witnesses, Andro Mayne, Andro Mudie, Robert Stewart.

29, Robert Currie and Jonet Cunynghame had Jonet; witnesses, Andro Mayne, Harie James, Thomas Stevinson.

29, Walter Sim and Jonet Anderson had Robert; witnesses, James Balfour of Baith, Robert Anderson, Thomas Stevinson.

M. 17, Robert Anderson to Jeane Brand.

20, Mr. James Tailyeour to Bessie Turnbull.

JULY.

B. 6, William Anderson and Katherine Wardlaw had James; witnesses, Robert Russell, David Scotland and James Anderson.

6, James Fisher and Christan Russell had Barbara; witnesses, Andro Wilson, Johne Lethem, Robert Lethem.

6, Alexander Hammell and Annas Legat had William; witnesses, William and James Legats and Patrik Legat.

6, David Chrystie and Issobell Mayne had Margaret ; witnesses, Andro Chrystie, Johne and Andro Maynes.

6, James Lamb and Nans Davidson had Johne ; witnesses, James Mudie, Robert Stirk, William Kinnens.

6, George Watt and Jonet Cubrugh had Bessie ; witnesses, George Turnbull, David Anderson and Walter Anderson.

8, Laurence Walls and Margaret Greive had Robert ; witnesses, Johne Greive, elder, Johne Greive, younger, Robert Mudie.

13, James Bryce and Jonet Allaster had James ; witnesses, Robert Angus, Robert Russell, William Rowan,

13, Johne Alexander and Margaret Spens had William ; witnesses, William Mudie, William Gotterston, Robert Bonar.

20, Adam Anderson and Katherine Gibbon had Johne ; witnesses, Robert Stevinson, James Anderson, Mr. Thomas Walker.

20, William Smert and Eupham Walls had Katherin ; witnesses, Thomas Wilson, Thomas Elder, Robert Stevinson.

20, James Peacok and Christan Alison had Eduart ; witnesses, Eduart Russell, George Wardlaw, James Short.

22, Adam Stevinson and Bessie Peirie had Magdalen ; witnesses, Adam Stanehous, James Baverage, Johne Dewar, Robert Mudie.

27, William Nicoll and Helen Mylne had Helen ; witnesses, James Andersons, elder and younger, and James Hadston.

27, Johne King and Margaret Trotter had Robert ; witnesses, James Trotter, Daniel Bryce and Johne Nicoll.

27, William Reid and Grissell Kirk had Marion ; witnesses, Frances Broun, James Huton, James Mudie, Thomas Tod.

M. 1, James Anderson to Issobell Dewar in the kirk of Baith.

8, James Bower to Margaret Nicoll.

10, Andro Belfrage to Nans Smert.

10, Johne Arky to Elspet Bax[   ].

11, Robert Kirk to Issobell Scot.

18, Mr. Thomas Dowglas to Margaret Kinynmont in Carnok.

24, William Walwood to Nans Huton in Carnok.

AUGUST.

B. 3, James Bryce and Katherine Bruce had James ; witnesses, Johne Currie, Andro Johnston, Johne Broun.

3, Patrik Sanders and Anna Elder had Helen ; witnesses, Johne Duncanson, Robert Huton, Johne Mackie.

10, David Anderson and Margaret Blak had David ; witnesses, William Gray, Walter Anderson, William M'Brek.

17, Henrie Meldrum and Jonet Inch had Jonet ; witnesses, George Walls, James Broun, William Inch.

17, Johne Hendirson and Margaret Watson had James ; witnesses, James Hendirson, Laurence Watson, Thomas Horne.

24, Eduart Burt and Jonet Hadston had Jonet ; witnesses, James Hadston, Johne Hadston, Laurence Trotter.

24, Andro Hannan and Grissell Boyd had Agnes ; witnesses, Johne Hamilton, Johne Hunnan, William Boyd.

31, Harie Anderson and Elspet Stanehous had Johne ; witnesses, Johne Stanehous, Robert Stanehous, Andro Smyth.

31, Johne M'Leish and Margaret Hutson had Thomas ; witnesses, Thomas Drysdaill, Thomas Elder, Thomas Horne.

M. 5, William Mudie to Nans Bryce.

14, Johne Creich to Margaret Flokart.

14, James Eason to Helen Walwood.

18, Adam Broun to Isobell Sim.

19, Robert Willy to Marion Russell.

19, Johne Smyth to Jonet Murray.

28, Eduart Dowglas to Margaret Shape in Sawline.

28, Patrik Norie to Jonet Young in Torrieburn.

SEPTEMBER.

B. 7, Thomas Meldrum and Margaret Robertson had Margaret; witnesses, James Balfour, Peter Walker, James Buist.

14, James Balfour and Marion Bruce had Eupham; witnesses, Sir Henrie Wardlaw of Pitreavie, Peter [Hay? see *infra*, Oct. 26, 1] of Naughton and James Mudie, land clerk.

14, Johne Dalgleish and Katherine Smyth had Margarett; witnesses, Johne Lawrie, Johne Dalgleish, James Bountorne.

14, Johne Blellok and Elspet Robertson had Margarett; witnesses, Robert Burn, David Robertson, Thomas Dowglas.

21, Robert Callendar and Helen Beatie had Jonet; witnesses, Johne Stanehous, Johne Anderson, James Anderson.

21, Johne Ker and Jonet Myllar had Anna; witnesses, James Legat, Johne Balfour, Johne Don, David Thomson.

21, Andro Broun and Margaret Stevinson had Patrik; witnesses, David Broun, Johne Broun, Thomas Stevinson.

21, Thomas Spens and Jonet Culros had Helen; witnesses, Johne Law, Johne Stevinson, Johne Aikin.

28, Johne Marshell and Margaret Anderson had Johne baptised in Carnok because of our minister's absence; witnesses, James Lowson, David Haigen, David Austie

30, Johne Lennoks and Nans Beany had Margaret baptized in Torryburn becaus of our minister's absence; witnesses, Johne Harrower, Robert Cunynghame, Andro Donald.

M. 2, James Duncanson to Margaret Wilson.

OCTOBER.

B. 12, David Blellok and Margaret Westwater had Johne; witnesses, Adam Turnbull, Thomas Mitchell, William Inglis.

12, Duncan Clerk and Margaret Horne had Duncan; witnesses, Thomas Horne, Johne Clerk, Robert Bonar.

12, Johne Dowgall and Margaret Eilson had Katherine; witnesses, Johne Eilson, Thomas Horne, Johne Neilson.

12, David Mayne and Margaret Peirson had James baptized in the kirk of Innerkething; witnesses, James Cunnan, James Balfour, James Paterson.

19, Thomas Drysdaill and Katherine Seton had twinnes, Johne and Elizabeth; witnesses, Johne and James Anderson, Johne Haliburton, William Walker, Michael Seton of Dumbarrow.

26, Thomas Elder and Issobell Simson had Helen; witnesses, Johne Hendirson of Fordell, Sir Henrie Wardlaw of Pitreavie, James Clerk of Pittincreiff, Peter Hay of Naughton, Mr. Robert Kay, minister, Harie James.

26, Johne Clow and Beatrix Bennet had Jonet; witnesses, Peter Walker, Thomas Elder, Robert Walwood.

26, Patrik Livingston and Jonet Rutherfoord (in fornication) had Robert; witnesses, Robert Walwood of Touch, James Legat and Robert Walwood, presenter of the childe.

26, James Gib and Elspet Marshell had William; witnesses, William Rowan, William Dewar, James Bryce.

M. 7, Alexander Harrower to Jonet Pullons in the kirk of Torrie.

23, Thomas Boyd to Barbara Russell.

30, Gawin Edison to Margaret Potter.

30, Robert Walwood to Jonet Nicoll.

NOVEMBER.

B. 2, Robert Burn and Jonet Sharp had Elspet; witnesses, David Currie, Henrie Dowglas, Andro Mitchell.

2, James Broun and Margaret George had Johne; witnesses, James Cunnan, Johne Broun, Andro Smyth.

2, Johne Simrell and Bessie Stevinson had Patrik; witnesses, Patrik Hall, Patrik Mudie, Thomas Stevinson.

2, William Clerk and Margaret Primros had Helen; witnesses, Robert Scotland, Eduard Dowglas, William Primros.

9, William Flokart and Issobell Mayne had Jonet; witnesses, Andro Mayne, David Flokart, Johne Broun.

23, James Robertson and Marion Greive had James; witnesses, Henrie Mitchell, Robert Scotland, James Broun.

23, William Hendirson and Mariorie Broun had Mariorie; witnesses, Andro Mayne, Johne Simrell, Andro Mudie.

25, Johne Hunter and Jonet Murgane had William; witnesses, Johne Broun, Robert Hog, James Murgane.

30, Patrik Norie and Jonet Young had William; witnesses, Johne Norie, William Lason, William Young.

30, Johne M'Farline and Jonet Horne had Johne; witnesses, Thomas Horne, Robert Bonar, Johne Watson.

30, David Drysdaill and Elspet Wilson had Margarett; witnesses, Andro Wilson, Eduart Rutherfoord, Thomas Wilson.

30, Donald Buchannan and Margaret Turnour had Margaret; witnesses, Eduart Dowglas, Johne Strachan, Johne Halkett.

M. 4, Robert Kellok to Issobell Kellok in Innerkething.

4, James Anderson to Eupham King.

4, Robert Anderson to Katherin Broun.

6, David Angus to Margaret Harrower.

13, Johne Flewear to Jonet Phillan.

27, Alexander M'Yowan to Jonet Neish.

DECEMBER.

B. 7, James Dowglas and Marie Faulds had Eduart; witnesses, Johne Faulds, Eduart Dowglas, Robert Dowglas.

7, James Marshell and Helen Faulds had Margaret; witnesses, William Lason, James Lason, William Huton.

7, Johne Myllar and Eupham M'Nere had James; witnesses, James Peirson, Andro Peirson, Richard Templeman.

7, Johne Dowgall and Margaret Young had Margaret; witnesses, James Anderson, Johne Heart, Johne Dalgleish.

7, James Hakston and Katherin Ewin had George; witnesses, James Lindsay, George Lindsay, James Broun.

7, William Anderson and Christan Mitchell had William; witnesses, William Huton, William Legat, James Legat.

14 Jonet Phillan in fornication to Abram Giro (as she affirmed) had Thomas; witnesses, David Hutton, Alexander Beane, and Thomas Beane, presenter of the childe. This childe was about a quarter old before he was baptized.

14, Harie Moreis and Elspet Tailyeour had Jeane; witnesses, Robert Walwood, William Walker, George Chalmers.

14, Patrik Legat and Issobell Stevinson had Margarett; witnesses, James Legat, William Legat, William Mudie.

14, William Purdie and Margaret Dowe had Johne; witnesses, Johne Colyear, Johne Belfrage, Johne Litlejohne.

21, Henrie Peirson and Helen Wilson had David; witnesses, James Cunnan, Thomas Stanehous, Andro Wilson.

21, Johne Smyth and Issobell Eadie had Elizabeth; witnesses, Johne Smyth, Johne Stirk and Thomas Eadie.

21, Johne Gibson and Elspet Hirdman had Jonet; witnesses, Robert Huton, Johne Wright, George Walls.

26, Peter Hay of Naughton and his ladie, Dame Margaret Hendirson had Elizabeth; witnesses, Thomas Bruce of Blairhall, Johne Scot of Spensirfeild, James Hoburn of Menstry.

28, Robert Cowston and Eupham Scot had Christan ; witnesses, James Broun, Henry Coventrie, Robert Cunynghame.

28, Robert Anderson and Katherine Broun had William ; witnesses, Johne Anderson, Robert Cunyngham, William Lethem.

28, Alexander Dunsyre and Katherine Brugh had Eupham ; witnesses William Smert, George Swinton, Robert Shortus.

28, Andro Cunyngham and Margaret Turnbull had James ; witnesses, James Cunnan, Mr James Tailyeour, James Mayne.

31, James Lawson and Issobell Robertson had Margaret ; witnesses, Laurence Watson, Johne Donald, Peter Buist.

M. 2, Johne Johneston to Margaret Lowson.

2, James White to Jonet Watson.

4, Andro Donald to Jonet Belfrage.

11, Thomas Thomson to Margaret Cullen.

16, William Wilson to Margaret Broun.

Robert Donald to Jonet Donald.

Thomas Sands to Helen Donald.

18, George Stirk to Margaret Lawrie.

JANUARY [1663].

B. 4, Robert Steward and Jonet Broun had David ; witnesses, David Broun, Andro Mayn, Johne Steward.

11, James Craig and Margaret Fergison had Elizabeth ; witnesses, James Clerk of Pittincreiff, George Stirk, Robert Stirk.

11, Thomas Mitchell and Margaret Mudie had Christan ; witnesses, James Legatt, Johne Potter, Gawin Edison.

11, William Alexander and Bessie Eadie had Jonet ; witnesses, Johne Potter, Andro Robertson, William Tailyeour.

11, Thomas Mitchell and Bessie Greive (in fornication) had Jonet, baptized in Saline ; witnesses, Robert Dalgleish, presenter of the childe, Thomas Hendirson, and Robert Greive.

18, Harie Philp and Jonet Toward had Marion ; witnesses, George Wardlaw, James Peacok, Johne Lindsay.

18, William Dewar and Issobell Fyff had David ; witnesses, James Dewar, David Dewar, David Peacok.

18, William Gotterstoun and Christan Strang had William ; witnesses, William Mudie, William Cunyngs, James Marshell.

25, James Weyld and Issobell Creich had William ; witnesses, James Baverage, Henrie Baverage, Johne Weyld.

25, Thomas Beane and Katherine Walker had Christan ; witnesses, Alexander Beane, Patrik Walker, Harie James.

25, Robert Stanehous and Bessie Huton had Robert ; witnesses, Robert Huton, Johne Cusine, James Broun.

25, Robert Sharp and Elspet Porteous had James ; witnesses, James Mudie, James Bountorne, James Richardson.

25, Robert Wilson and Grissell Toward (in fornication) had Johne baptized in Carnok ; witnesses, James Wilson, James Mudy, David Bad.

M. 27, Johne Wilson to Bessie Mudie. [Only one marriage recorded in January 1663.]

FEBRUARY.

B. 1, Johne Anderson and Margaret Macmirrie had Anna ; witnesses, James Anderson, Adam Anderson, Robert Colyear.

8, Robert Anderson and Margaret Cullen had Robert ; witnesses, Johne Cullen, Adam Anderson, Alexander Young.

8, Laurence Thomson and Eupham Mather had James ; witnesses, George Chalmers, Johne Turnbull, William Broun.

8, Alexander Anderson and Jonet Chrystie had Helen ; witnesses, James Anderson, William Anderson.

15, Johne Huton and Jonet Howie had William; witnesses, William Beany, William Robertson, Thomas Howie.

15, Andro Mudie and Issobell Mudie had James; witnesses, James Wilson, James Mudie, James Stevenson.

15, Eduart Overwhite and Grissell Dick had Johne; witnesses, Johne Anderson, Johne Cusine, Johne Broun.

15, Patrik Allan and Margaret Alison had Margaret; witnesses, David Turnbull, Johne Stevinson, Johne Park.

22, James Mudie, landclerk, had ane manchilde borne to him of his wyf Grissell Espline, the xi day of Februar about four in the morning, and baptized the 22 day and called James; witnesses, James Clerk of Pittincreif, Peter Hay of Naughton, George Wardlaw, and James Mudie, elder.

22, Johne Walwood and Katherine Coventrie had Robert; witnesses Robert Donald, Robert Lason, Robert Stirk.

22, Johne Allan and Jonet Ramsay had Johne; witnesses, Johne Stevinson, James Hadston, Eduart Burt.

22, Alexander Fairlie and Margaret Myllar had Alexander; witnesses, Robert Shortus, James Murgan, William Mudie.

22, Johne Peirson and Elspet Duff had Patrik; witnesses, Patrik Duff, Patrik Hall and Johne Thomson.

26, Robert Dewar and Issobell Alexander had Jeane; witnesses, Johne Thomson, Patrik Hall and James Bruce.

28, Johne Donn and Margaret Anderson had Margaret; witnesses, Robert Anderson, Johne Thomson, William Mercer.

M. 11, James Ruthven to Margaret Kay in Edinburgh.

26, Robert Sanders to Helen Walker.

MARCH.

B. 8, James Arkie and Bathia Dempstirton had James; witnesses, James Duncanson, James Anderson, George Wardlaw.

8, William Strachane and Margaret Marshell had James; witnesses, Robert Strachan, James Marshell, William Nicoll.

8, Andro Spear and Elspet Matheson had James; witnesses, James Cunnan, James Spear, James Buist.

8, James Crafoord and Margaret Walker had William; witnesses, William Walker, William Cunyngham, William Strachan.

15, Umquhile James Boyd and Bessie Belfrage had Christane; witnesses, William Belfrage, David Steward, Laurence Watson, and William Boyd, presenter of the childe.

17, Andro Wilson and Issobell Letham had Helen; witnesses, Henrie Peirson, Robert Donald, Robert Lethem.

17, George Gatt and Helen Gray had William; witnesses, David Anderson, Andro Johneston, William Anderson.

22, Johne Potter and Elspet Mullion had James; witnesses, Sir James Halket of Pitfirrane, James Legat, David Turnbull, William Potter.

22, Johne Spens and Issobell Walls had Jonet; witnesses, Eduart Dowglas, Johne Anderson, Johne Donalson.

22, Johne Lason and Nans Sanders had Bessie; witnesses, William Lason, Robert Lason, Johne Lason.

22, Umquhile Johne Hamilton and Bessie Anderson had Agnes; witnesses, James Anderson, younger, Alexander Anderson, Robert Huton and James Anderson, elder, presenter of the childe.

24, Harie Broun and Margaret Kingorne had William; witnesses, David Murray, Walter Anderson, Johne Lason.

24, Robert Dowglas and Elspet Peirson had Elspet; witnesses, William Lethem, William Hendirson, Robert Cant.

29, Andro Chrystie and Margaret Creich had Andro; witnesses, Andro Creich, Johne Creich, Andro Currie.

29, Robert Cheisly and Bessie Greg had Nanss; witnesses, Andro Hall, William Gotterston, Robert Walwood.

29, James Hew and Jonet Anderson had Geills; witnesses, Adam Currie, Andro Cunynghame, Johne Mudie.

29, David Thomson and Helen Johneston had Andro; witnesses, Johne Haliburton, Robert Haliburton, Thomas Horne.

29, George Wilson and Helen M'baith had George; witnesses, George Chapman, William Turnbull, Johne Chrystie.

31, Johne Cunynghame and Elspet Cant had Helen; witnesses, Andro Wilson, Johne Anderson, David Reid.

M. 6, James Kinynmont of that ilk to Margaret Wardlaw, dochter of Sir Henry Wardlaw of Pitreavie, knight, in the kirk of Baith.

10, Robert Meldrum to Jonet Weyld.

10, William Inglis to Jonet Burley.

12, Johne Walker to Jonet Hoburn.

APRIL.

B. 5, Robert Lason and Jonet Drysdaill had Jeane; witnesses, William Lason, James Lason, William Anderson.

5, Eduart Crowder and Marion Mitchell had George; witnesses, Peter Hay of Naughton, Alexander Innes, James Mitchell.

5, James Bower and Margaret Nicoll had Helen; witnesses, Robert Colyear, Andro Mayne, David Philp.

5, Johne Strachan and Katherin Mather had James; witnesses, James Clerk of Pittincreiff, Johne Strachan and Robert Shortus.

5, James Durham and Geills Livingston had James; witnesses, Johne Duncanson, James Duncanson, David Duncanson, Andro Hall.

5, Mr. James Tailyeour had ane womanchilde borne to him of his wyf Bessie Turnbull the 24 of March last, and baptized the said 5 day of Aprile and called Helen; witnesses, Peter Hay of Naughton, William Walker and Peter Walker.

7, Robert Myllar and Jonet Wood had David; witnesses, David Currie, Mr. David Dowglas, James Wood.

12, Adam Turnbull and Jonet Mitchell had James; witnesses, James Cunnan, James Mitchell, Johne Turnbull.

12, Alexander Cumyn and Jonet Steward had Thomas: witnesses, Thomas Mitchell, David Marshell, William Meldrum.

12, Johne M'Grew and Katherin M'Queene had Johne; witnesses, Peter Walker, George Chalmers, William Keir.

12, Mungo Johneston and Margaret Watson had Johne; witnesses, William Walwood, William Keir, Johne Keir.

12, James May and Nanss Gray (in fornication) had James; witnesses, William Turnbull, James Lindsay, George Chapman.

14, William Hadston and Annabel Blaiket had David; witnesses, James Lindsay, Henrie Mitchell, William Primros.

19, Henrie Dowglas and Katherin Brand had Anna; witnesses, James Scot of Spenserfeild, Mr. David Dowglas, Adam Brand.

19, Alexander Lowson and Margaret Keltie had Margaret; witnesses, Johne Johneston, Henrie Lowson, David Haigen.

19, Patrik Walker and Elspet Blaiket had twins, Bathia and Margaret; witnesses, William Walwood, William Keir, Johne Keir, Thomas Beane, William Potter, Gawin Edison, James Buist.

26, George Turnbull and Margaret Kellok had William; witnesses, William Walker, Adam and William Turnbulls.

26, Johne Chrystie and Christan Henryson had Johne; witnesses, Sir Henrie Wardlaw of Pitreavie, Johne Chrystie, Johne Henryson.

26, Robert Barclay and Jonet Richardson had Issobell; witnesses, William Gottetston, Andro Hall, James Lamb.

M. 16, Thomas Philp to Jonet Wright.

21, David Sharp to Jonet Watson.

30, Henrie Stevinson to Helen Chrystie.

MAY.

B. 3, James Anderson and Issobell Dewar had Margaret ; witnesses, David Dewar of Lassodie, Adam Anderson and Mr. Robert Anderson.

3, Henrie Wilson and Margaret Lindsay had Johne ; witnesses, Johne Dewar, Johne Cumyn, David Dowglas.

10, Duncan Campbell and Christan Dalgleish had Christan ; witnesses, Mr. Robert Kay, minister, James Ruthven, Mr. Thomas Walker.

10, William Mercer and Elspet Kellok had Bessie ; witnesses, James Cunnan, Robert Kellok, Adam Anderson.

10, Robert Kirk and Issobell Scot had Joseph ; witnesses, Henrie Davidson, Johne Stanehous, Eduart Russell.

10, Robert Willy and Marion Russell had Marion ; witnesses, Mr. George Walker, Peter Russell, David Steward.

10, Andro Galrik and Mariorie Williamson had Mariorie ; witnesses, Thomas Williamson, Johne Broun, Andro Broun.

14, Andro Stevinson and Christan Haigen had Margaret ; witnesses, David Haigen, Johne Stevinson, James Lowson.

24, James Duncanson and Margaret Wilson had James ; witnesses, Johne Duncanson, William Mudie, Johne Stevinson.

24, William Belfrage and Issobell Templeman had Johne ; witnesses, Johne Stirk, Henrie Meldrum, Andro Meldrum.

24, William Inch and Jonet Marshell had William ; witnesses, William Inch, James Marshell, Henry Meldrum.

26, Johne Cusine and Barbara Smeton (in fornication) had Nans ; witnesses, James Legat, Patrik Sanders, and Andro Hall, presenter of the childe.

29, Johne Harla and Jonet Rainy had Anna ; witnesses, James Hadstoun, David Haigen, James Anderson.

31, Thomas Stevinson and Alison Dowglas had Jonet ; witnesses, Mr. George Walker, Mr. David Dowglas and James Stevinson.

31, James Broun and Jonet Meldrum had Margaret ; witnesses, Johne Broun, Andro Broun, Johne Creich.

31, Johne Clerk and Anna Primros had Helen ; witnesses, Henrie Stevinson, Alexander Anderson, Johne Bad.

M. 18, Mr. Johne Udney to Margaret Kennedie.

28, Robert Hog to Elspet Barclay.

JUNE.

B. 7, James Paterson and Margaret Howe had Jeane ; witnesses, Henrie Mitchell, William Anderson, Robert Scotland.

7, Andro Wilson and Grissell Dewar had Johne ; witnesses, Johne Wright, Johne Mylne, James Wilson.

7, Walter Anderson and Agnes Smyth had Agnes ; witnesses, Johne Anderson, presenter of the childe, David Anderson, George Turnball.

7, Charles Graem and Issobell Harla had Margaret ; witnesses, Sir Henrie Wardlaw of Pitreavie, James Kinynmont of that Ilk, and William Harla.

7, Johne Drummond and Bessie Wardlaw had William ; witnesses, William Walker, William Smert, William Dowglas.

21, Johne Walloks and Margaret Broun had Bessie ; witnesses, Robert Cunynghame, Johne Harrower, James Donald.

21, Johne Barker and Issobell Clerk had Katherin ; witnesses, Adam Anderson, Robert Bonar, James Imrie.

23, Andro Greg and Elspet Malcom (in fornication) had Margaret ; witnesses, Thomas Couper, presenter of the childe, Johne Stevinson and Thomas Stevinson.

23, William Potter and Jeane Elder had Margaret ; witnesses, David Murray, Andro Johnston, Robert Colyear.

28, James Simson and Margaret Anderson had Issobell ; witnesses, Mr. Thomas Walker, William Broun, George Chalmers.

28, Johne Drumond and Katherin Reaburn had James ; witnesses, Peter Walker, Robert Walwood, David Jerman.

28, Thomas Hutson and Elspet Anstie had Issobell ; witnesses, Henrie Coventrie, Robert Lason, David Anstie.

M. 2, Johne Wood to Margaret Davidson.

4, Walter Potter to Katherin Meldrum.

4, Johne May to Margaret Peacok.

16, Robert Cunynghame to Margaret Donaldson.

18, Andro Wilson to Jonet Robertson.

23, Patrik Anderson to Jonet Primros.

25, Henrie Hendirson to Issobell Wightman.

30, Johne Stanchous to Nans Hendirson in the kirk of Innerkething.

JULY.

B. 5, Eduart Dowglas and Margaret Shape had Agnes ; witnesses, Eduart Dowglas, William Shape, Johne Shape.

5, Eduart Rutherfoord and Margaret Græm had Geills ; witnesses, James Durie, James Anderson, Robert Russell.

5, James Eason and Helen Walwood had William ; witnesses, William Eason, Johne Walwood, Johne Lason.

5, William Legat and Helen Kent had Christan ; witnesses, James Legat, William Kent, Johne Kent.

5, Johne Hunter and Margaret Burn had Robert ; witnesses, Robert Tailyeour, Andro Mayne, Patrik Hall.

5, Johne Arkie and Elspet Baxter had Margaret ; witnesses, Henrie Mitchell, James Broun, James Arkie.

5, Johne Halket and Bessie Miklejohne had James ; witnesses, William Huton, James Marshell, William Anderson.

12, James Sim and Nans Lason had Jeane ; witnesses, Robert Walwood, William Sim, Johne Stevinson.

12, James Sands and Bessie Touchie had Johne ; witnesses, Mr. Thomas Dowglas, Johne Creich, Andro Johnestoun.

19, Laurence Walker and Jeane Rae had Thomas ; witnesses, Thomas Belfrage, George Walls and David Steward.

26, Johne Turnbull and Anna Linton had Robert ; witnesses, William Walker, George Turnbull in Broomhall, and George Turnbull in Sillietoun.

26, Alexander Harrower and Jonet Pullons had Helen ; witnesses, George Turnbull, Andro Mitchell and Johne Anderson.

26, James Peirson and Margaret Peacok had Andro ; witnesses, Andro Peirson, William Cose, Johne Duncanson.

26, William Currie and Margaret Mayne had Margarett ; witnesses, David Currie, James Mayne, Johne Mayne.

26, James Fyg and Nans Dalgleish had George ; witnesses, George Turnbull, Robert Colyear, George Stirk.

30, James Clerk of Pittincreiff and Elizabeth Erskine had Alexander ; witnesses, Alexander Seton Lord ffyvie, Sir James Halket of Pitfirran, James Hoburn of Menstrie, and Sir Johne Couper of Gogar.

M. 7, Thomas Wilson to Margaret Donald.

9, Johne Mowbrey to Elspet Murebeck.

9, James Anderson to Issobell Anderson.

9, David Jerman to Elizabeth Elder.

23, James Lindsay to Bessie Thomson.

30, Andro Simson to Bessie Elder.

AUGUST.

B. 8, William Huton and Jeane Ker had William ; witnesses, James Huton, William Lason, James Marshell.

8, Patrik Sanders and Anna Elder had Elizabeth ; witnesses, David Jerman, Robert Huton, Johne Duncanson.

8, Abram Patrik and Marion Boyd had Jonet; witnesses, Robert Patrik, Patrik Sanders, Robert Huton.

8, Robert Bowie and Grissell Anderson had James; witnesses, Jerom Cowie, George Walls, James Anderson.

8, Johne Richardson and Jonet Strang had Margaret; witnesses, William Gotterston, Robert Sharp, Charles Græm.

15, James Anderson and Barbara Russell had Issobell; witnesses, Johne Anderson, William Anderson, Eduart Russell.

15, Johne Donald and Helen Reddie had James; witnesses, Johne Colyear, William Harla, Robert Donald.

15, Peter Currour and Barbara Hendirson had Johne; witnesses, Andro Mayne, Andro Mudie, James Stevinson.

15, William Ivat and Jeane Anderson had William; witnesses, Adam Anderson, David Jerman, Johne Wright.

23, Robert Baxter and Bessie Chapman had Bessie; witnesses, Andro Chapman, George Chapman, Johne Baxter.

23, Laurence Trotter and Jeane Hector had Cicell; witnesses, Eduart Burt, James Hadston, James Anderson.

30, James Mitchell and Margaret Mercer had Katherin; witnesses, Robert Dempster of Pitliver, Johne Turnbull, Henrie Dowglas.

30, Robert Smeton and Nans Moyes had Elizabeth: witnesses, James Moyes, Robert Mudie, Robert Russell.

30, William Miklejohn and Jonet Greg had Jonet; witnesses, Peter Russell, William Drylay, Johne Allan.

M. 6, Robert Dowglas to Issobell M'Craich.

11, Thomas Hamilton to Helen Lindsay in the kirk of Carnok.

18, James Alexander to Jonet Crambie in the kirk of Baith.

25, Robert Donald to Margaret Myllar.

27, Patrik Anderson to Bessie Belfrage.

SEPTEMBER.

B. 3, William Wilson and Katherin Lowson had Margarett; witnesses, Laurence Wilson, Andro Turnbull, Robert Bull.

6, William Dowglas and Margaret Huton had Robert; witnesses, James Anderson, Johne Thomson, Eduard Dowglas.

13, Johne Marshell and Helen Greg had Robert; witnesses, Robert Mudie, James Baverage, Johne Dewar.

13, Thomas Dowglas and Bessie Murie had Nans; witnesses, Eduard Dowglas, Adam Murie, James M'Yowan.

20, Alexander Young and Margaret Callendar had Johne; witnesses, Johne Anderson, Patrik Broun, Johne Bell.

20, William Peirson and Issobell Walwood had William; witnesses, William Broun, Johne Peirson, William Harla.

27, David Donaldson and Helen Donaldson had Thomas; witnesses, Johne Chrystie, Thomas Currour, David Young.

27, David Young and Margaret Drysdaill had Christan; witnesses, Johne Chrystie, Johne Walker, Robert Chrystie.

27, James Bountorne and Nans Laurie had ane manchilde the 14 day and baptized the 27 day and called George; witnesses, George Hay, lawfull sone to Peter Hay of Naughton, George Stirk, elder, and Johne Laurie.

29, Johne Hunnan and Katherin Yowan had Margarett; witnesses, James Anderson, elder, Robert Yowan, James Imrie.

M. [*None.*] [No marriages recorded for September 1663.]

OCTOBER.

B. 1, Henrie Mitchell and Grissell Lindsay had Andro; witnesses, Andro Mitchell, Mr. George Walker, Henrie Dowglas.

4, George Ewin and Elspet Potter had George; witnesses, David Turnbull, James Imrie, Thomas Wely.

4, William Wilson and Margaret Broun had William ; witnesses, William Broun, William Smert, William Mudie.

4, James Anderson and Eupham King had Jeane ; witnesses, Johne Mackie, William Anderson, Robert Scotland.

8, William Rowan and Margaret Allane had Issobell ; witnesses, Henrie Davidson, Johne Rowan, Robert Russell.

15, Andro Donald and Jonet Belfrage had Issobell ; witnesses, Robert Donald, Henrie Coventrie, James Donald.

15, David Reid and Katherin Scot had Grissell ; witnesses, Johne Stevinson, William Smert, George Walls.

18, Gawin Edison and Margaret Potter had Johne ; witnesses, Johne Potter, Walter Potter, Johne Lauthiane.

18, Robert Jak and Jonet Hall had Katherin ; witnesses, Andro Mudie, Johne Wardlaw, Robert Mayne.

25, James Stevinson and Margaret Anderson had Bessie ; witnesses, James Huton, James Anderson, William Stevinson.

25, William Lason and Nans Norie had James ; witnesses, James Donald, James Smyth, Johne Lason.

25, Johne Walker and Jonet Hoburn had Grissell ; witnesses, Johne Walker, David Walker, George Stirk, elder.

M. 1, William Donaldson to Rebecca Clow.

6, William Inch to Jonet Walls in the kirk of Baith.

22, Harie Anderson to Elizabeth Wightman in Edinburgh.

NOVEMBER.

B. 1, Robert Peirson and Elspet Mudie had William ; witnesses, Mr. Robert Anderson, William Mudie, William Gotterstoun.

1, William Donaldson and Issobell Malcom had Johne ; witnesses, Johne Mackie, William Mercer, Johne Colyear.

5, James Murgan and Jonet Inglis had Margaret ; witnesses, Andro Wilson, Johne Lethem, Robert Philp.

5, Andro Kirk and Issobell Coventrie had Issobell ; witnesses, Duncan Campbell, Thomas Elder, William Belfrage.

5, Robert Hogane and Bessie Potter had Elspet ; witnesses, Johne Potter David Steward, Laurence Watson.

5, Johne Weir and Jonet Hamilton had Jonet ; witnesses, William Walker, Johne Thomson, Johne Peirson.

8, Thomas Thomson and Margaret Cullen had Johne ; witnesses, Johne Chrystie, Robert Thomson.

12, Robert Shortus and Bessie Strachan had Margaret ; witnesses, Johne Strachan, Johne Cunyngham and Johne Stirk.

15, Robert Thomson and Issobel Dowglas had Henrie ; witnesses, Henrie Davidson, Robert Thomson, James Thomson.

19, Johne Wilson and Katherin Philp had Andro ; witnesses, Andro Wilson, Andro Johnestoun, Johne Lethem.

22, Andro Wardlaw and Issobell Murray had Issobell ; witnesses, James Anderson, William Douglas, Johne Burley.

22, Johne Aikin and Elspet Spens had David ; witnesses, Johne Law, David Turnbull, Johne Alexander.

26, Henrie Coventrie and Issobell Donald had Andro ; witnesses, Andro Donald, Andro Kirk, James Donald.

26, Johne Hadston and Issobell Pringle had Elspet ; witnesses, William Anderson, James Anderson, James Hadston.

29, George Stirk and Margaret Laurie had Elspet ; witnesses, George Stirk, Johne and Robert Stirks.

29, Andro Hannan and Grissell Boyd had Grissell ; witnesses, Johne Hunan, Patrik Sanders, Robert Huton.

M. 12, Henrie Lowson to Bessie Hall.

12, Mark Donald to Margaret Currie.

19, William Young to Elspet Broun.

Lightning Source UK Ltd.
Milton Keynes UK
UKHW050631160720
366640UK00013B/1159

9 789354 034213